Secure Multiparty Computation and Secret Sharing

In a data-driven society, individuals and companies encounter numerous situations where private information is an important resource. How can parties handle confidential data if they do not trust everyone involved? This text is the first to present a comprehensive treatment of unconditionally secure techniques for multiparty computation (MPC) and secret sharing. In a secure MPC, each party possesses some private data, whereas secret sharing provides a way for one party to spread information on a secret such that all parties together hold full information, yet no single party has all the information. The authors present basic feasibility results from the last thirty years, generalizations to arbitrary access structures using linear secret sharing, some recent techniques for efficiency improvements, and a general treatment of the theory of secret sharing, focusing on asymptotic results with interesting applications related to MPC.

RONALD CRAMER leads the Cryptology Group at CWI Amsterdam, the national research institute for mathematics and computer science in the Netherlands, and is Professor at the Mathematical Institute, Leiden University. He is Fellow of the International Association for Cryptologic Research and Member of the Royal Netherlands Academy of Arts and Sciences.

IVAN BJERRE DAMGÅRD leads the Cryptology Group in the Department of Computer Science, Aarhus University, and is a professor in the same department. He is a Fellow of the International Association for Cryptologic Research, and he received the RSA conference 2015 award for outstanding achievements in mathematics. He is a co-founder of the companies Cryptomathic and Partisia.

JESPER BUUS NIELSEN is an associate professor in the Department of Computer Science, Aarhus University. He is a co-founder of the company Partisia.

Secure Multiparty Computation and Secret Sharing

Ronald Cramer
CWI & Leiden University

Ivan Bjerre Damgård
Aarhus University

Jesper Buus Nielsen
Aarhus University

CAMBRIDGE
UNIVERSITY PRESS

CAMBRIDGE
UNIVERSITY PRESS

University Printing House, Cambridge CB2 8BS, United Kingdom

One Liberty Plaza, 20th Floor, New York, NY 10006, USA

477 Williamstown Road, Port Melbourne, VIC 3207, Australia

314-321, 3rd Floor, Plot 3, Splendor Forum, Jasola District Centre, New Delhi - 110025, India

79 Anson Road, #06-04/06, Singapore 079906

Cambridge University Press is part of the University of Cambridge.

It furthers the University's mission by disseminating knowledge in the pursuit of
education, learning and research at the highest international levels of excellence.

www.cambridge.org
Information on this title: www.cambridge.org/9781107043053

First published 2015

A catalogue record for this publication is available from the British Library

Library of Congress Cataloging in Publication data
Cramer, Ronald, 1968–
Secure multiparty computation and secret sharing / Ronald Cramer,
CWI & Leiden University, Ivan Damgård, Aarhus University, Jesper Buus Nielsen,
Aarhus University.
pages cm
Includes bibliographical references and index.
ISBN 978-1-107-04305-3 (hardback)
1. Computer networks–Security measures.   2. Computer security.   3. Computer network protocols.
4. Information theory.   I. Damgaard, Ivan, 1956–   II. Nielsen, Jesper Buus, 1973–   III. Title.
TK5105.59.C685 2015
005.8–dc23   2015002282

ISBN 978-1-107-04305-3 Hardback

Contents

Preface

This is a book on information theoretically secure multiparty computation (MPC) and secret sharing and about the intimate and fascinating relationship between the two notions. We decided to write this book because we felt that a comprehensive treatment of unconditionally secure techniques for MPC was missing in the literature. In particular, because some of the first general protocols were found before appropriate definitions of security had crystallized, proofs of those basic solutions have been missing so far.

We present the basic feasibility results for unconditionally secure MPC from the late 1980s, generalizations to arbitrary access structures using linear secret sharing, and a selection of more recent techniques for efficiency improvements. We also present our own simplified variant of the Universally Composable (UC) framework in order to be able to give complete and modular proofs for the protocols we present.

We also present a general treatment of the theory of secret sharing, in particular, secret-sharing schemes with additional algebraic properties, which is also a subject missing in textbooks. One of the things we focus on is asymptotic results for multiplicative secret sharing, which has various interesting applications that we present in the MPC part.

Our ambition has been to create a book that will be of interest to both computer scientists and mathematicians and can be used for teaching at several different levels. We have therefore tried to make Parts I and II self-contained units, even if this implies some overlap between the parts. This means that there are several different ways to read this book; we give a few suggestions in the following paragraphs. In particular, the concept of secret sharing, of course, appears prominently in both parts. In Part I, on MPC, however, it is introduced only as a tool on a "need-to-know" basis. In Part II, we reintroduce the notion, but as a general concept that is interesting in its own right and with a comprehensive treatment of the mathematical background.

This book is intended to be self-contained enough to be read by advanced undergraduate students, and the authors have used large parts of the material in the book for teaching courses at this level. By covering a selection of more advanced material, the book can also be used for a graduate course.

How to Use This Book

For a course on the advanced undergrad level for computer science students, we recommend covering Chapters 1 through 5. This will include the basic feasibility results for unconditionally secure MPC and the UC model. For some extra perspective, it may also be a good idea to cover Chapter 7, which is basically a survey of cryptographically secure solutions.

For a graduate-level computer science course, we recommend including also Chapters 8 and 9 because they contain several recent techniques and survey some open problems.

For a course in mathematics on secret sharing and applications, we recommend covering Chapters 1, 3, and 6 first. This will provide an intuition for what secret sharing is and how it is used in MPC. Then Part II should be covered to present the general theory of algebraic secret sharing. Finally, the last part of Chapter 9 can be used to present some of the more advanced applications.

Acknowledgments

We thank Alp Bassa, Morten D. Bech, Wieb Bosma, Ignacio Cascudo, Iwan Duursma, Morten Dahl Jørgensen, Serge Fehr, Helene Flyvholm Haagh, Irene Giacomelli, Lingfei Jin, Michiel Kosters, Carolin Lunemann, Antonio Macedone, Diego Mirandola, Carles Padró, Gabriele Spini, Anders Vinther, Chaoping Xing, and Sarah Zakarias for doing an enormous amount of work in proofreading and commenting. We also thank Sarah Zakarias for writing some of the simulation proofs and helping us to avoid many more mistakes than are present now.

RC would like to warmly thank the School of Mathematical Sciences at Nanyang Technological University in Singapore for its excellent hospitality during his frequent visits throughout the years for research and work on parts of this book.

Part I

Secure Multiparty Computation

1

Introduction

1.1 Private Information, Uses and Misuses

In a modern information-driven society, the everyday life of individuals and companies is full of cases where various kinds of private information are important resources. While a cryptographer might think of PIN codes and keys in this context, these types of secrets are not our main concern here. Rather, we will talk about information that is closer to the *primary business* of an individual or a company. For a private person, this may be data concerning his or her economic situation, such as income, loans, and tax data, or information about his or her health, such as diseases and medicine usage. For a company, it might be the customer database or information on how the business is running, such as turnover, profits, and salaries.

What is a viable strategy for handling private information? Finding a good answer to this question has become more complicated in recent years. When computers were in their infancy, in the 1950s and 1960s, electronic information security was to a large extent a military business. A military organization is quite special in that confidential information needs to be communicated almost exclusively between its own members, and the primary security goal is to protect this communication from being leaked to external enemies. While it may not be trivial to reach this goal, at least the overall purpose is simple to state and understand.

In modern society, things get much more complicated: using electronic media, we need to interact and do business with a large number of parties, some of whom we have never met and many of whom may have interests that conflict with ours. So how do you handle your confidential data if you cannot be sure that the parties you interact with are trustworthy?

One could save the sensitive data in a very secure location and never access it, but this is, of course, unreasonable. Our private data usually have value only because we want to use them for something. In other words, we have to have ways of controlling leakage of confidential data while these data are being stored, communicated, or computed on, *even in cases where the owner of the data does not trust the parties he or she communicates with.*

A very interesting fact that makes this problem even more important is that there are many scenarios in which a large amount of added value can be obtained by *combining confidential information from several sources* and from this computing some result that holds an interest for all parties. To illustrate what we mean by this, we look at a number of different example scenarios in the following subsections.

1.1.1 Auctions

Auctions exist in many variants and are used for all kinds of purposes, but we concentrate here on the simple variant where some item is for sale and the highest bid wins. We assume that the auction is conducted in the usual way, where the price starts at some preset amount and people place increasing bids until no one wants to bid more than the currently highest bid. When you enter such an auction, you usually have some (more or less precisely defined) idea of the maximum amount you are willing to pay and therefore when you will stop bidding. However, every bidder, of course, wants to pay as small a price as possible for the item. Indeed, the winner of the auction may hope to pay less than his or her maximum amount. This will happen if all other bidders stop participating long before the current bid reaches this maximum.

For such an auction to work in a fair way, it is obvious that the maximum amount you are willing to pay should be kept private. For instance, if the auctioneer knows your maximum and is working with another bidder, they can force the price to be always just below your maximum and so force you to pay more than if the auction had been honest. Note that the auctioneer has an incentive to do this to increase his or her own income, which is often a percentage of the price the item is sold for. However, the result of the auction could, in principle, be computed if one were given as input the true maximum value each bidder assigns to the item on sale.

1.1.2 Procurement

A procurement system is a sort of inverted auction, where some party (typically a public institution) asks companies to bid for a contract, that is, to make an offer on the price for doing a certain job. In such a case, the lowest bid usually wins. However, bidders are typically interested in getting as high a price as possible.

It is obvious that bids are private information: a participating company is clearly not interested in competitors learning its bid before it has to make its own bid. This would allow the competitors to beat the company's bid by always offering a price that is slightly lower than that offered by the company. This is also against the interests of the institution offering the contract because it will tend to make the winning bid higher. The result of the process, namely, who wins the contract, can, in principle, be computed given all the true values of the bids.

1.1.3 Benchmarking

Assume that you run a company. You will naturally be interested in how well you are doing compared with other companies in the same line of business as yours. The comparison may be concerned with a number of different parameters, such as profit relative to size, average salaries, and productivity. Other companies will most likely have similar interests in such a comparison, which is known as a *benchmark analysis*. Such an analysis takes input from all participating companies. Based on this, it tries to compute information on how well a company in the given line of business should be able to perform, and each company is told how its performance compares with this "ideal."

It is clear that each company will insist that its own data are private and must not be leaked to competitors. However, the desired results can be computed from the private data: there are several known methods from information economics for doing such an analysis efficiently.

1.1.4 Data Mining

In most countries, public institutions such as the tax authorities or the health care system keep databases containing information on citizens. In many cases, there are advantages one can get from coordinated access to several such databases. Researchers may be able to get statistics they could not get otherwise, or institutions might get an administrative advantage from being able to quickly gather the information they need on a certain individual.

However, there is clearly a privacy concern here: access to many different databases by a single party opens the possibility that complete dossiers could be compiled on particular citizens, which would be a violation of privacy. In fact, accessing data on the same person in several distinct databases is forbidden by law in some countries precisely because of this concern.

1.2 Do We Have to Trust Someone?

We are now in a position to extract some common features of all the scenarios we have looked at so far. One way to describe them all is as follows: we have a number of parties, and each possesses some private data. We want to do some computation that needs all the private data as input. The parties are interested in learning the result, or at least some part of it, but want to keep their private data as confidential as possible.

Hopefully, it is clear from the preceding section that if we can find a satisfactory solution to this problem, a very large number of applications would benefit. Moreover, this leads to an extremely intriguing theoretical question, as we now explain:

One possible – and trivial – solution would be to find some party T that everyone is willing to trust. All parties privately give their input to T, who does the required computation, announces the result to the parties, and forgets about the private data he or she has seen. A moment's thought will show that this is hardly a satisfactory solution: first, we have created a single point of attack from which all the private data can potentially be stolen. Second, the parties must all completely trust T with respect to both privacy and correctness of the results. The reason why there are privacy concerns is that the parties do not trust each other in the first place, so why should we believe that they can find a new party they all trust?

In some applications, one may pay a party T for doing the computation; if the amount paid is thought to be larger than what T could gain from cheating, the parties may be satisfied with the solution. This seems to work in some cases, for instance, when a consultancy house is paid a large fee for doing a benchmark analysis – but this is, of course, a very expensive solution.

Thus, we are left with a fundamental question: *can the problem be solved without relying on a trusted party?*

At first sight, it may seem that this cannot be possible. We want to compute a result that depends on private data from *all* involved parties. How could one possibly do this unless data from several parties become known to someone, and hence we have to trust that party?

Nevertheless, as we shall see, the problem is by no means impossible to solve, and solutions do exist that are satisfactory, both from theoretical and from practical points of view.

1.3 Multiparty Computation

Let us be slightly more precise about the problem we have to solve: the parties, or *players*, that participate are called $P_1, \ldots, P_n$. Each player P_i holds a secret input x_i, and the players agree on some function f that takes n inputs. Their goal is to compute $y = f(x_1, \ldots, x_n)$ while making sure that the following two conditions are satisfied:

- Correctness: the correct value of y is computed; and
- Privacy: y is the *only* new information that is released.

Regarding the latter property, note that because the purpose of the whole exercise is to learn y, the best we can hope for in terms of privacy is that nothing but y is leaked. Computing f such that privacy and correctness are achieved is referred to as computing f *securely*. Later in this book we will be precise about what secure computing is; for now, we will be content with the preceding intuitive idea. Note also that one may consider a more general case where each player gets his or her own private output. We will do so later; for now, we focus on a single, public output for simplicity.

As one example of how this connects to the scenarios from the preceding section, one may think of x_i as a number, namely, P_i's bid in an auction, and $f(x_1, ..., x_n) = (z, j)$, where $x_j = z$ and $z \geq x_i, i = 1, \ldots, n$; that is, f outputs the highest bid and the identity of the corresponding bidder. If we do not want the winner to pay his or her own bid but the bid of the second-highest bidder, we simply change z to be this value, which is again a well-defined function of the inputs. This would give us a function implementing a so-called second price auction.

In this section we give a first intuition on how one might compute a function securely without relying on trusted parties. This requires that we specify a *protocol*, that is, a set of instructions that players are supposed to follow to obtain the desired result. For simplicity, we will assume for now that players always follow the protocol. We will later address the case in which some parties may deviate from the protocol in order to get more information than they are supposed to or cause the result to be incorrect. We will also assume that any pair of players can communicate securely; that is, it is possible for P_i to send a message m to P_j such that no third party sees m, and P_j knows that m came from P_i. We discuss later how this can be realized in practice.

1.3.1 Secure Addition and Voting

Let us first look at a simple special case, namely, where each x_i is a natural number and $f(x_1, \ldots, x_n) = \sum_{i=1}^{n} x_i$. Secure computation of even such a simple function can have very meaningful applications. Consider the case where $P_1, ..., P_n$ want to vote on some yes/no decision. Then we can let x_i represent the vote of P_i, where $x_i = 0$ means "no" and $x_i = 1$

means "yes." If we can compute the sum of the x_i securely, this exactly means that we get a way to vote with the properties we usually expect: the result $\sum_{i=1}^{n} x_i$ is indeed the result of the vote, namely, the number of yes votes. Moreover, if the computation is secure, no information is leaked other than $\sum_{i=1}^{n} x_i$; in particular, no information is revealed on how a particular player voted.

We will now design a protocol for the voting application. To be consistent with the next example, we set $n = 3$. A later exercise shows how to construct a voting solution for any n.

Secret Sharing

Before we can solve the problem, we need to look at an important tool known as *secret sharing*. The term may seem self-contradictory at first sight: how can anything be secret if you share it with others? Nevertheless, the name makes good sense: the point is that secret sharing provides a way for a party, say P_1, to spread information on a secret number x across all the players such that they together hold full information on x, yet no player (except, of course, P_1) has any information on x. First, we choose a prime p, and we define $\mathbb{Z}_p$ as $\mathbb{Z}_p = \{0, 1, ..., p-1\}$.[1] In the following, we will think of the secret x as a number in $\mathbb{Z}_p$.

In order to *share the secret s*, P_1 chooses numbers r_1, r_2 uniformly at random in $\mathbb{Z}_p$ and sets

$$r_3 = x - r_1 - r_2 \bmod p$$

Put another way, P_1 chooses r_1, r_2, r_3 randomly from $\mathbb{Z}_p$, subject to the constraint that $x = r_1 + r_2 + r_3 \bmod p$. Note that this way of choosing r_1, r_2, r_3 means that each of the three numbers is uniformly chosen in $\mathbb{Z}_p$: for each of them, all values in $\mathbb{Z}_p$ are possible and equally likely. Now P_1 sends privately r_1, r_3 to P_2, r_1, r_2 to P_3, and keeps r_2, r_3 himself or herself. The r_js are called the *shares* of the *secret x*.

The process we have described satisfies two basic properties: First, the secret x is kept private in the sense that neither P_2 nor P_3 knows anything about that secret. As a result, if some hacker breaks into the machine of P_2 or P_3 (but not both), he or she will learn nothing about x. Second, x can be reconstructed if shares from at least two players are available. Let's argue that this is true in a more precise way:

Privacy. Even though P_1 has distributed shares of the secret x to the other players, neither P_2 nor P_3 has any idea what x is. For P_2, we can argue as follows: he or she knows r_1, r_3 (but not r_2) and that $x = r_1 + r_2 + r_3 \bmod p$. Take any $x_0 \in \mathbb{Z}_p$. From P_2's point of view, could it be that $x = x_0$? The answer is yes, for if $x = x_0$, it would have to be the case that $r_2 = x_0 - r_1 - r_3 \bmod p$. This is certainly a possibility. Recall that r_2 is uniformly chosen in $\mathbb{Z}_p$, so all values are possible. However, any other choice, say $x = x_0' \neq x_0$, is also a possibility. If this were the answer, we would have $r_2 = x_0' - r_1 - r_3 \bmod p$, which is a value that is different from $x_0 - r_1 - r_3 \bmod p$ but just as likely. We conclude that what has been sent to P_2 reveals nothing new about x. A similar argument shows that the same is true from P_3's point of view.

Correctness. If two of the three parties pool their information, the secret can be reconstructed because then all three shares will be known, and one can simply add them modulo p.

---

[1] To be more precise, $\mathbb{Z}_p$ is another name for $\mathbb{Z}/p\mathbb{Z}$, where we identify $i \in \mathbb{Z}_p$ with the residue class of numbers that are congruent to i modulo p. See more details in Chapter 2.

Note that the privacy property is *information theoretic*: as long as a party does not know all three summands, no amount of computing power can give that party any new information on the corresponding secret. In this book, we focus primarily on protocols with this type of security. The secret-sharing technique just shown is a special case of so-called replicated secret sharing. There are many ways to realize secret sharing with other desirable properties than the method we show here, and we look at several such techniques later, as well as a more general definition of what secret sharing is.

A Protocol for Secure Addition

The basic idea for secure addition is that all players P_1, P_2, and P_3 will distribute shares of their private values x_1, x_2, and x_3 in exactly the way we saw before. It turns out that one can now compute the sum securely by locally adding shares and announcing the result. The complete protocol is as follows:

Protocol Secure Addition

Participants are P_1, P_2, P_3; input for P_i is $x_i \in \mathbb{Z}_p$, where p is a fixed prime agreed on in advance.

1. Each P_i computes and distributes shares of his or her secret x_i as described in the text: he or she chooses $r_{i,1}, r_{i,2}$ uniformly at random in $\mathbb{Z}_p$ and sets $r_{i,3} = x_i - r_{i,1} - r_{i,2} \bmod p$.
2. Each P_i sends privately $r_{i,2}, r_{i,3}$ to P_1, $r_{i,1}, r_{i,3}$ to P_2, and $r_{i,1}, r_{i,2}$ to P_3 (note that this involves P_i sending "to himself or herself"). So P_1, for instance, now holds $r_{1,2}, r_{1,3}$, $r_{2,2}, r_{2,3}$, and $r_{3,2}, r_{3,3}$.
3. Each P_j adds corresponding shares of the three secrets – more precisely, he or she computes, for $\ell \neq j$, $s_\ell = r_{1,\ell} + r_{2,\ell} + r_{3,\ell} \bmod p$ and announces s_ℓ to all parties. Each party computes and announces two values.
4. All parties compute the result $v = s_1 + s_2 + s_3 \bmod p$.

To analyze the secure addition protocol, let us first see why the result v is indeed the correct result. This is straightforward:

$$v = \sum_j s_j \bmod p = \sum_j \sum_i r_{i,j} \bmod p = \sum_i \sum_j r_{i,j} \bmod p = \sum_i x_i \bmod p$$

This shows that the protocol computes the sum modulo p of the inputs, no matter how the x_i are chosen. However, if we let the parties choose $x_i = 1$ for "yes" and $x_i = 0$ for "no" and make sure that $p > 3$, then $\sum_i x_i \bmod p = \sum_i x_i$ because all x_i are 0 or 1, and so, their sum cannot be larger than p. So, in this case, v is indeed the number of yes votes.

Now why is it the case that no new information other than the result v is leaked to any player? Let us concentrate on P_1 for concreteness. In step 1, x_1, x_2, and x_3 are secrets shared, and we have already argued that this tells P_1 nothing whatsoever about x_2, x_3. In the final step, s_1, s_2, s_3 are announced. Note that P_1 already knows s_2, s_3, so s_1 is the only new piece of information. However, we can argue that seeing s_1 will tell P_1 what v is and nothing more. The reason for this is that if one is given s_2, s_3, and v, one can compute $s_1 = v - s_2 - s_3 \bmod p$. Put another way, given what P_1 is supposed to know, namely, v, we can already compute what he or she sees in the protocol, namely, s_1, and therefore, seeing the information from the protocol tells him or her nothing beyond v.

This type of reasoning is formalized later in this book and is called a *simulation argument*: given what a player is supposed to know, we show how to efficiently compute (simulate) everything he or she sees in the protocol, and from this, we conclude that the protocol tells the player nothing beyond what we wanted to tell him or her.

Note that given the result, P_1 is in fact able to compute some information about other people's votes. In particular, he or she can compute $v - x_1 = x_2 + x_3$, that is, the sum of the other players' votes. It is easy to get confused and think that because of this, something must be wrong with the protocol, but in fact, there is no problem: it is true that P_1 can compute the sum of the votes of P_2 and P_3, but this follows from information P_1 is *supposed to know*, namely, the result and his or her own input. There is nothing the protocol can do to deprive P_1 of such information – in other words, the best a protocol can do is to make sure that players only learn what they are supposed to learn, and this includes whatever can be derived from the player's own input and the intended result.

1.3.2 Secure Multiplication and Matchmaking

To do general secure computation, we will, of course, need to do more than secure addition. It turns out that the secret-sharing scheme from the preceding subsection already allows us to do more: we can also do secure multiplication.

Suppose that two numbers $a, b \in \mathbb{Z}_p$ have been secret shared as described earlier, so that $a = a_1 + a_2 + a_3 \bmod p$ and $b = b_1 + b_2 + b_3 \bmod p$, and we wish to compute the product $ab \bmod p$ securely. We obviously have

$$ab = a_1 b_1 + a_1 b_2 + a_1 b_3 + a_2 b_1 + a_2 b_2 + a_2 b_3 + a_3 b_1 + a_3 b_2 + a_3 b_3 \bmod p$$

It is now easy to see that if the a_is and b_is have been distributed as described earlier, it is the case that for each product $a_i b_j$, there is at least one player among the three who knows a_i and b_j and therefore can compute $a_i b_j$. For instance, P_1 has been given a_2, a_3, b_2, b_3 and can therefore compute $a_2 b_2, a_2 b_3, a_3 b_2$, and $a_3 b_3$. The situation is therefore that the desired result ab is the sum of some numbers where each summand can be computed by at least one of the players. But now we are essentially done because from Protocol Secure Addition we already know how to add securely!

The protocol resulting from these observations follows. To argue why it works, one first notes that correctness, namely, $ab = u_1 + u_2 + u_3 \bmod p$, follows trivially from the preceding. To show that nothing except $ab \bmod p$ is revealed, one notes that nothing new about a, b is revealed in the first step, and because Protocol Secure Addition is private, nothing except the sum of the inputs is revealed in the last step, and this sum always equals $ab \bmod p$.

It is interesting to note that even in a very simple case where both a and b are either 0 or 1, secure multiplication has a meaningful application: consider two parties, Alice and Bob. Suppose that Alice is wondering whether Bob wants to go out with her, and Bob is asking himself if Alice is interested in him. They would very much like to find out if there is mutual interest but without running the risk of the embarrassment that would result if, for instance, Bob tells Alice that he is interested, only to have Alice turn him down. The problem can be solved if we let Alice choose $a \in \mathbb{Z}_p$, where $a = 1$ if she is interested in Bob and $a = 0$ otherwise. In the same way, Bob chooses b to be 0 or 1. Then we compute the function $f(a, b) = ab \bmod p$ securely. It is clear that the result is 1 if and only

---

Protocol Secure Multiplication

Participants are P_1, P_2, and P_3; input for P_1 is $a \in \mathbb{Z}_p$; input for P_2 is $b \in \mathbb{Z}_p$, where p is a fixed prime agreed on in advance. P_3 has no input.

1. P_1 distributes shares a_1, a_2, a_3 of a, while P_2 distributes shares b_1, b_2, b_3 of b.
2. P_1 locally computes $u_1 = a_2 b_2 + a_2 b_3 + a_3 b_2 \bmod p$, P_2 computes $u_2 = a_3 b_3 + a_1 b_3 + a_3 b_1 \bmod p$, and P_3 computes $u_3 = a_1 b_1 + a_1 b_2 + a_2 b_1 \bmod p$.
3. The players use Protocol Secure Addition to compute the sum $u_1 + u_2 + u_3 \bmod p$ securely, where P_i uses u_i as input.

---

if there is mutual interest. However, if, for instance, Alice is not interested, she will choose $a = 0$, and in this case, she learns *nothing new* from the protocol. To see why, notice that security of the protocol implies that the only (possibly) new information Alice will learn is the result $ab \bmod p$. But she already knows that the result will be 0! In particular, she does not learn whether Bob was interested or not, so Bob is safe from embarrassment. By a symmetric argument, this is, of course, also the case for Alice.

This argument assumes, of course, that both players choose their inputs honestly according to their real interests. In the following section we discuss what happens if players do not follow the instructions and what we can do about the problems resulting from this.

From Protocol Secure Multiplication, we see that if Alice and Bob play the roles of P_1 and P_2, respectively, they just need to find a third party to help them to do the multiplication securely. Note that this third party is not a *completely trusted* third party of the kind we discussed earlier: he or she does not learn anything about a or b other than $ab \bmod p$. Alice and Bob do have to trust, however, that the third party does not share his or her information with Bob or with Alice.

It is an obvious question whether one can do secure multiplication such that *only* Alice and Bob have to be involved? The answer turns out to be yes, but then information-theoretic security is not possible, as we shall see. Instead, one has to use solutions based on cryptography. Such solutions can always be broken if one party has enough computing power, but this is an issue with virtually all the cryptographic techniques used in practice.

For completeness, we remark that Alice and Bob's problem is a special case of the so-called matchmaking problem that has somewhat more serious applications than secure dating. Consider a set of companies where each company has a set of other companies it would prefer to do business with. We want each pair of companies to find out whether there is mutual interest, but without forcing companies to reveal their strategy by announcing their interests in public.

EXERCISE 1.1 Consider the third party helping Alice and Bob to do secure multiplication. Show that the Protocol Secure Multiplication is indeed insecure if the third party reveals what he sees in the protocol to Alice or Bob.

EXERCISE 1.2 We have used replicated secret sharing, where each player receives two numbers in $\mathbb{Z}_p$, even though only one secret number is shared. This was done so that we would be able to do both secure addition and secure multiplication, but for secure addition only, something simpler can be done. Use the principle of writing the secret as a sum of random numbers to design a secret-sharing scheme for any number of parties, where each party gets as his or her share only a single number in $\mathbb{Z}_p$. Use your scheme to design a protocol for secure addition. How many players can go together and pool their information before the protocol becomes insecure?

EXERCISE 1.3 You may have asked yourself why Protocol Secure Multiplication uses Protocol Secure Addition as a subroutine. Why not just announce u_1, u_2, and u_3 and add them to get the result? The reason is that this would reveal too much information. Show that if P_1 was given u_2, he or she could – in some cases – compute P_2's input b. What is the probability that he or she will succeed?

1.3.3 What if Players Do Not Follow Instructions?

Until now we assumed that players always do what they are supposed to. But this is not always a reasonable assumption, since a party may have an interest in doing something different from what he or she is instructed to do.

There are two fundamentally different ways in which players could deviate from expected behavior: First, they could choose their inputs in a way different from what was expected when the protocol was designed. Second, while executing the protocol, they could do something different from what the protocol instructs them to do. We will consider the two issues separately.

Choice of Inputs

Consider the matchmaking application from earlier as an example. Let us assume that Alice is not really interested in Bob. We argued earlier that because her input should then be 0, the output is always 0, and she does not learn whether Bob was interested. The reader may have noticed that there seems to be a way Alice could cheat Bob if she is willing to choose an input that does not represent her actual interests: she could *pretend* to be interested by choosing $a = 1$, in which case the output will be $ab \bmod p = b$, so she now learns Bob's input and breaks his privacy.

A moment's thought will convince the reader that there is no way we could possibly solve this issue by designing a more secure protocol: whatever the protocol is, a player can, of course, always choose to execute it with any input he or she wants to. Because this book is about protocol design, this issue of choice of inputs is out of scope for us.

Therefore, if Bob is worried that Alice might behave as we just described, the only answer we can give is that then he should not play the game at all! If he goes ahead, this has to be based on an assumption that Alice (as well as he himself) has an interest in choosing inputs in a "reasonable way." A possible justification for such an assumption might be that if Alice really thinks Bob is a looser, then the prospect of being stuck with him the rest of the night should be daunting enough to make her choose her input according to her actual preference!

More seriously (and generally), to do secure computation, we have to assume that players have an incentive to provide inputs that will lead to a "meaningful" result they would like to learn. If one can describe and quantify these incentives, it is sometimes possible to analyze what will happen using a different mathematical discipline called game theory, but that is out of scope for this book.

Deviation from the Protocol

Regardless of how the inputs are chosen, it might be that deviating from the protocol could enable a player to learn more information than he or she was supposed to get, or it could allow the player to force the computation to give a wrong result. For instance, in this way the player could appoint himself or herself the winner of an auction at a low price. This is, of course, undesirable, but (in contrast to the issue of input choice) this is indeed an issue we can handle.

One solution is to add mechanisms to the protocol that ensure that any deviation from the protocol will be detected. To exemplify this, we look at Protocol Secure Addition.

In Protocol Secure Addition we first ask each party to distribute shares of their secret. Looking at P_1, we ask it to pick shares $r_{1,1}, r_{1,2}, r_{1,3}$ such that $x_1 = r_{1,1} + r_{1,2} + r_{1,3} \mod p$ and then send $r_{1,1}, r_{1,3}$ to P_2 and send $r_{1,1}, r_{1,2}$ to P_3. Here there are two ways to deviate.

First, P_1 could pick $r'_{1,1}, r'_{1,2}, r'_{1,3}$ such that $x_1 \neq r'_{1,1} + r'_{1,2} + r'_{1,3} \mod p$. This is not a problem because it just corresponds to having used the input $x'_1 \overset{\text{def}}{=} r'_{1,1} + r'_{1,2} + r'_{1,3} \mod p$, and as mentioned, we cannot (and should not) prevent P_1 from being able to pick any input it desires. The second way to deviate is that P_1 could send $r_{1,1}, r_{1,3}$ to P_2 and send $r'_{1,1}, r_{1,2}$ to P_3 with $r'_{1,1} \neq r_{1,1}$. This is more serious because now the input x_1 of P_1 is not well defined. This might or might not lead to an attack, but it is at least a clear deviation from the protocol. There is, however, a simple way to catch this deviation: when P_2 and P_3 receive their shares from P_1, then P_2 sends its value of $r_{1,1}$ to P_3 and P_3 sends its own value of $r_{1,1}$ to P_2. Then they check that they hold the same value. In a similar way, P_1 and P_3 can check that P_2 sends consistent shares, and P_1 and P_2 can check that P_3 sends consistent shares. In general, having players reveal more information to each other could make a protocol insecure. However, in this case, no new information leaks because a player only send information which the receiver should already have.

After the sharing phase, we then ask the parties to add their shares and make the sums public. Looking again at P_1, we ask it to compute s_2 and s_3 and make these public. Here P_1 might deviate by sending, for example, $s'_2 \neq s_2$. This could lead to a wrong result, $v = s_1 + s'_2 + s_3 \mod p$. Note, however, that P_3 will compute s_1 and s_2 and make these public. So both P_1 and P_3 are supposed to make s_2 public. Hence the players can simply check that P_1 and P_3 make the same value of s_2 public. And similarly, they can check that the two versions of s_1 and the two versions of s_3 are identical.

This means that Protocol Secure Addition has the following property: if any single party does not do what he or she is supposed to, the other two players will always be able to detect this. This idea of checking other players to ensure that the protocol is followed is something we will see many times in the following.

1.3.4 Toward General Solutions

We have now seen how to do secure multiplication and addition of numbers in $\mathbb{Z}_p$ – although under various rather strong assumptions. We have assumed that players always follow the protocol (although we have seen a partial answer on how to deal with deviations). Furthermore, we have only considered the harm that a *single* player can do to the protocol and not what happens if several players go together and try, for instance, to compute information on the other players' inputs.

Nevertheless, it is well known that multiplication and addition modulo a prime is sufficient to efficiently simulate any desired computation. This implies, on a very fuzzy and intuitive level, that we can hope to be able to do *any* computation securely if that computation was feasible in the first place – at least under certain assumptions.

It turns out that this is indeed the case, but of course, lots of questions remain. To name a few: How do we define security in a precise way? How do we scale solutions from three players to any number of players? What if players do not all follow the protocol? If several players pool their information to learn more than they were supposed to, how many such players can we tolerate and still have a secure protocol? On the following pages, we will arrive at answers to these questions.

2

Preliminaries

In this chapter we introduce some basic notions used throughout this book, such as random variables, families of random variables, interactive systems, and the statistical and computational indistinguishability of these objects. The primary purpose of this chapter is to fix and make precise our notation.

We use standard terminology from probability theory such as probability distributions, independence, and random variables. We will later introduce only a few specific notions that we need in the following and will assume that the reader is familiar with the remaining basic concepts.

A reader who has followed a course in basic cryptography will probably be familiar with most of the notions covered in this chapter but is encouraged to do a quick reading of the chapter to get familiar with the book's notation. A possible exception is the material on interactive systems. However, this part is not used until Chapter 4, so the reader unfamiliar with interactive agents and interactive systems can skip this material for now and later come back and read the part needed to understand Chapter 4.

2.1 Basic Notation

Let $\mathbb{F}$ be any ring. Vectors are given in boldface. If $\mathbf{a}$ is a vector in $\mathbb{F}^n$, then its coordinate vector is denoted $(a_1, \ldots, a_n)$. In expressions involving vectors and matrices, a vector $\mathbf{a}$ is considered to be a column vector. Let $\mathbf{a} = (a_1, \ldots, a_n) \in \mathbb{F}^n$, $\mathbf{b} = (b_1, \ldots, b_n) \in \mathbb{F}^n$, and $\alpha \in \mathbb{F}$. We use the following standard notation from linear algebra:

$$\mathbf{a} + \mathbf{b} = (a_1 + b_1, \ldots, a_n + b_n) \tag{2.1}$$

$$\alpha \mathbf{a} = (\alpha a_1, \ldots, \alpha a_n) \tag{2.2}$$

$$\mathbf{a} \cdot \mathbf{b} = \sum_{i=1}^{n} a_i b_i \tag{2.3}$$

$$\mathbf{a} * \mathbf{b} = (a_1 b_1, \ldots, a_n b_n) \tag{2.4}$$

The operator $\cdot$ is called the inner product, and $*$ is called the Schur product, or entrywise multiplication.

We use capitals to denote matrices. If A is a matrix, we use a_{ij} to denote the entry in row i, column j. We use $\mathbf{a}_i$ and $\mathbf{a}_{i*}$ to denote row i of matrix A and $\mathbf{a}_{*j}$ to denote column j of A. We use $A^\top$ for the matrix transpose and AB for matrix multiplication. For a matrix A, we write $\ker A$ for the kernel of the map defined by its columns.

For a nonnegative integer n, we use $\{0,1\}^n$ to denote the set of bit strings of length n. We let $\{0,1\}^* = \cup_{i=0}^{\infty}\{0,1\}^n$. We use $\{0,1\}^{\infty}$ to denote the set of all infinitely long bit strings.

We recall some basic terminology from probability theory. The purpose is not to give an introduction to probability theory, for such an introduction see, for instance, Hoel, Port, and Stone [110]. We only need to fix the terminology we use in this book.

A probability space is a triple (S, F, Pr), where S is a set called the sample space and F is a set called the event space and $\text{Pr} : F \to [0,1]$ is a probability measure. We call each element $E \in F$ an event and require that $E \subseteq S$. We call $\text{Pr}[E]$ the probability of the event E. We require that F is a σ-algebra, which just means that if $E \in F$, then $S \setminus E \in F$ and if $E_i \in F$ for $i = 1, \ldots, \infty$, then $\cup_{i=1}^{\infty} E_i \in F$. We require that $\text{Pr}[S] = 1$ and $\text{Pr}\left[\cup_{i=1}^{\infty} E_i\right] = \sum_{i=1}^{\infty} \text{Pr}[E_i]$ when the events E_i are pairwise disjoint. We call the last requirement countable additivity.

In this book, when S is a countable set we always assume that F is the set of all subsets of S, which means that all $E \subseteq S$ are events. In that case it always holds that $\text{Pr}[E] = \sum_{e \in E} \text{Pr}[e]$, where we use $\text{Pr}[e]$ to denote $\text{Pr}[\{e\}]$. Therefore, when S is countable, the probability space is fully specified by just giving S and $\text{Pr}[e]$ for each $e \in S$.

If S is finite we use the uniform distribution on S to denote the probability space with $\text{Pr}[e] = \frac{1}{|S|}$ for all $e \in S$. We use U_n to denote the uniform distribution on $\{0,1\}^n$. When the sample space S is a finite set, we will assume that $\text{Pr}[\cdot]$ is the probability measure given by the uniform distribution on S, unless explicitly stated otherwise. In that case, the probability space is fully specified by just giving S.

A random variable is a function $X : S \to A$ from the sample space S into a set A called the range. It is required that it holds for all $x \in A$ that $X^{-1}(x) \in F$, where $X^{-1}(x) = \{e \in S | X(e) = x\}$. For all $x \in A$ we use $X = x$ to denote the event $X^{-1}(x)$. This allows us to write $\text{Pr}[X = x]$ instead of the more cumbersome $\text{Pr}\left[X^{-1}(x)\right]$. If C is a countable subset of A, then $X \in C$ is used to denote the event $\cup_{x \in C} X^{-1}(x)$. It follows from countable additivity that $\text{Pr}[X \in C] = \sum_{x \in C} \text{Pr}[X = x]$.

The support of a random variable X is $\{x \in A \,|\, \text{Pr}[X = x] > 0\}$.

We use special notation for random variables which are predicates, that is, where the range is $\{\bot, \top\}$, where $\top$ denotes *true* and $\bot$ denotes *false*. In that case we use P to denote the event $P = \top$. This in particular means that $\text{Pr}[P] = \text{Pr}\left[P^{-1}(\top)\right]$. As an example, if $S = \{1,2,3,4,5,6\}$ and we consider the uniform distribution on S and $P : S \to \{\bot, \top\}$ is given by $P(1) = P(2) = \top$ and $P(x) = \bot$ otherwise, then $\text{Pr}[P] = \frac{1}{3}$.

We use standard shorthand notation to build random variables from other random variables. As an example, if $X : S \to A$ and $Y : S \to B$ are random variables and $g : A \times B \to C$ for a discrete set C, then we use $g(X, Y)$ to denote the random variable with $g(A, B) : S \to C$ and $g(X, Y)(s) = g(X(s), Y(s))$. As an example we have that $\text{Pr}[X = X] = 1$.

If Z is a variable or expression denoting a random variable, then we use $Y \leftarrow Z$ to denote that we assign the the random variable denoted by Z to the variable Y. Note that if Z denotes a random variable, it just denotes some function $S \to A$. It is this function we assign to Y such that Y now denotes the same random variable as Z. As an example, if we write that $Y \leftarrow 2 \cdot X^2$, then $\text{Pr}\left[X^2 = Y/2\right] = 1$.

DEFINITION 2.1 (STATISTICAL DISTANCE) *Let X_0 an X_1 be two random variables defined on the same probability space and with common range D. We call*

$$\delta(X_0, X_1) \stackrel{\text{def}}{=} \frac{1}{2} \sum_{d \in D} |\Pr[X_0 = d] - \Pr[X_1 = d]|$$

the statistical distance between X_0 and X_1.[1]

Statistical distance is also known as *total variation distance*.

2.2 Algorithms

We use probabilistic Turing machines (see Martin [138]) as our model of algorithmic computation. Specifically, when we say that A is an algorithm, we mean that it is a Turing machine with input alphabet $\{0, 1\}$ and a random tape with tape alphabet $\{0, 1\}$. If an algorithm takes several inputs, they are placed on separate input tapes. Recall that all tapes of Turing machines are infinite.

For inputs $x_1, \ldots, x_t \in \{0, 1\}^*$ and a random tape $r \in \{0, 1\}^\infty$, we use the notation $y = A(x_1, \ldots, x_t; r)$ to denote the output produced by running the algorithm A on the inputs $x_1, \ldots, x_t$ and random tape r. If A does not terminate on these inputs, we let $y = \bot$. We also need to run algorithms on finite random strings $r \in \{0, 1\}^n$. This means that the first n symbols of the random tape of A hold r and that the remaining symbols are all the empty symbol. If A terminates with output y without having read beyond position n on the random tape, then let $A(x_1, \ldots, x_t; r) = y$. Otherwise, let $A(x_1, \ldots, x_t; r) = \bot$; that is, now $\bot$ signals that A did not have enough randomness on the random tape or that A did not terminate.

We also want to be able to talk about random executions of an algorithm, that is, the result of running the algorithm with a uniformly random tape. For this purpose, we consider the random variable $r \mapsto A(x_1, \ldots, x_t; r)$ defined on the probability space U_n. This models an execution of A on a uniformly random $r \in \{0, 1\}^n$. We use $\Pr_n[\cdot]$ to denote the associated probability function. Note that

$$\Pr_n[A(x_1, \ldots, x_t) = y] = \frac{|\{r \in \{0, 1\}^n \mid A(x_1, \ldots, x_t; r) = y\}|}{2^n}$$

We extend this notion to a uniformly random tape $r \in \{0, 1\}^\infty$. This is more tricky than it might appear at first because $\{0, 1\}^\infty$ is an uncountable set, and there is no uniform distribution on $\{0, 1\}^\infty$ that assigns meaningful probabilities to all subsets of $\{0, 1\}^\infty$. Why this is the case and how to resolve it would divert us into measure theory. What is important is that we can define a probability space U_∞ with sample space $\{0, 1\}^\infty$ that behaves according to our intuition of running Turing machines with an unbounded supply of uniformly random bits.[2] Let $\Pr[\cdot]$ be the probability function defined by this probability

---

[1] Note that if the range D is countable infinite, this definition is only well defined if the sum converges. This is obviously the case because the series $\sum_{d \in D} \frac{1}{2} |\Pr[X_0 = d] - \Pr[X_1 = d]|$ is monotonously increasing and upper bounded by 1. Using this observation, it is easy to see that the value of the sum is the same, no matter the order of the terms. This, in turn, implies that Eq. (2.7), on characterization of statistical distance in terms of distinguishing advantage, holds also for countably-infinite ranges.

[2] We sketch the probability space. The reader with basic knowledge of probability spaces should be able to verify that it is indeed a probability space. For all $r \in \{0, 1\}^*$, let $E_r = \{r\} \times \{0, 1\}^\infty$. This is the event that "the $|r|$ first bits of the random tape are exactly the bits of r." Define the probability of this event to be $\Pr[E_r] = 2^{-|r|}$. The events of the probability space U_∞ are all E_r for $r \in \{0, 1\}^*$ and the sets obtained by taking closure under

space. If for all $x_1,\ldots,x_t \in \{0,1\}^*$ we let

$$A(x_1,\ldots,x_t) : \{0,1\}^\infty \to \{0,1\}^* \cup \{\bot\}$$

be the random variable $r \mapsto A(x_1,\ldots,x_t;r)$, then for all $y \in \{0,1\}^* \cup \{\bot\}$ it holds that $\{r \in \{0,1\}^\infty \mid A(x_1,\ldots,x_t;r) = y\}$ is an event. Furthermore, if A never reads beyond position n on the random tape on the inputs $x_1,\ldots,x_t$, then

$$\Pr[A(x_1,\ldots,x_t) = y] = \Pr_n[A(x_1,\ldots,x_t) = y]$$

Furthermore, it always holds that

$$\Pr[A(x_1,\ldots,x_t) = y] = \lim_{n\to\infty} \Pr_n[A(x_1,\ldots,x_t) = y]$$

We use $A(x_1,\ldots,x_t) : \{0,1\}^\infty \to \{0,1\}^* \cup \{\bot\}$ to denote the random variable described earlier. *For simplicity, all algorithms are tacitly assumed to terminate with probability* 1; that is, for all $x_1,\ldots,x_t \in \{0,1\}^*$, we have $\Pr[A(x_1,\ldots,x_t) = \bot] = 0$, making $A(x_1,\ldots,x_t)$ a random variable with support contained in $\{0,1\}^*$.

All objects on which we run algorithms in this book are from countable sets, such as integers or group elements from finite groups. We will tacitly assume that for all these objects, a unique representation as bit strings has been fixed, that is, a surjection into $\{0,1\}^*$ that can be computed efficiently in both directions, for instance, standard binary representation of positive integers. It is this representation on that we compute, and it is this representation that is sent between entities in protocols.

Note that because our Turing machines have unbounded input tapes over alphabet $\{0,1\}$ and all structures of our interest can be represented as bit strings, we can run all our algorithms on all discrete structures of interest. We call an algorithm that always gives an output in $\{0,1\}$ a distinguisher; that is, for all inputs $x_1,\ldots,x_t \in \{0,1\}^*$, it holds that $\Pr[A(x_1,\ldots,x_t) \in \{0,1\}] = 1$. If X is a random variable with range $D \subseteq \{0,1\}^*$ and A is an algorithm, then $A(X)$ denotes the random variable defined by the following process:

1. Let $x \leftarrow X$.
2. Let $a \leftarrow A(x)$.
3. Output a.

The notation extends naturally to the case of algorithms taking several inputs. We shall sometimes also use the notation $A(X)$ for random variables that do not have range $\{0,1\}^*$. In all such cases, a tacit representation of the range of X as bit strings is given, and A is run on the representation of X in $\{0,1\}^*$.

We call two random variables X_0 and X_1 with common range D disjoint random variables if it holds for all $x \in D$ that either $\Pr[X_0 = x] = 0$ or $\Pr[X_1 = x] = 0$. That is, we call them *disjoint* iff there is no element in the range that they can both output.

PROPOSITION 2.2 *Let A be any algorithm, and let X_0, X_1, X_2 be any random variables with common range D. Then the following properties hold:*

1. $\delta(X_0,X_1) \in [0,1]$.
2. $\delta(X_0,X_1) = 0$ *iff* $\Pr[X_0 = x] = \Pr[X_1 = x]$ *for all $x \in D$.*

---

complement in $\{0,1\}^\infty$ and union of countably many sets. The probability function is extended by $\Pr[\bar{E}] = 1 - \Pr[E]$ and countable additivity.

3. $\delta(X_0, X_1) = 1$ iff X_0 and X_1 are disjoint.
4. $\delta(X_0, X_1) = \delta(X_1, X_0)$.
5. $\delta(X_0, X_2) \le \delta(X_0, X_1) + \delta(X_1, X_2)$.
6. $\delta((X_0, X_2), (X_1, X_2)) \ge \delta(X_0, X_1)$ with equality if X_2 is independent of X_0 and X_1. Note that this makes sense only if X_0, X_1, X_2 are defined on the same probability space.
7. $\delta(A(X_0), A(X_1)) \le \delta(X_0, X_1)$.

These properties, in particular, mean that statistical distance is a metric on random variables with the same probability space and the same range. The last property shows that computation cannot make statistical distance increase.

EXERCISE 2.1 Prove Proposition 2.2.

2.2.1 Distinguishing Advantage of an Algorithm

For an algorithm A and two random variables X_0 and X_1, we need a measure of the ability of A to distinguish between X_0 and X_1. For this purpose, we play a game in which we give A either a sample from X_0 or a sample from X_1 and then ask it to guess from which random variable it received a sample. We can assume without loss of generality that A provides its guess by outputting a bit; that is, we assume that A is a distinguisher. The distinguishing game runs as follows:

1. Sample a uniformly random bit $b \leftarrow \{0, 1\}$.
2. Let $x \leftarrow X_b$.
3. Let $c \leftarrow A(x)$.

We think of c as A's guess at b. A fixed guess, $c = 0$, say, will allow A to be correct with probability $\frac{1}{2}$ as $b = 0$ with probability $\frac{1}{2}$. When we measure how good A is at distinguishing X_0 from X_1, we are therefore only interested in how much better than $\frac{1}{2}$ it does. For technical reasons, we consider the absolute value; that is, we use the measure $|\Pr[c = b] - \frac{1}{2}|$. Note that this is a value between 0 and $\frac{1}{2}$. Again, for technical reasons, we prefer the measure to be between 0 and 1, so we scale by a factor of 2, and we get the measure $2|\Pr[c = b] - \frac{1}{2}|$, which we call the advantage of A.

Note that if A guesses b correctly with probability 1, then $\Pr[c = b] = 1$, and the advantage will be 1. If A makes a random guess, a fixed guess or any other guess, independent of b, then $\Pr[c = b] = \frac{1}{2}$, and the advantage will be 0. We therefore think of the advantage of A as measuring how well A can distinguish X_0 and X_1, with 1 meaning *perfectly* and 0 meaning *not at all*.

Before we make a formal definition, it is convenient to rewrite the advantage. For this purpose, observe that because A always outputs a bit $c \in \{0, 1\}$, we have

$$\Pr[c = b] = \frac{1}{2} \Pr[c = b | b = 0] + \frac{1}{2} \Pr[c = b | b = 1]$$

$$= \frac{1}{2} (\Pr[c = 0 | b = 0] + \Pr[c = 1 | b = 1])$$

$$= \frac{1}{2}(\Pr[A(X_0) = 0] + \Pr[A(X_1) = 1])$$

$$= \frac{1}{2}(\Pr[A(X_0) = 0] + (1 - \Pr[A(X_1) = 0]))$$

$$= \frac{1}{2} + \frac{1}{2}(\Pr[A(X_0) = 0] - \Pr[A(X_1) = 0])$$

where the first equation is just an application of the law of total probability, and $\Pr[A(X_1) = 1] = 1 - \Pr[A(X_1) = 0]$ because A outputs either 0 or 1. This means that

$$2\left|\Pr[c = b] - \frac{1}{2}\right| = |\Pr[A(X_0) = 0] - \Pr[A(X_1) = 0]| \tag{2.5}$$

We can thus think of the advantage as the difference between the probability that A guesses 0 when it sees X_0 and the probability that A guesses 0 when it sees X_1. It is usual to use the right-hand side of Eq. (2.5) for defining the advantage.

DEFINITION 2.3 (ADVANTAGE) *Let X_0 and X_1 be two random variables. Let A be any distinguisher. The advantage of A in distinguishing X_0 and X_1 is*

$$Adv_A(X_0, X_1) \stackrel{\text{def}}{=} |\Pr[A(X_0) = 0] - \Pr[A(X_1) = 0]|$$

The reason why the right-hand side of Eq. (2.5) is typically used for the formal definition is that it is easily related to the statistical distance between the random variables $A(X_0)$ and $A(X_1)$, which is sometimes convenient when working with the notion of advantage. Note that

$$\delta(A(X_0), A(X_1)) = \frac{1}{2} \sum_{c=0,1} |\Pr[A(X_0) = c] - \Pr[A(X_1) = c]|$$

$$= \frac{1}{2}(|\Pr[A(X_0) = 0] - \Pr[A(X_1) = 0]| + |\Pr[A(X_0) = 1] - \Pr[A(X_1) = 1]|)$$

$$= \frac{1}{2}(|\Pr[A(X_0) = 0] - \Pr[A(X_1) = 0]| + |(1 - \Pr[A(X_0) = 0])$$

$$- (1 - \Pr[A(X_1) = 0])|)$$

$$= \frac{1}{2}(|\Pr[A(X_0) = 0] - \Pr[A(X_1) = 0]| + |\Pr[A(X_1) = 0] - \Pr[A(X_0) = 0]|)$$

$$= \frac{1}{2}(|\Pr[A(X_0) = 0] - \Pr[A(X_1) = 0]| + |\Pr[A(X_0) = 0] - \Pr[A(X_1) = 0]|)$$

$$= |\Pr[A(X_0) = 0] - \Pr[A(X_1) = 0]|$$

This shows that

$$Adv_A(X_0, X_1) = \delta(A(X_0), A(X_1)) \tag{2.6}$$

We can therefore think of the advantage of a distinguisher A as the statistical distance between its outputs when it gets X_0 as input and when it gets X_1 as input. It is clear that if we allowed A to output an arbitrarily long bit string, then it could simply output its input. In that case, $A(X_0) = X_0$ and $A(X_1) = X_1$, and we would have $Adv_A(X_0, X_1) = \delta(X_0, X_1)$. That is, the advantage would simply be the statistical distance. We have, however, required that

A outputs a single bit, which means that in general the advantage $\text{Adv}_A(X_0,X_1)$ could be smaller than the statistical distance $\delta(X_0,X_1)$.

The relation between advantage and statistical distance is convenient because it tells us that advantage inherits all the nice properties of statistical distance. In particular, Proposition 2.2 directly allows us to conclude the following:

COROLLARY 2.4 *Let A be any distinguisher, and let X_0,X_1,X_2 be any random variables. Then the following properties hold:*

1. $Adv_A(X_0,X_1) \in [0,1]$.
2. $Adv_A(X_0,X_1) = 0$ *if X_0 and X_1 are identically distributed.*
3. $Adv_A(X_0,X_1) = Adv_A(X_1,X_0)$.
4. $Adv_A(X_0,X_2) \le Adv_A(X_0,X_1) + Adv_A(X_1,X_2)$.
5. $Adv_A(X_0,X_1) \le \delta(X_0,X_1)$.

We have just seen that advantage can be phrased in terms of a statistical distance. Conversely, statistical distance can be phrased in terms of advantage. It can be shown that

$$\delta(X_0,X_1) = \sup_A \text{Adv}_A(X_0,X_1) \tag{2.7}$$

where the supremum is taken over all possible distinguishers. To show this, one considers the particular maximum likelihood distinguisher A_{ML}, which on input x outputs $c = 0$ if $\Pr[X_0 = x] \ge \Pr[X_1 = x]$ and otherwise outputs $c = 1$. One can argue that $\delta(A_{\text{ML}}(X_0),A_{\text{ML}}(X_1)) = \delta(X_0,X_1)$, which establishes Eq. (2.7) via Eq. (2.6).

EXERCISE 2.2 Prove Eq. (2.7) by working out the details of the argument following that equation.

2.2.2 Distinguishing Advantage

The notion of an algorithm distinguishing random variables can be extended to classes of algorithms simply by considering the best distinguisher in the class.

DEFINITION 2.5 (ADVANTAGE OF A CLASS OF ALGORITHMS) *Let X_0 and X_1 be two random variables. Let $\mathcal{A}$ be any class of distinguishers. The advantage of $\mathcal{A}$ in distinguishing X_0 and X_1 is*

$$Adv_{\mathcal{A}}(X_0,X_1) \stackrel{\text{def}}{=} \sup_{A \in \mathcal{A}} Adv_A(X_0,X_1)$$

From Eq. (2.7) we know that $\delta(X_0,X_1) = \text{Adv}_{\mathcal{A}}(X_0,X_1)$ when $\mathcal{A}$ is the class of all algorithms. In general, $\text{Adv}_{\mathcal{A}}$ can be much smaller than the statistical distance.

2.3 Families of Random Variables

By a family of random variables, we mean a function X that assigns a random variable to each nonnegative integer. That is, for each $\kappa \in \mathbb{N}$, $X(\kappa)$ is a random variable. We write a family of random variables as

$$X = \{X(\kappa)\}_{\kappa \in \mathbb{N}}$$

If $X = \{X(\kappa)\}_{\kappa \in \mathbb{N}}$ is a family of random variables and A is a two-input algorithm that takes the security parameter κ as its first input, then we let

$$A(X) \stackrel{\text{def}}{=} \{A(\kappa, X(\kappa))\}_{\kappa \in \mathbb{N}}$$

That is, $A(X)$ is again a family of random variables, and the random variable associated with κ is $A(\kappa, X(\kappa))$, which is defined by first sampling $x \leftarrow X(\kappa)$ and then running $A(\kappa, x)$ to define the output of $A(\kappa, X(\kappa))$.

2.3.1 Statistical Indistinguishability

We will say that two families of random variables X_0 and X_1 are statistically indistinguishable if the statistical distance between $X_0(\kappa)$ and $X_1(\kappa)$ tends to 0 very quickly as κ tends to infinity. By "very quickly," we mean that the statistical distance tends to 0 faster than any inverse polynomial; that is, it is a so-called negligible function, as defined next.

DEFINITION 2.6 (NEGLIGIBLE FUNCTION) *We call a function $\delta : \mathbb{N} \to [0,1]$ negligible if for all $c \in \mathbb{N}$ there exists $\kappa_c \in \mathbb{N}$ such that $\delta(\kappa) \leq \kappa^{-c}$ for all $\kappa \geq \kappa_c$.*

If an expression has several parameters, we use the terminology negligible in κ to specify that it is the expression as a function of κ that is negligible.

DEFINITION 2.7 (STATISTICAL INDISTINGUISHABILITY) *Let X_0 and X_1 be random variables with the same probability space and the same range. We say that X_0 and X_1 are statistically indistinguishable, written $X_0 \stackrel{\text{stat}}{\equiv} X_1$, if $\delta(X_0(\kappa), X_1(\kappa))$ is negligible in κ. If X_0 and X_1 are not statistically indistinguishable, we write $X_0 \stackrel{\text{stat}}{\not\equiv} X_1$.*

We say that X_0 and X_1 are perfectly indistinguishable, written $X_0 \stackrel{\text{perf}}{\equiv} X_1$, if $\delta(X_0(\kappa), X_1(\kappa)) = 0$ for all κ. If X_0 and X_1 are not perfectly indistinguishable, we write $X_0 \stackrel{\text{perf}}{\not\equiv} X_1$.

Two families of random variables that are perfectly indistinguishable cannot be distinguished by looking at their output because they make the same output with the same probability. Two families of random variables that are statistically indistinguishable are very close to being perfectly indistinguishable – by moving a negligible amount of probability mass on their output distributions, they can be made to be perfectly indistinguishable – and we therefore think of them as being essentially impossible to distinguish by looking at their output. We formalize this later.

When working with indistinguishability of families of random variables, it is convenient to know that the notion is an equivalence relation and preserved under computation.

PROPOSITION 2.8 *Let A be any algorithm, and let X_0, X_1, X_2 be any families of random variables. Then the following properties hold:*

1. $X_0 \stackrel{\text{stat}}{\equiv} X_0$.
2. *If $X_0 \stackrel{\text{stat}}{\equiv} X_1$, then $X_1 \stackrel{\text{stat}}{\equiv} X_0$.*
3. *If $X_0 \stackrel{\text{stat}}{\equiv} X_1$ and $X_1 \stackrel{\text{stat}}{\equiv} X_2$, then $X_0 \stackrel{\text{stat}}{\equiv} X_2$.*
4. *If $X_0 \stackrel{\text{stat}}{\equiv} X_1$, then $A(X_0) \stackrel{\text{stat}}{\equiv} A(X_1)$.*

The same properties hold for $\stackrel{\text{perf}}{\equiv}$.

EXERCISE 2.3 Prove Proposition 2.8 using Proposition 2.2.

2.3.2 Distinguishing Advantage of a Class of Algorithms

We now look at the advantage of an algorithm A in distinguishing two families of random variables $X_0 = \{X_0(\kappa)\}_{\kappa \in \mathbb{N}}$ and $X_1 = \{X_0(\kappa)\}_{\kappa \in \mathbb{N}}$. We are interested in how well A can distinguish $X_0(\kappa)$ and $X_1(\kappa)$ as κ grows. For this purpose, we define a function

$$\mathrm{Adv}_A(X_0, X_1) : \mathbb{N} \to [0, 1]$$

that for each $\kappa \in \mathbb{N}$ measures how well A distinguishes $X_0(\kappa)$ and $X_1(\kappa)$. That is,

$$\mathrm{Adv}_A(X_0, X_1)(\kappa) \stackrel{\mathrm{def}}{=} \mathrm{Adv}_{A(\kappa, \cdot)}(X_0(\kappa), X_1(\kappa))$$

where $A(\kappa, \cdot)$ is the algorithm that takes one input x and runs $A(\kappa, x)$.

We say that A statistically cannot distinguish X_0 and X_1 if $\mathrm{Adv}_{A(\kappa, \cdot)}(X_0(\kappa), X_1(\kappa))$ is negligible in κ. We say that A perfectly cannot distinguish X_0 and X_1 if $\mathrm{Adv}_{A(\kappa, \cdot)}(X_0(\kappa), X_1(\kappa)) = 0$ for all κ.

EXERCISE 2.4 Show that $\mathrm{Adv}_A(X_0, X_1)$ is negligible in κ iff $A(X_0) \stackrel{\mathrm{stat}}{\equiv} A(X_1)$ and that $\mathrm{Adv}_A(X_0, X_1)(\kappa) = 0$ for all κ iff $A(X_0) \stackrel{\mathrm{perf}}{\equiv} A(X_1)$.

The preceding exercise shows that we really do not need a notion of distinguishing advantage between families of random variables X_0 and X_1. We can simply work with statistical distance between families of random variables $A(X_0)$ and $A(X_1)$. It turns out that it is more convenient to work directly with statistical distance, so this is what we will do. For intuition it is, however, convenient to bear in mind that when A is a distinguisher (an algorithm outputting a single bit), then $A(X_0) \stackrel{\mathrm{perf}}{\equiv} A(X_1)$ essentially means that A perfectly cannot distinguish X_0 and X_1 and $A(X_0) \stackrel{\mathrm{stat}}{\equiv} A(X_1)$ means that A only has a negligible advantage in distinguishing X_0 and X_1.

Typically, in cryptography, we are not interested in whether one *specific* algorithm can distinguish two families of random variables. The distinguisher is typically modeling the adversary, which can have any behavior. We are therefore more interested in whether *some* algorithm can distinguish two families of random variables. We do, however, often restrict the adversary to performing some upper bound on realistic computation, such as at most 2^{100} basic operations. For this purpose and others, it is convenient to have a notion of indistinguishability for some *class* of distinguishers.

DEFINITION 2.9 (INDISTINGUISHABILITY BY A CLASS OF ALGORITHMS) *Let* $X_0 = \{X_0(\kappa)\}_{\kappa \in \mathbb{N}}$ *and* $X_1 = \{X_1(\kappa)\}_{\kappa \in \mathbb{N}}$ *be families of random variables, and let* $\mathcal{A}$ *be any class of distinguishers. We say that* X_0 *and* X_1 *are indistinguishable by* $\mathcal{A}$ *if* $A(X_0) \stackrel{\mathrm{stat}}{\equiv} A(X_1)$ *for all* $A \in \mathcal{A}$. *We write this as*

$$X_0 \stackrel{\mathcal{A}}{\equiv} X_1$$

If $X_0 \stackrel{\mathcal{A}}{\equiv} X_1$, *where* $\mathcal{A}$ *is the class of all polytime algorithms, then we say that* X_0 *and* X_1 *are computationally indistinguishable and write*

$$X_0 \stackrel{\mathrm{comp}}{\equiv} X_1$$

If X_0 *and* X_1 *are not computationally indistinguishable, we write* $X_0 \stackrel{\mathrm{comp}}{\not\equiv} X_1$.

EXAMPLE 2.10 The following example shows that two families of random variables might be perfectly distinguishable in the statistical sense yet computationally *in*distinguishable.

Let (G, E, D) be a public-key encryption scheme. On input of the security parameter κ, the key generator G generates a key pair $(pk, sk) \leftarrow G(\kappa)$, where pk is the public key and sk is the secret key, and κ specifies the desired security level of the key. On input of pk and a message m, the encryption algorithm outputs a ciphertext $C \leftarrow E_{pk}(m)$. Note the E is allowed to use internal randomness and that C depends on this randomness. On input C and sk, the decryption algorithm outputs a message $m \leftarrow D_{sk}(C)$. We require that $D_{sk}(C) = m$ when $C \leftarrow E_{pk}(m)$.

For $b \in \{0, 1\}$, let $X_b = \{X_b(\kappa)\}$, where $X_b(\kappa)$ is defined as follows: sample $(pk, sk) \leftarrow G(\kappa)$, samples $C \leftarrow E_{pk}(b)$, and let $X_b(\kappa) = (pk, C)$. In words, $X_b(\kappa)$ outputs a random public key and a random encryption of b using κ as the security level.

We first consider the statistical distance between X_0 and X_1. Because a given ciphertext C cannot be both an encryption of 0 and an encryption of 1, there is no value that both $X_0(\kappa)$ and $X_1(\kappa)$ could output; that is, they are disjoint random variables. By Proposition 2.2, this means that $\delta(X_0(\kappa), X_1(\kappa)) = 1$. This is, of course, trivial: the distinguisher is given (pk, C) and then simply checks whether C is an encryption of 0 or 1 and outputs the corresponding guess c. It might do this check by doing, for example, an exhaustive search for sk and then decrypting.

We then consider the "computational distance" between X_0 and X_1. For a public-key cryptosystem, a standard security notion is that of semantic security. Semantic secure cryptosystems are known to exist under a number of assumptions, such as the RSA assumption. The notion of semantic security essentially requires that no efficient algorithm can distinguish an encryption of 0 from an encryption of 1. Technically, this is defined by requiring that the distinguishing advantage of any polytime adversary is negligible in the security parameter. This directly implies that $X_0 \overset{\text{comp}}{\equiv} X_1$.

All in all, this shows that X_0 and X_1 have as large a statistical distance as possible, yet they are computationally indistinguishable. In particular, $X_0 \overset{\text{perf}}{\not\equiv} X_1$ and $X_0 \overset{\text{stat}}{\not\equiv} X_1$, yet $X_0 \overset{\text{comp}}{\equiv} X_1$. The explanation is that the statistical distance between X_0 and X_1 cannot be noticed by a polytime distinguisher. ∎

Let $\mathcal{A}$ be any class of algorithms. For any two algorithms A and B, let $A \circ B$ be the algorithm that runs as follows on input x:

1. Let $b \leftarrow B(x)$.
2. Let $a \leftarrow A(b)$.
3. Return a.

We let $\mathcal{A}^\circ$ be the class of algorithms B for which $A \circ B \subseteq \mathcal{A}$, by which we simply mean that it holds for all $A \in \mathcal{A}$ that $A \circ B \in \mathcal{A}$. In words, $\mathcal{A}^\circ$ are algorithms B for which it holds that if it is composed with an algorithm from $\mathcal{A}$, it is again an algorithm from $\mathcal{A}$. For example, if $\mathcal{A}$ is the set of all polytime algorithms, then $\mathcal{A}^\circ$ is also the class of all polytime algorithms.

THEOREM 2.11 *Let X_0 and X_1 be families of random variables, and let $\mathcal{A}$ be any class of distinguishers. Then the following properties hold:*

1. $X_0 \overset{\mathcal{A}}{\equiv} X_0$.
2. *If $X_0 \overset{\mathcal{A}}{\equiv} X_1$, then $X_1 \overset{\mathcal{A}}{\equiv} X_0$.*

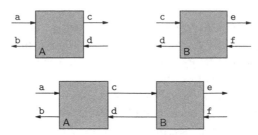

Figure 2.1 An interactive agent A with $\mathrm{In}(A) = \{\mathtt{a},\mathtt{d}\}$ and $\mathrm{Out}(A) = \{\mathtt{b},\mathtt{c}\}$; an interactive agent B with $\mathrm{In}(B) = \{\mathtt{c},\mathtt{f}\}$ and $\mathrm{Out}(B) = \{\mathtt{d},\mathtt{e}\}$; and the interactive system $\mathcal{IS} = A \diamond B$ with $\mathrm{Out}(\mathcal{IS}) = \{\mathtt{a},\mathtt{f}\}$ and $\mathrm{In}(\mathcal{IS}) = \{\mathtt{b},\mathtt{e}\}$.

3. *If* $X_0 \stackrel{A}{\equiv} X_1$ *and* $X_1 \stackrel{A}{\equiv} X_2$, *then* $X_0 \stackrel{A}{\equiv} X_2$.
4. *If* $X_0 \stackrel{A}{\equiv} X_1$ *and* $B \in \mathcal{A}^\circ$, *then* $B(X_0) \stackrel{A}{\equiv} B(X_1)$.

Proof The first three properties follows directly from Proposition 2.2. To show that $B(X_0) \stackrel{A}{\equiv} B(X_1)$, we have to show that $A(B(X_0)) \stackrel{stat}{\equiv} A(B(X_1))$ for all $A \in \mathcal{A}$. So let A be any algorithm from $\mathcal{A}$. Because $A \in \mathcal{A}$ and $B \in \mathcal{A}^\circ$, we have that $C \in \mathcal{A}$ when $C = A \circ B$. From $C \in \mathcal{A}$ and $X_0 \stackrel{A}{\equiv} X_1$ it follows that $C(X_0) \stackrel{stat}{\equiv} C(X_1)$. Combining this with $C(X_b) = (A \circ B)(X_b) = A(B(X_0))$, it follows that $A(B(X_0)) \stackrel{stat}{\equiv} A(B(X_1))$ for all $A \in \mathcal{A}$, as desired. ∎

EXERCISE 2.5 Show that if $X_0 \stackrel{comp}{\equiv} X_1$ and B is a polytime algorithm, then $B(X_0) \stackrel{comp}{\equiv} B(X_1)$.

2.4 Interactive Systems

An interactive agent A is a computational device that receives and sends messages on named ports and that holds an internal state (Figure 2.1). More formally, an interactive agent is a tuple, $A = (\mathrm{In}, \mathrm{Out}, \mathrm{State}, \mathrm{Msg}, T, \sigma_0)$, where In is a finite set of names of inports, Out is a finite set of names of outports, State is a set of possible states, Msg is a set of possible messages with at least $0, 1 \in \mathrm{Msg}$, and T is the transition algorithm: it is an algorithm that takes an input (κ, σ, I), where $\kappa \in \mathbb{N}$ is the security parameter, $\sigma \in \mathrm{State}$ is the current state, and $I \in \mathrm{Msg}$, or $I \in \mathrm{In}$, or $I \in \{\mathtt{EOQ}, \mathtt{SNT}, \mathtt{ILM}\}$. If the agent just tried to read on one of its inports, then it receives $I \in \mathrm{Msg}$ if there were messages ready and otherwise $I = \mathtt{EOQ}$. The input $I = \mathtt{SNT}$ is given to the agent when it just sent a message. The input $I \in \mathrm{In}$ is for the first activation of an agent, to tell it on which port it was activated – this is called the activation port. The input $I = \mathtt{ILM}$ indicates that the queue that was read contained an illegal message, that is, a message not from Msg. The output of T is of one of the following forms:

- $(\mathtt{send}, \mathtt{P}, m)$, where $\mathtt{P} \in \mathrm{Out}$ is the port to send on and $m \in \mathrm{Msg}$ is the message to send.
- $(\mathtt{read}, \mathtt{P})$, where $\mathtt{P} \in \mathrm{In}$ is the port to read on.
- $(\mathtt{return}, \mathtt{RP})$, where $\mathtt{RP} \in \mathrm{Out}$ is the return port.

The purpose of the return port is to specify which agent to activate next in a larger system. The agent connected to the return port will be activated next.

In the following, we let In(A) be the component In from A, we let Out(A) be the component Out from A, and we let

$$\text{Ports(A)} \stackrel{\text{def}}{=} \text{In(A)} \cup \text{Out(A)}$$

Running an agent is called an activation. In each activation, the agent can read on ports several times and send on ports several times and update its current state – the initial state is σ_0. At the end of the activation, it then specifies a return port. See Algorithm Activate Agent for the details.

Algorithm Activate Agent

The activation of an agent A takes as input the value κ of the security parameter, a current state σ, an activation port $AP \in \text{In}$, and a queue Q_P for each $P \in \text{Ports(A)}$.

1. Let $I = \text{AP}$.
2. Let $(\sigma', c) \leftarrow T(\kappa, \sigma, I)$.
3. Update the current state: $\sigma \leftarrow \sigma'$.
4. Process the command c as follows:

  send If $c = (\text{send}, P, m)$, then enter m to the end of the queue Q_P, let $I \leftarrow \text{SNT}$, and go to step 2.

  read If $c = (\text{read}, P)$, then let $I \leftarrow \text{EOQ}$ if the queue Q_P is empty. Otherwise, remove the first element from Q_P, and let I be this element. If $I \notin \text{Msg(A)}$, then let $I = \text{ILM}$. Then go to step 2.

  return If $c = (\text{return}, RP)$, then the activation returns. The output is the new current state σ and the return port RP. A side effect of the activation is that the queues $\{Q_P\}_{P \in \text{Ports(A)}}$ were updated.

When we describe agents, it is useful to use a little shorthand. If we say that an agent *sends the activation token on P*, we mean that it returns on P; that is, it outputs (return, P). If we say that an agent *sends m on P*, and we don't say anything else, we mean that it sends m on P and then sends the activation token on P. If we describe part of an agent by saying *on input m on P do A(m)*, we mean that when the agent is activated, it reads on P, and if it gets back $m \notin \{\text{EOQ}, \text{ILM}\}$, then it executes $A(m)$, where $A(m)$ is some action that depends on m.

We are often interested in how efficient it is to compute the behavior of an agent, for which the following definition is handy.

DEFINITION 2.12 (RESPONSIVE, POLYTIME) *We call an agent responsive if it holds for all contexts (i.e., all $\kappa \in \mathbb{N}$, all states $\sigma \in$ State, all activation ports $AP \in$ In, and all queues $\{Q_P\}_{P \in \text{Ports(A)}}$) that if we activate A in this context, then it returns with probability 1. We only allow responsive agents. We call an agent polyresponsive if it holds for all contexts that if we activate A in this context, then it will return after having executed at most a number of commands c that are polynomial in κ. We call an agent stepwise polytime if $\text{Msg} = \{0,1\}^{p(\kappa)}$ for a polynomial p, and T can be computed in expected polytime in κ. We call an agent polytime if it is stepwise polytime and polyresponsive.*

It is straightforward to see that the activation of a polytime agent can be computed in expected polynomial time.

We connect a set of interactive agents to become an interactive system simply by connecting outports and inports with the same name. For this procedure to be well defined, we need that no two agents have identically named inports and similarly for outports – we say that they are compatible.

DEFINITION 2.13 *We say that interactive agents* $A_1, \ldots, A_n$ *are port compatible if* $\forall i, j \in [n]$, $j \neq i : \operatorname{In}(A_i) \cap \operatorname{In}(A_j) = \emptyset \wedge \operatorname{Out}(A_i) \cap \operatorname{Out}(A_j) = \emptyset$. *If* $A_1, \ldots, A_n$ *are port compatible, we call* $IS = \{A_1, \ldots, A_n\}$ *an interactive system. We say that two or more interactive systems are port compatible if the set of all their interactive agents is port compatible. If two interactive systems* IS_1 *and* IS_2 *are port compatible, then we define their composition to be* $IS_1 \diamond IS_2 \stackrel{\text{def}}{=} IS_1 \cup IS_2$; *otherwise, we let* $IS_1 \diamond IS_2 = \bot$. *For any interactive system* IS, *we let* $IS \diamond \bot \stackrel{\text{def}}{=} \bot$ *and* $\bot \diamond IS \stackrel{\text{def}}{=} \bot$.

The following proposition is convenient when reasoning about composed interactive systems.

PROPOSITION 2.14 *The following properties hold for all interactive systems* IS_1, IS_2, IS_3:

1. $IS_1 \diamond IS_2 = IS_2 \diamond IS_1$.
2. $(IS_1 \diamond IS_2) \diamond IS_3 = IS_1 \diamond (IS_2 \diamond IS_3)$.

For an interactive system IS and a port name P that is an inport of an agent in IS, we use A_P to denote the agent from IS that has an inport named P.

For an interactive system IS, we let $\operatorname{In}(IS)$ be the inports that are not connected to outports, and we let $\operatorname{Out}(IS)$ be the outports that are not connected to inports. That is,

$$\operatorname{In}(IS) \stackrel{\text{def}}{=} (\cup_{A \in IS} \operatorname{In}(A)) \setminus (\cup_{A \in IS} \operatorname{Out}(A))$$

$$\operatorname{Out}(IS) \stackrel{\text{def}}{=} (\cup_{A \in IS} \operatorname{Out}(A)) \setminus (\cup_{A \in IS} \operatorname{In}(A))$$

We call $\operatorname{In}(IS)$ and $\operatorname{Out}(IS)$ the open ports of the system. We say that an interactive system is closed if $\operatorname{In}(IS) = \emptyset$ and $\operatorname{Out}(IS) = \emptyset$. We say that IS is executable if it is closed and there is some agent A in IS that has an inport named ϵ and an outport named ϵ – this is a technical requirement to have some well-defined initial activation port and final return port: the execution will begin by activating on the port ϵ and will end the first time an agent returns on the port ϵ.

The execution is activation driven. In each step we activate an agent. Initially we activate the agent A_ϵ with inport ϵ, and we do it on port ϵ. After this, the next agent to be activated is the one that has an inport with the name that the previous agent specified as return port, and the agent is activated on that port. We think of this as some activation token @ being passed around.

Algorithm Execute System

1. Initialize the current state of all agents to be the initial state: for all $A \in \mathcal{IS}$, do $\sigma_A \leftarrow \sigma_0(A)$.
2. Initialize an empty queue for all ports: for all $P \in \cup_{A \in \mathcal{IS}} \text{Ports}(A)$, do $Q_P \leftarrow \epsilon$.
3. Let the initial activation port be $AP = \epsilon$.
4. Let A_{AP} denote the agent with an inport named AP.
5. Activate A_{AP} on $(\kappa, \sigma_A, AP, \{Q_P\}_{P \in \text{Ports}(A_{AP})})$ – see Algorithm Activate Agent. This will update the queues $\{Q_P\}_{P \in \text{Ports}(A_{AP})}$ and make A_{AP} output a return port RP and a new current state σ'.
6. Update the current state of A_{AP}: $\sigma_{A_{AP}} \leftarrow \sigma'$.
7. Update the activation port: $AP \leftarrow RP$.
8. If $RP \neq \epsilon$, go to step 4. If $RP = \epsilon$, then the execution stops with output m, where $m = 0$ if Q_ϵ is empty and where m is the front element in Q_ϵ otherwise.

DEFINITION 2.15 (EXECUTION OF INTERACTIVE SYSTEM) *An interactive system is called executable if it is closed and contains an agent A with $\epsilon \in \text{In}(A)$ and $\epsilon \in \text{Out}(A)$. For an executable interactive system $\mathcal{IS}$ and a given value $\kappa \in \mathbb{N}$ of the security parameter, we use $\mathcal{IS}(\kappa)$ to denote the message m output in step 8 in Algorithm Execute System when executing $\mathcal{IS}$ as specified in Algorithm Execute System. If the execution does not stop, such that m is not defined, we let $\mathcal{IS}(\kappa) = \infty$ for some reserved symbol ∞. Note that this makes $\mathcal{IS}(\kappa)$ a random variable with range $\text{Msg} \cup \{\infty\}$, where Msg is the message space of A_ϵ. We sometimes use $\mathcal{IS}$ to denote the family of random variables $\{\mathcal{IS}(\kappa)\}_{\kappa \in \mathbb{N}}$.*

EXAMPLE 2.16 Let A be an interactive agent with $\text{In}(A) = \{\epsilon, 1\}$ and $\text{Out}(A) = \{\epsilon, 1\}$. On any input on ϵ or 1 it samples uniformly random $r \in \{0,1\}^\ell$ for $\ell = \lceil \log_2(\kappa) \rceil$ and interprets it as an integer $R \in \mathbb{Z}_{2^\ell}$. If $R < \kappa$, then it sends R on ϵ. Otherwise, it sends `retry` on 1. Let $\mathcal{IS} = \{A\}$. Then $\mathcal{IS}$ is executable and $\Pr[\mathcal{IS}(\kappa) = \infty] = 0$, so $\mathcal{IS}(\kappa)$ is a random variable with support $\mathbb{Z}_\kappa$, and it is uniformly random on that support. ∎

EXAMPLE 2.17 Let A_1 be an interactive agent with $\text{In}(A_1) = \{\epsilon, 1\}$ and $\text{Out}(A_1) = \{\epsilon, 2\}$. On any input on ϵ it samples a uniformly random bit $c \in \{0,1\}$ and sends c on 2. On input $e \in \{0,1\}$ on 1 it sends e on ϵ. Let A_2 be an interactive agent with $\text{In}(A_2) = \{2\}$ and $\text{Out}(A_2) = \{1\}$. On input $c \in \mathbb{N}$ on 2, it samples $d \leftarrow \{0,1\}$ and sends $c + d$ on 1. Let $\mathcal{IS} = \{A_1, A_2\}$. Then $\mathcal{IS}$ is executable and $\Pr[\mathcal{IS}(\kappa) = 0] = \frac{1}{4}$, $\Pr[\mathcal{IS}(\kappa) = 1] = \frac{1}{2}$, and $\Pr[\mathcal{IS}(\kappa) = \infty] = \frac{1}{4}$. ∎

We will not only be interested in the execution of closed systems. To allow us to talk about the execution of an open system, we introduce the notion of a closure.

DEFINITION 2.18 (CLOSURE) *Let $\mathcal{IS}$ be an interactive system. A closure of $\mathcal{IS}$ is an interactive system $\mathcal{Z}$ where $\mathcal{IS} \diamond \mathcal{Z} \neq \bot$ and for which $\mathcal{IS} \diamond \mathcal{Z}$ is executable. This, in particular, means that $\text{In}(\mathcal{Z}) = \text{Out}(\mathcal{IS})$ and $\text{Out}(\mathcal{Z}) = \text{In}(\mathcal{IS})$.*

We reserve the port name ϵ for closures; that is, we assume that normal interactive systems such as $\mathcal{IS}$ do not use this port name for internal communication. The reason is that we want the closure $\mathcal{Z}$ to be the one that defines the output of the execution.

Earlier we implicitly defined the output of an execution to be ∞ if the execution runs forever. In some of our later definitions, in particular, the definition of indistinguishability of interactive systems, handling systems that run forever is definitionally cumbersome. Since we do not need to study such systems, we will restrict our attention to systems that do not run forever. We call such systems *responsive*. Sometimes we also need to restrict systems to be polytime.

DEFINITION 2.19 (RESPONSIVE, POLYTIME) *We call an executable interactive system $\mathcal{IS}$ responsive if* $\Pr[\mathcal{IS}(\kappa) = \infty] = 0$ *for all κ.*

Let $\mathcal{IS}$ be an open interactive system not using the port name ϵ. We call $\mathcal{IS}$ responsive if it holds for all closures $\mathcal{Z}$ of $\mathcal{IS}$ and all values $\kappa \in \mathbb{N}$ of the security parameter that whenever the activation token is turned over from an agent in $\mathcal{Z}$ to an agent in $\mathcal{IS}$, in the execution $(\mathcal{IS} \diamond \mathcal{Z})(\kappa)$, then with probability 1 the activation token will later be turned over from an agent in $\mathcal{IS}$ to an agent in $\mathcal{Z}$. In words, the probability that $\mathcal{IS}$ at some point keeps the activation token forever is 0.

We say that $\mathcal{IS}$ is polyresponsive if there exists a polynomial $\tau : \mathbb{N} \to \mathbb{N}$ such that it holds for all closures $\mathcal{Z}$ of $\mathcal{IS}$ and all values $\kappa \in \mathbb{N}$ of the security parameter that whenever the activation token is turned over from an agent in $\mathcal{Z}$ to an agent in $\mathcal{IS}$, in the execution $(\mathcal{IS} \diamond \mathcal{Z})(\kappa)$, then the expected number of activations of agents in $\mathcal{IS}$ until the activation token is again turned over from an agent in $\mathcal{IS}$ to an agent in $\mathcal{Z}$ and is bounded by $\tau(\kappa)$. In other words, when $\mathcal{IS}$ is activated on an open inport, then the expected number of internal agent activations before it returns the activation token on an open outport is polynomial.

We say that $\mathcal{IS}$ is a polytime interactive system if all agents are polytime and $\mathcal{IS}$ is polyresponsive.

The main important fact to remember about this definition is the following:

PROPOSITION 2.20 *A polytime interactive system $\mathcal{IS}$ can be executed in expected polynomial time. More precisely, for any activation of $\mathcal{IS}(\kappa)$, the expected running time spent until the activation token is returned on an open port grows at most polynomially in κ.*

EXERCISE 2.6 Prove Proposition 2.20. The crucial step is the following:

Let $B(\kappa, \cdot)$ be a stateful algorithm taking the security parameter as input plus an additional input y. Stateful means, as usual, that B keeps a state that is stored between calls to B and that the output depends on the state as well as the input. Assume that B runs in expected polynomial time. That is, there exists a polynomial $q(\kappa)$ such that the expected running time of $B(\kappa, y)$ is bounded by $q(\kappa)$ for all states and inputs y.

Let $A(\kappa, \cdot)$ be an algorithm taking the security parameter as input plus an additional input x, and assume that $A(\kappa, \cdot)$ uses $B(\kappa, \cdot)$ as subroutine; that is, $A(\kappa, x)$ might call $B(\kappa, y)$, and it might do so several times and on different inputs y. Assume that $A(\kappa, \cdot)$ calls $B(\kappa, \cdot)$ an expected polynomial number of times. In other words, there exists a polynomial $p(\kappa)$ such that the expected number of times that $A(\kappa, x)$ calls $B(\kappa, \cdot)$ is bounded by $p(\kappa)$ for all inputs x. Let $t(\kappa, x)$ be the expected value of the sum of the running times of all the calls that $A(\kappa, x)$ makes to $B(\kappa, \cdot)$.

As a first step in your proof, you should show that there exists a polynomial $t(\kappa)$ such that $t(\kappa, x) \leq t(\kappa)$ for all inputs x.

2.4.1 Indistinguishable Interactive Systems

We say that two interactive systems are (behaviorly) *indistinguishable* if one cannot tell the difference between them by sending and receiving messages over the open ports of the systems. For this purpose, we work with the notion of an *environment*, which is just an interactive system that closes the system and makes it executable. We think of the execution as the environment playing with the system over the open ports. Its job is then to guess which system it is connected to. The closure therefore acts as a distinguisher. For this reason, we require that it outputs a bit c, which is its guess at which system it is playing with.

DEFINITION 2.21 *Let $\mathcal{IS}_0$ and $\mathcal{IS}_1$ be responsive interactive systems with $\mathrm{In}(\mathcal{IS}_0) = \mathrm{In}(\mathcal{IS}_1)$ and $\mathrm{Out}(\mathcal{IS}_0) = \mathrm{Out}(\mathcal{IS}_1)$. We call an interactive system $\mathcal{Z}$ an environment for $\mathcal{IS}_0$ and $\mathcal{IS}_1$ if $\mathcal{Z}$ is a closure of both $\mathcal{IS}_0$ and $\mathcal{IS}_1$ and $\mathcal{IS}_0 \diamond \mathcal{Z}$ and $\mathcal{IS}_1 \diamond \mathcal{Z}$ are responsive.[3] We also require that when $\mathcal{Z}$ produces an output on the port ϵ, then it is a bit c. We call c the guess of the environment. The responsiveness and the fact that $\mathcal{Z}$ outputs a bit on ϵ mean that $(\mathcal{IS}_0 \diamond \mathcal{Z})(\kappa)$ and $(\mathcal{IS}_1 \diamond \mathcal{Z})(\kappa)$ are random variables with support $\{0,1\}$.*

- *We say that the systems are perfectly indistinguishable, written $\mathcal{IS}_0 \overset{\mathrm{perf}}{\equiv} \mathcal{IS}_1$, if it holds that $\{(\mathcal{Z} \diamond \mathcal{IS}_0)(\kappa)\}_{\kappa \in \mathbb{N}} \overset{\mathrm{perf}}{\equiv} \{(\mathcal{Z} \diamond \mathcal{IS}_1)(\kappa)\}_{\kappa \in \mathbb{N}}$ for all environments $\mathcal{Z}$ for $\mathcal{IS}_0$ and $\mathcal{IS}_1$.*
- *We say that the systems are statistically indistinguishable, written $\mathcal{IS}_0 \overset{\mathrm{stat}}{\equiv} \mathcal{IS}_1$, if it holds that $\{(\mathcal{Z} \diamond \mathcal{IS}_0)(\kappa)\}_{\kappa \in \mathbb{N}} \overset{\mathrm{stat}}{\equiv} \{(\mathcal{Z} \diamond \mathcal{IS}_1)(\kappa)\}_{\kappa \in \mathbb{N}}$ for all environments $\mathcal{Z}$ for $\mathcal{IS}_0$ and $\mathcal{IS}_1$, such that $\mathcal{Z}$ makes a polynomial (in κ) number of activations of $\mathcal{IS}_0(\mathcal{IS}_1)$.*
- *For a class of interactive systems* Env, *we say that $\mathcal{IS}_0$ is indistinguishable from $\mathcal{IS}_1$ for* Env *(written $\mathcal{IS}_0 \overset{\mathrm{Env}}{\equiv} \mathcal{IS}_1$) if $\{(\mathcal{Z} \diamond \mathcal{IS}_0)(\kappa)\}_{\kappa \in \mathbb{N}} \overset{\mathrm{stat}}{\equiv} \{(\mathcal{Z} \diamond \mathcal{IS}_1)(\kappa)\}_{\kappa \in \mathbb{N}}$ for all $\mathcal{Z} \in$ Env for which $\mathcal{Z}$ is an environment for $\mathcal{IS}_0$ and $\mathcal{IS}_1$.*
- *We say that $\mathcal{IS}_0 \overset{\mathrm{comp}}{\equiv} \mathcal{IS}_1$ if $\mathcal{IS}_0 \overset{\mathrm{Env}}{\equiv} \mathcal{IS}_1$ for the class* Env *of polytime interactive systems.*

The case of statistical indistinguishability is meant to capture systems $\mathcal{IS}_0$, $\mathcal{IS}_1$ that behave "almost" in the same way, for instance, where the behavior is exactly the same except if some event E occurs where $\Pr[E]$ is negligible. To capture such cases, we need the restriction to a polynomial number of activations. Otherwise, an unbounded environment could distinguish easily: it would just keep activating the system until the "error event" occurs.

For a class of interactive systems Env, we let $\mathrm{Env}^\diamond$ be the class of interactive systems $\mathcal{IS}$ for which $\mathcal{Z} \diamond \mathcal{IS} \in$ Env whenever $\mathcal{Z} \in$ Env and $\mathcal{Z}$ and $\mathcal{IS}$ are port compatible.

PROPOSITION 2.22 *The following properties hold for all interactive systems $\mathcal{IS}_0, \mathcal{IS}_1, \mathcal{IS}_2$ and all classes of environments* Env:

1. *$\mathcal{IS}_0 \overset{\mathrm{Env}}{\equiv} \mathcal{IS}_0$.*
2. *If $\mathcal{IS}_0 \overset{\mathrm{Env}}{\equiv} \mathcal{IS}_1$, then $\mathcal{IS}_1 \overset{\mathrm{Env}}{\equiv} \mathcal{IS}_0$.*
3. *If $\mathcal{IS}_0 \overset{\mathrm{Env}}{\equiv} \mathcal{IS}_1$ and $\mathcal{IS}_1 \overset{\mathrm{Env}}{\equiv} \mathcal{IS}_2$, then $\mathcal{IS}_0 \overset{\mathrm{Env}}{\equiv} \mathcal{IS}_2$.*

---

[3] Since we require that $\mathcal{IS}_0$ and $\mathcal{IS}_1$ are responsive, the requirement that $\mathcal{IS}_0 \diamond \mathcal{Z}$ and $\mathcal{IS}_1 \diamond \mathcal{Z}$ are responsive just requires that $\mathcal{Z}$ does not make an infinite number of internal activations.

4. If $\mathcal{IS}_0 \overset{\text{Env}}{\equiv} \mathcal{IS}_1$ and $\mathcal{IS}_2 \in \text{Env}^\diamond$, then $\mathcal{IS}_2 \diamond \mathcal{IS}_0 \overset{\text{Env}}{\equiv} \mathcal{IS}_2 \diamond \mathcal{IS}_1$.

5. If $\mathcal{IS}_0 \overset{\text{Env}_1}{\equiv} \mathcal{IS}_1$ and $\mathcal{IS}_2 \diamond \text{Env}_2 \subseteq \text{Env}_1$, then $\mathcal{IS}_2 \diamond \mathcal{IS}_0 \overset{\text{Env}_2}{\equiv} \mathcal{IS}_2 \diamond \mathcal{IS}_1$.

The same properties hold for $\overset{\text{perf}}{\equiv}$, $\overset{\text{stat}}{\equiv}$, and $\overset{\text{comp}}{\equiv}$.

Proof The first three properties are straightforward. To show that $\mathcal{IS}_2 \diamond \mathcal{IS}_0 \overset{\text{Env}}{\equiv} \mathcal{IS}_2 \diamond \mathcal{IS}_1$, we have to show that $\mathcal{Z} \diamond (\mathcal{IS}_2 \diamond \mathcal{IS}_0) \overset{\text{stat}}{\equiv} \mathcal{Z} \diamond (\mathcal{IS}_2 \diamond \mathcal{IS}_1)$ for all $\mathcal{Z} \in \text{Env}$ that are environments for $\mathcal{IS}_2 \diamond \mathcal{IS}_0$ and $\mathcal{IS}_2 \diamond \mathcal{IS}_1$. Because $\mathcal{Z} \in \text{Env}$ and $\mathcal{IS}_2 \in \text{Env}^\diamond$, we have that $\mathcal{Z} \diamond \mathcal{IS}_2 \in \text{Env}$. From $\mathcal{Z} \diamond \mathcal{IS}_2 \in \text{Env}$ and $\mathcal{IS}_0 \overset{\text{Env}}{\equiv} \mathcal{IS}_1$, it follows that $(\mathcal{Z} \diamond \mathcal{IS}_2) \diamond \mathcal{IS}_0 \overset{\text{stat}}{\equiv} (\mathcal{Z} \diamond \mathcal{IS}_2) \diamond \mathcal{IS}_1$. The claim then follows from $(\mathcal{Z} \diamond \mathcal{IS}_2) \diamond \mathcal{IS}_b = \mathcal{Z} \diamond (\mathcal{IS}_2 \diamond \mathcal{IS}_b)$ for $b = 0, 1$. The proof of the last property follows in the same manner. ∎

EXERCISE 2.7 Prove Property 5 in Proposition 2.22.

We are particularly interested in Property 4 in the preceding proposition. It basically says that if two interactive systems are hard to distinguish, then this also holds if we use them in some context $\mathcal{IS}_2$, that is, as long as the context $\mathcal{IS}_2$ does not perform any computation that the class of distinguishers that we consider cannot perform on its own. This is very useful in comparing systems such as $\mathcal{IS}_2 \diamond \mathcal{IS}_0$ and $\mathcal{IS}_2 \diamond \mathcal{IS}_1$ because we only have to compare their noncommon parties, $\mathcal{IS}_0$ and $\mathcal{IS}_1$. This is sometimes called modularity of indistinguishability and sometimes called composability of indistinguishability.

In Property 4 we showed composability only for $\mathcal{IS}_2 \in \text{Env}^\diamond$. This is, in fact, the best general result we can hope for. If, for example, $\mathcal{Z}$ is the class of polytime environments and $\mathcal{IS}_2$ performs exponential time computations, then it might happen that $\mathcal{IS}_0 \overset{\text{Env}}{\equiv} \mathcal{IS}_1$ but $\mathcal{IS}_2 \diamond \mathcal{IS}_0 \overset{\text{Env}}{\not\equiv} \mathcal{IS}_2 \diamond \mathcal{IS}_1$: it might be that $\mathcal{IS}_0$ and $\mathcal{IS}_1$ are indistinguishable to polytime environments due to the use of cryptography but that $\mathcal{IS}_2$ breaks this cryptography using its exponential time computing power. The reason why this does not contradict the proposition is that when Env is the class of polytime environments and $\mathcal{IS}_2$ is an exponential time system, then $\mathcal{IS}_2 \notin \text{Env}^\diamond$.[4]

EXAMPLE 2.23 Let A be an interactive agent with $\text{In}(A) = \{a, d\}$ and $\text{Out}(A) = \{b, c\}$ and the following behavior: on input $x \in \mathbb{Z}$ on a, output $x + 1$ on c, and on input $x \in \mathbb{Z}$ on d, output $x + 1$ on b. Let B be an interactive agent with $\text{In}(B) = \{c\}$ and $\text{Out}(B) = \{d\}$ and the following behavior: on input $x \in \mathbb{Z}$ on c output $2x$ on d. Let C be an interactive agent with $\text{In}(C) = \{a\}$ and $\text{Out}(C) = \{b\}$ and the following behavior: on input $x \in \mathbb{Z}$ on a, output $2x + 3$ on b. Let $\mathcal{IS}_0 = \{A, B\}$, and let $\mathcal{IS}_1 = \{C\}$. Then $\mathcal{IS}_0 \overset{\text{perf}}{\equiv} \mathcal{IS}_1$. ∎

2.5 Public-Key Cryptosystems

This section precisely defines the security of public-key cryptosystems (we will use such systems later) and at the same time gives an example of how interactive systems and the

---

[4] Assume namely that $\mathcal{IS}_2 \in \text{Env}^\diamond$. By definition, this means that $\mathcal{IS}_2 \diamond \mathcal{IS} \in \text{Env}$ for all $\mathcal{IS} \in \text{Env}$. Since the empty interactive system $\mathcal{IS} = \emptyset$ is clearly polytime, we have that $\emptyset \in \text{Env}$, which implies that $\mathcal{IS}_2 \diamond \emptyset = \mathcal{IS}_2 \in \text{Env}$. This contradicts the premises that Env is the polytime systems and that $\mathcal{IS}_2$ is an exponential time system.

notion of indistinguishability of interactive systems can be used to make precise definitions. A public-key cryptosystem consists of three algorithms (G, E, D) called the key generator, the encryption algorithm, and the decryption algorithm, respectively.

We define security of a public-key cryptosystem by comparing two interactive agents. For $b = 0, 1$, let A_b be the following interactive agent:

- $\text{In}(A_b) = \{\texttt{keygen}, \texttt{msgs}, \texttt{dec}\}$.
- $\text{Out}(A_b) = \{\texttt{pk}, \texttt{target}, \texttt{plaintext}\}$.

It behaves as follows:

- The first time a message is input on $\texttt{keygen}$, it samples $(pk, sk) \leftarrow G(\kappa)$ and outputs pk on $\texttt{pk}$. It ignores all subsequent messages on $\texttt{keygen}$; that is, if it is later activated on this port, it will simply return the activation on $\texttt{pk}$ without reading or sending messages and without changing state.
- On the first message of the form (m_0, m_1) with $|m_0| = |m_1|$ on $\texttt{msgs}$ after (pk, sk) has been sampled, it samples a target ciphertext $c^* \leftarrow E_{pk}(m_b)$ and returns c^* on $\texttt{target}$. It ignores all subsequent messages on $\texttt{msgs}$.
- On each message c on $\texttt{dec}$, after (pk, sk) has been sampled, it returns $m \leftarrow D_{sk}(c)$ on $\texttt{plaintext}$. If c^* has been defined, then it ignores inputs with $c = c^*$.

The following definition captures the standard notions of indistinguishability under chosen ciphertext attack and indistinguishability under chosen plaintext attack.

DEFINITION 2.24 *We say that (G, E, D) is IND-CCA secure if $A_0 \overset{comp}{\equiv} A_1$. We say that (G, E, D) is IND-CPA secure if $A'_0 \overset{comp}{\equiv} A'_1$, where A'_b is A_b with the ports* $\texttt{dec}$ *and* $\texttt{plaintext}$ *removed.*

The notion of IND-CPA (which is sometimes called *semantic security*) says that it is impossible to distinguish encryptions of different messages in polytime, even if you get to pick the messages yourself, and even if you get to pick the messages after seeing the public key. The notion of IND-CCA says that the task remains hard even if you get access to a decryption oracle, unless, of course, you decrypt the ciphertext you were given as challenge (which would make the task trivial).

It is possible to build cryptosystems that are IND-CPA secure and IND-CCA secure under many assumptions, for example, the RSA assumption and the discrete logarithm assumption.

3

MPC Protocols with Passive Security

3.1 Introduction

In Chapter 1 we gave an introduction to the multiparty computation problem and explained what it intuitively means for a protocol to compute a given function securely, namely, we want a protocol that is correct and private. However, we only considered three players, we only argued that a single player does not learn more than he or she is supposed to, and finally, we assumed that all players would follow the protocol.

In this chapter we will consider a more general solution to multiparty computation, where we remove the first two restrictions: we will consider any number $n \geq 3$ of players, and we will be able to show that as long as at most $t < n/2$ of the players go together after the protocol is executed and pool all their information, they will learn nothing more than their own inputs and the outputs they were supposed to receive, even if their computing power is unbounded. We will still assume, however, that all players follow the protocol. This is known as *semihonest* or *passive security*.

To argue security in this chapter, we will use a somewhat weak but very simple definition that only makes sense for semihonest security. We then extend this in Chapter 4 to a fully general model of what protocols are and what security means.

Throughout this chapter we will assume that each pair of players can communicate using a perfectly secure channel, so if two players exchange data, a third player has no information at all about what is sent. Such channels might be available because of physical circumstances, or we can implement them relative to a computational assumption using cryptography. For more details on this, see Chapter 7.

We end the chapter by showing that the bound $t < n/2$ is optimal: if $t \geq n/2$, then some functions cannot be computed securely in the model mentioned, that is, obtaining perfect security by using only secure point-to-point communication as the communication resource.

3.2 Secret Sharing

Our main tool to build the protocol will be secret-sharing schemes. The theory of secret-sharing schemes is a large and interesting field in its own right with many applications to multiparty computation (MPC), and we look at this in more detail in Chapter 11, where a formal definition of the notion as well as a general treatment of the theory of secret sharing can be found.

Here we concentrate on a particular example scheme that will be sufficient for our purposes in this chapter, namely, Shamir's secret-sharing scheme. This scheme is based on polynomials over a finite field $\mathbb{F}$. The only necessary restriction on $\mathbb{F}$ is that $|\mathbb{F}| > n$, but we will assume for concreteness and simplicity that $\mathbb{F} = \mathbb{Z}_p$ for some prime $p > n$.

A value $s \in \mathbb{F}$ is *shared* by choosing a random polynomial $f_s(X) \in \mathbb{F}[X]$ of degree at most t such that $f_s(0) = s$ and then sending privately to player P_j the share $s_j = f_s(j)$. The basic facts about this method are that any set of t or fewer shares contains no information on s, whereas it can easily be reconstructed from any $t + 1$ or more shares. Both of these facts are proved using Lagrange interpolation.

Lagrange Interpolation

If $h(X)$ is a polynomial over $\mathbb{F}$ of degree at most l, and if C is a subset of $\mathbb{F}$ with $|C| = l + 1$, then

$$h(X) = \sum_{i \in C} h(i) \delta_i(X)$$

where $\delta_i(X)$ is the degree l polynomial such that, for all $i, j \in C$, $\delta_i(j) = 0$ if $i \neq j$ and $\delta_i(j) = 1$ if $i = j$. In other words,

$$\delta_i(X) = \prod_{j \in C,\, j \neq i} \frac{X - j}{i - j}$$

We briefly recall why this holds. Because each $\delta_i(X)$ is a product of l monomials, it is a polynomial of degree at most l. Therefore, the right-hand side $\sum_{i \in C} h(i) \delta_i(X)$ is a polynomial of degree at most l that on input i evaluates to $h(i)$ for $i \in C$. Therefore, $h(X) - \sum_{i \in C} h(i) \delta_i(X)$ is 0 on all points in C. Because $|C| > l$ and only the zero polynomial has more zeroes than its degree (in a field), it follows that $h(X) - \sum_{i \in C} h(i) \delta_i(X)$ is the zero polynomial, from which it follows that $h(X) = \sum_{i \in C} h(i) \delta_i(X)$.

Using the same argument, one easily sees that the Lagrange interpolation works, even if no polynomial is predefined. Given any set of values $\{y_i \in \mathbb{F} \mid i \in C\}$, $|C| = l + 1$, we can construct a polynomial h with $h(i) = y_i$ of degree at most l as

$$h(X) = \sum_{i \in C} y_i \delta_i(X)$$

A consequence of Lagrange interpolation is that there exist easily computable values $\mathbf{r} = (r_1, ..., r_n)$ such that

$$h(0) = \sum_{i=1}^{n} r_i h(i) \tag{3.1}$$

for all polynomials $h(X)$ of degree at most $n - 1$. Namely, $r_i = \delta_i(0)$. We call $(r_1, ..., r_n)$ the recombination vector. Note that $\delta_i(X)$ does not depend on $h(X)$, so neither does $\delta_i(0)$. Hence the *same* recombination vector $\mathbf{r}$ works for all $h(X)$. It is a public piece of information that all players can compute.

A final consequence is that for all secrets $s \in \mathbb{F}$ and all $C \subset \mathbb{F}$ with $|C| = t$ and $0 \notin C$, if we sample a uniformly random f of degree $\leq t$ and with $f(0) = s$, then the distribution of the t shares

$$(f(i))_{i \in C}$$

is the uniform distribution on $\mathbb{F}^t$. Because the uniform distribution on $\mathbb{F}^t$ clearly is independent of s, it in particular follows that given only t shares one gets no information on the secret.

One way to see that any t shares are uniformly distributed is as follows: one way to sample a polynomial for sharing of a secret s is to sample a uniformly random $a = (a_1, \ldots, a_t) \in \mathbb{F}^t$ and let $f_a(X) = s + \sum_{j=1}^{t} a_j X^t$ (because clearly $f_a(0) = s$). For a fixed s and fixed C as earlier, this defines an evaluation map from $\mathbb{F}^t$ to $\mathbb{F}^t$ by mapping $a = (a_1, \ldots, a_t)$ to $(f_a(i))_{i \in C}$. This map is invertible. That is, given any $(y_i)_{i \in C} \in \mathbb{F}^t$, we know that we seek $f_a(X)$ with $f_a(i) = y_i$ for $i \in C$. We furthermore know that $f_a(0) = s$. Thus we know $f_a(X)$ on $t + 1$ points, which allows us to compute $f_a(X)$ and $a \in \mathbb{F}^t$ using Lagrange interpolation. So the evaluation map is invertible. Any invertible map from $\mathbb{F}^t$ to $\mathbb{F}^t$ maps the uniform distribution on $\mathbb{F}^t$ to the uniform distribution on $\mathbb{F}^t$.

Example Computations

We look at an example. Assume that we have five parties $P_1, \ldots, P_5$ and that we want to tolerate $t = 2$ corrupted parties. Assume that we work in $\mathbb{F} = \mathbb{Z}_{11}$ and want to share $s = 7$. We pick $a_1, a_2 \in \mathbb{F}$ uniformly at random, say they become $a_1 = 4$ and $a_2 = 1$, and then we define

$$h(X) = s + a_1 X + a_2 X^2 = 7 + 4X + X^2 \tag{3.2}$$

Then we compute $s_1 = h(1) = 7 + 4 + 1 \bmod 11 = 1$, $s_2 = h(2) = 19 \bmod 11 = 8$, $s_3 = h(3) = 6$, $s_4 = h(4) = 6$, and $s_5 = h(5) = 8$. So the sharing is

$$[s] = (1, 8, 6, 6, 8)$$

We send s_i securely to P_i.

Assume now that someone is given just the shares s_3, s_4, s_5. Because $3 > 2$, that person can use Lagrange interpolation to compute the secret.

We first compute

$$\delta_3(X) = \prod_{j=4,5} \frac{X-j}{3-j} = \frac{(X-4)(X-5)}{(3-4)(3-5)} = (X^2 - 9X + 20)((3-4)(3-5))^{-1} \quad (\bmod \ 11)$$

We have that $(3-4)(3-5) = 2$ and $2 \cdot 6 \bmod 11 = 1$, so $((3-4)(3-5))^{-1} \bmod 11 = 6$. Thus,

$$\delta_3(X) = (X^2 - 9X + 20)6 = (X^2 + 2X + 9)6 = 6X^2 + 12X + 54 = 6X^2 + X + 10 \quad (\bmod \ 11)$$

We check that

$$\delta_3(3) = 6 \cdot 3^2 + 3 + 10 = 67 = 1 \quad (\bmod \ 11)$$
$$\delta_3(4) = 6 \cdot 4^2 + 4 + 10 = 110 = 0 \quad (\bmod \ 11)$$
$$\delta_3(5) = 6 \cdot 5^2 + 5 + 10 = 165 = 0 \quad (\bmod \ 11)$$

as it should be.

We then compute

$$\delta_4(X) = \prod_{j=3,5} \frac{X-j}{4-j} = \frac{(X-3)(X-5)}{(4-3)(4-5)}$$

$$= (X^2 - 8X + 15)(-1)^{-1}$$

$$= (X^2 + 3X + 4)10$$

$$= 10X^2 + 8X + 7$$

We can check that $\delta_4(3) = 121 = 0$ (mod 11), $\delta_4(4) = 199 = 1$ (mod 11), and $\delta_4(5) = 297 = 0$ (mod 11).

We then compute

$$\delta_5(X) = \prod_{j=3,4} \frac{X-j}{5-j} = \frac{(X-3)(X-4)}{(5-3)(5-4)}$$

$$= (X^2 - 7X + 12)(2)^{-1}$$

$$= (X^2 + 4X + 1)6$$

$$= 6X^2 + 2X + 6$$

We can check that $\delta_5(3) = 66 = 0$ (mod 11), $\delta_5(4) = 110 = 0$ (mod 11), and $\delta_5(5) = 166 = 1$ (mod 11).

It is now clear that if for any s_3, s_4, s_5 we let

$$h(X) = s_3 \cdot \delta_3(X) + s_4 \cdot \delta_4(X) + s_5 \cdot \delta_5(X)$$

then $h(3) = s_3 \cdot 1 + s_4 \cdot 0 + s_5 \cdot 0 = s_3$, $h(4) = s_3 \cdot 0 + s_4 \cdot 1 + s_5 \cdot 0 = s_4$, and $h(5) = s_3 \cdot 0 + s_4 \cdot 0 + s_5 \cdot 1 = s_5$, which implies that if $s_3 = f(3)$, $s_4 = f(4)$, and $s_5 = f(5)$ for some quadratic polynomial, then $h(X) = f(X)$. This allows us to compute $h(X)$ from the three shares.

More concretely, notice that

$$h(X) = s_3\delta_3(X) + s_4\delta_4(X) + s_5\delta_5(X)$$

$$= (6s_3 + 10s_4 + 6s_5)X^2 + (s_3 + 8s_4 + 2s_5)X + (10s_3 + 7s_4 + 6s_5)$$

Since we consider $h(X)$ of the form $h(X) = s + a_1 X + a_2 X^2$, we have that

$$s = 10s_3 + 7s_4 + 6s_5 \bmod 11$$

$$a_1 = s_3 + 8s_4 + 2s_5 \bmod 11$$

$$a_2 = 6s_3 + 10s_4 + 6s_5 \bmod 11$$

which is then the general formula for computing $h(X)$ from the three shares $s_3 = h(3), s_4 = h(4)$, and $s_5 = h(5)$.

In our concrete example we had the shares $s_3 = 6$, $s_4 = 6$, and $s_5 = 8$. If we plug this in, we get

$$s = 10 \cdot 6 + 7 \cdot 6 + 6 \cdot 8 \bmod 11 = 150 \bmod 11 = 7$$

$$a_1 = 6 + 8 \cdot 6 + 2 \cdot 8 \bmod 11 = 70 \bmod 11 = 4$$

$$a_2 = 6 \cdot 6 + 10 \cdot 6 + 6 \cdot 8 \bmod 11 = 144 \bmod 11 = 1$$

which gives exactly the polynomial in Eq. (3.2).

If we had only been interested in finding the secret s and not the entire polynomial, we would only need the equation $s = 10s_3 + 7s_4 + 6s_5 \bmod 11$. We see that $r = (10, 7, 6)$ is the recombination vector for finding $h(0)$ from $h(3), h(4)$, and $h(5)$ when $h(X)$ is a polynomial of degree at most 2.

3.3 A Passively Secure Protocol

3.3.1 Arithmetic Circuits

We will present a protocol that can securely evaluate a function with inputs and outputs in a finite field $\mathbb{F}$. For notational convenience, we construct the protocol for the case where each party has exactly one input and one output from $\mathbb{F}$. That is, $f: \mathbb{F}^n \to \mathbb{F}^n, (x_1, \ldots, x_n) \to (y_1, \ldots, y_n)$. We assume that the mapping $(y_1, \ldots, y_n) = f(x_1, \ldots, x_n)$ is described using an arithmetic circuit.

More formally, such a circuit is an acyclic directed graph, where each node is called a *gate*, and the edges are called *wires*. Each gate has at most two incoming wires. There are n input gates with no incoming and any number of outcoming wires, each such gate is labeled by i for the player P_i, who is going to supply the secret input value x_i for that gate, and that value is copied onto all outgoing wires. Then there are a number of internal addition and multiplication gates, with two input wires and any number of output wires; these add or multiply their two inputs onto the outgoing wires. We also have multiply-by-constant gates; they have one input wire and any number of output wires, each such gate is labeled by a constant $\alpha \in \mathbb{F}$ and does multiplication by α. Finally, there is for each P_i exactly one output gate labeled by i, with one input wire and no outgoing wires. The value eventually assigned to the input wire of this gate is going to be y_i.

Evaluating a circuit can be done as follows: we assume that the input values have been specified initially, and we think of this as assigning the value x_i to the wire(s) coming out of the input gate labeled i. We assume that the gates have been numbered in some (arbitrary) way. We then take the first gate for which values have been assigned to all its input wires, compute the output value, and assign it to the output wire(s) of the gate. Repeat this until all wires have had values assigned. This then also defines the output values. The order in which we visit the gates in this procedure will be called the computational ordering in the following.

Considering arithmetic circuits is without loss of generality: it is well known that any function that is feasible to compute at all can be specified as a polynomial-size Boolean circuit using *and* and *negation*. But any such circuit can be simulated by operations in $\mathbb{F}$: Boolean values `true` or `false` can be encoded as 1 resp. 0. Then the *negation* of bit b is $1 - b$, and the *and* of bits b and b' is $b \cdot b'$.

EXERCISE 3.1 Assume that you are given a protocol that securely computes any function $f: \mathbb{F}^n \to \mathbb{F}^n$ given by an arithmetic circuit. Show how it can be used to securely compute any function $g : \{0,1\}^n \to \{0,1\}^n$, where each party has a bit as input, and g can be any polytime computable function. Assume that you have a polysized Boolean circuit for g. We argued how to do that earlier, but the solution only works if players select inputs correctly. If parties may not do this, there is a problem when the Boolean circuit is coded as an arithmetic circuit: it is important that all parties input 0 or 1. If players may input any $x_i \in \mathbb{F}$, we may be in trouble: Consider a case with three parties, each with an input $x_i \in \{0,1\}$. Assume that $y_1 = (1 - x_1)x_2 + x_1x_3$. If $x_1 = 0$, then $y_1 = x_2$, and if $x_1 = 1$, then $y_1 = x_3$. That is, P_1 can choose to learn either x_2 or x_3 but not both.

1. Argue that a cheating P_i who inputs $x_1 \notin \{0,1\}$ can learn both x_2 and x_3.
2. Give a general construction that prevents this type of attack. [*Hint*: Assume that $\mathbb{F}$ is small, and try to map all possible inputs $x_i \in \mathbb{F}$ to an input $x_i' \in \{0,1\}$, and then do the actual computation on $(x_1', \ldots, x_n')$.]

An Assumption about the Structure of Circuits

In order to simplify the proofs of security in this book, we will assume throughout that a circuit that is to be computed securely contains a multiplication gate immediately before each output gate and that, furthermore, this multiplication gate has only one output wire. We can assume this without loss of generality – if the circuit does not satisfy the condition for output y_j, we can, for instance, introduce an extra input x'_j from P_j and then change to a new circuit that multiplies y_j by x'_j just before the output gate. This will make the circuit at most a constant factor larger, and by choosing $x'_j = 1$, P_j will still learn the same value.

We emphasize that the protocols we present are secure even without this assumption, but proofs become much more cumbersome. We will have more to say about this later, when we get to the concrete proofs.

3.3.2 The Protocol

We recall that we will give a protocol for the scenario where there are secure channels between all parties. We assume that some subset C of the players, of size at most t, will go together after the protocol and try to learn as much as they can from the data they have seen. We will say in the following that the players in C are corrupt, whereas players not in C are honest. Because the function we are to compute is specified as an arithmetic circuit over $\mathbb{F}$, our task is, loosely speaking, to compute a number of additions and multiplications in $\mathbb{F}$ of the input values (or intermediate results) while revealing nothing except for the final result(s).

We begin by defining some convenient notation

DEFINITION 3.1 *We define* $[a;f]_t$, *where* $a \in \mathbb{F}$ *and f is a polynomial over f with* $f(0) = a$ *and degree at most t:*

$$[a;f]_t = (f(1),....,f(n))$$

that is, the set of shares in secret a, computed using polynomial f. Depending on the context, we sometimes drop the degree or the polynomial from the notation, so we write $[a;f]$ *or just* $[a]$.

Notice that on one hand the notation $[a;f]$ *describes an object, namely, the set of shares* $(f(1),...,f(n))$. *On the other hand, it is also a statement. It states that* $f(0) = a$. *The notation* $[a;f]_t$ *describes the same object,* $(f(1),...,f(n))$, *but furthermore states that* $\deg(f) \leq t$.

Using the standard notation for entrywise addition, multiplication by a scalar, and the Schur product, we have for $\alpha \in \mathbb{F}$

$$[a;f]_t + [b;g]_t = (f(1)+g(1),...,f(n)+g(n)) \tag{3.3}$$

$$\alpha[a;f]_t = (\alpha f(1),...,\alpha f(n)) \tag{3.4}$$

$$[a;f]_t * [b;g]_t = (f(1)g(1),...,f(n)g(n)) \tag{3.5}$$

By the trivial observations that $f(i) + g(i) = (f+g)(i)$ and $f(i)g(i) = (fg)(i)$, the following very important facts are easy to see:

LEMMA 3.2 *The following holds for any $a, b, \alpha \in \mathbb{F}$ and any polynomials f, g over $\mathbb{F}$ of degree at most t with $f(0) = a$ and $g(0) = b$:*

$$[a;f]_t + [b;g]_t = [a+b;f+g]_t \tag{3.6}$$

$$\alpha[a;f]_t = [\alpha a; \alpha f]_t \tag{3.7}$$

$$[a;f]_t * [b;g]_t = [ab;fg]_{2t} \tag{3.8}$$

Because our notation for secret sharing both describes objects and makes statements, the equations in the lemma actually say more than might be obvious on a first reading. For example, the equation $[a;f]_t * [b;g]_t = [ab;fg]_{2t}$ states that the object $(f(1),\ldots,f(n)) * (g(1),\ldots,g(n))$ is identical to $((fg)(1),\ldots,(fg)(n))$. It also states that $(fg)(0) = ab$ and $\deg(fg) \leq 2t$.

The importance of the lemma is that it shows that by computing only on shares, we can – implicitly – compute on the corresponding secrets. For instance, the first of the preceding three relations shows that if secrets a, b have been shared, then if each player adds his or her shares of a and b, then we obtain shares in the secret $a + b$. It will be useful in the following to have language for this sort of thing, so we provide the following definition:

DEFINITION 3.3 *When we say that a player P_i distributes $[a;f_a]_t$, this means that he or she chooses a random polynomial $f_a(X)$ of degree $\leq t$ with $f_a(0) = a$ and then sends the share $f_a(j)$ to P_j, for $j = 1,\ldots,n$. Whenever players have obtained shares of a value a, based on polynomial f_a, we say that the players hold $[a;f_a]_t$.*

Suppose that the players hold $[a;f_a]_t$, $[b;f_b]_t$. Then, when we say that the players compute $[a;f_a]_t + [b;f_b]_t$, this means that each player P_i computes $f_a(i) + f_b(i)$, and by Lemma 3.2, this means that the players now hold $[a+b;f_a+f_b]_t$. In a similar way we define what it means for the players to compute $[a;f]_t * [b;g]_t$ and $\alpha[a;f]_t$.

Using the tools and terms defined so far, we can describe a protocol for securely evaluating an arithmetic circuit, see Protocol CEPS (Circuit Evaluation with Passive Security).

3.3.3 Analysis

We will now analyze the security of the CEPS protocol. We will require two conditions:

Perfect correctness. With probability 1, all players receive outputs that are correct based on the inputs supplied.

Perfect privacy. Any subset C of corrupt players, of size at most $t < n/2$, learns no information beyond $\{x_j, y_j\}_{P_j \in C}$ from executing the protocol, regardless of their computing power.

To be more precise about privacy, we will use the simulation paradigm that we also alluded to in the introduction: to show that someone learns only information X, we show that *everything* that he or she sees can be *efficiently* recreated, or simulated, given only X.

Protocol CEPS (Circuit Evaluation with Passive Security)

The protocol proceeds in three phases: the input-sharing, computation, and output-reconstruction phases.

Input sharing. Each player P_i holding input $x_i \in \mathbb{F}$ distributes $[x_i; f_{x_i}]_t$. We then go through the circuit and process the gates one by one in the computational order defined earlier. Just after the input-sharing phase, we consider all input gates as being processed. We will maintain the following:

Invariant. Recall that computing with the circuit on inputs $x_1, ..., x_n$ assigns a unique value to every wire. Consider an input or an output wire for any gate, and let $a \in \mathbb{F}$ be the value assigned to this wire. Then, if the gate has been processed, the players hold $[a; f_a]_t$ for a polynomial f_a.

We then continue with the last two phases of the protocol:

Computation phase. Repeat the following until all gates have been processed (then go to the next phase). Consider the first gate in the computational order that has not been processed yet. According to the type of gate, do one of the following:

Addition gate. The players hold $[a; f_a]_t, [b; f_b]_t$ for the two inputs a, b to the gate. The players compute $[a; f_a]_t + [b; f_b]_t = [a + b; f_a + f_b]_t$.

Multiply-by-constant gate. The players hold $[a; f_a]_t$ for the inputs a to the gate. The players compute $\alpha[a; f_a]_t = [\alpha a; \alpha f_a]_t$.

Multiplication gate. The players hold $[a; f_a]_t, [b; f_b]_t$ for the two inputs a, b to the gate.

1. The players compute $[a; f_a]_t * [b; f_b]_t = [ab; f_a f_b]_{2t}$.
2. Define $h \stackrel{\text{def}}{=} f_a f_b$. Then $h(0) = f_a(0) f_b(0) = ab$, and the parties hold $[ab; h]_{2t}$; that is, P_i holds $h(i)$. Each P_i distributes $[h(i); f_i]_t$.
3. Note that $\deg(h) = 2t \leq n - 1$. Let $\mathbf{r}$ be the recombination vector defined in Section 3.2, that is, the vector $\mathbf{r} = (r_1, ..., r_n)$ for which it holds that $h(0) = \sum_{i=1}^{n} r_i h(i)$ for any polynomial h of degree $\leq n - 1$. The players compute

$$\sum_i r_i[h(t); f_i]_t = [\sum_i r_i h(i); \sum_i r_i f_i]_t$$

$$= [h(0); \sum_i r_i f_i]_t = [ab; \sum_i r_i f_i]_t$$

Output reconstruction. At this point, all gates, including the output gates, have been processed. So do the following for each output gate (labeled i): the players hold $[y; f_y]_t$, where y is the value assigned to the output gate. Each P_j securely sends $f_y(j)$ to P_i, who uses Lagrange interpolation to compute $y = f_y(0)$ from $f_y(1), ..., f_y(t + 1)$ or any other $t + 1$ points.

To express what this exactly means in our case, we define view$_j$ to be all the values that P_j sees during execution of the protocol. More precisely, view$_j$ is a vector, where we first add x_j, and then each time P_j makes a random choice, we add it to view$_j$, and each time P_j receives a message, we add the message to view$_j$. Notice that view$_j$ is a random variable because it depends on the random choices made by P_j and the other parties (via their messages to P_j).

Privacy now means that there exists an efficient probabilistic algorithm – a simulator S – that, given $\{x_j, y_j\}_{P_j \in C}$, can produce an output whose distribution is exactly the same as the entire set of data seen by C during the protocol; that is, we want that

$$S(\{x_j, y_j\}_{P_j \in C}) \stackrel{\text{perf}}{\equiv} \{\text{view}_j\}_{P_j \in C}$$

The requirement that the distributions be exactly equal is the reason we talk about *perfect* privacy here.

We warn the reader already now that the general security definition we give in Chapter 4 looks quite different, although it too is based on the simulation paradigm. This is necessary because correctness and privacy are simply not sufficient to define security if corrupt players may deviate from the protocol.

Correctness

If the invariant defined in the CEPS protocol is maintained, it is clear that once all gates are processed, then in particular for every wire going into an output gate, players hold $[y; f_y]_t$, where y is the correct value for that wire. So the player who is to receive that value will indeed get y.

To check that the invariant holds, note that this is trivially true for the input gates after the first phase. In the computation phase, we easily see that the protocol for each type of gate maintains the invariant by Lemma 3.2 and (for multiplication) by definition of the recombination vector.

Privacy

We now argue that the values seen by t corrupted parties give them no information beyond their inputs and outputs. Note that the corrupted parties only receive two types of messages from the honest parties.

Type 1. In input-sharing and multiplication gate, they receive shares in the random sharings $[x_i; f_{x_i}]_t$ respectively $[h(i); f_i]_t$ made by honest parties.
Type 2. In output reconstruction, they receive all shares in $[y; f_y]_t$ for each output y that is for a corrupted party.

The privacy of the protocol now follows from the following two observations:

Observation 1. All values sent by honest parties to corrupted parties in input sharing and multiplication are shared using random polynomials, f_{x_i} respectively f_i, of degree at most t. Because there are at most t corrupted parties, the set of corrupted parties receives at most t shares of these polynomials, and t shares of random polynomials of degree at most t are just uniformly random values.

Observation 2. The values sent by honest parties to corrupted parties in output reconstruction to reconstruct $[y; f_y]_t$ could have been computed by the corrupted parties themselves given the values they know prior to output reconstruction plus the output y. The reason is that prior to output reconstruction, the corrupted parties already know $f_y(i)$ for each of the t corrupted parties P_i. This gives them t point on $f_y(X)$. If we give them the result y, they additionally know that $f_y(0) = y$. Thus, with their view prior to output reconstruction and the result y, they know $t + 1$ points on $f_y(X)$. Because $f_y(X)$

has degree at most t, this allows the corrupted parties to efficiently compute $f_y(X)$ using Lagrange interpolation. From $f_y(X)$ they can compute $f_y(i)$ for all honest parties P_i, and $f_y(i)$ is exactly the share in y sent by P_i in output reconstruction.

Let us first see why these two observations intuitively should make us consider the protocol secure. Recall that the goal is that the corrupted parties learn nothing extra beyond their own inputs and outputs. But clearly they don't! In input sharing and multiplication they just receive uniformly random values. This gives them nothing because they could have sampled such values themselves. In output reconstruction they then receive values that they could have computed themselves from their outputs y.

The observant reader will notice that this intuition is in fact also close to being a formal proof. Recall that our formal requirement to call a protocol perfectly private is that there exists a simulator S that given the inputs and outputs of the corrupted parties outputs a value with the same distribution as the view of the corrupted parties in the protocol. From this intuition it is clear how S would proceed:

1. It runs the corrupted parties on their own inputs according to the protocol. It can do so because it is given the inputs of the corrupted parties.
2. During input sharing and multiplication, it simulates the shares sent to the corrupted parties from the honest parties by simply sampling uniformly random values, which produces the right distribution by observation 1.
3. In output reconstruction, it will for each output y to a corrupted party compute the honest parties' shares in $[y; f_y]$ to be those consistent with the t simulated shares of the corrupted parties and $f_y(0) = y$. It can do so because y is the output of a corrupted party and hence was given as input to S. This gives the right distribution by observation 2.

We will now give the proof in more detail. It follows the preceding proof very closely. In the rest of this book, when we prove protocols secure, we will give proofs at the level of detail just provided. The purpose of the detailed proof that follows is to enable the reader interested in rigorous proofs to flesh out such proofs along the lines used in what follows.

Formalizing Observation 1

We start by formalizing observation 1. For this purpose, we define a function $\text{Strip}(\text{view}_j)$ that takes as input the view of a party $P_j \in C$ and removes from view_j the $n - t$ shares $f_{y_j}(i)$ sent to P_j in output reconstruction from parties $P_i \notin C$. The function outputs this stripped view. Notice that $\text{Strip}(\text{view}_j)$ still contains x_j, the random choices made by P_j, the shares sent to P_j in input sharing and multiplication, and the shares sent to P_j from *corrupted* parties in output reconstruction.

We can now formalize observation 1 as follows.

LEMMA 3.4 *Let $C \subset \{P_1, \dots, P_n\}$ be a set of corrupted parties, and assume for simplicity that $|C| = t$. Consider two global input vectors $\mathbf{x}^{(0)} = (x_1^{(0)}, \dots, x_n^{(0)})$ and $\mathbf{x}^{(1)} = (x_1^{(1)}, \dots, x_n^{(1)})$, where $x_j^{(0)} = x_j^{(1)}$ for $P_j \in C$; that is, the corrupted parties have the same inputs in both vectors. For $b = 0, 1$, let view_j^b be the view of P_j after running Protocol CEPS (Circuit Evaluation with Passive Security) on $\mathbf{x}^b$. Then it holds that*

$$\{\text{Strip}(\text{view}_j^{(0)})\}_{P_j \in C} \stackrel{\text{perf}}{\equiv} \{\text{Strip}(\text{view}_j^{(1)})\}_{P_j \in C} \tag{3.9}$$

Proof For each part of the protocol, we check that C sees the same distribution in case (0) and in case (1):

Input sharing. Each $P_i \in C$ distributes $[x_i^{(b)}]_t$. Because $x_i^{(0)} = x_i^{(1)}$, this clearly leads to the same distribution on the shares in the two cases.

Each $P_j \notin C$ distributes $[x_j^{(b)}]_t$. It might be the case that $x_j^{(0)} \neq x_j^{(1)}$, but parties in C see at most t shares, and these are uniformly random and independent of $x_j^{(b)}$. In particular, the distribution is the same when $b = 0$ and $b = 1$.

Addition. Here no party sends or receives anything, so there is nothing to show.

Multiplication. Follows as for input sharing: we can assume that all values held by parties in C before the current multiplication have the same distribution in case (0) and in case (1). This is trivially the case for the first multiplication and can be assumed by induction for the following ones. In particular, the values they are supposed to locally multiply have the same distribution. Therefore, all values generated and sent by parties in C have the same distribution. The honest parties only send shares of random sharings, and C only sees t shares of each sharing. These are just uniformly random values.

Output reconstruction. Here all shares in $[y_j^{(b)}; f_{y_j^{(b)}}]$ are securely sent to P_j, for $j = 1, \ldots, n$. If P_j is honest, parties in C see nothing. If $P_j \in C$ is corrupt, then parties in C see *all* shares in $[y_j^{(b)}; f_{y_j^{(b)}}]$. But Strip exactly deletes the shares sent from honest parties to corrupted parties. The shares sent from corrupted parties to corrupted parties are computed from their view prior to output reconstruction, which we, by induction, can assume are identically distributed when $b = 0$ and $b = 1$.

∎

Formalizing Observation 2

We then formalize observation 2. For this purpose, we need another function, Dress.

For any value $\mathbf{y}_C = \{y_j\}_{P_j \in C} \in \mathbb{F}^t$, we define a function $\text{Dress}_{\mathbf{y}_C}$ that takes an input $\{\text{view}'_j\}_{P_j \in C}$, where each view'_j is a stripped view of P_j; that is, $\text{view}'_j = \text{Strip}(\text{view}_j)$, where view_j is a possible view of P_j. The output is of the form $\{\text{view}''_j\}_{P_j \in C}$, where each view''_j is of the form of a full view of P_j. The purpose of $\text{Dress}_{\mathbf{y}_C}$ is to try to fill in those values that Strip removed. It attempts this as follows: for each $P_j \in C$, it takes the t shares that the corrupted parties hold in the output of P_j; then it assumes that the output of P_j is the value y_j given in $\mathbf{y}_C$, computes which shares the honest parties would hold in y_j in that case, and extends view'_j with these shares, as if they were sent to P_j. In more detail, first, $\text{Dress}_{\mathbf{y}_C}$ inspects each view'_j, $P_j \in C$, and reads off the shares of the output of P_j that were sent to P_j from corrupted parties $P_i \in C$ – recall that we did not delete these shares, only the shares sent by honest parties. Thus, for $P_j \in C$, it now knows the shares of the t corrupted parties in the output of P_j – call these $f_{y_j}(i)$ for $P_i \in C$. Then it takes the value y_j from $\mathbf{y}_C$ and defines $f_{y_j}(0) \overset{\text{def}}{=} y_j$. After this, $\text{Dress}_{\mathbf{y}_C}$ has defined $f_{y_j}(X)$ in $t + 1$ points and can hence compute the unique degree-t polynomial $f(X)$ consistent with these points. Then for $P_i \notin C$ it adds the share $f_{y_j}(i)$ to view'_j as if P_i sent $f_{y_j}(i)$ to P_j. Call the result view''_j, and let $\text{Dress}_{\mathbf{y}_C}(\{\text{view}'_j\}_{P_j \in C}) = \{\text{view}''_j\}_{P_j \in C}$.

We can now formalize observation 2 as follows:

LEMMA 3.5 *Let* $C \subset \{P_1, \ldots, P_n\}$ *be a set of corrupted parties, and assume for simplicity that* $|C| = t$. *Let* **x** *be any input vector, let* $(y_1, \ldots, y_n) = f(\mathbf{x})$, *let* $\mathbf{y}_C = \{y_j\}_{P_j \in C}$, *and let* view_j *be the view of* P_j *after running Protocol CEPS (Circuit Evaluation with Passive Security) on* **x**. *Then*

$$\text{Dress}_{\mathbf{y}_C}(\{\text{Strip}(\text{view}_j)\}_{P_j \in C}) = \{\text{view}_j\}_{P_j \in C}$$

Proof The view view_j contains n shares in the sharing $[y'_j; f_{y'_j}]_t$ of the output y'_j that P_j computes in the protocol. By perfect correctness of Protocol CEPS (Circuit Evaluation with Passive Security), we know that $y'_j = y_j$ for the y_j given by $(y_1, \ldots, y_n) = f(\mathbf{x})$. Thus view_j contains n shares in a sharing $[y_j; f_{y_j}]_t$ of y_j. Then Strip removes the shares of the honest parties. The function $\text{Dress}_{\mathbf{y}_C}$, however, recomputes the same shares because it computes them from the same correct y_j (the y_j in $\mathbf{y}_C$ was taken from $(y_1, \ldots, y_n)$) and the t shares of the corrupted parties, which were not deleted from view_j. By Lagrange interpolation, this gives exactly the shares back that Strip deleted. See Exercise 3.2 for the case where fewer than t parties are corrupted. ∎

Formalizing the Simulator

We can also formalize the simulator S via the two functions defined earlier. It proceeds as follows:

1. The input to S is $\{x_j, y_j\}_{j \in C}$.
2. It defines a global input vector $\mathbf{x}^{(0)} = (x_1^{(0)}, \ldots, x_n^{(0)})$, where $x_j^{(0)} = x_j$ for $P_j \in C$ and $x_j^{(0)} = 0$ for $P_j \notin C$. Here x_j for $P_j \in C$ are the values it received as input.
3. It runs Protocol CEPS (Circuit Evaluation with Passive Security) on $\mathbf{x}^{(0)}$ and lets $\text{view}_j^{(0)}$ be the view of P_j in this execution of the protocol.
4. It lets $\mathbf{y}_C = \{y_j\}_{P_j \in C}$, where y_j is the value it received as input.
5. It outputs $\text{Dress}_{\mathbf{y}_C}(\{\text{Strip}(\text{view}_j^{(0)})\}_{P_j \in C})$.

Notice that running the protocol on wrong inputs for the honest parties results in sending t shares of wrong values during the input-sharing and computation phase. Because the corrupted parties only receive t shares, this is the same as just sending them uniformly random values. Then Strip and $\text{Dress}_{\mathbf{y}_C}$ remove the shares sent by the honest parties in output reconstruction and replace them with shares consistent with the shares of the corrupted parties and the correct output. Thus the preceding way to specify the simulator is equivalent to the one given earlier.

Formally Analyzing the Simulator

We now prove that the simulator produces the right distribution.

THEOREM 3.6 *Let* $\mathbf{x} = (x_1, \ldots, x_n)$ *be a global input vector, and let* $(y_1, \ldots, y_n) = f(\mathbf{x})$ *and let* $C \subset \{P_1, \ldots, P_n\}$ *with* $|C| = t$. *For* $P_j \in C$, *let* view_j *be the view of* P_j *when running Protocol CEPS (Circuit Evaluation with Passive Security) on the input* **x**. *Then*

$$S(\{x_j, y_j\}_{P_j \in C}) \overset{\text{perf}}{\equiv} \{\text{view}_j\}_{P_j \in C}$$

Proof Let $\mathbf{y}_C = \{y_j\}_{P_j \in C}$ for the values y_j defined in the premise of the theorem. Define $\mathbf{x}^{(0)} = (x_1^{(0)}, \ldots, x_n^{(0)})$, where $x_j^{(0)} = x_j$ for the x_j given in the premise of the theorem for

$P_j \in C$ and $x_j^{(0)} = 0$ for $P_j \notin C$. Let $\text{view}_j^{(0)}$ be the view of P_j generated by S by running Protocol CEPS (Circuit Evaluation with Passive Security) on the input $\mathbf{x}^{(0)}$.

By construction of the simulator, we have that

$$S(\{x_j, y_j\}_{P_j \in C}) \stackrel{\text{perf}}{\equiv} \text{Dress}_{\mathbf{y}_C}(\{\text{Strip}(\text{view}_j^{(0)})\}_{P_j \in C}) \tag{3.10}$$

Because S generates $\text{view}_j^{(0)}$ by running Protocol CEPS (Circuit Evaluation with Passive Security) on the input $\mathbf{x}^{(0)}$, and because $x_j = x_j^{(0)}$ for $P_j \in C$ and $|C| = t$, it follows from Lemma 3.4 that

$$\{\text{Strip}(\text{view}_j^{(0)})\}_{P_j \in C} \stackrel{\text{perf}}{\equiv} \{\text{Strip}(\text{view}_j)\}_{P_j \in C} \tag{3.11}$$

We then apply Proposition 2.8, Property 4 to Eq. (3.11). This gives

$$A(\{\text{Strip}(\text{view}_j^{(0)})\}_{P_j \in C}) \stackrel{\text{perf}}{\equiv} A(\{\text{Strip}(\text{view}_j)\}_{P_j \in C}) \tag{3.12}$$

for all functions A. Let $A = \text{Dress}_{\mathbf{y}_C}$. Plugging this A into Eq. (3.12), we get

$$\text{Dress}_{\mathbf{y}_C}(\{\text{Strip}(\text{view}_j^{(0)})\}_{P_j \in C}) \stackrel{\text{perf}}{\equiv} \text{Dress}_{\mathbf{y}_C}(\{\text{Strip}(\text{view}_j)\}_{P_j \in C}) \tag{3.13}$$

By Lemma 3.5, we have that

$$\text{Dress}_{\mathbf{y}_C}(\{\text{Strip}(\text{view}_j)\}_{P_j \in C}) \stackrel{\text{perf}}{\equiv} \{\text{view}_j\}_{P_j \in C} \tag{3.14}$$

Using Eqs. (3.10), (3.13), and (3.14) and the transitivity of $\stackrel{\text{perf}}{\equiv}$ (Proposition 2.8, Property 3), we get

$$S(\{x_j, y_j\}_{P_j \in C}) \stackrel{\text{perf}}{\equiv} \{\text{view}_j\}_{P_j \in C}$$

as desired.   ∎

To formally prove that Protocol CEPS (Circuit Evaluation with Passive Security) is perfectly private, we have to prove Theorem 3.6 for all C with $|C| \le t$, not just $|C| = t$. There is a technical issue here that we need to take care of: suppose that the circuit computes $[a; f_a]_t, [b; f_b]_t$, and $[a + b, f_a + f_b]_t$ as intermediate values, and the corrupt players have output gates that let them learn a, b and $a + b$. If we would just open these directly, the corrupt players would see three polynomials where the sum of the first two equals the third, and so the simulator would have to ensure that this also happens in the simulation. This would require special care in the case where $|C| < t$ because there the output polynomials are not determined from the shares of corrupt players and the outputs; the simulator would have to make some random choices that would ensure the right relations between polynomials.

However, recall that we have assumed that a multiplication always happens immediately before we open an output. While doing the multiplication, players generate fresh random polynomials, and the sharing of the multiplication result is done using a linear combination of these polynomials. As a result, we can assume that whenever we open an output, the polynomial that is revealed is uniformly random, with the only constraint that it determines the correct output value. This allows the simulator to handle each output gate independently. Using this observation, the reader is invited to prove the general case.

EXERCISE 3.2 Give a rigorous proof for Theorem 3.6 for the case $|C| < t$. [*Hint*: Dress is going to be a probabilistic algorithm.]

3.3.4 Example Computations and Proofs by Example

The preceding argument for the output reconstruction shows that it does no harm to give all shares of an output to the corrupted parties. This, in particular, shows that the shares do not carry information about how the result was computed: if $c = a + b$ is reconstructed and the result is 6, then the n shares of c will be consistent with both $a = 2, b = 4$ and $a = 1, b = 5$ – otherwise, the protocol could not be secure. We will, however, look at two exercises to exemplify this phenomenon.

Consider a setting where variables a and b have been computed and where then a variable $c = a + b$ is computed and output to P_1. Assume that $n = 3$ and $t = 1$. That is, we have three parties P_1, P_2, P_3, and one can be corrupted. For the sake of example, say it is P_1. Because $t = 1$, we are using polynomials of the form $f(X) = \alpha_0 + \alpha_1 X$, a.k.a. lines.

Assume that $a = 2$ and that a is shared using the polynomial $a(X) = 2 + 2X$, and assume that $b = 4$ and that b is shared using the polynomial $b(X) = 4 + X$. This gives the following computation:

Variable	Value	P_1	P_2	P_3
a	2	**4**	6	8
b	4	**5**	6	7
$c = a + b$	6	**9**	**12**	**15**

We show the shares $a(1) = 4$, $a(2) = 6$, and $a(3) = 8$ and the shares $b(1) = 5$, $b(2) = 6$, and $b(3) = 7$ in the rows to the right of the variables and their values. When the parties compute the variable $c = a + b$, they simply add locally and compute the shares 9, 12, and 15. In the table, all shares that P_1 would see in this case are put in boldface.

We want that P_1 only learns that $c = 6$ and nothing about a and b except that $a + b = 6$. We demonstrate that this is the case by an example. We let the party P_1 make the hypothesis that $a = 1$ and $b = 5$. Hopefully, it cannot exclude this hypothesis. For starters, P_1 has the following view (not knowing the shares of P_1 and P_2):

Variable	Value	P_1	P_2	P_3
a	1	**4**	?	?
b	5	**5**	?	?
$c = a + b$	6	**9**	**12**	**15**

If $a(0) = 1$ and $a(1) = 4$, then it must be the case that $a(X) = 1 + 3X$, which would imply that $a(2) = 7$ and $a(3) = 10$. Furthermore, if $b(0) = 5$ and $b(1) = 5$, then it must be the case that $b(X) = 5 + 0X$, which would imply that $b(2) = 5$ and $b(3) = 5$. If P_1 fills these values into the table, he or she concludes that the network must be configured as follows for his or her hypothesis to hold:

Variable	Value	P_1	P_2	P_3
a	1	4	7	10
b	5	5	5	5
$c = a+b$	6	9	12	15

Note that this hypothesis is consistent with the protocol and what P_1 has seen because $7+5 = 12$ and $10+5 = 15$. Therefore, $a = 1$ and $b = 5$ are as possible as $a = 2$ and $b = 4$.

EXERCISE 3.3 In the preceding example, P_1 could also have made the hypothesis that $a = 0$ and $b = 6$. Show that P_1 cannot exclude this example by filling in the following table and noting that it is consistent.

Variable	Value	P_1	P_2	P_3
a	0	4	?	?
b	6	5	?	?
$c = a+b$	6	9	12	15

We now consider an example of a multiplication of variables $a = 2$ and $b = 3$. The polynomials used to share them are $a(X) = 2 + X$ and $b(X) = 3 - X$:

Variable	Value	P_1	P_2	P_3
a	2	3	4	5
b	3	2	1	0
$d = ab$	6	6	4	0
d_1	6	4	2	0
d_2	4	6	8	10
d_3	0	0	0	0
$c = 3d_1 - 3d_2 + d_3$	6	-6	-18	-30

We explain the lower part of the table soon, but first note that the shares of $d = ab = 6$ are not on a line because all the other shares are. The reason is that $d(X) = a(X)b(X)$ is not a line but a quadratic polynomial. In fact, $d(X) = (2 + X)(3 - X) = 6 + X - X^2$, which is consistent with $d(1) = 6$, $d(2) = 4$, and $d(3) = 0$.

After having computed the local products d_i, the next step in the multiplication algorithm uses the Lagrange formula for computing d from d_1, d_2, d_3, so we derive that one. Because $2t = 2$, we are looking at quadratic polynomials $y(X) = \alpha_0 + \alpha_1 X + \alpha_2 X^2$, where α_0 is the secret. Therefore, the shares are $y_1 = y(1) = \alpha_0 + \alpha_1 + \alpha_2$, $y_2 = y(2) = \alpha_0 + 2\alpha_1 + 4\alpha_2$, and $y_3 = y(3) = \alpha_0 + 3\alpha_1 + 9\alpha_2$. It follows that α_0 can always be computed from the shares because $\alpha_0 = 3y_1 - 3y_2 + y_3$. This formula was found using simple Gaussian elimination but is also given by the Lagrange interpolation formula. That is, in our case, the recombination vector is $r = (3, -3, 1)$.

In our example we have $d_1 = 6$, $d_2 = 4$, and $d_3 = 0$, and indeed, $3d_1 - 3d_2 + d_3 = 18 - 12 = 6 = ab$, as it should be. Each party now shares its value d_i. In the table, P_1 used the polynomial $d_1(X) = 6 - 2X$, P_2 used the polynomial $d_2(X) = 4 + 2X$, and P_3 used the polynomial $d_3(X) = 0 + 0X$. The parties then locally combine their shares by an inner product with the recombination vector $(3, -3, 1)$, leading to the shares in the table: for example, P_1 computed $-6 = 3 \cdot 4 + (-3) \cdot 6 + 1 \cdot 0$.

Again, an example will reveal that any other hypothesis, such as $a = 1$ and $b = 6$, would have given the exact same view to P_1. The reader is encourage to do this by solving the following exercise.

EXERCISE 3.4 Show that the values seen by P_1 are consistent with the hypothesis $a = 1$ and $b = 6$ by filling in the following table and noting that it is consistent.

Variable	Value	P_1	P_2	P_3
a	1	3	?	?
b	6	2	?	?
$d = ab$	6	6	?	?
d_1	6	4	2	0
d_2	?	6	?	?
d_3	?	0	?	?
$c = 3d_1 - 3d_2 + d_3$	6	−6	−18	−30

[To check the solution, it must say −42 and 84 somewhere.]

3.4 Optimality of the Corruption Bound

What happens if the number t of corrupt players is larger than what we assumed so far; that is, what if $t \geq n/2$? Then the CEPS protocol no longer works; the multiplication subprotocol breaks down. You may want to take a moment to see why this is the case. We will now show that this is no coincidence. In fact, there are functions that cannot be computed securely if $t \geq n/2$.

Toward a contradiction, suppose that there is a protocol π with *perfect privacy* and *perfect correctness* (as defined earlier) for two players P_1, P_2 to securely evaluate the logical AND of their respective private input bits b_1, b_2, that is, $b_1 \wedge b_2$. The set C of corrupt players from the definition may in this case be $C = \{P_1\}$ or $C = \{P_2\}$, that is, $n = 2, t = 1$.

We assume as usual that the players communicate using a perfect *error-free communication channel*. Without loss of generality, we may assume that the protocol is of the following form:

1. Each player P_i has a private input bit b_i. Before the protocol starts, the players select private random strings $r_i \in \{0,1\}^*$ of appropriate length. Their actions in the forthcoming protocol are now uniquely determined by these initial choices.
2. P_1 sends the first message m_{11}, followed by P_2's message m_{21}. This continues until P_2 has sent sufficient information for P_1 to compute $y = b_1 \wedge b_2$. Finally, P_1 sends y (and some halting symbol) to P_2. The transcript of an s-round conversation is

$$\mathcal{T} = (m_{11}, m_{21}, \ldots, m_{1s}, m_{2s}, y)$$

For $i = 1,2$, the view of P_i is

$$\mathrm{view}_i = (b_i, r_i, \mathcal{T})$$

To be concrete about the assumptions, perfect correctness here means that the protocol always halts (in a number of rounds s that may perhaps depend on the inputs and the random coins) and that the correct result is always computed. Perfect privacy means that the distribution of P_i's view of the protocol depends only on his or her input bit b_i and the result $r = b_1 \wedge b_2$.

Note that these conditions imply that if one of the players has an input bit equal to 1, then he or she learns the other player's input bit with certainty, whereas if his or her input bit equals 0, the player should have no information at all about the other player's input bit.

Let $\mathcal{T}(c,d)$ denote the set of transcripts $\mathcal{T}$, which can arise when $b_1 = c$ and $b_2 = d$. That is, if $\mathcal{T} = (m_{11}, m_{21}, \ldots, m_{1s}, m_{2s}, y)$, then there exist r_1 and r_2 such that running P_1 with input $b_1 = c$ and randomness r_1 along with P_2 with input $b_2 = d$ and randomness r_2 will result in $\mathcal{T}$ being generated. Namely, if we assume that P_1 receives the message m_{2i} in round i for $i = 1, \ldots, s$, then with $b_1 = c$ and randomness r_1, P_1 would send exactly the message m_{1i+1} in round $i + 1$ and similarly for P_2.

It follows from perfect privacy that

$$\mathcal{T}(0,1) = \mathcal{T}(0,0)$$

Assume that P_1 has input $b_1 = 0$ and P_2 has input $b_2 = 0$ and that P_1 sees a transcript $\mathcal{T}$ that is not from $\mathcal{T}(0,1)$. Then P_1 can conclude that $b_2 = 0$, contradicting perfect privacy. Similarly, we have that

$$\mathcal{T}(1,0) = \mathcal{T}(0,0)$$

This gives

$$\mathcal{T}(1,0) \cap \mathcal{T}(1,0) = \mathcal{T}(0,0) \cap \mathcal{T}(0,0) = \mathcal{T}(0,0) \tag{3.15}$$

However, we also have

$$\mathcal{T}(1,0) \cap \mathcal{T}(1,0) \subset \mathcal{T}(1,1) \tag{3.16}$$

This is simply by definition of the sets. Thus, if $\mathcal{T} \in \mathcal{T}(1,0) \cap \mathcal{T}(1,0)$, then in particular $\mathcal{T} \in \mathcal{T}(1,0)$. Hence there exists r_1 such that running P_1 with input $b_1 = 1$ and randomness r_1 is consistent with $\mathcal{T} = (m_{11}, m_{21}, \ldots, m_{1s}, m_{2s}, y)$; that is, if we assume that P_1 receives the message m_{2i} in round i for $i = 1, \ldots, s$, then with $b_1 = 1$ and randomness r_1, P_1 would send exactly the message m_{1i+1} in round $i + 1$. Similarly, we get from $\mathcal{T} \in \mathcal{T}(0,1)$ that there exists exists r_2 such that running P_2 with input $b_2 = 1$ and randomness r_2 is consistent with *the same* transcript $\mathcal{T}$. Hence, by definition, $\mathcal{T} \in \mathcal{T}(1,1)$.

From Eqs. (3.15) and (3.16), we get

$$\mathcal{T}(0,0) \subset \mathcal{T}(1,1)$$

From perfect correctness, we have that all transcripts from $\mathcal{T}(0,0)$ have output bit $y = 0$. From perfect correctness, we also have that all transcripts from $\mathcal{T}(1,1)$ have output bit $y = 1$. Hence

$$\mathcal{T}(0,0) \cap \mathcal{T}(1,1) = \emptyset$$

so because $\mathcal{T}(0,0) \neq \emptyset$, we get

$$\mathcal{T}(0,0) \not\subset \mathcal{T}(1,1)$$

a contradiction.

The argument can be generalized to show the impossibility of two-party protocols where privacy or correctness may fail with small but negligible probability or even with small constant probability. To show that a similar impossibility results for $n > 2$ players, assume that there exist an n-player protocol π where each P_i has an input bit b_i, and the protocol computes $b_1 \wedge \cdots \wedge b_n$ as output for everyone, with perfect security against $t \geq n/2$ corrupted players. Such a protocol would imply the existence of a protocol for two players A, B computing the AND, which we have just seen is impossible. We construct this protocol by letting A and B emulate π such that A runs $n/2$ players in π "in his or her head" and B runs the others. A and B exchange message when a message in π is sent between the two sets of $n/2$ players. We can make this protocol compute the AND of two input bits from A and B, and security follows from the security of π. The details are straightforward and are left to the reader.

EXERCISE 3.5 Show that there is no two-party perfectly secure and perfectly correct protocol for the OR function $(b_1, b_2) \mapsto b_1 \vee b_2$.

EXERCISE 3.6 Show that the following protocol is a perfectly secure (in the sense of polytime simulation) and perfectly correct protocol for the XOR function $(b_1, b_2) \mapsto b_1 \oplus b_2$. Party P_1 sends b_1 to P_2 and P_2 sends b_2 to P_1. Then they both output $b_1 \oplus b_2$.

EXERCISE 3.7 Any binary Boolean function $B : \{0,1\} \times \{0,1\} \to \{0,1\}$ can be given by a vector $(o_{00}, o_{01}, o_{10}, o_{11}) \in \{0,1\}^4$ by letting $B(b_1, b_2) = o_{b_1 b_2}$. The AND function is given by $(0,0,0,1)$, the OR function is given by $(0,1,1,1)$, the XOR function is given by $(0,1,1,0)$, and the NAND function is given by $(1,1,1,0)$. Show that all functions specified by a vector with an even number of 1s can be securely computed as defined earlier and that none of the other functions can.

Computational Security

The assumptions about the players' unbounded computational resources and the communication channel are essential for the impossibility results. It can be shown that any of the following conditions is sufficient for the existence of a secure two-party protocol for the AND function (as well as OR):

1. Existence of trapdoor one-way permutations.
2. Both players are memory bounded.
3. The communication channel is noisy.

We sketch a secure AND protocol based on the assumption that there exists a public-key cryptosystem where the public keys can be sampled in two different ways. There is the usual key generation that gives an encryption key ek and the corresponding decryption key dk. The other method only generates ek, and even the party having generated ek cannot decrypt ciphertexts under ek. We assume that these two key generators give encryption keys with the same distribution.

If $b_1 = 0$, then P_1 samples ek uniformly at random without learning the decryption key. If $b_1 = 1$, then P_1 samples ek in such a way that it learns the decryption key dk. It sends ek to P_2. Then P_2 sends $C = E_{pk}(b_2)$ to P_1. If $b_1 = 0$, then P_1 outputs 0 and sends $y = 0$ to P_2, which outputs y. If $b_1 = 1$, then P_1 decrypts C to learn b_2, outputs b_2, and sends $y = b_2$ to P_2, which outputs y.

Because the two ways to sample the public key gives the same distribution, the protocol is perfectly secure for P_1. The security of P_2 depends on the encryption hiding b_2 when $b_1 = 0$ and is therefore computational. In particular, a computationally unbounded P_1 could just use brute force to decrypt C and learn b_2 even when $b_1 = 0$.

This protocol can in principle be made secure against deviations by letting the parties use generic zero-knowledge proofs to show that they followed the protocol. This in principle leads to secure two-party protocols for any function.

EXERCISE 3.8

1. Use the special cryptosystem from earlier to give a secure protocol for the OR function.
2. Try to generalize to any two-party function, where one of the parties has a constant number of input bits and the other party might have an arbitrary number of inputs. [*Hint*: The party with a constant number of inputs will have perfect security and will not send just a single encryption key.]

4

Models

4.1 Introduction

The protocol we described in Chapter 3 is perfectly correct and perfectly private, but it cannot tolerate that any of the parties deviate from the protocol. In later chapters we will present protocols that are correct and private even if some parties do not follow the protocol. Such protocols are called robust. Before we can prove that these protocols are robust, we need a good definition of what we mean by that.

In this section we will describe a security model for cryptographic protocols known as the UC model. Here *UC* stands for *universally composable*. The name was adopted because a protocol proven secure in this model remains secure regardless of the context in which it is used. In other words, it can be "universally" composed with any set of other protocols. Our formulation of the UC model differs in several respects from the way it was originally formalized in the literature. We will hint at these differences as we go; some additional comments can be found in the Notes section of this chapter.

Before we look at the formal details, let us start by discussing the basic ideas of how to define privacy and robustness of a protocol and last, but not least, why and how these two concepts should be defined via one common definition because they are closely entangled.

4.1.1 Defining Privacy

It is convenient to first look back on how we defined privacy in Chapter 3. Informally, we defined a protocol to be private (against corruptions of size t) as follows: first, pick an input $(x_1, \ldots, x_n)$ for the protocol, and make a run of the protocol on this input. Then pick some $C \subset \{P_1, \ldots, P_n\}$ with $|C| \leq t$ and consider the values $\{\text{view}_j\}_{P_j \in C}$, where view_j is the view of party P_j in the execution. The values $\{\text{view}_j\}_{P_j \in C}$ constitute exactly the information leaked to the corrupted parties, C, during an execution. In the following we therefore call the values $\{\text{view}_j\}_{P_j \in C}$ the leaked values.

We then want to say that the leaked values do not allow the corrupted parties to learn anything that they should not learn. It is clear that the corrupted parties necessarily must learn their own inputs and outputs; in fact, this is the entire purpose of the protocol. We therefore call the values $\{x_j, y_j\}_{P_j \in C}$ the allowed values.

In these new terms we can give the following informal definition of what it means for a protocol to be private:

A protocol is private if it always holds that the leaked values contain no more information than the allowed values.

This leaves us with the problem of defining what it means for one value V_1 to contain no more information than some other value V_2. One very convenient way to define this is to note that if V_1 can be computed from (only) V_2, then clearly V_1 cannot contain more information than V_2. However, this definition would be a bit too liberal for our use, in particular, if we consider security that is guaranteed using cryptography. Suppose, for instance, that we make $V_2 = n$ public, where $n = pq$ is an integer that is the product of two large primes p, q. And let us define $V_1 = (p, q)$. Now, since the prime factors of integers are unique, it is certainly *possible* to compute $V_1 = (p, q)$ from $V_2 = n$. Nevertheless, if factoring large integers is a hard problem (as we hope if we use the RSA public-key cryptosystem), we could make n public and expect that, in practice, p, q will remain secret.

From this point of view, one would claim that $V_2 = (p, q)$ contains more than $V_1 = n$ because given V_2 we can efficiently compute much more than if we were given only V_1. We therefore say that a value V_1 contains no more knowledge than V_2 if V_1 can be computed *efficiently* from V_2.

Following this line of thought, we get the following more developed definition of privacy:

> *A protocol is private if it always holds that the leaked values can be computed efficiently from the allowed values.*

To prove that a protocol is private, one therefore has to show that there exists an efficient algorithm that takes the allowed values as input and outputs the leaked values. This program, which demonstrates that it is possible to efficiently compute the leaked values from the allowed values, is what we called the simulator. By our latest attempt at a definition, the simulator would be required to efficiently compute the leaked values from the allowed values. Note, however, that the views $view_i$ are generated by the parties in the protocol, and they are allowed to make random choices. Therefore $\{view_j\}_{P_j \in C}$ is not a fixed value but actually a random variable. Therefore, the simulator also will have to output a random variable, that is, use internal random choices. This is why the actual definition of privacy says the following:

> *There exists an efficient simulator S such that the simulated values $S(\{x_j, y_j\}_{P_j \in C})$ and the leaked values $\{view_j\}_{P_j \in C}$ have the same distribution.*

4.1.2 Defining Robustness

We now sketch how we define robustness. Robustness has to do with how an attack influences the protocol and achieves some effect, in that the outputs may be different. In other words, an attack on robustness tries to achieve influence rather than knowledge. For the definition, we will therefore play exactly the same game as we did with privacy, just using influence as the basic currency instead of knowledge.

When we consider robustness, we assume that the corrupted parties are what we call Byzantine. This just means that we make absolutely no assumptions on how they behave. Concretely, we assume that an adversary has taken control over the corrupted parties, and every time the protocol instructs them to send some message, which is supposed to be computed in a particular way according to the protocol, the adversary may instruct them send any other message. Our job, as protocol designer, is then to design the protocol to work correctly regardless of how the adversary behaves.

Before discussing influence in more general terms, it is instructive to see two examples of what constitutes influence.

EXAMPLE 4.1 Consider Protocol CEPS (Circuit Evaluation with Passive Security), and let us run it with three parties and $t = 1$. Let us compute the function $f(x_1,x_2,x_3) = (x_1x_2x_3,x_2,x_3)$. That is, P_1 is to learn $x_1x_2x_3$, and the other parties are only to learn their own input. Let us now assume that P_1 is corrupted and show an example of how P_1 can influence the protocol. Suppose that P_1 replaces its input x_1 by $x_1' = 1$; that is, in the input-sharing phase, it does a secret sharing of 1. Then it follows the rest of the protocol honestly. As a result, P_1 will learn $y_1 = x_1'x_2x_3 = 1x_2x_3 = x_2x_3$. ∎

The preceding example shows that Protocol CEPS (Circuit Evaluation with Passive Security) allows P_1 to influence the protocol in such a way that he or she always learns x_2x_3. The reader should take a moment to contemplate whether we should consider this a security problem, and if so, why?

EXAMPLE 4.2 Consider again Protocol CEPS (Circuit Evaluation with Passive Security) with three parties, $t = 1$, and $f(x_1,x_2,x_3) = (x_1x_2x_3,x_2,x_3)$. Suppose that we order the gates in the corresponding circuit such that we first compute $[u]_t = [x_1x_2]_t$ and then $[y_1]_t = [ux_3]_t$. Finally, in the output phase, players send all their shares in $[y_1]_t$ to P_1.[1] Let us again assume that P_1 is corrupt. Now, however, we assume that P_1 follows the protocol during the input-sharing phase using the input $x_1' = 0$. Then, during the multiplication protocol, where $[u]_t = [x_1'x_2]_t$ is computed, players locally compute products that define a polynomial h with $h(0) = x_1'x_2$. However, P_1 does not distribute $[h(1)]_t$ as he or she is supposed to but instead distributes $[r_1^{-1} + h(1)]$, where we recall that r_1 is the first entry in the reconstruction vector. This means that the result becomes

$$[u]_t = r_1[r_1^{-1} + h(1)]_t + \sum_{i=2}^{n} r_i[h(i)]_t$$

$$= [r_1r_1^{-1} + r_1h(1) + \sum_{i=2}^{n} r_ih(i)]_t$$

$$= [1 + \sum_{i=1}^{n} r_ih(i)]_t$$

$$= [1 + x_1'x_2]_t$$

$$= [1]_t$$

where the last equality follows because $x_1' = 0$. Then P_1 follows the protocol honestly in the multiplication protocol for $[y_1]_t = [ux_3]_t$ and in the reconstruction phase. As a result, P_1 will learn $y_1 = ux_3 = 1x_3 = x_3$. ∎

---

[1] Note that the other parties can just output their input, though the generic protocol would secret share their inputs and then reconstruct them toward the parties.

The preceding example shows that Protocol CEPS (Circuit Evaluation with Passive Security) allows P_1 to influence the protocol in such a way that P_1 always learns x_3. Should we consider this a security problem, and if so, why?

It seems natural to say that a protocol is robust if the adversary cannot gain anything from influencing the protocol. Note, however, that if the adversary is able to take over a party P_i, then some influence is inevitable, namely, input substitution. If, for example, the adversary is controlling party P_1, then it can, of course, force P_1 to use some value x_1' as the input to the protocol instead of x_1. As a result, the protocol would compute $f(x_1', x_2, \ldots, x_n)$ instead of $f(x_1, x_2, \ldots, x_n)$. There is no way to combat this because it is identical to the situation in which an honest P_1 is running with input x_1', which is, of course, a perfectly allowable situation. We therefore have an allowed influence that we must accept. In the secure function evaluation protocol, the only allowed influence is input substitution.

In general, we decide on what the allowed influence is by specifying an ideally secure way to solve the problem at hand. Then we say that any influence that is possible in this ideal world is allowed influence. To specify an ideal world for secure function evaluation, we could imagine a perfectly trusted hardware box that allows each P_i to securely input x_i to the box without the other parties learning anything about x_i. Then the box computes $(y_1, \ldots, y_n) = f(x_1, \ldots, x_n)$ and outputs y_i to P_i in such a way that the other parties learn nothing about y_i. After this, the box blows up such that its internal state is lost forever. Except for the explosion, it is hard to imagine a more secure way to do function evaluation. And it is easy to see that the only power a set of corrupted parties has in this ideal world is to pool their inputs and then compute some alternative inputs to the box; that is, they can only do input substitution.

The influence that the attacker has on the actual protocol execution is called the actual influence. For a secure function evaluation protocol that runs on a network with secure channels, the actual influence of the adversary is that he or she can send arbitrary values to the honest parties on behalf of one or more of the corrupted parties.

We then say that a protocol is robust if no matter how the adversary uses his or her actual influence, the effect will always correspond to an effect of an allowed influence. This would, namely, show that whatever effect the actual influence has, the attacker could have obtained the same using an allowed influence, so the effect is, by definition, allowed. This leads to the following first attempt at defining robustness.

> *A protocol is robust if it always holds that the effect of an actual influence can also be obtained using an allowed influence.*

To make this more precise, recall that when we considered privacy, we said that a protocol was private if the actual values leaked by the protocol could be efficiently simulated given the allowed values. We will reuse this approach. So we will require that for every adversary attacking the protocol, we can efficiently compute an allowed way to influence the protocol that has the same effect. The efficient algorithm computing this allowed influence is called a *simulator*.

> *A protocol is robust if there exists an efficient simulator S such that for every adversary attacking the protocol, S can efficiently compute an allowed influence with the same effect.*

For the secure function evaluation protocol, this definition just means that for each attack on the protocol resulting in outputs $(y'_1, \ldots, y'_n)$, one should be able to efficiently compute an input substitution for the corrupted parties that makes the ideal box for function evaluation give the same outputs $(y'_1, \ldots, y'_n)$.

Let us return to the preceding two examples of possible attacks. In the first example, P_1 influences the protocol as to always learn $x_2 x_3$. This is not a problem because P_1 can obtain this simply by using $x_1 = 1$ as input, which is an allowed influence. Therefore, this is not an attack on the robustness. In the second example, P_1 influences the protocol as to always learn x_3. This *is* an attack on the robustness because there is no input substitution that allows P_1 to always learn x_3. To see this, suppose that we are in a case where P_2 has input 0. This means, of course, that no matter how the other inputs are chosen, the result will be 0. In particular, no matter how P_1 chooses his or her input, he or she will learn nothing about x_3. However, in the actual attack, P_1 learns x_3 with certainty.

4.1.3 Combining Privacy and Robustness

The last attack we just saw looks at first like an attack on the correctness only: P_1 makes the result be different from what it should be. However, it actually turns out to be an attack on the privacy as well: the incorrectness makes the protocol leak the input of P_3 in cases where it should be perfectly hidden from P_1. The fact that correctness and privacy can be entangled in this way makes it impossible to consider them in isolation. They are really two sides of the same coin.

What this concretely means for our full formal definition is that we must require existence of *one single simulator* that simultaneously demonstrates both privacy and robustness. In other words, this means that the simulator receives information on how the adversary tries to influence the real protocol, and it must translate this efficiently into an allowed influence. In the "opposite" direction, it receives the allowed values and must efficiently simulate the leaked values. If this can be done, it essentially shows that anything that an adversary could obtain in an attack could also be obtained using an attack that is by definition harmless.

4.1.4 A Sketch of UC Security

In this subsection we will sketch how our intuitive ideas on privacy and correctness materialize when we move toward a formal definition by considering players as computational entities. In Section 4.2 we then give the full formal model and definition of security.

The UC model was originally phrased in terms of interactive Turing machines. We will take a slightly more abstract approach and model protocols using so-called interactive systems, which, in turn, consist of a number of so-called interactive agents that can communicate by sending messages on so-called ports. Interactive systems are defined in Chapter 2. Here we recall briefly the main terminology.

The ports of an agent are named and are divided into inports and outports. This is a simple mechanism for describing how the agents are connected. If some agent A_1 outputs a message m on an outport named P and some agent A_2 has an inport also named P, then m will be input to A_2 on port P.

An interactive agent A can be thought of as a computer that has some open connections, or ports, on which it can receive and send messages. The main technical differences are that an agent only changes state when it is explicitly activated and that the activation happens on an inport. Let AP be the name of an inport of A. An activation starts by inputting AP to A to tell it which port it was activated on – the port AP is called the activation port. Now A might read some of the messages waiting on its inports, possibly change state, and possibly sends messages on some of its outports. This is called an activation of the agent. At the end of an activation, the agent also outputs the name RP of one of its outports – the port RP is called the return port. In a larger system, the return port specifies the next activation port. We think of this as some activation token @ being passed around between the agents.

An interactive system $\mathcal{IS}$ is just a set of agents, where no two agents have inports with the same name and no two agents have outports with the same name – this is to ensure that it is uniquely given how the ports should be connected.

If some agent A has an outport named P and some agent B has an inport named P, then we say that A and B are connected by P. Technically, when the interactive system is executed, a message queue will be associated with P. When A sends a message on P, it is entered to the end of the queue. When B reads from P, it pops the front element of the queue or receives EOQ if the queue is empty.

If some agent A in an interactive system $\mathcal{IS}$ has a inport named P and no agent in $\mathcal{IS}$ has an outport named P, then we call P an open inport of the system $\mathcal{IS}$. In the same way, if some agent A in $\mathcal{IS}$ has an outport named P and no agent in $\mathcal{IS}$ has an inport named P, then we call P an open outport of the system $\mathcal{IS}$.

An interactive system $\mathcal{IS}$ can receive messages from its environment on its open inports – these are just entered into the message queues for the open inports. An interactive system with open inports also can be activated. This happens by specifying an open inport AP of the system. The system is activated as follows: first, the agent who has AP as input is activated with activation port AP. As a result, it reads messages on some of its inports, changes state, and sends messages on some of its outports. It also specifies a return port RP. The agent with an inport named RP is then activated next, with the activation port being RP, and so on. When at some point an agent specifies a return port RP that is an open outport of the system (such that there is no agent in the system with an inport named RP), activation of the system stops. We say that $\mathcal{IS}$ returned with return port RP. As a result, the system might have read some messages on its open inports, might have changed state, might have output messages on some of its open outports, and will have specified a return port RP. Hence an interactive system is much like an interactive agent – it just has more internal structure.

Behavioral Equivalence

Seen from outside the system (not having access to the internal structure of $\mathcal{IS}$), the only observable events in an activation of $\mathcal{IS}$ are that some values were input on some open inports and that later some values appeared on some open outports. We are often not interested in the internal structure of a system (because it will correspond to how a protocol is implemented) but only this externally observable input-output behavior (because it will correspond to the inputs and outputs of the protocol, the allowed influence on the protocol, and the leakage from the protocol). We therefore have a notion of two systems being indistinguishable if they give the same outputs on the same open outports whenever they get the same inputs on the same open inports. Because two indistinguishable systems need not have the same internal structure, as long as they behave in the same way, we sometimes call them *behaviorally equivalent*.

Security by Behavioral Equivalence

In the UC model, the security of a protocol is based on the notion of behaviorally equivalent systems. The first step in the formalization is to model the protocol using an interactive system π. The system π will contain an agent P_i for each party in the protocol and some agent $\mathcal{R}$ modeling the communication resource that the parties have access to, such as an agent securely moving messages between the parties. The party P_i will have an inport in_i on which it receives inputs for the protocol and an outport out_i on which it delivers outputs from the protocol. It also has ports connecting it to the resource $\mathcal{R}$. The resource $\mathcal{R}$ takes care of moving messages between parties. In addition to moving messages, $\mathcal{R}$ also models the leakage of the communication network and the possible influence that an attacker might have on the communication network.

EXAMPLE 4.3 If we want $\mathcal{R}$ to model authenticated communication without order preservation of the messages, it could have an outport R.leak on which it would output all messages sent via $\mathcal{R}$ to model that authenticated channels do not necessarily hide the messages sent, and it could have an inport R.infl on which it takes instruction about the order in which to deliver the messages to model that it does not preserve the ordering of messages. This is exactly the allowed leakage and the allowed influence on an authenticated channel without order preservation. ■

To specify how a protocol is *supposed* to work, a potentially much simpler system F is formulated. The system F is formulated such that it always has the intended input-output behavior, it only leaks the allowed values, and it only allows the allowed influence. We sometimes call F the intended functionality, and sometimes we call F the ideal functionality. The ideal functionality F is often without internal structure (just a single agent) because its only job is to have the correct input-output behavior such that we can compare the protocol π to F.

EXAMPLE 4.4 For the secure function evaluation problem, F could simply take one input x_i from each party on some inport in_i designated for that party, and then it internally computes $(y_1, \ldots, y_n) = f(x_1, \ldots, x_n)$ and outputs each y_i on an outport out_i designated for the party who is to learn y_i. Its only leakage would be that it reveals *when* a party provides input. The only influence would be that it allows the attacker to specify when the outputs are to be delivered.[2] To model this leakage and the influence, we give F an outport F.leak and an inport F.infl. When it receives x_i on in_i, it outputs "party i gave input" on F.leak. After computing $(y_1, \ldots, y_n) = f(x_1, \ldots, x_n)$, if it receives an input "deliver to party i" on F.infl, it outputs y_i on out_i unless it already gave output to party number i. ■

---

[2] Creating protocols in which it is not visible when a party gives input and an attacker with some control over the communication network cannot influence when the parties are ready to give outputs is hard. Hence we can turn this into allowed leakage and influence by adding it to F to make F easier to realize.

Notice that if there existed such a thing as F in the real world and party number i were magically and locally connected to in_i and out_i on F, then secure function evaluation would be easy: each party inputs x_i to F and then at some point gets back y_i. The adversary would learn when and if F was used and determine when it delivers messages, but the parties would always be guaranteed that the results are correct and that their inputs are kept secret by F. It does not get better than this, which is why we call F the *ideal* functionality.

A protocol π is then said to be secure if the system π behaves "in the same way" as the ideal functionality F. This means that the security of a protocol π is always relative to another system F. We therefore cannot speak about a protocol π being secure. We can only say that π is at least as secure as F. This is natural, because a statement of the form π *is secure* is actually absurd: it claims that the protocol π is secure without even stating what problem the protocol π is supposed to solve. The statement π *is at least as secure as F*, however, can be made precise. The job of F in this statement is to specify the task that π is supposed to solve by having the required input-output behavior, by allowing only the allowed influence, and by leaking only the allowed leakage. When π is as secure as the intended functionality F, then we also say that π securely implements F.

The Simulator

When comparing a protocol π and an ideal functionality F, we are left with the following problem: the ideal functionality F has a leakage port F.leak and an influence port F.infl, and it typically allows very limited leakage and influence. The protocol π will consist of n parties $\text{P}_1, \ldots, \text{P}_n$, and these will be connected using an agent $\mathcal{R}$ that models the communication network used by the protocol. All these agents will have their own leakage ports and influence ports, say, R.leak, and R.infl for $\mathcal{R}$.

Hence we cannot expect π and F to be behaviorally equivalent; the sets of available ports are completely different. To make matters worse, the ports of the players and of $\mathcal{R}$ will typically allow much more leakage and influence than does F.

We therefore introduce the simulator, whose job it is to fix this problem. The simulator is another interactive agent $\mathcal{S}$ meant to be connected to F. It connects to the leakage port F.leak of F and the influence port F.infl of F; that is, it sees the leakage of F and gets to influence F. At the same time, it has all the leakage and influence ports of the players in π and of $\mathcal{R}$. Thus, if we connect $\mathcal{S}$ and F, then $\text{F} \diamond \mathcal{S}$ has the same set of open ports as π. Now at least it makes sense to ask for π and $\text{F} \diamond \mathcal{S}$ to be behaviorally equivalent.

Here we used the notion $\mathcal{IS}_0 \diamond \mathcal{IS}_1$ for composing interactive systems. This notation is defined in detail in Chapter 2; here we just remind the reader that the two systems are composed by connecting open inports in one system with the open outports in the other system *with the same name*, if they exist. Open outports that do not have an identically named inport in the other system remain open. Correspondingly, we also leave open inports that do not have an outport with the same name in the other system. The ports that are not matched by name hence becomes the open ports of the composed system. If the two systems have two inports or two outport with the same name, the composition is defined to be an erroneous system denoted by $\perp$.

Notice that whether π and $\text{F} \diamond \mathcal{S}$ are behaviorally equivalent depends heavily on the simulator $\mathcal{S}$. The job of $\mathcal{S}$ is to make the systems look the same to any distinguisher. That is, it translates commands on the influence ports corresponding to the protocol into commands on the influence port of the ideal functionality, and it sees the values output on the leakage port of the ideal functionality and must then output values on the leakage ports corresponding to the protocol. It must do so in such a way that $F \diamond S$ behaves like π. In other words, the simulator simulates the leakage of the protocol using the leakage from the ideal functionality, and it simulates influence on the protocol using its influence on the ideal functionality. This is exactly according to our informal definitions of privacy and robustness from earlier. Note that we have not yet talked about how we model corruption of players; we will return to this shortly when we give the complete definition.

Universal Composition

A primary reason for the popularity of the UC model is its universal composition theorem (UC theorem). The UC theorem says that if π is a secure protocol for some task (specified by an intended functionality F), then it is safe to use the protocol π as a subprotocol in any context where one needs to solve the task at hand. More precisely, if some protocol is secure when it uses F as a communication resource, then that protocol is also secure if F is replaced by the protocol π. This allows us to analyze a complex protocol π_{CMPLX} in an easier way by abstracting away some subprotocol π: we replace calls to π by calls to an ideal functionality F with the intended input-output behavior of π. We then prove two claims that are reduced in complexity, namely, that (1) π_{CMPLX} is secure when it uses the ideal subsystem F as resource, and we prove that (2) the protocol π securely implements F. From this we get for free, using the UC theorem, that π_{CMPLX} is also secure when it uses π as subprotocol instead of calling F.

4.2 The UC Model

We now proceed to give the formal details of our version of the UC framework.

4.2.1 Clock-Driven Execution

One minor deviation we make from the way the UC framework was originally formulated is that we use a clock-driven execution, where we introduce a very abstract notion of local clocks in most entities. The original formulation of the UC framework was more message driven. The reason for choosing clock-driven activation is that we want our framework to handle both synchronous and asynchronous protocols. We can do this by either letting the local clocks be synchronized or by allowing them to drift apart. The original formulation of the UC framework was targeted against asynchronous protocols only and hence does not capture synchronous protocols in a convenient way.

By a clocked entity in our framework, we mean an interactive agent with some extra properties as specified below. Recall that in Chapter 2 we defined interactive systems that are composed of interactive agents. When executing such a system, an agent passes control to another by handing it an activation token. An interactive system of clocked entities will simply be a special case where the token is passed according to certain rules that we will specify in a moment.

All clocked entities in our framework are going to have one or more inports with a name ending in `infl` or `infl`$_i$. This could, for example, be an inport named `N.infl` or `N.infl`$_i$. If a clocked entity has an inport named `N.infl`, then it must have a matching outport named

N.leak, called a *leakage port*. And vice versa, if a clocked entity has an *outport* named N.infl, then it must have a matching *inport* named N.leak. Among many other things, these ports will be used to drive the execution of the interactive systems we consider.

A clocked entity receives a clocking signal (we say it is clocked) if it receives the activation token on an inport with a name of the form N.infl (or N.infl$_i$). When it is clocked, it must eventually return the activation on the matching outport N.leak (or N.leak$_i$). We introduce this rule, and other rules for passing the activation around, for technical reasons, which we discuss later. Before returning the activation token on N.leak or N.leak$_i$, a clocked entity C is allowed to do recursive calls to other clocked entities. Concretely, if C has an outport with a name of the form R.infl (or R.infl$_i$), it is allowed to send the activation token on that port. When it later receives the activation token back on R.leak (or R.leak$_i$), it must either return the activation token on N.leak (or N.leak$_i$ if it was originally received on N.infl$_i$) or do another recursive call to a clocked entity. Summarizing, a clocked entity must obey the following rules for activation.

Initialization. A clocked entity holds as part of its state a bit active $\in \{0, 1\}$, which is initially set to 0. When active $= 0$, the clocked entity is said to be inactive. When active $= 1$, the clocked entity is said to be active. It also holds a bit calling $\in \{0, 1\}$, which is initially set to 0. When calling $= 1$, the clocked entity is said to be calling.

Activation bounce during inactivity. If an inactive clocked entity receives the activation token on any port with a name not of the form N.infl or N.infl$_i$, then it returns the activation token on the matching outport without doing anything else; that is, it does not read messages, it does not change state, and it does not send messages.

Clocking. If an inactive clocked entity receives the activation token on an open inport with a name of the form N.infl or N.infl$_i$, then it sets active $\leftarrow 1$ and stores the name CP of the inport on which it was activated. We say that it was called on CP.

Return or clock. An active clocked entity is only allowed to send the activation token on an outport matching the inport CP on which it was called or an open outport with a name of the form R.infl or R.infl$_i$.

Return the call. If an active clocked entity sends the activation token on the outport matching the inport CP on which it was called, then it sets active $\leftarrow 0$. In this case, we say that it returned the call.

Recursive call. If an active clocked entity sends the activation token on an open outport named R.infl or R.infl$_i$, it first sets calling $\leftarrow 1$ and stores the name RP of the port on which it did the recursive call. We say that it did a recursive call on RP.

Activation bounce during calls. If a *calling* clocked entity receives the activation token on any inport P that does not match the outport RP on which it did the recursive call, then it returns the activation token on the outport matching P without doing anything else.

Result. If a *calling* clocked entity receives the activation token on the inport matching the outport RP on which it did the recursive call, then it sets calling $\leftarrow 0$.

Together these rules ensure that all clocked entities pass the activation token in a simple recursive manner over matching influence and leakage ports and that they only do work when they are called on their influence ports or after having returned a recursive call.

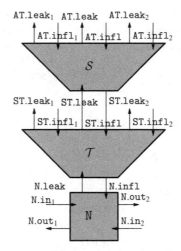

Figure 4.1 Diagram used for explaining the rules for activation.

For example, see Figure 4.1. If we call S on AT.infl$_1$, then it must return the activation on AT.leak$_1$. Before it does so, though, it is allowed to make a number of calls to T on ST.infl.[3] Whenever S does a recursive call to T, the clocked entity T must return the activation on ST.leak, but before it does so, it is allowed to make a number of calls to the agent named N on N.infl.[4] Whenever T does a recursive call to N, the clocked entity N must return the activation on N.leak. And because N has no outport ending in infl or infl$_i$, it is not allowed to do recursive calls before returning the activation. The net result of this is that when $S \diamond T \diamond N$ is called on AT.infl$_1$, it may send messages on some of its outports, and it eventually returns the activation on AT.leak$_1$.

As another example, assume that we call T on ST.infl$_1$. In this case, T must eventually return the call on ST.leak$_1$. Before doing so, it is allowed to do recursive calls to N. It is, however, not allowed to do recursive calls to S because it is connected to S by an outport that is a leakage and not an influence port, so this would be against the rule *return or clock*.

We can extend the definition of a clocked entity to an interactive system IS composed of several clocked entities. A system IS composed of clocked entities is defined to be active if and only if at least one of its constituents is active. It is calling if one its constituents is calling and has called an agent that it not part of IS. It is now trivial to check that if IS consists of clocked entities, then IS itself also obeys all the preceding rules for clocked entities. That is, we have

LEMMA 4.5 *A composition of clocked entities is a clocked entity.*

Another advantage of only having simple recursive calls is that we can define a notion of polynomial time that is maintained under composition.

---

[3] Note that S is *not* allowed to send the activation on any other outport because it is only allowed to do recursive calls on ports ending in infl or infl$_i$.

[4] Note that T is *not* allowed to send the activation on any other outport.

DEFINITION 4.6 *We say that a clocked entity is recursive polytime if all its internal computation is expected polynomial time (in the security parameter κ), and it does at most an expected polynomial (in κ) number of recursive calls before it returns it own call.*

LEMMA 4.7 *A composition of recursive polytime clocked entities is a recursive polytime clocked entity.*

Proof Consider a system $\mathcal{IS}$ composed of recursive polytime agents. It follows from Lemma 4.5 that $\mathcal{IS}$ is a clocked entity. It is also clear that $\mathcal{IS}$ is responsive; that is, an activation is eventually returned. Now let us see that the total number of internal activations in any execution of $\mathcal{IS}$ is expected polynomial. This follows by induction on the number of agents. If $\mathcal{IS}$ has only one agent, the claim is trivial. Thus, assume that we have i agents, and consider an activation of $\mathcal{IS}$, and say that agent A is the first one activated. Note that by the clocking rules, the activation of $\mathcal{IS}$ ends when A returns its call. The expected number of calls A makes is bounded by a polynomial $p(\kappa)$ by definition. By the clocking rules, each such call is actually an activation of a composed clocked entity with $i - 1$ agents. By induction hypothesis, the expected number of internal calls in the smaller system is bounded by a polynomial $q(\kappa)$. This means that the total expected number of calls in $\mathcal{IS}$ is at most $p(\kappa)q(\kappa)$, which is polynomial. The fact that $\mathcal{IS}$ is responsive and has an expected polynomial number of internal activations exactly means that $\mathcal{IS}$ is a polytime interactive system in the sense we defined in Chapter 2. Hence, by Proposition 2.20, the expected running time spent in any activation of $\mathcal{IS}$ is polynomial. ∎

In the following, we describe various types of agents we need in our framework, namely, players in protocols, ideal functionalities, and simulators. These will all be clocked entities and are therefore assumed to follow the rules for clocked entities. In particular, when an agent is activated, we assume that it will read some of its incoming message queues, treat the incoming messages according to its specification, and then return the call on the appropriate leakage port. This is required behavior, so we will not always explicitly state that the activation is returned in this manner.

4.2.2 Ideal Functionalities

Formally, an ideal functionality will be an interactive agent, as defined in Section 2.4. To name ports uniquely throughout the framework, each ideal functionality has a name F. The interface of F is as follows: F has n inports named $F.in_1, \ldots, F.in_n$ and n outports named $F.out_1, \ldots, F.out_n$. These $2n$ ports are called the protocol ports. In addition to the protocol ports, F has two special ports, an inport F.infl called the influence port and an outport F.leak called the leakage port.

EXAMPLE 4.8 As an example, we specify an ideal functionality F_{ST} for secure transfer as in Agent F_{ST}. Only the port structure for two parties is shown. The code is general enough to handle any number of parties. Each time the ideal functionality is clocked, we apply the rules until all message queues are empty and then return on ST.leak. The commands on the influence port are used to determine the order in which the messages are delivered. The leakage of $(mid, i, j, |m|)$ specifies that also an implementation of F_{ST} is allowed to leak the message identifier and the length of m. Leaking $|m|$ is important because no

Agent F$_{ST}$

The ideal functionality for secure transfer between n parties.

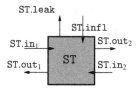

- On input (mid, j, m) on ST.in$_i$ (where $j \in \{1, \dots, n\}$), output $(mid, i, j, |m|)$ on ST.leak and store (mid, i, j, m). Ignore any later input of the form $(mid, j, \cdot)$ on ST.in$_i$. Here mid is a message identifier used to distinguish different messages from i to j.
- On input $(\texttt{deliver}, mid, i, j)$ on ST.infl, where some (mid, i, j, m) is stored, delete (mid, i, j, m), and output (mid, i, m) on ST.out$_j$.

cryptosystem can fully hide the size of the information being encrypted. Leaking mid allows implementations to do the same, which might make implementation easier. ∎

Modeling Corruption

The special ports of an ideal functionality are also used to model which information is allowed to leak when a party is corrupted and which control an adversary gets over a party when that party is corrupted. There are many choices, but we will assume in this book that all ideal functionalities have the following standard corruption behavior.

- On input (passive corrupt, i) on F.infl, the ideal functionality F outputs (state, i, σ) on F.leak, where σ is called the ideal internal state of party i and is defined to be all previous inputs on F.in$_i$ plus those in the message queue of F.in$_i$, along with all previous outputs on F.out$_i$.[5]
- On input (active corrupt, i) on F.infl, the ideal functionality F records that the party i is corrupted and outputs the ideal internal state of party i on F.leak. Then it starts ignoring all inputs on F.in$_i$ and stops giving outputs on F.out$_i$. Instead, whenever it gets an input (input, i, x) on F.infl, it behaves exactly as if x had arrived on F.in$_i$, and whenever F is about to output some value y on F.out$_i$, it instead outputs (output, i, y) on F.leak.

One way to think of a passive corruption is that if a party is corrupted, the adversary only learns the inputs and outputs of that party.[6] One way to think about active corruption is that after a party has become actively corrupted, all its inputs are chosen by the adversary

---

[5] Formally, we do not require that the ideal functionality empties its input queues and outputs all messages on the leakage tape because this would not be polytime behavior and we do not have an upper bound on how long the queues might be. We can solve this technical problem by instead saying that it outputs only the next message from F.in$_i$. The adversary then can just input (passive corrupt, i) several times in a row to empty the input queue, if so desired. This is considered polytime because the ideal functionality responds in polytime on each activation. Note, in particular, that all messages are assumed to be of polynomial length; otherwise, they are replaced by ILM, so one message can clearly be copied in polynomial time. Similar tricks are used later, but we stop mentioning them explicitly.

[6] A nonstandard corruption behavior could be to only leak the last input or output. This would model an even more ideal situation, where an adversary cannot learn previous inputs and outputs when it breaks into a party.

(via F.infl), and all its outputs are leaked to the adversary (via F.leak). Since it is impossible to protect against input substitution (even an otherwise honest party could do this), and it is inevitable that outputs intended for some party are seen by an adversary controlling that party, the standard corruption behavior models an ideal situation in which an adversary gets only these inevitable powers.

4.2.3 Protocols

A simple protocol π consists of just n parties $P_1, \ldots, P_n$, where each P_i is an agent; that is, the protocol is the interactive system $\pi = \{P_1, \ldots, P_n\}$. A simple protocol has a protocol name F. For reasons that will become obvious, we let a protocol π and the ideal functionality F that π is supposed to implement have the same name. A simple protocol also has a resource name R. This is the name of the resource that π uses for communication. The agent P_i is called a simple party, and it has six ports. The port structure of P_i is derived from the names F and R. It has an inport F.in$_i$ and an outport F.out$_i$, exactly as the ideal functionality F that π will be compared with later. Those two ports are called the protocol ports. In addition, it has an outport named R.in$_i$ and an inport named R.out$_i$. Those two ports are called the resource ports. Finally, P_i has an inport named R.infl$_i$ and an outport named R.leak$_i$. These are called the special ports and are used to model corruption of P_i (and to clock P_i). This is detailed later, but first we discuss how the parties in a protocol communicate.

Let $\pi = \{P_1, \ldots, P_n\}$ be a protocol with resource name R, and let $\mathcal{R}$ be an ideal functionality with name R. Then $\mathcal{R}$ has an inport named R.in$_i$ and P_i has an outport named R.in$_i$, and $\mathcal{R}$ has an outport named R.out$_i$ and P_i has an inport named R.out$_i$. This means that in the system $\pi \diamond \mathcal{R} = \{P_1, \ldots P_n, \mathcal{R}\}$, the resource ports of the parties are connected to the protocol ports of $\mathcal{R}$. Hence the only open ports in $\pi \diamond \mathcal{R}$ are the protocol ports of π and the special ports of π and $\mathcal{R}$. We call $\pi \diamond \mathcal{R}$ a protocol using resource $\mathcal{R}$. Notice that in this way ideal functionalities can play two roles: they can be specifications of intended behavior, but they also can play the role of network resources, that is, the means by which parties communicate. As we will see, this duality is central in formulating the UC theorem.

Agent F_{AT}

The ideal functionality for authenticated transfer between n parties.

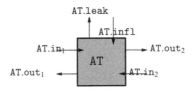

- On receiving a value (mid, j, m) on AT.in$_i$ (where $j \in \{1, \ldots, n\}$), output (mid, i, j, m) on AT.leak and store (mid, i, j, m). Ignore any later input of the form $(mid, j, \cdot)$ on AT.in$_i$.
- On an input $(\texttt{deliver}, mid, i, j)$ on AT.infl, where some (mid, i, j, m) is stored, delete (mid, i, j, m) and output (mid, i, m) on AT.out$_j$.

This is known as forward security and is a desirable property in some cases but not a concern we will have in this book.

Agent P$_1$

1. On input $(mid, 2, m)$ on ST.in$_1$, and output $(mid, 2, \texttt{hello})$ on AT.in$_1$.
2. On a later input $(mid, 2, ek)$ on AT.out$_1$, sample a random encryption $c \leftarrow E_{ek}(m)$, and output $(mid, 2, c)$ on AT.in$_1$.

Agent P$_2$

1. On input $(mid, 1, \texttt{hello})$ on AT.out$_2$, sample a random key pair (ek, dk) for an IND-CPA secure public-key cryptosystem and output $(mid, 1, ek)$ on AT.in$_2$.
2. On a later input $(mid, 1, c)$ on AT.out$_2$, output $(mid, 1, D_{dk}(c))$ on ST.out$_2$.

EXAMPLE 4.9 We continue with the secure transfer example. We want to implement F_{ST} using an authenticated channel and a public-key encryption scheme. For starters, let us consider a sender P$_1$ and a receiver P$_2$. These will communicate using an authenticated channel. To do a secure transfer from P$_1$ to P$_2$, one can use the following protocol:

1. First, P$_1$ announces over the authenticated channel to P$_2$ that it wants to send a message securely.
2. Then P$_2$ samples a key pair (ek, dk) and sends the encryption key ek to P$_1$ over the authenticated channel.
3. Then P$_1$ encrypts the message, $c \leftarrow E_{ek}(m)$, and returns c over the authenticated channel.
4. Then P$_2$ outputs $m = D_{dk}(c)$.

We want to formally model this protocol within the UC model.

To model the preceding protocol for secure transfer, we need an ideal functionality F_{AT} for authenticated transfer to use as resource for the protocol (see Agent F_{AT}). The only difference from F_{ST} is that m is leaked and not just $|m|$. This models that m is allowed to leak in an authenticated channel. The protocol π_{ST} is given by Agent P$_1$ and Agent P$_2$ (Figure 4.2). Similar code is included for the direction from P$_2$ to P$_1$ and similarly between each other pair of parties. Figure 4.2 shows the protocol $\pi_{ST} \diamond F_{AT}$ next to the ideal functionality F_{ST} that it tries to implement. ∎

Modeling Corruption

Back to how corruption is modeled. Again, there are many choices, but we will assume in this book that all parties have the following standard corruption behavior:

- If a party P$_i$ receives a special symbol (passive corrupt) on R.infl$_i$, then P$_i$ returns its internal state σ on R.leak$_i$. The internal state σ consists of all randomness used by the party so far along with all inputs sent and received on its ports and the messages in the message queues of its inports.
- If a party P$_i$ receives a special symbol (active corrupt) on R.infl$_i$, then P$_i$ outputs it current state on R.leak$_i$ and starts executing the following rules and only these rules:

Models

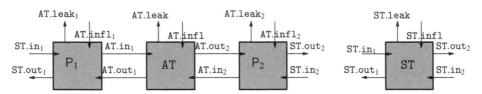

Figure 4.2 The protocol π_{ST} for secure transfer and the ideal functionality F_{ST} for secure transfer.

- On input $(\texttt{read}, \mathsf{P})$ on $\mathsf{R.infl}_i$, where P is an inport of P_i, it reads the next message m on P and returns m on $\mathsf{R.leak}_i$.
- On input $(\texttt{send}, \mathsf{P}, m)$ on $\mathsf{R.infl}_i$, where P is an outport of P_i, it sends m on P.

By passive corrupting a party in a protocol $\pi \diamond \mathcal{R}$ using resource $\mathcal{R}$, we mean that $(\texttt{passive corrupt})$ is input on $\mathsf{R.infl}_i$ and then $(\texttt{passive corrupt}, i)$ is input on $\mathsf{R.infl}$ on the communication device $\mathcal{R}$. By active corrupting a party in $\pi \diamond \mathcal{R}$, we mean that $(\texttt{active corrupt})$ is input on $\mathsf{R.infl}_i$ and then $(\texttt{active corrupt}, i)$ is input on $\mathsf{R.infl}$ on $\mathcal{R}$. After that, P_i can be controlled using read and send commands.

4.2.4 The Simulator

If we inspect Fig. 4.2, we see that we have the problem discussed in the introduction to this chapter that a protocol, such as $\pi_{\mathrm{ST}} \diamond \mathsf{F}_{\mathrm{AT}}$, and the ideal functionality specifying its intended behavior, such as F_{ST}, have different open-port structures and hence cannot be behaviorally equivalent. We also discussed that we solve this by introducing a simulator $\mathcal{S}$ that gives $\pi_{\mathrm{ST}} \diamond \mathsf{F}_{\mathrm{AT}}$ and $\mathsf{F}_{\mathrm{ST}} \diamond \mathcal{S}$ the same open-port structure. An example is shown in Figure 4.3.

In general, a simulator $\mathcal{S}$ for a simple protocol π with protocol name F and resource name R is defined as follows: It is a polytime[7] interactive system with an open inport named $\mathsf{F.leak}$ and an open outport named $\mathsf{F.infl}$. These two ports allow it to connect to an ideal functionality F with name F because such an F has an open outport named $\mathsf{F.leak}$ and an open inport named $\mathsf{F.infl}$. In addition to these two ports, $\mathcal{S}$ has ports corresponding to the special ports of π; that is, for $i = 1, \ldots, n$, it has inports named $\mathsf{R.infl}_i$ and outports named $\mathsf{R.leak}_i$, like the parties of π. Finally, $\mathcal{S}$ has an inport named $\mathsf{R.infl}$ and an outport named $\mathsf{R.leak}$, like a resource $\mathcal{R}$ used by π. As a consequence, $\mathsf{F} \diamond \mathcal{S}$ and $\pi \diamond \mathcal{R}$ have the same open ports.

We call the open ports of $\mathcal{S}$ that connect to F the ideal functionality ports of $\mathcal{S}$. We call the other open ports of $\mathcal{S}$ the simulation ports of $\mathcal{S}$.

We additionally require that $\mathcal{S}$ is corruption preserving in the sense that it does not corrupt a party on F unless that party was corrupted in the simulation. That is, $\mathcal{S}$ does not output $(\texttt{passive corrupt}, i)$ on $\mathsf{F.infl}$ unless at some point it received $(\texttt{passive corrupt})$ on $\mathsf{R.infl}_i$, and $\mathcal{S}$ does not output $(\texttt{active corrupt}, i)$ on $\mathsf{F.infl}$ unless at some point it received $(\texttt{active corrupt})$ on $\mathsf{R.infl}_i$. We also require that if $\mathcal{S}$ receives

---

[7] A polytime interactive system is a system that returns on an open outport within expected polytime when it is activated on an open inport. For the interested reader, a formal definition is given in Definition 2.19.

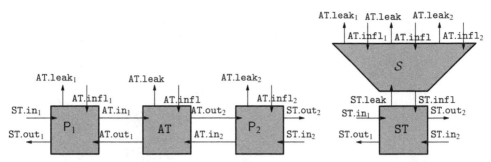

Figure 4.3 Port structure of the protocol $\pi_{ST} \diamond F_{AT}$ for secure transfer and the ideal functionality F_{ST} for secure transfer composed with a simulator S for π_{ST}.

(passive corrupt) on $R.infl_i$, then its next action is to output (passive corrupt, i) on $F.infl$ and similarly for active corruptions. This last requirement is a technicality needed when we later define so-called static security.

Finally, we require that S is clock preserving. This is a technicality needed when we later define synchronous security. What we need is that S outputs (clockin, i) on $F.infl$ if and only if it just received (clockin, i) on $R.infl_i$ and that S outputs (clockout, i) on $F.infl$ if and only if it just received (clockout, i) on $R.infl_i$. We shall return to the use of these commands later.

4.2.5 The Environment

Having introduced the simulator, we can now compare a protocol π using resource R with an ideal functionality F with an attached simulator S for the protocol. We will do that by requiring that $\pi \diamond R$ is "hard" to distinguish from $F \diamond S$. Indistinguishability of interactive systems was defined in Definition 2.21 in Chapter 2. The technical details can be found there. Here we remind the reader of the main ideas; this will be sufficient to understand our discussion in this chapter.

The notion of indistinguishability requires that we consider an interactive system Z that must be an environment for $\pi \diamond R$ and $F \diamond S$. This notion was defined for general interactive systems in Definition 2.21, and we now describe what it means in our concrete context of protocols and resources.

An environment Z for a simple protocol π with protocol name F and resource name R is an interactive system Z that has the dual open ports of $\pi \diamond R$, where R is a resource with name R. Concretely, for each open inport P of $\pi \diamond R$, the system Z has an open outport named P, and for each open outport P of $\pi \diamond R$, the system Z has an open inport named P, and Z has no other open ports. As a consequence, $\pi \diamond R \diamond Z$ is a closed system, and so is $F \diamond S \diamond Z$. A closed system is just one with no open ports. Figure 4.4 provides two examples. Note that S, being a simulator, must be such that the port structures of $\pi \diamond R$ and $F \diamond S$ are the same, and therefore, Z is an environment for both systems.

We call the open ports of Z that connect to the protocol ports of π the protocol ports of Z. We call the other open ports of Z the special ports of Z.

Two systems are indistinguishable to an environment Z if Z cannot tell them apart (except with negligible advantage) by sending and receiving messages on the open ports

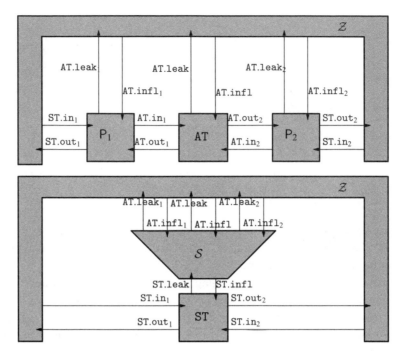

Figure 4.4 Example of two systems closed using the same environment $\mathcal{Z}$.

of the systems. Formally, the environment gets to play with a random one of the two systems and must then not be able to guess which one it is, except with probability negligibly close to $\frac{1}{2}$. How much better than $\frac{1}{2}$ the guess is we call the advantage of the guess. Two systems such as $\pi \diamond \mathcal{R}$ and $\mathsf{F} \diamond \mathcal{S}$ are called *indistinguishable* to a class Z of environments if they are indistinguishable to all $\mathcal{Z} \in Z$. This is written $\pi \diamond \mathcal{R} \overset{Z}{\equiv} \mathsf{F} \diamond \mathcal{S}$. If, for instance, Z is the class of polynomial time environments, we speak about *computational indistinguishability* and write $\pi \diamond \mathcal{R} \overset{\text{comp}}{\equiv} \mathsf{F} \diamond \mathcal{S}$. If Z contains all environments (that activate the system only a polynomial number of times), we speak about *statistical indistinguishability* (written $\pi \diamond \mathcal{R} \overset{\text{stat}}{\equiv} \mathsf{F} \diamond \mathcal{S}$). Finally, if all environments have zero advantage in distinguishing, we speak about *perfect indistinguishability* (written $\pi \diamond \mathcal{R} \overset{\text{perf}}{\equiv} \mathsf{F} \diamond \mathcal{S}$).

4.2.6 Comparing Protocols to Their Ideal Functionalities

We are now finally ready to define what it means that a protocol π using, for instance, resource F_{AT} does "the same" as an ideal functionality, say, F_{ST}. The definition is general, but we reuse the names from the example for concreteness.

DEFINITION 4.10 (SECURITY FOR SIMPLE PROTOCOLS) *Let ST and AT denote arbitrary protocol names. Let F_{ST} be any ideal functionality with name ST, let π_{ST} be any simple protocol with protocol name ST and resource name AT, and let F_{AT} be any ideal functionality with name AT. We say that $\pi_{ST} \diamond \mathsf{F}_{AT}$ securely implements F_{ST} in environments from Z if there exists a simulator S for π_{ST} such that $\pi_{ST} \diamond \mathsf{F}_{AT} \overset{Z}{\equiv} \mathsf{F}_{ST} \diamond S$. We will also write this* as $\pi_{ST} \diamond F_{AT} \overset{Z}{\geq} F_{ST}$. We will sometimes say that $\pi_{ST} \diamond F_{AT}$ is at least as secure as F_{ST} in environments from Z.

By defining Z appropriately, we can use the definition to talk about perfect, statistical, computational security of π_{ST}. We give many more details on this later.

For simplicity, this definition only considers protocols using a single resource. It is trivial to extend it to several resources by allowing multiple resource names as long as the port structure of simulators and environments are required to match this.

Agent S

A simulator for π_{ST}. This is how to simulate a secure transfer from P_1 to P_2. All other directions are handled similarly.

1. On input $(mid, 1, 2, l)$ on ST.leak (from F_{ST}, and with $l = |m|$), it outputs $(mid, 1, 2, \texttt{hello})$ on AT.leak.
2. On a later input $(\texttt{deliver}, mid, 1, 2)$ on AT.infl, it samples a key pair (ek, dk) and outputs $(mid, 2, 1, ek)$ on AT.leak.
3. On a later input $(\texttt{deliver}, mid, 2, 1)$ on AT.infl it samples a random encryption $c \leftarrow E_{ek}(m')$ and outputs $(mid, 1, 2, C)$ on AT.leak. Here $m' = 0^l$ is an all-zero message of length l.
4. On a later input $(\texttt{deliver}, mid, 1, 2)$ on AT.infl it outputs $(\texttt{deliver}, mid, 1, 2)$ on ST.infl, which makes F_{ST} output $(mid, 1, m)$ on ST.out$_2$.

EXAMPLE 4.11 As an example, we prove that $\pi_{ST} \diamond F_{AT}$ securely implements F_{ST} in polynomial time environments. As a first step, we first consider a polytime environment Z that does not corrupt any of the parties.

As we describe the simulator S, it is instructive to look at Figure 4.4. Recall that we try to construct some S for that setting such that Z cannot see which of the two systems it is playing with. The simulator is described in the box Agent S.

The reason why S uses m' and not the real m is that F_{ST} only outputs $l = |m|$ to S. Giving m to S would make the simulation trivial, but remember that the whole idea of S is to demonstrate that the real leakage can be simulated given only the leakage allowed by the ideal functionality, and m is not allowed to leak in a secure transfer.

Consider now some distinguisher Z that gets to play with either $\pi_{ST} \diamond F_{AT}$ or $F_{ST} \diamond S$. For now, we assume that Z does not use the special ports of the parties – that is, it makes no corruptions. Furthermore, for simplicity, we only allow Z to do one secure transfer and to do it only from P_1 to P_2. Then Z works as follows:

1. It picks some message m and inputs $(mid, 2, m)$ on ST.in$_1$.
2. Then it sees $(mid, 1, 2, \texttt{hello})$ on AT.leak and inputs $(\texttt{deliver}, mid, 1, 2)$ on AT.infl.
3. Then it sees some $(mid, 2, 1, ek)$ on AT.leak and inputs $(\texttt{deliver}, mid, 2, 1)$ on AT.infl.
4. Then it sees some $(mid, 1, 2, c'')$ on AT.leak and inputs $(\texttt{deliver}, mid, 1, 2)$ on AT.infl.
5. In response to this, it sees some $(mid, 1, m'')$ output on ST.out$_2$.

It could, of course, refuse some of the deliveries. This would, however, only have Z see fewer messages and thus make the distinguishing of the systems harder.

Note that by design of the simulator $\mathcal{S}$, the distinguisher $\mathcal{Z}$ will see both systems behave as specified earlier. The only difference between the two systems is that

- If $\mathcal{Z}$ is playing with $\mathsf{F}_{\text{ST}} \diamond \mathcal{S}$, then $c'' \leftarrow E_{ek}(0^{|m|})$, and m'' is the message $m'' = m$ output by F_{ST}.
- If it is playing with $\pi_{\text{ST}} \diamond \mathsf{F}_{\text{AT}}$, then $c'' \leftarrow E_{ek}(m)$, and $m'' = D_{dk}(c'')$ is the message output by P_2.

If the encryption scheme has perfect correctness, then $D_{dk}(E_{ek}(m)) = m$, so $\pi_{\text{ST}} \diamond \mathsf{F}_{\text{AT}}$ and $\mathsf{F}_{\text{ST}} \diamond \mathcal{S}$ always output the same m''. Thus, the only difference between the two systems is that $c'' \leftarrow E_{ek}(m)$ or $c'' \leftarrow E_{ek}(0^{|m|})$. Also, a distinguisher $\mathcal{Z}$ essentially has the following job: pick m and receive $(ek, E_{ek}(m'))$, where ek is random and $m' = m$ or $m' = 0^{|m|}$. Then try to distinguish which m' was used. The definition of IND-CPA security more or less exactly says that no polytime system can distinguish $(ek, E_{ek}(m))$ and $(ek, E_{ek}(0^{|m|}))$. Hence it follows that $\pi_{\text{ST}} \diamond \mathsf{F}_{\text{AT}} \diamond \mathcal{Z} \overset{\text{stat}}{\equiv} \mathsf{F}_{\text{ST}} \diamond \mathcal{S} \diamond \mathcal{Z}$ for all polytime environments $\mathcal{Z}$ that do not corrupt parties and that do only one transfer, from P_1 to P_2. More formally, we can turn a polytime system $\mathcal{Z}$ that distinguishes the two systems $\pi_{\text{ST}} \diamond \mathsf{F}_{\text{AT}}$ and $\mathsf{F}_{\text{ST}} \diamond \mathcal{S}$ into a polytime system $\mathcal{Z}'$ that wins in the IND-CPA game in Section 2.5 as follows:

1. The system $\mathcal{Z}'$ will play with A_0 or A_1 as defined in Section 2.5.
2. First $\mathcal{Z}'$ receives ek from A_b (here $b = 0$ or $b = 1$).
3. Then $\mathcal{Z}'$ runs $\mathcal{Z}$ to see which message $(mid, 2, m)$ it outputs on $\mathsf{ST.in}_1$.
4. Then $\mathcal{Z}'$ inputs $(m, 0^{|m|})$ to A_b and gets back an encryption c^*, where c^* is an encryption of m if $b = 0$ and c^* is an encryption of $0^{|m|}$ if $b = 1$.
5. Then $\mathcal{Z}'$ runs $\mathcal{Z}$ and shows it the messages $(mid, 1, 2, \texttt{hello})$, $(mid, 2, 1, ek)$, and $(mid, 1, 2, c^*)$ on $\mathsf{AT.leak}$ and $(mid, 1, m)$ on $\mathsf{ST.out}_2$.
6. Then $\mathcal{Z}'$ runs $\mathcal{Z}$ until it outputs its guess c, and then $\mathcal{Z}'$ outputs c.

If $b = 0$, then c^* is a random encryption of m, and if $b = 1$, then c^* is a random encryption of $0^{|m|}$. Thus, if $b = 0$, then $\mathcal{Z}$ see exactly the interaction it would see when interacting with $\pi_{\text{ST}} \diamond \mathsf{F}_{\text{AT}}$, and if $b = 1$, then $\mathcal{Z}$ sees exactly the interaction it would see when interacting with $\mathsf{F}_{\text{ST}} \diamond \mathcal{S}$. Thus, if $\mathcal{Z}$ can distinguish $\pi_{\text{ST}} \diamond \mathsf{F}_{\text{AT}}$ and $\mathsf{F}_{\text{ST}} \diamond \mathcal{S}$, then $c = b$ with probability significantly better than $\frac{1}{2}$. But this exactly means that $\mathcal{Z}'$, who also outputs c, will guess b with probability significantly better than $\frac{1}{2}$. If the encryption scheme is IND-CPA secure, then this is a contradiction, because $\mathcal{Z}'$ is polytime when $\mathcal{Z}$ is polytime, and IND-CPA security means that no polytime system can distinguish A_0 and A_1.

It is fairly easy to extend the argument to polytime environments $\mathcal{Z}$ that do not corrupt parties but are allowed to do any number of transfers. Each transfer is simulated as earlier, and the security follows from the fact that IND-CPA security is maintained even if you get so many encryptions. Later we will extend the analysis to polytime environments that are allowed to corrupt parties. $\blacksquare$

4.2.7 Composed Protocols

An important property of the UC framework is that when $\pi_{\text{ST}} \diamond \mathsf{F}_{\text{AT}}$ implements F_{ST} with computational security, then F_{ST} can securely be replaced by $\pi_{\text{ST}} \diamond \mathsf{F}_{\text{AT}}$ in any polytime protocol.

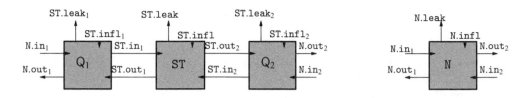

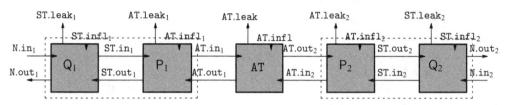

Figure 4.5 The protocol $\pi_N \diamond F_{ST}$, the ideal functionality F_N, and the protocol $\pi_N \diamond (\pi_{ST} \diamond F_{AT})$.

Consider some third ideal functionality F_N doing some interesting task that is ideally secure. Assume that we can design a protocol π_N with protocol name N and resource name ST that securely implements F_N when it uses F_{ST} as a communication resource. Designing a secure implementation of F_N using secure transfer as a communication resource is potentially much easier than designing a protocol using only authenticated transfer as a communication resource. The structure of such a protocol is shown in the top row of Figure 4.5, along with F_N.

To get an implementation using only authenticated transfer, we can replace the use of F_{ST} in $\pi_N \diamond F_{ST}$ by the use of the protocol $\pi_{ST} \diamond F_{AT}$, resulting in the protocol $\pi_N \diamond (\pi_{ST} \diamond F_{AT})$. This is possible because F_{ST} and $\pi_{ST} \diamond F_{AT}$ have the same structure of protocol ports. The result is shown in the bottom row of Figure 4.5.

We have that $\pi_N \diamond (\pi_{ST} \diamond F_{AT}) = (\pi_N \diamond \pi_{ST}) \diamond F_{AT}$ because interactive systems are just sets of agents and $\diamond$ is just the union operator on sets. We call $\pi_N \diamond \pi_{ST}$ a composed protocol. In general, a composed protocol is just an interactive system composed of simple protocols. We use the term protocol to cover both simple protocols and composed protocols.

The protocol name of a composed protocol is the protocol name of the outer simple protocol because it is this outer protocol that provides the open protocol ports. For example, the protocol name of $\pi_N \diamond \pi_{ST}$ is N.

The resource name of a composed protocol is the protocol name of the inner simple protocol because it is this inner protocol that provides the open resource ports. For example, the resource name of $\pi_N \diamond \pi_{ST}$ is AT.

We can also compose protocols that are already composed, as long as the resource name of the outer composed protocol matches the protocol name of the inner composed protocol.

Composed Parties

We consider Q_1 and P_1 as one party and consider P_2 and Q_2 as one party. This leads to a notion of a composed party, which is just an interactive system consisting of simple parties. In other words, a composed protocol π simply consists of n composed parties $\mathcal{P}_1, \ldots, \mathcal{P}_n$, that is, $\pi = \mathcal{P}_1 \diamond \cdots \diamond \mathcal{P}_n$. We use the term party to cover both simple parties and composed parties.

For example, $\mathcal{P}_1 = \{Q_1, P_1\}$ is just an interactive system with open ports $\texttt{AT.in}_1$ and $\texttt{AT.out}_1$ connecting it to the protocol's communication device F_{AT} and with open protocol ports $\texttt{N.in}_1$ and $\texttt{N.out}_1$ named as the ideal functionality F_{N} that the protocol is trying to implement. The ports inside $\mathcal{P}$ are just particularities of how the party is implemented.

In addition $\mathcal{P}_1$ has some special ports that allow us to corrupt it. We could insist on somehow joining these ports, but allowing us to corrupt the components of $\mathcal{P}_1$ separately just gives more power to the attacker. A passive corruption of $\mathcal{P}_1$ is done by inputting ($\texttt{passive corrupt}$) on both $\texttt{ST.infl}_1$ and $\texttt{AT.infl}_1$ and inputting ($\texttt{passive corrupt}, 1$) on $\texttt{AT.infl}$, in response to which we receives the internal state of both components of the party plus the internal state of the party on the communication device. An active corruption of $\mathcal{P}_1$ is done by inputting ($\texttt{active corrupt}$) on both $\texttt{ST.infl}_1$ and $\texttt{AT.infl}_1$ and inputting ($\texttt{active corrupt}, 1$) on $\texttt{AT.infl}$.

Security of Composed Protocols

We define security of composed protocols as we did for simple protocols. Consider the protocol $\pi_{\mathrm{N}} \diamond \pi_{\mathrm{ST}} \diamond \mathsf{F}_{\mathrm{AT}}$ in the bottom row of Figure 4.5. If we want to ask if it is a secure implementation of F_{N} in the upper right corner of Figure 4.5, we have the usual problem that the port structures are different. We therefore introduce a simulator $\mathcal{U}$. As usual, this simulator has an open outport $\texttt{N.infl}$ and an open inport $\texttt{N.leak}$, so it can connect to F_{N} to exploit the allowed leakage and influence of this ideal functionality. Its job is then to simulate the leakage and influence of the protocol $\pi_{\mathrm{N}} \diamond \pi_{\mathrm{ST}} \diamond \mathsf{F}_{\mathrm{AT}}$. Therefore, $\mathcal{U}$ must have an open port for each of the special ports in $\pi_{\mathrm{N}} \diamond \pi_{\mathrm{ST}} \diamond \mathsf{F}_{\mathrm{AT}}$ (see Figure 4.6).

In general, a simulator for a composed protocol π with protocol name F and resource name R is just an interactive system S with an open outport $\texttt{F.infl}$ and an open inport $\texttt{F.leak}$ so that it can connect to the special ports of F_{F}. It must further have open ports that match the special ports of all simple parties and resources used in the composed protocol. With this extension of the simulator, we can reuse Definition 4.10 to say what it means for a composed protocol to implement a functionality.

4.2.8 The UC Theorem

We are now ready to phrase and prove the UC theorem. Before doing so, it is instructive, however, to give a pictorial proof using our secure transfer example.

EXAMPLE 4.12 Let Env be the set of polytime environments. We assumed that $\pi_{\mathrm{N}} \diamond \mathsf{F}_{\mathrm{ST}} \overset{\text{Env}}{\geqslant} \mathsf{F}_{\mathrm{N}}$, and we argued that $\pi_{\mathrm{ST}} \diamond \mathsf{F}_{\mathrm{AT}} \overset{\text{Env}}{\geqslant} \mathsf{F}_{\mathrm{ST}}$, though we still did not consider all cases in the analysis. These two security guarantees allow us to conclude that $\pi_{\mathrm{N}} \diamond \pi_{\mathrm{ST}} \diamond \mathsf{F}_{\mathrm{AT}} \overset{\text{Env}}{\geqslant} \mathsf{F}_{\mathrm{N}}$. Notice that if all the systems where real numbers, $\diamond$ was addition, and $\overset{\text{Env}}{\geqslant}$ was $\geq$, then our assumptions would be that $\pi_{\mathrm{N}} + \mathsf{F}_{\mathrm{ST}} \geq \mathsf{F}_{\mathrm{N}}$ and $\pi_{\mathrm{ST}} + \mathsf{F}_{\mathrm{AT}} \geq \mathsf{F}_{\mathrm{ST}}$. From this we could conclude as follows: $\pi_{\mathrm{N}} + \pi_{\mathrm{ST}} + \mathsf{F}_{\mathrm{AT}} = \pi_{\mathrm{N}} + (\pi_{\mathrm{ST}} + \mathsf{F}_{\mathrm{AT}}) \geq \pi_{\mathrm{N}} + \mathsf{F}_{\mathrm{ST}} \geq \mathsf{F}_{\mathrm{N}}$. Then it follows from the transitivity of $\geq$ that $\pi_{\mathrm{N}} + \pi_{\mathrm{ST}} + \mathsf{F}_{\mathrm{AT}} \geq \mathsf{F}_{\mathrm{N}}$, which would correspond to $\pi_{\mathrm{N}} \diamond \pi_{\mathrm{ST}} \diamond \mathsf{F}_{\mathrm{AT}} \overset{\text{Env}}{\geqslant} \mathsf{F}_{\mathrm{N}}$. The proof of the UC theorem follows this line of arguing. The proof goes as follows:

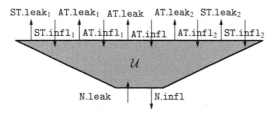

Figure 4.6 Open-port structure of a simulator for the composed protocol $\pi_N \diamond \pi_{ST} \diamond F_{AT}$.

From $\pi_{ST} \diamond F_{AT} \overset{Env}{\geqslant} F_{ST}$ we know that there exists a simulator S such that the two systems in the top row of Figure 4.7 cannot be told apart by playing with their open ports. Thus, if we connect π_N to both systems, where π_N is represented by Q_1 and Q_2 in the figure, we know that the two bottom systems in Figure 4.7 cannot be told apart. That is, if some environment Z plays with the open ports of one of the bottom systems, it is really just playing with one of the systems in the top row via π_N. Here, $Z \diamond \pi_N$ is playing with one of the systems in the top row. Thus, if Z distinguishes the bottom systems, then $Z \diamond \pi_N$ distinguishes the top systems. Since these systems cannot be told apart by any environment, it follows that no Z can distinguish the bottom systems.

From $\pi_N \diamond F_{ST} \overset{Env}{\geqslant} F_N$ we know that there exists a simulator T such that the two systems in the top row of Figure 4.8 cannot be told apart by playing with their open ports. Thus, if we connect S to both systems, we know that the two bottom systems cannot be told apart by playing with their open ports using the same logic as earlier. Here we turn a successful distinguisher Z for the bottom systems into a successful distinguisher $Z \diamond S$ for the top systems and reach a contradiction.

Now, if IS_0 cannot be told apart from IS_1 and IS_1 cannot be told apart from IS_2, it follows that IS_0 cannot be told apart from IS_2. This follows from transitivity of indistinguishability, as shown in Chapter 2. We use this transitivity to finish the proof. The protocol $\pi_N \diamond \pi_{ST} \diamond F_{AT}$ is the middle system in Figure 4.7. We concluded that this system cannot be told apart from the system in the bottom row of Figure 4.7. The same system is found as the bottom-left system in Figure 4.8, and we concluded that this system cannot be told apart from the bottom-right system in Figure 4.8. The bottom-right system in Figure 4.8 is $F_N \diamond T \diamond S$. So we can conclude this $\pi_N \diamond \pi_{ST} \diamond F_{AT}$ cannot be told apart from $F_N \diamond T \diamond S$. If we let $U = T \diamond S$, then it follows that $\pi_N \diamond \pi_{ST} \diamond F_{AT}$ cannot be told apart from $F_N \diamond U$. But this means that U successfully simulates $\pi_N \diamond \pi_{ST} \diamond F_{AT}$ given F_N,[8] so $\pi_N \diamond \pi_{ST} \diamond F_{AT}$ is a secure implementation of F_N. ∎

We are now almost ready to phrase and prove the UC theorem. The last definition we need is the notion of a class of environments. The purpose of this notion is clear from the preceding example. Recall that we said that if some environment Z can tell apart the two bottom systems of Figure 4.7, then $\pi_N \diamond Z$ can tell apart the two systems in the top row of Figure 4.7. We said that this leads to a contradiction because no environment can tell

---

[8] Notice, in particular, that $T \diamond S$ is a system that can connect to the special ports of F_N and that has open special ports corresponding to $\pi_N \diamond \pi_{ST}$, so it qualifies as a simulator.

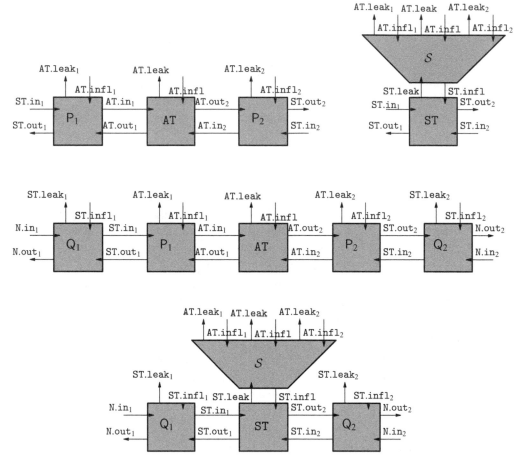

Figure 4.7 Extending π_{ST} and $\mathsf{F}_{\mathsf{ST}} \diamond \mathcal{S}$ with Q_1 and Q_2.

apart the two systems in the top row of Figure 4.7 by assumption. Notice, however, that this requires that $\pi_{\mathsf{N}} \diamond \mathcal{Z}$ *is an environment*. We assume that *no environment* can tell apart the two systems in the top row of Figure 4.7. Thus, if $\pi_{\mathsf{N}} \diamond \mathcal{Z}$ is not an environment, we do not get a contradiction. So we need to require that if we take a protocol π and an environment $\mathcal{Z}$ for π, then $\mathcal{Z} \diamond \pi$ is again an environment. For similar reasons, we need to assume that if we take an environment $\mathcal{Z}$ and a simulator $\mathcal{S}$, then $\mathcal{Z} \diamond \mathcal{S}$ is again an environment. For example, if we work with the class of environments that are polytime, then we need that if we take such an environment $\mathcal{Z}$ and a protocol π, then $\mathcal{Z} \diamond \pi$ is again polytime. If we define polytime environments in a proper way and only consider polytime protocols, then this will be the case, as we demonstrate next.

DEFINITION 4.13 *We let* Pro *be the set of simple and composed protocols in which all simple parties follows the rules for clocked entities and are recursive polytime.*

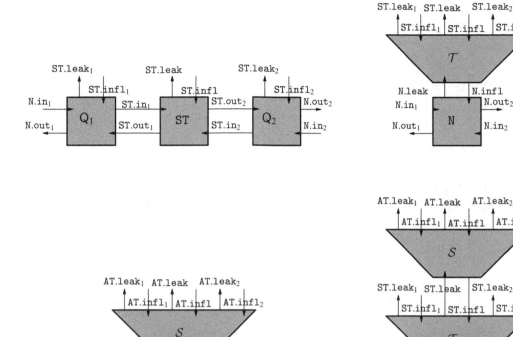

Figure 4.8 Extending π_N and $F_N \diamond \mathcal{T}$ with $\mathcal{S}$.

It is straightforward to verify the following lemma:

LEMMA 4.14 *If $\pi_F \in$ Pro is a protocol with protocol name F and resource name R and $\pi_R \in$ Pro is a protocol with protocol name R and $\pi_F \diamond \pi_R \neq \perp$, then $\pi_F \diamond \pi_R \in$ Pro.*

DEFINITION 4.15 *We let* Sim *be the set of interactive systems $\mathcal{S}$ that are a simulator for some protocol. We remind the reader that this means that for $\mathcal{S} \in$ Sim, it holds that*

1. *There exists a protocol π_F (composed or simple) with protocol name F and an ideal functionality F_F with name F such that π_F and $F_F \diamond \mathcal{S}$ have the same special ports.*
2. *$\mathcal{S}$ follows the rules for clocked entities and is recursive polytime.*
3. *$\mathcal{S}$ is corruption preserving.*
4. *$\mathcal{S}$ is clock preserving.*

It is straightforward to verify the following lemma:

LEMMA 4.16 *If $\mathcal{S} \in$ Sim and $\mathcal{T} \in$ Sim and $\mathcal{T}$ has two open special ports that connect it to the ideal functionality ports of $\mathcal{S}$ and $\mathcal{S} \diamond \mathcal{T} \neq \perp$, then $\mathcal{S} \diamond \mathcal{T} \in$ Sim.*

DEFINITION 4.17 *We say that* Env *is an environment class if the following hold:*

1. *Each* $\mathcal{Z} \in$ Env *has the open port structure of an environment for some simple or composed protocol.*
2. *For all* $\mathcal{Z} \in$ Env *and all* $\pi \in$ Pro, *where* $\pi \diamond \mathcal{Z} \neq \perp$ *and the protocol ports of* π *connect to the protocol ports of* $\mathcal{Z}$ *in* $\pi \diamond \mathcal{Z}$, *it holds that* $\pi \diamond \mathcal{Z} \in$ Env.
3. *For all* $\mathcal{Z} \in$ Env *and all* $\mathcal{S} \in$ Sim, *where* $\mathcal{S} \diamond \mathcal{Z} \neq \perp$ *and the simulation ports of* $\mathcal{S}$ *connect to the special ports of* $\mathcal{Z}$, *it holds that* $\mathcal{S} \diamond \mathcal{Z} \in$ Env.

In the following we call an environment $\mathcal{Z}$ recursive polytime if it is polytime and it makes at most an expected polynomial number of calls before it makes its guess.

PROPOSITION 4.18 *Let* Env^{poly} *be the set of all recursive polytime systems that have an open port structure of an environment for some simple or composed protocol. Then* Env^{poly} *is an environment class.*

Proof

1. The first property of an environment class is fulfilled by definition.
2. If $\mathcal{Z} \in \mathrm{Env}^{poly}$ and $\pi \in$ Pro and the protocol ports of π connect to the protocol ports of $\mathcal{Z}$ in $\pi \diamond \mathcal{Z}$, then $\pi \diamond \mathcal{Z}$ has an open port structure of an environment for some simple or composed protocol. Note that this is true because when we compose $\mathcal{Z}$ with only π, we explicitly do not include the resource used by π; that is, we compose with π and not a system of the form $\pi \diamond \mathcal{R}$. Hence, if π has resource name R, $\pi \diamond \mathcal{Z}$ has an open port structure matching a protocol with protocol name R. Thus, to show that $\pi \diamond \mathcal{Z} \in \mathrm{Env}^{poly}$, we just have to show that $\pi \diamond \mathcal{Z}$ is recursive polytime. But, since $\mathcal{Z} \in \mathrm{Env}^{poly}$, it is recursive polytime. Moreover, $\pi \in$ Pro is also recursive polytime by definition, so $\pi \diamond \mathcal{Z}$ is recursive polytime, as desired.
3. If $\mathcal{Z} \in \mathrm{Env}^{poly}$ and $\mathcal{S} \in$ Sim and the simulation ports of $\mathcal{S}$ connect to the special ports of $\mathcal{Z}$, it holds that $\mathcal{S} \diamond \mathcal{Z}$ has an open port structure of an environment for some simple or composed protocol. Thus, to show that $\mathcal{S} \diamond \mathcal{Z} \in \mathrm{Env}^{poly}$, we just have to show that $\mathcal{S} \diamond \mathcal{Z}$ is recursive polytime. This follows as for $\pi \diamond \mathcal{Z}$ because $\mathcal{S} \in$ Sim implies that $\mathcal{S}$ is recursive polytime. ∎

EXERCISE 4.1 Show that if Env_1 and Env_2 are environment classes, then $\mathrm{Env}_1 \cap \mathrm{Env}_2$ is an environment class and $\mathrm{Env}_1 \cup \mathrm{Env}_2$ is an environment class.

The following definition is very similar to Definition 4.10, but we now also consider composed protocols, and we make all the demands on environments that are necessary to prove the UC theorem.

DEFINITION 4.19 (UC SECURITY FOR PROTOCOLS) *Let* F_F *be an ideal functionality with name F, let* π_F *be a protocol with protocol name F and resource name R, and let* F_R *be an ideal functionality with name R. Let* Env *be an environment class. We say that* $\pi_F \diamond F_R$ *securely implements* F_F *in environments* Env *if there exists a simulator* $\mathcal{S} \in$ Sim *for* π_F *such that* $\pi_F \diamond F_R \overset{\mathrm{Env}}{\equiv} F_F \diamond \mathcal{S}$. *We will also write this as* $\pi_F \diamond F_R \overset{\mathrm{Env}}{\geqslant} F_F$, *and we will sometimes say that* $\pi_F \diamond F_R$ *is at least as secure as* F_F *for environments in Z.*

THEOREM 4.20 (THE UC THEOREM) *Let* Env *be an environment class. Let $\pi_F \in$ Pro be a protocol with protocol name F and resource name G. Let π_G be a protocol with protocol name G and resource name H and for which $\pi_F \diamond \pi_G \neq \perp$. Let F_F, F_G, and F_H be ideal functionalities with names F, G, and H. If $\pi_F \diamond F_G \overset{\text{Env}}{\geq} F_F$ and $\pi_G \diamond F_H \overset{\text{Env}}{\geq} F_G$, then $(\pi_F \diamond \pi_G) \diamond F_H \overset{\text{Env}}{\geq} F_F$.*

Proof We start by writing out the premises of the theorem to make them easier to use. We assume that $\pi_F \diamond F_G \overset{\text{Env}}{\geq} F_F$. This means that there exists a simulator $\mathcal{S} \in$ Sim for π_F such that

$$\pi_F \diamond F_G \diamond \mathcal{Z}_1 \overset{\text{stat}}{\equiv} F_F \diamond \mathcal{S} \diamond \mathcal{Z}_1 \tag{4.1}$$

for all $\mathcal{Z}_1 \in$ Env for which the compositions make sense. Note that this is just a convenient (and equivalent) way to say that $\pi_F \diamond F_G \overset{\text{Env}}{\equiv} F_F \diamond \mathcal{S}$

We also assume that $\pi_G \diamond F_H \overset{\text{Env}}{\geq} F_G$. This means that there exists a simulator $\mathcal{T} \in$ Sim for π_G such that

$$\pi_G \diamond F_H \diamond \mathcal{Z}_2 \overset{\text{stat}}{\equiv} F_G \diamond \mathcal{T} \diamond \mathcal{Z}_2 \tag{4.2}$$

for all $\mathcal{Z}_2 \in$ Env for which the compositions make sense.

We then write out the conclusion to better see what we have to prove. We want to prove that $\pi_F \diamond \pi_G \diamond F_H \overset{\text{Env}}{\geq} F_F$. This means that there should exist a simulator $\mathcal{U} \in$ Sim for $\pi_F \diamond \pi_G$ such that

$$\pi_F \diamond \pi_G \diamond F_H \diamond \mathcal{Z} \overset{\text{stat}}{\equiv} F_F \diamond \mathcal{U} \diamond \mathcal{Z} \tag{4.3}$$

for all $\mathcal{Z} \in$ Env for which the compositions make sense.

The flow of the proof is as follows: we first show that

$$\pi_F \diamond \pi_G \diamond F_H \diamond \mathcal{Z} \overset{\text{stat}}{\equiv} \pi_F \diamond F_G \diamond \mathcal{T} \diamond \mathcal{Z} \tag{4.4}$$

Then we show that

$$\pi_F \diamond F_G \diamond \mathcal{T} \diamond \mathcal{Z} \overset{\text{stat}}{\equiv} F_F \diamond \mathcal{S} \diamond \mathcal{T} \diamond \mathcal{Z} \tag{4.5}$$

Then we use the transitivity of $\overset{\text{stat}}{\equiv}$ on Eqs. (4.4) and (4.5) to conclude that

$$\pi_F \diamond \pi_G \diamond F_H \diamond \mathcal{Z} \overset{\text{stat}}{\equiv} F_F \diamond \mathcal{S} \diamond \mathcal{T} \diamond \mathcal{Z} \tag{4.6}$$

Then we observe that if we have $\mathcal{U} \overset{\text{def}}{=} \mathcal{S} \diamond \mathcal{T}$, then $\mathcal{U} \in$ Sim. Plugging this into Eq. (4.6), we get exactly Eq. (4.3). What remains is therefore just to show Eqs. (4.4) and (4.5).

Consider first Eq. (4.4) and let $\mathcal{Z}_2 \overset{\text{def}}{=} \pi_F \diamond \mathcal{Z}$. Then

$$\pi_G \diamond F_H \diamond \mathcal{Z}_2 = \pi_G \diamond F_H \diamond \pi_F \diamond \mathcal{Z} = \pi_F \diamond \pi_G \diamond F_H \diamond \mathcal{Z}$$

$$F_G \diamond \mathcal{T} \diamond \mathcal{Z}_2 = F_G \diamond \mathcal{T} \diamond \pi_F \diamond \mathcal{Z} = \pi_F \diamond F_G \diamond \mathcal{T} \diamond \mathcal{Z}$$

Thus, to prove Eq. (4.4), we just have to prove that

$$\pi_G \diamond F_H \diamond \mathcal{Z}_2 \overset{\text{stat}}{\equiv} F_G \diamond \mathcal{T} \diamond \mathcal{Z}_2 \ . \tag{4.7}$$

This, however, follows directly from Eq. (4.2), because $\mathcal{Z}_2 \in$ Env when $\pi_F \in$ Pro and $\mathcal{Z} \in$ Env.

Consider then Eq. (4.5), and let $\mathcal{Z}_1 \overset{\text{def}}{=} \mathcal{T} \diamond \mathcal{Z}$. Then, to prove Eq. (4.5), we just have to prove that

$$\pi_F \diamond F_G \diamond \mathcal{Z}_1 \overset{\text{stat}}{\equiv} F_F \diamond \mathcal{S} \diamond \mathcal{Z}_1 \tag{4.8}$$

This, however, follows directly from Eq. (4.1), because $\mathcal{Z}_1 \in$ Env when $\mathcal{T} \in$ Sim and $\mathcal{Z} \in$ Env.   ∎

4.2.9 Extensions

It is possible to extend the UC theorem in several ways. For example, we say (with the same notation as in the UC theorem) that π_F is a perfect secure implementation of F_F in environments Env if there exist a simulator $\mathcal{S} \in$ Sim for π_F such that

$$\pi_F \diamond F_R \diamond \mathcal{Z} \overset{\text{perf}}{\equiv} F_F \diamond \mathcal{S} \diamond \mathcal{Z}$$

for all $\mathcal{Z} \in$ Env instead of just

$$\pi_F \diamond F_R \diamond \mathcal{Z} \overset{\text{stat}}{\equiv} F_F \diamond \mathcal{S} \diamond \mathcal{Z}$$

The following theorem follows directly from the proof of Theorem 4.20:

THEOREM 4.21 *Let* Env *be an environment class. Let* $\pi_F \in$ Pro *be a protocol with protocol name F and resource name G. Let* π_G *be a protocol with protocol name G and resource name H and for which* $\pi_F \diamond \pi_G \neq \perp$. *Let* F_F, F_G, *and* F_H *be ideal functionalities with names F, G, and H. If* $\pi_F \diamond F_G$ *is a perfect secure implementation of* F_F *in the environments* Env *and* $\pi_G \diamond F_H$ *is a perfect secure implementation of* F_G *in the environments* Env, *then* $(\pi_F \diamond \pi_G) \diamond F_H$ *is a perfect secure implementation of* F_F *in the environments* Env.

It is also possible to show the following theorem:

THEOREM 4.22 *Let* Env_1 *and* Env_2 *be environment classes. Let* $\pi_F \in$ Pro *be a protocol with protocol name F and resource name G. Let* π_G *be a protocol with protocol name G and resource name H. Let* F_F, F_G, *and* F_H *be ideal functionalities with names F, G, and H. Assume that if* $\mathcal{Z} \in \text{Env}_1$, *then* $\mathcal{Z} \diamond \pi_F \in \text{Env}_2$. *If* $\pi_F \diamond F_G \overset{\text{Env}_1}{\geqslant} F_F$ *and* $\pi_G \diamond F_H \overset{\text{Env}_2}{\geqslant} F_G$, *then* $(\pi_F \diamond \pi_G) \diamond F_H \overset{\text{Env}_1}{\geqslant} F_F$.

Intuitively $\pi_G \diamond F_H \overset{\text{Env}_2}{\geqslant} F_G$ say that it is secure to use $\pi_G \diamond F_H$ instead of F_G in environments from the class Env_2. And the assumption that if $\mathcal{Z} \in \text{Env}_1$, then $\mathcal{Z} \diamond \pi_F \in \text{Env}_2$ says that if π_F is run in an environment from the class Env_1, then it provides an environment from the class Env_2 for its resource. Thus, replacing F_G by $\pi_G \diamond F_H$ inside π_F is secure as long as π_F is run in an environment from the class Env_1.

EXERCISE 4.2 Give a formal proof of Theorem 4.22 along the lines of the proof of Theorem 4.20.

Another important generalization is that we can consider protocols π that use more than one communication resource. In this case, π has one set of protocol ports named like the ideal functionality F it tries to implement, but it has a separate set of resource ports for each of the ideal functionalities $F_{R,1}, \ldots, F_{R,N}$ that it uses as communication resources. It is still secure to replace some resource by a secure implementation of the resource. That is, $\pi \diamond F_{R,1} \diamond \cdots \diamond F_{R,N} \overset{\text{Env}}{\geqslant} F$ and $\pi_{R,I} \overset{\text{Env}}{\geqslant} F_{R,I}$ imply that $\pi \diamond F_{R,1} \diamond \cdots \diamond F_{R,I-1} \diamond \pi_{R,I} \diamond F_{R,I+1} \diamond \cdots \diamond F_{R,N} \overset{\text{Env}}{\geqslant} F$. Using this N times, we can replace all the resources by secure implementations.

For the preceding to hold, some changes have to be made to the definition of Env because $\mathcal{Z}_2$ in the proof will be $\pi \diamond \mathsf{F}_{\mathsf{R},1} \diamond \cdots \diamond \mathsf{F}_{\mathsf{R},\mathsf{I}-1} \diamond \mathsf{F}_{\mathsf{R},\mathsf{I}+1} \diamond \cdots \diamond \mathsf{F}_{\mathsf{R},\mathsf{N}} \diamond \mathcal{Z}$. We therefore need that this $\mathcal{Z}_2$ is in Env. If Env is the set of all recursive polytime environments and each $\mathsf{F}_{\mathsf{R},\mathsf{J}}$ for $J = 1,\ldots,n$, $J \neq I$ are recursive polytime, then it can be seen that Env is an environment class under this definition.

EXERCISE 4.3 Prove the UC theorem for protocols using several resources, and make the needed modifications to the definitions involved if you have to. Argue that all the changes are needed.

4.3 Adversaries and Their Powers

In secure multiparty computation, it is often impossible to prove security in all environments. We therefore work with a large number of restricted classes of environments. In this section we list some of these restrictions, discuss why they have been considered, and model them using an environment class. In doing this, we always let Env be the environment class consisting of all interactive systems and then discuss how to restrict it.

4.3.1 Threshold Security

Our Protocol CEPS (Circuit Evaluation with Passive Security) from Chapter 3 is only secure against $t < n/2$ corrupted parties because $n/2$ parties have enough shares in all secret sharings to allow them to reconstruct. This is called threshold security, and in this case the threshold is $\lfloor n/2 - 1 \rfloor$. For any t, we let Env^t be the set of $\mathcal{Z} \in \mathrm{Env}$ that corrupts at most t parties. To prove that this is an environment class, the crucial observation is that if $\mathcal{Z} \in \mathrm{Env}^t$ and $\mathcal{S} \in \mathrm{Sim}$, then also $\mathcal{Z} \diamond \mathcal{S}$ corrupts at most t parties because $\mathcal{S}$ is corruption preserving.

4.3.2 Adaptive Security versus Static Security

Environments in Env are allowed to corrupt parties when they desire. This is called adaptive corruption, and the environment is called an adaptive adversary because it can adapt its corruption pattern to the communication that it observes in the protocol. Protocols that can be proven secure against adaptive adversaries are called adaptively secure.

Sometimes adaptive corruption makes security proofs hard or impossible. We therefore also work with the notion of a static adversary that must specify which parties it is going to corrupt *before the protocol execution starts*. This is called static corruption, and a protocol that is only proven secure against static adversaries is called statically secure.

Recall that when we proved Protocol CEPS (Circuit Evaluation with Passive Security) secure, we gave the set of corrupted parties as input to the simulator S because we gave it $\{x_i, y_i\}_{\mathsf{P}_i \in C}$. So what we did in Chapter 3 was actually a static simulation. It turns out that Protocol CEPS (Circuit Evaluation with Passive Security) is also adaptively secure; we just did not want to go into the details of this in Chapter 3. However, as we will see in a later example, there exist protocols that are statically but not adaptively secure. For now, we concentrate on modeling the notion of a static adversary.

Technically, what we want is that the simulator knows which parties are going to be corrupted before the simulation starts. We ensure this by restricting Env to the set of

$\mathcal{Z} \in$ Env, which behaves as follows: before $\mathcal{Z}$ sends any other messages, it does a corruption of some subset C of the parties, either passively or actively. This is called the preamble. In the simulation, $\mathcal{S}$ sees the initial corruptions done by $\mathcal{Z}$ and can therefore learn the set C before it has to simulate any leakage or influence. We use $\mathrm{Env}^{\mathtt{static}}$ to denote this set of environments. To prove that this is an environment class, the crucial observation is that if $\mathcal{Z} \in \mathrm{Env}^{\mathtt{static}}$ and $\mathcal{S} \in$ Sim, then also $\mathcal{Z} \diamond \mathcal{S}$ does static corruptions because $\mathcal{S}$ is corruption preserving.

EXAMPLE 4.23 To demonstrate the difference between adaptive corruption and static corruption, we return to our secure transfer example (Example 4.11) and consider how we simulate corruption. Assume first that we allow one static, active corruption. This means that at most one party gets corrupted and that the simulator $\mathcal{S}$ is told which party it is before the protocol is run.

Assume first that it is P_1 who is corrupted. Technically, this means that before it does anything else, the environment $\mathcal{Z}$ outputs (active corrupt) on $\mathtt{AT.infl}_1$ and then outputs (active corrupt, 1) on $\mathtt{AT.infl}$. Now, since $\mathcal{S}$ is corruption preserving, it will then output (active corrupt, 1) on $\mathtt{ST.infl}$. More important, $\mathcal{S}$ is now allowed to send $(\mathtt{send}, 1, (mid, 2, m'))$ on $\mathtt{ST.infl}$ at any point, in response to which F_{ST} stores $(mid, 1, 2, m')$ as if $(mid, 2, m')$ had arrived on $\mathtt{ST.in}_1$. Then $\mathcal{S}$ can send $(\mathtt{deliver}, mid, 1, 2)$ on $\mathtt{ST.infl}$, in response to which F_{ST} outputs $(mid, 1, m')$ on $\mathtt{ST.out}_2$. Thus, all in all, $\mathcal{S}$ can make F_{ST} output any message of the form $(mid, 1, m')$ on $\mathtt{ST.out}_i$. The simulator uses this to simulate as follows: it runs a copy of $\pi_{\mathsf{ST}} \diamond \mathsf{F}_{\mathsf{AT}}$ internally, where it corrupts party 1. It connects the special ports of $\pi_{\mathsf{ST}} \diamond \mathsf{F}_{\mathsf{AT}}$ to $\mathcal{Z}$ such that $\mathcal{Z}$ is interacting with a copy of $\pi_{\mathsf{ST}} \diamond \mathsf{F}_{\mathsf{AT}}$ exactly as in the real world. Whenever the party P_2 in the internal copy of $\pi_{\mathsf{ST}} \diamond \mathsf{F}_{\mathsf{AT}}$ outputs a message of the form $(mid, 1, m')$ on $\mathtt{ST.out}_2$, then $\mathcal{S}$ makes F_{ST} output $(mid, 1, m')$ on $\mathtt{ST.out}_2$. As a result, $\mathcal{Z}$ will receive $(mid, 1, m')$ on $\mathtt{ST.out}_2$ exactly as in the real world, where it interacts with $\pi_{\mathsf{ST}} \diamond \mathsf{F}_{\mathsf{AT}}$. It is easy to see that this gives a perfect simulation.[9]

If it is P_2 who is corrupted, then $\mathcal{S}$ simulates as follows: whenever $\mathcal{S}$ is activated, it checks whether it received some $(mid, 1, 2, |m|)$ on $\mathtt{ST.leak}$. If so, it inputs $(\mathtt{deliver}, mid, 1, 2)$ on $\mathtt{ST.leak}$. In response to this, F_{ST} outputs $(mid, 1, m)$ on $\mathtt{ST.leak}$ because outputs of corrupted parties are redirected to the simulator. This means that as soon as $\mathcal{Z}$ sends $(mid, 2, m)$ to F_{ST} on $\mathtt{ST.in}_1$, the simulator can learn m. This again makes the simulation trivial because $\mathcal{S}$ now knows the input, so it can just run the protocol on m and connect the special ports of the protocol to $\mathcal{Z}$.   ∎

The preceding example shows that $\pi_{\mathsf{ST}} \diamond \mathsf{F}_{\mathsf{AT}}$ securely implements F_{ST} in polytime environments, doing one active corruption. It is trivial to give a simulator for environments that do a static corruption of both P_1 and P_2 because the simulator then sees all inputs of

---

[9] The argument here was easy because we only consider two parties. If we look at the larger protocol for n parties, other things could go wrong. Suppose, for instance, that $\mathcal{Z}$ could make P_2 output a message of the form $(mid, 3, m')$ in a setting where P_3 is honest and where $(mid, 2, m')$ was not input on $\mathtt{ST.in}_3$, that is, make P_2 think it received a message from P_3 even though P_3 did not send it. Then $\mathcal{S}$ cannot simulate because it cannot make F_{ST} output a message of the form $(mid, 3, m)$ on $\mathtt{ST.out}_2$ unless F_{ST} received $(mid, 2, m)$ on $\mathtt{ST.in}_3$ or P_3 is corrupted. It is, however, easy to see that $\mathcal{Z}$ cannot create such a situation because the protocol uses authenticated transfer as a resource.

P_1 and P_2 and determines which outputs F_{ST} gives on behalf of P_1 and P_2 as in a complete breakdown. Thus,

$$\pi_{ST} \diamond F_{AT} \overset{Env^{poly,static}}{\geqslant} F_{ST}$$

To demonstrate that there is a difference between static and adaptive security, we now argue that $\pi_{ST} \diamond F_{AT}$ does not implement F_{ST} even against just one adaptive corruption, at least if the encryption scheme is a normal encryption scheme such as RSA. Assume, namely, that both parties are honest from the beginning of the protocol, and that Z sends a uniformly random bit string $m \in \{0,1\}^k$ and finishes the protocol and then corrupts P_1. When playing with $\pi_{ST} \diamond F_{AT}$, it will see pk and $c = E_{pk}(m;r)$ during execution of the protocol, and when it corrupts P_1, it receives the internal state of P_1, which includes m and r. Then it checks whether $c = E_{pk}(m;r)$. If so, it outputs 1; otherwise, it outputs 0. It is clear that $\Pr[(\pi_{ST} \diamond F_{AT}) \diamond Z = 1] = 1$. Consider then the simulation $F_{ST} \diamond S$. As before, Z sends uniformly random $m \in \{0,1\}^\kappa$. Since P_1 is honest during the execution, S only learns $|m| = \kappa$. Then S must show some pk and some c to Z. Then Z corrupts P_1, and S must simulate this by giving an internal state of P_1 that includes some m and r. Sending the correct m is easy because S receives m from F_{ST} when P_1 is corrupted. The simulator must cook up the value r, itself. Now Z checks whether $c = E_{pk}(m;r)$. The claim is that the probability that $c = E_{pk}(m;r)$ is at most $2^{-\kappa}$. Thus, $\Pr[(F_{ST} \diamond S) \diamond Z = 1] = 2^{-\kappa}$, no matter which strategy S is using. The reason is that as soon as S sends pk and c, there exists at most one m' for which there exists some r' such that $c = E_{pk}(m';r')$ because a ciphertext c can be an encryption of at most one plaintext. When S sent (pk,c), it did not know m, only $|m|$. Thus, the m' that is fixed by (pk,c) is independent of the uniformly random m sent by Z; hence the probability that $m = m'$ is exactly $2^{-\kappa}$, and if $m \neq m'$, then S cannot produce r such that $c = E_{pk}(m;r)$, even if it had infinite computing power – such an r simply does not exist. If Z does an adaptive corruption of P_2 instead of P_1, the situation gets even worse because the simulator would also have to show the secret key to Z.

Non-committing Encryption

The basic problem just demonstrated is that as soon as S shows the simulated pk and c to Z, it is committed to the m' inside c, and hence it gets caught if m' is not the message that Z gave to F_{ST}. There actually exist encryption schemes that avoid this problem, called a *non-committing encryption schemes*. A non-committing encryption scheme is an encryption scheme that in normal mode works as a normal encryption scheme. It is possible, however, to produce a simulated public key pk and a simulated ciphertext c that are indistinguishable from a real public key and a real ciphertext but where it is possible to take any message m and then efficiently compute r and sk such that r is indistinguishable from a uniformly random randomizer for the encryption scheme, sk is indistinguishable from a secret for pk, and $c = E_{pk}(m;r)$ and $D_{sk}(c) = m$. Using a non-committing encryption scheme in π_{ST} will produce a protocol that is secure also against adaptive corruptions. However, we do, not know any efficient construction of non-committing encryption – all known schemes use at least κ bits to encrypt just one plaintext bit, where κ is the security parameter. Finding a non-committing encryption scheme that can encrypt κ bits using the order of κ bits of ciphertext is an important open problem in the theory of adaptive secure multiparty computation.

4.3.3 Active Security versus Passive Security

We already saw that protocols can be secure against passive corruptions but not active corruptions, where the environment takes complete control over the corrupted party. By definition, environments $\mathcal{Z} \in \text{Env}$ are allowed active corruptions. We use $\text{Env}^{\texttt{passive}}$ to denote the set of $\mathcal{Z} \in \text{Env}$ that only does passive corruptions. That it is an environment class follows from all simulators being corruption preserving. This defines notions of a passive adversary and passively secure and active adversary and active secure. We also call a protocol that is active secure robust, and we call a protocol that is passively secure private.

4.3.4 Unconditional Security versus Computational Security

Recall that our Protocol CEPS (Circuit Evaluation with Passive Security) from Chapter 3 was proven perfectly secure. This means that even an environment $\mathcal{Z}$ with unbounded computing power cannot distinguish the protocol from the simulation. When we use cryptography in a protocol, as in π_{ST}, then we can only expect to prove security against polytime environments because stronger environments, for example, can distinguish encryptions of different messages. When security can be proven against a computationally unbounded adversary, we talk about unconditional security. When security can only be proven against a polytime adversary, we talk about computational security.

We use $\text{Env}^{\texttt{poly}}$ to denote the set of recursive polytime environments. We already saw that this is an environment class.

If it is possible to prove security against unbounded environments and it in addition holds for all $\mathcal{Z}$ that

$$\pi_{\text{F}} \diamond \text{F}_{\text{R}} \diamond \mathcal{Z} \stackrel{\text{perf}}{\equiv} \text{F}_{\text{F}} \diamond \mathcal{S} \diamond \mathcal{Z}$$

instead of just

$$\pi_{\text{F}} \diamond \text{F}_{\text{R}} \diamond \mathcal{Z} \stackrel{\text{stat}}{\equiv} \text{F}_{\text{F}} \diamond \mathcal{S} \diamond \mathcal{Z}$$

then we talk about perfect security.

4.3.5 Synchronous versus Asynchronous

In our framework, we have chosen to clock the parties via the influence ports, which means that it is the environment that determines the order in which the parties are clocked. The environment therefore can either choose to clock the parties an equal number of times, modeling that they have synchronized clocks, or can choose to clock parties a different number of times, modeling that the parties do not have synchronized clocks. This, in particular, means that we have to model clock synchronization simply as a restriction on the environment. Another approach could have been to add clock synchronization as an ideal functionality $\text{F}_{\text{CLOCK-SYNC}}$. This would have allowed us to talk about securely realizing clock synchronization by giving a protocol securely realizing $\text{F}_{\text{CLOCK-SYNC}}$. One disadvantage of our approach of letting clock synchronization be a restriction on the environment is that we cannot talk about how to securely realize it, at least not via the UC theorem. An advantage of our approach is that it is technically much simpler. Specifying $\text{F}_{\text{CLOCK-SYNC}}$ in a usable and implementable way is technically very challenging. Since the topic of securely realizing clock synchronization is not a topic of this book, we have chosen the simpler approach.

When talking about synchronous computation, we talk in terms of rounds. Each round will actually consist of two clockings of each party. The first clocking, called *inward clocking*, allows the party to send its messages to the ideal functionality for that round. The second clocking, called *outward clocking*, allows the party to receive its messages from the ideal functionality for that round.

We explain inward and outward clocking using an example. Consider the composed party $\mathcal{P}_1 = \{Q_1, P_1\}$ in Figure 4.5 using the resource F_{AT}. When we say that $\mathcal{P}_1$ is inward clocked, we mean that $\mathcal{Z}$ first clocks Q_1 and then P_1, and then $\mathcal{Z}$ sends (inclock, i) on AT.infl and clocks F_{AT}. Note that this allows $\mathcal{P}_1$ to deliver a message to F_{AT} and allows F_{AT} to process it.

When we say that $\mathcal{P}_1$ is outward clocked, we mean that $\mathcal{Z}$ first sends (outclock, i) on AT.infl, then clocks F_{AT}, then clocks P_1, and then clocks Q_1. Note that this allows F_{AT} to deliver a message to $\mathcal{P}_1$.

We say that $\mathcal{Z}$ is a synchronous environment if it proceeds in rounds, where in each round it behaves as follows:

1. First, it does an inward clocking of all parties that are not actively corrupted. It is up to $\mathcal{Z}$ to set the order in which the parties are inward clocked.
2. Then it possibly interacts with F_{AT} by sending messages on AT.infl, clocking F_{AT}, and looking at the messages output on AT.leak.
3. Then it does an outwards clocking of all parties which are not actively corrupted. It is up to $\mathcal{Z}$ in which order the parties are outwards clocked.

In each round we call the phase from the point at which the first party P_i that is not actively corrupted is clocked in until the point at which the last party P_i that is not actively corrupted is clocked in the clock-in phase. We call the phase from the point at which the last party P_i that is not actively corrupted is clocked in until the point at which the first party P_i that is not actively corrupted is clocked out the negotiation phase. We call the phase from the point at which the first party P_i that is not actively corrupted is clocked out until the point at which the last party P_i that is not actively corrupted is clocked out the clock-out phase. We call the phase from the point in round r at which the last party P_i that is not actively corrupted is clocked out until the point in round $r+1$ at which the first party P_i that is not actively corrupted is clocked in the transition phase. We say that the transition phase belongs to round r.

The environment $\mathcal{Z}$ is allowed to do corruptions in all phases. Notice that a phase can end by a corruption. Assume, for example, that all parties that are not actively corrupted have been clocked in, except P_1. If then P_1 is actively corrupted by $\mathcal{Z}$, it now holds that *all* parties that are not actively corrupted have been clocked in, so the clock-in phase ended and the negotiation phase began.

We use $\mathrm{Env}^{\mathrm{sync}}$ to denote the class of synchronous environments. It is not hard to see that if $\mathcal{Z} \in \mathrm{Env}^{\mathrm{sync}}$, $\pi \in \mathrm{Pro}$, and $\pi \diamond \mathcal{Z}$ connects the protocol ports of the two systems, then $\pi \diamond \mathcal{Z} \in \mathrm{Env}^{\mathrm{sync}}$. It is also true that if $\mathcal{Z} \in \mathrm{Env}^{\mathrm{sync}}$, $\mathcal{S} \in \mathrm{Sim}$, and $\mathcal{S} \diamond \mathcal{Z}$ connects the special ports of the two systems, then $\mathcal{S} \diamond \mathcal{Z} \in \mathrm{Env}^{\mathrm{sync}}$. This follows from $\mathcal{S}$ being clock preserving.

Synchronous Communication

If n parties $\mathcal{P}_1, \ldots, \mathcal{P}_n$ are using F_{AT} as communication resource, then even though the parties are synchronized, the communication is not. It might happen that $\mathcal{P}_1$ sends a message to

$\mathcal{P}_2$ in round r during its inward clocking, and still $\mathcal{P}_2$ does not receive it in round r during its outward clocking. This is so because we formulated F_{AT} in an inherently asynchronous manner, which made it easier to talk about how to securely implement it because we did not have to deal with synchronization issues. If we also want to guarantee that messages sent in round r are received in round r, then we talk about synchronous communication, which is technically different from clock synchronization. In fact, implementing synchronous communication securely requires that you have both good clock synchronization and an upper bound on message delivery time on the network such that you can use timeouts. Again, we are not going to talk about how to implement synchronous communication; we are simply going to assume it when we need it. It is simple to turn F_{AT} into an ideal functionality for synchronous communication by adding the following two rules:

1. On $(\texttt{inclock}, i)$, process all messages on $\texttt{AT.in}_i$ as F_{AT} does.
2. On $(\texttt{outclock}, i)$, for all stored values (mid, j, i, m), delete (mid, j, i, m), and output (mid, j, m) on $\texttt{AT.out}_i$.

The first rule ensures that when $\mathcal{P}_i$ is inward clocked, all the messages (mid, j, m) sent in that round will be processed, and hence (mid, i, j, m) will be stored. The second rule ensures that when $\mathcal{P}_i$ is outward clocked, all the messages sent to it in that round will be delivered first such that they are available to $\mathcal{P}_i$. In a synchronous environment, this implies that all honest parties get to deliver all their messages to all parties in all rounds.

When we talk about a synchronous protocol, we mean a protocol using an ideal functionality for synchronous communication run in synchronous environment; that is, a synchronous protocol uses both clock synchronization and synchronous communication.

In this book we will mainly work with synchronous protocols. Assuming synchronous communication is not a very good model of reality, but we allow ourselves to assume it because the problems we look at are hard enough already in this model and because most of the techniques of multiparty computation are easier to present in the synchronous model.

As an example of an advantage of assuming synchronous communication, assume that we want to tolerate that up to t of the n parties are corrupted, and assume that we only have asynchronous communication. Since t parties can be corrupted, it is easy to see that if an honest party at some point in the protocol waits for messages from more than $n - t$ parties, then it might potentially be waiting for a message from a corrupted party. If this corrupted party is Byzantine, it might not have sent its message at all, and since no upper bound on message delivery is guaranteed, an unsent message cannot be distinguished from a slow message.[10] The party therefore might end up waiting forever for the unsent message, and the protocol deadlocks. Thus, in an asynchronous protocol that must tolerate t corruptions and must be deadlock-free, the honest parties cannot wait for messages from more than $n - t$ parties in each round. If the adversary delivers the messages of the corrupted parties faster than the messages of the honest parties, some honest parties must proceed without having heard from up to t of the other honest parties. But this means that *some of the honest parties might not even be able to send their inputs to the other honest parties*, let alone have their

---

[10] In fact, it is easy to see that the ability to distinguish an unsent message from a sent-but-slow message requires that you know an upper bound on delivery time.

inputs securely contribute to the result. Therefore, any asynchronous protocol allows input deprivation in the sense that in some executions, up to t of the honest parties might not be able to make the result depend on their inputs. In some application, such as voting, this is, of course, intolerable.

4.3.6 Consensus Broadcast versus Point-to-Point Communication

For active adversaries, there is a problem with broadcasting; namely, if a protocol requires a player to broadcast a message to everyone, it does not suffice to just ask him or her to send the same message to all players. If he or she is corrupt, he or she may say different things to different players, and it may not be clear to the honest players if he or she did this or not. And in some protocols, if a party sends different messages to different parties when it should not, it can make the protocol give incorrect results or make it fail in such a way that the adversary learns more than it should. Hence we sometimes need a mechanism that forces a party to send the same message to all parties. This is known as a consensus broadcast or Byzantine agreement.[11]

In a consensus broadcast, all honest receivers are guaranteed to receive the same message *even if the sender and some of the other parties are corrupted*. This problem is so hard that sometimes it is impossible to implement. One therefore in general has to make a distinction between the case where a consensus broadcast channel is given for free as a part of the model and whether such a channel has to be securely implemented by a subprotocol. We return to this issue in more detail later and look at an implementation of consensus broadcast.

What is important here is that consensus broadcast is not hard to model as an ideal functionality. We therefore do not model it as an environment class. We mention the problem in this section only because it fits into the discussion of the powers of adversaries.

4.3.7 Combining Environment Classes

We can combine the preceding notions and, for example, talk about a synchronous, polytime bounded, t-threshold adversary only doing static (and active) corruptions. The corresponding environment class is

$$\mathrm{Env}^{\mathrm{sync,poly},t,\mathrm{static}} \stackrel{\mathrm{def}}{=} \mathrm{Env}^{\mathrm{sync}} \cap \mathrm{Env}^{\mathrm{poly}} \cap \mathrm{Env}^{t} \cap \mathrm{Env}^{\mathrm{static}}$$

Since the intersection of environment classes produces an environment class, we have that $\mathrm{Env}^{\mathrm{sync,poly},t,\mathrm{static}}$ is an environment class.

4.4 Some Ideal Functionalities

In this section we describe some standard ideal functionalities that we will use later.

---

[11] Sometimes it is also just known by broadcast, but in the distributed computing literature, the term *broadcast* is sometimes used to refer to a communication mechanisms that does not necessarily guarantee consistency if the sender is corrupted. We want to avoid this possible confusion and therefore use the term *consensus broadcast*.

4.4.1 Complete Break Down

Before describing the functionalities, it is useful to introduce the notion of a complete breakdown. When we say that an ideal functionality F_F does a complete breakdown, we mean that it starts behaving as if all parties were actively corrupted. More specifically, it starts ignoring all its other code and only executes the following rules:

- It first outputs the ideal internal state of *all* parties on F.leak.
- On all subsequent inputs (send, i, m) on F.infl, it outputs m on F.out$_i$.
- On all subsequent inputs m on F.in$_i$, it outputs (i, m) on F.leak.

Notice that if F_F is used as a communication resource and does a complete breakdown, then the adversary sees all inputs given to F_F, and it is the adversary who specifies all outputs delivered by F_F. This is an ultimately useless and insecure communication resource. However, if F_F is acting as an ideal functionality and does a complete breakdown, then the simulator sees all inputs given to F_F, and it is the simulator S that specifies all outputs delivered by F_F. This makes simulation trivial. Assume that S is trying to simulate a protocol $\pi_F \diamond R$. The simulator S will simply run a copy of $\pi_F \diamond R$ internally and connect the special ports of $\pi_F \diamond R$ to the environment Z. Whenever Z inputs m on some inport F.in$_i$ of F_F, S is given (i, m). In response to this, S inputs m on the port F.in$_i$ of its internal copy of $\pi_F \diamond R$. And whenever the copy of $\pi_F \diamond R$ that S is running outputs a value m on some port F.out$_i$, then S inputs (send, i, m) to F_F, in response to which F_F sends m to Z on F.out$_i$. This means that Z is essentially just playing with the copy of $\pi_F \diamond R$ run by S, so clearly Z cannot distinguish this from a situation in which it is playing with $\pi_F \diamond R$. In fact, $\pi_F \diamond R$ and $F_F \diamond S$ will be perfectly indistinguishable to any Z.

With the preceding discussion in mind, we can think of a complete breakdown of an ideal functionality as a technical way to say that from the point in time of the complete breakdown, we require no security properties of an implementation of F_F.

4.4.2 Secure Synchronous Communication and Broadcast

In the box Agent F_{SC} we give an ideal functionality for secure *synchronous* communication and *consensus* broadcast. In each round, each party P_i specifies one message $m_{i,j}$ for each of the other parties P_j plus a message m_i that P_i wants to broadcast. At the end of the round, each P_j receives the messages $m_{i,j}$ and m_i from each P_i. The message m_i output to different parties P_j and P_k is guaranteed to be the same. This means that all messages are guaranteed to be delivered and that there is no way to send different broadcast messages to different parties.

Notice that we allow the corrupted parties to see their messages first, and we allow them to change their mind on their own messages until the round is over. This allows them to choose their own messages based on what the honest parties are sending. This is called rushing. If we do not allow rushing, then it is very hard and sometimes impossible to securely implement F_{SC}, the reason essentially being that some party must send its messages first, and the corrupted parties can always wait a little longer than the honest parties.

Observe also that if an honest party sends a message and gets corrupted before the round is over, then the adversary might replace the messages of the now-corrupted party. This

Agent F$_{SC}$

The ideal functionality for secure communication and consensus broadcast between n parties (drawing shows only two for simplicity).

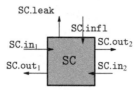

Initialization The ideal functionality keeps track of three sets, A, P, and C, which are all initially empty. When party i is actively corrupted, it adds i to A and C. When party i is passively corrupted, it adds i to P and C.

Honest inputs On input $(\texttt{clockin}, i)$ on $\texttt{SC.infl}$, read a message from $\texttt{SC.in}_i$. If there was a message on $\texttt{SC.in}_i$, then parse it on the form $(m_{i,1}, \ldots, m_{i,n}, m_i)$. Here $m_{i,j}$ is the message that P_i sends to P_j, and m_i is the message P_i is broadcasting. It then outputs $(\{m_{i,j}\}_{j \in C}, m_i)$ on $\texttt{SC.leak}$ (this means that as soon as a honest party sends messages, the adversary learns the messages intended for the corrupted parties). Finally, it stores $(m_{i,1}, \ldots, m_{i,n}, m_i)$. Furthermore, if at some point during the round the set C grows, then output $(i, j, m_{i,j})$ occurs on $\texttt{SC.leak}$ for the new $j \in C$.

Corrupted inputs On input $(\texttt{change}, i, (m_{i,1}, \ldots, m_{i,n}, m_i))$ on $\texttt{SC.infl}$, where $i \in A$ and at a point before the clock-out phase started, store $(m_{i,1}, \ldots, m_{i,n}, m_i)$, overriding any previous input from the actively corrupted party i in this round (this means that as long as no passively corrupted party or honest party received outputs, the corrupted parties are allowed to change their inputs).

Delivery On input $(\texttt{clockout}, i)$ on $\texttt{SC.infl}$, if there is a party P_i for which no $(m_{i,1}, \ldots, m_{i,n}, m_i)$ is stored, then store $(m_{i,1}, \ldots, m_{i,n}, m_i) = (\epsilon, \ldots, \epsilon)$ for all such parties. Then output $(m_{1,i}, \ldots, m_{n,i}, (m_1, \ldots, m_n))$ on $\texttt{SC.out}_i$.

makes it easier to implement the functionality because an implementation does not have to ensure that parties are committed to their inputs until the round is over.

Notice that if a party fails to send a message in some round, we simply set all its messages to be the empty string ϵ. This holds for both the honest parties and the corrupted parties. In terms of implementation, this just means that if you do not receive a message from some party before the timeout for a given round, you define the message to be ϵ. For an implementation to be secure, it is therefore essential that the timeout is so long that any honest party who tries to deliver a message will always have it delivered before the timeout, and this should hold in the worst case and except with negligible probability. This can make a secure implementation of synchronous communication very inefficient because each round suffers a delay that is at least as long as the worst-case delivery time of the network.

4.4.3 Secure Synchronous Function Evaluation

In the box Agent F_{SFE}^f we give an ideal functionality for secure synchronous function evaluation. For simplicity, we focus on the case in which each party gives just one input, and we give an ideal functionality that can be used only once.

Agent F_{SFE}^{f}

The ideal functionality for one secure function evaluation between n parties of a function $f : \mathbb{F}^n \to \mathbb{F}^n$ for a finite field $\mathbb{F}$ (drawing shows only two parties for simplicity).

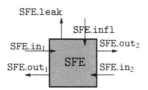

Initialize The ideal functionality keeps track of three sets A, P, and C as F_{SC}. It also keeps bits `delivery-round`, `evaluated`, `inputs-ready`, `input-ready`$_1$, ..., `input-ready`$_n \in \{0,1\}$, initially set to 0.

Honest inputs On input (`clockin`, i) on `SFE.infl` for $i \notin A$, read a message from `SFE.in`$_i$. If there was a message x_i on `SFE.in`$_i$, $x_i \in \mathbb{F}$ and `input-ready`$_i = 0$, then set `input-ready`$_i \leftarrow 1$, store (i, x_i), and output (`input`, i) on `SFE.leak`.

Corrupted inputs On input (`change`, i, x_i) on `SFE.infl`, where $i \in A$, $x_i \in \mathbb{F}$, and `evaluated` $= 0$, set `input-ready`$_i \leftarrow 1$, and store (i, x_i), overriding any such previous value stored for party i (this means that as long as the function has not been evaluated on the inputs, the corrupted parties are allowed to change their inputs).

Simultaneous inputs If it holds in some round that after the clock-in phase ends there exist $i, j \notin A$ such that `input-ready`$_i = 0$ and `input-ready`$_j = 1$, then do a complete breakdown. If it happens in some round that after the clock-in phase ends, `input-ready`$_i = 1$ for all $i \notin A$ and `inputs-ready` $= 0$, then set `inputs-ready` $\leftarrow 1$, and for each $i \in A$ where `input-ready`$_i = 0$, store $(i, x_i) = (i, 0)$.

Evaluate function On input (`evaluate`) on `SFE.infl` where `inputs-ready` $= 1$ and `evaluated` $= 0$, set `evaluated` $\leftarrow 1$, let $(x_1, \ldots, x_n)$ be the values defined by the stored values (i, x_i) for $i = 1, \ldots, n$, and compute $(y_1, \ldots, y_n) = f(x_1, \ldots, x_n)$. Then output $\{(i, y_i)\}_{i \in C}$ on `SFE.leak`, and if C later grows, then output (j, y_j) on `SFE.leak` for the new $j \in C$.

Simultaneous output On input (`delivery-round`) on `SFE.infl`, where `evaluated` $= 1$ and `delivery-round` $= 0$, proceed as follows: if we are at a point where not party $i \notin A$ was clocked out yet, then set `delivery-round` $\leftarrow 1$.

Delivery On input (`clockout`, i) on `SFE.infl`, where `delivery-round` $= 1$, output y_i on `SFE.out`$_i$.

As for F_{SC}, we allow that actively corrupted parties can change their inputs as long as the function was not evaluated, and we give all corrupted parties their outputs as soon as they are defined. This rushing behavior makes it easier to implement F_{SFE}^{f} as a protocol that is allowed to have the same influence and leakage (see box).

We allow that the adversary determines when the function is evaluated, but we require that it waits until all parties that are not actively corrupted have given their inputs, or we would implicitly have allowed the adversary to set the inputs of honest parties or passively corrupted parties to 0.

Notice that until the ideal functionality provides outputs, it sends no messages on its outports `SFE.out`$_i$. This means that some larger protocol using F_{SFE}^{f} will just observe silence from F_{SFE}^{f} during most of the rounds.

Simultaneous Input

Notice also that we implicitly require that all honest parties provide their inputs in the same round. That is, if they do not do this, we make F_{SFE}^f do a complete breakdown. This allows a secure implementation of F_{SFE}^f to do the same. In other words, we do not require any security properties from an implementation if the parties in the protocol do not get inputs in the same round. This makes implementation much easier because the implementation can just assume that all parties get inputs from the environment in the same round and ignore what happens if this is not true: any behavior of the protocol in case the simultaneous input assumption is broken can be trivially simulated as the ideal functionality does a complete breakdown.

Assuming that all parties that are not actively corrupted get their inputs in the same round is called simultaneous input. The reason why we do not require security of a protocol when there is nonsimultaneous input is that it is very hard to securely handle this and sometimes impossible.

As an example of this, consider the Protocol CEPS (Circuit Evaluation with Passive Security). Assume that honest parties only start running the protocol when they get inputs from the environment, and say that, for instance, party P_1 gets input in round 42 and party P_2 gets input in round $1,042$. This means that when P_1 starts running the protocol π_{CEPS}, the party P_2 will not be running the protocol yet, so P_1 will not receive shares of the input of P_2, and P_2 will not be ready to receive and store the share of the input of P_1. And it is provably impossible to do anything about this if we do not want input deprivation and if we want to tolerate active corruptions and want to guarantee that the protocol terminates. From the point of view of P_1, the party P_2 either might be an honest party that did not get its input yet or P_2 might be a corrupted party who is deviating from the protocol. Any subprotocol that tries to resolve this must have the property that it does not start the protocol until all honest parties received their inputs. However, this should allow the honest parties to proceed even if some corrupted party claims that it is honest but just did not get its input yet. These two requirements are clearly contradictory.

Simultaneous Output

Notice that the way we handle delivery means that all parties that are not actively corrupted will receive their outputs in the *same* round. This is called simultaneous output.

Having simultaneous output is very convenient in a synchronous environment. To see why, consider a synchronous protocol π_N that uses F_{SFE}^f as a subroutine in some larger protocol. Consider the following plausible behavior: at some point, the parties $Q_1, \ldots, Q_n$ call F_{SFE}^f. Then they wait until F_{SFE}^f delivers outputs, and in that round they then continue with the outer protocol, where the next step is to invoke some other subprotocol π_{SUB}. Now, if F_{SFE}^f delivers outputs to different parties in different rounds, then the parties $Q_1, \ldots, Q_n$ would continue with the outer protocol in different rounds. This would make them give inputs to π_{SUB} in different rounds. Thus, if π_{SUB} assumes simultaneous inputs, the overall protocol will now break down. Put briefly, we need simultaneous outputs to guarantee simultaneous inputs in later parts of the protocol. This means that simultaneous outputs are an important *security property*.

It is instructive to see how this property is captured by the UC framework. Let us say that π_N is secure when it uses F_{SFE}^f, and that π_N depends on F_{SFE}^f having simultaneous output. If we then replace F_{SFE}^f with a protocol π_{SFE} that does not have simultaneous output, then the overall protocol would break.

Fortunately, our framework would exactly catch such a bad protocol before we substitute it for F_{SFE}^f because it cannot be proven to be a secure implementation of F_{SFE}^f. Assume that F_{SFE}^f has simultaneous output and that π_{SFE} does not. Then it will be very easy to distinguish the two: no matter which simulator we attach to F_{SFE}^f, the system $F_{SFE}^f \diamond \mathcal{S}$ will have simultaneous output when run in a synchronous environment because $\mathcal{S}$ is clock preserving. And we assumed that the protocol π_{SFE} does not have simultaneous output. Thus, $\mathcal{Z}$ just looks at whether the outputs are delivered in the same round and outputs 1 if and only if they are. Then $\pi_{SFE} \diamond \mathcal{Z}$ will output 0, and $F_{SFE}^f \diamond \mathcal{S} \diamond \mathcal{Z}$ will output 1. The same distinguishing strategy works even if π_{SFE} fails to have simultaneous outputs with some nonnegligible probability.

It might seem that simultaneous output is easy to achieve. This is true, but only if consensus broadcast is given for free by the communication model. If consensus broadcast is to be implemented using a secure protocol that only uses point-to-point communication, then it is possible to prove the following two claims:

1. Any secure realization of consensus broadcast that can tolerate up to t actively corrupted parties and that has simultaneous output uses at least $t + 1$ communication rounds, even when no parties are corrupted.
2. There exist a secure realization of consensus broadcast that can tolerate up to t actively corrupted parties and that has nonsimultaneous output that uses only $\min(t + 1, f + 2)$ communication rounds, where $f \in \{0, \ldots, t\}$ is the number of parties who were actually corrupted during execution of the protocol.

Thus, if we have $n = 1{,}001$ parties and want to tolerate $t = 500$ actively corrupted parties, but in typical executions of the protocol no parties are actually deviating from the protocol, then requiring simultaneous output would make each consensus broadcast cost 501 communication rounds, whereas tolerating nonsimultaneous output typically would allow us to run each consensus broadcast in two communication rounds. If we are in a network where the worst-case delivery time of a message is 1 minute, this would make the difference between each consensus broadcast taking 2 minutes, or more than 8 hours. That is, with nonsimultaneous output, we only pay a high price when there are many parties who deviate from the protocol. If we insist on simultaneous output, then we pay a high price even if no parties deviate from the protocol.

It should be added that there exist frameworks for taking several protocols that expect simultaneous input but that give outputs in different rounds and still compose them securely with a minimal overhead in round complexity by massaging the constituent protocols into tolerating a small deviation in the round in which they are started at different parties.

Adversarially Chosen Output Round

Finally, notice that we allow the environment to specify the round in which the outputs are delivered. We call this the adversarially chosen output round. First of all, the reason why we do not just compute and give the outputs already in the round where the inputs are ready is that we want to allow an implementation to use several rounds of communication. If outputs were delivered immediately by the ideal functionality, a secure implementation would be allowed to use only one round of communication: the environment can observe the number of rounds that pass between inputs and outputs, so if the ideal functionality uses one round and the protocol uses two or more rounds, then the environment could trivially distinguish. However, secure multiparty computation is impossible in one round of communication. This opens the question of which round we should then specify as the output round. If we choose round seven, then for the same reasons as earlier, only protocols with exactly seven rounds would be deemed secure. Furthermore, if we pick any fixed-round as the output round, then only protocols with a fixed-round complexity would be secure. However, some protocols naturally have a varying output round. In fact, some of our MPC protocols will use more rounds when there is adversarial behavior because subprotocols must be run to deal with this adversarial behavior. We could, of course, pad the runs where there is no adversarial behavior with some dummy rounds to ensure that all executions take the same number of rounds, but introducing such inefficiency just because the model artificially asks for a fixed output round would not be desirable nor elegant. The correct solution is to note that if the adversary in the protocol has influence on which round is the output round, and we want to tolerate such influence, then we should add it to the ideal functionality as allowed influence.

EXAMPLE 4.24 We now argue that our Protocol CEPS (Circuit Evaluation with Passive Security) is secure in the UC model. Let π_{CEPS}^f denote the Protocol CEPS (Circuit Evaluation with Passive Security) for a function f with the addition that all parties wait on outputting their output y_i until the results y_j have been reconstructed toward all parties. Then all parties output their y_i in the same round. We show that

$$\pi_{\text{CEPS}}^f \diamond \mathsf{F}_{\text{SC}} \overset{\text{Env}^{t,\text{static,sync}}}{\geqslant} \mathsf{F}_{\text{SFE}}^f$$

for all $t < n/2$.

For this purpose, we construct the simulator Agent $\mathcal{S}_{\text{CEPS}}$ shown in the following box. By inspecting $\mathcal{S}_{\text{CEPS}}$, we can see that the views produced are distributed as in the real world. Actually, $\mathcal{S}_{\text{CEPS}}$ is producing the exact same views as the simulator S from the box in Section 3.3.3. (Repeating the argument, $\mathcal{S}_{\text{CEPS}}$ runs the corrupt players on their true inputs, so this has the exact same distribution. During the protocol, the environment will never see more than t shares of values belonging to honest players. No information on these values is given because they are shared using random polynomials of degree t. In output reconstruction, the environment sees for each corrupted player's output y_i all the shares sent by the honest parties. But these are already given as those consistent with the output being y_i and the t shares held by the corrupted parties. If fewer than t players are corrupted, the simulator chooses the missing shares at random. This can indeed be done independently for each output: recall that we assume that every output is produced by a multiplication gate and that the protocol for such a gate produces a fresh random set of shares with the only constraint that they determine the correct value. Furthermore, both $\pi_{\text{CEPS}}^f \diamond \mathsf{F}_{\text{SC}}$ and $\mathsf{F}_{\text{SFE}}^f$ output the correct y_i and hence *the same y_i*. Finally, $\mathcal{S}_{\text{CEPS}}$ makes $\mathsf{F}_{\text{SFE}}^f$ give output on SFE.out$_i$ exactly when P_i would give output on SFE.out$_i$. Hence the perfect security follows.

We now describe how to modify $\mathcal{S}_{\text{CEPS}}$ to handle the case where the environment does not give inputs to all parties in the same round. Again, $\mathcal{S}_{\text{CEPS}}$ learns the set of corrupted parties C in the preamble. If, in some round, $\mathcal{Z}$ gives inputs to some parties and not others, then $\mathsf{F}_{\text{SFE}}^f$

Agent $\mathcal{S}_{\text{CEPS}}$

A simulator for $\pi_{\text{CEPS}}^f \diamond \mathsf{F}_{\text{SC}}$ for the static case and when the environment gives inputs to all parties in the same round.

Initialize: In the preamble, the environment $\mathcal{Z}$ specifies the set C of passively corrupted parties. After this, the simulator sets up a copy of $\pi_{\text{CEPS}}^f \diamond \mathsf{F}_{\text{SC}}$ where it passively corrupts the players in C and connects the special ports of $\pi_{\text{CEPS}}^f \diamond \mathsf{F}_{\text{SC}}$ to $\mathcal{Z}$.

Input sharing: After the clock-in phase in the round where all inputs are given, $\mathcal{S}_{\text{CEPS}}$ does passive corruptions of $\mathsf{P}_i \in C$ on $\mathsf{F}_{\text{SFE}}^f$, which makes $\mathsf{F}_{\text{SFE}}^f$ leak the corresponding inputs x_i to $\mathcal{S}_{\text{CEPS}}$. Now $\mathcal{S}_{\text{CEPS}}$ does the input-sharing steps of π_{CEPS}^f with the true inputs for the corrupted parties and with 0 as input for honest parties. That is, for each player P_j, $\mathcal{S}_{\text{CEPS}}$ distributes $[x_j^{(0)}; f_{x_j^{(0)}}]_t$, where $x_j^{(0)} = x_j$ for $\mathsf{P}_j \in C$ and $x_j^{(0)} = 0$ for $\mathsf{P}_j \notin C$.

Computation phase: In the computation phase, the simulator simply follows the protocol steps of π_{CEPS}^f according to the gates that need to be processed.

Output reconstruction: First, $\mathcal{S}_{\text{CEPS}}$ instructs $\mathsf{F}_{\text{SFE}}^f$ to evaluate the function, thereby learning the outputs y_j for all $\mathsf{P}_j \in C$.

For each $\mathsf{P}_j \in C$, π_{CEPS}^f takes the $|C|$ shares that the corrupted parties hold in the output of P_j and defines $f_{y_j}(0) \stackrel{\text{def}}{=} y_j$. Also, for $t - |C|$ honest players P_i, it defines $f_{y_j}(i)$ to be a random value. After this, $f_{y_j}(\mathtt{X})$ is defined in $t + 1$ points and hence $\mathcal{S}_{\text{CEPS}}$ can use Lagrange interpolation to compute the unique degree-t polynomial consistent with these points. Then, for $\mathsf{P}_i \notin C$ it computes the share $f_{y_j}(i)$ and sends it to P_j on behalf of P_i.

When $\mathcal{Z}$ clocks out P_i in the copy of $\pi_{\text{CEPS}}^f \diamond \mathsf{F}_{\text{SC}}$ so that P_i should produce an output, the simulator first inputs $(\texttt{delivery-round})$ to $\mathsf{F}_{\text{SFE}}^f$ if it has not done so already. Then $\mathcal{S}_{\text{CEPS}}$ inputs $(\texttt{clock-out}, i)$ to $\mathsf{F}_{\text{SFE}}^f$ to make it output y_i on $\mathtt{SFE.out}_i$, exactly as P_i would have done in the protocol.

---

does a complete break down, so $\mathcal{S}$ learns all inputs $(x_1, \ldots, x_n)$. It then runs $\pi_{\text{CEPS}}^f \diamond \mathsf{F}_{\text{SC}}$ on these inputs and connects the special ports of $\pi_{\text{CEPS}}^f \diamond \mathsf{F}_{\text{SC}}$ to $\mathcal{Z}$. Whenever $\mathcal{Z}$ makes a party P_i output some value y_i' on $\mathtt{SFE.out}_i$, the simulator instructs $\mathsf{F}_{\text{SFE}}^f$ to do the same, which it is allowed to do because $\mathsf{F}_{\text{SFE}}^f$ is in a complete breakdown. This perfectly simulates the protocol, no matter how it behaves when there is nonsimultaneous input. There is one little twist, though. In the round where $\mathcal{Z}$ gives inputs x_i to some P_i and not to others, $\mathsf{F}_{\text{SFE}}^f$ does not do a complete breakdown until there is some P_i that does not get an input, and $\mathcal{Z}$ might choose to, for example, first give input to P_2 and then to P_5 and then fail to give input to P_3 during the clock-in of P_3. In this case, the simulator would have to simulate P_2 and P_5 while $\mathsf{F}_{\text{SFE}}^f$ is not in complete breakdown. This is easy, however. If, for example, P_2 is corrupted, then $\mathcal{S}$ learns x_2 from $\mathsf{F}_{\text{SFE}}^f$ and inputs x_2 to P_2 in $\pi_{\text{CEPS}}^f \diamond \mathsf{F}_{\text{SC}}$. If, for example, P_5 is honest, then $\mathcal{S}$ does not learn x_5 from $\mathsf{F}_{\text{SFE}}^f$, so it just inputs 0 to P_5 in $\pi_{\text{CEPS}}^f \diamond \mathsf{F}_{\text{SC}}$, which makes P_5 do a sharing of 0, and this will show at most t shares to $\mathcal{Z}$, namely, those sent to P_i for $i \in C$. When $\mathcal{Z}$ then fails to give input to P_3, the complete breakdown will give the true value of x_5 to $\mathcal{S}$. Then $\mathcal{S}$ computes the secret sharing of x_5 that is consistent with $f(0) = x_5$ and the t shares already shown to $\mathcal{Z}$. From $f(\mathtt{X})$ it computes the shares that P_5 would have sent to the other honest parties, and then it updates the internal state of P_5 and F_{SC} to be consistent with P_5 having sent these shares – this is possible because the internal state of the honest P_5 was not shown to $\mathcal{Z}$ at this point and because F_{SC} only leaked what P_5 sent to the corrupted parties. Now the state of $\pi_{\mathrm{CEPS}}^{f} \diamond \mathsf{F}_{\mathrm{SC}}$ is consistent with P_5 having run with x_5. The simulator patches the state this way for all honest parties that received inputs before the complete breakdown, and then $\mathcal{S}_{\mathrm{CEPS}}$ finishes the simulation as earlier simply by running the protocol on the true inputs of the parties. ∎

EXERCISE 4.4 Argue that

$$\pi_{\mathrm{SFE}}^{f} \diamond \mathsf{F}_{\mathrm{SC}} \stackrel{\mathrm{Env}^{t,\mathrm{sync}}}{\geqslant} \mathsf{F}_{\mathrm{SFE}}^{f}$$

for all $t < n/2$. That is, argue that the protocol is also adaptively secure. [*Hint*: Look at how the simulator in the preceding example handled the case where it first had to simulate P_5 without knowing its input and then had to patch the state of P_5 to be consistent with x_5 when the total breakdown occurred.]

4.5 Adaptive versus Static Security Revisited

In this section we again consider the relation between static and adaptive security and show a general strategy for proving adaptive security that generalizes what we saw in the preceding section (Example 4.24 and Exercise 4.4). The idea is to first prove static security and then construct, from the simulator $\mathcal{S}$ we built, a new simulator $\mathcal{S}'$ for the adaptive case. Roughly speaking, the strategy for $\mathcal{S}'$ is to follow the algorithm of $\mathcal{S}$, but every time a new player P_i is corrupted, $\mathcal{S}'$ cooks up a view for P_i that "looks convincing," gives this to the environment, patches the state of $\mathcal{S}$ accordingly, and continues.

It turns out that there is a class of unconditionally secure protocols and functionalities in which this idea works, and our goal will be to characterize this class and to point out what the procedure run by $\mathcal{S}'$ to handle corruptions must satisfy. This will mean that it becomes easier to give proofs for adaptive security later in the book. We will consider the case of perfect security first and later show that the results are also true in some cases for statistical security.

Thus we will assume that we are given protocol π, communication resource $\mathcal{R}$, ideal functionality F, and simulator $\mathcal{S}$ such that $\pi \diamond \mathcal{R} \stackrel{\mathrm{perf}}{\equiv} \mathcal{S} \diamond \mathsf{F}$ with respect to static, unbounded environments that corrupt at most t players. We will assume synchronous protocols only for simplicity.

We will need some notation in the following:

DEFINITION 4.25 *For an agent A that is part of an interactive system $\mathcal{IS}$, the view of A is a random variable, written $V_A(\mathcal{IS})$, and is defined to be the ordered concatenation of all messages exchanged on the ports of A and of the random choices of A. We use $V_A(\mathcal{IS}|E)$ to denote the view when conditioned on some event E occurring and $V_A(\mathcal{IS})_j$ to denote the view truncated to contain only the first j rounds.*

DEFINITION 4.26 *For a player P_i in a protocol π running with communication resource $\mathcal{R}$ and environment $\mathcal{Z}$, the conversation of P_i is a random variable, written $\mathrm{Conv}_{\mathsf{P}_i}(\mathcal{Z} \diamond \pi \diamond \mathcal{R})$, and is defined to be the ordered concatenation of all messages P_i exchanged with honest players and $\mathcal{R}$. The conversation of $\mathcal{Z}$, written $\mathrm{Conv}_{\mathcal{Z}}(\mathcal{Z} \diamond \pi \diamond \mathcal{R})$, is the ordered concatenation of all messages exchanged on the special ports of $\mathcal{Z}$. For conversations, we denote truncation and conditioning on events in the same way as for views.*

Note that the conversation of a party is a substring of its view. Also note that when a player P_i is corrupted, its view becomes a substring of the conversation of Z because Z learns the entire view of P_i up to the corruption and then decides (or sees) all messages P_i sends and receives. We may think of $\text{Conv}_Z(Z \diamond \pi \diamond \mathcal{R})$ as the total information Z gets from attacking the protocol. Recall, however, that Z also learns the inputs and outputs of the honest players.

We will need to assume that the ideal functionality has a certain behavior. First, it must ensure that whenever it receives input or gives output, the time at which this happens is publicly known; that is, it is indicated on the leakage port of the ideal functionality which party just received an input. The second demand is meant to capture the idea that the functionality should treat players who are corrupt but behave honestly in the same way as if they were honest. The formulation may look strange at first sight, but we give an intuitive explanation after the definition.

DEFINITION 4.27 *The ideal functionality F is said to be input-based if the following are satisfied:*

> ***Honest behavior equivalence:*** *Consider executions of F where some set A is corrupted from the start and where a fixed (ordered) set of inputs I_F is given to F during the execution.[12] In any such execution, the outputs produced by F and its state at the end have the same distribution; in particular, the distribution does not depend on the corruptions that occur during the execution.[13]*
>
> ***Publicly known input-output provision:*** *Each time F receives an input from P_i, F sends a message on its leakage port specifying that some input from P_i has been received. Each time F sends a private output to P_i, it also leaks a message specifying that an output was given, but not the value.*

The "honest behavior equivalence" condition can be explained intuitively as follows: an ideal functionality knows which players are corrupt, and its actions may in general depend arbitrarily on this information. The condition puts a limitation on this: consider first an execution in which all players outside A remain honest and F gets I_F as input. Compare this with a case in which $P_i \notin A$ is corrupted, but F still gets the same inputs. This means in particular that P_i sends the same inputs, so it "behaves honestly" toward F. Therefore, the demand we make, loosely speaking, means that as long as a corrupt player behaves honestly toward the functionality, the actions it takes will be the same as if that player had been honest.

Our results also will be valid for a slightly more general case in which the outputs produced by F do not have to be the same in all executions, but the outputs in one execution can be efficiently computed from I_F and the outputs in any other execution. For simplicity, we do not treat this general case explicitly in the following.

---

[12] Notice that these inputs may arrive on the protocol port or on the influence port depending on which players happen to be corrupted in the given execution.

[13] Note that technically F must keep track of which parties are corrupted to know which parties can be controlled via the leakage port, so the state cannot be exactly the same in all cases. However, we require that up to the fact that the different sets of corrupted players are stored, the state is exactly the same.

We also need to make some assumptions on how the simulator S behaves and more precisely on how it decides on the inputs it sends to F on behalf of corrupted players (recall that once a player is corrupted, the simulator gets to decide which inputs this player provides to F). We will assume that S uses a standard technique to decide on these inputs; namely, at the time when the input is given, it looks at the conversation of the corrupt player and decides on the input based on this. This is formalized as follows:

DEFINITION 4.28 *The simulator S is conversation-based if the following are satisfied:*

Conversation-based inputs: *If S sends an input x to F on behalf of P_i in round j, it computes x as $x = \mathrm{Inp}_i(c)$, where Inp_i is a function specified by the protocol and $c = \mathrm{Conv}_{P_i}(\mathcal{Z} \diamond S \diamond F)_j$.*[14]

Honest behavior implies correct inputs: *If P_i is corrupt but has followed the protocol honestly, then it is always the case that $\mathrm{Inp}_i(c_i)$ equals the corresponding input P_i was given from the environment. By a corrupt P_i following the protocol honestly, we mean that the environment decides the actions of P_i by running a copy of the code of the honest P_i on the inputs and messages that P_i receives in the protocol.*

Corruption-consistent input functions: *Consider a conversation c of P_i. Form a new conversation c' by deleting the messages exchanged with some of the honest players but such that at least $n - t$ honest players remain. For all such c, c' and all input functions Inp_i, it must be the case that $\mathrm{Inp}_i(c) = \mathrm{Inp}_i(c')$.*

Note that input functions only have to be defined on conversations that actually occur in π. Also note that the corruption consistency of the input functions model the following reasonable intuition: consider a run of π that leads to certain inputs. Now suppose that we run π again with the same random coins, but some players that were honest before are now corrupted but are told to play honestly. Since all players make the same moves in the two cases, it is reasonable to expect that the resulting inputs should be the same, and this is what corruption consistence of the input functions implies.

A typical example of an input function is where P_i provides inputs by secret sharing them using polynomials of degree at most t. Here the input function reconstructs the input from the shares held by honest players using Lagrange interpolation. If the protocol guarantees that the shares are consistent with some polynomial of degree at most t, even if P_i is actively corrupt, then the input function only has to be defined on such sets of shares and is indeed corruption consistent.

Now suppose that we are given an adaptive environment $\mathcal{Z}$, and we want to show that the protocol is secure with respect to this environment. For this, we need to think about how we can use a static simulator S. Of course, we cannot just run it against $\mathcal{Z}$ because S does not know how to handle corruptions that occur in the middle of the protocol. Instead, therefore, we will construct a family of static environments from $\mathcal{Z}$: for each set A that $\mathcal{Z}$ may corrupt, we construct environment $\mathcal{Z}_A$. Informally, what $\mathcal{Z}_A$ does is that it corrupts set A, but initially

---

[14] It is possible to generalize the notion of conversation-based inputs to allow x to be computed from the conversation between *all* corrupted parties and the honest parties and not just the conversation between the single corrupted party P_i and the honest parties. However, in this book, we do not need the generalized notion, and the simpler notion gives slightly simpler definitions and proofs. The interested reader can consult Damgård and Nielsen [74] for details on the generalized notion.

it lets all players in A play honestly. It runs internally a copy of $\mathcal{Z}$ and lets it interact with the protocol as usual, where the only difference is that players in A are run honestly by $\mathcal{Z}_A$ instead of running by themselves. When $\mathcal{Z}$ corrupts a player in A, $\mathcal{Z}_A$ gives control of that player to $\mathcal{Z}$ and continues; if the corrupted player is not in A, $\mathcal{Z}_A$ outputs guess 0 and terminates. If $\mathcal{Z}$ outputs a guess $c \in \{0, 1\}$ without corrupting anyone outside A, then $\mathcal{Z}_A$ outputs the same guess c. A formal description is given later.

We know that $\mathcal{S}$ can do perfect simulation against any of the $\mathcal{Z}_A$ we just defined, and this will be the basis of the adaptive simulator we construct later. Before we can construct the adaptive simulator, we need some auxiliary lemmas on how $\mathcal{S}$ behaves when interacting with the $\mathcal{Z}_A$s.

Agent $\mathcal{Z}_A$

Static environment constructed from $\mathcal{Z}$. It has the same port structure as $\mathcal{Z}$.

1. In the preamble, corrupt set A. Set up internally a (honest) copy P'_j of each player $\mathsf{P}_j \in A$. Also set up internally a copy of $\mathcal{Z}$. Connect the special ports of $\mathcal{Z}$ corresponding to each player $\mathsf{P}_j \in A$ to the special ports of P'_j. Connect all other special ports and the protocol ports of $\mathcal{Z}$ to the corresponding external ports.
2. When the system executes and some $\mathsf{P}_j \in A$ is activated, then if P_j has not been corrupted by $\mathcal{Z}$ (see next item), $\mathcal{Z}_A$ does the following: in case of passive corruption, a copy of the messages received by P_j is read from its leakage port, and a copy of its state is kept inside P'_j. In case of active corruption, the messages received by P_j are read from its leakage port and are given to the (honest) P'_j, who determines the messages to send. $\mathcal{Z}_A$ makes P_j send these messages via its influence port. In both cases, leakage from P'_j is sent to $\mathcal{Z}$ as if P'_j was uncorrupted.
3. If $\mathcal{Z}$ decides to corrupt $\mathsf{P}_j \in A$, $\mathcal{Z}_A$ gives the current state of P'_j to $\mathcal{Z}$ and gives (passive or active) control of P_j to $\mathcal{Z}$.
4. If $\mathcal{Z}$ decides to corrupt $\mathsf{P}_j \notin A$, $\mathcal{Z}_A$ halts and outputs the guess 0.
5. If $\mathcal{Z}$ halts (having corrupted no player outside A) with guess $c \in \{0, 1\}$, $\mathcal{Z}_A$ halts and outputs guess c.

Some notation: in the following, $\mathbf{s}$ will denote an ordered sequence of players, and $A(\mathbf{s})$ will denote the set of players that occur in $\mathbf{s}$. $E_{\mathbf{s}}$ will be the event that the first $|\mathbf{s}|$ corruptions done by the environment are exactly those in $\mathbf{s}$ (in the specified order). Later, when we write views or conversations with subscript $\mathbf{s}$, for instance, as in $V_{\mathcal{Z}}(\mathcal{Z} \diamond \pi \diamond \mathcal{R} | E_{\mathbf{s}})_{\mathbf{s}}$, this means that if a corruption outside $\mathbf{s}$ occurs, we truncate the view at the point where this corruption happens.

Finally, consider the copy of $\mathcal{Z}$ that is run internally by $\mathcal{Z}_{A(\mathbf{s})}$, where we execute $\mathcal{Z}_{A(\mathbf{s})} \diamond \mathcal{IS}$ for some interactive system $\mathcal{IS}$ (such as $\pi \diamond \mathcal{R}$). We then let $V_{\mathcal{Z}}(\mathcal{Z}_{A(\mathbf{s})} \diamond \mathcal{IS} | E_{\mathbf{s}})$ be its view, conditioned on $E_{\mathbf{s}}$. Since $\mathcal{Z}_{A(\mathbf{s})}$ runs $\mathcal{Z}$ "in the head," it is clear that $V_{\mathcal{Z}}(\mathcal{Z}_{A(\mathbf{s})} \diamond \mathcal{IS} | E_{\mathbf{s}})$ can be deterministically and easily extracted from $V_{\mathcal{Z}_{A(\mathbf{s})}}(\mathcal{Z}_{A(\mathbf{s})} \diamond \mathcal{IS} | E_{\mathbf{s}})$. We will write this as

$$V_{\mathcal{Z}}(\mathcal{Z}_{A(\mathbf{s})} \diamond \mathcal{IS} | E_{\mathbf{s}}) = \mathrm{Extr}(V_{\mathcal{Z}_{A(\mathbf{s})}}(\mathcal{Z}_{A(\mathbf{s})} \diamond \mathcal{IS} | E_{\mathbf{s}}))$$

We can now show that assuming that $E_{\mathbf{s}}$ occurs, then $\mathcal{S}$ can be used to perfectly simulate (a part of) the view $\mathcal{Z}$ sees in the protocol because it can simulate the view of $\mathcal{Z}_{A(\mathbf{s})}$.

LEMMA 4.29 *Assuming that $\mathcal{R}$ is input based, we have*

$$V_{\mathcal{Z}}(\mathcal{Z}_{A(\mathbf{s})} \diamond \mathcal{S} \diamond \mathsf{F}|E_{\mathbf{s}}) \overset{\text{perf}}{\equiv} V_{\mathcal{Z}}(\mathcal{Z} \diamond \pi \diamond \mathcal{R}|E_{\mathbf{s}})_{\mathbf{s}}$$

Proof We have $V_{\mathcal{Z}_{A(\mathbf{s})}}(\mathcal{Z}_{A(\mathbf{s})} \diamond \mathcal{S} \diamond \mathsf{F}) \overset{\text{perf}}{\equiv} V_{\mathcal{Z}_{A(\mathbf{s})}}(\mathcal{Z}_{A(\mathbf{s})} \diamond \pi \diamond \mathcal{R})$ because $\mathcal{S}$ is a good static simulator. Thus the two distributions are also the same when conditioning on $E_{\mathbf{s}}$, that is, we have

$$V_{\mathcal{Z}_{A(\mathbf{s})}}(\mathcal{Z}_{A(\mathbf{s})} \diamond \mathcal{S} \diamond \mathsf{F}|E_{\mathbf{s}}) \overset{\text{perf}}{\equiv} V_{\mathcal{Z}_{A(\mathbf{s})}}(\mathcal{Z}_{A(\mathbf{s})} \diamond \pi \diamond \mathcal{R}|E_{\mathbf{s}}) \qquad (4.9)$$

The two distributions remain equal if we apply the same deterministic function to both of them, so if we apply Extr on both sides of Eq. (4.9), we get

$$V_{\mathcal{Z}}(\mathcal{Z}_{A(\mathbf{s})} \diamond \mathcal{S} \diamond \mathsf{F}|E_{\mathbf{s}}) \overset{\text{perf}}{\equiv} V_{\mathcal{Z}}(\mathcal{Z}_{A(\mathbf{s})} \diamond \pi \diamond \mathcal{R}|E_{\mathbf{s}}) \qquad (4.10)$$

Moreover, from the point of view of $\mathcal{Z}$ (and still conditioning on $E_{\mathbf{s}}$), the only difference between $\mathcal{Z}_{A(\mathbf{s})} \diamond \pi \diamond \mathcal{R}$ and $\mathcal{Z} \diamond \pi \diamond \mathcal{R}$ is that in the first case the parties in A are run honestly by $\mathcal{Z}_{A(\mathbf{s})}$ until $\mathcal{Z}$ wants to corrupt them, whereas in the second case they run as honest players in π. This makes no difference to $\mathcal{R}$ because it is input based (by the honest behavior equivalence property), and hence it makes no difference to $\mathcal{Z}$ either. So we have

$$V_{\mathcal{Z}}(\mathcal{Z}_{A(\mathbf{s})} \diamond \pi \diamond \mathcal{R}|E_{\mathbf{s}}) \overset{\text{perf}}{\equiv} V_{\mathcal{Z}}(\mathcal{Z} \diamond \pi \diamond \mathcal{R}|E_{\mathbf{s}})_{\mathbf{s}} \qquad (4.11)$$

The lemma now follows from Eqs. (4.10) and (4.11). ∎

We also need to consider a connection between simulation against several different $\mathcal{Z}_{A(\mathbf{s})}$s: for a sequence of players $\mathbf{s}$, we can append a player P_i (who is not in $\mathbf{s}$) at the end of the sequence. We write this new sequence as $\mathbf{s}, i$, and define $E_{\mathbf{s},i}$ and $A(\mathbf{s}, i)$ as before.

LEMMA 4.30 *Assuming that $\mathcal{R}$ is input based, we have*

$$V_{\mathcal{Z}}(\mathcal{Z}_{A(\mathbf{s})} \diamond \mathcal{S} \diamond \mathsf{F}|E_{\mathbf{s},i}) \overset{\text{perf}}{\equiv} V_{\mathcal{Z}}(\mathcal{Z}_{A(\mathbf{s},i)} \diamond \mathcal{S} \diamond \mathsf{F}|E_{\mathbf{s},i})_{\mathbf{s}}$$

Proof Since $\mathcal{S}$ is a good static simulator, we have by an argument similar to that in the proof of Lemma 4.29 that

$$V_{\mathcal{Z}}(\mathcal{Z}_{A(\mathbf{s})} \diamond \mathcal{S} \diamond \mathsf{F}|E_{\mathbf{s},i}) = \mathrm{Extr}(V_{\mathcal{Z}_{A(\mathbf{s})}}(\mathcal{Z}_{A(\mathbf{s})} \diamond \mathcal{S} \diamond \mathsf{F}|E_{\mathbf{s},i})) \qquad (4.12)$$

$$\overset{\text{perf}}{\equiv} \mathrm{Extr}(V_{\mathcal{Z}_{A(\mathbf{s})}}(\mathcal{Z}_{A(\mathbf{s})} \diamond \pi \diamond \mathcal{R}|E_{\mathbf{s},i})) \qquad (4.13)$$

$$= V_{\mathcal{Z}}(\mathcal{Z}_{A(\mathbf{s})} \diamond \pi \diamond \mathcal{R}|E_{\mathbf{s},i}) \qquad (4.14)$$

Note that assuming that $E_{\mathbf{s},i}$ occurs, the only difference between $\mathcal{Z}_{A(\mathbf{s})} \diamond \pi \diamond \mathcal{R}$ and $\mathcal{Z}_{A(\mathbf{s},i)} \diamond \pi \diamond \mathcal{R}$ is that in the latter case P_i is run honestly by $\mathcal{Z}_{A(\mathbf{s},i)}$, whereas in the former it plays honestly as a party in the protocol. Because $\mathcal{R}$ is input based, this makes no difference to $\mathcal{R}$ and hence also no difference to the view of $\mathcal{Z}$ as long as we only consider what happens up to the point where P_i is corrupted. So we have

$$V_{\mathcal{Z}}(\mathcal{Z}_{A(\mathbf{s})} \diamond \pi \diamond \mathcal{R}|E_{\mathbf{s},i}) \overset{\text{perf}}{\equiv} V_{\mathcal{Z}}(\mathcal{Z}_{A(\mathbf{s},i)} \diamond \pi \diamond \mathcal{R}|E_{\mathbf{s},i})_{\mathbf{s}} \qquad (4.15)$$

Using again that $\mathcal{S}$ is a good static simulator, it follows in that same way as before that

$$V_{\mathcal{Z}}(\mathcal{Z}_{A(\mathbf{s},i)} \diamond \pi \diamond \mathcal{R}|E_{\mathbf{s},i})_{\mathbf{s}} \overset{\text{perf}}{\equiv} V_{\mathcal{Z}}(\mathcal{Z}_{A(\mathbf{s},i)} \diamond \mathcal{S} \diamond \mathsf{F}|E_{\mathbf{s},i})_{\mathbf{s}} \qquad (4.16)$$

The lemma now follows from Eqs. (4.14) through (4.16). ∎

We now want to show that if we consider both the view of $\mathcal{Z}$ and the inputs and outputs that F exchanges, we still have a similar result as in the previous lemma. This does not have to be true in general but is indeed true if $\mathcal{S}$ is conversation-based, and if F is input based. Then we can prove the following:

LEMMA 4.31 *Let* $\mathrm{St}_F(\cdot)$ *be the state of F after running in some interactive system. Then, if* $\mathcal{S}$ *is conversation based and F is input based, we have*

$$(V_{\mathcal{Z}}(\mathcal{Z}_{A(\mathbf{s})} \diamond \mathcal{S} \diamond F|E_{\mathbf{s},i}), \quad \mathrm{St}_F(\mathcal{Z}_{A(\mathbf{s})} \diamond \mathcal{S} \diamond F|E_{\mathbf{s},i}))$$

$$\stackrel{\mathrm{perf}}{\equiv} (V_{\mathcal{Z}}(\mathcal{Z}_{A(\mathbf{s},i)} \diamond \mathcal{S} \diamond F|E_{\mathbf{s},i})_{\mathbf{s}}, \quad \mathrm{St}_F(\mathcal{Z}_{A(\mathbf{s},i)} \diamond \mathcal{S} \diamond F|E_{\mathbf{s},i})_{\mathbf{s}})$$

Proof We already have from Lemma 4.30 that the view of $\mathcal{Z}$ has the same distribution in the two systems. We then prove the lemma by arguing that because $\mathcal{S}$ is conversation based, all inputs sent to F follow deterministically from the view of $\mathcal{Z}$ and will be the same in both systems, so because F is input based, the distribution of its state must be the same as well.

In more detail, consider a view v for $\mathcal{Z}$ that occurs with nonzero probability (in both systems). Note first that by public input-output provision of F, one can infer from v in which rounds inputs were provided to F or outputs were sent, so these must be the same in the two systems. Consider a particular input and say that it comes from player P_j. We do a case analysis:

$P_j \notin A(\mathbf{s},i)$. In this case, P_j is honest throughout in both systems. This means that $\mathcal{Z}$ provides the input directly to F, so the input occurs in v and is the same in both systems.

$P_j = P_i$. In the system $\mathcal{Z}_{A(\mathbf{s})} \diamond \mathcal{S} \diamond F$, P_i is honest, and $\mathcal{Z}$ provides directly to F the input, say, x, that occurs in v. In $\mathcal{Z}_{A(\mathbf{s},i)} \diamond \mathcal{S} \diamond F$, P_i is corrupt but is told to play honestly on input x as provided by $\mathcal{Z}$. Then $\mathcal{S}$ decides on the input to F based on the conversation of P_i, and this will result in x by the "honest behavior implies correct input" property.

$P_j \in A(\mathbf{s})$ *and has not been corrupted by* $\mathcal{Z}$ *when the input is provided.* In this case, in both systems $\mathcal{Z}$ provides input x to P_j, who plays honestly, and $\mathcal{S}$ decides the input to F based on the conversation, which will be x, again by the "honest behavior implies correct input" property.

$P_j \in A(\mathbf{s})$ *and has been corrupted by* $\mathcal{Z}$ *when the input is provided.* In this case, $\mathcal{S}$ will decide in both systems on the input based on the conversation of P_j. Note first that the messages P_j has exchanged with all players that $\mathcal{Z}$ has not corrupted yet are part of v and therefore are the same in both systems (this includes at least all players outside $A(\mathbf{s})$). However, from the point of view of $\mathcal{S}$, the conversation of P_j is *not* the same in the two systems: in $\mathcal{Z}_{A(\mathbf{s})} \diamond \mathcal{S} \diamond F$, it consists of messages exchanged with players outside $A(\mathbf{s})$, whereas in $\mathcal{Z}_{A(\mathbf{s},i)} \diamond \mathcal{S} \diamond F$, it consists of a subset of these messages, namely, those exchanged with players outside $A(\mathbf{s},i)$. However, since the input functions are corruption consistent, the input computed by $\mathcal{S}$ is nevertheless the same in the two systems. ∎

In the following we will consider a situation in which we execute the system $\mathcal{Z}_{A(\mathbf{s})} \diamond \mathcal{S} \diamond F$ until a point where $E_{\mathbf{s},i}$ has occurred. At this point, $\mathcal{Z}_{A(\mathbf{s})}$ would halt. However, by Lemma 4.31, as far as $\mathcal{Z}$ and the state of F are concerned, we might as well have been running $\mathcal{Z}_{A(\mathbf{s},i)} \diamond \mathcal{S} \diamond F$, and unlike $\mathcal{Z}_{A(\mathbf{s})}$, $\mathcal{Z}_{A(\mathbf{s},i)}$ would be able to continue even after P_i is corrupted. Thus if we could somehow "pretend" that in fact it was the latter system we ran, we would not have to stop when P_i is corrupted.

To help us do this trick, we consider an execution of $\mathcal{Z}_{A(s,i)} \diamond \mathcal{S} \diamond F$ in which $E_{s,i}$ occurs. Say that the values of $V_{\mathcal{Z}}(\mathcal{Z}_{A(s,i)} \diamond \mathcal{S} \diamond F|E_{s,i})_s$ and $\mathrm{St}_F(\mathcal{Z}_{A(s,i)} \diamond \mathcal{S} \diamond F|E_{s,i})_s$ are v and w. We then define $D_{v,w}$ to be the joint distribution of the states of $\mathcal{Z}_{A(s,i)}$ and $\mathcal{S}$ at the point where P_i is corrupted, given v and w. Note that because we assume that $E_{s,i}$ occurred, the state of $\mathcal{Z}_{A(s,i)}$ consists of a state of $\mathcal{Z}$ that is fixed by v and a view of P_i who has been playing honestly so far. Thus we can think of the output of $D_{v,w}$ as a view of P_i plus a state of $\mathcal{S}$.

LEMMA 4.32 *Consider an execution of the system $\mathcal{Z}_{A(s,i)} \diamond \mathcal{S} \diamond F$ until a point where $E_{s,i}$ has occurred. Let*

$$V_{\mathcal{Z}}(\mathcal{Z}_{A(s,i)} \diamond \mathcal{S} \diamond F|E_{s,i})_s = v \quad and \quad \mathrm{St}_F(\mathcal{Z}_{A(s,i)} \diamond \mathcal{S} \diamond F|E_{s,i})_s = w$$

Let io_S be the string of inputs and outputs $\mathcal{S}$ has exchanged with F, and let $\mathrm{Conv}_{\mathcal{Z}}$ be the conversation of $\mathcal{Z}$ in the execution. Then one can sample from the distribution $D_{v,w}$ if given io_S and $\mathrm{Conv}_{\mathcal{Z}}$. In particular, $D_{v,w}$ depends only on io_S and $\mathrm{Conv}_{\mathcal{Z}}$.

Proof Recall that $\mathcal{Z}_{A(s,i)}$ consists of a copy of $\mathcal{Z}$ and copies of players in $A(s,i)$. However, since $E_{s,i}$ occurs, all players in $A(s)$ have been corrupted earlier by $\mathcal{Z}$, so their entire view until they were corrupted by $\mathcal{Z}$ is part of $\mathrm{Conv}_{\mathcal{Z}}$.

The sampling procedure we claim is now very simple: for each possible set of coins for P_i and for $\mathcal{S}$, we will test whether these coins are consistent with the values of io_S and $\mathrm{Conv}_{\mathcal{Z}}$ we are given. We do the test by simulating P_i and $\mathcal{S}$ running as part of the system $\mathcal{Z}_{A(s,i)} \diamond \mathcal{S} \diamond F$. This is possible because the given values io_S and $\mathrm{Conv}_{\mathcal{Z}}$ specify the entire communication that P_i and $\mathcal{S}$ should have with F and $\mathcal{Z}$. If the current random coins lead to P_i or $\mathcal{S}$ sending a message that is inconsistent with io_S, and $\mathrm{Conv}_{\mathcal{Z}}$, we throw away this set of coins. Finally, we choose randomly a set of coins among those that survived and output the resulting view of P_i and state of $\mathcal{S}$. ∎

In view of the result of Lemma 4.32, we will write $D_{\mathrm{io}_S,\mathrm{Conv}_{\mathcal{Z}}}$ instead of $D_{v,w}$ in the following. We can now specify the final tool we need to build an adaptive simulator, namely, the sampling we have just seen must be possible to do efficiently:

DEFINITION 4.33 *Consider a probabilistic algorithm* Patch *that takes as input strings io_S and $\mathrm{Conv}_{\mathcal{Z}}$ of the form as specified in Lemma 4.32.* Patch *is said to be a good sampling function if it satisfies the following:*

- *It is polynomial time computable.*
- *The output* Patch$(\mathrm{io}_S,\mathrm{Conv}_{\mathcal{Z}})$ *is distributed according to $D_{\mathrm{io}_S,\mathrm{Conv}_{\mathcal{Z}}}$.*

We are now finally ready to specify the main result of this section:

THEOREM 4.34 *Assume that we are given a simulator $\mathcal{S}$ for protocol π and functionality F such that $\mathcal{Z}_{\mathtt{static}} \diamond \pi \diamond \mathcal{R} \overset{\mathrm{perf}}{\equiv} \mathcal{Z}_{\mathtt{static}} \diamond \mathcal{S} \diamond F$ for any static and synchronous environment $\mathcal{Z}_{\mathtt{static}}$ corrupting at most t parties. Assume further that $\mathcal{S}$ is conversation based, F and $\mathcal{R}$ are input based, and we are given a good sampling function* Patch. *Then there exists a simulator $\mathcal{S}'$ such that $\mathcal{Z} \diamond \pi \diamond \mathcal{R} \overset{\mathrm{perf}}{\equiv} \mathcal{Z} \diamond \mathcal{S} \diamond F$ for any adaptive and synchronous environment $\mathcal{Z}$ corrupting at most t parties.*

Proof We specify the algorithm of our adaptive simulator S'. To do this, suppose that we are given a string io_S containing inputs and outputs that S has exchanged with F on behalf of corrupted players in a set A. Suppose that we are also given the inputs and outputs io_i that some honest player P_i has exchanged with F in the same execution. Then we can merge these strings in a natural way: we define $\text{Merge}(io_S, io_i)$ to be the string that contains, for every protocol round, the inputs to F that occur in either io_S or io_i and also outputs from F that occur in either io_S or io_i. Note that $\text{Merge}(io_S, io_i)$ is a string of inputs and outputs that S might have exchanged with F if $A \cup \{P_i\}$ had been the corrupted set (and P_i had behaved honestly).

To see that this simulation works, note first that it is obvious that $\text{Conv}_{\mathcal{Z}}$ contains at all times the conversation of $\mathcal{Z}$ so far and that io_S contains at all times the inputs and outputs we have exchanged with F so far.

Agent S'

Adaptive simulator constructed from S.

1. Let **s** be the empty sequence. Set $io_S, \text{Conv}_{\mathcal{Z}}$ to be the empty strings. Set up a copy of S in its initial state. Tell S as input (in the preamble) that the empty set is the corrupted set.
2. Whenever S' is activated, if the input is a request to corrupt a new player P_i, it goes to the next step. Otherwise, it runs S on the input received and sends the output S produces on the corresponding output port of its own. Messages exchanged with $\mathcal{Z}$ are appended to $\text{Conv}_{\mathcal{Z}}$; inputs and outputs exchanged with F are appended to io_S.
3. Set $\mathbf{s} = \mathbf{s}, i$. Send a request to corrupt P_i to F and get a string io_i back. Set $io_S = \text{Merge}(io_S, io_i)$. Compute $(v_i, \text{St}') = \text{Patch}(io_S, \text{Conv}_{\mathcal{Z}})$. Put S in state St', send v_i to the environment, append v_i to $\text{Conv}_{\mathcal{Z}}$, and go to step 2.

We can now show the following:

Claim: Whenever S' enters step 2 in the box Agent S', the states of $\mathcal{Z}, S$, and F are distributed exactly as in a run of $\mathcal{Z}_{A(\mathbf{s})} \diamond S \diamond \mathsf{F}$ where $E_{\mathbf{s}}$ occurs.

We show this by induction: the claim is trivial when we enter step 2 the first time because here **s** is empty. So consider a later stage where we enter step 2, and write the current **s** as $\mathbf{s} = \mathbf{s}', i$. The previous time we entered step 2, by induction hypothesis, the states of $\mathcal{Z}, S$, and F were distributed exactly as in a run of $\mathcal{Z}_{A(\mathbf{s}')} \diamond S \diamond \mathsf{F}$ where $E_{\mathbf{s}'}$ occurs. During the following execution of step 2, S' simply ran S, so when the ith player is corrupted, the states of $\mathcal{Z}, S$, and F were distributed exactly as in a run of $\mathcal{Z}_{A(\mathbf{s}')} \diamond S \diamond \mathsf{F}$ where $E_{\mathbf{s}', i}$ occurs. Now, by Lemma 4.31, the views (and hence state) of $\mathcal{Z}$ and the state of F are distributed as in a run of $\mathcal{Z}_{A(\mathbf{s}', i)} \diamond S \diamond \mathsf{F}$ where $E_{\mathbf{s}, i}$ occurs.

Then Patch was run, and the claim now follows by assumption on Patch, if we show that the inputs $\text{Conv}_{\mathcal{Z}}$ and io_S we use have the distribution they would have in $\mathcal{Z}_{A(\mathbf{s}', i)} \diamond S \diamond \mathsf{F}$, given the current values of the view of $\mathcal{Z}$ and the state of F. This is trivially true for $\text{Conv}_{\mathcal{Z}}$ because it follows deterministically from the view of $\mathcal{Z}$. For io_S, note that the inputs to F that occur in this string also follow deterministically from the view of $\mathcal{Z}$; we argued this in the proof of Lemma 4.31. But since F is input based, the resulting outputs from F will be the same regardless of whether we run $\mathcal{Z}_{A(\mathbf{s})}$ or $\mathcal{Z}_{A(\mathbf{s}', i)}$, so io_S has the desired distribution.

We can now argue that $V_{\mathcal{Z}}(\mathcal{Z} \diamond \pi \diamond \mathcal{R}) \stackrel{\text{perf}}{=} V_{\mathcal{Z}}(\mathcal{Z} \diamond \mathcal{S}' \diamond \mathsf{F})$, which clearly implies the theorem. We will consider the executions of step 2 one by one. In the first execution, by the preceding claim, the states of $\mathcal{Z}, \mathcal{S}$, and F are distributed exactly as in a run of $\mathcal{Z}_{A(\mathbf{s})} \diamond \mathcal{S} \diamond \mathsf{F}$ where $E_{\mathbf{s}}$ occurs. But here $\mathbf{s}$ is the empty sequence, so $E_{\mathbf{s}}$ always occurs. In step 2, we simply run $\mathcal{S}$, so by Lemma 4.29 we obtain a perfect simulation of $\mathcal{Z}$'s view until the point where it halts or corrupts the first player. In particular, in the latter case, that player is chosen with the distribution we would also see in a real execution of the protocol. When we have executed step 3, again by the claim, the states of $\mathcal{Z}, \mathcal{S}$, and F are distributed exactly as in a run of $\mathcal{Z}_{A(\mathbf{s})} \diamond \mathcal{S} \diamond \mathsf{F}$ where $E_{\mathbf{s}}$ occurs and where $\mathbf{s}$ now contains one player. Again by Lemma 4.29, while executing step 2, we obtain a perfect simulation of $\mathcal{Z}$'s view from the point where it corrupts the first player until the point where it halts or corrupts the second player.

Repeating this argument at most t times (because $\mathcal{Z}$ can corrupt only so many players), we see that we get a perfect simulation of the entire view of $\mathcal{Z}$. ∎

Using Theorem 4.34

In order to use Theorem 4.34 on a concrete protocol, one has to first construct a static simulator $\mathcal{S}$ and verify that is conversation based and that the target functionality F is input based. This is usually quite easy. Then one has to construct an efficient procedure Patch. This may seem harder because the formal definition is quite technical and involves two static environments constructed from an arbitrary adaptive environment.

We therefore give an explanation in more "human" language of what Patch must be able to do. Recall that when Patch is called, players in the sequence $\mathbf{s}$ were corrupted earlier, and a new player P_i has just been corrupted. We know $\mathrm{io}_{\mathcal{S}}$, that is, all the inputs and outputs that players in $\mathbf{s}, i$ have exchanged with the functionality F, and we know $\mathrm{Conv}_{\mathcal{Z}}$, that is, the protocol execution as seen by $\mathcal{Z}$ until now. Patch now has two tasks that must be solved efficiently:

The first one is to construct a complete view of P_i playing honestly in the protocol until now, and this must be consistent with $\mathrm{io}_{\mathcal{S}}$ and $\mathrm{Conv}_{\mathcal{Z}}$. In particular, $\mathrm{io}_{\mathcal{S}}$ contains the inputs and outputs P_i has exchanged with F, and $\mathrm{Conv}_{\mathcal{Z}}$ contains the messages that P_i has sent to players who were corrupted earlier. The reason why this can be feasible, for example, for protocols based on secret sharing is that the corrupted players (actually, $\mathcal{Z}$) have seen fewer than t shares of the secrets of P_i. This leaves the secrets undetermined, so when we now learn the actual secret values of P_i (from $\mathrm{io}_{\mathcal{S}}$), we are able create a full set of shares that is consistent with the secrets and the shares of the corrupt players.

The second task is to create a new state for the simulator $\mathcal{S}$. This must be the state as it would have looked if we had run $\mathcal{S}$ with all players in $\mathbf{s}, i$ being corrupt from the start but where P_i plays honestly until the current point in time. In this book, we will often consider a strategy for building $\mathcal{S}$ that makes both tasks easier: Initially, $\mathcal{S}$ sets up a copy of the honest players in the protocol and gives them dummy inputs. It now simulates by essentially letting these "virtual players" do the protocol with the corrupt players (controlled by $\mathcal{Z}$). The state of $\mathcal{S}$ is simply the state of the virtual players. Now, when P_i is corrupted, Patch will compute how the view of the virtual copy of P_i should change, now that we know its actual inputs, and will then update the state of the other virtual players to make everything consistent, including io$_S$ and Conv$_Z$. This creates the required view of P$_i$, and the new state of S is the state of the updated virtual players, except for P$_i$.

In the following, we will use the method given in Theorem 4.34 in most cases when proving adaptive security. But we will not always explicitly verify that the functionality is input based and the static simulator is conversation based because this would be rather tedious reading.

Extension to Statistical Security

It is not clear that Theorem 4.34 is true for statistical security in general. But it not hard to see that it holds in an important special case: suppose that we can define an "error event" E such that E occurs with negligible probability, and we can make a static simulator S that simulates perfectly if E does not occur. Then we can redo the proof of Theorem 4.34 while conditioning throughout on E not occurring. We leave the details to the reader.

4.6 Notes

In hindsight, it can seem quite surprising that at the time when the first completeness results for multiparty computation were established, we did not have generally accepted definitions of security for multiparty computation protocols. These crystallized only much later after a lot of research work. There are many reasons for this, but a main complication was the issue of composition: It is a natural requirement that protocols should remain secure even when composed with other protocols, and for a long time it was not clear how a definition should be put together to ensure this.

In 1991, Micali and Rogaway [144] as well as Beaver [8] put forward definitions. It was realized already at this point that simulation-based security is the way to go, but it was not until the work around 2000 of Canetti [33] and independently Pfitzmann, Schunter, and Waidner [156] that security under arbitrary concurrent composition could be expressed. A related but different approach known as *constructive cryptography* was initiated recently by Ueli Maurer [141]. This framework is also simulation based and gives security under composition but is technically different from the UC model in several ways.

It is natural to ask if the early protocols actually turned out to be secure under these later definitions? It turns out that all the protocols with unconditional security underlying the completeness results from the late 1980s are in fact secure in the strongest sense: they are UC secure against adaptive adversaries (see later for more on the history of the security definitions). In contrast, the computationally secure protocols, for instance, that of Goldreich, Micali, and Wigdersen [100], are only known to be statically secure. This is mainly due to a technical problem related to the fact that when simulating encrypted communication, the simulator will implicitly commit itself to some plaintext that it would have to change if the sender or receiver are corrupted. Adaptive security can be obtained using so-called non-committing encryption [36], but only at the cost of significant technical complications.

It may seem superficially that all the technical problems that prevent us from proving adaptive security in the computational case go away in the information-theoretic setting. This is not true, however; there are natural examples of information-theoretically secure protocols that are statically secure but not adaptively secure [61].

The model and security definitions in this book are based on Canetti's work on universal composition, the UC model. We depart somewhat, however, from his original model. Basically, we sacrifice some generality to have a simpler model that is easier to explain and use. For instance, we demand that agents pass control in a certain nicely structured way in order to preserve polynomial running time when we compose agents. We also define our agents as the more abstract input-output (IO) automata rather than interactive Turing machines. The modifications make our model somewhat similar to the constructive cryptography model [142], although several technical differences remain.

It also should be mentioned that several variants of the UC model have been proposed more recently in the literature, see, for instance, the GUC framework by Canetti et al. [34] and the GNUC framework by Hofheinz and Shoup [109].

For more details on the round complexity of consensus broadcast and the price of requiring parties to terminate a protocol in the same round, see Dolev, Reischuk, and Strong [85], Lamport, Shostak, and Pease [124] and Canetti et al. [34]. On how to compose a protocol with simultaneous input but non-committing output, see, for instance, Nielsen [149, section 3.11].

5

Information-Theoretic Robust MPC Protocols

5.1 Introduction

In this chapter we show how to modify the protocol from Chapter 3 to make it secure against active attacks. In the terms introduced in Chapter 4, the goal is to implement F_{SFE}^f, where we will assume that we have available the ideal functionality F_{SC} for secure communication and consensus broadcast and also another ideal commitment functionality F_{COM} that we explain in detail later. In Section 5.4 we show how the commitment functionality can be implemented based only on F_{SC} under appropriate assumptions on t, the number of corrupted players.

The final results are collected in Section 5.5. We note already, however, that if $t < n/3$, then F_{SFE}^f can be implemented with perfect security without using broadcast but assuming secure channels between each pair of the players. If we additionally assume broadcast and we allow a nonzero error probability, then $t < n/2$ will be sufficient. These bounds are tight, as we shall see later.

5.2 Model for Homomorphic Commitments and Some Auxiliary Protocols

We will assume that each player P_i can commit to a value $a \in \mathbb{F}$ while keeping his or her choice secret. The player may, however, choose to reveal a later. We shall see how this can be implemented by distributing and/or broadcasting some information to other players. We model this here by assuming that we have an ideal functionality F_{COM}. To commit, one simply sends a to F_{COM}, who will then keep it until P_i asks to have it revealed. Formally, we assume that F_{COM} is equipped with commands commit and open as described in the box.

Some general remarks on the definition of F_{COM}: because the implementation of any of the commands may require all (honest) players to take part actively, we require that all honest players in a given round send the same commands to F_{COM} in order for the command to be executed. In some cases, such as a commitment, we can, of course, not require that all players send exactly the same information because only the committing players knows the value to be committed to. Thus, in such a case, we require that the committer sends the command and his or her secret input, while the others just send the command. If F_{COM} is not used as intended by the honest parties (e.g., the honest players do not agree on the command to execute), F_{COM} will do a complete breakdown. It also will do a complete breakdown if an honest party commits under the same cid twice or uses the same cid_3 twice in an addition command or a multiplication command. This is to ensure that all values are stored under unique identifiers. It also will do a complete breakdown if the honest parties use some cid_1 or cid_2 that has not been defined yet, that is, if they, for instance, input $(add, i, cid_1, cid_2, cid_3)$, but no (i, cid_1, a) is stored.

104

We will use the following convention for specifying F_{COM}:

- When we say that a command gives a particular output, then this output is not delivered immediately. Instead, it will be specified via COM.infl in which round to deliver, and in that round, the output to all parties will be given; that is, F_{COM} guarantees simultaneous output with an adversarially chosen output round (see Section 4.4.3 for a motivation for these choices).

Agent F_{COM}

Ideal functionality for homomorphic commitment. The functionality does a complete breakdown if inputs from honest players are not given as specified. Output from a command is sent once the round in which to deliver it is specified on the influence port.

Commit. This command is executed if in some round honest player P_i sends $(\text{commit}, i, cid, a)$ and in addition all other honest players send $(\text{commit}, i, cid, ?)$. Leak $(\text{commit}, i, cid, ?)$,[a] and store the triple (i, cid, a). Here cid is just a commitment identifier, and a is the value committed to.[b] Output $(\text{commit}, i, cid, \text{success})$ to all parties. The command is also executed if P_i is corrupt and all honest players send $(\text{commit}, i, cid, ?)$. In this case, leak $(\text{commit}, i, cid, ?)$. Then, if P_i sends $(\text{commit}, i, cid, a)$ before the output is delivered, store data and output success as if P_i were honest. Otherwise, store nothing, and output $(\text{commit}, i, cid, \text{fail})$ to all parties.

Public commit. This command is executed if in some round all honest parties send $(\text{pubcommit}, i, cid, a)$. In this case, F_{COM} records the triple (i, cid, a). Leak $(\text{pubcommit}, i, cid, a)$, and output $(\text{pubcommit}, i, cid, \text{success})$ to all parties.[c]

Open. This command is executed if in some round all honest players send (open, i, cid), and some (i, cid, a) is stored. Leak (open, i, cid) or, if any party is corrupted, leak (open, i, cid, a). If P_i is honest, output (open, i, cid, a) to all parties. If P_i is corrupted and inputs (open, i, cid) before the output is delivered, output a to all parties as earlier. Otherwise, output $(\text{open}, i, cid, \text{fail})$ to all parties.

Designated open. This command is executed if in some round all honest players send (open, i, cid, j), and some (i, cid, a) is stored. Leak (open, i, cid, j), or if P_j is corrupted, leak $(\text{open}, i, cid, j, a)$. If P_i is honest, output $(\text{open}, i, cid, j, a)$ to P_j and also output $(\text{open}, i, cid, j, \text{success})$ to all other parties. If P_i is corrupted and inputs (open, i, cid, j), send the output as if P_i were honest. Otherwise, output $(\text{open}, i, cid, \text{fail})$ to all parties.

Add. This command is executed if in some round all honest players send $(\text{add}, i, cid_1, cid_2, cid_3)$, and some (i, cid_1, a_1) and some (i, cid_2, a_2) are stored. Leak $(\text{add}, i, cid_1, cid_2, cid_3)$. As a result, F_{COM} stores $(i, cid_3, a_1 + a_2)$. The output to all parties is $(\text{add}, i, cid_1, cid_2, cid_3, \text{success})$.

Mult by constant. This command is executed if in some round all honest players send $(\text{mult}, i, \alpha, cid_2, cid_3)$, and $\alpha \in \mathbb{F}$ and some (i, cid_2, a_2) is stored. As a result, F_{COM} stores $(i, cid_3, \alpha a_2)$. The output to all parties is $(\text{mult}, i, \alpha, cid_2, cid_3, \text{success})$. Leak $(\text{mult}, i, \alpha, cid_2, cid_3)$.

---

[a] We leak $(\text{commit}, i, cid, ?)$ to say that an implementation need not hide that a commitment is being made. More technically, in the simulation $S \diamond F_{COM}$, the simulator will in this way learn that it should start simulating a commitment. If all parties are honest, the simulator has no other way to learn this essential fact.

[b] We require that all honest players agree to the fact that a commitment should be made because an implementation will require the active participation of all honest players.

[c] The difference here is that all parties input a, and P_i is forced to commit. In an implementation, the other parties can, in principle, just remember that P_i is committed to the known a, but it is convenient to have an explicit command for this.

Agent F_{COM} (continued)

Advanced manipulation commands for the functionality F_{COM}:

transfer. This command is executed if in some round all honest players send $(\text{transfer}, i, cid, j)$, and some (i, cid, a) is stored. Leak $(\text{transfer}, i, cid, j)$ or, if P_j is corrupted, leak $(\text{transfer}, i, cid, j, a)$. If P_i is honest, store (j, cid, a). Output $(\text{transfer}, i, cid, j, \text{success})$ to all parties except P_j, and $(\text{transfer}, i, cid, j, a)$ to P_j. If P_i is corrupted and inputs $(\text{transfer}, i, cid, j)$, store data and output as if P_i were honest. Otherwise, store nothing, and output $(\text{transfer}, i, cid, j, \text{fail})$ to all parties.

mult. This command is executed if in some round all honest players send $(\text{mult}, i, cid_1, cid_2, cid_3)$, and some (i, cid_1, a_1) and some (i, cid_2, a_2) are stored. Leak $(\text{mult}, i, cid_1, cid_2, cid_3)$. If P_i is honest, store $(i, cid_3, a_1 a_2)$, and output $(\text{mult}, i, cid_1, cid_2, cid_3, \text{success})$ to all parties. If P_i is corrupt and inputs $(\text{mult}, i, cid_1, cid_2, cid_3)$, output success as if P_i were honest. Otherwise, no value is stored, and the output to all parties is $(\text{mult}, i, cid, j, \text{fail})$.

- If a party P_i is corrupted in between a command given to F_{COM} and the output delivery round, then we allow that the input of P_i to the command is changed via COM.infl, and the outputs will be recomputed accordingly. For example, if P_i becomes corrupted in **commit** before the output is delivered, then we allow the environment to delete the input of P_i, thereby making the output $(\text{commit}, i, cid, \text{fail})$. This models the idea that if a committer P_i becomes (adaptively) corrupted during implementation of the commitment protocol, it is allowed that the now corrupted P_i can make the protocol fail. This is important for being able to prove adaptive security: requiring that the protocol will always terminate correctly if just the first round was run honestly is often impossible to implement.

- When we say that a command leaks a value, then the value is output on COM.leak in the round where inputs to the command are given, not in the delivery round. For a discussion of this rushing behavior, see the specification and discussion of F_{SC}.

The final part of the description of F_{COM} includes two *advanced manipulation* commands. The transfer command transfers a committed value from one party to another. The idea is that even if P_i has committed to a value a, after a transfer to P_j, we are in a situation equivalent to what we would have if P_j had committed to a in the first place – except, of course, that P_i also knows a. The mult command is used by a player to create, given commitments to a_1 and a_2, a new commitment that is guaranteed to contain $a_1 a_2$.

Later we will use the following shorthand for describing interactions with F_{COM}. The symbol $\langle \cdot \rangle_i$ denotes a variable in which F_{COM} keeps a committed value received from player P_i. Thus, when we write $\langle a \rangle_i$, this means that player P_i has committed to a. We also need the following notation:

$\langle a \rangle_i \leftarrow a$: the commit command is executed to let P_i commit to a.

$\langle a \rangle_i \Leftarrow a$: the pubcommit command is used to force P_i to commit to a.

$a \leftarrow \langle a \rangle_i$: the open command is executed to let all parties learn a.

$(P_j) a \leftarrow \langle a \rangle_i$: the designated open command is executed to let P_j learn a.

$\langle a \rangle_j \leftarrow \langle a \rangle_i$: the transfer command from P_i to P_j.

$\langle a_3 \rangle_i \leftarrow \langle a_1 \rangle_i \langle a_2 \rangle_i$: the mult command.

It is clear from these descriptions that all players know at any point which committed values have been defined. Of course, the value committed to is not known to the players (except the committer), but nevertheless, they can ask F_{COM} to manipulate committed values, namely, to add committed values and multiply them by public constants, as long as the involved variables belong to the same party. This is done by issuing the add or mult commands. The following notation will stand for execution of these commands:

$$\langle a_3 \rangle_i \leftarrow \langle a_1 \rangle_i + \langle a_2 \rangle_i \qquad \langle a_3 \rangle_i \leftarrow \alpha \langle a_2 \rangle_i$$

where it is understood that $a_3 = a_1 + a_2$ and $a_3 = \alpha a_2$.

Implementing Advanced Commands Using Basic Commands

The first step toward using F_{COM} for secure function evaluation is to implement the advanced manipulation commands from the basic set of operations. Formally speaking, we can think of this as follows: we are given a functionality $F_{COM\text{-}SIMPLE}$ that has all the commands of F_{COM} except the advanced manipulation commands. We then build protocols that will implement F_{COM} when given access to $F_{COM\text{-}SIMPLE}$. Once we show that these protocols work as defined in Chapter 4, the UC theorem allows us to assume in the following that we have F_{COM} available. However, when it comes to implementing commitments, we will only need to implement $F_{COM\text{-}SIMPLE}$.

Protocol Transfer

If any command fails in steps 1–3, it will be clear that either P_i or P_j is corrupt. In this case, go to step 4.

1. $(P_j) a \leftarrow \langle a \rangle_i$.
2. $\langle a \rangle_j \leftarrow a$.
3. For $k = 1, \ldots, n$ do[a]

    (a) P_i picks a uniformly random $r \in_R \mathbb{F}$ and sends it privately to P_j.
    (b) Execute $\langle r \rangle_i \leftarrow r$ and $\langle r \rangle_j \leftarrow r$.
    (c) P_k broadcasts a random challenge $e \in \mathbb{F}$.
    (d) The parties execute $\langle s \rangle_i \leftarrow e \langle a \rangle_i + \langle r \rangle_i$ and $\langle s \rangle_j \leftarrow e \langle a \rangle_j + \langle r \rangle_j$.
    (e) $s \leftarrow \langle s \rangle_i$ and $s' \leftarrow \langle s \rangle_j$ (we use s' here to indicate that the opened values may be different if P_i or P_j is corrupt).
    (f) If $s \neq s'$, all players go to step 4.

    If all n iterations of the loop were successful, parties output success, except P_j, who outputs a.
4. This is the "exception handler." It is executed if it is known this P_j or P_i is corrupt. First, execute $a \leftarrow \langle a \rangle_i$. If this fails, all parties output fail. Otherwise, do $\langle a \rangle_j \Leftarrow a$ (this cannot fail). Parties output success, except P_j, who outputs a.

[a] The description of this step assumes that $1/|\mathbb{F}|$ negligible in the security parameter. If this is not the case, we repeat the step u times in parallel, where u is chosen such that $(1/|\mathbb{F}|)^u$ is negligible.

Protocol Perfect Transfer

If any command fails in steps 1–4, it will be clear that either P_i or P_j is corrupt. In this case, go to step 5

1. $(P_j)a \leftarrow \langle a \rangle_i$.
2. $\langle a \rangle_j \leftarrow a$.
3. To check that P_i and P_j are committed to the same value, we do the following:
   P_i selects a polynomial $f(X) = a + \alpha_1 X + \cdots + \alpha_t X^t$ for uniformly random $\alpha_1, \ldots, \alpha_t$ and executes $\langle \alpha_l \rangle_i \leftarrow \alpha_l$ for $l = 1, \ldots, t$. We invoke the `add` and `mult` commands so that all players collaborate to compute, for $k = 1, \ldots, n$,

$$\langle f(k) \rangle_i = \langle a \rangle_i + k \langle \alpha_1 \rangle_i + \cdots + k^t \langle \alpha_t \rangle_i$$

   and then $(P_k)f(k) \leftarrow \langle f(k) \rangle_i$. Then P_i sends $\alpha_1, \ldots, \alpha_t$ privately to P_j, and we execute $\langle \alpha_l \rangle_j \leftarrow \alpha_l$ for $l = 1, \ldots, t$. In the same way as earlier, we compute $\langle f(k) \rangle_j$ and execute $(P_k)f(k) \leftarrow \langle f(k) \rangle_j$.
4. For $k = 1, \ldots, n$, P_k compares the two values that were opened toward him or her. If they agree, he or she broadcasts `accept`; otherwise, he or she broadcasts `reject`.
   For every P_k who said reject, execute $a_k \leftarrow \langle f(k) \rangle_i$ and $a'_k \leftarrow \langle f(k) \rangle_j$. If $a_k = a'_k$ for all k, all players output `success` except P_j, who outputs a. Otherwise, go to step 5.
5. This is the "exception handler." It is executed if it is known that P_j or P_i is corrupt. First, execute $a \leftarrow \langle a \rangle_i$. If this fails, all parties output `fail`. Otherwise, do $\langle a \rangle_j \Leftarrow a$ (this cannot fail). Parties output `success` except P_j, who outputs a.

5.2.1 Implementations of the `transfer` Command

We will present two implementations of this command. One is only statistically secure but makes no assumption on t, the number of corrupted players, whereas the other is perfectly secure but requires $t < n/2$.

The basic idea in both cases is that $\langle a \rangle_i$ will be opened to P_j only, and then P_j commits to a. If P_j is corrupt and fails to do a commitment, then we make a public and force a commitment to a for P_j. This is secure because when P_j is corrupted, a also becomes know to the adversary in the ideal world (because a is output to P_j). Thus, the simulator learns a and can simulate the protocol simply by running it on the correct a.

This is, however, not sufficient. If P_j is corrupted, it could do $\langle a' \rangle_j \leftarrow a'$ for $a' \neq a$. This cannot be solved by doing $(P_i)a' \leftarrow \langle a' \rangle_j$ and letting P_i check that $a' = a$ because P_i could be corrupted as well. The ideal functionality ensures that $a' = a$ even if P_i and P_j are corrupted; therefore, this also should hold for the protocol. The final step in both protocols is therefore that P_i and P_j prove to the other parties that $a' = a$.

We sketch the argument why Protocol Transfer is secure as follows: it is clear that if P_i and P_j are honest, then all proofs will be accepting. Second, if P_i and P_j are honest, then r is random, and the only value leaked to the other parties is $ea + r$, which is just a uniformly random field element. This is secure because the simulator can simulate $ea + r$ using a uniformly random value. If either P_i or P_j is corrupted, there is nothing to simulate because the simulator learns a in the ideal world. What remains is to argue if that if $a' \neq a$, then the proof will fail with high probability. This ensures that a case where $a' \neq a$ but parties still output `success` will occur with only negligible probability. This is necessary because such a case would constitute a chance to distinguish between the ideal case and the protocol execution.

Thus, assume that $a' \neq a$. That is, P_j made a commitment $\langle a + \Delta_a \rangle_j$ for $\Delta_a \neq 0$. Then P_i and P_j makes commitments $\langle r \rangle_i$ and $\langle r + \Delta_r \rangle_j$. Again, P_j could pick $\Delta_r \neq 0$ but also could use $\Delta_r = 0$ – we do not know which. We do know, however, that $s = ea + r$ and $s' = e(a + \Delta_a) + (r + \Delta_r) = s + (e\Delta_a + \Delta_r)$. Therefore, the proof is accepted if and only if $e\Delta_a + \Delta_r = 0$, which is equivalent to $e = \Delta_a^{-1}(-\Delta_r)$ (recall that $\Delta_a \neq 0$ and thus is invertible.) Since e is uniformly random when P_k is honest and picked after Δ_a and Δ_r are fixed, the probability that $e = \Delta_a^{-1}(-\Delta_r)$ is exactly $1/|\mathbb{F}|$. If this is not negligible, the whole process can be repeated a number of times in parallel, as mentioned in the protocol description.

Note that if the proof fails, it could be due to P_j being corrupted, so we run the "exception handler" to give P_i a chance to reveal a and let the other parties do a forced commitment of P_j to a.

In Protocol Perfect Transfer, the idea is to check in a different way that the values committed by P_i and P_j are the same; that is, we ask them to commit also to two polynomials that should be the same. Furthermore, these polynomial both determine the value a in question. We then check that the two polynomials agree in so many points that they must be equal, and this, in turn, implies that the values committed by P_i and P_j are indeed the same. A more detailed argument can be found in the proof of Theorem 5.1.

Protocol Commitment Multiplication

If any command used during this protocol fails, all players output `fail`.

1. $P_i : \langle c \rangle_i \leftarrow ab$.
2. For $k = 1, \ldots, n$, do[a]

   (a) P_i chooses a uniformly random $\alpha \in \mathbb{F}$.
   (b) $\langle \alpha \rangle_i \leftarrow \alpha$; $\langle \gamma \rangle_i \leftarrow \alpha b$.
   (c) P_k broadcasts a uniformly random challenge $e \in \mathbb{F}$.
   (d) $\langle A \rangle_i \leftarrow e\langle a \rangle_i + \langle \alpha \rangle_i$; $A \leftarrow \langle A \rangle_i$.
   (e) $\langle D \rangle_i \leftarrow A\langle b \rangle_i - e\langle c \rangle_i - \langle \gamma \rangle_i$; $D \leftarrow \langle D \rangle_i$.
   (f) If $D \neq 0$, all players output `fail`.

3. If we arrive here, no command failed during the protocol, and all D values were 0. All players output `success`.

[a] The description of this step assumes that $1/|\mathbb{F}|$ is negligible in the security parameter. If this is not the case, we repeat the step u times in parallel, where u is chosen such that $(1/|\mathbb{F}|)^u$ is negligible.

5.2.2 Implementations of the `mult` *Command*

For the `mult` command, we will follow a similar pattern as for `transfer`: we present an implementation that is not only statistically secure but also makes no assumption on t, the number of corrupted players, while the other implementation is perfectly secure but requires $t < n/3$.

The idea in Protocol Commitment Multiplication is that P_i commits to what he or she claims is the product ab and then proves to each other player P_k that this was done correctly.

It is easy to show that if P_i remains honest, then the proof succeeds, and all values opened are random (or fixed to 0). Thus they reveal no extra information to the adversary and are easy to simulate. Using an analysis similar to the one for Protocol Transfer, it can be shown that if $c = ab + \Delta$ for $\Delta \neq 0$, then for each P_k, the proof fails except with probability $1/|\mathbb{F}|$.

Protocol Perfect Commitment Multiplication

If any command used during this protocol fails, all players output `fail`.

1. $\langle c \rangle_i \leftarrow ab$.
2. P_i chooses polynomials $f_a(X) = a + \alpha_1 X + \cdots + \alpha_t X^t$ and $f_b(X) = b + \beta_1 X + \cdots + \beta_t X^t$, for random α_j, β_j. He or she computes $h(X) = f_a(X)f_b(X)$ and writes $h(X)$ as $h(X) = c + \gamma_1 X + \cdots + \gamma_{2t} X^{2t}$. Then establish commitments as follows:

$$\langle \alpha_j \rangle_i \leftarrow \alpha_j \qquad \text{for } j = 1, \ldots, t$$
$$\langle \beta_j \rangle_i \leftarrow \beta_j \qquad \text{for } j = 1, \ldots, t$$
$$\langle \gamma_j \rangle_i \leftarrow \gamma_j \qquad \text{for } j = 1, \ldots, 2t$$

3. The `add` and `mult` commands are invoked to compute, for $k = 1, \ldots, n$,

$$\langle f_a(k) \rangle_i = \langle a \rangle_i + k\langle \alpha_1 \rangle_i + \cdots + k^t \langle \alpha_t \rangle_i$$
$$\langle f_b(k) \rangle_i = \langle b \rangle_i + k\langle \beta_1 \rangle_i + \cdots + k^t \langle \beta_t \rangle_i$$
$$\langle h(k) \rangle_i = \langle b \rangle_i + k\langle \gamma_1 \rangle_i + \cdots + k^{2t} \langle \gamma_{2t} \rangle_i$$

   Then $(P_k)a_k \leftarrow \langle f_a(k) \rangle_i$, $(P_k)b_k \leftarrow \langle f_b(k) \rangle_i$, and $(P_k)c_k \leftarrow \langle h(k) \rangle_i$ are executed.
4. For $k = 1, \ldots, n$, do: P_k checks that $a_k b_k = c_k$ and broadcasts `accept` if this is the case; otherwise he or she broadcast `reject`.
5. For each P_k who said `reject`, do $a_k \leftarrow \langle f_a(k) \rangle_i$, $b_k \leftarrow \langle f_b(k) \rangle_i$, and $c_k \leftarrow \langle h(k) \rangle_i$; all players check whether $a_k b_k = c_k$ holds. If this is not the case, all players output `fail`.
6. If we arrive here, no command failed during the protocol, and all relations $a_k b_k = c_k$ that were checked hold. All players output `success`.

The idea in Protocol Perfect Commitment Multiplication is to have P_i commit to polynomials f_a, f_b (determining a, b) and to what he or she claims is the product $h = f_a f_b$ of the polynomials. Then players check that $h(k) = f_a(k)f_b(k)$ in a number of points sufficient to guarantee that indeed $h = f_a f_b$. A more detailed argument can be found in the proof of Theorem 5.1.

Let $\pi_{\text{TRANSFER,MULT}}$ be the protocol that implements the basic commands by simply relaying the commands to $F_{\text{COM-SIMPLE}}$ and that implements the transfer and multiplication commands by running Protocol Transfer and Protocol Commitment Multiplication on $F_{\text{COM-SIMPLE}}$. Let $\pi_{\text{PTRANSFER,PMULT}}$ be the protocol that implements the basic commands by relaying the commands to $F_{\text{COM-SIMPLE}}$ and that implements the transfer and multiplication commands by running Protocol Perfect Transfer and Protocol Perfect Commitment Multiplication on $F_{\text{COM-SIMPLE}}$.[1] We can then summarize the protocols and results we have shown so far as follows:

---

[1] The protocols for advanced commands should pick commitment identifiers for intermediary values so as not to collide with the identifiers used by the basic commands.

THEOREM 5.1 *Let $F_{COM\text{-}SIMPLE}$ be a functionality that has all the commands of F_{COM} except the advanced manipulation commands. Then $\pi_{TRANSFER,MULT} \diamond F_{SC} \diamond F_{COM\text{-}SIMPLE}$ implements F_{COM} in $\mathrm{Env}^{t,sync}$ with statistical security for all $t < n$. Moreover, $\pi_{PTRANSFER}, \pi_{PMULT} \diamond F_{SC} \diamond F_{COM\text{-}SIMPLE}$ implements F_{COM} in $\mathrm{Env}^{t,sync}$ with perfect security for all $t < n/3$.*

Proof We prove here in detail the case for perfect security. The case of statistical security can be proved along the same lines, based on the arguments we gave earlier. This is straightforward (but quite tedious) and is left to the reader.

The first step is constructing the simulator S_{COM}. On a high level, the idea is that the simulator will relay messages connected to the basic commitment commands, while for `transfer` and `mult`, it will run internally a copy of $\pi_{PTRANSFER,PMULT} \diamond F_{SC} \diamond F_{COM\text{-}SIMPLE}$, where it uses its instance of $F_{COM\text{-}SIMPLE}$ for basic commitment commands related to executing $\pi_{PTRANSFER,PMULT}$. Here the simulator will as usual play the roles of the honest parties.

The details are given in the box Agent S_{COM}. We argue in the following that the distribution produced by S_{COM} is the same as in the real case.

Agent S_{COM}

A simulator for $\pi_{PTRANSFER,PMULT} \diamond F_{SC} \diamond F_{COM\text{-}SIMPLE}$ for the static case.

Basic commands. When any of the basic commands are executed, the simulator will just forward messages back and forth between the environment and F_{COM}.[a] When a corrupted player commits to a value, S_{COM} will store it.

Transfer. When F_{COM} is executing a `transfer` of some value a from P_i to P_j, then P_i has already committed to that value. Therefore, if P_i is corrupted, the simulator has stored a. However, if P_j is corrupt, then a is leaked from F_{COM} as soon as `transfer` is initiated. Now S_{COM} can run its copy of $\pi_{PTRANSFER} \diamond F_{SC} \diamond F_{COM\text{-}SIMPLE}$ with the environment using as input the correct value a and where it simulates the parts of the honest players. If the simulated protocol terminates correctly, the simulator inputs $(\mathtt{transfer}, i, cid, j)$ and asks for delivery of outputs on COM.infl. If P_i is corrupt and makes some command fail, the simulator will ask for delivery of outputs without inputting $(\mathtt{transfer}, i, cid, j)$, which will make F_{COM} output `fail`, matching the real scenario. If both parties are honest, then the transfer protocol is simulated with some random value.

Multiplication. When F_{COM} is executing a `mult` for P_i of some values a, b, then P_i has already committed to these values. Hence, if P_i is corrupted, the simulator has already stored a, b and can do $\pi_{PMULT} \diamond F_{SC} \diamond F_{COM\text{-}SIMPLE}$ with the correct values. If P_i is honest, $\pi_{PMULT} \diamond F_{SC} \diamond F_{COM\text{-}SIMPLE}$ is done with random values. If the simulated protocol terminates correctly, the simulator inputs $(\mathtt{mult}, i, cid_1, cid_2, cid_3)$ and asks for delivery of outputs on COM.infl. If P_i is corrupt and makes some command fail, the simulator will ask for delivery of outputs on COM.infl without inputting $(\mathtt{mult}, i, cid_1, cid_2, cid_3)$, which will make F_{COM} output fail, matching the real scenario.

[a] Note here that this does *not* include the basic commands needed for executing $\pi_{PTRANSFER,PMULT}$. This is only for the basic commands that F_{COM} will execute.

Since messages concerning the basic commands are just relayed between the environment and F_{COM}, this is exactly the same. During `transfer`, if either P_i or P_j is corrupt, the simulator learns the value to be transferred. Similarly, in `mult`, if P_i is corrupt, the simulator knows the values to be multiplied. Hence, in these cases, the protocol $\pi_{PTRANSFER,PMULT}$ is run on the true values. If, however, the players are honest, then for both `transfer` and `mult` the environment sees at most t points of polynomials of degree at least t. Thus no information on the actual values is given.

What remains to argue is that the protocol execution is consistent with the inputs-outputs to and from F_{COM}. That is, if the protocol finishes successfully, then the output is correct, meaning that the players have indeed transferred a commitment or multiplied values correctly. However, if the simulated protocol fails, then this is also consistent with the state of F_{COM}.

First, during `transfer`, if P_i and P_j are honest, it is clear that all the proofs will be accepting. Moreover, if one or both are corrupted but we still reach the point where values are compared, no command failed earlier. At this point, we know that we have strictly more than $2t$ honest players. Hence, if at most t players said `reject`, then at least $t+1$ honest players said `accept`, which implies that indeed P_i and P_j are committed to the same polynomials. In particular, their degree 0 terms are also the same, so it follows that $\langle a \rangle_i$ and $\langle a \rangle_j$ do contain the same value.

As for `mult`, it is clear from the way the polynomials are committed to that even if P_i is corrupt, we have $f_a(0) = a, f_b(0) = b, h(0) = c$ and that $\deg(f_a), \deg(f_b) \le t$, and $\deg(h) \le 2t$. Moreover, if the players output `success` at the end, it follows that $f_a(k)f_b(k) = h(k)$ for every player P_k who remains honest. The assumption that $t < n/3$ implies that there are at least $2t+1$ honest players. Since $2t+1$ points determine any polynomial of degree at most $2t$ uniquely, it follows that $f_a(X)f_b(X) = h(X)$ and hence that $ab = f_a(0)f_b(0) = h(0) = c$. It is also easy to check that if P_i remains honest, then the protocol will always be successful.

Finally, if the simulated protocol fails at some point because of a corrupted P_i, the simulator outputs `fail`, which is consistent with the internal state of F_{COM} because, in this case, S_{COM} also makes F_{COM} fail.

Adaptive Corruption

We now show how to modify S_{COM} to handle adaptively corrupted players. Hence we allow a player P_k to be corrupted in the beginning of any round during the protocol. If this happens, the simulator learns the true values of P_k's inputs, and then it has to show the internal state of P_k to the environment. For this, the simulator must patch the state so that it is consistent with the rest of the values shown to the environment during the execution. After creating a correctly patched state of the simulation, we give the state of the newly corrupted P_k to the environment, and then simulation continues exactly as described in S_{COM}.

We describe how to patch up for the advanced commands. The basic commands are executed by an ideal functionality, so nothing needs to be handled there.

First, assume that a player different from P_i or P_j for `transfer` or different from P_i for `mult` becomes corrupted. Here nothing needs to be patched; the simulator simply shows the environment the values that were used in the execution. This is perfectly fine because for both `transfer` and `mult`, the environment has seen fewer than t points of polynomials of degree at least t. Therefore, showing the set of points that was used is still consistent with what has already been shown, and since at most t points are shown for each polynomial, still no information is given on the actual inputs to the command.

Similarly, for `transfer`, no patching is needed if at a point where one of P_i and P_j is corrupted the other player gets corrupted. The protocol $\pi_{PTRANSFER}$ was run with the correct value, so the simulator simply shows the environment the values that were used in the execution.

However, if in mult P_i gets corrupted or in transfer either P_i or P_j gets corrupted where before both were honest, then the state needs to be patched. When the player becomes corrupted, the simulator will learn the true value of the player's input. That is, for transfer, S_{COM} will learn the true value to be transferred, and for mult, S_{COM} will learn the values to be multiplied.

Now S_{COM} patches the state by recomputing the steps of the protocol with the true values. For the steps that involve secret sharing, S_{COM} recomputes new polynomials that are consistent with the degree 0 term equaling the true values and the (strictly less than t) shares already shown to the environment. For example, for transfer, this means that the polynomial $f(X)$ from step 3 is recomputed such that it is consistent with the shares already shown to the environment and $f(0) = a$, where a is the true value to be transferred. Note that this patching can be done easily even if a player gets corrupted in the middle of a command. The steps are simply recomputed up the point where the player gets corrupted. ∎

5.3 A Secure Function–Evaluation Protocol for Active Adversaries

In this section we show how to implement F_{SFE}^f given access to F_{SC} and F_{COM}. The basic idea is to do the same as in our passively secure protocol but in addition make sure that all parties are committed to all the shares they hold.

We note for future reference that the definition of F_{COM} implies that if one of its commands fails, this is always because a particular corrupt player has caused this to happen by not providing the correct input. Therefore, the honest players can always conclude from failure of a command that some particular player is corrupt.

We will need the following notation for $a \in \mathbb{F}$ and f a polynomial of degree at most t over $\mathbb{F}$:

$$[[a;f]]_t = (\langle f(1) \rangle_1, \ldots, \langle f(n) \rangle_n)$$

Thus this notation refers to n variables held by F_{COM} and claims that the ith variable contains the appropriate value $f(i)$ owned by P_i.

When we say that P_i distributes $[[a;f_a]]_t$, this means the following: P_i chooses a polynomial $f_a(X) = a + a_1 X + \cdots + a_t X^t$ with $a_j \in \mathbb{F}$ at random; then P_i commits to the coefficients of f_a, the addition and multiplication commands are used to compute a commitment to $f_a(k)$ owned by P_i, for $k = 1, \ldots, n$, and finally, this commitment is transferred to P_k. More formally, the following sequence of commands of F_{COM} is executed:

1. $\langle a \rangle_i \leftarrow a, \langle a_j \rangle_i \leftarrow a_j, j = 1, \ldots, t.$
2. $\langle f_a(k) \rangle_i \leftarrow \langle a \rangle_i + \sum_{j=1}^t k^j \langle a_j \rangle_i, k = 1, \ldots, n.$
3. $\langle f_a(k) \rangle_k \leftarrow \langle f_a(k) \rangle_i, k = 1, \ldots, n.$

It is very easy to see that when P_i distributes $[[a;f_a]]_t$, this does in fact create the object $[[a;f_a]]_t$, or all players agree that one of the commands failed, in which case they can conclude that P_i is corrupt. Note that this fact is not a result of proving the preceding sequence of commands secure as a protocol; it simply follows by definition of F_{COM}. Earlier, we said that P_i should commit to a as a part of the process, but P_i could instead use an already

Protocol CEAS (Circuit Evaluation with Active Security)

The protocol assumes that $t < n/3$ and proceeds in three phases: the input-sharing, computation, and output-reconstruction phases.

Input sharing. Each player P_i holding input $x_i \in \mathbb{F}$ distributes $[\![x_i; f_{x_i}]\!]_t$. If this fails, P_i is corrupt, so we will instead assign 0 as default input for P_i: execute $\langle 0 \rangle_k \Leftarrow 0$ for $k = 1, \ldots, n$, thus creating $[\![0; o]\!]_t$, where o is the zero polynomial.

We then go through the circuit and process the gates one by one in the computational order. Just after the input-sharing phase, we consider all input gates as being processed. We will maintain the following:

Invariant. Consider an input or an output wire for any gate, and let $a \in \mathbb{F}$ be the value assigned to this wire. Then, if the gate has been processed, the players hold $[\![a; f_a]\!]_t$ for a polynomial f_a.

We then continue with the last two phases of the protocol:

Computation phase. Repeat the following until all gates have been processed (then go to the next phase). Consider the first gate in the computational order that has not been processed yet. According to the type of gate, do one of the following:

Addition gate. The players hold $[\![a; f_a]\!]_t, [\![b; f_b]\!]_t$ for the two inputs a, b to the gate. The players compute $[\![a + b; f_a + f_b]\!]_t = [\![a; f_a]\!]_t + [\![b; f_b]\!]_t$.[a]

Multiply-by-constant gate. The players hold $[\![a; f_a]\!]_t$ for the input a to the gate. The players compute $[\![\alpha a; \alpha f_a]\!]_t = \alpha [\![a; f_a]\!]_t$.

Multiplication gate. The players hold $[\![a; f_a]\!]_t, [\![b; f_b]\!]_t$ for the two inputs a, b to the gate.

1. The players compute $[\![ab; f_a f_b]\!]_{2t} = [\![a; f_a]\!]_t * [\![b; f_b]\!]_t$. Note that this involves each P_j committing to $f_a(j) f_b(j)$ and proving that this was done correctly by using the multiplication command. So this may fail for up to t players.
2. Define $h \overset{\text{def}}{=} f_a f_b$. Then $h(0) = f_a(0) f_b(0) = ab$, and the parties hold $[\![ab; h]\!]_{2t}$, where P_i is committed by $\langle h(i) \rangle_i$. Each P_i distributes $[\![h(i); f_i]\!]_t$ from $\langle h(i) \rangle_i$. Also, this step may fail for up to t players.
3. Let S be the indices of at the (at least $n - t$) players for which the preceding two steps did not fail. Note that since $t < n/3$, $\deg(h) = 2t < n - t$. Let $\mathbf{r}_S$ be a recombination vector for S, that is, a vector $\mathbf{r}_S = (r_1, \ldots, r_n)$ for which it holds that $h(0) = \sum_{i \in S} r_i h(i)$ for any polynomial h of degree $\leq 2t$. The players compute

$$\sum_{i \in S} r_i [\![h(i); f_i]\!]_t = [\![\sum_{i \in S} r_i h(i); \sum_{i \in S} r_i f_i]\!]_t$$

$$= [\![h(0); \sum_{i \in S} r_i f_i]\!]_t = [\![ab; \sum_{i \in S} r_i f_i]\!]_t$$

Output reconstruction: At this point all gates, including the output gates, have been processed. So do the following for each output gate (labeled i): the players hold $[\![y; f_y]\!]_t$, where y is the value assigned to the output gate. Now we open $[\![y; f_y]\!]_t$ toward P_i.

---

[a] Whenever we say that the parties compute a command, we implicitly say that they wait until F_{COM} returns `success` or `fail` before they proceed with the next command.

existing commitment $\langle a \rangle_i$ to some value a. In this case, we say that P_i distributes $[[a;f_a]]_t$ from $\langle a \rangle_i$. Again, by definition of F_{COM}, it is guaranteed that the new object determines the same value that the existing commitment contains.

Distributing $[[a;f_a]]_t$ is actually a concept known from the literature as verifiable secret sharing: a dealer (here P_i) distributes shares of a secret to the players in such a way that the honest players are guaranteed to get consistent shares of a well-defined secret or they will agree that the dealer failed. Moreover, the correct secret can always be reconstructed, even if the dealer does not participate. This is easily seen to be the case for $[[a;f_a]]_t$ if $t < n/2$. In the following, when we say that $[[a;f_a]]$ is opened, this means that we execute

$$f_a(k) \leftarrow \langle f_a(k) \rangle_k \qquad \text{for } k = 1, \ldots, n$$

This will result in up to t failures but also in at least $n - t > t$ correct values, from which all players can compute a by Lagrange interpolation (see Section 3.2). We can also open $[[a;f_a]]$ toward P_j. This means that we execute $(P_j) f_a(k) \leftarrow \langle f_a(k) \rangle_k$, for $k = 1, \ldots, n$, so that only P_j learns a.

We can also do arithmetic on objects of form $[[a;f_a]]_t$ in much the same way as we did for $[a, f_a]_t$ when we did passively secure protocols. Now, however, we have to do arithmetic on committed values. Hence, for $\alpha, a, b \in \mathbb{F}$, and f_a, f_b polynomials of degree at most t, we define $[[a;f_a]]_t + [[b;f_b]]_t$, $\alpha [[a;f_a]]_t$, and $[[a;f_a]]_t * [[b;f_b]]_t$ to denote sequences of commands from F_{COM} as follows:

- $[[a;f_a]]_t + [[b;f_b]]_t$ means that we execute $\langle f_a(k) + f_b(k) \rangle_k \leftarrow \langle f_a(k) \rangle_k + \langle f_b(k) \rangle_k$, for $k = 1, \ldots, n$.
- $\alpha [[a;f_a]]_t$ means that we execute $\langle \alpha f_a(k) \rangle_k \leftarrow \alpha \langle f_a(k) \rangle_k$, for $k = 1, \ldots, n$.
- $[[a;f_a]]_t * [[b;f_b]]_t$ means that we execute $\langle f_a(k) f_b(k) \rangle_k \leftarrow \langle f_a(k) \rangle_k \langle f_b(k) \rangle_k$, for $k = 1, \ldots, n$.

Again, by definition of F_{COM}, it is easy to see that these command sequences create objects of the form we naturally would expect, namely, $[[a + b; f_a + f_b]]_t$, $[[\alpha a; \alpha f_a]]_t$, and $[[ab; f_a f_b]]_{2t}$, respectively, again unless one of the commands fails. Therefore, by a slight abuse of notation, in the following we will write

$$[[a + b; f_a + f_b]]_t = [[a;f_a]]_t + [[b;f_b]]_t$$

$$[[\alpha a; \alpha f_a]]_t = \alpha [[a;f_a]]_t$$

$$[[ab; f_a f_b]]_{2t} = [[a;f_a]]_t * [[b;f_b]]_t$$

to denote that we execute the command sequence on the right side to create the object on the left side.

The notation we have defined is used in Protocol CEAS (Circuit Evaluation with Active Security), whose security follows almost directly from the security of the passive secure protocol. In particular, since the manipulation commands of F_{COM} are used, all parties compute all shares exactly as in the passively secure protocol, and F_{COM} keeps the shares secret. Therefore, as we see next, essentially the same simulator works in this case as well. Letting π_{CEAS} denote Protocol CEAS, we have

THEOREM 5.2 $\pi_{CEAS}^f \diamond F_{SC} \diamond F_{COM}$ *implements* F_{SFE}^f *in* $\text{Env}^{t,\text{sync}}$ *with perfect security for any f and for all $t < n/3$.*

Proof   We construct a simulator for $\pi^f_{\mathsf{CEAS}} \diamond \mathsf{F_{SC}} \diamond \mathsf{F_{COM}}$ where the idea is very similar to the simulator $\mathcal{S}_{\mathsf{CEPS}}$ for the passive case. The simulator runs a copy of $\pi^f_{\mathsf{CEAS}} \diamond \mathsf{F_{SC}} \diamond \mathsf{F_{COM}}$ where it plays the role of the honest parties and executes the protocol with the environment that is controlling the actively corrupted players. Since the simulator is running, $\mathsf{F_{COM}}$, it is able to keep track of all the corrupted parties' values. We present first the simulator Agent $\mathcal{S}_{\mathsf{CEAS}}$ for the static case and when the environment provides inputs to all parties in the same round. The case where not all parties receive inputs in the same round is handled as in the passive case. After arguing static security, we show how to modify the simulator to achieve adaptive security as well.

Agent $\mathcal{S}_{\mathsf{CEAS}}$

A simulator for $\pi^f_{\mathsf{CEAS}} \diamond \mathsf{F_{SC}} \diamond \mathsf{F_{COM}}$ for the static case where the environment gives inputs to all parties in the same round.

Initialize. In the preamble, the environment $\mathcal{Z}$ specifies the set C of actively corrupted parties. After this, the simulator sets up a copy of $\pi^f_{\mathsf{CEAS}} \diamond \mathsf{F_{SC}} \diamond \mathsf{F_{COM}}$ where it actively corrupts the players in C and connects the special ports of $\pi^f_{\mathsf{CEAS}} \diamond \mathsf{F_{SC}} \diamond \mathsf{F_{COM}}$ to $\mathcal{Z}$. $\mathcal{S}_{\mathsf{CEAS}}$ also does active corruptions of $\mathsf{P}_i \in C$ on $\mathsf{F}^f_{\mathsf{SFE}}$, which means that $\mathsf{F}^f_{\mathsf{SFE}}$ will ignore all inputs on $\mathsf{SFE.in}_i$ and stop giving outputs on $\mathsf{SFE.out}_i$. Instead, the simulator must now provide the input to $\mathsf{F}^f_{\mathsf{SFE}}$ on behalf of the corrupt players.

Input sharing. The simulator performs the steps of input sharing with the environment (which runs the corrupted parties). That is, $\mathcal{S}_{\mathsf{CEAS}}$ runs the honest parties, so it will for each $\mathsf{P}_i \notin C$ distribute a sharing of 0. When the corrupt parties share their inputs, the simulator will receive all the values they want to commit to (since the simulator is running $\mathsf{F_{COM}}$). In particular, $\mathcal{S}_{\mathsf{CEAS}}$ will for each $\mathsf{P}_j \in C$ receive x_j, which it can then pass on to $\mathsf{F}^f_{\mathsf{SFE}}$.

Computation phase. In the computation phase, the simulator simply performs the protocol steps of π^f_{CEAS} together with the environment according to the gates that need to be processed.

Output reconstruction. First, $\mathcal{S}_{\mathsf{CEAS}}$ instructs $\mathsf{F}^f_{\mathsf{SFE}}$ to evaluate the function, thereby learning the outputs y_j for all $\mathsf{P}_j \in C$. For each output of a corrupted party P_j, it takes the t shares that the corrupted parties hold, it defines $f_{y_j}(0) \stackrel{\text{def}}{=} y_j$, and if $t' < t$ players are corrupted, then for $t - t'$ honest players, P_i sets $f_{y_j}(i)$ to be a random value. After this, $f_{y_j}(X)$ is defined in $t + 1$ points, and hence $\mathcal{S}_{\mathsf{CEAS}}$ can compute the unique degree t polynomial consistent with these points. Then, for $\mathsf{P}_i \notin C$ it sets the committed share of P_i to be $f_{y_j}(i)$ and opens it to P_j on behalf of P_i. When $\mathcal{Z}$ clocks out P_i in the copy of $\pi^f_{\mathsf{CEAS}} \diamond \mathsf{F_{SC}} \diamond \mathsf{F_{COM}}$ so that P_i should produce an output, the simulator first inputs $(\mathtt{delivery\text{-}round})$ to $\mathsf{F}^f_{\mathsf{SFE}}$ if it has not done so already. Then $\mathcal{S}_{\mathsf{CEAS}}$ inputs $(\mathtt{clock\text{-}out}, i)$ to $\mathsf{F}^f_{\mathsf{SFE}}$ to make it output y_i on $\mathsf{SFE.out}_i$, exactly as P_i would have done in the protocol. (Since the environment is running the corrupted parties, this will only happen for the honest parties.)

Perfect security is argued similarly to the passive case. First, the shares sent by honest players to corrupt players in the input distribution and computation phase are distributed exactly as in the simulation, namely, t uniformly random shares for each shared value. Furthermore, since the commands of $\mathsf{F_{COM}}$ are used, the shares computed by local computation are the same as in the passively secure protocol. This follows from the definition of $\mathsf{F_{COM}}$, which guarantees that either the players are committed to the correct shares or they all agree that a command failed because a particular player P_i is corrupt. However, this can happen for at most t players, which by construction we can tolerate when $t < n/3$. Therefore, the invariant in the protocol holds, which implies that the output is correct and hence *the same* in both $\pi_{\mathrm{CEAS}}^f \diamond \mathsf{F_{SC}} \diamond \mathsf{F_{COM}}$ and $\mathsf{F_{SFE}^f}$. Furthermore, $\mathcal{S}_{\mathrm{CEAS}}$ makes $\mathsf{F_{SFE}^f}$ give output on $\mathsf{SFE.out}_i$ at the same point where P_i would. Finally, note that in the case where fewer than $t' < t$ players are corrupted, the simulator makes random choices for the remaining $t - t'$ shares, independently for each output. This matches the distribution of a real execution because each output comes from a multiplication gate (by the assumption on the circuit we made in Chapter 3). The protocol for a multiplication gate produces a random polynomial that determines the correct output from the gate. We conclude that the views produced by $\mathcal{S}_{\mathrm{CEAS}}$ are distributed exactly as in the real case.

Adaptive Corruption

We now show how to modify $\mathcal{S}_{\mathrm{CEAS}}$ such that it can handle adaptively corrupted players. Hence we allow a player P_k to be corrupted in the beginning of any round during the protocol. If this happens, the simulator learns the true value of x_k, and then it has to show the internal state of P_k to the environment. For this, the simulator must patch the state of P_k so that it is consistent with x_k and the rest of the values shown to environment during the execution. After creating a correctly patched state of the simulation, we give the state of the newly corrupted P_k to the environment, and then simulation continues exactly as described in $\mathcal{S}_{\mathrm{CEAS}}$.

We describe here the case where P_k gets corrupted after the protocol is completed. Then handling corruption at an earlier stage will consist simply of doing a smaller part of the patching steps (namely, up to the point where the player gets corrupted). Basically, the way to patch the state is to recompute every honest player's share that is affected by the input of P_k. This is done as follows[2]:

Input sharing. When $\mathcal{S}_{\mathrm{CEAS}}$ learns x_k, it can compute a new random secret sharing of x_k that is consistent with the (strictly fewer than t) shares shown to the environment and $f_{x_k}(0) = x_k$. From $f_{x_k}(\mathrm{X})$, the simulator recomputes the steps of the input distribution, not involving other corrupt parties. That is, first $\mathcal{S}_{\mathrm{CEAS}}$ sets up the commitments to the new coefficients of $f_{x_k}(\mathrm{X})$ (by modifying the values held by its internal copy of $\mathsf{F_{COM}}$). Then it sets up new commitments of shares to honest parties and transfers the commitments to them, obtaining $\langle f_{x_k}(i) \rangle_i$.

Addition or multiplication by a constant. Here the players only do local computations, so $\mathcal{S}_{\mathrm{CEAS}}$ can simply adjust the commitments of all honest parties' shares that were affected by $f_{x_k}(\mathrm{X})$.

Multiplication. The first round in the processing of a multiplication gate only has local computations, and hence the simulator adjusts as earlier commitments of the affected shares of honest parties. Then, in the second round, new shares are distributed of the product of two polynomials $f_a f_b$. If $f_{x_k}(\mathrm{X})$ is involved in one of these polynomials, $\mathcal{S}_{\mathrm{CEAS}}$ must compute a new random secret sharing of $f_a(0)f_b(0)$, as it did for x_k in input sharing. In the third and last round, the simulator is again able to recompute the shares

---

[2] It might be a good idea to have the protocol π_{CEAS} in mind when reading this.

of the honest parties by local computations. Recall that the recombination vector is independent of $f_a f_b(\mathtt{X})$; it is the same for all polynomials of degree at most $n - t$, so it is indeed possible to redo this step with the new product.

Output reconstruction. We will get from the ideal functionality the output value y_k belonging to the player that was just corrupted. We then create shares for honest players such that the total set of shares determines y_k, exactly as in the output step of $\mathcal{S}_{\text{CEAS}}$, and list these shares as those sent to P_k in the round where he or she was to learn y_k.

Now let C be the set of already corrupted players. For every y_j belonging to a player $\mathsf{P}_j \in C$, note that the environment has already seen (points on) a polynomial f_{y_j} that $\mathcal{S}_{\text{CEAS}}$ created earlier. Therefore, we must patch the state such that P_k ends up holding $f_{y_j}(k)$ as his or her share. Recall that f_{y_j} is produced by the multiplication gate protocol. Our patching procedure applied to this gate produces a polynomial f_i for each player, and then the local recombination step determines a polynomial $f = \sum_{i \in S} r_i f_i$. Since the patching never changes the shares of players in C, we have $f_{y_j}(i) = f(i)$ for each $\mathsf{P}_i \in C$. But we also need that $f_{y_j}(k) = f(k)$, and this is not guaranteed.

To correct for this, note that there must exist an honest player P_{i_0} such that $r_{i_0} \neq 0$; otherwise, the corrupt players could reconstruct the product on their own. We now choose a random polynomial g of degree at most t subject to

$$g(0) = 0, \quad g(i) = 0 \quad \text{for all } \mathsf{P}_i \in C, \quad \text{and} \quad g(k) = r_{i_0}^{-1}(f_{y_j}(k) - f(k))$$

This is possible because at most $t - 1$ players could be corrupted before P_k, so we fix the value of g in at most $t + 1$ points. We now adjust the state of (the simulator's copy of) P_{i_0} such that we replace its polynomial f_{i_0} with $f_{i_0} + g$. This keeps the state of P_{i_0} internally consistent because $f_{i_0}(0) = (f_{i_0} + g)(0)$, and the shares of players in C are unchanged. However, we have now replaced f by $f + r_{i_0} g$, and clearly, $(f + r_{i_0} g)(k) = f_{y_j}(k)$ as desired.

As mentioned earlier, if a player gets corrupted earlier, patching is done only up to that point. Note that this is also possible even if the player gets corrupted before a round in the middle of some command that has more than one round. Patching is simply done up to the round just before the player gets corrupted, and then the simulation proceeds as in the static case. Also, if a player gets corrupted just before the input-sharing phase but after the environment has provided the inputs, the simulation is essentially the same as before. The only difference is that giving $\mathsf{F}_{\text{SFE}}^f$ the input of a corrupted party now means overriding any previous value stored for that party. ∎

We note that it is possible to modify Protocol CEAS to make it also work for $t < n/2$. The difficulty in this case is that if a player fails during processing of a multiplication gate, we cannot proceed because all players are needed to determine a polynomial of degree $2t$ when we only assume $t < n/2$. The simplest way to handle such failures is to go back to the start of the computation and open the input values of the players that have just been disqualified. Now we restart the protocol while the honest players simulate the disqualified players. Note that we can use default random choices for these players, so no communication is needed for the honest players to agree on the actions of the simulated ones. This allows the adversary to slow down the protocol by a factor at most linear in n. In doing this, it is important that we do not have to restart the protocol after some party received its output – this is ensured by starting the output-reconstruction phase only after all multiplication gates have been handled. If we allowed some party P_i to see its output before all multiplication gates were handled, then it could, for instance, first run with $x_i = 1$ to let the corrupted parties learn their parts of the output $f(x_1, \ldots, x_n)$ when $x_i = 1$. Then it could make the next multiplication gate fail. Then the parties would rerun, but now using the dummy input $x_i = 0$ for P_i. This would let the corrupted parties learn their parts of the output $f(x_1, \ldots, x_n)$ when $x_i = 0$. Seeing f evaluated on two points might let the corrupted parties learn more about the inputs of the honest parties than is possible in the ideal world. It is, however, clear that it is secure to rerun as long as no party received its output because the prefix of the protocol not including the reconstruction phase leaks no information to any party.

EXERCISE 5.1 The preceding way to handle corrupted parties allows the corrupted parties to delay the computation by a factor t because they might one by one refuse to participate in the last multiplication gate, forcing yet another rerun. It is possible to ensure that they can delay by at most a factor $O(\log(t))$. We sketch the first part of how this is done, and the exercise is to realize how to generalize. Assume that in the first execution of the protocol all parties follow the protocol, except that P_n at some point refuses to participate in the execution of the protocol for a multiplication gate. Then we can let $n' = n - 1$, $t' = t - 1$, and $f'(x_1, \ldots, x_{n'}) = (y_1, \ldots, y_{n'})$, where the outputs are given by $(y_1, \ldots, y_{n'}, y_n) = f(x_1, \ldots, x_{n'}, 0)$. Then we can let the parties $P_1, \ldots, P_{n'}$ run the protocol for securely evaluating f' among themselves using secret sharings of degree t' instead of t. It is secure to use only degree t' because at most t' of the remaining parties are corrupted given that we started with at most t corrupted parties and just excluded P_n. This approach also leads to a correct result because the honest parties learn their part of the output $f(x_1, \ldots, x_{n-1}, 0)$. Thus, all P_n got out of cheating was that it was forced to use input $x_n = 0$ and that it does not learn its output. Notice, however, that if we started with $2t + 1 \leq n$, we now have that $2t' + 1 \leq n' - 1$ because $2t' + 1 = 2(t - 1) + 1 = (2t + 1) - 2 \leq n - 2$ and $n' = n - 1$. Since $2t' + 1 \leq n' - 1$ and we are running the protocol with polynomials of degree at most t' and have n' parties that are holding shares, it follows that we can run the protocol for a multiplication gate even if one party does not share its $h(i)$ value – we will still have $n' - 1$ of the values $h(i)$, which is enough to interpolate $h(0)$ because $h(X)$ has degree at most $2t'$. This means that to force a rerun of the protocol, at least two of the remaining corrupted parties have to stop participating. In this case, we exclude those two parties and restart with $n'' = n' - 2$ parties and at most $t'' = t' - 2$ corrupted parties. Thus, we can use polynomials of degree at most $t'' = t - 3$ and hence tolerate that even more corrupted parties stop participating before we need to do the next rerun.

1. In the first execution, we can tolerate that 0 corrupted parties refuse to participate in the protocol for a multiplication gate. In the second execution, we can tolerate that one corrupted party refuses to participate in the protocol for a multiplication gate. Argue that in the third execution we can tolerate that three corrupted parties refuse to participate in the protocol for a multiplication gate and that we hence can exclude four more parties before the fourth execution if we are forced to do a fourth execution.
2. How many refusing parties can we tolerate in the fourth execution?
3. How many refusing parties can we tolerate in the ith execution?
4. If we start with $2t + 1 = n$, what is the worst-case number of reruns that the corrupted parties can force? Try to give an exact answer.

Let $\pi^f_{\text{CEAS-N/2}}$ be π^f_{CEAS} modified to handle $t < n/2$, as we just discussed. We then have the following theorem, the proof of which we leave to the reader:

THEOREM 5.3 $\pi^f_{\text{CEAS-N/2}} \diamond F_{SC} \diamond F_{COM}$ *implements* F^f_{SFE} *in* $\text{Env}^{t,\text{sync}}$ *with perfect security for any f and for all $t < n/2$.*

5.3.1 Reactive Functionalities

So far our results for general secure computing have only been about secure function evaluation. It is easy to define a *reactive functionality* that is much more general than F^f_{SFE}, namely, a functionality that keeps internal state and offers to repeatedly do the following: compute some function that depends on both the state and inputs from the players, and update the state as well as deliver outputs to players.

Using the way we represent data in π_{CEAS}, it is easy to design a secure implementation of such a functionality: we can represent the state as a number of objects of form $[[a; f_a]]$. We can assume that we get the inputs from players represented in the same form, and then we evaluate whatever function we need using the subprotocols for addition and multiplication. When we have representations of the outputs, we keep those that represent the new state and open those that contain output to the players.

It is straightforward to formalize this construction; we leave the details to the reader.

5.4 Realization of Homomorphic Commitments

We assume throughout this section that we are in the information-theoretic scenario with secure point-to-point channels and consensus broadcast. Most of the time we assume that $t < n/3$, although we will look at the case $t < n/2$ at the end of this section. We show how to implement a commitment scheme with the desired basic commands and simple manipulation commands.

The idea that immediately comes to mind in order to have a player D commit to a is to ask him or her to secret share a. At least this will hide a from the adversary if D is honest and will immediately ensure the homomorphic properties we need; namely, to add commitments, each player just adds his or her shares, and to multiply by a constant, all shares are multiplied by the constant.

However, if D is corrupt, he or she can distribute inconsistent shares and then can easily "open" a commitment in several ways, as detailed in the following exercise:

EXERCISE 5.2 A player D sends a value a_i to each player P_i (also to himself or herself). D is supposed to choose these such that $a_i = f(i)$ for all i, for some polynomial $f(X)$ of degree at most t, where $t < n/3$ is the maximal number of corrupted players. At some later time, D is supposed to reveal the polynomial $f(X)$ he or she used, and each P_i reveals a_i. The polynomial is accepted if values of at most t players disagree with $f(X)$ (we cannot demand fewer disagreements because the corrupted parties might send wrong values, so we may get t of them even if D were honest).

1. We assume here (for simplicity) that $n = 3t + 1$. Suppose that the adversary corrupts D. Show how to choose two different polynomials $f(X), f'(X)$ of degree at most t and

values $\tilde{a}_i$ for D to send such that D can later reveal and have accepted both $f(X)$ and $f'(X)$.

2. Suppose for a moment that we would settle for computational security and that D must send to P_i not only a_i, but also his or her digital signature s_i on a_i. We assume that we can force D to send a valid signature even if he or she is corrupt. We can now demand that to be accepted, a polynomial must be consistent with *all* revealed and properly signed shares. Show that now the adversary cannot have two different polynomials accepted, even if up to $t \le n/3$ players may be corrupted before the polynomial is to be revealed. [*Hint*: First argue that the adversary must corrupt D before the a_i, s_i are sent out (this is rather trivial). Then assume that $f_1(X)$ is later successfully revealed, and let C_1 be the set that is corrupted when f_1 is revealed. Assume that the adversary also could choose to let D reveal $f_2(X)$, in which case C_2 is the corrupted set. Note that if we assume that the adversary is adaptive, we cannot assume that $C_1 = C_2$. But you can still use the players outside C_1, C_2 to argue that $f_1(X) = f_2(X)$.]

3. (Optional) Does the security just proved still hold if $t > n/3$? Why or why not?

To prevent the problems just outlined, we must find a mechanism to ensure that the shares of all uncorrupted players after committing consistently determine a polynomial $f(X)$ of degree at most t without harming privacy, of course.

Minimal Distance Decoding

Before we do so, it is important to note that n shares out of which at most t are corrupted still uniquely determine the committed value a, even if we don't know which t of them is corrupted. This is based on an observation also used in error-correcting codes.

Concretely, let $f(X)$ be a polynomial of degree at most t and define the shares

$$\mathbf{s}_f \overset{\text{def}}{=} (f(1), \ldots, f(n))$$

and let $\mathbf{e} \in \mathbb{F}^n$ be an arbitrary "error vector" subject to

$$w_H(\mathbf{e}) \le t$$

where w_H denotes the Hamming weight of a vector (i.e., the number of its non-zero coordinates) and define

$$\tilde{\mathbf{s}} \overset{\text{def}}{=} \mathbf{s} + \mathbf{e}$$

Then a is uniquely defined by $\tilde{\mathbf{s}}$.

In fact, more is true because the entire polynomial $f(X)$ is true. This is easy to see from Lagrange interpolation and the fact that $t < n/3$.

That is, suppose that $\tilde{\mathbf{s}}$ can also be "explained" as originating from some other polynomial $g(X)$ of degree at most t together with some other error vector $\mathbf{u}$ with Hamming weight at most t. In other words, suppose that

$$\mathbf{s}_f + \mathbf{e} = \mathbf{s}_g + \mathbf{u}$$

Since $w_H(\mathbf{e}), w_H(\mathbf{u}) \le t$, we have that $w_H(\mathbf{e} + \mathbf{u}) \le 2t$, so since $n > 3t$, there are at least $n - 2t > t$ positions in which the coordinates of both are simultaneously zero. Thus, for at least $t + 1$ values of i, we have

$$f(i) = g(i)$$

Since both polynomials have degree at most t, this means that

$$f(X) = g(X)$$

The conclusion is that if a player P_i has distributed shares of some value $a \in \mathbb{F}$ and we can somehow guarantee that the shares are consistent with one polynomial f of degree at most $t < n/3$, then this can serve as a commitment to a. P_i can open by broadcasting the polynomial, and then each player can state whether his or her share agrees with the polynomial claimed by P_i. The opening is accepted if at most t players disagree. By the preceding discussion, if P_i tries to open a polynomial that is different from f, at least $t + 1$ players would disagree.

Note that we do not rely on Lagrange interpolation or any efficient method for decoding in the presence of errors: we rely on the committer to supply the correct polynomial, and we are fine as long as it is uniquely defined.

EXERCISE 5.3 This exercises asks you to realize how minimal-distance decoding can be used to make a noisy channel reliable. Assume that we have a sender S and a receiver R that are connected by a noisy channel that allows us to transfer bit strings. The effect of the noise is that sometimes a bit sent as 0 will be received as 1, and vice versa. If the errors are probabilistic in nature and not too common, then the first step in handling them is to send long bit strings. Then, even though individual bits might flip, most of the bit string will be received correctly. The next step is then to send a redundant string such that receiving most of the string correctly will allow us to compute the original string. This exercise focuses on the second step.

Let t be some fixed parameter, let $n = 3t + 1$ and $\ell = \lceil \log_2(n) \rceil$, and let $\mathbb{F}$ be the finite field with 2^ℓ elements. This allows us to consider a bit string $m_i \in \{0, 1\}^\ell$ as an element from $\mathbb{F}$, and it allows us to consider a bit string $m \in \{0, 1\}^{(t+1)\ell}$ as an element from $\mathbb{F}^{t+1}$ as follows: split m into $t + 1$ blocks $m = (m_0, \ldots, m_t)$, each being ℓ bits long. Then consider m_i as an element from $\mathbb{F}$. Now $m \in \mathbb{F}^{t+1}$. Finally, given an element $(m_0, \ldots, m_t) \in \mathbb{F}^{t+1}$, we can define the polynomial $f_m(X) \stackrel{\text{def}}{=} \sum_{i=0}^t m_i X^i$ over $\mathbb{F}$; that is, for each bit string $m \in \{0, 1\}^{(t+1)\ell}$, we have a unique polynomial $f_m(X)$ of degree at most t, and for each polynomial $f(X)$ of degree at most t, we have a bit string $m \in \{0, 1\}^{(t+1)\ell}$. To send a bit string from $\{0, 1\}^{(t+1)\ell}$, we can hence focus on sending a polynomial of degree at most t.

Show that when S is given a bit string $m \in \{0, 1\}^{(t+1)\ell}$, it can send a bit string $c \in \{0, 1\}^{n\ell}$ to R that allows R to recover m even if up to t of the bits of c are flipped during transmission.

A Perfect Commitment Protocol

Based on the preceding observation, what we need is a protocol ensuring that all honest parties end up holding consistent shares of some value, of course, while preserving privacy if the committer is (remains) honest. The idea for ensuring consistent behavior is to have the committer P_i not only secret share the value he or she commits to but also distribute some extra "redundant" information that the other players can check.

Redundant Sharing Using Bivariate Polynomials

To do a redundant sharing, P_i chooses a polynomial in two variables; that is,

$$f_a(X, Y) = \sum_{\sigma, \tau = 0}^t \alpha_{\sigma, \tau} X^\sigma Y^\tau$$

where the $\alpha_{\sigma,\tau}$ are random, subject to two constraints: First, $\alpha_{0,0} = a$ or, put differently, $f_a(0,0) = a$. Second, the polynomial is *symmetric*; that is, $\alpha_{\sigma,\tau} = \alpha_{\tau,\sigma}$. The committer then will send a polynomial in one variable to each player P_k, namely,

$$f_k(X) = f_a(X,k) = \sum_{\sigma=0}^{t} \left(\sum_{\tau=0}^{t} \alpha_{\sigma,\tau} k^{\tau} \right) X^{\sigma},$$

where by sending a polynomial we simply mean sending its coefficients.

Interpretation in Terms of Standard Secret Sharing

Let us first explain how this connects to the more standard form of secret sharing we have seen before: consider the polynomial

$$g_a(X) = f_a(X,0) = \sum_{\sigma=0}^{t} \alpha_{\sigma,0} X^{\sigma}$$

which is clearly a polynomial of degree at most t such that $g_a(0) = a$. Furthermore, because f_a is symmetric, we have $g_a(k) = f_a(k,0) = f_a(0,k) = f_k(0)$. In other words, by distributing the information we described, the committer has in particular secret shared a in the standard way, using the polynomial $g_a(X)$, where the kth share is $f_k(0)$.

Furthermore, the coefficients in $f_k(X)$ are $c_{\sigma} = \sum_{\tau=0}^{t} \alpha_{\sigma,\tau} k^{\tau}$, for $\sigma = 0, \ldots, t$. Note that each c_{σ} can be interpreted as the value of a degree t polynomial evaluated at point k, that is, the polynomial with coefficients $\alpha_{\sigma,0}, \ldots, \alpha_{\sigma,t}$. Thus each c_{σ} is in fact also a share of a secret, namely, the degree 0 coefficient $\alpha_{\sigma,0}$. Note that $\alpha_{\sigma,0}$ is also a coefficient in $g_a(X)$.

This means that the process of choosing $f_a(X,Y)$ and sending $f_k(X)$ to P_k also can be interpreted as follows: first, secret share a in the standard way using polynomial $g_a(X)$, and then secret share all the coefficients in $g_a(X)$, also in the standard way, and send shares to the respective players. To make this be exactly equivalent to what we described earlier, the polynomials for the last step must be chosen such that their coefficients satisfy the symmetry condition. One might think that this could hurt privacy because then coefficients are not independent. But this is not the case, as we show next.

Consistency Check

The key to checking consistency of the information P_i distributes is to observe that by the symmetry of $f_a(X,Y)$, we have for any two players P_k, P_j that

$$f_k(j) = f_a(j,k) = f_a(k,j) = f_j(k)$$

The idea for the protocol is then as follows: after each player P_k has received $f_k(X)$, he or she will check with each other player P_j whether it is the case that $f_k(j) = f_j(k)$. If all pairwise checks go through for a set of at least $t+1$ honest players, their information is sufficient to determine a polynomial of degree at most t on which all honest players eventually agree. Of course, the protocol has to take care of what should happen if the checks are not satisfied; here the idea is to ask P_i to help resolve any conflicts.

The complete protocol for implementing the commit command from $F_{\text{COM-SIMPLE}}$ is described in Protocol Commit. The implementation of the other commands is specified in Protocol Perfect-Com-Simple.

Protocol Commit

1. On input $(\texttt{commit}, i, cid, a)$, P_i samples a bivariate symmetric polynomial $f_a(X, Y)$ of degree at most t such that $f_a(0,0) = a$. He or she sends the polynomial $f_k(X) = f_a(X, k)$ to each P_k (therefore P_k also learns $\beta_k = f_k(0)$).

2. Each P_j computes $\beta_{kj} = f_j(k)$ and sends β_{kj} to each P_k.

3. Each P_k checks that $\deg(f_k) \leq t$ and that $\beta_{kj} = f_k(j)$, for $j = 1, \ldots, n$. If so, he or she broadcasts $\texttt{success}$. Otherwise, he or she broadcasts $(\texttt{dispute}, k, j)$ for each inconsistency.

4. For each dispute reported in the preceding step, P_i broadcasts the correct value of β_{kj}.

5. If any P_k finds a disagreement between what P_i has broadcast and what he or she received privately from P_i, he or she knows that P_i is corrupt and broadcasts $(\texttt{accuse}, k)$.

6. For any accusation from P_k in the preceding step, P_i broadcasts $f_k(X)$.

7. If any P_k finds a new disagreement between what P_i has now broadcast and what he or she received privately from P_i, he or she knows P_i is corrupt and broadcasts $(\texttt{accuse}, k)$.

8. If the information broadcast by P_i is not consistent, or if more than t players have accused P_i, players output $\texttt{fail}$. Otherwise, players who accused P_i and had a new polynomial $f_k(X)$ broadcast will accept it as their polynomial. All others keep the polynomial they received in the first step. Now each P_k outputs $\texttt{success}$ and stores $(cid, i, \beta_k = f_k(0))$. In addition, P_i stores the polynomial $g_a(X) = f_a(X, 0)$.

Protocol Perfect-Com-Simple

Commit: See Protocol Commit.

Public commit. On input $(\texttt{pubcommit}, i, cid, a)$, a party P_k lets $a_k = a$ (this is a share of the polynomial $a(X) = a$), outputs $(\texttt{pubcommit}, i, cid, \texttt{success})$, and stores (cid, i, a_k).

Open. On input $(\texttt{open}, i, cid)$ where some $(cid, i, a(X))$ is stored, the party P_i broadcasts $(cid, i, a(X))$. On input $(\texttt{open}, i, cid)$ where some (cid, i, a_k) is stored, a party $P_k \neq P_i$ broadcasts (cid, i, a_k). If $\deg(a(X)) \leq t$ and $a_k = a(k)$ for at least $n - t$ parties, then all parties output $(\texttt{open}, i, cid, a(0))$. Otherwise, they output $(\texttt{open}, i, cid, \texttt{fail})$.

Designated open. As earlier, but the polynomial and the shares are only sent to P_j. If P_j rejects the opening, it broadcasts a public complaint, and P_i must then do a normal opening. If this one fails too, all parties output $\texttt{fail}$.

Add. On input $(\texttt{add}, i, cid_1, cid_2, cid_3)$, where some $(i, cid_1, a(X))$ and $(i, cid_2, b(X))$ are stored, the party P_i stores $(i, cid_3, a(X) + b(X))$ and outputs $(\texttt{add}, i, cid_1, cid_2, cid_3, \texttt{success})$. On input $(\texttt{add}, i, cid_1, cid_2, cid_3)$, where some (i, cid_1, a_k) and (i, cid_2, b_k) are stored, a party $P_k \neq P_i$ stores $(i, cid_3, a_k + b_k)$ and outputs $(\texttt{add}, i, cid_1, cid_2, cid_3, \texttt{success})$.

Multiplication by constant. On input $(\texttt{mult}, i, \alpha, cid_2, cid_3)$, where some $(i, cid_2, b(X))$ is stored, the party P_i stores $(i, cid_3, \alpha b(X))$ and outputs $(\texttt{mult}, i, \alpha, cid_2, cid_3, \texttt{success})$. On input $(\texttt{mult}, i, \alpha, cid_2, cid_3)$, where some (i, cid_2, b_k) is stored, a party $P_k \neq P_i$ stores $(i, cid_3, \alpha b_k)$ and outputs $(\texttt{mult}, i, \alpha, cid_2, cid_3, \texttt{success})$.

Before arguing the security of the protocols, we show two simple results:

LEMMA 5.4 *If P_i remains honest throughout Protocol Commit, the view of any t corrupted players is independent of the committed value a, and all players who are honest at the end of the protocol will output shares consistent with a and the polynomial $g_a(X)$ that P_i distributed.*

Proof We first argue that the information revealed in the first step is independent of a: by Lagrange interpolation, let $h(X)$ be a polynomial of degree at most t such that $h(0) = 1$ and $h(k) = 0$ for all corrupt P_k. Then $h(X)h(Y)$ is a symmetric polynomial with value 1 in $(0,0)$. Suppose that P_i used polynomial $f_a(X,Y)$. Let $f_0(X,Y) = f_a(X,Y) - ah(X)h(Y)$. Clearly, $f_0(0,0) = 0$, and each corrupt P_k will receive the same information whether f_a or f_0 is used. Moreover, adding $-ah(X)h(Y)$ is a bijection between symmetric polynomials consistent with a and those consistent with 0. Since P_i chooses a uniformly random polynomial consistent with a, it follows that any t corrupt players in step 1 see the same distribution regardless of a, namely, the one that follows from sharing 0.

In the following steps, one easily sees that the set of corrupt players is told nothing they did not already know: there can be no dispute unless at least one of P_j, P_k is corrupt, so they already know all β_{kj} broadcast. Likewise, only a corrupt P_k will accuse an honest P_i, so the corrupt players already know all polynomials and values broadcast. The fact that an honest player never accuses P_i also means that honest players will always output the shares they got in the first step. This implies the last conclusion of the lemma because $g_a(k) = f_a(k,0) = f_a(0,k) = f_k(0) = \beta_k$ and $g_a(0) = f_a(0,0) = a$. ∎

LEMMA 5.5 *If $t < n/3$, then no matter how corrupt players behave in Protocol Commit, players who are honest at the end of the protocol will all output* fail *or will output a set of shares in some value a' all consistent with a polynomial $g_{a'}(X)$ of degree at most t.*

Proof The decision to output fail is based on public information, so it is clear that players who remain honest will either all output fail or all output some value, so assume that the latter case occurs. This means that at least $n - t$ players did not accuse P_i, and hence by assumption in the lemma, at least $n - 2t \geq t + 1$ players who remained honest did not accuse P_i. Let S be the set of indices of such honest players, and consider an honest P_j. We claim that for every $k \in S$ with P_k holding polynomial $f_k(X)$, we have that the β_{kj} that follows from the polynomial $f_j(X)$ held by P_j at the end satisfies

$$f_k(j) = \beta_{kj}$$

We argue this as follows: if P_j had a new polynomial broadcast for him or her in step 6, then he or she keeps that one, and the claim is true because otherwise P_k would have accused in step 7, and then we would not have that $k \in S$. However, suppose that no new values were broadcast for P_j. Then he or she keeps the values he or she was given in the step 1, as does P_k, and we can also assume that neither P_j nor P_k accused in step 5. But our claim holds for the values sent in step 1 because if not, a (dispute,k,j) would have been reported, and either P_j or P_k would have accused P_i, and by assumption, this did not happen.

Now let $(r_k)_{k \in S}$ be the recombination vector for reconstructing a secret from shares of players in S. That is, for any polynomial f of degree at most t, we have $f(0) = \sum_{k \in S} r_k f(k)$; such a vector exists because $|S| \geq t + 1$.

Now define the polynomial $g_{a'}(X)$ as

$$g_{a'}(X) = \sum_{k \in S} r_k f_k(X)$$

and set $a' = g_{a'}(0)$. Since an honest P_j outputs β_j, we see that in order to show the lemma, we need to show that $g_{a'}(j) = \beta_j$ for all honest P_j. Recall that P_j computes β_{kj} as $\beta_{kj} = f_j(k)$.

Now, by the preceding claim, we can compute as follows:

$$g_{a'}(j) = \sum_{k \in S} r_k f_k(j) = \sum_{k \in S} r_k \beta_{k,j} = \sum_{k \in S} r_k f_j(k) = f_j(0) = \beta_j$$

■

From the preceding lemmas, we get the following theorem:

THEOREM 5.6 $\pi_{PERFECT\text{-}COM\text{-}SIMPLE} \diamond F_{SC}$ *implements* $F_{COM\text{-}SIMPLE}$ *in* $\text{Env}^{t,\text{sync}}$ *with perfect security for all* $t < n/3$.

Proof A simulator for the case of static corruption is given as $S_{PERFECT\text{-}COM\text{-}SIMPLE}$. We argue that this is a perfect simulator: all commit commands are simulated perfectly; this follows from Lemma 5.4 if the committer is honest and from the fact that we just follow the protocol if the committer is corrupt. Furthermore, each open command will reveal the shares the environment already knew in case the committer is corrupt (note that the existence of these shares for all honest players is guaranteed by Lemma 5.5). If the committer is honest, it will be a set of shares consistent with what the corrupt players have and the opened value. This holds in both the real protocol and the simulation.

It follows that the views of corrupt players are identically distributed in the real protocol and in the execution, so the only way the environment can distinguish is if the input-output behavior of honest players is different in the simulation and in the real execution. This cannot happen for an honest committer because the simulator gets the correct values to open and the open protocol always succeeds for an honest committer. It cannot happen for a corrupt committer either: if the open protocol fails, the simulator makes the functionality fail as well, and if it succeeds, the opened value must be the one that follows from earlier committed values and therefore equals the one output by the functionality. This is so because Lemma 5.5 guarantees that all honest players have consistent shares of each committed value; therefore, by our discussion on minimal-distance decoding, an incorrect polynomial will disagree with at least $t + 1$ honest players, and the opening will fail.

Adaptive Corruption

To simulate for adaptive corruption, we start $S_{PERFECT\text{-}COM\text{-}SIMPLE}$ in the state where all players are honest. Recall that $S_{PERFECT\text{-}COM\text{-}SIMPLE}$ works with virtual players $\bar{P}_i$. When we get to a point where a new player P is corrupted, we corrupt P on $F_{COM\text{-}SIMPLE}$ and get the set of values he or she committed to from its leakage port. Using these data, we then adjust (if needed) the views of the virtual players so that they are consistent with the new values we learned and everything the environment has seen so far. We give the view of $\bar{P}$ to the environment and continue the simulation following the algorithm of $S_{PERFECT\text{-}COM\text{-}SIMPLE}$, giving it the adjusted state of the virtual players (except for that of P, who is now corrupt).

We will see that the view of P that we give to the environment always has exactly the correct distribution, and furthermore, the state of virtual players is distributed exactly as if we had run $S_{PERFECT\text{-}COM\text{-}SIMPLE}$ with P being corrupt from the start but where the environment let it behave honestly up to this point. Therefore, it follows from the result for static corruption that the simulation after the corruption is perfect.

Agent $\mathcal{S}_{\text{PERFECT-COM-SIMPLE}}$

Simulator for $\pi_{\text{PERFECT-COM-SIMPLE}}$ for the case of static corruption.

Initialize. In the preamble, the environment $\mathcal{Z}$ specifies the set C of actively corrupted players. Then the simulator sets up an internal copy of F_{SC} where it corrupts players in C and connects the special ports of F_{SC} to $\mathcal{Z}$. It also corrupts C on $\mathsf{F}_{\text{COM-SIMPLE}}$. Finally, it sets up a copy of every honest player. These "virtual" players are called $\bar{\mathsf{P}}_i, \bar{\mathsf{P}}_k$ and $\bar{\mathsf{P}}_j$; their internal variables will be called $\bar{a}, \bar{\beta}_k$, and so on. The basic idea is to let the virtual players execute the protocol with the corrupt players (controlled by $\mathcal{Z}$), letting the virtual players commit to dummy values. Below we describe in more detail how this is done for each command.

For every committed value a (dummy or not), the simulator stores a polynomial $f_a(X, Y)$ determining the complete set of shares of a held by the (corrupt and virtual) players.

For every honest player P_i, we maintain an invariant. Note that every value b that P_i opened via an **open** command is a linear combination of all his or her committed values so far $a_1, \ldots, a_T$: $b = \gamma_1 a_1 + \cdots + \gamma_T a_T$, where the γ_is are public because they follow from the executed sequence of **add** and **mult** commands. The invariant now is that the set of "committed" dummy values $\{\bar{a}_j\}$ held by $\bar{\mathsf{P}}_i$ is a random set of values consistent with every b that has been opened; that is, it holds that $b = \gamma_1 \bar{a}_1 + \cdots + \gamma_T \bar{a}_T$, and furthermore, each polynomial $f_{\bar{a}_j}$ held by the virtual player is a random symmetric polynomial of degree at most t that is consistent with $\bar{a}_j$ and the shares held by corrupt players.

Commit. If P_i is honest, execute the **commit** protocol giving a random $\bar{a}$ as input to $\bar{\mathsf{P}}_i$. This maintains the invariant because no opened value depends on the value we commit now. The simulator stores the polynomial $f_{\bar{a}}$ used by $\bar{\mathsf{P}}_i$. If P_i is corrupt, we execute the **commit** protocol; if it fails, we make $\mathsf{F}_{\text{COM-SIMPLE}}$ fail as well; otherwise, we use Lemma 5.5 to compute the committed value a' and give this as input to $\mathsf{F}_{\text{COM-SIMPLE}}$. The simulator also stores the polynomial $g_{a'}(X)$ guaranteed by the lemma.

Add, mult. There is no communication to simulate; we just let the virtual players do the local computation prescribed in the protocol.

Open. If the committer is honest, we get the value z to be revealed from leakage of $\mathsf{F}_{\text{COM-SIMPLE}}$. We now adjust the views of the virtual players so that they are consistent with the value z, and hence the invariant is maintained. We do this by considering all equations of form $b = \gamma_1 a_1 + \cdots + \gamma_T a_T$ for revealed values b (including the new equation for z) and set $(\bar{a}_1, \ldots, \bar{a}_t)$ to be a random solution to this system of equations. Note that a solution must exist, namely, $(\bar{a}_1, \ldots, \bar{a}_t) = (a_1, \ldots, a_t)$, the set of values actually input by $\mathcal{Z}$. The set of committed values held by the virtual player is set to be the new solution we found, and we adjust each polynomial $f_{\bar{a}_j}(X, Y)$ so that the invariant is maintained. This is done by computing the new polynomial as $f_{\bar{a}_{j,new}}(X, Y) = f_{\bar{a}_{j,old}}(X, Y) + (\bar{a}_{j,new} - \bar{a}_{j,old})h(X)h(Y)$, where h is a degree at most t polynomial that is 1 in 0 and 0 in points of corrupt players. This always works because there are at most t corrupt players. Now all virtual players are still in a consistent state, and we can execute the **open** protocol. If the committer is corrupt, we simply execute the **open** protocol; if it fails, we make $\mathsf{F}_{\text{COM-SIMPLE}}$ fail as well.

We now describe the procedure for adjusting views: we will be given every value committed by P. For every such value a, the state of $\mathcal{S}_{\text{PERFECT-COM-SIMPLE}}$ contains a polynomial $f_{\bar{a}}(X, Y)$ that is part of its state for the virtual player $\bar{\mathsf{P}}$. We now replace $f_{\bar{a}}(X, Y)$ by $f_{\bar{a}}(X, Y) + (a - \bar{a})h(X)h(Y)$, where $h(\cdot)$ is a polynomial that is 1 in 0 and 0 in all points of players that were corrupted earlier, and we adjust the view of all virtual players accordingly. By the invariant of $\mathcal{S}_{\text{PERFECT-COM-SIMPLE}}$, $f_{\bar{a}}(X, Y)$ is a random polynomial consistent with $\bar{a}$ and the views of corrupt players. The adjustment we do will maintain this but now with $\bar{a}$ replaced by a.　　　　　　　　　　　　　　　　　　　　　　　　　　　■

5.4.1 Commitments in Case of Honest Majority

In this section we present a protocol that implements $F_{\text{COM-SIMPLE}}$ with statistical security for the case of honest majority, that is, when $t < n/2$. We will use the same idea as before of committing by secret sharing the value to which to commit. But the problem we face is that even if we force the committer to give us consistent shares, the resulting commitment will not be binding.

The problem is that there may only be $t + 1$ honest players. Even if they all have consistent shares, the adversary can easily cook up a different polynomial that is consistent with t of these players and any value of the secret he or she desires. If he or she opens such a value using the open protocol we have seen, only one honest player would disagree, and this may as well be a corrupt player who is complaining for no good reason.

Agent F_{ICSIG}

Ideal functionality for IC signatures. Each instance of this functionality provides service to two special players P_D and P_{INT}. The functionality does a complete breakdown if both are corrupt or if inputs from honest players are not given as specified. Whenever a command is received, the functionality leaks the name of the command and whatever public input is given. Output from a command is sent once the round in which to deliver is specified on the influence port.

Sign. This command is executed if in some round player P_D sends (sign, sid, a) and in addition all honest players send $(\text{sign}, sid, ?)$. In this case, F_{ICSIG} records the pair (sid, a). Here sid is just an identifier, and a is the value that is "signed."[a] The output to all parties is $(\text{sign}, sid, \text{success})$; in addition, a is sent to P_{INT}.

Reveal. This command is executed if in some round all honest players send (reveal, sid) and some (sid, a) is stored. The output to all parties is (reveal, sid, a).

If P_{INT} is corrupted and does not input (reveal, sid), then $(\text{reveal}, sid, \text{fail})$ is output to all parties.

Designated reveal. This command is executed if in some round all honest players send (reveal, j, sid) and some (sid, a) is stored. The command behaves exactly as reveal, except that only P_j gets output.

Add. This command is executed if in some round all honest players send $(\text{add}, sid_1, sid_2, sid_3)$ and some (sid_1, a_1) and some (sid_2, a_2) are stored. As a result, F_{ICSIG} stores $(sid_3, a_1 + a_2)$. The output to all parties is $(\text{add}, sid_1, sid_2, sid_3, \text{success})$.

Mult by constant. This command is executed if in some round all honest players send $(\text{mult}, c, sid_2, sid_3)$ and $c \in \mathbb{F}$ and some (i, sid_2, a_2) is stored. As a result, F_{ICSIG} stores (i, sid_3, ca_2). The output to all parties is $(\text{mult}, c, sid_2, sid_3, \text{success})$.

[a] We require that all honest players agree to the fact that a value should be signed because an implementation will require the active participation of all honest players.

The problem could be solved if the unhappy honest player could *prove* that his or her inconsistent share was in fact what he or she received from the committer. This would require something similar to a signature scheme.

Protocol ICSign

Initialize. This step is carried out before any commands are executed. For $i = 1, \ldots, n$, P_D chooses $\alpha_i \in \mathbb{F}$ at random and sends α_i to P_i; both players store the value.

Sign. On input $(\texttt{sign}, sid, a)$ to P_D and $(\texttt{sign}, sid, ?)$ to other players, do the following: for $i = 1, \ldots, n$, P_D chooses $\beta_{i,a} \in \mathbb{F}$ at random and sets $K_{i,a} = (\alpha_i, \beta_{i,a})$. He or she sends $\beta_{i,a}$ to P_i and $a, \{m_{i,a} = \mathrm{MAC}_{K_{i,a}}(a)\}_{i=1,\ldots,n}$ to P_{INT}. We now check that P_D has sent correctly formed data. First, P_D chooses $a' \in \mathbb{F}$ and $\beta_{i,a'} \in \mathbb{F}$ at random, sets $K_{i,a'} = (\alpha_i, \beta_{i,a'})$, and sends $\beta_{i,a'}$ to P_i. He or she also sends $a', \{m_{i,a'} = \mathrm{MAC}_{K_{i,a'}}(a')\}_{i=1,\ldots,n}$ to P_{INT}. P_{INT} chooses $e \in \mathbb{F}$ at random and broadcasts $e, a' + ea$.

Then do the following loop for $i = 1, \ldots, n$:

1. P_{INT} broadcasts $m_{i,a'} + em_{i,a} = \mathrm{MAC}_{K_{i,a'} + eK_{i,a}}(a' + ea)$.

2. P_D checks the broadcast message from P_{INT}. If it is correct; he or she broadcasts `accept`; otherwise, he or she broadcasts "P_{INT} is corrupt," and we exit the loop.

3. P_i checks that $m_{i,a'} + em_{i,a} = \mathrm{MAC}_{K_{i,a'} + eK_{i,a}}(a' + ea)$ and broadcasts `accept` or `reject` accordingly. P_D checks that P_i acted correctly; if so, he or she broadcasts `accept`; otherwise, he or she broadcasts "P_i is corrupt: $K_{i,a}$." This broadcasted key value will be used in the following, and P_{INT} adjusts his or her values so that it holds that $m_{i,a} = \mathrm{MAC}_{K_{i,a}}(a)$. If P_i said `reject` and P_D said `accept`, we exit the loop (this can only happen if P_D is corrupt).

If this loop were terminated by an exit, P_D would broadcast $a, \{m_{i,a}\}_{i=1,\ldots,n}$. These values will be used in the following, and each P_i adjusts his or her $\beta_{i,a}$ value so that it holds that $m_{i,a} = \mathrm{MAC}_{K_{i,a}}(a)$.

P_{INT} outputs $(\texttt{sign}, sid, a, \texttt{success})$ where he or she uses the last value for a that he or she received from P_D and stores $a, \{m_{i,a}\}_{i=1,\ldots,n}$ under sid. Each P_i outputs $(\texttt{sign}, sid, \texttt{success})$ and stores $K_{i,a}$ under sid.

(Designated) reveal. On input $(\texttt{reveal}, sid)$ to all players, P_{INT} broadcasts $a, \{m_{i,a}\}_{i=1,\ldots,n}$ as stored under sid. Each P_i retrieves $K_{i,a}$ stored under sid and checks that $m_{i,a} = \mathrm{MAC}_{K_{i,a}}(a)$. If this holds, he or she outputs $(\texttt{reveal}, sid, a)$; otherwise, he or she outputs $(\texttt{reveal}, sid, \texttt{fail})$. If the command was designated $(\texttt{reveal}, j, sid)$, P_{INT} only sends $a, m_{j,a}$ to P_j, who checks the MAC as in the normal `reveal` command.

Add. On input $(\texttt{add}, sid_1, sid_2, sid_3)$ to all players, P_{INT} retrieves the values $(a_1, m_{1,a_1}, \ldots, m_{n,a_1}), (a_2, m_{1,a_2}, \ldots, m_{n,a_2})$ that were stored under sid_1, sid_2 and stores $(a_1 + a_2, m_{1,a_1} + m_{1,a_2}, \ldots, m_{n,a_1} + m_{n,a_2})$ under sid_3. Each P_i retrieves the values $\beta_{i,a_1}, \beta_{i,a_2}$ stored under sid_1, sid_2 and stores $\beta_{i,a_1} + \beta_{i,a_2}$ under sid_3. All players output $(\texttt{add}, sid_1, sid_3, sid_3, \texttt{success})$.

Multiplication by constant. On input $(\texttt{mult}, c, sid_2, sid_3)$ to all players, P_{INT} retrieves the values $(a_2, m_{1,a_2}, \ldots, m_{n,a_2})$ that were stored under sid_2 and stores $(c \cdot a_2, c \cdot m_{1,a_2}, \ldots, c \cdot m_{n,a_2})$ under sid_3. Each P_i retrieves the value β_{i,a_2} stored under sid_2 and stores $c \cdot \beta_{i,a_2}$ under sid_3. All players output $(\texttt{mult}, c, sid_2, sid_3, \texttt{success})$.

IC Signatures

We therefore begin with an important tool known as *information checking* or *IC signatures*. The idea is to provide a functionality similar to digital signatures but with information-theoretic security. The basic version of this idea involves two players that we call P_D and P_{INT} for dealer and intermediary. The basic idea is that P_D can give a secret message s to P_{INT}, and at any later time, P_{INT} can choose to reveal s and prove to the other players that s really was the value he or she got from P_D. We specify what we want more formally as a functionality F_{ICSIG}. The main properties we get are that if both P_D and P_{INT} are honest, then s will always be successfully revealed, but no corrupt player knows s before it is revealed. If P_{INT} is corrupt (but P_D is honest), he or she can refuse to reveal s but cannot reveal a wrong value successfully. Finally, if P_D is corrupt (but P_{INT} is honest), it will still be possible for P_{INT} to convince the other players about the correct value of s. In addition, we want that linear operations can be done on signed values so that if P_D has given $a, b \in \mathbb{F}$ to P_{INT}, then P_{INT} can later convince everyone about the correct value of $ca + b$ for a publicly known constant c.

The protocol for implementing F_{ICSIG} is based on the well-known notion of unconditionally secure message authentication codes (MACs). Such a MAC uses a key K, a random pair $K = (\alpha, \beta) \in \mathbb{F}^2$, and the authentication code for a value $a \in \mathbb{F}$ that is $MAC_K(a) = \alpha a + \beta$.

We will apply the MACs by having P_D give a key $K_{i,a} = (\alpha_i, \beta_{i,a})$ to each P_i and a set of values $a, MAC_{K_{i,a}}(a), i = 1, \ldots, n$, to P_{INT}. The idea is to use the MACs to prevent P_{INT} from lying about a when he or she broadcasts it. Given a and $K_{i,a}$, each P_i can compute the MAC value he or she expects to see and compare it with the MAC sent by P_{INT}.

It will be very important in the following that if we keep α constant over several different MAC keys, then one can add two MACs and get a valid authentication code for the sum of the two corresponding messages. More concretely, two keys $K = (\alpha, \beta)$ and $K' = (\alpha', \beta')$ are said to be *consistent* if $\alpha = \alpha'$. For consistent keys, we define $K + K' = (\alpha, \beta + \beta')$; it is then trivial to verify that $MAC_K(a) + MAC_{K'}(a') = MAC_{K+K'}(a + a')$.

If P_{INT} is corrupt (but P_D is honest), it is also easy to see (as detailed in the following proof) that P_{INT} will be able to lie about the values he or she was given (or about any linear combination of them) with probability at most $1/|\mathbb{F}|$. Also, a key clearly reveals no information on the authenticated value. However, if P_D is corrupt (but P_{INT} is honest), he or she may not give consistent information to players, so the protocol must do an interactive verification when a value is signed in order to check this.

THEOREM 5.7 $\pi_{ICSIG} \diamond F_{SC}$ *implements* F_{ICSIG} *in* $\mathrm{Env}^{t,\mathrm{sync}}$ *with statistical security for all* $t < n$.

Proof As usual, we construct a simulator S_{ICSIG} for the protocol. The simulator shown deals with static corruption and considers separately the three cases where both P_D and P_{INT} are honest, P_D is corrupt, and P_{INT} is corrupt. At the same time, any number of other players may be corrupt. If P_D and P_{INT} are both corrupt, there is nothing to show because the functionality does a complete breakdown in that case. We show next how to deal with adaptive corruption, but first we argue why the simulation is statistically close to a real execution.

Both P_D and P_{INT} Are Honest

In this case, S_{ICSIG} runs the protocol on behalf of the honest players using random dummy inputs. Note that this also involves generating keys to be held by each player P_i (whether he or she is corrupt or not). Now, by the random choice of a', the view of the sign protocol is independent of the signed values, so the simulation of this part is perfect. So is the simulation

Agent $\mathcal{S}_{\text{ICSIG}}$

Simulator for π_{ICSIG} for the case of static corruption.

Initialize. In the preamble, the environment $\mathcal{Z}$ specifies the set C of actively corrupted players. Then the simulator sets up an internal copy of F_{SC}, where it corrupts players in C and connects the special ports of F_{SC} to $\mathcal{Z}$. It also corrupts C on $\mathsf{F}_{\text{ICSIG}}$. Finally, it sets up a copy of every honest player. These "virtual" players are called $\bar{\mathsf{P}}_i, \bar{\mathsf{P}}_D$, and $\bar{\mathsf{P}}_{INT}$. Their internal variables will be called $\bar{a}, \bar{a}'$, and so on. The basic idea is to let the virtual players execute the protocol with the corrupt players (controlled by $\mathcal{Z}$). Below, we describe in more detail how this is done for each command.

We consider three "modes": (1) both P_D and P_{INT} are honest, (2) P_D is corrupt, and (3) P_{INT} is corrupt. If both P_D and P_{INT} are corrupt, simulation becomes trivial because $\mathsf{F}_{\text{ICSIG}}$ does a complete breakdown in that case.

In mode 1, we maintain an invariant: Note that every value b that is revealed in a `reveal` command is a linear combination of all signed values so far $a_1, \ldots, a_t$: $b = \gamma_1 a_1 + \cdots + \gamma_t a_t$, where the γ_is are public because they follow from the executed sequence of `add` and `mult` commands. The invariant now is that the set of "signed" values $\{\bar{a}_j\}$ held by $\bar{\mathsf{P}}_D$ is a random set of values consistent with every b that has been revealed; that is, it holds that $b = \gamma_1 \bar{a}_1 + \ldots + \gamma_t \bar{a}_t$.

Sign. In mode 1, execute the `sign` protocol giving a random $\bar{a}$ as input to $\bar{\mathsf{P}}_D$. This maintains the invariant because, no revealed value depends on the input we sign now. In mode 2, we get a value a that the corrupt P_D sends via F_{SC}. We give a as input to $\mathsf{F}_{\text{ICSIG}}$ on behalf of P_D and then execute the `sign` protocol. In mode 3, we get a value a from leakage of $\mathsf{F}_{\text{ICSIG}}$ (since P_{INT} is corrupt), and we execute the `sign` protocol giving a as input to $\bar{\mathsf{P}}_D$.

Add, mult. There is no communication to simulate; we just let the virtual players do the local computation prescribed in the protocol.

(Designated) reveal. For a public `reveal` in mode 1, we get the value z to be revealed from leakage of $\mathsf{F}_{\text{ICSIG}}$. We now adjust the views of the virtual players so that they are consistent with the value z, and hence the invariant is maintained. We do this by considering all equations of form $b = \gamma_1 a_1 + \cdots + \gamma_t a_t$ for revealed values b (including z) and set $(\bar{a}_1, \ldots, \bar{a}_t)$ to be a random solution to this system of equations. Note that a solution must exist, namely, $(\bar{a}_1, \ldots, \bar{a}_t) = (a_1, \ldots, a_t)$, the set of values actually input by $\mathcal{Z}$. If this requires a previous value of $\bar{a}_j$ to be changed, we compensate for this by adjusting the value of $\bar{a}'_j$ (and hence the MAC on $\bar{a}'_j$) such that all broadcasted values remain the same. Now all virtual players are still in a consistent state, and we can execute the `reveal` command. The same is done for a designated reveal where the receiver is corrupt. If the receiver is honest, the corrupt players see no communication; the simulator just executes the designated `reveal` internally to keep a consistent state.

In modes 2 and 3, we have executed the protocol with the correct signed values, and we therefore execute the `reveal` or `designated reveal` protocol.

of the `add` and `mult` commands because no communication is done. Furthermore, when a value b is opened, the simulator adjusts the views of its virtual players so that they are consistent with b. This includes computing from $K_{i,b}$ a MAC on b to show to each P_i. Since the key held by P_i has the correct distribution and the MAC follows deterministically from b and $K_{i,b}$, the joint distribution of everything seen by $\mathcal{Z}$ in the `reveal` command is correct.

P_{INT} Is Corrupt

In this case, $\mathcal{S}_{\texttt{ICSIG}}$ knows each a to be signed from the start and now simulates by simply following the protocol. Therefore, the only way in which the simulation can deviate from the real execution comes from the fact that in the simulation, when a value is revealed, honest players get the value from the functionality, which, by definition, always reveals the value sent by P_D, whereas this may not be the case in the real protocol. It *is* the case except with negligible probability, however: if P_{INT} is about to reveal a value a to honest player P_i, he or she knows the correct MAC $m_{i,a} = \alpha_i a + \beta_{i,a}$. This reveals no information on α_i by random choice of $\beta_{i,a}$, and neither does any other MACs known to P_{INT} by the same argument. Now if P_{INT} produces $a' \neq a$ and $m_{i,a'}$ that P_i would accept, we know that $m_{i,a} = \alpha_i a + \beta_{i,a}$ and $m_{i,a'} = \alpha_i a' + \beta_{i,a}$. Subtracting one equation from the other, we obtain $\alpha_i = (m_{i,a} - m_{i,a'})/(a - a')$, which makes sense because $a - a' \neq 0$. In other words, P_{INT} must guess α_i to cheat, and this can done with probability at most $1/|\mathbb{F}|$. If a MAC is rejected and the protocol continues, P_{INT} knows that a certain value is not the correct α_i. In a polynomial time protocol, though, he or she will only be able to exclude a polynomial number of values, so the probability to cheat remains negligible. The simulation is therefore statistically close in this case.

P_D Is Corrupt

In this case, $\mathcal{S}_{\texttt{ICSIG}}$ knows each a to be signed from the start and simulates by following the protocol. This means that the only way the simulation can deviate from the real protocol comes from the fact that in the simulation the functionality on a `reveal` command always reveals the value it got from P_D to the honest players. In the protocol, it may happen that the honest P_{INT} attempts to reveal the correct value but has it rejected by an honest P_i; however, this only happens with negligible probability: in the cases where in the `sign` phase P_D broadcasts a and a set of MACs or broadcasts the key for some P_i, the problem never occurs because all honest P_i are guaranteed to have data that are consistent with P_{INT}. Therefore, the only remaining case is where P_i says `accept` in the sign phase, and P_D does not claim that P_i or P_{INT} is corrupt. Now P_i only accepts if it holds that

$$m_{i,a'} + e m_{i,a} = \text{MAC}_{K_{i,a'} + e K_{i,a}}(a' + ea) = \alpha_i(a' + ea) + \beta_{i,a'} + e\beta_{i,a}$$

If P_D gave an incorrect MAC to P_{INT} in the first place, then $m_{i,a} \neq \alpha_i a + \beta_{i,a}$. This would mean that we could rearrange the preceding equation as

$$e = (\alpha_i a' + \beta_{i,a'} - m_{i,a'})/(m_{i,a} - \alpha_i a - \beta_{i,a})$$

and compute e from the values generated by P_D before e is chosen; in other words, P_D must guess e to successfully distribute inconsistent data. This happen with only negligible probability $1/|\mathbb{F}|$, and the simulation is also statistically close in this case.

Adaptive Corruption

To construct a simulator for adaptive corruption, we start $\mathcal{S}_{\texttt{ICSIG}}$ in the mode where all players are honest. Recall that $\mathcal{S}_{\texttt{ICSIG}}$ works with virtual players $\bar{P}_i, \bar{P}_D$, and $\bar{P}_{INT}$. When a new player P is corrupted, we corrupt P on $F_{\texttt{ICSIG}}$ and get some data from the leakage port of $F_{\texttt{ICSIG}}$. Using these data, we then adjust (if needed) the views of the virtual players so that they are consistent with everything the environment has seen so far, we give the view of $\bar{\mathsf{P}}$ to the environment, and we continue the simulation following the algorithm of $\mathcal{S}_{\mathtt{ICSIG}}$. If $\mathsf{P} = \mathsf{P}_D$ or P_{INT}, we switch to the simulation mode, where P_D or P_{INT} is corrupt. We will see that the view of P that we give to the environment always has exactly the correct distribution. Therefore, we can argue, as for $\mathcal{S}_{\mathtt{ICSIG}}$, that the only case where simulation and real execution differ is if a corrupt P_D or P_{INT} succeeds in cheating, which happens with negligible probability, as we saw earlier.

We now describe the procedure for adjusting views: if P is not P_D or P_{INT}, we use the view of $\bar{\mathsf{P}}$ with no change. This works because the simulator gets no new input-output information when such a player is corrupted, and the view of such a player consists of keys (that we chose with the right distribution) and possibly some revealed values and MACs that were already broadcast.

If P is not P_D or P_{INT}, we are given all values that were privately revealed to this player in the designated `reveal`. If $\mathsf{P} = \mathsf{P}_D$ or P_{INT}, we are given every signed value. In any case, we then run the procedure used by $\mathcal{S}_{\mathtt{ICSIG}}$ during the simulation of `reveal` to adjust the views of $\bar{\mathsf{P}}_D$ and $\bar{\mathsf{P}}_{INT}$ to be consistent with each value we got from $\mathsf{F}_{\mathtt{ICSIG}}$ (by doing the same as if each value was revealed). This gives a correctly distributed history for every value we consider: given the correct set of a values to sign (and random e values), we can either choose the a' values at random and compute the broadcasted values from this (this is what the real protocol does), or we can choose the broadcasted values with the correct distribution and compute matching a' values. This is what the simulation does. Both methods clearly lead to the same distribution. Note that all keys are chosen independently, and the MACs follow deterministically from keys and authenticated values. Keys and MACs therefore make no difference to this argument.

Finally, if both P_D and P_{INT} are corrupted, we do as just explained: give the views of $\bar{\mathsf{P}}_D$, and $\bar{\mathsf{P}}_{INT}$ to $\mathcal{Z}$, and let $\mathcal{Z}$ decide what happens hereafter (since $\mathsf{F}_{\mathtt{ICSIG}}$ now breaks down). ∎

A Statistically Secure Commitment Scheme

The basic idea in the implementation of $\mathsf{F}_{\mathtt{COM\text{-}SIMPLE}}$ for $t < n/2$ is to do essentially the same protocol as for $t < n/3$ but ask the committer to sign every value he or she sends to players. This actually makes the `commit` protocol simpler because accusations against the committer can be proved: the accuser can demonstrate that the message he or she claims to have received from the committer is correct, and everyone then can check that it indeed contradicts what the committer has broadcast.

Protocol Statistical Commit and Protocol Com-Simple specify the solution in detail. The protocols assume access to $\mathsf{F}_{\mathtt{ICSIG}}$.

The following theorem is easy to show using the same principles we have seen many times by now. We leave the details to the reader.

THEOREM 5.8 $\pi_{COM\text{-}SIMPLE} \diamond \pi_{ICSIG} \diamond \mathsf{F}_{SC}$ *implements* $\mathsf{F}_{COM\text{-}SIMPLE}$ *in* $\mathrm{Env}^{t,sync}$ *with statistical security for all* $t < n/2$.

5.5 Final Results and Optimality of Corruption Bounds

In this section we put together all the results we have seen in this chapter and show that the resulting bounds on the number of actively corrupted parties we can tolerate with our

---

Protocol Statistical Commit

1. On input $(\mathtt{commit}, i, cid, a)$, P_i samples a bivariate symmetric polynomial $f_a(X, Y)$ of degree at most t such that $f_a(0,0) = a$. For each coefficient of the polynomial $f_k(X) = f_a(X, k)$, players call $\mathtt{sign}$ on F_{ICSIG} with $P_D = P_i, P_{INT} = P_k$, and the coefficient being the value to sign. This means that P_k learns all the coefficients, including $\beta_k = f_k(0)$.

2. Each P_j computes $\beta_{kj} = f_j(k)$ and sends β_{kj} to each P_k.

3. Each P_k checks that $\beta_{kj} = f_k(j)$, for $j = 1, \ldots, n$. If so, he or she broadcasts $\mathtt{success}$. Otherwise, he or she broadcasts $(\mathtt{dispute}, k, j)$ for each inconsistency.

4. For each dispute reported in the preceding step, P_i broadcasts the correct value of β_{kj}.

5. If any P_k finds a disagreement between what P_i has broadcast and what he or she received privately from P_i, he or she knows that P_i is corrupt and broadcasts $(\mathtt{accuse}, k)$, as well as the offending value β'. This value is always a linear combination of values received directly from P_i.

6. For any accusation from P_k in the preceding step, players call an appropriate sequence of $\mathtt{add}$ and $\mathtt{mult}$ commands to have F_{ICSIG} compute β' internally. Then they call $\mathtt{reveal}$ to make that value public. If the revealed value is indeed the β' broadcast by P_k and β' differs from the corresponding value broadcast by P_i, players output $\mathtt{fail}$, and the protocol ends here.

7. If we reach this step, no accusations were proved. Each P_k outputs $\mathtt{success}$ and stores (cid, i, β_k). In addition, P_i stores the polynomial $g_a(X) = f_a(X, 0)$.

---

protocols are in fact optimal. We emphasize that all the negative results hold even if we only require security for static corruption, whereas the positive results hold for adaptive security.

Let F_{PPC} be a functionality that provides a secure point-to-point channel between every pair of players. That is, it is defined exactly as F_{SC}, except that broadcast is not provided. A first important fact is that Lamport et al. [124] have shown a result that in our terminology is as follows:

THEOREM 5.9 *There exists a protocol $\pi_{BROADCAST}$ such that $\pi_{BROADCAST} \diamond F_{PPC}$ implements F_{SC} in $\mathrm{Env}^{t,\mathrm{sync}}$ with perfect security for all $t < n/3$.*

They have also shown that the bound on t is optimal; that is,

THEOREM 5.10 *There exists no protocol $\pi_{BROADCAST}$ such that $\pi_{BROADCAST} \diamond F_{PPC}$ implements F_{SC} in $\mathrm{Env}^{t,\mathrm{sync}}$ with perfect or statistical security if $t \geq n/3$.*

We do not give the proofs here because the techniques are somewhat out of scope for this book. But the intuition is not hard to understand. Consider the case where $n = 3$, $t = 1$, and P_1 wants to broadcast a value x. Let us assume that P_2 is honest. Now, if P_1 is honest, P_2 must output x. However, if P_1 is corrupt and may send different values to different players, P_2 must agree with P_3 on some value. Of course, we can ask P_1 to send x to both P_2 and P_3. But now the only thing that P_2 can do to ensure that he or she agrees with P_3 is to ask him or her what he or she heard from P_1. If he or she is told a value $x' \neq x$, he or she knows, of course, that one of P_1 or P_3 is corrupt, but there is no way to tell who is lying and therefore no way to decide if the output should be x or x'. The proof of Theorem 5.10 is basically a formalization of this argument. However, if $n = 4$ and $t = 1$, there are two other players P_2 can ask what they heard from P_1, and if P_1 is honest, we are guaranteed that the correct

Protocol Com-Simple

Commit. See Protocol Statistical Commit.

Public commit. On input $(\text{pubcommit}, i, cid, a)$, a party P_k lets $a_k = a$ (this is a share on the polynomial $a(\mathsf{X}) = a$), outputs $(\text{pubcommit}, i, cid, \text{success})$, and stores (cid, i, a_k). Players call sign on $\mathsf{F}_{\text{ICSIG}}$ with $\mathsf{P}_D = \mathsf{P}_i, \mathsf{P}_{INT} = \mathsf{P}_k$, and a as the value to sign (this is just for consistency so that every value stored after a commitment is signed by the committer).[a]

Open. On input (open, i, cid), where some $(cid, i, a(\mathsf{X}))$ is stored, the party P_i broadcasts $(cid, i, a(\mathsf{X}))$. On input (open, i, cid), where some (cid, i, a_k) is stored, each party $\mathsf{P}_k \neq \mathsf{P}_i$ broadcasts (cid, i, a_k). Players call reveal on $\mathsf{F}_{\text{ICSIGN}}$ to confirm that a_k is correct. If the reveal fails or the revealed value is not a_k, P_k is *ignored*. If $\deg(a(\mathsf{X})) \leq t$ and $a_k = a(k)$ for all parties that were not ignored, then all parties output $(\text{open}, i, cid, a(0))$. Otherwise, they output $(\text{open}, i, cid, \text{fail})$.

Designated open. As earlier, but the polynomial and the shares are only sent to P_j, and the designated reveal is called on $\mathsf{F}_{\text{ICSIG}}$. If P_j rejects the opening, it broadcasts a public complaint, and P_i must then do a normal opening. If that one fails too, all parties output fail.

Add. On input $(\text{add}, i, cid_1, cid_2, cid_3)$, where some $(i, cid_1, a(\mathsf{X}))$ and $(i, cid_2, b(\mathsf{X}))$ are stored, the party P_i stores $(i, cid_3, a(\mathsf{X}) + b(\mathsf{X}))$ and outputs $(\text{add}, i, cid_1, cid_2, cid_3, \text{success})$. On input $(\text{add}, i, cid_1, cid_2, cid_3)$, where some (i, cid_1, a_k) and (i, cid_2, b_k) are stored, a party $\mathsf{P}_k \neq \mathsf{P}_i$ stores $(i, cid_3, a_k + b_k)$. Players call add on $\mathsf{F}_{\text{ICSIG}}$ to have it add a_k and b_k internally. P_k outputs $(\text{add}, i, cid_1, cid_2, cid_3, \text{success})$.

Multiplication by constant. On input $(\text{mult}, i, \alpha, cid_2, cid_3)$, where some $(i, cid_2, b(\mathsf{X}))$ is stored, the party P_i stores $(i, cid_3, \alpha b(\mathsf{X}))$ and outputs $(\text{mult}, i, \alpha, cid_2, cid_3, \text{success})$. On input $(\text{mult}, i, \alpha, cid_2, cid_3)$, where some (i, cid_2, b_k) is stored, a party $\mathsf{P}_k \neq \mathsf{P}_i$ stores $(i, cid_3, \alpha b_k)$. Players call mult on $\mathsf{F}_{\text{ICSIG}}$ to have it multiply α and b_k internally. P_k outputs $(\text{mult}, i, \alpha, cid_2, cid_3, \text{success})$.

[a] Formally, we would extend $\mathsf{F}_{\text{ICSIG}}$ with a "public sign" command *a la* the pubcommit command of F_{COM} and implement the signature simply by letting all parties store a. We leave the formal details as an exercise.

---

output can be found by taking the majority decision among the three values P_2 has seen. This is the basic reason why a broadcast protocol as claimed in Theorem 5.9 can be built.

Putting all our results for the case of $t < n/3$ together using the UC theorem, we get that Theorems 5.1, 5.2, 5.6, and 5.9 imply that any function can be computed with perfect active security if fewer than $n/3$ players are corrupt, given access to secure point-to-point channels. More formally, we have

THEOREM 5.11 $\pi^f_{CEAS} \diamond \pi_{PTRANSFER, PMULT} \diamond \pi_{PCOM\text{-}SIMPLE} \diamond \pi_{BROADCAST} \diamond F_{PPC}$ *implements* F^f_{SFE} *in* $\text{Env}^{t, \text{sync}}$ *with perfect security for all* $t < n/3$.

We now argue that the bound $t < n/3$ is optimal. First, note that the problem of implementing broadcast can be phrased as a problem of computing a function securely, namely, a function f that takes an input x from a single player and outputs x to all players. In this language, Theorem 5.10 says that if $t \geq n/3$, there exist functions (such as f) that cannot be computed given only F_{PPC}, not even if we want only statistical rather than perfect security.

In other words, Theorem 5.11 is false for $t \geq n/3$ even if we only ask for statistical security. We shall see in a moment that if we assume that broadcast is given (i.e., access to F_{SC} rather than F_{PPC}) and only ask for statistical security, we can tolerate $t < n/2$. Thus the obvious remaining question is what happens if we have access to F_{SC} but insist on perfect security. The answer turns out to be negative: let F_{COMMIT} be the functionality defined as $F_{COM-SIMPLE}$ but with only the commit and open commands. Then

THEOREM 5.12 *There exists no protocol π_{COMMIT} such that $\pi_{COMMIT} \diamond F_{SC}$ implements F_{COMMIT} in $\text{Env}^{t,\text{sync}}$ with perfect security if $t \geq n/3$.*

Proof We demonstrate that no such protocol exists for $n = 3$ and $t = 1$. Assume, for contradiction, that we have a protocol π_{COMMIT}. Suppose that P_1 commits to a bit b. Let $V_i(b, R)$ be the view of the execution of the commit command seen by player P_i, where we assume that all players follow the protocol and R is the random coins used by all players. By perfect security, the distribution of $V_2(b, R)$ is independent of b (P_2 learns nothing about b before opening). It follows that given a sample $V_2(0, R)$, there must exist R' such that $V_2(0, R) = V_2(1, R')$. Now consider the following two cases:

Case 0. P_1 is corrupt. He or she commits to $b = 0$ following the protocol, so he or she sees $V_1(0, R)$ for some R. Now he or she tries to guess R' such that $V_2(0, R) = V_2(1, R')$ and computes $V_1(1, R')$. He or she then executes the open command following the protocol but pretending that his or her view of the commit command was $V_1(1, R')$.

Case 1. P_1 is honest, but P_3 is corrupt. P_1 commits to $b = 1$, and P_3 follows the protocol during execution of the commit command. R' are the random coins used. Now P_3 tries to guess R as defined in Case 0, computes $V_3(0, R)$, and then executes the open command following the protocol but pretending that his or her view of the commit command was $V_3(0, R)$.

Obviously, both cases may happen with (possibly small but) nonzero probability. Furthermore, the views that are input to the open command are exactly the same in the two cases, so the distribution of the bit that P_2 will output is the same in both cases. However, by perfect security, P_2 must *always* output (or reject) 0 in Case 0 and 1 in Case 1, which is clearly not possible. ∎

The reader might complain that what we have shown to be impossible here is a reactive functionality, and this is a more advanced tool than secure evaluation of a function, which is what the positive results talk about. However, first the protocols we have shown also can be used to implement general reactive functionalities, as discussed earlier. Second, Theorem 5.12 also can be shown for secure evaluation of a function, although this is a bit more cumbersome. Consider the function that takes inputs x from P_1 and y from P_2 and outputs x, y to all players. If we require that the ideal functionality for computing this function does not output anything before its gets both inputs, we can show a result similar to Theorem 5.12 for this function. The point is that even if P_1 is corrupt, he or she must decide on x before he or she gets any output, and the same holds for P_2. Hence the protocol must commit P_1 to x but without revealing any information on x to the corrupt players if P_1 is honest. This is the same property we need for commitments, so the result can be shown along the same lines. We leave the details to the reader.

The final result in this chapter concerns the case where we assume access to F_{SC} and go for statistical security. In this case, putting previous results together using the UC theorem, we get that Theorems 5.1, 5.3, and 5.8 imply that any function can be computed with statistical active security if fewer than $n/2$ players are corrupt, given access to secure point-to-point channels and broadcast. More formally, we have

THEOREM 5.13 $\pi^f_{CEAS\text{-}N/2} \diamond \pi_{TRANSFER,MULT} \diamond \pi_{COM\text{-}SIMPLE} \diamond F_{SC}$ *implements* F^f_{SFE} *in* $\mathrm{Env}^{t,\mathrm{sync}}$ *with statistical security for all* $t < n/2$.

Here $\pi^f_{CEAS\text{-}N/2}$ is π^f_{CEAS} modified to handle $t < n/2$, as discussed in Section 5.3. The bound $t < n/2$ is optimal: we have already seen in Chapter 3 that secure computation with information-theoretic security is not even possible with passive corruption if $t \geq n/2$.

5.6 Notes

The history of multiparty computation starts in 1986 with the work of Yao [180], who suggested the famous Yao garbling technique. This technique can actually not be found in the paper but was apparently mentioned in an oral presentation of that work. The garbling technique is described and proven secure in Lindell and Pinkas [131]. The garbling technique shows that any function can be securely evaluated with computational security by two players.

In 1987, Goldreich, Micali, and Wigderson [100] showed the same result for any number of players and an honest majority, based on the existence of one-way trapdoor permutations. This result also was obtained independently, but later, by Chaum, Damgård, and van de Graaf [47], based on the quadratic residuosity assumption. It should be mentioned that Yao garbling leads to constant-round protocols, which is not the case for either of the preceding references. Constant round for an arbitrary number of players was obtained in 1990 by Beaver, Micali, and Rogaway [9].

While all the work mentioned so far was based on computational assumptions, the work that large parts of this book is based on was started in 1988 by Ben-Or, Goldwasser, and Wigderson [14] and independently by Chaum, Crépeau, and Damgård [46]. They showed that in a model with secure point-to-point channels, any function can be securely evaluated with unconditional security against t corrupted players, where $t < n/2$ for a passive adversary and $t < n/3$ for an active adversary. In 1989, Rabin and Ben-Or [157] showed that if broadcast is given for free and a small error probability is allowed, $t < n/2$ can be obtained even for an active adversary.

One also can consider so-called mixed adversaries that may corrupt some players passively and others actively. Also for this case one can show optimal bounds on the number of corruptions that can be tolerated; this was done in 1998 by Fitzi, Hirt, and Maurer [91]. If t_p and t_a are the number of passively and actively corrupted players, respectively, then perfectly secure general multiparty computation is possible if and only if $2t_p + 3t_a < n$.[3]

Concerning the material in this book, the passively secure protocol we give in Chapter 3 is essentially the protocol from Ben-Or, Goldwasser, and Wigderson [14], except that the

---

[3] The reader should note that the proceedings version of Fitzi, Hirt, and Maurer [91] states a different, incorrect result; the authors proved the correct result later.

way we do multiplications is different. The approach we use, where players multiply shares locally and reshare the product, was suggested by Michael Rabin shortly after ref. 14 was published.

The actively secure protocol from Chapter 5 is again similar to ref. 14 in spirit but with some major differences in how multiplications are handled. We do verifiable secret sharing by having players commit to the shares they hold in the basic secret-sharing scheme, and then we implement the commitments using secret sharing again. This approach is from Cramer, Damgård, and Maurer [61]. It makes the presentation more modular, and it also allows a simple generalization to linear secret sharing. The resulting protocol is, however, less efficient than that of Ben-Or, Goldwasser, and Wigderson [14], who do verifiable secret sharing directly, without passing through a construction of commitments. This is possible because the protocol for commitment is actually already a verifiable secret sharing when the underlying secret-sharing scheme is Shamir's: if a sufficiently small number of incorrect shares are submitted when we try to reconstruct, then the secret can be efficiently computed. This is not true for linear secret-sharing schemes in general, so in Chapter 6 on linear secret sharing, our modular approach is actually necessary.

6

MPC from General Linear Secret-Sharing Schemes

6.1 Introduction

In this chapter we will show how the protocols we have seen so far can be generalized to be based on general linear secret-sharing schemes. Doing this generalization has several advantages: first, it allows us to design protocols that protect against general adversary structures, a concept we explain later, and second, it allows us to consider protocols in which the field that is used in defining the secret-sharing scheme can be of size independent of the number of players. This turns out to be an advantage for the applications of multiparty computation (MPC) that we consider later but cannot be done for the protocols that we have seen so far: to use Shamir's scheme for n players based on polynomials as we have seen, the field must be of size at least $n + 1$.

For now, we will only consider the theory for linear secret sharing that we need to construct the protocols in this chapter. However, we note already that to get full mileage from the more general applications of secret sharing and MPC, we need additional theory, in particular, about the asymptotic behavior of secret-sharing schemes. This material can be found in Chapter 11.

6.2 General Adversary Structures

The corruption tolerance of the protocols that we have seen so far has been characterized by only a single number t, the maximal number of corruptions that can be tolerated. This is also known as the *threshold-t model*. One way to motivate this might be to think of corruption of a player as something that requires the adversary to invest some amount of resource, such as time or money. If the adversary has only bounded resources, there should be a limit on the corruptions he or she can do. However, characterizing this limit by only an upper bound implicitly assumes that all players are equally hard to corrupt. In reality, this may be completely false: some players may have much better security than others, so a more realistic model might be that the adversary can corrupt a small number of well-protected players or a large number of poorly protected players. However, the threshold model does not allow us to express this.

Another way to interpret corruptions is to see them as a result of some subset of players working together to cheat the others. Also from this point of view, it seems quite restrictive to assume that any subset of a given size might form such a collaboration. Which subsets we should actually worry about may depend on the composition of the set of players and their relation to each other more than on the size of the subsets.

To solve these issues, we consider the more general concept of an adversary structure. This is a family $\mathcal{A}$ of subsets of the set of players $P = \{P_1, \ldots, P_n\}$. The idea is that this is a complete list of the subsets that the adversary is able to corrupt. In the threshold-t model, $\mathcal{A}$ would contain all subsets of size at most t. But, in general, any list of subsets is possible, with one constraint, however: we require that $\mathcal{A}$ be antimonotone, namely, $A \subseteq B$ and $B \in \mathcal{A}$ imply that $A \in \mathcal{A}$. The meaning of this is that if the adversary is powerful enough to corrupt set B, he or she also can choose to corrupt any smaller set. We characterize two important classes of adversary structures as follows:

DEFINITION 6.1 *An adversary structure $\mathcal{A}$ is said to be Q2 if for all $A_1, A_2 \in \mathcal{A}$ it holds that $A_1 \cup A_2 \neq P$. It is said to be Q3 if for all $A_1, A_2, A_3 \in \mathcal{A}$ it holds that $A_1 \cup A_2 \cup A_3 \neq P$.*

The $Q2$ and $Q3$ conditions are natural generalizations of the threshold-t model for $t < n/2$ and $t < n/3$, respectively. For instance, the union of two sets that are both smaller than $n/2$ cannot be the entire player set P.

We can then define what it means that a protocol implements some functionality securely against an adversary structure $\mathcal{A}$. This is done in exactly the same way as we defined security for at most t corruptions, except that we now consider environments that corrupt only subsets in $\mathcal{A}$.

We have seen that multiparty computation with perfect, passive security in the threshold-t model is possible if and only if $t < n/2$ and with active security if and only if $t < n/3$. The following theorem is then easy to prove:

THEOREM 6.2 *For any adversary structure $\mathcal{A}$ that is not Q2, there are functions that cannot be securely computed with passive and perfect security against $\mathcal{A}$. Moreover, for any adversary structure $\mathcal{A}$ that is not Q3, there are functions that cannot be securely computed with active and perfect security against $\mathcal{A}$.*

To prove this, one notices that the corresponding proofs for $t \geq n/2$ and $t \geq n/3$ actually only use the fact the the underlying adversary structures are not $Q2$ and $Q3$. This is straightforward and is left to the reader (see, e.g., Section 3.4).

We shall see later that the converse is also true: multiparty computation with perfect, passive security against adversary structure $\mathcal{A}$ is possible if $\mathcal{A}$ is $Q2$ and with active security if $\mathcal{A}$ is $Q3$.

The following examples illustrate that we can achieve strictly more with general adversary structures than what can be done in the threshold case:

EXAMPLE 6.3 Suppose that we have six players and consider the adversary structure containing the sets $\{P_1\}, \{P_2, P_4\}, \{P_2, P_5, P_6\}, \{P_3, P_5\}, \{P_3, P_6\}, \{P_4, P_5, P_6\}$, and all smaller sets. It is trivial to see that this structure is $Q3$, so we can do multiparty computation with active security in this case. Note that if the threshold-t model with $t < n/3$ was all we could do, we could only tolerate corruption of a single player. ∎

EXAMPLE 6.4 Here is an infinite family of examples: suppose that our player set is divided into two disjoint sets X and Y of m players each ($n = 2m$), where the players are on friendly terms within each group but tend to distrust players in the other group. Hence a coalition of active cheaters might consist of almost all players from X or from Y, whereas a mixed coalition with players from both groups is likely to be quite small. Concretely, suppose that we assume that a corrupted set can consist of at most $9m/10$ players from only X or only Y, *or* it can consist of fewer than $m/5$ players coming from both X and Y. This defines a $Q3$ adversary structure, so multiparty computation with active security is possible in this scenario. Nevertheless, no threshold solution exists because the largest coalitions of corrupt players have size more than $n/3$. The intuitive reason why multiparty computation is nevertheless possible is that although some corruptible sets are larger than $n/3$, we do not need to protect against corruption of *all* sets larger than $n/3$. ∎

6.3 Linear Secret Sharing

Let us consider how we can realize multiparty computation that is secure if the adversary may corrupt subsets of players in some adversary structure that is not necessarily threshold. One might think that a solution could be to use Shamir secret sharing, generate more shares than there are players, and give a different number of shares to different players. At least this will imply that we can tolerate corruption of a larger number of those players that received only a small number of shares. This approach would allow us to handle some, but not all, relevant adversary structures, and it will often be suboptimal in terms of efficiency.

A much better solution is to generalize Shamir's scheme further: say we share the secret s among n players in the usual way using a polynomial $f_s(X)$. We compute shares by evaluating f_s in points $1, 2, \ldots, n$. This computation of the shares can be rephrased as follows: consider a Van der Monde matrix M that by definition is a matrix in which the rows are of form $(i^0, i^1, i^2, \ldots, i^t)$, for $i = 1, \ldots, n$. Now define a column vector $\mathbf{r}_s$ whose entries are the coefficients of f_s, with s (the degree 0 coefficient) as the first entry. Now, computing the product $M \cdot \mathbf{r}_s$ is clearly equivalent to evaluating f_s at points $1, \ldots, n$. Therefore, we can rephrase Shamir's scheme as follows: choose a random vector with $t + 1$ entries subject to the secret s appearing as the first coordinate. Compute $M\mathbf{r}_s$, and give the ith entry of the result to player P_i.

A generalization now quite naturally suggests itself: first, why not consider other matrices than Van der Monde, in particular, with more than n rows? Second, once we do this, we can assign more than one row to each player, so they may receive more than one value in the field. This generalization exactly leads to the linear secret-sharing schemes we consider in this chapter.

Before we define these schemes formally, some notation: for consistency in the following, vectors are column vectors unless we state otherwise, and we will sometimes use $\cdot$ to denote matrix multiplication. Thus we will sometimes write the inner product of $\mathbf{a}$ and $\mathbf{b}$ as $\mathbf{a}^\top \cdot \mathbf{b}$.

DEFINITION 6.5 *A linear secret-sharing scheme $\mathcal{S}$ over a field $\mathbb{F}$ for n players is defined by a matrix M and a function ϕ. M has $m \geq n$ rows and $t + 1$ columns, and ϕ is a labeling function $\phi : \{1, \ldots, m\} \to \{1, \ldots, n\}$. We say that M is the matrix for $\mathcal{S}$. We can apply ϕ to the rows of M in a natural way, and we say that player $P_{\phi(i)}$ owns the ith row of M. For a subset A of the players, we let M_A be the matrix consisting of the rows owned by players in A.*

To secret share $s \in \mathbb{F}$ using $\mathcal{S}$, one forms a column vector $\mathbf{r}_s$ with s as the first coordinate, while the other coordinates are $r_1, \ldots, r_t$, where each r_i is uniformly random in $\mathbb{F}$. Finally, one computes the vector of shares $M\mathbf{r}_s$ and distributes them among players by giving $(M\mathbf{r}_s)_i$ to player $\mathsf{P}_{\phi(i)}$. Note that in this way, a player may get more than one value as his or her share. Note also that for a subset A of players, $M_A\mathbf{r}_s$ is the set of values received by players in A when s is shared.

DEFINITION 6.6 *The adversary structure of S is a family of subsets of players. A set A is in the adversary structure if and only if the distribution of $M_A\mathbf{r}_s$ is independent of s. Such a set is called unqualified. The access structure of S is also a family of subsets of players. A set A is in the access structure if and only if s is uniquely determined from $M_A\mathbf{r}_s$. Such a set is called qualified.*

It follows from Theorem 6.8 that every player subset is either qualified or unqualified.

We will let $\mathbf{m}_k$ denote the kth row of M. When we need to talk about individual entries in M, it turns out to be convenient to number the columns from 0, and hence the kth row of M also can be written as

$$\mathbf{m}_k = (M_{k,0}, M_{k,1}, \ldots, M_{k,t})$$

This also gives an alternative way to address single shares that will sometimes be convenient; that is, we have

$$(M \cdot \mathbf{r}_a)_k = \mathbf{m}_k \cdot \mathbf{r}_a$$

We will need the following basic fact from linear algebra, where we recall that $\mathrm{im}(N)$ for a matrix N is the set of all vectors of form $N\mathbf{v}$ or, put differently, the set of vectors obtained as linear combinations of the columns of N.

LEMMA 6.7 *For any matrix M and vector $\mathbf{e}$, we have that $\mathbf{e} \notin \mathrm{im}(M^\intercal)$ if and only if there exists $\mathbf{w}$ with $\mathbf{w} \in \ker(M)$ and $\mathbf{w}^\intercal \cdot \mathbf{e} \neq 0$.*

Proof For a subspace V of any vector space over $\mathbb{F}$, $V^\perp$ denotes the orthogonal complement of V, the subspace of vectors that are orthogonal to all vectors in V. Now notice that $\mathrm{im}(M^\intercal)$ is the space spanned by the rows of M. Therefore, it is clear that $\ker(M) = \mathrm{im}(M^\intercal)^\perp$ because computing $M \cdot \mathbf{a}$ for some $\mathbf{a}$ is equivalent to computing the inner product of $\mathbf{a}$ with every row of M. From this and $V = (V^\perp)^\perp$ for any subspace V, it follows that $\ker(M)^\perp = \mathrm{im}(M^\intercal)$. So $\mathbf{e} \notin \mathrm{im}(M^\intercal)$ if and only if $\mathbf{e} \notin \ker(M)^\perp$, and this holds if and only if $\mathbf{w}$ as in the statement of the lemma exists. ∎

THEOREM 6.8 *Let S be a linear secret-sharing scheme, and let M be the matrix for S. A player subset A is qualified in S if and only if $\mathbf{e} = (1, 0, \ldots, 0)^\intercal \in \mathrm{im}(M_A^\intercal)$; that is, the subspace spanned by the rows of M_A contains $\mathbf{e}^\intercal$. In this case, there exists a recombination vector $\mathbf{u}$ such that $\mathbf{u}^\intercal(M_A\mathbf{r}_s) = s$ for all s. A is unqualified in S if and only if $\mathbf{e} \notin \mathrm{im}(M_A^\intercal)$. In this case, there exists a vector $\mathbf{w}$ that is orthogonal to all rows in M_A and has first coordinate 1.*

Proof If $\mathbf{e} \in \mathrm{im}(M_A^\intercal)$, there exists a vector $\mathbf{u}$ such that $M_A^\intercal \cdot \mathbf{u} = \mathbf{e}$, or $\mathbf{u}^\intercal \cdot M_A = \mathbf{e}^\intercal$. But then we have

$$\mathbf{u}^\intercal \cdot (M_A \cdot \mathbf{r}_s) = (\mathbf{u}^\intercal \cdot M_A) \cdot \mathbf{r}_s = \mathbf{e}^\intercal \cdot \mathbf{r}_s = s$$

If $\mathbf{e}$ is not in the span of the rows of M_A, then by Lemma 6.7 there exists a vector $\mathbf{w}$ that is orthogonal to all rows of M_A but not orthogonal to $\mathbf{e}$. This can be used as the $\mathbf{w}$ claimed in the theorem because we may assume without loss of generality that the inner product $\mathbf{w}^{\mathsf{T}} \cdot \mathbf{e}$ is 1. Let s, s' be any two possible values of the secret to be shared. For any $\mathbf{r}_s$, let $\mathbf{r}_{s'} = \mathbf{r}_s + (s' - s)\mathbf{w}$. Then the first coordinate of $\mathbf{r}_{s'}$ is s', and we have

$$M_A \cdot \mathbf{r}_{s'} = M_A \cdot \mathbf{r}_s$$

That is, for each set of random coins used to share s, there is exactly one set of coins for sharing s' such that the players in A receive the same shares. Since the randomness is chosen uniformly, it follows that the distribution of shares received by A is the same for all values of the secret, so A is in the adversary structure. ■

In the following we will refer to m, the number of rows in M, as the size of the secret-sharing scheme defined by M. The reason it makes sense to ignore t (the number of columns) in this connection is that we can assume without loss of generality that $t + 1 \leq m$: given any M, we could always consider a new matrix M' containing only a maximal independent set of columns from M (including the first column). Because the column rank equals the row rank for any matrix, such a set will have size at most m. Moreover, it will lead to a secret-sharing scheme with the same access structure. This follows from Theorem 6.8, which says that a set A is qualified exactly if the rows of M_A span the first basis vector. This happens if and only if the rows of M'_A span the first basis vector because the columns in M_A can all be obtained as linear combinations of the columns in M'_A. In the following we will always assume that the columns of M are independent.

In the following we will reuse some notation from earlier chapters and write

$$M\mathbf{r}_s = [s; \mathbf{r}_s]_{\mathcal{S}}$$

Using the standard entrywise addition and multiplication by a scalar, the following vectors are well defined (for $\alpha, a, b \in \mathbb{F}$):

$$[a; \mathbf{r}_a]_{\mathcal{S}} + [b; \mathbf{r}_b]_{\mathcal{S}} \qquad \alpha[a; \mathbf{r}_a]_{\mathcal{S}}$$

We now want to consider multiplication of shared values. To understand how this works, recall how we handled secure multiplication with Shamir's secret-sharing scheme in previous chapters: say that $[a; f_a]_t$, and $[b; f_b]_t$ have been distributed, and we want to compute ab in shared form. The main observation that we used for this was that if each player locally multiplies his or her share of a and b, then the local products form a set of shares in ab; that is, they form $[ab; f_a f_b]_{2t}$. This new sharing is of a different type, however; it is formed by a polynomial of degree $2t$ and not t.

It turns out that something similar happens for general linear secret sharing. Assume that $[a; \mathbf{r}_a]_{\mathcal{S}}$ and $[b; \mathbf{r}_b]_{\mathcal{S}}$ have been distributed. We now want to define what it means for players to locally multiply their shares of a and b. This gets more complicated than in the case of polynomials because a player may have more than one field value as his or her share of a (and of b). Therefore, there may be several different pairwise products that he or she can compute, and we need notation to capture all of these. We therefore define a special type of product, written

$$[a; \mathbf{r}_a]_{\mathcal{S}} \odot [b; \mathbf{r}_b]_{\mathcal{S}}$$

This vector is constructed so that it contains all products of a share of a and a share of b that some player can compute locally. More formally,

$$[a; \mathbf{r}_a]_{\mathcal{S}} \odot [b; \mathbf{r}_b]_{\mathcal{S}} = (((([a; \mathbf{r}_a]_{\mathcal{S}})_{\{P_1\}} \otimes ([b; \mathbf{r}_b]_{\mathcal{S}})_{\{P_1\}}), \ldots, ((([a; \mathbf{r}_a]_{\mathcal{S}})_{\{P_n\}} \otimes ([b; \mathbf{r}_b]_{\mathcal{S}})_{\{P_n\}})$$

where $([a; \mathbf{r}_a]_S)_{\{P_i\}}$ denotes the vector containing all shares of a given to P_i, and where for $\mathbf{a}, \mathbf{b} \in \mathbb{F}^\ell$, $\mathbf{a} \otimes \mathbf{b}$ is the tensor product of vectors; that is, $\mathbf{a} \otimes \mathbf{b} \in \mathbb{F}^{\ell^2}$ and contains all (ordered) pairwise products of entries in the two vectors.

Note that if $n = m$ and every player owns one value, we can set $\phi(i) = i$. In this case, $[a; \mathbf{r}_a]_S \odot [b; \mathbf{r}_b]_S$ is just the Schur product $[a; \mathbf{r}_a]_S * [b; \mathbf{r}_b]_S$. In the following, $\hat{m}$ will denote the length of $[a; \mathbf{r}_a]_S \odot [b; \mathbf{r}_b]_S$.

6.3.1 Multiplicative secret sharing

As we hinted at earlier, if values a, b have been secret shared using S, it turns out that the vector $[a; \mathbf{r}_a]_S \odot [b; \mathbf{r}_b]_S$ forms a set of shares of ab, albeit in a different linear secret-sharing scheme, which we will denote $\hat{S}$. We specify $\hat{S}$ by directly constructing its matrix $\hat{M}$: consider the rows of M owned by P_i, that is, $M_{\{P_i\}}$. We now define $\hat{M}_{\{P_i\}}$ to be a matrix consisting of all rows of form $\mathbf{u} \otimes \mathbf{v}$, where $\mathbf{u}$ and $\mathbf{v}$ are rows in $M_{\{P_i\}}$. Then $\hat{M}$ is built by putting all the $\hat{M}_{\{P_i\}}$ together in one matrix. The labeling function is defined such that P_i owns exactly the rows that came from $\hat{M}_{\{P_i\}}$.

With this extension of the labeling function, we get the following simple fact that we will use later:

LEMMA 6.9 *Let c_k be the kth entry in $[a; \mathbf{r}_a]_S \odot [b; \mathbf{r}_b]_S$. Then there exist (fixed) indices u, v such that $c_k = a_u b_v$, where a_u is the uth entry in $[a; \mathbf{r}_a]_S$, b_v is the vth entry in $[b; \mathbf{r}_b]_S$, and $\phi(k) = \phi(u) = \phi(v)$.*

The main reason we introduce $\hat{S}$ is that it can be used to implement multiplication of shared secrets:

LEMMA 6.10 *For any linear secret-sharing scheme S, we have*

$$[a; \mathbf{r}_a]_S \odot [b; \mathbf{r}_b]_S = [ab; \mathbf{r}_a \otimes \mathbf{r}_b]_{\hat{S}}$$

Proof Notice first that if $\mathbf{u}, \mathbf{v}$ are rows in $M_{\{P_i\}}$, then $\mathbf{u} \cdot \mathbf{r}_a$ and $\mathbf{v} \cdot \mathbf{r}_b$ are values P_i will receive when secrets a an b are shared; that is, they are entries in $([a; \mathbf{r}_a]_S)_{\{P_i\}}$ and $([b; \mathbf{r}_b]_S)_{\{P_i\}}$, respectively. Therefore, the entries in $([a; \mathbf{r}_a]_S)_{\{P_i\}} \otimes ([b; \mathbf{r}_b]_S)_{\{P_i\}}$ are of form

$$(\mathbf{u} \cdot \mathbf{r}_a) \cdot (\mathbf{v} \cdot \mathbf{r}_b) = (\mathbf{u} \otimes \mathbf{v}) \cdot (\mathbf{r}_a \otimes \mathbf{r}_b) .$$

The lemma now follows by definition of $\hat{M}$.   ∎

Note that the adversary structure of $\hat{S}$ contains that of S. This is so because any player set A can locally compute its part of $[ab; \mathbf{r}_a \otimes \mathbf{r}_b]_{\hat{S}}$ after secrets a and b have been shared. If players in A could reconstruct ab from this, this reveals information on a and b, which cannot be the case if A is in the adversary structure of S.

DEFINITION 6.11 *If the access structure of $\hat{S}$ contains the set of all players, S is said to be multiplicative. If the access structure of $\hat{S}$ contains the complement of every set in the adversary structure $\mathcal{A}$ of S, then S is said to be strongly multiplicative.*

Note that if S is multiplicative, then there exists a recombination vector $\mathbf{u}$ such that

$$\mathbf{u} \cdot ([a; \mathbf{r}_a]_S \odot [b; \mathbf{r}_b]_S) = \mathbf{u} \cdot [ab; \mathbf{r}_a \otimes \mathbf{r}_b]_{\hat{S}} = ab$$

A way to think about the strong multiplication property is as follows: if an adversary is able to corrupt a set of players in $\mathcal{A}$ (but not more than that), then the set of honest players is always the complement of a set in $\mathcal{A}$. And then strong multiplication says that the set of honest players on its own can reconstruct ab from $[ab; \mathbf{r}_a \otimes \mathbf{r}_b]_{\hat{S}}$.

The reader should take a moment to understand that the multiplication property indeed generalizes in a natural way what we know about secret sharing using polynomials, as we promised earlier: the secret-sharing scheme S corresponds to sharing using polynomials of degree at most t, whereas $\hat{S}$ corresponds to sharing using polynomials of degree at most $2t$. Likewise, $\mathbf{r}_s$ corresponds to the coefficients of a polynomial that evaluates to s in 0, and $\mathbf{r}_a \otimes \mathbf{r}_b$ corresponds to multiplication of polynomials.

Summarizing what we have seen, we have the following:

LEMMA 6.12 *The following holds for any $a, b, \alpha \in \mathbb{F}$, and any multiplicative linear secret-sharing scheme S:*

$$[a; \mathbf{r}_a]_S + [b; \mathbf{r}_b]_S = [a + b; \mathbf{r}_a + \mathbf{r}_b]_S \tag{6.1}$$

$$\alpha[a; \mathbf{r}_a]_S = [\alpha a; \alpha \mathbf{r}_a]_S \tag{6.2}$$

$$[a; \mathbf{r}_a]_S \odot [b; \mathbf{r}_b]_S = [ab; \mathbf{r}_a \otimes \mathbf{r}_b]_{\hat{S}} \tag{6.3}$$

6.3.2 On the Existence of Linear Secret-Sharing Schemes

We start with the most basic facts on the existence of linear secret-sharing schemes:

THEOREM 6.13

- *For every adversary structure $\mathcal{A}$, there exists a linear secret-sharing scheme S whose adversary structure is $\mathcal{A}$.*
- *For every Q2 structure $\mathcal{A}$, there exists a multiplicative linear secret-sharing scheme S whose adversary structure is $\mathcal{A}$.*
- *For every Q3 structure $\mathcal{A}$, there exists a strongly multiplicative linear secret-sharing scheme S whose adversary structure is $\mathcal{A}$.*

This theorem can be shown using just a single scheme, namely replicated secret sharing, which works as follows: given adversary structure $\mathcal{A}$ and secret $s \in \mathbb{F}$ to share, do the following: for each set $A \in \mathcal{A}$, choose $r_A \in \mathbb{F}$ at random, subject to the constraint that $s = \sum_{A \in \mathcal{A}} r_A$. Then, for all $A \in \mathcal{A}$, give r_A to all players *not* in A. We will call this scheme $\mathcal{R}_{\mathcal{A}}$. Note that it can be defined over any field independent of the number of players.

EXERCISE 6.1 Show that $\mathcal{R}_{\mathcal{A}}$ is a linear secret-sharing scheme with adversary structure $\mathcal{A}$.

EXERCISE 6.2 Show that $\mathcal{R}_{\mathcal{A}}$ is multiplicative if $\mathcal{A}$ is Q2.

EXERCISE 6.3 Show that $\mathcal{R}_{\mathcal{A}}$ is strongly multiplicative if $\mathcal{A}$ is Q3.

Of course, $\mathcal{R}_{\mathcal{A}}$ is in general very inefficient in the sense that most adversary structures contain a number of sets that is exponential in the number of players, so players will receive a very large number of shares. However, Shamir's scheme with threshold t is linear and is easily seen to be multiplicative and strongly multiplicative if $t < n/2$ and $t < n/3$, respectively. In this scheme, players get only a single field element as their share, so we see that the share size does not have to depend on the size of the adversary structure, even if we also require (strong) multiplication.

It would therefore be great if we could characterize those access structures that admit efficient linear schemes, that is, of size polynomial in the number of players. However, this question is completely open. But we can at least say that asking for multiplication does not incur a large cost over just asking for a linear scheme. This is formalized in Theorem 6.16. However, we first need a new notion.

DEFINITION 6.14 *Let $\mathcal{F}$ be an access structure. Then the dual access structure $\bar{\mathcal{F}}$ is defined as follows: a set A is in $\bar{\mathcal{F}}$ if and only if the complement $\bar{A}$ is not in $\mathcal{F}$.*

For instance, if $\mathcal{F}$ contains all sets of size larger than t, then $\bar{\mathcal{F}}$ contains all sets of size larger than $n - t$.

EXERCISE 6.4 Let $\mathcal{S}$ be a secret-sharing scheme with adversary structure $\mathcal{A}$ and access structure $\mathcal{F}$. Show that if $\mathcal{A}$ is $Q2$, then $\bar{\mathcal{F}} \subseteq \mathcal{F}$.

LEMMA 6.15 *Given any linear secret-sharing scheme $\mathcal{S}$ with access structure $\mathcal{F}$, one can construct a linear secret-sharing scheme $\bar{\mathcal{S}}$ with access structure $\bar{\mathcal{F}}$ in time polynomial in the size of $\mathcal{S}$. Moreover, the matrices M and $\bar{M}$ of $\mathcal{S}$ and $\bar{\mathcal{S}}$ satisfy $M^\tau \bar{M} = E$, where E is a matrix with 1 in the top-left corner and 0 elsewhere.*

Proof Let M be the matrix of $\mathcal{S}$, let $\mathbf{v}_0$ be a solution to $M^\tau \cdot \mathbf{v}_0 = \mathbf{e}$, and let $\mathbf{v}_1, \ldots, \mathbf{v}_{m-(t+1)}$ be a basis for $\ker(M^\tau)$. We now let the matrix $\bar{M}$ for $\bar{\mathcal{S}}$ be the matrix with columns $\mathbf{v}_0, \mathbf{v}_1, \ldots, \mathbf{v}_{m-(t+1)}$ and with the same labeling function as for $\mathcal{S}$. We also define for later $\bar{\mathbf{e}} \in \mathbb{F}^{m-(t+1)+1}$ to be $(1, 0, \ldots, 0)^\tau$. Then $M^\tau \bar{M} = E$ follows immediately by construction of $\bar{M}$.

We now want to show that $\bar{\mathcal{F}}$ is indeed the access structure of $\bar{\mathcal{S}}$; that is, $A \in \mathcal{F}$ if and only if $\bar{A}$ is not in the access structure of $\bar{\mathcal{S}}$. If $A \in \mathcal{F}$, the rows of M_A span $\mathbf{e}$, or equivalently, there exists $\mathbf{v}$ such that $\mathbf{v}_{\bar{A}} = 0$ and $M^\tau \cdot \mathbf{v} = \mathbf{e}$, where $\mathbf{v}_{\bar{A}}$ is the vector we obtain by selecting from $\mathbf{v}$ the coordinates owned by players in $\bar{A}$. By construction of $\mathbf{v}_0, \mathbf{v}_1, \ldots, \mathbf{v}_{m-(t+1)}$, any such $\mathbf{v}$ can be written as $\mathbf{v}_0$ plus some linear combination of $\mathbf{v}_1, \ldots, \mathbf{v}_{m-(t+1)}$, or equivalently, there exists a vector $\mathbf{w}$ with 1 as its first coordinate such that $\mathbf{v} = \bar{M} \cdot \mathbf{w}$. But then $\bar{M}_{\bar{A}} \cdot \mathbf{w} = \mathbf{v}_{\bar{A}} = 0$, and $\mathbf{w}^\tau \cdot \bar{\mathbf{e}} = 1 \neq 0$. By Lemma 6.7, the existence of such a $\mathbf{w}$ shows that the rows of $\bar{M}_{\bar{A}}$ do not span $\bar{\mathbf{e}}$, so $\bar{A}$ is not in the access structure of $\bar{\mathcal{S}}$.

Conversely, if $\bar{A}$ is not in the access structure of $\bar{\mathcal{S}}$, there exists $\mathbf{w}$ with $\bar{M}_{\bar{A}} \cdot \mathbf{w} = 0$ and $\mathbf{w}^\tau \cdot \bar{\mathbf{e}} = 1$. If we set $\mathbf{v} = \bar{M} \cdot \mathbf{w}$, then $\mathbf{v}_{\bar{A}} = 0$, so

$$M_A^\tau \cdot \mathbf{v}_A = M^\tau \cdot \mathbf{v} = M^\tau \cdot \bar{M} \cdot \mathbf{w} = E \cdot \mathbf{w} = \mathbf{e}$$

This shows that A is in $\mathcal{F}$.   ∎

THEOREM 6.16 *From every linear secret-sharing scheme $\mathcal{S}$ with $Q2$ adversary structure $\mathcal{A}$, we can construct a multiplicative linear secret-sharing scheme $\mathcal{S}'$ whose adversary structure is $\mathcal{A}$ in time polynomial in the size of $\mathcal{S}$. The size of $\mathcal{S}'$ is at most twice that of $\mathcal{S}$.*

Proof We begin by using Lemma 6.15 to construct $\bar{\mathcal{S}}$ with access structure $\bar{\mathcal{F}}$. We can now start describing the desired new scheme $\mathcal{S}'$. As a first step, consider a secret-sharing scheme where we share a secret s according to both $\mathcal{S}$ and $\bar{\mathcal{S}}$. More formally, we generate vectors $\mathbf{r}_s$ and $\bar{\mathbf{r}}_s$ at random but with s as the first coordinate, compute $M \cdot \mathbf{r}_s$, $\bar{M} \cdot \bar{\mathbf{r}}_s$, and distribute shares according to the labeling function. Now, from Exercise 6.4, we know that $\bar{\mathcal{F}} \subseteq \mathcal{F}$, and this implies that the access structure of our new scheme is $\mathcal{F}$.

Now assume that we have shared secrets a and b according to this scheme. In particular, this means that players hold $M \cdot \mathbf{r}_a$ and $\bar{M} \cdot \bar{\mathbf{r}}_b$. Note that because we use the same labeling function for M and $\bar{M}$, the entries in the vector $(M \cdot \mathbf{r}_a) * (\bar{M} \cdot \bar{\mathbf{r}}_b)$ can be computed locally by the players. We claim that the sum of all these entries is actually ab. Since the sum of the entries in the $*$ product is just the inner product, this can be seen from

$$(M \cdot \mathbf{r}_a)^{\mathsf{T}} \cdot (\bar{M} \cdot \bar{\mathbf{r}}_b) = \mathbf{r}_a^{\mathsf{T}} \cdot (M^{\mathsf{T}} \cdot \bar{M}) \cdot \bar{\mathbf{r}}_b = \mathbf{r}_a^{\mathsf{T}} \cdot E \cdot \bar{\mathbf{r}}_b = ab \tag{6.4}$$

by Lemma 6.15

We can now finally specify $\mathcal{S}'$ by directly constructing its matrix M', which will have $2m$ rows and $2(t+1)$ columns. First, build a matrix M'' filled in with M in the upper-left corner, $\bar{M}$ in the lower-right corner, and 0s elsewhere. Let $\mathbf{k}$ be the column in M'' that passes through the first column of $\bar{M}$. Add $\mathbf{k}$ to the first column of M'', and delete $\mathbf{k}$ from M''. Let M' be the result of this. The labeling of M' is carried over in the natural way from M and $\bar{M}$.

It is now clear that secret sharing according to $\mathcal{S}'$ will generate shares from both $\mathcal{S}$ and $\bar{\mathcal{S}}$, as described earlier, and hence by Eq. (6.4), the set of all players will be qualified in $\hat{\mathcal{S}}'$, and this is exactly the requirement for $\mathcal{S}'$ to be multiplicative. ∎

We end this section by showing that multiplicative schemes can only exist for $Q2$ structures.

THEOREM 6.17 *Let $\mathcal{S}$ be a multiplicative linear secret-sharing scheme. Then the adversary structure for $\mathcal{S}$ is $Q2$.*

Proof Suppose for contradiction that the adversary structure $\mathcal{A}$ is not $Q2$. Then there are two sets $A_1, A_2 \in \mathcal{A}$, such that $A_1 \cup A_2 = \mathsf{P}$. By Lemma 6.7, there exists vectors $\mathbf{w}_1, \mathbf{w}_2$ with $\mathbf{w}_1 \in \ker(M_{A_1})$ and $\mathbf{w}_2 \in \ker(M_{A_2})$ and with nonzero first coordinates that we can assume without loss of generality are both 1. We can think of $M \cdot \mathbf{w}_1$ and $M \cdot \mathbf{w}_2$ as two sets of shares of the secret 1. Hence, by the multiplicative property, we should be able to reconstruct the product 1 as a linear combination of the entries in $(M \cdot \mathbf{w}_1) \odot (M \cdot \mathbf{w}_2)$. But since $(M \cdot \mathbf{w}_1)_{A_1}$ and $(M \cdot \mathbf{w}_2)_{A_2}$ are both 0 and $A_1 \cup A_2 = \mathsf{P}$, $(M \cdot \mathbf{w}_1) \odot (M \cdot \mathbf{w}_2)$ is in fact the all-zero vector, and we have a contradiction. ∎

EXERCISE 6.5 Let $\mathcal{S}$ be a strongly multiplicative linear secret-sharing scheme. Show that the adversary structure for $\mathcal{S}$ is $Q3$.

An obvious question is whether a result similar to Theorem 6.16 holds for strongly multiplicative secret sharing; that is, from a linear secret-sharing scheme for a $Q3$ adversary structure, can one construct a strongly multiplicative scheme of similar size? This question is wide open. It has resisted attempts to solve it for more than a decade, and no clear evidence is known either way as to what the answer might be.

Protocol GCEPS (General Circuit Evaluation with Passive Security)

The protocol proceeds in three phases: the input-sharing, computation, and output-reconstruction phases.

Input sharing. Each player P_i holding input $x_i \in \mathbb{F}$ distributes $[x_i; \mathbf{r}_{x_i}]_S$. We then go through the Circuit and process the gates one by one in the computational order. Just after the input-sharing phase, we consider all input gates as being processed. We will maintain the following:

Invariant. Recall that computing with the circuit on inputs $x_1, \ldots, x_n$ assigns a unique value to every wire. Consider an input or an output wire for any gate, and let $a \in \mathbb{F}$ be the value assigned to this wire. Then, if the gate has been processed, the players hold $[a; \mathbf{r}_a]_S$ for some vector $\mathbf{r}_a$.

We then continue with the last two phases of the protocol.

Computation phase. Repeat the following until all gates have been processed (then go to the next phase): Consider the first gate in the computational order that has not been processed yet. According to the type of gate, do one of the following

> **Addition gate.** The players hold $[a; \mathbf{r}_a]_S$, $[b; \mathbf{r}_b]_S$ for the two inputs a, b to the gate. The players compute $[a; \mathbf{r}_a]_S + [b; \mathbf{r}_b]_S = [a + b; \mathbf{r}_a + \mathbf{r}_b]_S$.
>
> **Multiply-by-constant gate.** The players hold $[a; \mathbf{r}_a]_S$ for the input a to the gate. The players compute $\alpha[a; \mathbf{r}_a]_S = [\alpha a; \alpha \mathbf{r}_a]_S$.
>
> **Multiplication gate.** The players hold $[a; \mathbf{r}_a]_S$, $[b; \mathbf{r}_b]_S$ for the two inputs a, b to the gate.
>
> 1. The players compute $[a; \mathbf{r}_a]_S \odot [b; \mathbf{r}_b]_S = [ab; \mathbf{r}_a \otimes \mathbf{r}_b]_{\hat{S}}$.
> 2. Define $\mathbf{s} \stackrel{\text{def}}{=} \mathbf{r}_a \otimes \mathbf{r}_b$. Then the parties hold $[ab; \mathbf{s}]_{\hat{S}}$. Let $[ab; \mathbf{s}]_{\hat{S}} = (c_1, \ldots, c_{\hat{m}})$. For each P_i and each c_j he or she owns, P_i distributes $[c_j; \mathbf{r}_{c_j}]_S$.
> 3. Let $\mathbf{u} = (u_1, \ldots, u_{\hat{m}})$ be the recombination vector defined earlier and guaranteed by the fact that S is multiplicative. The players compute
>
> $$\sum_j u_j [c_j; \mathbf{r}_{c_j}]_S = \left[\sum_j u_j c_j; \sum_j u_j \mathbf{r}_{c_j} \right]_S = \left[ab; \sum_j u_j \mathbf{r}_{c_j} \right]_S$$

Output reconstruction. At this point, all gates, including the output gates have been processed. So do the following for each output gate (labeled i): the players hold $[y; \mathbf{r}_y]_S$, where y is the value assigned to the output gate. Each P_j securely sends every share he or she holds of y to P_i, who can then compute $y = \omega_P \cdot [y; \mathbf{r}_y]_S$, where ω_P is the recombination vector for the set of all players P.

6.4 A Passively Secure Protocol

In this section we show a natural generalization of the passively secure protocol we have seen earlier, Protocol CEPS (Circuit Evaluation with Passive Security). We basically replace polynomials by linear secret sharing and do "the same thing." First, a definition:

DEFINITION 6.18 *When we say that a player P_i distributes $[s; r_s]_S$, we mean that he or she calculates $[s; r_s]_S$ as described earlier and distributes the shares to the players according to the labeling function ϕ. Whenever players have obtained shares of a value a, based* on polynomial $\mathbf{r}_a$, we say that the players hold $[s; \mathbf{r}_s]_S$. Suppose the players hold $[a; \mathbf{r}_a]_S$, $[b; \mathbf{r}_b]_S$. Then, when we say that the players compute $[a; \mathbf{r}_a]_S + [b; \mathbf{r}_b]_S$, this means that each player P_i computes the sum of corresponding shares of a and b that he or she holds, and by Lemma 6.12, this means that the players now hold $[a + b; \mathbf{r}_a + \mathbf{r}_b]_S$. In a similar way, we define what it means for the players to compute $[a; \mathbf{r}_a]_S \odot [b; \mathbf{r}_b]_S$ and $\alpha \cdot [a; \mathbf{r}_a]_S$.

We can now describe the protocol for securely evaluating an arithmetic circuit using a general linear secret-sharing scheme S; see Protocol GCEPS (General Circuit Evaluation with Passive Security). The only condition we need is that S is multiplicative.

We can then show the following result, where we let π_{GCEPS}^f denote protocol GCEPS instantiated for computing an arithmetic circuit for the function f and $\mathrm{Env}^{\mathrm{sync},\mathcal{A}}$ denote environments that corrupt subsets in adversary structure $\mathcal{A}$. We do not give the proof in detail here. It is very easy to derive from the corresponding proof for π_{CEPS}^f found in Example 4.24. As in that proof, the simulator runs the protocol with the environment while internally running copies of the honest players using dummy inputs. Since the environment only sees shares from a set of players in $\mathcal{A}$, this makes no difference. In the final output step, the simulator patches the sets of shares of outputs known by the environment to match the real outputs. This is easy by adding an appropriate multiple of the vector $\mathbf{w}$ constructed in the proof of Theorem 6.8. Likewise, adaptive security follows because correct views for newly corrupted honest players can be constructed by patching the dummy views in the same way.

THEOREM 6.19 $\pi_{GCEPS}^f \diamond F_{SC}$ implements F_{SFE}^f in $\mathrm{Env}^{\mathrm{sync},\mathcal{A}}$ with perfect security whenever the protocol is based on a multiplicative linear secret-sharing scheme S with adversary structure $\mathcal{A}$.

It is easy to see that to have security against $\mathrm{Env}^{\mathrm{sync},\mathcal{A}}$, we do not actually need to have a linear scheme S whose adversary structure exactly equals $\mathcal{A}$; it is enough if it contains $\mathcal{A}$. We still have to demand, however, that the adversary structure of S be $Q2$ because otherwise we cannot compute all functions securely, by Theorem 6.2. This implies that $\mathcal{A}$ must be $Q2$ as well. Therefore, by also invoking Theorem 6.16, we get the following:

COROLLARY 6.20 *Any function can be computed with perfect and passive security against an environment corrupting subsets in adversary structure $\mathcal{A}$, provided that $\mathcal{A}$ is $Q2$. The complexity of the protocol can be made polynomial in the size of the smallest linear secret-sharing scheme whose adversary structure is $Q2$ and contains $\mathcal{A}$.*

6.5 Actively Secure Protocols

In this section we show how to get actively secure protocols from general linear secret sharing. We do not give all the details because many of them are trivial to derive from the corresponding results and protocols in Chapter 5.

We will first assume that we are given the functionality F_{COM} for homomorphic commitment. We must show how to evaluate functions securely from this and then consider how to implement commitments based on linear secret sharing.

We first define some notation. Let S be a linear secret-sharing scheme, and recall that for an appropriately chosen vector $\mathbf{r}_a$ with a the first coordinate, $g(\mathbf{r}_a) = M_{\mathcal{A}} \cdot \mathbf{r}_s$ is the vector of

Protocol GCEAS (Generalized Circuit Evaluation, Active Security)

The protocol assumes a strongly multiplicative linear secret-sharing scheme S with adversary structure A and proceeds in three phases: the input-sharing, computation, and output-reconstruction phases.

Input sharing. Each player P_i holding input $x_i \in \mathbb{F}$ distributes $[[x_i; \mathbf{r}_{x_i}]]_S$. If this fails, P_i is corrupt, so we will instead assign 0 as default input for P_i, by distributing $[[0; \mathbf{r}_0]]_S$ for a fixed default value of $\mathbf{r}_0$, say, the all-zero vector. This can be done by a number of public commit to 0s.

We then go through the circuit and process the gates one by one in the computational order. Just after the input-sharing phase, we consider all input gates as being processed. We will maintain the following:

Invariant. Consider an input or an output wire for any gate, and let $a \in \mathbb{F}$ be the value assigned to this wire. Then, if the gate has been processed, the players hold $[[a; \mathbf{r}_a]]_S$.

We then continue with the last two phases of the protocol.

Computation phase. Repeat the following until all gates have been processed (then go to the next phase). Consider the first gate in the computational order that has not been processed yet. According to the type of gate, do one of the following

Addition gate. The players hold $[[a; \mathbf{r}_a]]_S, [[b; \mathbf{r}_b]]_S$ for the two inputs a, b to the gate. The players compute $[[a + b; \mathbf{r}_a + \mathbf{r}_b]]_S = [[a; \mathbf{r}_a]]_S + [[b; \mathbf{r}_b]]_S$.

Multiply-by-constant gate. The players hold $[[a; \mathbf{r}_a]]_S$ for the input a to the gate. The players compute $[[\alpha a; \alpha \mathbf{r}_a]]_S = \alpha [[a; \mathbf{r}_a]]_S$.

Multiplication gate. The players hold $[[a; \mathbf{r}_a]]_S, [[b; \mathbf{r}_b]]_S$ for the two inputs a, b to the gate.

1. The players compute $[[ab; \mathbf{r}_a \otimes \mathbf{r}_b]]_{\hat{S}} = [[a; \mathbf{r}_a]]_S \odot [[b; \mathbf{r}_b]]_S$. Note that this involves each P_j committing to his or her local products and proving that this was done correctly. So this may fail for some subset of players $A \in \mathcal{A}$.

2. Define $\mathbf{s} \overset{\text{def}}{=} \mathbf{r}_a \otimes \mathbf{r}_b$. Then the parties hold $[[ab; \mathbf{s}]]_{\hat{S}}$. Let $[[ab; \mathbf{s}]]_{\hat{S}} = (c_1, \ldots, c_{\hat{m}})$. For each P_i and each c_j he or she owns, he or she distributes $[[c_j; \mathbf{r}_{c_j}]]_S$ from $\langle c_j \rangle_i$. Also, this step may fail for a subset $A \in \mathcal{A}$.

3. Let S be the indices of the players for which the preceding two steps did not fail. By strong multiplicativity of S, there exists $\mathbf{r}_S$, a recombination vector for S, that is, a vector $\mathbf{r}_S = (r_1, \ldots, r_{\hat{m}})$, that players in S can use to reconstruct secrets generated by $\hat{S}$. In particular, we have $ab = \sum_{\phi(j) \in S} r_j c_j$. The players compute

$$\sum_{\phi(j) \in S} r_j [[c_j; \mathbf{r}_{c_j}]]_S = [[\sum_{\phi(j) \in S} r_j c_j; \sum_{\phi(j) \in S} r_j \mathbf{r}_{c_j}]]_S = [[ab; \sum_{\phi(j) \in S} r_j \mathbf{r}_{c_j}]]_S$$

Output reconstruction. At this point, all gates, including the output gates, have been processed. So do the following for each output gate (labeled i): the players hold $[[y; f_y]]_S$, where y is the value assigned to the output gate. Now we open $[[y; f_y]]_S$ toward P_i.

---

shares of a. Also recall that ϕ is the labeling function that tells us which players receive the individual shares. Then we define

$$[[a; \mathbf{r}_a]]_S = (\langle g(\mathbf{r}_a)_1 \rangle_{\phi(1)}, \ldots, \langle g(\mathbf{r}_a)_m \rangle_{\phi(m)})$$

This is just the natural generalization of the concept we defined earlier: the secret a has been shared, and players are committed to the shares they hold. We can then also define

$$[\![a; \mathbf{r}_a]\!]_\mathcal{S} + [\![b; \mathbf{r}_b]\!]_\mathcal{S}, \ \alpha[\![a; \mathbf{r}_a]\!]_\mathcal{S}, \ [\![a; \mathbf{r}_a]\!]_\mathcal{S} \odot [\![b; \mathbf{r}_b]\!]_\mathcal{S}$$

similarly to Definition 6.18, but in addition to computing on shares locally, the corresponding commands from F_{COM} are also invoked. Then the following lemma is easy to show:

LEMMA 6.21 *The following holds for any* $a, b, \alpha \in \mathbb{F}$, *and any multiplicative linear secret-sharing scheme* $\mathcal{S}$:

$$[\![a; \mathbf{r}_a]\!]_\mathcal{S} + [\![b; \mathbf{r}_b]\!]_\mathcal{S} = [\![a + b; \mathbf{r}_a + \mathbf{r}_b]\!]_\mathcal{S} \tag{6.5}$$

$$\alpha[\![a; \mathbf{r}_a]\!]_\mathcal{S} = [\![\alpha a; \alpha \mathbf{r}_a]\!]_\mathcal{S} \tag{6.6}$$

$$[\![a; \mathbf{r}_a]\!]_\mathcal{S} \odot [\![b; \mathbf{r}_b]\!]_\mathcal{S} = [\![ab; \mathbf{r}_a \otimes \mathbf{r}_b]\!]_{\hat{\mathcal{S}}} \tag{6.7}$$

Similar to what we saw in Chapter 5, when we say that P_i distributes $[\![a; \mathbf{r}_a]\!]_\mathcal{S}$, we mean that P_i commits to all entries in $\mathbf{r}_a$; we then use the add and mult commands to compute commitments to the shares in a and finally use transfer commands to ensure that the party holding a share is committed to that share.

It is now straightforward to show the following:

THEOREM 6.22 $\pi_{GCEAS}^f \diamond F_{SC} \diamond F_{COM}$ *implements* F_{SFE}^f *in* $\text{Env}^{A,\text{sync}}$ *with perfect security for any* f *whenever the protocol is based on a strongly multiplicative linear secret-sharing scheme* $\mathcal{S}$ *with adversary structure* $\mathcal{A}$.

We note that it is possible to modify Protocol GCEAS to make it also work for a $Q2$ adversary structure and a multiplicative scheme $\mathcal{S}$. As in Chapter 5, the difficulty in this case is that if a player fails during processing of a multiplication gate, we cannot proceed because all players are needed to reconstruct in $\hat{\mathcal{S}}$ since we do not assume strong multiplication. We can handle such failures by going back to the start of the computation and opening the input values of the players that have just been disqualified. Now we restart the protocol while the honest players simulate the disqualified players. Note that we can use default random choices for these players, so no communication is needed for the honest players to agree on the actions of the simulated ones. This allows the adversary to slow down the protocol by a factor at most linear in n. In doing this, it is important that we do not have to restart the protocol after some party received its output – this is ensured by starting the output-reconstruction phase only after all multiplication gates have been handled.

Let $\pi_{GCEAS\text{-}Q2}^f$ be π_{GCEAS}^f modified to handle $Q2$ structures as we just discussed. We then have the following theorem, the proof of which we leave to the reader:

THEOREM 6.23 $\pi_{GCEAS\text{-}Q2}^f \diamond F_{SC} \diamond F_{COM}$ *implements* F_{SFE}^f *in* $\text{Env}^{A,\text{sync}}$ *with perfect security for any* f *when based on a multiplicative secret-sharing scheme with adversary structure* $\mathcal{A}$.

6.5.1 Implementation of Homomorphic Commitment from Linear Secret Sharing

Let us first consider how we can implement F_{COM} from $F_{COM\text{-}SIMPLE}$. Note first that from the results in Chapter 5, we already have the following:

Protocol Generalized Perfect Commitment Multiplication

This protocol is based on a strongly multiplicative secret-sharing scheme $\mathcal{S}$. If any command used during this protocol fails, all players output `fail`.

1. $\langle c \rangle_i \leftarrow ab$.
2. P_i chooses vectors $\mathbf{r}_a, \mathbf{r}_b$ with coordinates $a, \alpha_1, \ldots, \alpha_t$ and $b, \beta_1, \ldots, \beta_t$ for random α_j, β_j. He or she computes $\mathbf{r}_c = \mathbf{r}_a \otimes \mathbf{r}_b$ and lets $c, \gamma_1, \ldots, \gamma_{(t+1)^2} - 1$ be the coordinates of $\mathbf{r}_c$. Then he or she establishes commitments as follows:

$$\langle \alpha_j \rangle_i \leftarrow \alpha_j \quad \text{for } j = 1, \ldots, t$$

$$\langle \beta_j \rangle_i \leftarrow \beta_j \quad \text{for } j = 1, \ldots, t$$

$$\langle \gamma_j \rangle_i \leftarrow \gamma_j \quad \text{for } j = 1, \ldots, (t+1)^2 - 1$$

3. Recall that the matrices of $\mathcal{S}$ and $\hat{\mathcal{S}}$ are called M and $\hat{M}$. Then, for $k = 1, \ldots, m$, the `add` and `mult` commands are invoked to compute

$$\langle a_k \rangle_i = M_{k,0} \langle a \rangle_i + M_{k,1} \langle \alpha_1 \rangle_i + \cdots + M_{k,t} \langle \alpha_t \rangle_i$$

$$\langle b_k \rangle_i = M_{k,0} \langle b \rangle_i + M_{k,1} \langle \beta_1 \rangle_i + \cdots + M_{k,t} \langle \beta_t \rangle_i$$

and for $k = 1, \ldots, \hat{m}$, we compute

$$\langle c_k \rangle_i = \hat{M}_{k,0} \langle b \rangle_i + \hat{M}_{k,1} \langle \gamma_1 \rangle_i + \cdots + \hat{M}_{k,(t+1)^2 - 1} \langle \gamma_{2t} \rangle_i$$

Note that by this computation we have that a_k is the kth share in a; that is, $a_k = \mathbf{m}_k \cdot \mathbf{r}_a$. Similarly, b_k, c_k are the kth shares in b and c, respectively. Then, for all k, we execute $(P_{\phi(k)}) a_k \leftarrow \langle a_k \rangle_i$, $(P_{\phi(k)}) b_k \leftarrow \langle b_k \rangle_i$, and $(P_{\phi(k)}) c_k \leftarrow \langle c_k \rangle_i$.

4. For $k = 1, \ldots, \hat{m}$, do $P_{\phi(k)}$ checks that $a_u b_v = c_k$ for the appropriate u, v with $\phi(u) = \phi(v) = \phi(k)$ (see Lemma 6.9). He or she broadcasts `accept` if this is the case; otherwise, he or she broadcasts $(\texttt{reject}, k)$.

5. For each $P_{\phi(k)}$ who said $(\texttt{reject}, k)$, do $a_u \leftarrow \langle a_u \rangle_i$, $b_v \leftarrow \langle b_v \rangle_i$, and $c_k \leftarrow \langle c_k \rangle_i$; all players check whether $a_u b_v = c_k$ holds. If this is not the case, all players output `fail`.

6. If we arrive here, no command failed during the protocol, and all relations $a_u b_v = c_k$ that were checked hold. All players output `success`.

THEOREM 6.24 *There exists a protocol $\pi_{TRANSFER,MULT}$ such that $\pi_{TRANSFER,MULT} \diamond F_{SC} \diamond F_{COM\text{-}SIMPLE}$ implements F_{COM} in $\text{Env}^{t,\text{sync}}$ with statistical security for all $t < n$.*

This is just a restatement of part of Theorem 5.1. The result can be used in this context because $\pi_{TRANSFER,MULT}$ only uses commands from $F_{COM\text{-}SIMPLE}$ and no secret sharing and because tolerating any number of corruptions less than n is, of course, good enough to handle any nontrivial adversary structure. Furthermore, we also have the following:

THEOREM 6.25 *There exists a protocol $\pi_{GPTRANSFER,GPMULT}$ such that $\pi_{GPTRANSFER,GPMULT} \diamond F_{SC} \diamond F_{COM\text{-}SIMPLE}$ implements F_{COM} in $\text{Env}^{A,\text{sync}}$ with perfect security when based on a strongly multiplicative secret-sharing scheme $\mathcal{S}$ with adversary structure $\mathcal{A}$.*

The idea for constructing $\pi_{GPTRANSFER,GPMULT}$ is to start from $\pi_{PTRANSFER,PMULT}$, as presented in Section 5.2, replace secret sharing based on polynomials by $\mathcal{S}$, and otherwise "do the same." We show here how the multiplication proof can be done in this way. We argue informally why Protocol Generalized Perfect Commitment Multiplication is secure and leave a formal simulation proof to the reader.

If the prover P_i is honest, the adversary gets no information on a or b; some values a_k, b_k, and c_k are revealed to corrupt players, but the corrupted set is in the adversary structure, so the a_k, b_k give no information and c_k always equals $a_u b_v$ for the relevant values of k, u, v. Furthermore, all honest players will say accept after the check, so only values the adversary already knows are broadcast. If P_i is corrupt, note that the computation on commitments ensures that the sets $\{a_k\} = [a, \mathbf{r}_a]_S, \{b_k\} = [b, \mathbf{r}_b]_S$, and $\{c_k\} = [c, \mathbf{r}_c]_{\hat{S}}$ are consistent sets of shares computed under S, S, and $\hat{S}$, respectively, and they therefore determine well-defined secrets a, b, c. Furthermore, the set of shares $[a, \mathbf{r}_a]_S \odot [b, \mathbf{r}_b]_S$ is a valid set of secrets under $\hat{S}$ and determines the secret ab. By the checks done, we know that if success is output, the sets of shares $[a, \mathbf{r}_a]_S \odot [b, \mathbf{r}_b]_S$ and $[c, \mathbf{r}_c]_{\hat{S}}$ agree in all entries owned by honest players. But the set of honest players is the complement of a set in the adversary structure of S. It is therefore in the access structure of $\hat{S}$ by the strong multiplication property; hence it is large enough to determine a secret in $\hat{S}$ uniquely. It follows that $c = ab$ as desired.

EXERCISE 6.6 Construct the rest of protocol $\pi_{\text{GPTRANSFER,GPMULT}}$, that is, construct a perfectly secure protocol for transferring a commitment from one player to another based on a linear secret-sharing scheme S, and use this to prove Theorem 6.25.

We now turn to the question of how to implement $F_{\text{COM-SIMPLE}}$ from linear secret sharing. Of course, it is not surprising that the solution is similar to what we have seen in Chapter 5, but some issues need to be addressed.

Note first that if players hold $[s, \mathbf{r}_s]_S$, the adversary structure $\mathcal{A}$ is $Q3$, and players broadcast their shares. Then the correct value of s is uniquely determined: we can in principle simply search for some $s', \mathbf{r}_{s'}$ such that $[s'; \mathbf{r}_{s'}]_S$ agrees with the set of shares broadcast except in some set of entries owned by some unqualified set $A' \in \mathcal{A}$. We claim that then s' always equals the correct secret s. The set A' may not be the set of players that are actually corrupted, but this does not matter: if we start from the set of all shares and then take away entries owned by corrupted players (say, in set A) and also take away all entries in A', then $[s'; \mathbf{r}_{s'}]_S$ agrees with $[s, \mathbf{r}_s]_S$ in the remaining entries because these all correspond to honest players. This set of entries is in the access structure of S by the $Q3$ property, so $s = s'$ as desired. However, the search will always stop because $(s', \mathbf{r}_{s'}) = (s, \mathbf{r}_s)$ is, of course, a good solution. Note that if this is used as a commitment scheme, players would not have to do the search (this would be inefficient in most cases); we could just ask the committer to point out the right solution.

To make a perfect homomorphic commitment scheme, it is therefore sufficient to force a committer to hand out consistent shares of the value he or she has in mind; that is, we want something of form $[a; \mathbf{r}_a]_S$. This ensures privacy against corruption of any unqualified set, and if we require the committer to reveal $\mathbf{r}_a$ at opening time, it follows from what we just saw that he or she cannot change to a different value of a.

To enforce consistency, we reuse the approach from earlier and have the committer secret share his or her value but then also secret share the randomness he or she used for this. This introduces the possibility of other players cross-checking what they have, ultimately enforcing consistency. We can phrase this as a redundant version of the original linear secret-sharing scheme, similar to the bivariate polynomials we saw earlier.

Therefore, to commit to a value $a \in \mathbb{F}$, based on secret-sharing scheme S, P_i chooses a random symmetric $(t+1) \times (t+1)$ matrix R_a with a in the upper-left corner. Note that by symmetry, we have $R_a = R_a^{\top}$. Then, for each index k, he or she sends $\mathbf{u}_k = R_a \cdot \mathbf{m}_k^{\top}$ to $P_{\phi(k)}$ (recall that $\mathbf{m}_k$ is a row vector taken from the matrix of S).

Note that the product of the first row of R_a with $\mathbf{m}_k^{\top}$ is a normal share of a according to S, so the share β_k of a is defined to be the first entry in $\mathbf{u}_k$. Note that for any pair of indices k,j, we have (because R_a is symmetric)

$$\mathbf{m}_j \cdot \mathbf{u}_k = \mathbf{m}_j \cdot R_a \cdot \mathbf{m}_k^{\top} = (R_a \cdot \mathbf{m}_j^{\top})^{\top} \cdot \mathbf{m}_k^{\top} = \mathbf{m}_k \cdot \mathbf{u}_j$$

Thus, if we define $\beta_{kj} = \mathbf{m}_j \cdot \mathbf{u}_k = \mathbf{m}_k \cdot \mathbf{u}_j$, this is a value that both $P_{\phi(k)}$ and $P_{\phi(j)}$ can compute, so this can be used as a consistency check on the information P_i distributes. We have the following:

LEMMA 6.26 *If honest player P_i chooses R_a and sends $\mathbf{u}_k = R_a \cdot \mathbf{m}_k^{\top}$ to $P_{\phi(k)}$, then the information given to any unqualified set A has distribution independent of a.*

Proof The information given to the set A can be written as $M_A \cdot R_a$. Since A is unqualified, there exists a vector $\mathbf{w}$ that has first coordinate 1 and is orthogonal to all rows in M_A. Now, if we interpret the tensor product $\mathbf{w} \otimes \mathbf{w}$ as a matrix in the natural way, this matrix is symmetric and has 1 in the upper-left corner. Therefore, if we define $R_0 = R_a - a \cdot (\mathbf{w} \otimes \mathbf{w})$, then R_0 is symmetric and has 0 in the upper-left corner. Furthermore, $M_A \cdot R_a = M_A \cdot R_0$, so for any set of shares that A might receive, the number of random choices that could lead to these shares is the same for any value of a, namely, the number of possible choices for $a = 0$. The lemma follows. ∎

Protocol Generalized Commit

1. On input $(\texttt{commit}, i, cid, a)$, P_i chooses a uniformly random symmetric matrix R_a with a in the top-left corner and sends $\mathbf{u}_k = R_a \cdot \mathbf{m}_k^{\top}$ to $P_{\phi(k)}$. Then $P_{\phi(k)}$ sets β_k to be the first entry in $\mathbf{u}_k$.
2. For each j, $P_{\phi(j)}$ computes $\beta_{kj} = \mathbf{m}_k \cdot \mathbf{u}_j$ and sends β_{kj} to $P_{\phi(k)}$.
3. Each $P_{\phi(k)}$ checks that $\beta_{kj} = \mathbf{m}_j \cdot \mathbf{u}_k$. If so, it broadcasts $\texttt{success}$. Otherwise, it broadcasts $(\texttt{dispute}, k, j)$ for each inconsistency.
4. For each dispute reported in the preceding step, P_i broadcasts the correct value of β_{kj}.
5. If any $P_{\phi(k)}$ finds a disagreement between what P_i has broadcast and what he or she received privately from P_i, he or she knows that P_i is corrupt and broadcasts $(\texttt{accuse}, k)$.
6. For any accusation from $P_{\phi(k)}$ in the preceding step, P_i broadcasts all vectors he or she sent to $P_{\phi(k)}$.
7. If any P_k finds a new disagreement between what P_i has now broadcast and what he or she received privately from P_i, he or she knows that P_i is corrupt and broadcasts $(\texttt{accuse}, k)$.
8. If the information broadcast by P_i is not consistent or if a set of players not in the adversary structure has accused P_i, players output $\texttt{fail}$. Otherwise, players who accused P_i and had new vectors broadcast will accept these. All others keep the vectors they received in the first step. Now, for each j, $P_{\phi(j)}$ stores (cid, i, β_j). In addition, P_i stores the first row of R_a. All players output $\texttt{success}$.

Now, to show the security of Protocol Generalized Commit, we need two main lemmas.

LEMMA 6.27 *If P_i remains honest throughout Protocol Generalized Commit, the view of any set $A \in \mathcal{A}$ players is independent of the committed value a, and all players who are honest at the end of the protocol will output the shares in a that P_i distributed.*

This follows immediately from Lemma 6.26 and the fact that if P_i remains honest, then the values that are broadcast are only values that players in A already know from the first step.

LEMMA 6.28 *If the adversary structure is Q3, then no matter how corrupt players behave in Protocol Generalized Commit, players who are honest at the end of the protocol will all output* fail *or will output a set of shares in some value a' that are all consistent with a vector $\mathbf{r}_{a'}$.*

Proof The decision to output fail is based on public information, so it is clear that players who remain honest will either all output fail or all output some value. Thus assume that the latter case occurs. If we take the set of all players and subtract the set A' of players who accused P_i and also subtract the set of players who are corrupt at the end of the protocol, then since A, A' are unqualified and the adversary structure is Q3, the remaining set S must be qualified. Note that S consists of honest players who did not accuse P_i. Let H be the set of all honest players.

We make the following *claim*: consider any j with $P_{\phi(j)} \in H$ and any k with $P_{\phi(k)} \in S$. Then the two players agree on the β_{kj} they have in common, that is, $\mathbf{m}_k \cdot \mathbf{u}_j = \mathbf{m}_j \cdot \mathbf{u}_k$.

We argue this as follows: if $P_{\phi(j)}$ had a new vector broadcast for him or her in step 6, then the claim is true because otherwise $P_{\phi(k)}$ would have accused in step 7. However, suppose that no new values were broadcast for $P_{\phi(j)}$. Then he or she keeps the values he or she was given in step 1, as does $P_{\phi(k)}$. It also means that neither $P_{\phi(j)}$ nor $P_{\phi(k)}$ accused at any time. But our claim holds for the values sent in step 1, because if not, a (dispute, k,j) would have been reported, and either $P_{\phi(j)}$ or $P_{\phi(k)}$ would have accused P_i in step 5, and this did not happen.

Now form two matrices U_H and U_S in which the columns consist of all $\mathbf{u}_k$ vectors held by players in H and S. If M is the matrix of the secret-sharing scheme $\mathcal{S}$, then $M_S \cdot U_S$ is a matrix containing all β_{kj} values that players in S can compute. The preceding claim on agreement between players in S and all players in H can be compactly written as $M_H \cdot U_S = (M_S \cdot U_H)^\top$.

Let $\mathbf{v}$ be the recombination vector for S that we know exists by Theorem 6.8. We claim that the vector $\mathbf{r}_{s'} = U_S \cdot \mathbf{v}$ defines the sharing that P_i has effectively distributed. More precisely, as s' we can take the first entry in $\mathbf{r}_{s'}$, and furthermore, if we build a vector containing the shares output by players in H, this is indeed formed correctly from $\mathbf{r}_{s'}$, that is, it equals $M_H \cdot \mathbf{r}_{s'}$. To show this, we can use the preceding claim to compute

$$M_H \cdot \mathbf{r}_{s'} = M_H \cdot U_S \cdot \mathbf{v} = (M_S \cdot U_H)^\top \cdot \mathbf{v} = U_H^\top \cdot M_S^\top \cdot \mathbf{v} = U_H^\top \cdot \mathbf{e}$$

where the last step follows from the property the recombination vector has (as can be seen in the proof of Theorem 6.8), and $\mathbf{e}$ is the first canonical basis vector. Clearly, the entries in the vector $U_H^\top \cdot \mathbf{e}$ are the first entries in all the $\mathbf{u}_j$ vectors held by players in H, and these entries are exactly what they output as their shares by specification of the protocol. ∎

Based on what we have seen, it is now straightforward to construct a complete protocol $\pi_{\text{GEN-PERFECT-COM-SIMPLE}}$ for implementing $F_{\text{COM-SIMPLE}}$ based on a secret-sharing scheme S. This, as well as the simulation proof of security, follows the same recipe we used for the proof of Theorem 5.6. We therefore have the following:

THEOREM 6.29 $\pi_{\text{GEN-PERFECT-COM-SIMPLE}} \diamond F_{SC}$ *implements* $F_{\text{COM-SIMPLE}}$ *in* $\text{Env}^{A,\text{sync}}$ *with perfect security when based on a linear secret-sharing scheme S with $Q3$ adversary structure A.*

EXERCISE 6.7 Construct the rest of protocol $\pi_{\text{GEN-PERFECT-COM-SIMPLE}}$, and show Theorem 6.29.

If we only go for statistical security in the end and assume that we have a broadcast functionality given, then assuming access to the F_{ICSIG} functionality from Section 5.4.1, we can implement $F_{\text{COM-SIMPLE}}$ even for $Q2$ adversary structures. The resulting protocol $\pi_{\text{GEN-COM-SIMPLE}}$ can be constructed in exactly the same way as we did $\pi_{\text{COM-SIMPLE}}$ for the threshold case earlier: to commit, we do the same as in Protocol Generalized Commit, except that the committer must sign everything he or she sends using F_{ICSIG}. All accusations against the committer now can be proved because the accuser can demonstrate that he or she indeed received a particular message from the committer. This leads to the following:

THEOREM 6.30 $\pi_{\text{GEN-COM-SIMPLE}} \diamond \pi_{\text{ICSIG}} \diamond F_{SC}$ *implements* $F_{\text{COM-SIMPLE}}$ *in* $\text{Env}^{A,\text{sync}}$ *with statistical security when based on a linear secret-sharing scheme S with $Q2$ adversary structure A.*

6.5.2 General Results on MPC from Linear Secret Sharing

If we combine everything we have seen so far, we obtain a number of results for general adversary structures that are natural generalizations of the results for threshold adversaries. We first note that broadcast can be implemented securely from secure point-to-point channels if the actively corrupted set of players is from a $Q3$ adversary structure [92]:

THEOREM 6.31 *There exists a protocol $\pi_{\text{GEN-BROADCAST}}$ such that $\pi_{\text{GEN-BROADCAST}} \diamond F_{PPC}$ implements F_{SC} in $\text{Env}^{A,\text{sync}}$ with perfect security when A is $Q3$.*

Then Theorems 6.25, 6.22, 6.29, and 6.31 imply that any function can be computed with perfect, active security against $Q3$ adversary structures given access to secure point-to-point channels. More formally, we have the following:

THEOREM 6.32 $\pi^f_{\text{GCEAS}} \diamond \pi_{\text{GPTRANSFER, GPMULT}} \diamond \pi_{\text{GEN-PERFECT-COM-SIMPLE}} \diamond \pi_{\text{GEN-BROADCAST}} \diamond F_{PPC}$ *implements* F^f_{SFE} *in* $\text{Env}^{A,\text{sync}}$ *with perfect security when based on a strongly multiplicative linear secret-sharing scheme S with $Q3$ adversary structure A.*

The final result in this chapter concerns the case in which we assume access to F_{SC}; that is, we assume secure channels and broadcast and go for statistical security. In this case, putting previous results together, we get that Theorems 6.24, 6.23, and 6.30 imply that any function can be computed with statistical, active security if the adversary is limited to Q2 corruptions given access to secure point-to-point channels and broadcast. More formally, we have the following:

THEOREM 6.33 $\pi^f_{GCEAS\text{-}Q2} \diamond \pi_{TRANSFER,MULT} \diamond \pi_{ICSIG} \diamond \pi_{GEN\text{-}COM\text{-}SIMPLE} \diamond F_{SC}$ *implements* F^f_{SFE} *in* $\text{Env}^{A,\text{sync}}$ *with statistical security when based on a multiplicative linear secret-sharing scheme* S *with Q2 adversary structure* A.

These results show what can be done for active security with a given secret-sharing scheme. We might also ask, what is the best protocol we can have for a given adversary structure A?

One can first note that in general it is clearly sufficient for security to come up with a secret-sharing scheme S whose adversary structure *contains* A. The protocol built from S then would protect against an even stronger adversary.

Now, for perfect security, we know that A must be $Q3$ to allow any function to be computed with perfect active security, and finally, any $Q3$ structure admits a strongly multiplicative secret-sharing scheme. Therefore, we have the following:

COROLLARY 6.34 *Any function can be computed with perfect, active security against an environment corrupting subsets in adversary structure* A, *provided that* A *is Q3, and we have access to* F_{PPC}. *The complexity of the protocol can be made polynomial in the size of the smallest strongly multiplicative linear secret-sharing scheme whose adversary structure contains* A.

For the case of statistical security, it is sufficient to have any linear scheme with a $Q2$ adversary structure containing A, by Theorem 6.16. Thus, for this case, we get the following:

COROLLARY 6.35 *Any function can be computed with statistical active security against an environment corrupting subsets in adversary structure* A, *provided that* A *is Q2, and we have access to* F_{SC}. *The complexity of the protocol can be made polynomial in the size of the smallest linear secret-sharing scheme whose adversary structure contains* A.

One also can note in this last corollary that if A happens to be $Q3$, then we can replace access to F_{SC} by access to F_{PPC} and simulate broadcast using Theorem 6.31. This gives a statistical version of the first corollary, and this can be significant for efficiency because the smallest linear scheme for an adversary structure may (for all we know) be much smaller than the best strongly multiplicative one.

6.6 Notes

Multiparty computation with security against general adversary structures was first considered by Hirt and Maurer [107], who showed that the basic completeness theorems for unconditional security generalize from $t < n/2$ and $t < n/3$ to $Q2$ and $Q3$ adversary structures, respectively.

In 2000, Cramer, Damgård, and Maurer [61] showed that passive and active multiparty computation follows from multiplicative and strongly multiplicative linear secret-sharing schemes, respectively, where the complexity of the protocol is polynomial in the size of the secret-sharing scheme.

One may wonder if this result is the most general one possible; that is, can one base unconditionally secure multiparty computation on *any* secret-sharing scheme? An answer to this was given by Cramer, Damgård, and Dziembowski [59], who showed that although verifiable secret sharing does follow by an efficient black-box reduction from any secret-sharing scheme, no such reduction exists for multiparty computation, at least not one that would be efficient for any access structure. Therefore, some extra property (such as linearity) must be assumed for a general reduction to exist.

The results on linear secret sharing in this chapter are from Cramer, Damgård, and Maurer [61], except the efficient construction of secret sharing for the dual-access structure, which is by Serge Fehr. The model of linear secret sharing that we use in this chapter is essentially that of monotone span programs, which were introduced by Karchmer and Wigderson [119]. We do not, however, introduce the full formalism of span programs; this is more relevant if one wants to see span programs as a model of computation, which is not our focus here.

7

Cryptographic MPC Protocols

7.1 Introduction

The main focus of this book is information-theoretic solutions, and therefore, we cover the case of computational security only very superficially. Basically, we survey some of the main results and give pointers for further reading.

7.2 The Case of Honest Majority

A main completeness result for computationally secure multiparty computation is that any function can be computed with computational security in a model where authenticated point-to-point channels are given. The adversary may corrupt $t < n/2$ players actively. Recall that computational security is defined just like statistical security, except that the simulator is only required to work for polynomial time-bounded environments. More formally, the result is as follows:

THEOREM 7.1 *If non-committing encryption schemes exist, then there exists a protocol $\pi^f_{COMPSEC}$ such that $\pi^f_{COMPSEC} \diamond F_{AT}$ implements F^f_{SFE} in $\text{Env}^{t,\text{sync},\text{poly}}$ with computational security for all $t < n/2$.*

We will explain what non-committing encryption is in a moment (see also Section 4.3). For now, we note that the assumption that $t < n/2$ is necessary to guarantee that the protocol terminates and gives output to honest players. In the two-party case, for instance, it is clear that we cannot terminate if one of the players simply stops playing. We discuss later what can be done if we do not assume an honest majority.

Note that we have already seen *statistically* secure protocols for the case $t < n/2$, but there we had to assume access to secure channels and broadcast (F_{SC}), so the preceding result says that we can make do with only authenticated channels (F_{AT}) if we settle for computational security.

The reader might complain about the fact that we assume authenticated channels – if we are willing to assume computationally secure cryptography, we can both public-key encrypt and authenticate messages with signatures, so can we not get a protocol that starts from nothing? This, however, is not possible, at least in most practical scenarios. One issue is that even in a two-player protocol, an honest player would need to make sure that he or she is talking to the player he or she wants to do the protocol with and not a third party. Otherwise, the protocol would not be secure against an external attacker in the case where both players are honest, and this is a property one would often need. We can, however, minimize the use of authenticated channels, namely, by using signatures. This will mean that we only need authenticated channels in an initial phase to communicate public keys.

To show Theorem 7.1, one notes that from Theorem 5.13 we already know that we can implement F'_{SFE} with statistical security if we are given access to F_{SC}. It will therefore be sufficient to implement F_{SC} given access to F_{AT}, that is, implement secure communication based on authenticated communication. Signatures plus authenticated channels to communicate public keys is enough to get the broadcast we need to implement for F_{SC}. The only remaining thing is to also provide confidentiality. This can be done using encryption – recall that this is a running example in Chapter 4. To get adaptive security, though, one needs a solution that is secure even if both players are corrupted after some communication has happened. One can do this using non-committing encryption, where the simulator is able to construct "ciphertexts" that are not the result of properly encrypting something but can later be claimed to contain any plaintext the simulator desires. In this way, the simulator can handle the case where it must simulate a conversation between two honest players and where one or both of these players is later corrupted. Non-committing encryption from one-way trapdoor permutations with certain extra properties was constructed by Canetti et al. [35], with efficiency improvements under specific assumptions provided by Damgård et al. [71]. Informally speaking, what one needs is that one can generate a permutation (a public key) obliviously, that is, while learning nothing about the corresponding trapdoor (secret key). This is also sometimes known as a simulatable trapdoor permutations (STP).

Even the best non-committing encryption schemes known are very inefficient compared with regular public-key encryption. The size of a ciphertext is a factor κ larger than the plaintext, where κ is the security parameter. However, if we are only after static security, any chosen-ciphertext-secure (CCA-secure) cryptosystem can be used instead, and this will lead to a much more efficient protocol with current state of the art.

Note also that this approach gives a completely different proof of Theorem 7.1 than the first one given in Goldreich, Micali, and Wigderson [100], which only showed static security, assuming the existence of one-way trapdoor permutations. The approach used there was to build a protocol for oblivious transfer (OT) from trapdoor permutations and then to base the rest of the protocol on OT and zero-knowledge proofs.

Oblivions transfer is a primitive that one may think of as an ideal functionality that gets two input bits b_0, b_1 from a sender and one input bit c from a receiver and then returns b_c to the receiver. In fact, given only OT as a black box, one can evaluate any function securely for any number of players; this was shown by Kilian [121].

It is instructive to note the difference in efficiency between the two approaches we have outlined and where it comes from. The first approach combines a statistically secure protocol π_{STAT} based on secret sharing with a computationally secure implementation of F_{SC}. Since π_{STAT} requires only that we do linear algebra in a relatively small field, it can be implemented very efficiently. In fact, the complexity can be close to linear in the security parameter. The implementation of F_{SC} does require public-key cryptography, which is much less efficient, but since we only need the cryptography as a secure transport mechanism, we can combine the public-key systems with much more efficient symmetric cryptosystems, at least if we settle for static security. Such an implementation of F_{SC} corresponds closely to the kind of service offered on the Internet by the well-known (and very efficient) SSL and TLS protocols. In contrast, the approach from Goldreich, Micali, and Wigderson [100] uses public-key techniques throughout to do the actual computation and is therefore less efficient when used directly. The reader should note, however, that with a more recent technique for implementing the OTs needed in the preceding work [100], the difference in efficiency becomes much smaller. This technique is known as OT-extension [112, 150], and the idea is do a small number of OTs using expensive public-key cryptography and then extend them to a much larger number of OTs by cheaper techniques based on special types of hash functions.

However, regardless of the approach used, if we want adaptive security and resort to non-committing encryption, we will get an impractical protocol. It is therefore interesting to note that we can have adaptively secure solutions that are more efficient if we use public-key cryptosystems with stronger properties. For instance, some cryptosystems are additively homomorphic (i.e., the plaintexts come from some ring), and given ciphertexts c_1 and c_2 that are encryptions of m_1 and m_2 and the public key (but not the secret key), one can easily compute c_3 that looks exactly like a fresh encryption of $m_1 + m_2$. It was shown in Cramer, Damgård, and Nielsen [58] that we can compute arithmetic circuits over the plaintext ring securely if the secret key is secret shared among the players. This only gives static security, but in Damgård and Nielsen [72] it was shown that if we base the protocol on Paillier's public-key cryptosystem [154], adaptive security can be obtained at a cost only a constant factor over that of the static solution.

Even stronger properties are offered by fully homomorphic encryption, where we can also compute a new ciphertext that contains the product of the plaintexts. The first such schemes were constructed by Gentry [99]. With such a scheme, multiparty computation is easy in principle: players publish ciphertexts (under a single public key) containing their input, everyone can now evaluate a ciphertext containing the desired output, and if we assume that the secret key has been secret shared among the players, then they can collaborate to decrypt the result. This solution is extremely efficient in terms of communication, in particular, we need only a constant number of rounds, and the amount of communication is independent of the circuit we compute. However, with the current state of the art, the computational overhead is very large.

7.3 The Case of Dishonest Majority

When t is not assumed to be less than $n/2$, we have already seen that we cannot have information-theoretic security at all, and we also cannot guarantee that the protocol terminates (unless we only go for passive security). This means that the best we can hope for is a computationally secure solution of a weaker version of F_{SFE}^f where the environment gets the output first and then can tell the functionality whether the honest players should get the result or not. Let $F_{\text{SFE}}^{f,\text{abort}}$ be this weaker variant.

Even if we only go for a UC-secure implementation of $F_{\text{SFE}}^{f,\text{abort}}$, this turns out to be impossible is most cases, as shown by Canetti, Kushilevitz, and Lindell [36]. Basically, to do anything nontrivial in the UC model for dishonest majority, one needs a setup assumption, some ideal functionality that is assumed to be available but is not implemented. Popular such assumptions are the common reference string (CRS) model, where we assume a functionality that outputs a string to all players with a certain distribution, and the key-registration model [3], where it is assumed that parties have public keys and are guaranteed to know their secret keys. Of course, one can argue that this makes the model less realistic, but all results up to now have assumed at least access to F_{AT}, and this is also a type of setup assumption, even if it is often not considered as such in the literature.

The basic reason why simulation arguments do not always go through in the plain UC model is that the simulator needs to be able to do "something" that an adversary could not do in a real attack. For example, suppose that a protocol instructs a player P_i to send a ciphertext and prove to another player P_j that he or she knows the plaintext of without revealing it. A simulator for this procedure is typically required to simulate what a corrupt P_j would see in this game. The simulation must be done without knowing the plaintext, this is exactly how we argue that the plaintext stays hidden from P_j. However, assume that instead P_i is corrupt and sends a ciphertext in which he or she does not know the plaintext. Now, why can he or she not do what the simulator does and in this way cheat P_j? In the so-called stand-alone model, where we do not consider composition of protocols, the answer usually is that the simulator is allowed to rewind its "opponent" (the adversary) to a previous state, and rewinding the other player is, of course, not something one could do in a real protocol execution.

However, rewinding does not work in the UC model: to have security under arbitrary concurrent composition, we cannot allow the simulator to rewind the adversary (the environment in this case). Therefore, we need to be able to give the simulator an edge in some other way. In the CRS model, the edge is that the simulator gets to choose the reference string – in fact, it *must* do so because it has to simulate everything the environment sees in the protocol. The point is that it may be able to generate the CRS together with some trapdoor relating to the CRS that a real-life adversary does not get to see, and this is why the simulator can fake a convincing view of the protocol, whereas an adversary cannot do so.

Using such a setup assumption, we can indeed also do general multiparty computation with dishonest majority. In Canetti et al. [37], the following was shown:

THEOREM 7.2 *Assuming that STPs exist, there exists a protocol $\pi^f_{COMPSEC\text{-}DM}$ in the CRS model such that $\pi^f_{COMPSEC\text{-}DM} \diamond F_{AT}$ implements $F^{f,abort}_{SFE}$ in $\mathrm{Env}^{t,poly}$ with computational security for all $t \leq n$.*

Based on the fact that information-theoretic security is not possible for a dishonest majority, one might think that information-theoretic methods for protocol design are not useful in this setting. This is very far from true, however, and we will have more to say about this in Chapter 8.

8

Some Techniques for Efficiency Improvements

8.1 Introduction

In this chapter we cover some techniques for improving the efficiency of the protocols we have seen earlier in this book, but some of the techniques also apply to secure computing protocols in general.

8.2 Circuit Randomization

Recall the way we represented secret data when we constructed the first multiparty computation (MPC) protocol for passive security: for $a \in \mathbb{F}$, we defined the object $[a; f_a]_t$ to be the set of shares $f_a(1), \ldots, f_a(n)$ where $f_a(0) = a$ and the degree of f_a is at most t. At the same time it was understood that player P_i holds $f_a(i)$.

One of the most important properties of this way to represent data is that it is linear; that is, given representations of values a and b, players can compute a representation of $a + b$ by only local computation. This is what we denoted by $[a; f_a]_t + [b; f_b]_t = [a + b; f_a + f_b]_t$, which for this particular representation means that each P_i locally computes $f_a(i) + f_b(i)$.

Of course, this linearity property is not only satisfied by this representation. The representation $[[a; f_a]]_t$ we defined, based on homomorphic commitments to shares, is also linear in this sense.

A final example can be derived from additively homomorphic encryption: if we represent $a \in \mathbb{F}$ by $E_{pk}(a)$, where pk is a public key and the corresponding secret key is shared among the players, then the additive homomorphic property exactly ensures that players can add ciphertexts and obtain an encryption of the sum; that is, it holds that $E_{pk}(a) + E_{pk}(b) = E_{pk}(a + b)$, where the addition of ciphertexts is an operation that can be computed efficiently given only the public key.

In the following, for simplicity, we will use the notation $[a]$ to denote any representation that is linear in the sense we just discussed. In doing so, we suppress the randomness that is usually used to form the parts held by the players (such as the polynomial f_a in $[a; f_a]_t$).

We assume some main properties of a linear representation that we only define informally here. For any of the examples we mentioned, it is easy to see what they concretely mean is each of the cases.

163

DEFINITION 8.1 *A linear representation* $[\cdot]$ *over a finite field* $\mathbb{F}$ *satisfies the following properties:*

1. *Any player* P_i *can collaborate with the other players to create* $[r]$, *where* $r \in \mathbb{F}$ *is chosen by* P_i. *If* P_i *is honest, the process reveals no information on* r. *Furthermore,* $[r]$ *will be correctly formed no matter whether* P_i *is honest or not.*
2. *If players hold representations* $[a], [b]$ *and a public constant* α, *they can locally compute new representations* $[a] + [b] = [a+b]$ *and* $\alpha[a] = [\alpha a]$ *of the same form as* $[a]$ *and* $[b]$.
3. *Given* $[a], [b]$, *the players can interact to compute a new representation* $[a][b] = [ab]$ *of the same form as* $[a]$ *and* $[b]$ *while revealing nothing new about* a *or* b.
4. *The players can collaborate with open any representation, in particular, also representations of form* $[a + b]$ *or* $[ab]$. *This will reveal* $a + b$ *and* ab *but will reveal no other information on* a, b.

Following the pattern of several protocols we have already seen, it is clear how one could do secure function evaluation with a linear representation; namely, players first create representations of their inputs, then they work their way through a circuit representing the desired function using the procedures for addition and multiplication, and finally, they open the representations of the outputs.

There is, however, a way to push a lot of the work needed into a preprocessing phase, and this technique is known as circuit randomization. The idea is to preprocess a number of secure multiplications on random values and then later to use these to multiply more efficiently the actual values occurring in the desired computation. This not only leads to a more efficient online phase but also can lead to better efficiency overall because it is often more efficient to generate a lot of multiplications on random values in parallel than to perform the multiplications on real data as they are needed.

More concretely, we first create a number of multiplication triples. Such a triple has form $[a], [b], [c]$, where a, b are uniformly random, unknown to all players, and $c = ab$. One way to create such triples is to have each player P_i create $[a_i], [b_i]$ for random a_i, b_i and use the assumed operations to compute

$$[a] = [a_1] + \cdots + [a_n], \quad [b] = [b_1] + \cdots + [b_n], \quad \text{and finally} \quad [c] = [ab]$$

We note that this is not the most efficient method, and we look at better solutions later. In any case, though, it is clear that whatever protocol we use should create many triples in parallel. This opens the possibility of using techniques specialized for this purpose in which the amortized cost per triple can be minimized. Moreover, this can usually be done in a constant number of rounds and hence be quite efficient.

We can then revisit the MPC protocol we sketched earlier: in a preprocessing phase, we would create a large number of multiplication triples. Once we know the function to compute and the inputs are fixed, we execute the online phase. Here we have players create representations of their inputs, and then any linear computation on represented values can be done by only local operations. For multiplication, however, we would make use of the preprocessing:

Assume that we are given $[a], [b]$ and want to compute $[ab]$ securely. To do this, we take the next unused triple $[x], [y], [z]$ from the preprocessing. We then compute

$$[a] - [x] = [a - x] \quad \text{and} \quad [b] - [y] = [b - y]$$

and open $e = a - x$ and $d = b - y$. Note that because we assume x, y to be uniformly random in the view of the environment, this is secure to do: e, d will be uniformly random and hence easy to simulate. Moreover, it is easy to see that we have

$$ab = xy + eb + da - ed = z + eb + da - ed$$

and hence players can compute locally

$$[ab] = [z] + e[b] + d[a] - ed$$

This will reduce the work we need in the online phase to opening two representations per secure multiplication plus some local computation, whereas doing $[x][y]$ directly typically would require more interaction. Since communication is usually more costly in practice than local computation, this gives a significant performance improvement for many concrete representations. In addition, for the case of a dishonest majority, where we know that we need to use public-key cryptography in some form, it turns out to be possible to push the use of such expensive cryptography into the preprocessing phase and use a more efficient representation in the online phase. We return to this later.

Protocol Online Phase summarizes the protocol we have just sketched. It is straightforward to formalize it by first specifying the representation as an ideal functionality with operations for creation, arithmetic, and opening. One can then show that the protocol implements $\mathsf{F}_{\mathrm{SFE}}^{f}$ when the circuit used computes f.

8.3 Hyperinvertible Matrices

A hyperinvertible matrix M over a finite field $\mathbb{F}$ is a matrix with the property that all its minors are nonzero; that is, any square submatrix is invertible. More precisely, we have the following:

DEFINITION 8.2 *A matrix M is hyperinvertible if the following holds: let R be a subset of the rows, and let M_R denote the submatrix of M consisting of rows in R. Likewise, let C be a subset of columns, and let M^C denote the submatrix consisting of columns in C. Then we require that M_R^C is invertible whenever $|R| = |C| > 0$.*

The term *hyperinvertible* was coined by Beerliová-Trubíniová and Hirt [10] in the context of MPC. Hyperinvertible matrices are known in several other places than MPC and are also known as regular matrices and MDS matrices, and are equivalent to linear interpolation codes and MDS codes. See Chapter 11 for more on interpolation codes and MDS codes.

Hyperinvertible matrices have nice properties that make them very useful in MPC. We will look at this shortly. First, we show that they actually exist, at least if the underlying field is large enough. Some notation that will be useful later: when C is a set of indices designating some of the entries in $\mathbf{x}$, we let $\mathbf{x}_C$ denote the vector containing only the coordinates designated by C.

THEOREM 8.3 *Let $\alpha_1, \ldots, \alpha_n, \beta_1, \ldots, \beta_m \in \mathbb{F}$ be arbitrary but distinct (so that we assume $|\mathbb{F}| \geq n + m$). Consider the function that maps $(x_1, \ldots, x_n)$ to $(y_1, \ldots, y_m)$ as follows: first, compute the unique polynomial f of degree at most $n - 1$ such that $f(\alpha_i) = x_i, i = 1, \ldots, n$. Then output $f(\beta_1), \ldots, f(\beta_m)$. This is clearly a linear mapping. The matrix M of this mapping is hyperinvertible.*

Protocol Online Phase

This protocol computes an arithmetic circuit securely over a field $\mathbb{F}$. It assumes a linear representation of values in the field, written $[a]$, with properties as described in the text. We assume also a preprocessing phase that creates a number of random multiplication triples of form $[a], [b], [c]$, with $ab = c$. We assume for simplicity that all outputs are public.

Input sharing. Each player P_i holding input $x_i \in \mathbb{F}$ creates a representation $[x_i]$. We then go through the circuit and process the gates one by one in the computational order. Just after the input-sharing phase, we consider all input gates as being processed. We will maintain the following:

Invariant. Computing with the circuit on inputs $x_1, \ldots, x_n$ assigns a unique value to every wire. Consider an input or an output wire for any gate, and let $a \in \mathbb{F}$ be the value assigned to this wire. Then, if the gate has been processed, the players hold $[a]$.

Computation phase. Repeat the following until all gates have been processed (then go to the next phase): Consider the first gate in the computational order that has not been processed yet. According to the type of gate, do one of the following:

> **Addition gate.** The players hold $[a], [b]$ for the two inputs a, b to the gate. The players compute $[a] + [b] = [a + b]$.
>
> **Multiply-by-constant gate.** The players hold $[a]$ for the input a to the gate, and public constant α. The players compute $\alpha[a] = [\alpha a]$.
>
> **Multiplication gate.** The players hold $[a], [b]$ for the two inputs a, b to the gate. Take the next unused triple $[x], [y], [z]$ from the preprocessing phase.
>
> 1. Players compute $[a] - [x] = [a - x]$ and $[b] - [y] = [b - y]$ and open $e = a - x$ and $d = b - y$.
> 2. Players compute locally $[ab] = [z] + e[b] + d[a] - ed$.

Output reconstruction. At this point all gates, including the output gates, have been processed. So, for each output gate, the players hold $[y]$, where y is the value assigned to the output gate. We open $[y]$ to reveal y to all players.

Proof   First, consider any input $\mathbf{x} = (x_1, \ldots, x_n)$ and corresponding output $\mathbf{y} = (y_1, \ldots, y_m)$. Then given a total of n of the x_is and y_is, we can compute all the other x_is and y_is. This just follows from the fact that knowing the value f takes when evaluated on n distinct inputs is enough to compute f by Lagrange interpolation, and then we evaluate f in the other points to get the remaining x_is and y_is.

Now assume that we are given sets R, C designating rows and columns with $|C| = |R|$, and let $\bar{C}$ be the complement of C. Then, clearly, $|\bar{C}| + |R| = n$. Therefore, it follows from what we just observed that given $\mathbf{x}_{\bar{C}}, \mathbf{y}_R$, we can compute $\mathbf{x}_C$.

We now use this to show that M_R^C is invertible. We do so by demonstrating how $\mathbf{x}_C$ can be computed from $\mathbf{y}_R = M_R^C \mathbf{x}_C$. Suppose that we are given just $\mathbf{y}_R$. Then we set $\mathbf{x}_{\bar{C}}$ to be the all-zero vector. The preceding observation says that we can now compute full vectors $\mathbf{x}, \mathbf{y}$ with $\mathbf{y} = M\mathbf{x}$. But this and $\mathbf{x}_{\bar{C}} = 0$ imply that in particular we have found $\mathbf{x}_R$ such that $\mathbf{y}_R = M_R^C \mathbf{x}_C$ because $\mathbf{y} = M\mathbf{x} = M^C \mathbf{x}_C + M^{\bar{C}} \mathbf{x}_{\bar{C}} = M^C \mathbf{x}_C$. ∎

We now state two useful properties of hyperinvertible matrices:

LEMMA 8.4 *Let M be hyperinvertible, let C be a subset of the columns, and let R be a subset of the rows, with $|\bar{C}| = |R|$; that is, $|C| + |R| = n$. Consider any $\mathbf{x}, \mathbf{y}$ with $\mathbf{y} = M\mathbf{x}$. Then, given $\mathbf{x}_C, \mathbf{y}_R$, one can efficiently compute $\mathbf{x}_{\bar{C}}, \mathbf{y}_{\bar{R}}$. Furthermore, the map $\mathbf{x}_C, \mathbf{y}_R \mapsto \mathbf{x}_{\bar{C}}, \mathbf{y}_{\bar{R}}$ is linear.*

Proof It is easy to see that

$$\mathbf{y}_R = M_R \mathbf{x} = M_R^C \mathbf{x}_C + M_R^{\bar{C}} \mathbf{x}_{\bar{C}}$$

Since M is hyperinvertible, $M_R^{\bar{C}}$ is invertible, so rearranging the preceding, we have

$$\mathbf{x}_{\bar{C}} = (M_R^{\bar{C}})^{-1}(\mathbf{y}_R - M_R^C \mathbf{x}_C)$$

Now we have all of $\mathbf{x}$, so $\mathbf{y}$ is trivial to compute. It is clear that the map is linear. ∎

LEMMA 8.5 *Let M be hyperinvertible, and consider the linear mapping $\phi_M : \mathbb{F}^n \rightarrow \mathbb{F}^m$ induced by M. Suppose that we fix k of the input coordinates to arbitrary values. Then consider the linear mapping ϕ' naturally induced by ϕ_M from the remaining $n - k$ coordinates to any $n - k$ coordinates of the output (so we assume that $m \geq n - k$). Then ϕ' is a bijection.*

Proof The $n - k$ input coordinates correspond naturally to a subset C of the columns of M and the selection of output coordinates naturally to a subset R of the rows. Given an input vector $\mathbf{z} \in \mathbb{F}^{n-k}$ for ϕ', we can construct a vector $\mathbf{x} \in \mathbb{F}^n$ such that $\mathbf{x}_C = \mathbf{z}$ and $\mathbf{x}_{\bar{C}}$ contains the k fixed coordinates. Then

$$\phi'(\mathbf{z}) = M_R \mathbf{x} = M_R^C \mathbf{x}_C + M_R^{\bar{C}} \mathbf{x}_{\bar{C}}$$

Since $M_R^{\bar{C}} \mathbf{x}_{\bar{C}}$ is a fixed vector and M_R^C is invertible, this is clearly a bijection. ∎

Randomness Extraction and Efficient Secure Multiplication

We now look at how the preceding properties of hyperinvertible matrices can be used in multiparty computation. In particular, we have seen the concept of a linear representation of secret data, and we have seen that, for instance, to create multiplication triples, it is very useful to be able to create a representation of a random field element that is unknown to the environment. We also saw a trivial way to do this in which each player creates a representation of his or her own random element, and then we add all contributions. This works but seems wasteful because each of the $n - t$ honest players contributes a random element, but we end up with only one random representation.

Hyperinvertible matrices offer a better solution, as shown in Protocol Extract Random Representations. The protocol uses an n by n hyperinvertible matrix M and creates first a set of representations $[x_i]$, $i = 1, \ldots, n$. Now note that since we can do linear computation on representations, we can consider these as a vector with entries $[x_i]$, $i = 1, \ldots, n$. Now multiply M on this vector and obtain in a natural way a vector of representations $[y_i]$, $i = 1, \ldots, n$. More precisely, $[y_i] = M_{i,1}[x_1] + \cdots + M_{i,n}[x_n]$. Note that by our assumptions on linear representations, the $[y_i]$ can be computed by only local computation.

Protocol Extract Random Representations

This protocol produces a number of random representations based on contributions from each player.

1. Each player P_i creates $[x_i]$, where x_i is uniformly random.
2. The players apply matrix M to this vector $[x_1], \ldots, [x_n]$ of representations (as explained in the text) to get via local computation representations $[y_1], \ldots, [y_n]$.
3. Output the representations $[y_1], \ldots, [y_{n-t}]$.

We claim that the y_is contained in the output $[y_1], \ldots, [y_{n-t}]$ are uniformly random in the view of the environment. To see this, note that if we let $\mathbf{x} \in \mathbb{F}^n$ be the vector with the x_is as entries and define a vector $\mathbf{y}$ from the y_is in a similar way, then $\mathbf{y} = M\mathbf{x}$. Now let C be the set of indices designating the $n - t$ honest players, and let R be the set of indices $1, \ldots, n - t$. Now, by Lemma 8.5, for any set of values in $\mathbf{x}_{\bar{C}}$ chosen by the corrupt players, the values taken by $y_1, \ldots, y_{n-t}$ are in one-to-one correspondence with the entries in $\mathbf{x}_C$. But these are uniformly random and independent of the view of the environment because they were chosen by the honest players and hence so are $y_1, \ldots, y_{n-t}$.

In this way, the amortized cost of outputting a representation of a random value is, up to a constant factor, only that of having a single player create a representation and hence a factor n more efficient than the naive method.

It is instructive to consider that this idea also can be seen as follows: we are given $x_1, \ldots, x_n$, and we know that $n - t$ of these values are random but not which ones. Now, using a hyperinvertible matrix, we can compute $n - t$ new values that are guaranteed to be random, so in other words we can extract all the randomness that is available.

EXERCISE 8.1 In this exercise we assume passive corruption, and we use representations of form $[a; f_a]_t$, where $t < n/2$.

Using Protocol Extract Random Representations as a starting point, construct a protocol that will produce as output a number of pairs $[r; f_r]_t, [r, g_r]_{2t}$, where r is random and unknown to all players, and f_r, g_r are independent and randomly chosen polynomials. Show that the total communication done in your protocol is $O(n)$ field elements per pair that is output.

The result of the exercise can be used to construct an efficient protocol that starts from $[a; f_a]_t, [b; f_b]_t$ and outputs $[ab; f_{ab}]_t$, still assuming passive (adaptive) corruption. To see this, recall that players can compute using local computation $[ab; f_a f_b]_{2t}$. Now, if we assume that we have a pair $[r; f_r]_t, [r; g_r]_{2t}$ available, then by further local computation, players can compute $[ab - r; g_r - f_a f_b]_{2t}$. This representation we can safely open because r and g_r are random, so all players now know $ab - r$. We can then make a default representation of $ab - r$ using the polynomial that is constantly $ab - r$: $[ab - r; ab - r]_t$. Adding this to $[r; f_r]_t$ will produce $[ab; f_{ab}]_t$, where $f_{ab} = f_r + ab - r$.

An important detail about this protocol is that to open $[ab - r; g_r - f_a f_b]_{2t}$, there is no reason to have all players send their share to all other players. It is sufficient to send to just one player, say, P_1. He or she can then reconstruct $ab - r$ and send this value to all players. Note that this works because we assume passive corruption (so P_1 will follow the protocol) and that this only requires sending $O(n)$ field elements.

Together with the exercise, we see that we now have a protocol for doing many secure multiplications that costs communication $O(n)$ field elements per multiplication. In comparison, the first protocol we saw in Chapter 3 required $O(n^2)$ field elements.

EXERCISE 8.2 The efficient opening described earlier can be made active secure at almost the same price. We will only sketch how this is done. The parties start with t secret sharings that need to be opened; call the secret-shared values $(v_1, \ldots, v_t)$. Then they apply a linear error-correcting code C over $\mathbb{F}$, producing secret sharings of the entries in the codeword $(w_1, \ldots, w_n) = C(v_1, \ldots, v_t)$, which is possible by just locally applying C to the shares of all values because C is linear. Then each $[w_i]$ is opened efficiently as earlier, with P_i playing the role of P_1. The corrupted P_is might lie about their w_i, but the honest P_is will distribute the correct w_is. This ensures that $n - t$ of the values w_i received by all parties are correct. If $n < 3t$, then a linear interpolation code C (see Chapter 11) will allow us to recover the t original values even in the presence of the t errors (see Section 11.8.2). Work out the exact details of this.

Checking Consistency of Secret Sharings and Other Linear Properties

In the first part of this subsection we concentrate on linear representations based on secret sharing. The simplest form we have seen is $[a;f_a]_t$, where player P_j holds $f_a(j)$ and $f_a(0) = a$. Having player P_i create such a representation is simple if we settle for passive security: P_i just selects f_a and sends $f_a(j)$ to each P_j.

This does not work for active security because we have no guarantee that what P_i sends is consistent with a polynomial of degree at most t. We have seen a protocol in Chapter 5 that can be used to force even a corrupt P_i to select consistent shares (Protocol Commit). This protocol has perfect security if $t < n/3$ but requires a lot of interaction and communicates much more data than the simple solution where P_i just sends one value to all players.

We now show in Protocol Check Consistent Secret Shares that hyper-invertible matrices can be used to verify whether P_i has behaved correctly, and this method will be much more efficient if we want to create many random shared values. We will assume for simplicity that $n = 3t + 1$.

In the following we will say that a representation $[a;f_a]_t$ is well formed if the values held by honest players are consistent with a polynomial of degree at most t. Note that we abuse notation slightly by writing $[a;f_a]_t$ with subscript t even if there is no guarantee that the degree of f_a is at most t until this has been checked.

The claim is now that if all players say accept, then $[y_{2t+1};f_{y_{2t+1}}]_t, \ldots, [y_n;f_{y_n}]_t$ are well formed even if P_i is corrupt; that is, the degree of f_{x_j} for $j = 2t + 1, \ldots, n$ is at most t. Then, if P_i is honest, $y_{2t+1}, \ldots, y_n$ are uniformly random in the view of the environment.

To show the first claim, notice that if all players say accept, then of the $2n$ representations $[x_1;f_{x_1}]_t, \ldots, [x_n;f_{x_n}]_t, [y_1;f_{y_1}]_t, \ldots, [y_n;f_{y_n}]_t$, we know that at least n of them are well formed, namely, the $2t + 1$ $[x_j;f_{x_j}]_t$s that were checked by honest players and the t $[y_j;f_{y_j}]_t$s that were checked by honest players. Then it follows from Lemma 8.4 that all the other representations can be computed from these n well-formed ones. In particular, $[y_{2t+1};f_{y_{2t+1}}]_t, \ldots, [y_n;f_{y_n}]_t$ can be computed as a linear combination of well-formed representations, so it immediately follows that they are well formed as well. This is so because a linear combination of polynomials of degree at most t is again of degree at most t.

Protocol Check Consistent Secret Shares

This protocol checks that a set of shares of values distributed by player P_i are well formed.

1. P_i distributes $[x_1; f_{x_1}]_t, \ldots, [x_n; f_{x_n}]_t$ for random $x_1, \ldots, x_n$.
2. The players apply matrix M to this vector of representations (in the same way as in the preceding subsection) to get via local computation representations $[y_1; f_{y_1}]_t, \ldots, [y_n; f_{y_n}]_t$.
3. For $j = 1, \ldots, 2t$, all players send their share in $[x_j; f_{x_j}]_t$ and $[y_j; f_{y_j}]_t$ to P_j. Furthermore, for $j = 2t+1, \ldots, n$, all players send their share in $[x_j; f_{x_j}]_t$ to P_j. Player P_j checks that all sets of shares that he or she receives are consistent with a polynomial of degree at most t and broadcasts `accept` or `reject` accordingly.
4. If all players said `accept`, then output $[y_{2t+1}; f_{y_{2t+1}}]_t, \ldots, [y_n; f_{y_n}]_t$.

To show the second claim, note that the environment knows t of the values $x_1, \ldots, x_n$, namely, those for which the corresponding representations were "checked" by a corrupt player. It now follows from Lemma 8.5 that the remaining $n - t$ x_j's (which are unknown to the environment) are in one-to-one correspondence with any subset of $n - t$ of the y_js. We form such a subset as the union of $y_{2t+1}, \ldots, y_n$ and t y_js that were checked by honest players (at least t such y_js must be available). All these y_js are uniformly random in the view of the environment, so in particular this is true for $y_{2t+1}, \ldots, y_n$.

Note that if Protocol Check Consistent Secret Shares has success, then it outputs a constant fraction of the representations that were created initially. Hence, up to a constant fraction, the cost of the protocol is the same as simply sending one share to each player per representation.[1]

It is, of course, a natural to ask, what we do if Protocol Check Consistent Secret Shares is not successful? The protocol as it stands would just not generate any output. However, there are more productive ways of dealing with such a situation. The basic observation is that if some P_j says `reject`, then either P_i or P_j must be corrupt. One option is to simply eliminate both players from the global protocol. Note that if we had less than one-third corrupted players before the elimination, this is also the case after, so we can still hope to finish the computation eventually. Also note that such a problem can occur at most t times, so this upper bounds the extra work we do as a result of eliminations. See the Notes at the end of this chapter for pointers to literature on this issue.

It is not hard to see that the principle from Protocol Check Consistent Secret Shares can be used to check other properties of values inside representations as long as these properties are preserved under linear transformations. For example, suppose that we use representations of form $[a; f_a]_t$, and we want to check that a player has created a number of representations $[0; f_1]_t, \ldots, [0; f_n]_t$. This can be done with a simple variation of Protocol Check Consistent Secret Shares in which players who verify representations also should verify that the value in the checked representation is 0. This works exactly because the property of containing a 0 is preserved under linear mappings on representations.

---

[1] Here we conveniently ignore the broadcasts toward the end of the protocol, and these will usually not come for free. However, if we created enough representations in parallel and only do one set of broadcasts, then the amortized cost of these will become insignificant.

EXERCISE 8.3 Specify the protocol sketched earlier, and prove that if $n = 3t + 1$, your protocol can output t random sharings of 0. Specify and prove a protocol for producing a number of pairs of representations of form $([a;f_a]_t, [a;g_a]_{2t})$; that is, the same element is contained in both representations.

8.4 Packed Secret Sharing

In this section we present a technique that allows us to secret share several field elements in one go in such a way that each player receives only one field element as his or her share. We must pay for this by being able to tolerate a smaller number of corrupted players, but the idea nevertheless can be used in combination with other techniques to get better efficiency in many cases.

The idea is a simple twist on Shamir secret sharing. We will assume for simplicity of notation that the underlying field is $\mathbb{F} = \mathbb{Z}_p$ for a prime p, where $p > \ell + n$, and n is the number of players. This means that the numbers $-\ell + 1, \ldots, 0, 1, \ldots, n$ can be interpreted as distinct field elements in a natural way. To share a vector of elements $\mathbf{s} = (s_1, \ldots, s_\ell) \in \mathbb{F}^\ell$, tolerating up to t corrupted players, one selects a random polynomial $f_{\mathbf{s}}(X)$ of degree at most $d = \ell - 1 + t$ with the property that $f_{\mathbf{s}}(-j + 1) = s_j$, for $j = 1, \ldots, \ell$. Then the share given to P_i is $f_{\mathbf{s}}(i)$. We can now easily prove the following:

LEMMA 8.6 *Let the secret vector* $\mathbf{s}$ *and random polynomial* $f_{\mathbf{s}}$ *be defined as earlier. Then any subset of at most t shares has a distribution independent of* $\mathbf{s}$, *and from any set of at least $\ell + t$ shares, one can reconstruct* $\mathbf{s}$.

Proof The last statement on reconstruction follows trivially from Lagrange interpolation. As for the first statement, assume without loss of generality that we consider the shares $f_{\mathbf{s}}(1), \ldots, f_{\mathbf{s}}(t)$. Note that by Lagrange interpolation, we can construct a polynomial h of degree at most $d = \ell - 1 + t$ such that $h(1) = \cdots = h(t) = 0$ and $h(-j + 1) = -s_j$, for $j = 1, \ldots, \ell$. Hence for each polynomial $f_{\mathbf{s}}(X)$ for sharing $\mathbf{s}$, there exists exactly one polynomial, namely, $f_{\mathbf{s}}(X) + h(X)$, for sharing the vector $(0, \ldots, 0)$, generating the same first t shares. Since polynomials are chosen uniformly, it follows that for every secret vector, the distribution of the t shares is the same, namely, the one resulting from sharing the all-zero vector. ∎

We now show how to use packed secret sharing to get passively secure computation on vectors while only having players operate on single field elements. We will need to assume that the degree d of the polynomials is such that $2d < n$. We also will assume that t and ℓ are both in $\Theta(n)$; this is clearly possible while still ensuring that the demand on d is satisfied.

We can first define a linear representation of vectors with ℓ coordinates, denoted

$$[\mathbf{a};f_{\mathbf{a}}]_d = (f_{\mathbf{a}}(1), \ldots, f_{\mathbf{a}}(n))$$

And if we define addition of representations by coordinate-wise addition as usual, one easily sees that we have

$$[\mathbf{a};f_{\mathbf{a}}]_d + [\mathbf{b};f_{\mathbf{b}}]_d = [\mathbf{a} + \mathbf{b};f_{\mathbf{a}} + f_{\mathbf{b}}]_d$$

In other words, if the n players hold representations of two vectors, we can add them securely by each player doing just one local addition.

In the same way, we define $[\mathbf{a};f_\mathbf{a}]_d * [\mathbf{b};f_\mathbf{b}]_d$ as the coordinate-wise product of the two sets of shares, and we have

$$[\mathbf{a};f_\mathbf{a}]_d * [\mathbf{b};f_\mathbf{b}]_d = [\mathbf{a} * \mathbf{b};f_\mathbf{a}f_\mathbf{b}]_{2d}$$

This means that if $2d < n$, we can do a multiplication protocol in much the same way as we have seen before; this can be seen in Protocol Packed Secure Multiplication.

The protocol assumes that auxiliary representations $[\mathbf{r};f_\mathbf{r}]_{2d}, [\mathbf{r};g_\mathbf{r}]_d$ for a random vector $\mathbf{r}$ are available. Such pairs can be constructed using the techniques we have seen in the preceding section (see Exercise 8.4). Note that it is secure to send all shares of $\mathbf{a} * \mathbf{b} - \mathbf{r}$ to P_1 because $\mathbf{r}$ and $f_\mathbf{r}$ are random.

Protocol Packed Secure Multiplication

This protocol takes as input two representations $[\mathbf{a};f_\mathbf{a}]_d$, $[\mathbf{b};f_\mathbf{b}]_d$. It is assumed that we have available a pair of auxiliary representations $[\mathbf{r};f_\mathbf{r}]_{2d}, [\mathbf{r};g_\mathbf{r}]_d$ for a random vector $\mathbf{r}$.

1. $[\mathbf{a} * \mathbf{b};f_\mathbf{a}f_\mathbf{b}]_{2d} = [\mathbf{a};f_\mathbf{a}]_d * [\mathbf{b};f_\mathbf{b}]_d$ by local multiplication.
2. The difference $[\mathbf{a} * \mathbf{b};f_\mathbf{a}f_\mathbf{b}]_{2d} - [\mathbf{r};f_\mathbf{r}]_{2d}$ is computed by local computation, and all shares are sent to player P_1.
3. P_1 reconstructs $\mathbf{a} * \mathbf{b} - \mathbf{r}$ from the shares received, then forms $[\mathbf{a} * \mathbf{b} - \mathbf{r};h]_d$, and sends a share to each player.
4. Players compute by local operations $[\mathbf{a} * \mathbf{b} - \mathbf{r};h]_d + [\mathbf{r};g_\mathbf{r}]_d = [\mathbf{a} * \mathbf{b};h + g_\mathbf{r}]$.

EXERCISE 8.4 Using the randomness extraction techniques from the preceding section, build a protocol that outputs a set of pairs of form $[\mathbf{r};f_\mathbf{r}]_{2d}, [\mathbf{r};g_\mathbf{r}]_d$ for random $\mathbf{r}$, as required in the multiplication in the box. Assuming that t and ℓ are $\Theta(n)$, show that your protocol uses communication of $O(n)$ field elements per pair produced.

Let us consider what these ideas actually achieve: we have seen that if $2d = 2(t + \ell - 1) < n$, then we can do secure addition and multiplication of ℓ vectors using the same communication (and computational work) that we used in the preceding subsection to do addition and multiplication on *single* field elements; that is, we send $O(n)$ field elements per operation. Thus we get ℓ operations "for the price of one." Of course, this only works in a so-called same-instruction, multiple-data fashion (SIMD); that is, we always have to do the *same* operation on all ℓ entries in a block. Moreover, SIMD operations do not come for free; we have to accept a smaller threshold value for the number of corruptions we can tolerate, but we can still tolerate corruption of a constant fraction of the players.

An obvious application of this is to compute securely ℓ instances in parallel of the same arithmetic circuit C. Since we chose ℓ to be $\Theta(n)$, the communication we need computed per gate is a *constant number* of field elements.

It is natural to ask if we can use this approach to also save on computation and work when computing a *single* circuit securely and whether we can get active security as well? The answer turns out to be yes in both cases, and this leads to protocols that are close to optimal, at least in some respects. The Notes section at the end of this chapter has more information on this.

8.5 Information-Theoretic Protocols in the Preprocessing Model

In this section we show how some of the techniques we have seen can be used for the case of a *dishonest majority*; that is, we assume up to t active corruptions and that $t \leq n - 1$. We have already seen in Chapter 7 that for this case we have to use public-key machinery that is typically quite expensive. In comparison, the information theoretically secure primitives we have seen are computationally simpler and more efficient.

It therefore may seem that we cannot have really efficient solutions for a dishonest majority. This is not entirely true, however. What we can do is to assume a preprocessing phase (using public-key cryptography) in which the function to compute and the inputs are not yet known. This phase will produce some "raw material" to be used in an online phase in which the actual computation is done and we can use the more efficient primitives. More concretely, we will use the pattern we saw in the section on circuit randomization, so the idea will be to define an appropriate linear representation and assume a preprocessing that outputs multiplication triples in this representation.

To define our linear representation, we will again use a technique that we saw in the implementation of F_{ICSIG}, namely, to use information-theoretic message authentication codes (MACs). This will lead to statistical security, and in general, the protocols we will see have error probability $1/|\mathbb{F}|$. We assume for simplicity that the field is so large that this is negligible, but there are also solutions that work for small fields (see the Notes for details on this).

A key K for our MACs is a random pair $K = (\alpha, \beta) \in \mathbb{F}^2$, and the authentication code for a value $a \in \mathbb{F}$ is $\text{MAC}_K(a) = \alpha a + \beta$. We recall briefly how these MACs are to be used: one party P_i will hold a and $\text{MAC}_K(a)$, and another party P_j will hold K. The idea is to use the MAC to prevent P_i from lying about a when he or she is supposed to reveal it to P_j. It will be very important in the following that if we keep α constant over several different MAC keys, then one can add two MACs and get a valid authentication code for the sum of the two corresponding messages. More concretely, two keys $K = (\alpha, \beta), K' = (\alpha', \beta')$ are said to be *consistent* if $\alpha = \alpha'$. For consistent keys, we define $K + K' = (\alpha, \beta + \beta')$ so that it holds that $\text{MAC}_K(a) + \text{MAC}_{K'}(a') = \text{MAC}_{K+K'}(a + a')$.

In the Protocol Operations on [.] Representations, we will give to P_i several different values $m_1, m_2, \ldots$ with corresponding MACs $\gamma_1, \gamma_2, \ldots$ computed using keys $K_i = (\alpha, \beta_i)$ that are random but consistent. It is then easy to see that if P_i claims a false value for any of the m_is (or a linear combination of them), he or she can guess an acceptable MAC for such a value with probability at most $1/|\mathbb{F}|$. This follows by an argument similar to what we saw in the proof of Theorem 5.7.

To represent a value $a \in \mathbb{F}$, we will give a share a_i to each party P_i, where the a_is are randomly chosen, subject to $a = \sum_i a_i$. In addition, P_i will hold MAC keys $K_{a_1}^i, \ldots, K_{a_n}^i$. He or she will use key $K_{a_j}^i$ to check the share of P_j if we decide to make a public. Finally, P_i also holds a set of authentication codes $\text{MAC}_{K_{a_i}^j}(a_i)$. We will denote $\text{MAC}_{K_{a_i}^j}(a_i)$ by $m_j(a_i)$ from now on. Party P_i will use $m_j(a_i)$ to convince P_j that a_i is correct if we decide to make a public. Summing up, we have the following way of representing a:

$$[a] = (a_i, \{K_{a_j}^i, m_j(a_i)\}_{j=1}^n)_{i=1}^n$$

where $a_i, \{K_{a_j}^i, m_j(a_i)\}_{j=1}^n$ is the information held privately by P_i.

We say that $[a] = (a_i, \{K^i_{a_j}, m_j(a_i)\}^n_{j=1})^n_{i=1}$ is *consistent*, with $a = \sum_i a_i$, if $m_j(a_i) = \text{MAC}_{K^j_{a_i}}(a_i)$ for all i,j. Two representations

$$[a] = (a_i, \{K^i_{a_j}, m_j(a_i)\}^n_{j=1})^n_{i=1} \quad \text{and} \quad [a'] = (a'_i, \{K^i_{a'_j}, m_j(a'_i)\}^n_{j=1})^n_{i=1}$$

are said to be *key consistent* if they are both consistent and if for all i,j the keys $K^i_{a_j}, K^i_{a'_j}$ are consistent. We will want *all* representations in the following to be key consistent: this is ensured by letting P_i use the same α_j value in keys toward P_j throughout. Therefore, the notation $K^i_{a_j} = (\alpha^i_j, \beta^i_{a_j})$ makes sense, and we can do linear computations with these representations, as detailed in Protocol Operations on $[\cdot]$ Representations.

Protocol Operations on $[\cdot]$ Representations

Opening. We can reliably open a consistent representation to P_j: each P_i sends $a_i, m_j(a_i)$ to P_j. Then P_j checks that $m_j(a_i) = \text{MAC}_{K^j_{a_i}}(a_i)$ and broadcasts `accept` or `fail` accordingly. If all is okay, P_j computes $a = \sum_i a_i$; otherwise, we abort. We can modify this to opening a value $[a]$ to all parties by opening as earlier to every P_j.

Addition. Given two key-consistent representations as earlier we get that

$$[a + a'] = (a_i + a'_i, \{K^i_{a_j} + K^i_{a'_j}, m_j(a_i) + m_j(a'_i)\}^n_{j=1})^n_{i=1}$$

is a consistent representation of $a + a'$. This new representation can be computed by only local operations.

Multiplication by constants. In a similar way, we can multiply a public constant δ "into" a representation. This is written $\delta[a]$ and is taken to mean that all parties multiply their shares, keys, and MACs by δ. This gives a consistent representation $[\delta a]$.

Addition of constants. We can add a public constant δ into a representation. This is written $\delta + [a]$ and is taken to mean that P_1 will add δ to his or her share a_1. Also, each P_j will replace his or her key $K^j_{a_1} = (\alpha^j_1, \beta^j_{a_1})$ by $K^j_{a_1+\delta} = (\alpha^j_1, \beta^j_{a_1} - \delta\alpha^j_1)$. This will ensure that the MACs held by P_1 will now be valid for the new share $a_1 + \delta$, so we now have a consistent representation $[a + \delta]$.

We now specify what exactly we need the preprocessing phase to do for us: it must implement the ideal functionality F_{TRIP}. For multiplication and input sharing later, we will need it to output both random single values $[a]$ and triples $[a], [b], [c]$, where a, b are random, and $c = ab \mod p$. Also, all singles and triples produced must be key consistent so that we can freely add them together.

The specification of the functionality follows an important general principle that is very useful whenever a functionality is supposed to output shares of secret data to the players: the environment is allowed to specify to the functionality all the data that the corrupted parties should hold, including all shares of secrets, keys, and MACs. Then the functionality chooses the secrets to be shared and constructs the data for honest parties so that they are consistent with the secrets and the data specified by the environment.

At first sight this may seem overly complicated: why don't we just let the functionality choose all shares and output them to the players? However, it is important to understand that if we had specified the functionality this way, it could not be implemented! The point is that the simulator we need to construct to prove an implementation secure needs to show

---

Agent F$_{\mathrm{TRIP}}$

Ideal functionality specifying the preprocessing needed for the [·] representation. Whenever a command is received, the functionality leaks the name of the command and whatever public input is given. Output from a command is sent once the round in which to deliver is specified on the influence port.

Initialize. On input (init, $\mathbb{F}$) from all parties, the functionality stores a description of the field $\mathbb{F}$. For each corrupted party P_i, the environment specifies values $\alpha_j^i, j = 1, \ldots, n$, except those α_j^i where both P_i and P_j are corrupt. For each honest P_i, the functionality chooses $\alpha_j^i, j = 1, \ldots, n$, at random.

Singles. On input (singles, u) from all parties P_i, the functionality does the following for $v = 1, \ldots, u$:

1. It waits to get from the environment either stop or some data as specified later. In the first case, it sends fail to all honest parties and stops. In the second case, the environment specifies for each corrupt party P_i a share a_i and n pairs of values $(m_j(a_i), \beta_{a_j}^i), j = 1, \ldots, n$, except those $(m_j(a_i), \beta_{a_j}^i)$ where both P_i and P_j are corrupt.

2. The functionality chooses $a \in \mathbb{F}$ at random and creates the representation $[a]$ as follows:

   a. First, it chooses random shares for the honest parties such that the sum of these and those specified by the environment is correct: let A be the set of corrupt parties; then a_i is chosen at random for $P_i \notin A$, subject to $a = \sum_i a_i$.

   b. For each honest P_i and $j = 1, \ldots, n$, $\beta_{a_j}^i$ is chosen as follows: if P_j is honest, $\beta_{a_j}^i$ is chosen at random; otherwise, it sets $\beta_{a_j}^i = m_i(a_j) - \alpha_j^i a_j$. Note that the environment already specified $m_i(a_j), a_j$, so what is done here is to construct the key to be held by P_i to be consistent with the share and MAC chosen by the environment.

   c. For all $i = 1, \ldots, n, j = 1, \ldots, n$, it sets $K_{a_j}^i = (\alpha_j^i, \beta_{a_j}^i)$ and computes $m_j(a_i) = \mathrm{MAC}_{K_{a_i}^j}(a_i)$.

   d. Now all data for $[a]$ are created. The functionality sends $a_i, \{K_{a_j}^i, m_j(a_i)\}_{j=1,\ldots,n}$ to each honest P_i (no need to send anything to corrupt parties, the environment already has the data).

Triples. On input (triples, u) from all parties P_i, the functionality does the following for $v = 1, \ldots, u$:

1. Step 1 is done as in "Singles."
2. For each triple to create, it chooses a, b at random and sets $c = ab$. Now it creates representations $[a], [b], [c]$, each as in step 2 in "Singles."

---

to the environment a simulated execution of the protocol we use to create the triples. The shares, keys, and MACs for the corrupt parties created here must be consistent with the data that F$_{\mathrm{TRIP}}$ creates for honest parties because this will always be the case for a real execution. This consistency is only ensured if the functionality is willing to be consistent with what the simulator wants. Also, most natural protocols actually allow the corrupted parties to influence or choose their outputs. If, for example, the output is the sum of contributions chosen by individual parties, a corrupted party can pick his or her contribution last and hence use his or her own share of his or her own representation to make the sum of his or her shares exactly the value he or she wants.

Protocol Online Phase, MAC-Based

The protocol assumes access to F_{TRIP}, and we assume that a field $\mathbb{F}$ and a circuit C to compute securely are given at some point after F_{TRIP} has been invoked. Protocol Operations on $[\cdot]$ Representations is used for linear operations on representations.

Initialize. The parties first invoke $F_{TRIP}(\texttt{init}, \mathbb{F})$. Then they invoke $F_{TRIP}(\texttt{triples}, u)$ and $F_{TRIP}(\texttt{singles}, u)$ to create enough singles and triples. Here only an upper bound on the size of the circuit to compute needs to be known. At some later stage when C and the inputs are known, do the following:

Input sharing. To share P_i's input $[x_i]$, P_i takes a single $[a]$ from the set of unused ones. Then the following is performed:

1. $[a]$ is opened to P_i.
2. P_i broadcasts $\delta = x_i - a$.
3. The parties compute $[x_i] = [a] + \delta$.

We then go through the circuit and process the gates one by one in the computational order. Just after the input-sharing phase, we consider all input gates as being processed. We will maintain the following:

Invariant. Computing with the circuit on inputs $x_1, \ldots, x_n$ assigns a unique value to every wire. Consider an input or an output wire for any gate, and let $a \in \mathbb{F}$ be the value assigned to this wire. Then, if the gate has been processed, the players hold $[a]$.

Computation phase. Repeat the following until all gates have been processed (then go to the next phase). Consider the first gate in the computational order that has not been processed yet. According to the type of gate, do one of the following:

Addition gate. The players hold $[a], [b]$ for the two inputs a, b to the gate. The players compute $[a] + [b] = [a + b]$.

Multiply-by-constant gate. The players hold $[a]$ for the input a to the gate and public constant α. The players compute $\alpha[a] = [\alpha a]$.

Multiplication gate. The players hold $[a], [b]$ for the two inputs a, b to the gate. Take the next unused triple $[x], [y], [z]$ from the preprocessing phase.

1. Players compute $[a - x] = [a] - [x]$ and $[b - y] = [b] - [y]$ and open $e = a - x$ and $d = b - y$.
2. Players can compute locally $[ab] = [z] + e[b] + d[a] - ed$.

Output reconstruction. At this point, all gates, including the output gates, have been processed. So, for each output gate, the players hold $[y]$, where y is the value assigned to the output gate. If P_i is to learn this value, we open $[y]$ to P_i.

Note also that F_{TRIP} may get input stop from the environment and in this case will not generate any output. This is so because we work with a dishonest majority, where termination cannot be guaranteed.

Since F_{TRIP} outputs random multiplication triples, we can securely compute multiplications exactly as we saw in the section on circuit randomization. This leads to Protocol Online Phase, MAC-Based, which is essentially Protocol Online Phase specialized for the MAC-based representation we use here. Note that since we allow a majority of the players to be corrupt, that we cannot guarantee that the protocol terminates and gives output to the honest players. This means that we can only hope to implement a weaker version

---

Agent Simulator $\mathcal{S}_{\texttt{ONLINE}}$

In the following, C and H represent the set of corrupted and honest parties, respectively.

Initialize. The simulator initializes a copy of $\mathsf{F}_{\texttt{TRIP}}$ with $\mathbb{F}$ as the field to use and creates the desired number of triples. Note that the simulator can read all data that corrupted parties specify to the copy of $\mathsf{F}_{\texttt{TRIP}}$.

Input. If $\mathsf{P}_i \in H$, the protocol is run honestly but with dummy input, for example, 0. If in step 1 during input the MACs are not correct, the protocol is aborted. If $\mathsf{P}_i \in C$, the input step is done honestly, and then the simulator waits for P_i to broadcast δ. Given this, the simulator can compute $x'_i = a + \delta$ because it knows (all the shares of) a. This is the supposed input of P_i, which the simulator now gives to the ideal functionality $\mathsf{F}_{\texttt{SFE}}^{f,\texttt{abort}}$.

Add/multiply-by-constant. The simulator runs the protocol honestly.

Multiply. The simulator runs the protocol honestly and, as before, aborts if some share from a corrupted party is not correct.

Output. If the receiving party $\mathsf{P}_i \in H$, the output step is run, and the protocol is aborted if some share from a corrupted party is not correct. Otherwise, the simulator tells $\mathsf{F}_{\texttt{SFE}}^{f,\texttt{abort}}$ to give output to P_i. If $\mathsf{P}_i \in C$, the simulator asks $\mathsf{F}_{\texttt{SFE}}^{f,\texttt{abort}}$ for output. Since P_i is corrupted, the ideal functionality will provide the simulator with y, which is the output to P_i. Now it has to simulate shares y_j of honest parties such that they are consistent with y. This is done by changing one of the internal shares of an honest party. Let P_k be that party. The new share is now computed as $y'_k = y - \sum_{i \neq k} y_i$. Next, a valid MAC for y'_k is needed. This the simulator can compute from scratch as $\mathrm{MAC}_{K^i_{y_k}}(y'_k)$ because it knows from the beginning the keys of P_i. This enables it to compute $K^i_{y_k}$ by the computations on representations done during the protocol. Now the simulator sends the internal shares and corresponding MACs to P_i.

---

of secure function evaluation $\mathsf{F}_{\texttt{SFE}}^{f,\texttt{abort}}$, where the functionality can be aborted before honest players get output (but where corrupted players may have received theirs).

Let $\pi_{\texttt{ONLINE}}$ denote Protocol Online Phase, MAC-Based. Then we have the following theorem:

THEOREM 8.7 $\pi_{ONLINE} \diamond \mathsf{F}_{TRIP}$ *implements* $\mathsf{F}_{SFE}^{f,\texttt{abort}}$ *in* $\mathrm{Env}^{t,\texttt{sync,static}}$ *with statistical security for all* $t < n$.

Proof We construct a simulator $\mathcal{S}_{\texttt{ONLINE}}$ such that a polytime environment $\mathcal{Z}$ cannot distinguish between $\pi_{\texttt{ONLINE}} \diamond \mathsf{F}_{\texttt{TRIP}}$ and $\mathsf{F}_{\texttt{SFE}}^{f,\texttt{abort}} \diamond \mathcal{S}_{\texttt{ONLINE}}$. We assume here static, active corruption. The simulator will internally run a copy of $\mathsf{F}_{\texttt{TRIP}}$ composed with $\pi_{\texttt{ONLINE}}$ in which it corrupts the parties specified by $\mathcal{Z}$. The simulator relays messages between parties $\mathsf{F}_{\texttt{TRIP}}$ and $\mathcal{Z}$ such that $\mathcal{Z}$ will see the same interface as when interacting with a real protocol. During the run of the internal protocol, the simulator will keep copies of the shares, MACs, and keys of both honest and corrupted parties and update them according to the execution.

The idea is that the simulator runs the protocol with the environment, where it plays the role of the honest parties. Since the inputs of the honest parties are not known to the simulator, these will be random values (or zero). However, the environment will not be able to tell the difference.

In general, the openings in the protocol do not reveal any information about the actual values in the computation. Whenever we open a value during Input or Multiply, we mask it by subtracting with a new random value. Therefore, the distribution of the view of the corrupted parties is exactly the same in the simulation as in the real case. Then the only method left for the environment to distinguish between the two cases is to compare the protocol execution with the inputs and outputs of the honest parties and check for inconsistency.

If the simulated protocol fails at some point because of a wrong MAC, the simulator aborts, which is consistent with the internal state of the ideal functionality because, in this case the simulator also makes the ideal functionality fail.

If the simulated protocol succeeds, the ideal functionality is always told to output the result of the function evaluation. This result is, of course, the correct evaluation of the input matching the shares that were read from the corrupted parties in the beginning. Therefore, if the corrupted parties during the protocol successfully cheat with their shares, this would not be consistent. However, as we saw earlier, the probability of a party being able to claim a wrong value for a given MAC is $1/|\mathbb{F}|$. Therefore, since we abort as soon as a check fails, we conclude that if the protocol succeeds, the computation is correct except with probability $1/|\mathbb{F}|$. ∎

EXERCISE 8.5 Show that $\pi_{\text{ONLINE}} \diamond F_{\text{TRIP}}$ implements $F_{\text{SFE}}^{f,\text{abort}}$ in $\text{Env}^{t,\text{sync}}$ with statistical security for all $t < n$; that is, π_{ONLINE} is in fact adaptively secure.

By inspection of the protocol, we see that the work invested by each player in π_{ONLINE} amounts to $O(n|C|)$ elementary field operations, where $|C|$ is the size of the circuit computed. This basically follows from the fact that the cost of doing the multiplications dominates, and for each of these, a player needs to check $O(n)$ MACs. Thus, for a constant number of players, the work one needs to invest to do the protocol is comparable with the work one would need to just compute the circuit in the clear with no security properties ensured. Using a more complicated protocol, one can improve this to $O(|C|)$ operations independent of how many players are in the protocol (see the Notes section for more on this).

Also note that π_{ONLINE} is only really efficient if the circuit C is defined over a large field $\mathbb{F}$, where large means that $1/|\mathbb{F}|$ is an acceptable error probability. If this is not the case, we could have more than one MAC on each value. This would make the error smaller, but the protocol would be less efficient. There are, however, solutions that are as efficient as π_{ONLINE}, even for the field with two elements, that is, for Boolean circuits (see the Notes section for more details).

Of course, in order to actually use a protocol such as π_{ONLINE} in practice, one needs to also implement the preprocessing. This will require use of computationally secure cryptography (because otherwise we would contradict the fact that information-theoretic security is not possible with a dishonest majority); the details of this are not the main focus of this book. We just mention that it can be done quite efficiently using public-key cryptosystems with homomorphic properties. It is not hard to see why an additively homomorphic scheme would help here: suppose that player P_i has a key pair (sk,pk) and holds the secret key sk, whereas other players have the public key pk. Suppose further that the encryption function is linearly homomorphic over $\mathbb{F}$; that is, from ciphertexts $E_{pk}(a)$ and $E_{pk}(b)$ and constant α, one can efficiently compute a new ciphertext $E_{pk}(a + \alpha b)$ (where we suppress the randomness involved in the encryption for simplicity).

Now, if P_i has a message a and P_j holds a MAC key (α, β), then P_i can send $E_{pk}(a)$ to P_j, who can then compute and return to P_i a new ciphertext $E_{pk}(\alpha a + \beta)$. Decrypting this, P_i will get a MAC on a under P_j's key. If P_j is able to do his or her operations such that the ciphertext he or she returns is a *random* ciphertext containing $\alpha a + \beta$, we are sure that P_i learns nothing except for the MAC and hence cannot beak the MAC scheme later. However, to have active security, we still need to ensure that players send well-formed ciphertexts computed according to the protocol. The Notes section has pointers to literature with details on how this can be done.

8.6 Open Problems in Complexity of MPC

In this section we give a short and very informal overview of some things we know about the complexity of multiparty computation with unconditional security and mention some open problems. We begin with the model that we consider in most of this book. We assume secure point-to-point channels (and broadcast in case more than $n/3$ players are corrupt) and fewer than $n/2$ corruptions. For this case, the ideas of circuit randomization, hyper-invertible matrices, packed secret sharing, and more lead to protocols where the total work players need to invest in to compute circuit C securely is essentially $|C|$ field operations (where we ignore some factors that depend logarithmically on n and $|C|$; the Notes section has more details). Since computing C securely in particular means that you compute it, we cannot hope to do better. It should be noted, however, that this result only holds in an asymptotic sense for a large number of players and large circuits, and the underlying protocols are not practical even if they are asymptotically efficient. The upper bound on the computational work also implies a similar bound on the communication complexity of the protocol. However, it is completely open whether we actually need to send $\Omega(|C|)$ field elements to compute C. For computational security, we know that fully homomorphic encryption (FHE) allows us to have protocols in which the communication does not depend on $|C|$, but we do not know if something like FHE for unconditional security exists.

Another issue is the number of messages we need to send to compute C or, in the case of synchronous networks, the number of rounds we need. All the general protocols we have seen require a number of rounds that is linear in the depth of C. We do not know if this is inherent; in fact, we do not even know which functions can be computed with unconditional security and a constant number of rounds. We do know large classes of functions that can indeed be computed with unconditional security and a constant number of rounds, but there is nothing to suggest that these functions are the only ones with this property.

If we go to the preprocessing model, we know protocols that require total computational work of essentially $\Omega(n|C|)$ field operations. These protocols also require communication of $\Omega(n|C|)$ field elements, and the players also need to store this many fields elements from the preprocessing. It can be shown that the storage requirement is optimal and that the computational work per player is optimal in the following sense: for any player P_i, there exists a circuit C for which secure computing of it in the preprocessing model would require P_i to do $\Omega(|C|)$ operations, but it is not guaranteed that other players also would have to work this hard when computing C. It is intuitively quite reasonable that each player needs to invest $\Omega(|C|)$ operations: the circuit needs to be computed, so it is clear that the *total* number of field operations done by the players should be $\Omega(|C|)$. However, it might be the case that only one player is honest and everybody else works against him or her, so it would be quite surprising if this player would not have to do work at least equivalent to computing the circuit on his or her own. We emphasize, however, that such a result is not known in full generality at the time of this writing.

As for communication and rounds, also in the preprocessing model, it is completely open as to what the optimal complexities are.

8.7 Notes

The circuit randomization idea from this first section of this chapter was suggested by Beaver [7]. The hyperinvertible matrices and applications of these was suggested by Beerliová-Trubíniová and Hirt [10], improving on the use of so-called superinvertible matrices in Damgård and Nielsen [73]. Packed secret sharing was suggested by Franklin and Yung [93].

The work by Beerliová-Trubíniová and Hirt [10] is one of many results in a line of research known as *scalable MPC*, where one tries to build protocols that scale well as the number of players increase. Beerliová-Trubíniová and Hirt [10] show how circuit randomization and hyperinvertible matrices lead to perfectly secure evaluation of a circuit C for fewer than $n/3$ corrupted players and secure point-to-point channels with total communication complexity $O(n|C|)$ field elements plus an additive overhead that depends polynomially on the number of players and linearly on the depth of C but not on the size of C. To reach this goal, the authors [10] also do an indepth treatment of how one deals with the case where Protocol Check Consistent Secret Shares is not successful.

Ben-Sasson, Fehr, and Ostrovsky [15] show a similar result for fewer than $n/2$ corruptions when broadcast is also given for free. They show a protocol with statistical security (we cannot do better in this model) and communication complexity $O((n\log n + k/n^c)|C|)$ field elements, where k is the security parameter and c is an arbitrary constant. Here there is again an additive term that depends polynomially on n and k and the depth of C but not $|C|$.

A closely related line of research also tries to minimize the computational work as a function of the number of players. The latest work in this line is by Damgård, Ishai, and Krøigaard [69], who show a perfectly secure protocol for fewer than $(1/3 - \epsilon)n$ corruptions, where $\epsilon > 0$ is an arbitrary constant. In this protocol, the total number of field operations players need to do is $O(|C|\log|C|\log^2 n)$ plus an additive term that depends polynomially on n and the depth of C but only logarithmically on $|C|$. On the one hand, this is stronger than that of Beerliová-Trubíniová and Hirt [10] because the dependency on n is reduced, and it is the computational work that is optimized. On the other hand, the corruption tolerance is not quite optimal (because of the ϵ).

The protocol in Damgård, Ishai, and Krøigaard [69] is based on packed secret sharing and therefore needs to work with only blockwise operations, where the same operation is done on all positions in a block, but still one needs to compute an arbitrary Boolean circuit. This is handled using a technique by which an arbitrary circuit can be restructured so that it computes the same function, but the new circuit only uses blockwise operations and a small number of intrablock permutations and is a logarithmic factor larger. We have already seen passively secure protocols for packed secret sharing; active security is obtained using error correction, which works if the number of honest players is large enough. The use of error correction and packed secret sharing means that the basic protocol π is only secure against a small (but constant) fraction of corrupted players. This is then boosted to the almost optimal threshold of $(1/3 - \epsilon)n$ using the *committees technique*. Here we form a number of committees, each consisting of a constant number of players. Each committee emulates a player in π. The emulation is done using an expensive protocol with optimal threshold (but this does not hurt overall asymptotic efficiency because committees have constant size). If at most $(1/3 - \epsilon)n$ players are corrupt, we can choose the committees in such a way that only a small constant fraction of them contains more than a third corrupted players. This means that the (emulated) execution of π will be secure.

The committees approach was suggested by Bracha [28] for the purpose of broadcast and was introduced in multiparty computation in Damgård et al. [70]. We emphasize that all the results on scalable MPC that we mentioned hold asymptotically for a large number of players and even larger circuits. This is so because the protocols typically use the approach we saw in Protocol Check Consistent Secret Shares, where one runs a protocol that very efficiently handles a large number of secret sharings and works correctly as long as players follow the protocol. However, honest players can verify that the protocol has been followed and complain if this is not the case. If complaints occur, we need to resolve the conflicts, and this usually requires doing something very expensive. This approach makes sense if the computation we do is large enough that it makes sense to do many secret sharings in parallel *and* if we can make sure that complaints will not occur very often relative to the size of the computation, in which case the cost of handling them will be insignificant compared with the rest of the work.

The material in the section on preprocessing is from Bendlin et al. [19]. This paper also introduces the notion of semihomomorphic public-key encryption and shows that it is sufficient for implementing the preprocessing specified in $\mathsf{F_{TRIP}}$. In a subsequent paper, Damgård et al. [75] showed that the total computational complexity can be improved from quadratic in n to $O(n|C| + n^3)$ field operations, where the error probability is $1/|\mathbb{F}|$. The amount of data players have to store from the preprocessing as well as the communication complexity is also $O(n|C| + n^3)$ field elements. It is also shown in this paper that the required storage from the preprocessing is optimal and the computational work is optimal in the sense explained earlier: for any player P_i, there exists a circuit C for which secure computing of it in the preprocessing model would require P_i to do $\Omega(|C|)$ operations, but it is not guaranteed that other players also would have to work this hard. Finally, Damgård et al. [75] show how to implement the preprocessing more efficiently based on somewhat homomorphic encryption. Informally, this is a weaker form of fully homomorphic encryption in which many additions but only a small bounded number of multiplications can be performed.

9

Applications of MPC

In this chapter we will look at two different applications of information-theoretic multiparty computation (MPC), a practical application and a theoretical application. The example of a practical application is the use of MPC to clear a commodity derivative market. The focus will be on the algorithmic tricks used to implement the auction efficiently. The theoretical application is the use of MPC to realize so-called zero-knowledge proofs. A zero-knowledge proof is a way for a prover to convince a verifier about the validity of a statement without leaking any information on why the statement is true. This can be seen as an MPC problem with $n = 2$ parties. However, since the minimal requirement for information-theoretic MPC is that fewer than $n/2$ parties are corrupted, information-theoretic MPC does not seem to help in constructing zero-knowledge proofs. However, as we shall see, a technique sometimes called MPC in the head can be used to turn an efficient, secure MPC for a given relation into an efficient zero-knowledge proof for the same relation.

9.1 A Double Auction

In this section we look at a concrete application of MPC, with a main focus on the algorithmic tricks needed to efficiently do a secure auction. Along the way, we will look at how to efficiently and securely compare two integers secret shared among the parties.

9.1.1 Introduction

The algorithmic techniques we will look at are fairly general, but it is instructive to view them in a practical context. We will look at how they have been used to clear the Danish market for contracts on sugar beets from 2008 and until the time of this writing. This was the first industrial application of MPC. More historical details on this can be found later and in the Notes section at the end of this chapter.

In the economic field of mechanism design, the concept of a trusted third party has been a central assumption since the 1970s. The field has grown in momentum since it was initiated and has turned into a truly cross-disciplinary field. Today, many practical mechanisms require a trusted third party. In particular, several research projects on combining mechanism design and MPC have concentrated on two types of applications:

- **Various types of auctions.** This is not limited to only standard highest-bid auctions with sealed bids but also includes, for instance, variants with many sellers and buyers, so-called double auctions: essentially scenarios in which one wants to find a fair-market price for a commodity given the existing supply and demand in the market.

• **Benchmarking,** where several companies want to combine information on how their businesses are running in order to compare themselves with best practice in the area. The benchmarking process is used either for learning, planning, or motivation purposes. This, of course, has to be done while preserving confidentiality of companies' private data.

When looking at such applications, one finds that the computation needed is basically elementary arithmetic on integers of moderate size, typically around 32 bits. More concretely, quite a wide range of the cases requires only addition, multiplication, and comparison of integers. The known generic MPC protocols usually can handle addition and multiplication very efficiently by using the field $\mathbb{F} = \mathbb{Z}_p$ for a prime p chosen large enough compared with the input numbers to avoid modular reductions. This gives integer addition and multiplication by doing addition and multiplication in $\mathbb{F}$.

This is efficient because each number is shared "in one piece" as opposed to, for example, a bitwise sharing. Unfortunately, this input representation also implies that comparison of shared values is much harder. A generic solution would express the comparison operation as an arithmetic circuit over $\mathbb{Z}_p$, but this would be far too large to give a practical solution because the circuit would not have access to the binary representation of the inputs. Instead, special-purpose techniques for comparison have been developed. We will have a closer look at these in Section 9.1.5.

9.1.2 A Practical Application Scenario

In this section we describe the history behind the practical case in which a secure auction was deployed in 2008, as mentioned earlier. In Denmark, several thousand farmers produce sugar beets, which are sold to a company called Danisco, which is the only sugar-producing company on the Danish market. Farmers have contracts that give them production rights; that is, a contract entitles a farmer to produce a certain amount of beets per year. These contracts can be traded between farmers, but trading historically has been very limited and has been done only via bilateral negotiations. In the years up to 2008, however, the European Union drastically reduced the support for sugar beet production. This and other factors meant that there was now an urgent need to reallocate contracts to farmers whose productions payed off best. It was realized that this was best done via a nationwide exchange, a double auction.

Briefly, the goal is to find the market-clearing price, which is a price per unit of the commodity that is traded. In the specific case, the commodity is a contract for producing sugar beets, and the unit is tons of beets. What happens is that each buyer specifies, for each potential price, how much he or she is willing to buy at that price. Similarly, all sellers say how much they are willing to sell at each price. All bids go to an auctioneer, who computes, for each price, the total supply and demand in the market. Since we can assume that supply grows and demand decreases with increasing price, there is a price where total supply equals total demand, at least approximately, and this is the price we are looking for. Finally, all bidders who specified a nonzero amount to trade at the market-clearing price get to sell/buy the amount at that price.

This could, in principle, be implemented with a single trusted party as the auctioneer. However, in the given scenario, there are some additional security concerns implying that this is not a satisfactory solution: bids clearly reveal information on a farmer's economic position and his or her productivity, and therefore, farmers would be reluctant to accept Danisco acting as auctioneer, given its position in the market. Even if Danisco would never misuse its knowledge of the bids in future price negotiations, the mere fear of this happening could affect the way farmers bid and lead to a suboptimal result of the auction. However, contracts in some cases act as security for debt that farmers have to Danisco, and hence the farmers' organization DKS running the auction independently would not be acceptable to Danisco. Finally, the common solution of delegating the legal and practical responsibility by paying, for example, a consultancy house to be the trusted auctioneer would have been a very expensive solution. It was therefore decided to implement an electronic double auction, in which the role of the auctioneer would be played by a multiparty computation done by representatives for Danisco, DKS, and the research project implementing the auction.

A three-party solution was selected partly because it was natural in the given scenario but also because it allowed using efficient information-theoretic tools such as secret sharing rather than more expensive cryptographic methods needed when there are only two parties.

9.1.3 The Auction System

In the system that was deployed, a Web server was set up for receiving bids, and three servers were set up for doing the secure computation. Before the auction started, a public/private key pair was generated for each computation server, and a representative from each involved organization stored the private key on a USB stick, protected under a password.

Encrypt and Share Curve

Each bidder logged onto the Web server, and an applet was downloaded to his or her PC together with the public keys of the computation servers. After the user typed in his or her bid, the applet secret shared the bids, creating one share for each server, and encrypted the shares under the respective server's public key. Finally, the entire set of ciphertexts was stored in a database by the Web server.

As for security precautions on the client side, the system did not explicitly implement any security against cheating bidders other than verifying their identities. The reason for this was that the method used for encrypting bids implicitly gives some protection: it is a variant of a technique called *noninteractive VSS* based on pseudorandom secret sharing. We will not look at the details of this method, but using it, an encrypted bid is either obviously malformed or is guaranteed to produce consistently shared values. This means that the only cheating that is possible is to submit bids that are not monotone, that is, bids in which, for instance, the amount you want to buy does not decrease with increasing price, as it should. It is easy to see that this cannot be to a bidder's economic advantage.

Secure Computation

After the deadline for the auction had passed, the servers were connected to the database and each other, and the market-clearing price was securely computed, as well as the quantity each bidder would buy/sell at that price. The representative for each of the involved parties triggered the computation by inserting his or her USB stick and entering his or her password on his or her own machine.

The computation was based on standard Shamir secret sharing over $\mathbb{F} = \mathbb{Z}_p$, where p was a 64-bit prime. The system worked with a set of 4,000 possible values for the price, meaning that after the total supply and demand had been computed for all prices, the market-clearing price could be found using binary search over 4,000 values, which means about twelve secure comparisons.

9.1.4 Practical Evaluation

The bidding phase was done in the beginning of 2008. It ran smoothly, with only a small number of technical questions asked by users. The only issue observed was that the applet on some PCs took up to a minute to complete the encryption of the bids. It is not surprising that the applet needed a nontrivial amount of time because each bid consisted of 4,000 numbers that had to be handled individually. A total of 1,200 bidders participated in the auction, and each had the option of submitting a bid for selling, for buying, or for both.

The actual secure computation was done January 14, 2008, and lasted about thirty minutes. Most of this time was spent on decrypting shares of the individual bids, which is not surprising, because the input to the computation consisted of about 9 million individual numbers. As a result of the auction, about 25,000 tons of production rights changed owner.

9.1.5 Implementation Details

In this section we describe the technical details of how the secure computation of the market-clearing price was performed. We assume that there are P different prices $p_1, \ldots, p_P$, B buyers, S sellers, and n servers. We start at a point where each buyer $j = 1, \ldots, B$ for each price p_i shared an integer d_{ij} among the servers. We denote the sharing by $[d_{i,j}]$. The integer $d_{i,j}$ specifies how much the buyer is willing to buy if the price turns out to be p_i. Similarly, we assume that each seller $j = 1, \ldots, S$ for each price p_i shared an integer s_{ij} among the servers. We denote the sharing by $[s_{i,j}]$. The integer s_{ij} specifies how much the seller is willing to sell if the price turns out to be p_i.

Discrete Market-Clearing Price

The goal, given by economic mechanism design, is now to find the price where most goods are moved. For this, the servers first run the following code:

1. For all prices p_i, compute sharings

$$[d_i] = \sum_{j=1}^{B} [d_{i,j}]$$

and

$$[s_i] = \sum_{j=1}^{S} [s_{i,j}]$$

by locally adding shares; that is, use the protocol for adding shared values.

2. The output is a secret-shared demand "curve" $[d_1], \ldots, [d_P]$ and a secret-shared supply "curve" $[s_1], \ldots, [s_P]$.

If the demand d and supply s were continuous functions of the price p and were monotonously decreasing and monotonously increasing, respectively, then the price p_{MCP} where most goods would be traded is given by $d(p_{\mathrm{MCP}}) = s(p_{\mathrm{MCP}})$. Below this price, the supply is smaller (or at least not larger), and above this price, the demand is smaller (or at least not larger), which leads to a lower amount being traded (or at least not more).

We assume that the curves computed in shared form are monotone, as specified earlier. They are, however, not continuous. We will therefore first compute

$$i_{\mathrm{MCP}} = \max\{i : d_{i_{\mathrm{MCP}}} > s_{i_{\mathrm{MCP}}}\}$$

We can assume that $d_1 > s_1$ (by, e.g., setting $p_1 = 0$), which ensures that i_{MCP} is well defined.[1] It is then easy to see that the price trading most goods is $p_{i_{\mathrm{MCP}}}$ or $p_{i_{\mathrm{MCP}}+1}$. For our purpose here, we simply define the discrete market-clearing price to be $p_{i_{\mathrm{MCP}}}$. If the price grid is fine enough, we expect the amount of goods being traded at $p_{i_{\mathrm{MCP}}}$ and $p_{i_{\mathrm{MCP}}+1}$ to be the same for all practical purposes. In the practical application, more involved choices were used to choose between the two possible clearing prices.

Binary Search

To find i_{MCP}, the servers simply do a binary search on $i \in \{1, \ldots, P\}$. They start with $i = \lceil P/2 \rceil$ and securely test whether $d_i > s_i$. If so, they go to a higher price; if not, they go to a lower price. In this way, they arrive at i_{MCP} using $\log_2(P)$ secure comparisons. By securely testing, we mean that they leak whether $d_i > s_i$ and nothing else.

Note that doing a binary search does not violate the security goal of leaking only i_{MCP}. Given i_{MCP}, one knows that $d_i > s_i$ for all $i \le i_{\mathrm{MCP}}$ and $d_i \le s_i$ for all $i > i_{\mathrm{MCP}}$. Therefore, the outcome of all the comparisons done during the computation can be simulated given just the result i_{MCP}.

The binary search was important for the feasibility of the system because each secure comparison was relatively expensive, meaning that the difference between, for example, $4,000$ comparison and $\lceil \log_2(4,000) \rceil = 12$ comparisons would have been a difference between running for minutes and running for hours.

After i_{MCP} is found, the individual values $d_{i_{\mathrm{MCP}},j}$ and $s_{i_{\mathrm{MCP}},j}$ are reconstructed, and the goods are traded at price $p_{i_{\mathrm{MCP}}}$ and in the revealed amounts.

9.1.6 Secure Comparison

The preceding approach leaves us only with the problem of taking two secret-shared integers $[a]$ and $[b]$ and securely computing a bit $c \in \{0, 1\}$, where $c = 1$ if and only if $a > b$. We write

$$c = [a]\overset{?}{>}[b]$$

Unfortunately, there is no efficient algorithm for computing c from a and b using only addition and multiplication modulo p. Instead, we will take an approach that involves first

---

[1] Alternatively, we can introduce some dummy price p_0 and define $s_0 = 0$ and d_0 to be the maximal amount and create some dummy sharings $[s_0]$ and $[d_0]$.

securely computing sharings of the individual bits of a and b and then performing the comparison on the bitwise representations.

Protocol Compare

Input. Sharings $[a]$ and $[b]$.
Output. A sharing $[c]$, where $c = 1$ if $a > b$ and $c = 0$ otherwise.
Algorithm.

1. $([a_\ell], \ldots, [a_0]) = \text{Bits}([a])$.
2. $([b_\ell], \ldots, [b_0]) = \text{Bits}([b])$.
3. For $i = 0, \ldots, \ell$, $[c_i] = [a_i] + [b_i] - 2[a_i][b_i]$.
4. $([d_\ell], \ldots, [d_0]) = \text{MS1}([c_\ell], \ldots, [c_0])$.
5. For $i = 0, \ldots, \ell$, $[e_i] = [a_i][d_i]$.
6. $[c] = \sum_{i=0}^{\ell} [e_i]$.

Assume first that we have a Protocol Bits that given a sharing $[a]$ securely computes sharings $[a_\ell], \ldots, [a_0]$, where $\ell = \lfloor \log_2(p) \rfloor$ and $a_\ell \cdots a_0$ is the binary representation of a, with a_0 being the least significant bit. That is, $a = \sum_{i=0}^{\ell} 2^i a_i$. Assume furthermore that we have a Protocol MS1 that given sharings $[c_\ell], \ldots, [c_0]$ of bits computes sharings $[d_\ell], \ldots, [d_0]$ of bits, where $d_i = 1$ for the largest i for which $c_i = 1$ and where $d_i = 0$ for all other i – if all $c_i = 0$, then let all $d_i = 0$. That is, $[d_\ell], \ldots, [d_0]$ can be seen as a unary representation of the index i of the most significant 1 in c.

We assume that it never happens that $a = b$. That is, $a > b$ or $b > a$. This can be guaranteed by introducing some dummy different least significant bits. The comparison is then performed as in Protocol Compare. A computation such as $[a_i] + [b_i] - 2[a_i][b_i]$ means that the parties first run the multiplication protocol to compute a sharing of $a_i b_i$. Then they run the multiplication protocol with the result of this and a dummy sharing of -2 to get a sharing of $-2a_i b_i$. Then they run the addition protocol twice to get a sharing of $a_i + b_i - 2a_i b_i$.

It is easy to see that $c_i \in \{0, 1\}$ and $c_i = 1$ if and only if $a_i \neq b_i$. Thus, the i for which $d_i = 1$ is the most significant bit position in which a and b differ. Therefore, $a > b$ if and only if $a_i > b_i$ for the i where $d_i = 1$, and since $a_i \neq b_i$ we have that $a_i > b_i$ if and only if $a_i = 1$. So the result is $c = a_i$ for the i where $d_i = 1$, which can be computed as $\sum_j a_j d_j$ because $d_j = 0$ for all other positions. Thus, the value of c is correct.

Clearly, the protocol is secure because no values are opened during the computation – all computations are done on secret-shared values using secure subprotocols. Note that we computed a sharing of c. When c is needed, one can simply reconstruct $[c]$ toward all parties. If the comparison is done as a part of a larger secure computation, it is, however, in some cases necessary to not leak c. We will see an example of this later.

We also use a version Protocol BitCompare that starts with bitwise sharings of the numbers $([a_L], \ldots, [a_0])$ and $([b_L], \ldots, [b_0])$ and computes $[c]$.[2] Such a protocol is a special case of Protocol Compare, and does not need Bits as a subprotocol.

Since Protocol MS1 starts with a binary representation of the inputs, it is straightforward to construct a secure protocol with the desired functionality. A general approach is to start with a Boolean circuit for the desired functionality and then simulate this circuit using

---

[2] We use L as bound because it might be the case that $L \neq \ell$.

Protocol MS1

Input. Sharings $[c_\ell], \ldots, [c_0]$ of bits.
Output. Sharings $[d_\ell], \ldots, [d_0]$, where $d_\ell \cdots d_0 = \text{MS1}(c_\ell \cdots c_0)$.
Algorithm.

    1. Let $[f_{\ell+1}]$ be a dummy sharing of 1.
    2. For $i = \ell, \ldots, 0$, $[f_i] \leftarrow [f_{i+1}](1 - [c_i])$.
    3. For $i = \ell, \ldots, 0$, $[d_i] \leftarrow [f_{i+1}] - [f_i]$.

---

addition and multiplication. However, sometimes a carefully constructed protocol can do slightly better. One approach to computing a unary representation of the most significant 1 is given in Protocol MS1. Note that it uses only addition and multiplication of shared values as it should. As for the correctness, note that f_i is always a value from $\{0, 1\}$ and that it is 0 if and only if $f_{i+1} = 0$ or $c_i = 1$. In particular, when $f_j = 0$, then $f_k = 0$ for all $k < j$. Furthermore, since we start with $f_{\ell+1} = 1$, it follows that $f_i = 1$ for $i = \ell, \ldots, i_0$, where i_0 is the smallest index such that all the bits $c_\ell, \ldots, c_{i_1}$ are 0. For an example, if $c = c_7 \cdots c_0 = 00010010$, then $f_8 f_7 \cdots f_0 = 111100000$. Note, then, that $f_{i+1} - f_i$ is 0 if $f_{i+1} f_i = 11$ or $f_{i+1} f_i = 00$ and that $f_{i+1} - f_i$ is 1 if $f_{i+1} f_i = 10$. Thus, d_i will be 0 everywhere, except where the sequence 111100000 changes from 1 to 0. In our example, where $f_8 f_7 \cdots f_0 = 111100000$, we get that $d_7 \cdots d_0 = 00010000$. In general, d_i will be 1 exactly where the first 1 is found in c, as it should be.

Using similar techniques, we can also develop an efficient and secure Protocol BitAdd, which takes bitwise sharings $([a_L], \ldots, [a_0])$ and $([b_L], \ldots, [b_0])$ and produces a bitwise sharing $([c_{L+1}], [c_L], \ldots, [c_0])$ of $c = a + b$ (without any modular reduction). And we can produce a secure Protocol BitSub, which takes bitwise sharings $([a_L], \ldots, [a_0])$ and $([b_L], \ldots, [b_0])$ of $a \geq b$ and produces a bitwise sharing $([c_L], \ldots, [c_0])$ of $c = a - b$. For these protocols, we also use versions in which some inputs might be known bits instead of shared bits, for example, b_0 instead of $[b_0]$: simply first do a dummy sharing $[b_0]$ of b_0, and then run the corresponding protocol for shared values.

EXERCISE 9.1 Implement BitAdd and BitSub securely using on the order of ℓ secure multiplications. The number of secure additions is not important because they are cheap in that they do not require communication. [*Hint*: Iterate from the least significant bit to the most significant one, and keep a carry bit. The challenge is to use only addition and multiplication.] How few multiplications can you do with?

We then turn our attention to Protocol Bits. At first, this seems to be a hard challenge because it is not clear how to access an individual bit using only addition and multiplication, but as is often the case in MPC, a random self-reduction will do the job. That is, we generate a random solved instance of the problem, and then use it to solve the original problem. In doing this, we use the randomness of the solved instance to mask the original instance, which allows us to reveal the masked values and do most of the hard operations on plaintext. This is a very common technique.

Assume that we have a secure Protocol RandomSolvedBits that outputs a random sharing $[r]$ of a random number r from $\mathbb{Z}_p$, along with sharings of the bits $([r_\ell], \ldots, [r_0])$ of r. As we show later, producing such a random solved instance is fairly easy. The protocol then proceeds as described in Protocol Bits.

Protocol Bits

Input. A sharing $[a]$ of $a \in \mathbb{Z}_p$.
Output. Sharings $[f_\ell], \ldots, [f_0]$ of the bits of a.
Algorithm.

1. $([r], [r_\ell], \ldots, [r_0]) \leftarrow \text{RandomSolvedBits}$.
2. $[c] = [a] - [r]$.
3. $c \leftarrow \text{Reconstruct}([c])$.
4. Write c in binary $c_\ell, \ldots, c_0$.
5. $([d_{\ell+1}], \ldots, [d_0]) \leftarrow \text{BitAdd}(([r_\ell], \ldots, [r_0]), (c_\ell, \ldots, c_0))$.
6. Write p in binary $(p_{\ell+1}, p_\ell, \ldots, p_0)$.
7. $[e] = \text{BitCompare}(([d_{\ell+1}], \ldots, [d_0]), (p_{\ell+1}, \ldots, p_0))$.
8. For $i = 0, \ldots, \ell + 1$, $[ep_i] = [e][p_i]$.
9. $([f_{\ell+1}], \ldots, [f_0]) \leftarrow \text{BitSub}(([d_{\ell+1}], \ldots, [d_0]), ([ep_{\ell+1}], \ldots, [ep_0]))$.

The protocol reconstructs only one value, namely, c. Since $c = a - r \bmod p$ and r is an unknown uniformly random value in $\mathbb{Z}_p$ independent of a, the value c is a uniformly random number in $\mathbb{Z}_p$ independent of a, so it is secure to let all parties learn c. Therefore, the protocol is secure. It takes a little more work to see that it is correct.

First, note that $d = c + r$. Since $c = a - r \bmod p$, this means that $d = a$ or $d = a + p$. The later case happens when $r > a$ such that $a - r \bmod p$ gives a wrap-around. We find out which case we are in by (securely) comparing d to p: the bit e is 1 if $d = a + p$ and it is 0 if $d = a$ – we can write this as $d = a + ep$. The next step then (securely) subtracts ep from d. In the for loop, we compute a bitwise sharing of ep. Then we use a secure subtraction. It follows that $f_{\ell+1}, f_\ell, \ldots, f_0$ is the bitwise representation of $d - ep = a$. Since a is an ℓ-bit number, we in particular know that $f_{\ell+1} = 0$, so we only have to use $[f_\ell], \ldots, [f_0]$ as the result.

Protocol RandomSolvedBits

Output. Sharing $[r]$ of a random unknown field element $r \in \mathbb{Z}_p$.
Output. Sharings $[r_\ell] \ldots, [r_0]$ of the bits of r.
Algorithm.

1. For $i = 0, \ldots, \ell$, $[r_i] \leftarrow \text{RandomBit}(\cdot)$.
2. Write p in binary $p_\ell, \ldots, p_0$.
3. $[c] \leftarrow \text{BitCompare}((p_\ell, \ldots, p_0), ([r_\ell], \ldots, [r_0]))$.
4. $c \leftarrow \text{Reconstruct}([c])$.
5. If $c = 0$, go to step 1.
6. $[r] \leftarrow \sum_{i=0}^{\ell} 2^i [r_i]$.

We are then stuck with Protocol RandomSolvedBits. For a last time, we push some of the burden into the future by assuming that we have a Protocol RandomBit that generates a sharing of a random bit. Then a random solved instance is generated as in Protocol RandomSolvedBits. We essentially generate a random element $r \in \mathbb{Z}_p$ by using rejection sampling. Since $r < p$ with probability at least $\frac{1}{2}$, by the definition of ℓ, this protocol terminates after an expected two iterations, and on termination, r is clearly a uniformly random integer from $[0, p)$, as desired.

Note that the reason why generating a random solved instance is easier than solving a given instance is that we do not solve the random instance – we generate the solution (the bits) and then compute the instance from the solution.

All that is left is then to implement Protocol RandomBit. One inefficient way of doing this is to let all parties generate a sharing of a random bit and then, for example, take the secure XOR of these bits.[3] The reason why this is inefficient is that it would require $n - 1$ multiplications for each of the generated bits. With three servers, this is fine, but in general it can be rather inefficient. Furthermore, it is not actively secure because the servers might not all contribute bits, and as can be seen, all the preceding protocols are indeed active secure if the subprotocols are active secure, so we should try to also make the generation of random bits active secure too.

Protocol RandomBit

Output. A sharing $[r]$ of a uniformly random bit r.
Algorithm.

1. $[a] \leftarrow$ RandomFieldElement.
2. $[a^2] = [a][a]$.
3. $A \leftarrow$ Reconstruct $([a^2])$
4. If $A = 0$, go to step 1.
5. $b \leftarrow \sqrt{A} \bmod p$.
6. $[c] = (b^{-1} \bmod p)[a]$.
7. $[r] = 2^{-1}([c] + 1)$.

Our active secure protocol is based on the fact that squaring a nonzero element modulo an odd prime is a two-to-one mapping, and given $b = a^2$, one has no idea if the preimage was a or $-a$. We will let the "sign" of such an a be our random bit. We use a subprotocol RandomFieldElement that generates a sharing of a random field element. It is implemented by each server sharing a random field element and then adding all of them. Here there is no room to cheat: as long as just one server contributes a random field element, the result is random.

The protocol is given in Algorithm RandomBit. It rejects when $A = 0$ to ensure that we started with $a \in \mathbb{Z}_p^*$. When the loop terminates, then $A = a^2 \bmod p$ for a uniformly random $a \in \mathbb{Z}_p^*$. Since A only has two square roots, because we are computing modulo a prime, and since a is one of them, it follows that $b = a$ or $b = -a \bmod p$. Since $A = a^2 \bmod p$ and $A = (-a)^2 \bmod p$, the value $b = \sqrt{A} \bmod p$ is clearly independent of whether A was computed as $A = a^2 \bmod p$ or $A = (-a)^2 \bmod p$, no matter which algorithm is used for computing the square root. Since a was chosen uniformly at random, it follows that $\Pr[b = a] = \frac{1}{2}$ and $\Pr[b = -a \bmod p] = \frac{1}{2}$. If $b = a$, then $b^{-1}a \bmod p = 1$, and thus $r = 1$. If $b = -a \bmod p$, then $b^{-1}a \bmod p = -1 \bmod p$, and thus $r = 0$. Therefore, $\Pr[r = 1] = \frac{1}{2}$ and $\Pr[r = 0] = \frac{1}{2}$. Since $[a]$ is not reconstructed, no party knows whether $r = 0$ or $r = 1$.

---

[3] The XOR of bits a and b can be expressed via addition and multiplication as $a + b - 2ab$.

Conclusion

By inspection of the preceding protocols, and given a solution to Exercise 9.1, it can be seen that all protocols use a number of multiplications on the order of $\log_2(p)$, and the unmentioned constant is fairly small. This allows us to perform comparisons of shared integers relatively efficiently. The ability to split a shared number has many other applications. One is to move a number x shared modulo one prime p into a sharing modulo another prime q. If q is smaller than p, this computes a modulo reduction of x modulo q. Many similar tricks exists and are constantly being produced to allow efficient secure computation of specific operations.

EXERCISE 9.2 Earlier we had to compute $\sqrt{A} \bmod p$. When p is a prime and A is a square modulo p, this can be done efficiently. The algorithm depends on whether $p \bmod 4 = 1$ or $p \bmod 4 = 3$. Note that if $p > 2$, then p is odd, so it cannot be the case that $p \bmod 4 \in \{0,2\}$. If $p \bmod 4 = 3$, then $\sqrt{A} \bmod p = A^{(p+1)/4} \bmod p$. That is, if you let $b = A^{(p+1)/4} \bmod p$, then $b^2 \bmod p = A$. Notice that $A^{(p+1)/4}$ is well defined because $p \bmod 4 = 3$ implies that $p = 4m + 3$ for some integer. Therefore, $p + 1 = 4m + 4 = 4(m+1)$, and $(p+1)/4 = m+1$ is an integer, as it should be for $A^{(p+1)/4}$ to be defined. Prove that $b^2 \bmod p = A$. [*Hint*: Use that $A = a^2 \bmod p$ for some a and that $p + 1 = (p-1) + 2$ and a little theorem.]

EXERCISE 9.3 Assume that you are given a sharing $[a]$ of an element $a \neq 0$, and assume also that you can generate a sharing $[r]$ of a uniformly random element $r \neq 0$. Argue that it is secure to compute $[ar] = [a][r]$ and reveal ar. Show how to securely compute $[a^{-1}]$ from $[a]$.

EXERCISE 9.4 In a Vickrey auction, there is a single item and a number of buyers B_i. Each buyer B_i bids a price p_i. The winner is the buyer with the highest bid, and the winner gets to buy the item, but at the second-highest bid. Assume that all prices are different, and describe a protocol that computes the winner and the price and that leaks noting else. You are allowed to assume that you have access to some servers of which more than half are honest. Try to make the system as efficient as possible.

9.2 Zero-Knowledge Proofs via MPC in the Head

In this section we explain how efficient multiparty computation can be used to construct efficient zero-knowledge proofs of knowledge. In a zero-knowledge proof of knowledge, a prover convinces a verifier that he or she knows a particular secret without revealing anything about the secret. For example, consider a prover P who sends his or her public key pk to a verifier V and claims that he or she knows the secret key sk corresponding to pk. Of course, P could prove this simply by sending sk to V, but this would not be secure in most settings, so we seek a way to prove such knowledge without leaking any information.

Generally, the problem is parametrized by a binary relation $R \subset \{0,1\}^* \times \{0,1\}^*$. For a pair $(x,w) \in R$, we call x an instance, and we call w the witness. The prover knows $(x,w) \in R$ and sends x to the verifier, claiming to know w such that $(x,w) \in R$. In the preceding example, we would have $x = pk$ and $w = sk$, and R would consist of the pairs (pk, sk) for which sk is the secret key corresponding to pk. We seek a way for P to substantiate his or her claim without leaking anything about w to V. Phrased as an ideal functionality, the problem can be captured using Agent ZKPOK^R.

Agent ZKPOK^R

The ideal functionality ZKPOK^R for zero knowledge is for two parties, a prover P and a verifier V. It is parametrized by a polynomial time binary relation $R \subset \{0,1\}^* \times \{0,1\}^*$.

Proof. On input (x,w) from P, where $(x,w) \in R$, output x on `leak`, and store (proved,x).

Delivery. On input $(\text{deliver},x)$ on `infl` when some (proved,x) is stored, output x to V.

A related problem is that of implementing a "processing channel." Here a sender S sends some message x to a receiver R. However, instead of receiving x, the receiver is to receive some processed version of x, where the processing is given by some function f. If security were not an issue, the sender could just send x and let R compute the processed value $y = f(x)$. However, we seek a way to let R learn y without learning anything extra about x. Phrased as an ideal functionality, the problem can be captured using Agent PC^f.

Agent PC^f

The ideal functionality PC^f for a processing channel is for two parties, a sender S and a receiver R. It is parametrized by a polynomial time function $f : \{0,1\}^* \to \{0,1\}^*$.

Send. On input x from S, compute $y = f(x)$, output y on `leak`, and store $(\text{sending},y)$.

Delivery. On input $(\text{deliver},y)$ on `infl` when some $(\text{sending},y)$ is stored, output y to R.

For a given binary relation R, consider the function $f_R(x,w)$, where $f_R(x,w) = x$ if $(x,w) \in R$ and $f_R(x,w) = \bot$ if $(x,w) \notin R$, where $\bot \notin \{0,1\}^*$. It should be clear that if we can securely implement PC^{f_R}, then we can also securely implement ZKPOK^R. This, in fact, follows from the UC theorem because it is trivial to securely implement ZKPOK^R in the hybrid model with access to PC^{f_R}. The prover will input (x,w) to PC^{f_R}, acting as S with respect to PC^{f_R}. The verifier V will act as R with respect to PC^{f_R}. If it receives $x \neq \bot$ from PC^{f_R}, it output x. If it receives $x = \bot$, it does nothing. Constructing a simulator is trivial.

We can therefore focus on implementing PC^{f_R} for the given R. We will, in fact, show something stronger. We will show how to securely implement PC^f for any polytime function f.

The first step is to consider a related problem in a setting with n parties. For a given f, consider the corresponding function $g(x_1, x_2, \ldots, x_n) = (y_1, \ldots, y_n)$, where $y_1 = y_2 = \cdots = y_n = f(x_1)$. We know from Chapter 5 that there exists a perfectly secure protocol π implementing g given secure point-to-point channels and broadcast, tolerating $t < n/3$ corrupted parties. We are going to massage this π into a protocol for two parties that securely implements PC^f.

Our first step will be to assume that π is in so-called canonical form, which means that it is defined as a function:

$$\pi : \mathbb{N} \times \mathbb{N} \times \{0,1\}^{n+1} \to \{0,1\}^{n+1}$$

Concretely, this means that we assume that π proceeds in ℓ rounds, where in each round each party sends one secure message to each of the other parties and broadcasts one message. Then the execution of a given party in a given round is given by

$$(x_{i,1}^r, \ldots, x_{i,n}^r, x_i^r) = \pi\,(r, i, y_{1,i}^{r-1}, \ldots, y_{n,i}^{r-1}, \rho_i)$$

where r specifies the round number, $i \in \{1, \ldots, n\}$ specifies the index of the party that is being computed, $(y_{1,i}^{r-1}, \ldots, y_{n,i}^{r-1})$ are the incoming messages from $(P_1, \ldots, P_n)$, respectively, and ρ_i is a randomizer from which, for example, shares are drawn. The output $x_{i,j}^r$ is the message sent securely from P_i to P_j in round r, and x_i^r is the message broadcast by P_i in round r. The party P_i can pass an internal state to the next round by "securely sending it to itself" as $x_{i,i}^r$. In detail, an honest execution of a protocol π in canonical form runs as described in the next box.

Honest Execution of Canonical form Protocol (ℓ, π)

1. The input for P_i is x_i.
2. For $i = 1, \ldots, n$, set $y_{i,i}^0 = x_i$, and set $y_{i,j \neq i}^0 = 0$. Sample uniformly random ρ_i.
3. For $r = 1, \ldots, \ell$,

   a. For $i = 1, \ldots, n$, compute $(x_{i,1}^r, \ldots, x_{i,n}^r, x_i^r) = \pi\,(r, i, y_{1,i}^{r-1}, \ldots, y_{n,i}^{r-1}, \rho_i)$.
   b. For $j = 1, \ldots, n$, $y_{i,j}^r = (x_{i,j}^r, x_i^r)$.

4. The output of P_i is $y_i = y_{i,i}^\ell$.

A global transcript of such a protocol π consist of the values

$$G = (\{x_i\}_{i=1}^n, \{\rho_i\}_{i=1}^n, \{x_i^r\}_{i=1,r=1}^{n,\ell}, \{x_{i,j}^r\}_{i=1,j=1,r=1}^{n,n,\ell}) \tag{9.1}$$

That is, it is all the inputs, all the random choices, all the broadcast messages, and all the secret messages exchanged.

We can restrict a global transcript to a single party P_k, giving a local view

$$L_k = P_k(G) = (x_k, \rho_k, \{x_i^r, x_{i,k}^r\}_{i=1,i \neq k,r=1}^{n,\ell}) \tag{9.2}$$

That is, L_k consists of the inputs of P_k, the random choices of P_k, and all broadcast messages and all secret messages P_k received from other players. Note that from L_k we can use π to compute (deterministically) all messages that P_k would send in an execution in which its local view is L_k. Note also that the preceding way to generate a global transcript only makes sense if all parties follow the protocol. If some players are actively corrupted, the concept of a local view still makes sense and is well defined for honest parties, but the corrupted parties will, of course, not necessarily compute their messages according to π.

We say that two local views L_k, L_j are consistent if the messages P_k sends to P_j according to L_k are those that occur as received from P_k in L_j and vice versa. Accordingly, we define a predicate $\text{Consistent}(L_k, L_j) \in \{\top, \bot\}$, computed as in Algorithm Consistent.

Algorithm Consistent

1. The input is L_k, L_j, where $k \neq j$.
2. Use π to compute from L_k all messages P_k sends, and extract those that P_j would see, namely, $\{\tilde{x}_k^r, \tilde{x}_{j,k}^r\}_{r=1}^\ell$. If these messages differ from the corresponding messages $\{x_k^r, x_{j,k}^r\}_{r=1}^\ell$ occurring in L_j, output $\perp$ and stop.
3. Use π to compute from L_j all messages P_j sends, and extract those that P_k would see, namely, $\{\tilde{x}_j^r, \tilde{x}_{k,j}^r\}_{r=1}^\ell$. If these messages differ from the corresponding messages $\{x_j^r, x_{k,j}^r\}_{r=1}^\ell$ occurring in L_k, output $\perp$ and stop.
4. Output $\top$.

We now sketch how S and R will use protocol π: first, S simulates a run of π on input $x_1 = x$ and gives the output $y = f(x)$ of P_2 to R. In other words, S computes locally $(y, \dots, y) = (y_1, \dots, y_n) \leftarrow \pi(x, 0, \dots, 0)$ and shows the outcome y to R. To convince R that y is the correct output, S will be asked to show the local view of a random selection of t of the parties in the protocol π. The only restriction is that R does not get to see the view of P_1. Note that it is secure to show the view of t parties to R because the protocol is secure against t corrupted parties, so seeing the view of t parties will not leak the input x of P_1.

Protocol Zero-Knowledge Proof of Knowledge via MPC in the Head

The protocol is for two parties S and R. It runs in the hybrid model with access to an ideal functionality COM for commitment to strings.

1. First, S runs π on input $x_1 = x$:

   a. Run π on $(x_1, \dots, x_n) = (x, 0, \dots, 0)$ as in the "Honest Execution" box, defining a global transcript G as in Eq. (9.1).
   b. Commit to $P_i(G)$ for $i = 1 \dots n$, using one call to the ideal functionality for each of the n local views. This means that the local views can be individually opened.

2. R waits until the commitment functionality reports that all commitments were done.
3. Then R asks to see the local views of t random parties.

   a. Pick a uniformly random subset $E \subset \{1, \dots, n\}$, with $|E| = t$ and $1 \notin E$.
   b. Send E to S.

4. S reveals the local views of the t chosen parties. For $i \in E$, open the commitment to $P_i(G)$.
5. Then R checks that the revealed values are consistent with the parties P_i having followed the protocol π: for any pair $k, j \in E$, let L_k, L_j be the views opened in the preceding step. If Consistent$(L_k, L_j) = \perp$, then terminate the protocol.
6. Check that all inspected players output the same value y; that is, for all $i \in E$, check that the output value $y_{i,i}^\ell$ in L_i equals y.
7. If all the preceding checks go through, then R outputs y.

To avoid that a cheating S modifies the views depending on who R wants to inspect, we first ask S to commit to all the local views in the protocol. Then R picks who to inspect, and S must open the corresponding commitments. If the views of the t inspected parties are all consistent, then except with very small probability the views of at least $n - t$ of the parties were all consistent, as we shall see later. But, if this is the case, then the trace of the protocol that has been committed is one that actually could occur in real life, where at most t parties are corrupt. This means that all the consistent parties must have computed the correct output because the protocol can tolerate up to t corrupted parties. The details are given in Protocol Zero-Knowledge Proof of Knowledge via MPC in the Head. For the protocol to be secure, we need that the underlying protocol is private and robust, as defined now.

9.2.1 Perfect Privacy of MPC

We define privacy simply by specializing the definition from Chapter 3.

DEFINITION 9.1 (PERFECT PRIVACY) *We say that π is a perfectly t-private implementation of g if there exists a polytime function* Sim *such that the following condition holds for all input vectors $(x_1,\ldots,x_n)$. Compute $(y_1,\ldots,y_n) = g(x_1,\ldots,x_n)$, and execute π on inputs $(x_1,\ldots,x_n)$ as in the "Honest Execution" box. Then, for all $C \subset \{1,\ldots,n\}$ with $|C| \leq t$, it holds that*

$$\text{Sim}(\{x_j,y_j\}_{j\in C}) \overset{\text{perf}}{\equiv} \{P_j(G)\}_{j\in C}$$

It follows in general that a protocol that is perfectly secure in the sense the we proved π to be in Chapter 5 is also t-private in the preceding sense for $t < n/3$.

9.2.2 Perfect Robustness of MPC

We say that a protocol π is perfectly t-robust if it always computes the correct result even if t parties deviated from the protocol. The correct result is defined by requiring that from the view of just the honest parties we can also extract a well-defined input for the corrupt parties, and the correct result is then defined based on these inputs. Note that this notion of robustness is not sufficient for or equivalent to security in general; we will have more to say about this later. The notion will suffice, however, for our application here.

Recall that the output of a party is just the message it sends to itself in the last round. We write

$$\text{Output}(L_i) = y_{i,i}^\ell$$

where L_i is the local view of an honest party P_i. We use $\text{Input}(L_i)$ to denote the input of P_i.

DEFINITION 9.2 (PERFECT ROBUSTNESS) *We say that π is a perfectly t-robust implementation of g if there exists a polytime function* Inputs *that returns values of the form $(x_1,\ldots,x_n)$ satisfying the following: let $L_H = \{L_i | P_i \in H\}$ be any set of local views that may result from an execution of π where a set H of at least $n - t$ parties are honest. Set*

$$(x_1,\ldots,x_n) = \text{Inputs}(L_H)$$

$$(y_1,\ldots,y_n) = g(x_1,\ldots,x_n)$$

Then the following two conditions hold:

1. $x_i = \text{Input}(L_i)$ *for $P_i \in H$.*
2. $\text{Output}(L_i) = y_i$ *for $P_i \in H$.*

As mentioned earlier, this notion of robustness is tailored to our application in this section and is in fact incomparable with standard notions. On the one hand, it is not sufficient for security in general because it might allow the extracted inputs of the corrupted parties to depend on the inputs of the honest parties. On the other hand, it does not follow in general that a protocol that is perfectly secure in the sense we proved for π Chapter 5 is also *t*-robust in the preceding sense.

The reason is that the preceding definition asks that the inputs of inconsistent parties be computed from just the transcript of the consistent parties. When proving security in the sense that we did in Chapter 5, the simulator potentially has more power, in that it is the simulator itself that *produces* the transcript of the consistent parties – it might even simulate in a way that does not involve explicitly defining these transcripts.

However, it can be easily verified that the protocol π produced in Chapter 5 is indeed *t*-robust in the preceding sense, for $t < n/3$. This is so because the way we extracted an input x_i for a corrupted P_i in Chapter 5 was to take the shares of x_i seen by the honest parties and interpolate x_i from them. For this we needed only $n - t$ shares, so this way to extract inputs is exactly of the form required by the preceding definition. Then these inputs were submitted to the ideal functionality, which computed $(y_1, \ldots, y_n) = f(x_1, \ldots, x_n)$, where x_i for the honest P_i was the value sent directly to the ideal functionality by the environment. Then the ideal functionality sent y_i to each honest P_i.

9.2.3 Analysis

We now proceed to prove that Protocol Zero-Knowledge Proof of Knowledge via MPC in the Head is secure. We will only prove static security, but the protocol is in fact adaptive secure. Simulating the case where both parties are honest is simple: if we run the protocol over a secure channel, there is no view to simulate. It therefore suffices to describe the simulators for the case where S and R are corrupted. To simulate when S is corrupted, we use $\bar{S}$. To simulate when R is corrupted, we use $\bar{R}$.

Agent $\bar{R}$

To simulate against a corrupted receiver, run as follows:

1. The simulator receives $y = f(x)$ from PC^f but does not know x.
2. The simulator (who is simulating COM) commits to n dummy values on COM.
3. Receive E from R, and check that $|E| = t$ and $1 \notin E$.
4. Then simulate the local transcripts to be revealed.

   a. For $i \in E$, let $x_i = 0$.
   b. Let $y_1 = y$.
   c. For $i \in E \setminus \{1\}$, let $y_i = 0$.
   d. Use the simulator Sim from Definition 9.1 to sample

   $$\{P_j(G)\}_{j \in E} \leftarrow \text{Sim}(\{x_j, y_j\}_{i \in E})$$

5. For $j \in E$, change the values stored in COM such that the commitments are consistent with the values computed in the preceding step for $j \in E$. This goes unnoticed by the environment because it is the simulator that simulates COM and so far no commitments were opened.
6. For $j \in E$, open the commitments to the $P_j(G)$ values we just prepared.

Agent $\bar{\mathsf{S}}$

To simulate against a corrupted sender, run as follows:

1. Simply simulate the protocol honestly by running as the honest R in Protocol Zero-Knowledge Proof of Knowledge via MPC in the Head. This is possible because R has no input.
2. The only challenge is that if during the preceding simulation R produces an output y. In this case, the simulator needs to make the ideal functionality PC^f output y on behalf of R. This can only be done by inputting some $x \in f^{-1}(y)$ to PC^f on behalf of the corrupted S. This x is computed as follows:

   a. If R outputs y in the protocol, then S already committed to a set of local views. Inspect COM to extract these values $L_1, \ldots, L_n$ (this is possible because it is the simulator that simulates COM).
   b. Construct a set T of players as follows: initially let T be the set of all players. Now, if there exists a pair of players $\mathsf{P}_i, \mathsf{P}_j \in T$ for which L_i, L_j are not consistent, that is, Consistent$(L_i, L_j) = \bot$, then remove P_i and P_j from T. Continue this way until no more pairs can be removed.
   c. If $|T| < n - t$, set $x = 0$. Otherwise, compute $(x_1, \ldots, x_n) = \text{Inputs}(\{L_i\}_{i \in T})$, and use $x = x_1$.

It easily follows from t-privacy that the view produced by $\bar{\mathsf{R}}$ is identical to the view in the protocol. To analyze $\bar{\mathsf{S}}$, consider first the case where the set T of players constructed by $\bar{\mathsf{S}}$ has size less than $n - t$. We claim that R would abort with overwhelming probability in such a case. To see this, note that at least $t/2$ pairs of players have been deleted from the full set of players to obtain T. If any such pair is in the set of t players checked by R, he or she will abort.

Let t' be the number of players not in T; then we know that $t' \geq t$. Let us assume that $t/n = c$ for a constant c. Then $t'/n \geq c$, so we expect that at least ct among the t players checked by R are not in T. In fact, by a standard Chernoff bound, except with negligible probability (as a function of n), there will be at least $c't$ such players for $c' < c$. Now, if selecting the first $c't/2$ players not in T misses all inconsistent pairs, this means that the "partners" of these first players have not been selected. But then each time a new player is selected after this point, an inconsistent pair is found with at least constant probability $c't/(2n) = c'/(2c)$. Overall, R finds an inconsistent pair except with negligible probability in n. Therefore, when T is smaller than $n - t$, it does not matter that $\bar{\mathsf{S}}$ does not compute the correct x.

Then we consider the case where T has size at least $n - t$. Since the local views of players in T are all pairwise consistent, this collection of local views could have resulted from a real execution of π. Indeed, consider an environment that corrupts the players not in T and instructs them to send exactly those messages to players in T that occur in their local views. It therefore follows from t-robustness that evaluating the Inputs function results in an input x for P_1 such that all honest players output $y = f(x)$. Since R inspects t players, he or she will inspect at least one honest player except with negligible probability and therefore will output y or reject. Hence, in this case, $\bar{\mathsf{S}}$ indeed computes the correct value of x.

We have proved the following:

THEOREM 9.3 *Consider functionality* PC^f, *and construct a function g with n outputs from f as described earlier. Suppose that protocol* π *is a perfect t-private and t-robust implementation of g, where* $n = ct$ *for a constant c. Then Protocol Zero-Knowledge Proof of Knowledge via MPC in the Head composed with functionality* COM *implements* PC^f *with statistical security.*

Implementation and Efficiency Considerations

We note first that protocols that can be used as π in the preceding theorem do exist. Indeed, we have seen protocols that can evaluate any function with perfect active security assuming $t < n/3$. Such a protocol more than satisfies the conditions. However, it is clear that the resulting two-player protocol becomes more efficient the more efficient π is.

To get a protocol that implements PC^f from scratch, we could attempt to implement COM, but this would require the implementation to be UC secure and hence cannot be done without some setup assumption (see Chapter 7). An approach leading to better efficiency that does not require setup assumptions is to use a non-UC commitment scheme and prove directly that that the composed protocol is a zero-knowledge proof that the prover knows x such that $y = f(x)$. The standard definitions of this (which are out of scope for this book) do not require universal composability, so in a sense this allows us to trade composability for efficiency.

This is important because the main motivation for the MPC-in-the-head approach is indeed efficiency – it was already well known that very general zero-knowledge proofs follow from commitment schemes, but with MPC-in-the-head we can make the proofs smaller. This improvement comes from several sources, and we sketch here what the main ideas are.

- In Protocol Zero-Knowledge Proof of Knowledge via MPC in the Head, only n commitments need to be produced. Now, except for a small additive overhead that depends on the security parameter, commitments can be implemented such that a commitment has size equal to the string committed to. Therefore, the communication needed in the two-player protocol is essentially the communication complexity of π.
- The communication complexity of π can be optimized using some of the techniques we saw in Chapter 8. In particular, we saw that using packed secret sharing, we can implement many parallel instances of the same computation almost "for the price of one." This is very useful in connection with zero knowledge: here we need to evaluate the function $f_R(x, w)$ for NP relation R, as defined earlier. Imagine that we write down a Boolean circuit that evaluates f_R. Now the prover (who knows x, w) can compute the inputs and outputs that occur for every gate in the circuit when we input x, w. He or she then can supply these as extra input to the computation. Now all π needs to do is to check that the claimed output from every gate is the correct function of its inputs, and this can be done for all gates in parallel.
- Packed secret sharing can be done based on Shamir's scheme, as we have seen, but the price is that the size of field we use must grow linearly with the number of players n because each player must have his or her own evaluation point. As a result, we get an overhead factor of $\log(n)$. This can be avoided using asymptotically good, strongly multiplicative secret-sharing schemes (see Chapter 12). The overhead disappears because those schemes can be constructed using a constant-size field.

Using all the preceding ideas, one can get zero-knowledge proofs for NP relations R with communication complexity linear in a circuit computing f_R. It is even possible to construct two-party protocols for secure function evaluation using the MPC-in-the-head approach (see the Notes section for details). This further emphasizes the interesting fact that it is important to study secure protocols for many players, even if the final goal is two-party protocols.

9.3 Notes

The sugar beets double auction was developed as part of two research projects SCET (Secure Computing, Economy, and Trust) and SIMAP (Secure Information Management and Processing) carried out at Aarhus University. These projects aimed at improving the efficiency of SMC, with an explicit focus on a range of economic applications that were believed to be particularly interesting for practical use. At the time of this writing, the auction is still run once a year by the spinoff company Partisia Market Design. The final implementation of the auction was reported on by Bogetoft et al. [27]. The algorithmic ideas behind the secure comparison that we describe here are based on work by Damgård et al. [68].

The general idea of designing two-party protocols from multiparty computation using the MPC-in-the-head approach is from Ishai, Kushilevitz, Ostrovsky, Sahai [118], and the construction we give here is also from that paper. The proof is slightly different because we prove the two-party protocol to be a proof of knowledge, whereas the original proof only shows that it is a proof of language membership. Ishai, Prabhakaran, and Sahai [115] show how to design secure two-party computation from multiparty protocols.

Part II

Secret Sharing

10

Algebraic Preliminaries

10.1 Introduction

Throughout, the reader is assumed to already have a good (working) knowledge of basic undergraduate algebra.[1] For ease of reference, we shall first recall some central definitions and useful elementary results concerning groups, rings, fields, modules, vector spaces, and algebras. For additional basic theory, full details and more, please refer, for example, to Serge Lang's *Algebra* [126].[2]

Furthermore, at some points we shall need some results from field theory and algebraic number theory, as well as from multilinear algebra, specifically concerning cyclotomic number fields and tensor products. In each of these cases we shall give a brief introduction and state the required results. For full details and more, please refer to references 125, 126, 127. Our exposition of these topics (loosely) follows Lang [126], except where stated otherwise.

Finally, we shall need results from the theory of algebraic function fields (in one variable) over finite fields, that is, algebraic curves over finite fields.[3] This is deferred to Section 12.7. Specifically, the focus there will be on families of curves with asymptotically many rational points. We will give a bird's-eye introduction to this topic that is self-contained in that it assumes as background only the material on basic algebra covered earlier on. For a full treatment of the basic theory of algebraic function fields, as well as such results as the ones referred to earlier, we refer to Henning Stichtenoth's *Algebraic Function Fields and Codes* [172].[4] Except when stated differently, our exposition follows Stichtenoth [172], specifically parts of Chapters 1, 3, 5, and 7. Full proofs are mostly beyond the scope of this introduction. Sometimes a sketch is given. Yet we shall state all results needed for our purposes.

---

[1] Our goal here is to refresh knowledge, to quickly expand it in some more advanced directions relevant to our main cryptographic topic, and to issue an invitation to more in-depth study from specialized sources, for instance, those referenced here.

[2] Lang's classic book [126] is a standard reference work for basic algebra. See also for example, Lang's *Undergraduate Algebra* [127], which is of introductory nature.

[3] More precisely, projective smooth absolutely irreducible algebraic curves over finite fields.

[4] Stichtenoth's book is one of a few that makes a number of important concepts and (modern) developments on algebraic function fields over finite fields rather quickly accessible to readers with just a firm command of basic commutative algebra (as covered, e.g., by parts of Lang's book [126]). Some prior exposure to Galois theory and algebraic number theory is useful but not strictly necessary. It also features an in-depth treatment of asymptotically good towers of algebraic function fields over finite fields. See also Niederreiter and Xing [148], Moreno [146], and Tsfasman, Vlăduţ, and Nogin [177].

Basic definitions and results that are covered in full detail by most standard introductory textbooks are mentioned without reference (but sometimes a proof is given). In case we suspect that a result we quote is not so easy to look up elsewhere in full detail (say, if it is disguised as a special case of more advanced theory or hidden in exercises), we give an explicit reference to a suitable text.

In a few places in the text we will give appropriate references when discussing certain specific (advanced) algorithmic aspects. For an introduction to computational aspects of number theory and algebra, the reader is referred to Shoup [168], and for an introduction to computational algebraic number theory, the reader is referred to Cohen [53].

10.2 Groups, Rings, Fields

10.2.1 Monoids

A monoid is a set G together with a map $\bullet : G \times G \longrightarrow G$, a law of composition, such that

1. For all $a, b, c \in G$, it holds that $a \bullet (b \bullet c) = (a \bullet b) \bullet c$ (associativity).
2. There is $e \in G$ such that, for all $a \in G$, it holds that $e \bullet a = a \bullet e = a$ (neutral element).

The neutral element e (sometimes denoted e_G) is unique: if e' is another neutral element, then $e = e \bullet e' = e'$. A monoid is commutative if $a \bullet b = b \bullet a$ for all $a, b \in G$.

A submonoid of G is a subset G' such that the neutral element e is contained in G' and G' is closed under the composition. The restricted composition makes it a monoid. In what follows we write ab instead of $a \bullet b$.

Let G, H be monoids. A morphism from G to H is a function $\phi : G \longrightarrow H$ such that $\phi(e_G) = e_H$ and $\phi(ab) = \phi(a)\phi(b)$ for all $a, b \in G$. Note that the composition on the l.h.s. (resp., r.h.s.) corresponds to the one in G (resp., in H). If $G = H$, we speak of an endomorphism.

A morphism $\phi : G \to H$ of monoids is an isomorphism if there is a morphism $\phi' : H \to G$ such that $\phi' \circ \phi$ is the identity on G and $\phi \circ \phi'$ is the identity on H. Here $\circ$ denotes composition as functions. A morphism is an isomorphism if and only if it is bijective.[5] If $G = H$, we speak of an automorphism.

10.2.2 Groups

A group is a monoid G such that for each $a \in G$, there is $a' \in G$ with $aa' = a'a = e_G$ (an inverse). For each $a \in G$, its inverse is unique. A subgroup is a subset H such that it contains the neutral element, it is closed under the composition, and it is closed under taking inverses. The restricted composition makes H a group. Equivalently, a subgroup H is a submonoid that is closed under taking inverses.

An abelian group is a group whose composition is commutative (i.e., as a monoid, it is commutative). If G is abelian, it is common to use additive notation (i.e., $+$) for its composition. The neutral element is then denoted as 0_G (or simply as 0) and the inverse of $a \in G$ as $-a$. In particular, for all $a, b \in G$, it holds that $a + b = b + a$ and

---

[5] That is, both *injective* (each element in the range has *at most* one preimage) and *surjective* (each element in the range has *at least* one preimage).

$a - a := a + (-a) = 0$. If G is a nonabelian group, it is common to use multiplicative notation (i.e., $\cdot$) for its composition. The neutral element is then denoted as 1_G (or simply as 1) and the inverse of $a \in G$ as a^{-1} (or $1/a$). If it is not specified whether G is abelian or not, the notation pertaining to the nonabelian case is used. The order of a group G is the cardinality $|G|$. A group is finite if its order is finite. Otherwise, a group is infinite. A group is trivial if its order equals 1; that is, it consists of the neutral element only.

If G is a group and $x \in G$, then $\mathrm{ord}(x)$ is the smallest positive integer m such that $x^m = 1$ (if it exists). If such m does not exist, then $\mathrm{ord}(x) = \infty$. The subgroup of G consisting of all elements of finite order is the torsion subgroup. If G is finite, then for all $x \in G$ it holds that $\mathrm{ord}(x)$ is finite and divides $|G|$. Moreover, if $p > 0$ is a prime number such that p divides $|G|$, then there is $x \in G$ with $\mathrm{ord}(x) = p$. A group G is cyclic if there is $x \in G$ such that for each $y \in G$ it holds that $x^d = y$ for some integer d. In this case, such element x is a generator (of G).

A morphism of groups is just a morphism of the corresponding monoids. However, it is no longer necessary to require $\phi(1_G) = 1_H$ of a group morphism $\phi : G \longrightarrow H$ because this is implied here. Indeed, since $\phi(1_G) = \phi(1_G 1_G) = \phi(1_G)\phi(1_G)$, left multiplication by $\phi(1_G)^{-1} \in H$ on the l.h.s. as well as on the r.h.s. shows the desired implication.

For example, the integers $\mathbb{Z}$ under addition constitute an infinite abelian group. Also, "the integers modulo n" ($n > 0$ an integer), denoted $\mathbb{Z}/n\mathbb{Z}$, constitute a finite group (of order n) under addition.[6] The set $\{-1, 1\} \subset \mathbb{Z}$ under multiplication is a finite abelian group. Note that these examples are cyclic as well. Write $(\mathbb{Z}/n\mathbb{Z})^*$ for the subset of $\mathbb{Z}/n\mathbb{Z}$ ($n > 1$) consisting of those (nonzero) classes $\bar{x}$ with x coprime to n. Then $(\mathbb{Z}/n\mathbb{Z})^*$ is an abelian group under multiplication. In fact, it is not hard to show that if $p > 0$ is a prime number, then $(\mathbb{Z}/p\mathbb{Z})^*$ is a cyclic group of order $p - 1$. If G is a monoid, then the set consisting of its automorphisms together with functional composition constitutes a group, the *automorphism group* of G, and its neutral element is the identity morphism.[7] For example, the automorphism group of the additive group $\mathbb{Z}/p\mathbb{Z}$ ($p > 0$ prime) is a cyclic group of order $p - 1$.[8] The automorphism group of the additive group $\mathbb{Z}$ is cyclic of order 2 because it only consists of the identity and the automorphism sending $x \in \mathbb{Z}$ to $-x \in \mathbb{Z}$, for all $x \in \mathbb{Z}$.[9]

10.2.3 Rings

A ring is a set R with a law of addition $+ : R \times R \longrightarrow R$ and a law of multiplication $\cdot : R \times R \longrightarrow R$ such that the following hold:

---

[6] If $n = 0$, this would give $\mathbb{Z}$ itself, and if $n = 1$, this gives the trivial group.

[7] In case of a cyclic group G, the automorphisms are easy to describe. Fix a generator $x \in G$. Since an endomorphisms on G is determined by the image of x, the automorphisms are in one-to-one correspondence with the generators of G.

[8] Namely, each nonzero element in $\mathbb{Z}/p\mathbb{Z}$ is a generator, including 1, of course. Hence, each automorphism of the additive group $\mathbb{Z}/p\mathbb{Z}$ corresponds to multiplication by a nonzero constant in $\mathbb{Z}/p\mathbb{Z}$. This leads to the conclusion that the automorphism group is essentially $(\mathbb{Z}/p\mathbb{Z})^*$.

[9] Indeed, since 1 is a generator, it holds that $\sigma(\mathbb{Z}) = \sigma(1) \cdot \mathbb{Z}$. Therefore, such σ is not surjective (and, hence, not an automorphism) if $\sigma(1) \neq -1, 1$.

1. $(R, +)$ is an abelian group.
2. $(R, \cdot)$ is a monoid; that is, multiplication is associative, and there is a neutral element.[10]
3. $a(b + c) = ab + ac$ and $(a + b)c = ac + bc$ for all $a, b, c \in R$ (distributivity).

The neutral element for multiplication is denoted 1_R (or simply 1). Note that multiplication is not necessarily commutative. Moreover, it is not required that $0 \neq 1$. However, it holds that $0 = 1$ if and only if R is the trivial ring; that is, R consists of a single element 0 ($= 1$) only.[11]

Let R be a ring. The ring R is commutative if $ab = ba$ for all $a, b \in R$ (i.e., the multiplicative monoid is commutative). A subring is a subset $R' \subset R$ that is closed under addition and closed under multiplication such that the restricted compositions give an additive subgroup and a multiplicative submonoid, respectively. Under the restricted operations, a subring is a ring. Note that, by definition, $1 \in R'$ because R' is, in particular, a multiplicative submonoid of R. If R' is a subring of R, we also say equivalently that R is an extension ring of R'. An element $u \in R$ is a unit if there is $u' \in R$ such that $uu' = u'u = 1$. The units in a ring form a group under multiplication.

A morphism of rings is a function that is both a morphism of the corresponding addition monoid and a morphism of the corresponding multiplication monoid. Equivalently, $\phi : R \longrightarrow R'$ is a ring morphism if it holds that $\phi(a + b) = \phi(a) + \phi(b)$ and $\phi(ab) = \phi(a)\phi(b)$ for all $a, b \in R$, and if $\phi(1_R) = 1_{R'}$. As noted earlier, it is not necessary to require $\phi(0_R) = 0_{R'}$ separately.

For example, there is a unique ring morphism ϕ from $\mathbb{Z}$ to R. Let $a \in \mathbb{Z}$. If $a \geq 0$, define $\phi(a) = 1_R + \cdots + 1_R$ (a times). By convention, the empty sum yields 0_R and thus $\phi(0) = 0_R$. If $a < 0$, define $\phi(a) = (-1_R) + \cdots + (-1_R)$ ($-a$ times). This is a ring morphism. By definition, any ring morphism from $\mathbb{Z}$ to R maps 0 to 0_R and 1 to 1_R, and this uniquely determines the morphism.

Throughout this chapter, let A be a commutative ring.

An ideal of A is a subgroup I under addition that is closed under multiplication by scalars from A, that is, if $a \in A$ and $x \in I$, then $ax \in I$. Note that A is an ideal of A, as is the null ideal consisting of 0 only. These are special cases of principal ideals. An ideal I of A is principal if there is $x \in A$ such that $I = xA := \{xa \mid a \in A\}$; that is, it consists of all A multiples of x. We also sometimes use the notation (x) instead of xA. In particular, $A = (1)$, and the null ideal corresponds to (0). As another example, the ideal (2) of $\mathbb{Z}$ consists of all even integers.

Let I, J be ideals of A. Their sum is defined as

$$I + J = \{x + y \mid x \in I, y \in J\} \subset A$$

which is an ideal of A. Their product is defined as

$$IJ = \{x_1 y_1 + \cdots + x_m y_m \mid m \geq 1, x_1, \ldots, x_m \in I, y_1, \ldots, y_m \in J\} \subset A$$

which is also an ideal of A. Equivalently, IJ is the ideal generated by the products xy with $x \in I$ and $y \in J$. These definitions extend trivially for ≥ 2 ideals.

---

[10] As to multiplication in R, it is often more convenient to write ab instead of $a \cdot b$.

[11] In the forward direction: if $0 = 1$, then $0 = 0a = 1a = a$ for all $a \in R$. The statement in the other direction is trivial.

The ideal I is a prime ideal if $I \neq A$ and if for all $x, y \in A$ it holds that $xy \in I$ implies $x \in I$ or $y \in I$. The ideal I is a maximal ideal if $I \neq A$ and if there is no ideal J of A with $I \subsetneq J \subsetneq A$. If I is a maximal ideal, then I is also a prime ideal. By an application of Zorn's Lemma, each nontrivial ring contains a maximal ideal. In fact, the stronger result holds that each proper ideal in a nontrivial ring is contained in some maximal ideal.

A zero divisor is an element $z \in A$ with $z \neq 0$ such that $zz' = 0$ for some $z' \in A$ with $z' \neq 0$. The set consisting of all $z \in A$ such that $z = 0$ or z is a zero divisor in A is denoted $Z(A)$. It is convenient to state the following trivial lemma for later use:

LEMMA 10.1 *The complement $A \setminus Z(A)$ is multiplicatively closed.*

Proof Let $a, a' \in A \setminus Z(A)$. Suppose that $b \in A$ is such that $(aa')b = 0$. Since $(aa')b = a(a'b) = 0$, it follows that $a'b = 0$. This implies that $b = 0$. Hence, $aa' \in A \setminus Z(A)$. ∎

An element $x \in A$ is a nilpotent if there exists a positive integer m such that $x^m = 0$. The nilpotent elements form an ideal, the nilradical. The nilradical is the intersection of all prime ideals of A.[12]

The ring A is a domain if $0 \neq 1$ and if it has no zero divisors or, equivalently, if the ideal (0) is a prime ideal. If A is a domain, $x, y \in A$, and $xy \neq 0$, then y divides x, denoted $y|x$, if there is $z \in A$ such that $yz = x$. Furthermore, if A is a domain, then $x \in A$ ($x \neq 0$) is irreducible if it is not a unit and for all $y, z \in A$ it holds that if $x = yz$, then y is a unit or z is a unit. The ring A is factorial if it is a domain and it has "unique factorization." This means that if $x \in A$ is nonzero, then there exist irreducible elements $\pi_1, \ldots, \pi_\ell \in A$ and a unit $u \in A$ such that

$$x = u\pi_1 \cdots \pi_\ell$$

This factorization is unique in the following sense: if $x = u'\pi_1' \cdots \pi_{\ell'}'$ is another such factorization, then $\ell = \ell'$, and there are units $u_1, \ldots, u_\ell \in A$ such that, after applying a permutation on the indices if necessary, it holds that $\pi_i' = u_i \pi_i$, for $i = 1, \ldots, \ell$. If A is factorial, then an irreducible element is called a prime.

The ring A is a principal ideal domain (PID) if it is a domain and if each of its ideals is principal. Each PID is factorial. An example of a PID is the ring of integers $\mathbb{Z}$. All nonzero prime ideals in a PID are maximal, and a nonzero ideal $J = (x)$ with $x \in A$ is a prime ideal if and only if $x \in A$ is a prime element. For example, if $A = \mathbb{Z}$, then the nonzero prime ideals (= maximal ideals) are the ones of the form (p), where p is prime.

By $A[X]$ we denote the commutative ring of polynomials with coefficients in A. The usual definition of the degree of a polynomial applies, but recall that the degree of the zero polynomial $f = 0$ is $-\infty$ by definition. Note that A is naturally included in $A[X]$. Namely, A corresponds to the *constants* in $A[X]$, that is, the polynomials of degree ≤ 0. For any integer $m \geq 1$, by extension, $A[X_1, \ldots, X_m]$ denotes the commutative ring of m-variate polynomials with coefficients in A.

Finally, A is Noetherian if each of its ideals is finitely generated. In other words, if I is an ideal of A, then there exist some $c_1, \ldots, c_k \in I$ such that each element of I can be expressed as an A-linear combination of $c_1, \ldots, c_k$.

---

[12] See, for example, Lang [126], Chapter X, paragraph 2, page 417.

10.2.4 Fields

Let A be a commutative ring. If $0 \neq 1$ and each of its nonzero elements is a unit, then A is a field. Note that a field has no zero divisors. The only ideals of a field are (0) (a maximal ideal) and (1), that is, the whole field. A subfield is a subring that is a field. A finite field is one with finite cardinality (i.e., the set has finite cardinality). Recall that for each positive integer q of the form $q = p^m$, where $p \geq 2$ is a prime number and $m \geq 1$ is an integer, there exists a finite field of cardinality q. Any two given finite fields of the same cardinality are isomorphic.[13] For all other finite cardinalities q, there is no finite field with that cardinality.[14] We typically denote a finite field with cardinality q by $\mathbb{F}_q$.

Suppose that K is a field, and consider the intersection of all its subfields, which is a field as well. If this is the field of rational numbers $\mathbb{Q}$, we say that the characteristic of K is 0. If it is a finite field $\mathbb{F}_p$ for some prime number $p > 0$, we say that the characteristic of K is p. This covers all the possibilities. Indeed, if $n \cdot 1 = 0$ for some integer $n \geq 2$, then the smallest such integer must be a prime number p; otherwise, there would be zero divisors. Hence, $\mathbb{F}_p$ is the "smallest" subfield in this case. Otherwise, if there is no such integer n, then the field contains $\mathbb{Z}$, and hence, $\mathbb{Q}$ is the "smallest" subfield.

In the other direction, if K, L are subfields of some given field Ω, then KL denotes their compositum, that is, the intersection of all subfields of Ω having both K and L as a subfield.[15]

It should be noted that a field K is a PID[16] because its only ideals are (0) and (1). Moreover, $K[X]$ is a PID. The primes of $K[X]$ are the irreducible polynomials, that is, the polynomials $P(X) \in K[X]$ of degree ≥ 1 such that for all $f(X), g(X) \in K[X]$ with $P(X) = f(X)g(X)$ it holds that $f(X)$ is constant or $g(X)$ is constant.

10.2.5 The Field of Fractions and Localization

If A is a domain, then $Q(A)$ denotes the field of fractions of A, that is, "the smallest field that contains A." This is formalized as follows: consider the set U consisting of all pairs $(a, b) \in A \times A$ with $b \neq 0$. For all $(a, b), (c, d) \in U$, declare

$$(a, b) \sim (c, d) \quad \text{if} \quad ad = bc$$

This is an equivalence relation on U in the usual sense. The field of fractions $Q(A)$ is defined as $U/\sim$ (that is, U taken modulo this equivalence). The class of $(a, b) \in U$ is denoted a/b. Addition and multiplication are defined by $a/b + c/d = (ad + bc)/bd$ and $a/b \cdot c/d = ac/bd$, respectively. We write $1 := 1/1$ and $0 := 0/1$. These definitions do not depend on the choice of representatives.

---

[13] However, the choice of an isomorphism between them is *not unique* (except in the case of a prime field).

[14] A finite field of characteristic p (defined later; see also Section 10.4) is, trivially, a finite-dimensional $\mathbb{F}_p$ vector space. Hence, its cardinality is a prime power.

[15] From a more constructive perspective, the compositum consists of all elements $x \cdot y^{-1}$ where both x and y are finite sums of terms of the form ab with $a \in K$ and $b \in L$ and where $y \neq 0$.

[16] But the implied unique factorization does not mean much in the case of a field because all its nonzero elements are units.

If P is a prime ideal of the domain A, the localization of A at P is the subring A_P of $Q(A)$ consisting of all elements in $Q(A)$ representable as a/b with $b \notin P$.[17] This is well defined because the complement $A \setminus P$ is multiplicatively closed (owing to the fact that P is prime). This is an example of a local ring, a commutative ring with a unique maximal ideal, namely, the ideal consisting of all $a/b \in Q(A)$ with $a \in P$ and $b \notin P$. Note that each nonzero element not contained in the maximal ideal is a unit; that is, the units in A_P are those elements $a/b \in Q(A)$ such that $a, b \notin P$.

For example, let $p \in \mathbb{Z}$ be a prime number. Then $\mathbb{Z}_{(p)}$ is the subring of $\mathbb{Q}$ consisting of those $a/b \in \mathbb{Q}$ such that p does not divide b. Its unique maximal ideal consists of all elements of the form $a/b \in Q(A)$ such that p divides a and p does not divide b. The units in $\mathbb{Z}_{(p)}$ are those elements $a/b \in \mathbb{Q}$ such that p divides neither b nor a. Note that, moreover, $\mathbb{Z}_{(p)}$ is a PID: if I is a nonzero ideal, then $I = (p^m)$ for some nonnegative integer m. As an aside, each nonzero element $z \in \mathbb{Q}$ can be uniquely expressed as $z = up^m$ with $m \in \mathbb{Z}$ and u a unit in $\mathbb{Z}_{(p)}$. Localization also can be defined when A is not a domain, but we will not need it and do not treat it here.

10.3 Modules and Vector Spaces

We now give the definition of modules and vector spaces.

10.3.1 Basic Definitions

We give a concise definition of a module that avoids a "long list" of axioms. It gives the user a good vantage point, especially in situations where showing the module property would otherwise come across as "complicated" as a result of the "gravitational pull" of such listings.

First, we define the endomorphism ring of an abelian group G. The set of endomorphisms $\mathrm{End}(G)$ has a natural ring structure as follows: its 0 element corresponds to the function that sends each element of G to 0_G, and its 1 element is the identity function on G. Let $\phi, \phi' \in \mathrm{End}(G)$. The endomorphism $\phi + \phi' \in \mathrm{End}(G)$ is defined by $(\phi + \phi')(a) := \phi(a) + \phi'(a)$ for all $a \in G$. The endomorphism $\phi \cdot \phi' \in \mathrm{End}(G)$ is defined by $(\phi \cdot \phi')(a) := \phi(\phi'(a))$ for each $a \in G$. Thus, multiplication is given by functional composition. Note that $-\phi \in \mathrm{End}(G)$, the additive inverse of ϕ, is given by the rule $(-\phi)(a) := \phi(-a) = -\phi(a)$ for each $a \in G$. It is easy to check that this indeed gives a ring structure on $\mathrm{End}(G)$.

An R-module M consists of an abelian group M, a ring R, and a ring morphism

$$\psi : R \longrightarrow \mathrm{End}(M)$$

In particular, the (left) multiplication rm of a group element $m \in M$ by a scalar $r \in R$ is defined as the application to m of the endomorphism corresponding to r. Formally, $rm := \psi_r(m)$, where $\psi_r := \psi(r) \in \mathrm{End}(M)$. A submodule is a subgroup M' under addition that is closed under (left) multiplication by scalars from R. Define

$$\psi' : R \longrightarrow \mathrm{End}(M')$$

---

[17] Since A is a domain, the ideal $P = (0)$ is prime. Thus, the localization at (0) is well defined, and it coincides with $Q(A)$.

such that for each $r \in R$ its image ψ'_r under this map equals the restriction of ψ_r to M'. This is indeed an element of $\text{End}(M')$; since M' is a submodule, it holds that $\psi_r(M') \subset M'$, for each $r \in R$. Under this restriction, M' is a module. A morphism $\phi : M \longrightarrow N$ of R-modules is a morphism of the additive groups such that $\phi(rm) = r\phi(m)$ for all $r \in R$, $m \in M$.

For example, let G be an abelian group. Then G is a $\mathbb{Z}$-module in a natural (and unique) way. As remarked earlier, for any given ring R, there is a unique ring morphism from $\mathbb{Z}$ to R. Now simply take $R = \text{End}(G)$; the element $\lambda \in \mathbb{Z}$ is sent to the multiplication-by-λ map on G.

As another example, if R' is a subring of a ring R, then R is an R'-module. Write R^+ for the additive group of R, and simply define the ring morphism $\phi : R' \longrightarrow \text{End}(R^+)$ by sending $r' \in R'$ to the multiplication-by-r' map, which is clearly an endomorphism of R^+. In particular, R is an R-module. Finally, an ideal I of a commutative ring A is nothing else than a submodule of the A-module A.

If A is a commutative ring and M is an A-module, then M is Noetherian if each of its submodules is generated by a finite number of elements. In other words, if N is a submodule, then there are some elements $c_1, \ldots, c_k \in N$ such that each element of N can be written as an A-linear combination of $c_1, \ldots, c_k$. Thus, A is Noetherian as a ring if and only if A is Noetherian as an A-module.

If K is a field and V is a K-module, we speak of a K-vector space V. Also, in the case of K-vector spaces, we speak of K-vector space morphisms (a.k.a. linear maps).

We will also use the notion of the dual of a vector space. Let K be a field, and let V be a finite-dimensional K-vector space. Then V^* is the K-vector space consisting of all K-vector space morphisms $\phi : V \longrightarrow K$ (the space of *K-linear forms* on V). It is isomorphic to V. Without loss of generality, suppose that $V = K^n$ for some positive integer n. Let $\langle \cdot, \cdot \rangle$ denote the *standard inner product* on K^n; that is,

$$\langle \mathbf{x}, \mathbf{y} \rangle = x_1 y_1 + \cdots + x_n y_n$$

for all $\mathbf{x} = (x_i), \mathbf{y} = (y_i) \in K^n$.[18] Then an isomorphism between V and V^* is given by the map

$$\phi : V \longrightarrow V^*$$

$$\mathbf{a} \mapsto \langle \cdot, \mathbf{a} \rangle$$

that is, the vector $\mathbf{a} \in V$ is mapped to the K-linear form that consists of taking the inner product with $\mathbf{a}$.

Let V, W, Z be A-modules. An *A-bilinear map* $\phi : V \times W \longrightarrow Z$ is a map such that it is A-linear in each of its two arguments.[19] This means that fixing any $v \in V$ (or any $w \in W$), the map $\phi(v, \cdot) : W \longrightarrow Z$ (or the map $\phi(\cdot, w) : V \longrightarrow Z$) is a morphism of A-modules.

If K is a field and V is a finite-dimensional K-vector space, then a *bilinear form* on V is a bilinear map $\psi : V \times V \longrightarrow K$. It is *nondegenerate* if the map

$$V \longrightarrow V^*$$

$$v \mapsto \psi(\cdot, v)$$

---

[18] Note that if K has positive characteristic, then, unlike in the case of (say) $K = \mathbb{Q}$, it may hold that $\langle \mathbf{x}, \mathbf{x} \rangle = 0$ for some $\mathbf{x} \neq \mathbf{0}$ (*self-orthogonality*).

[19] This extends naturally to the notion of n-multilinear maps.

is an isomorphism.[20] Otherwise, it is degenerate. Since the dimensions on the left and right are the same (and finite), nondegeneracy is equivalent to injectivity; that is, no nonzero $v \in V$ is mapped to the 0 form. For example, the standard inner product on K^n is a nondegenerate bilinear form on K^n.

10.3.2 Free Modules and Bases

Let R be a ring, and let M be an R-module. Suppose that $S \subset M$ is a subset. Then S is a basis if

1. S generates M over R; that is, each element of M can be written as an R-linear combination of a finite number of elements of S.
2. S is R-linearly independent; that is, if some R-linear combination of finitely many distinct elements of S yields 0, then each of the R coefficients equals 0.

We allow $S = \emptyset$ as "the basis of the trivial module." This simplifies certain statements where otherwise an exception for the trivial module is made. Note that if $S \neq \emptyset$ is a basis, then M is not the trivial module if R is not the trivial ring.

A free R-module M is one that admits a basis. Note that if M is free and a basis S is given, then each element of M is uniquely expressed as an R-linear combination of finitely many elements of S.[21] See also Remark 10.3.

10.3.3 Free Modules over PIDs

Suppose that A is a nontrivial commutative ring. Then the cardinality of any two bases of a free A-module M is the same. As an aside, this is easy to reduce to the case of vector spaces, for which this is a well-known fact. We argue this later. For quotients, please refer to Section 10.4. Choose some maximal ideal P of A. Let PM denote the submodule of M generated by the terms of the form rm with $r \in P$ and $m \in M$. Observe that M/PM is an A/P-vector space and that a basis of the A-module M, after reduction modulo PM, is a basis of the A/P-vector space M/PM.[22] The claim follows.

The rank of M is the cardinality of any basis. If the rank is infinite, then a basis involves infinitely many elements. Yet each element of M is expressed as an A-linear combination of finitely many of them. If $A = K$ for some field K, we speak of the dimension of the K-vector space M. It is denoted by $\dim_K M$.

If A is a PID, more is true. If M' is a submodule of a free A-module M, then it is free as well, and its rank is at most that of M. If $A = K$ for some field K, $M' \subsetneq M$ is a subspace, and the dimension of M is finite, then the dimension of M' is strictly smaller than that of M. If A is a PID that is not a field, the rank of M' may equal that of M, yet $M' \subsetneq M$. For example, $\mathbb{Z}^n$ has rank n as a free $\mathbb{Z}$ module and $2 \cdot \mathbb{Z}^n$ is a free submodule of rank n as well, yet $2 \cdot \mathbb{Z}^n \subsetneq \mathbb{Z}^n$. Notable examples of PIDs include $A = \mathbb{Z}, K[X], K$ (K a field).

---

[20] One may equivalently define the map as $v \mapsto \psi(v, \cdot)$, as follows from linear algebra.

[21] That is, each element of M admits exactly one such expression in a given basis, and all expressions occur. Trivially, distinct elements of M have distinct expressions.

[22] Suppose that $m_1, \ldots, m_\ell \in M$ constitute an A basis of M. Since PM consists of P-linear combinations of finitely many elements in M, it holds that PM is the P span of $m_1, \ldots, m_\ell$. Therefore, $a_1 m_1 + \cdots + a_\ell m_\ell \in PM$ with the a_is in A if and only if the a_is are in P.

As an example of a vector space, if n is a positive integer, then K^n is a K-vector space of dimension n, with the usual vector addition and scalar multiplication. As another example, if a ring R contains a field K as a subring, then R is a K-vector space. If L is a field that contains K as a subfield, then we say that L is an extension field of K. The degree of the extension, denoted $[L : K]$, is the dimension of L as a K-vector space.

The main result on free modules of finite rank over PIDs is as follows[23]:

THEOREM 10.2 (STRUCTURE THEOREM FOR FREE MODULES OVER A PID) *Let A be a PID. Let M be a free A-module of finite rank $n \geq 1$, and let M' be a submodule. Then M' is a free A-submodule, and it has rank ℓ with $0 \leq \ell \leq n$. Moreover, if M' is nontrivial, then there is an A-basis $e_1, \ldots, e_n$ of M, and there are nonzero elements $a_1, \ldots, a_\ell \in A$ such that*

- $a_1 e_1, \ldots, a_\ell e_\ell$ *is an A-basis of M'.*
- $a_i \mid a_{i+1}$ $(i = 1, \ldots, \ell - 1)$, *for $i = 1, \ldots, \ell - 1$.*

The ideals $(a_1), \ldots, (a_\ell)$ of A are uniquely determined by M and M'.

10.4 Quotients

Suppose that $\phi : X \longrightarrow Y$ is a morphism of groups. The image of ϕ, denoted imϕ, is the set $\phi(X) \subset Y$. The kernel of ϕ, denoted kerϕ, is the set $\phi^{-1}(e_Y) \subset X$, that is, the set of elements in X sent to e_Y by ϕ, where e_Y is the neutral element of Y. A morphism $\phi : X \longrightarrow Y$ is an isomorphism if there is a morphism $\phi' : Y \longrightarrow X$ such that $\phi' \circ \phi$ is the identity morphism on X and $\phi \circ \phi'$ is the identity morphism on Y. A morphism is an isomorphism if and only if it is bijective. The notation $X \simeq Y$ means that X and Y are isomorphic; that is, there is an isomorphism $X \longrightarrow Y$. These definitions carry over naturally to the cases of rings, modules, and vector spaces.[24]

We now define quotient groups and quotient rings. Let G be an abelian group and let H be a subgroup. Then G/H denotes the quotient group consisting of the classes $\bar{a} := \{a + H\}$ with $a \in G$. This is an abelian group with addition defined by $\bar{a} + \bar{b} = \overline{a + b}$ for all $a, b \in G$. The definition of this operation does not depend on the choice of the class representatives a, b. The map from G to G/H that sends $g \in G$ to its class $\bar{g} \in G/H$ is the canonical morphism. This remark carries over naturally to the cases of commutative rings and modules later, and we shall not repeat it there.

We shall not need the notion of a quotient in the case of nonabelian groups or noncommutative rings.[25] If $\phi : G \longrightarrow G'$ is a group morphism, then kerϕ is a subgroup[26] of G and imϕ is a subgroup of G'. The assignment $a + \text{ker}\phi \mapsto \phi(a)$ defines a group isomorphism $G/\text{ker}\phi \longrightarrow \text{im}\phi$. In particular, if ϕ is surjective, then $G/\text{ker}\phi \simeq G'$ as groups.

---

[23] For a proof, see, for example, Lang [126], pages 153–4.

[24] Note that, in these cases, the kernel of a morphism is defined with respect to the neutral element 0_Y of the respective additive group.

[25] It suffices to recall that if G is a nonabelian group, then the construction of the quotient group G/H works in essentially the same way as in the abelian case under the additional requirement that the subgroup H in question is normal; that is, $gHg^{-1} \subset H$ for all $g \in G$. In the abelian case, normal subgroups and subgroups coincide.

[26] In fact, kerϕ is a normal subgroup of G whether G is abelian or not.

As before, let A be a commutative ring. Let I be an ideal of A. Considering A as an abelian group and I as a subgroup, the quotient A/I is formed, which is an abelian group by the preceding discussion. By virtue of the fact that I is an ideal, it holds that $\overline{a}\overline{b} = \overline{ab}$ for all $a, b \in A$ independent of the class representatives a, b. This turns A/I into a commutative ring, the quotient ring. It holds that A/I is a domain if and only if I is a prime ideal, whereas A/I is a field if and only if I is a maximal ideal.

For example, consider the ring of integers $\mathbb{Z}$. As remarked earlier, this is a PID. Each of its ideals is of the form $n\mathbb{Z}$ for some integer $n \geq 0$. Furthermore, the ring $\mathbb{Z}/n\mathbb{Z}$ is the "ring of integers modulo n," which has cardinality n if $n \neq 0$. The maximal ideals of $\mathbb{Z}$ are of the form $p\mathbb{Z}$, with $p > 0$ a prime number. Hence, $\mathbb{F}_p := \mathbb{Z}/p\mathbb{Z}$ is the field of cardinality p.[27] The polynomial ring $\mathbb{F}_p[X]$ is a PID. If $f(X) \in \mathbb{F}_p[X]$ is an irreducible polynomial of degree $d \geq 1$, then $\mathbb{F}_p[X]/(f(X))$ is a finite field with $q := p^d$ elements. Recall that every finite field may be constructed in this way. Note that, in particular, $\mathbb{F}_q$ is an extension field of $\mathbb{F}_p$ of degree d.

If $\phi : A \longrightarrow A'$ is a morphism of commutative rings, then $\ker \phi$ is an ideal of A and $\operatorname{im} \phi$ is a subring of A'. Moreover, the assignment $a + \ker \phi \mapsto \phi(a)$ defines a ring isomorphism $A/\ker \phi \longrightarrow \operatorname{im} \phi$. In particular, if ϕ is surjective, then $A/\ker \phi \simeq A'$ as rings.

For example, we can now give a more satisfactory definition of the *characteristic of a field* (see Section 10.2.4). Recall that for each ring R, there is a (unique) morphism of the ring of integers $\mathbb{Z}$ to the ring R. Namely, a morphism sends 0 to 0_R and 1 to 1_R, and this uniquely determines its action on all of $\mathbb{Z}$. Suppose that this ring R is in fact a field. If this morphism is injective, its image may be identified with $\mathbb{Z}$ itself (characteristic 0). If its kernel is nontrivial, it must be a nonzero prime (= maximal) ideal in $\mathbb{Z}$; otherwise, its image contains zero divisors, which is nonsense. Hence, its image is isomorphic to the finite field $\mathbb{Z}/p\mathbb{Z}$ for some prime number $p > 0$ (characteristic p). Note that there is a unique injective field morphism of $\mathbb{Z}/p\mathbb{Z}$ into a field R of characteristic p.[28]

Let R be a ring, let M be an R-module, and let $N \subset M$ be a submodule. Considering M as an abelian group and N as a subgroup, the quotient M/N is formed, which is an abelian group. By definition, $RN \subset N$. Hence, the ring morphism $\psi : R \longrightarrow \operatorname{End}(M/N)$, where $\psi_r(\overline{m}) = \overline{rm}$ for all $r \in R, m \in M$, is well defined and does not depend on the choice of class representative. In conclusion, M/N is an R-module as well. Vector spaces do not require a separate treatment because they form a subclass. If $\phi : M \longrightarrow M'$ is a module morphism, then $\ker \phi$ is a submodule of M and $\operatorname{im} \phi$ is a submodule of M'. Moreover, the map $a + \ker \phi \mapsto \phi(a)$ defines an R-module isomorphism $M/\ker \phi \longrightarrow \operatorname{im} \phi$. In particular, if ϕ is surjective, then $M/\ker \phi \simeq M'$ as R-modules.

10.5 Direct Products and Direct Sums

10.5.1 Direct Products

We now very briefly discuss direct products. Let $\mathcal{I}$ be a nonempty index set, and for each $i \in \mathcal{I}$, let X_i be a group. Then there is a natural group structure on the Cartesian product

---

[27] In the cryptographic literature, the notation $\mathbb{Z}_p$ is sometimes used instead of $\mathbb{Z}/p\mathbb{Z}$. We adhere to the latter because the notation $\mathbb{Z}_p$ is more commonly used in the mathematical literature to designate the ring of p-adic integers.

[28] Namely, this morphism is determined by the images of $\overline{0}$ and $\overline{1}$, which are sent to 0_R and 1_R, respectively.

$\prod_{i \in \mathcal{I}} X_i$ given by component-wise compositions. For example, in such a product $X \times Y$, the X composition is taken in the X part and the Y composition is taken in the Y part. Concretely, for all $(x,y), (x',y') \in X \times Y$, define the composition

$$(x,y) \cdot (x',y') := (xx', yy') \in X \times Y$$

where the product xx' (and yy') is taken in X (and Y).

This basic idea extends naturally to the case of rings (modules/vector spaces). For example, suppose that A, A' are rings. Then $A \times A'$ is a ring with A addition (and A multiplication) in the A part and, independently, A' addition (and A' multiplication) in the A' part. Note that if X, Y are fields, then their direct product is *not* a field: each nonzero element with 0 in some part lacks a multiplicative inverse. That said, their product *is* a commutative ring. These remarks are also valid if the index set is infinite.

10.5.2 *Direct Sums*

A direct sum is a constrained direct product as follows: a direct sum of abelian groups G_i is their direct product under the condition that for each element of the product, almost all entries are zero; that is, at most, a finite number of entries are nonzero. A direct sum is denoted $\bigoplus G_i$ instead of $\prod G_i$. In the case of a finite number of factors, a direct sum is the same as a direct product. If $n \geq 1$ is an integer and G is a group, then G^n denotes the group $\bigoplus_{i=1}^{n} G$ (or equivalently, $\prod_{i=1}^{n} G$). This definition extends to rings and modules as well.

For example, if S is a set, then the free abelian group generated by S is the direct sum $\bigoplus_{i \in S} \mathbb{Z}$. If $S = \emptyset$, this is the null module.

REMARK 10.3 As another example of the use of direct sums, let R be a ring, and let M be a (nontrivial) R-module. Then M is free of *finite* rank $n \geq 1$ if and only if there are $e_1, \ldots, e_n \in M$ such that the map

$$R^n \longrightarrow M$$

$$(\lambda_1, \ldots, \lambda_n) \mapsto \lambda_1 e_1 + \cdots + \lambda_n e_n$$

is an isomorphism of R-modules; that is, $e_1, \ldots, e_n$ constitute a basis. This is easily generalized to the *infinite* rank case using the fact that the direct sum definition requires almost all coefficients to be equal to zero.

An important example is the main result on finite abelian groups, which gives a direct sum decomposition.

THEOREM 10.4 (STRUCTURE THEOREM FOR FINITE ABELIAN GROUPS) *Let G be a finite abelian group. Then there are (unique) integers $\ell \geq 1$ and $a_1, \ldots, a_\ell \geq 2$ such that $a_1 \mid \cdots \mid a_\ell$ and*

$$G \simeq \bigoplus_{i=1}^{\ell} \mathbb{Z}/a_i\mathbb{Z}$$

In particular, a finite abelian group is a direct sum of cyclic groups.

This can be verified as follows: suppose that $g_1, \ldots, g_n$ generate G. Consider the surjective morphism

$$\phi : \mathbb{Z}^n \longrightarrow G$$

$$(\lambda_1, \ldots, \lambda_n) \mapsto \lambda_1 g_1 + \cdots + \lambda_n g_n$$

of $\mathbb{Z}$ modules. Then its kernel is a free submodule of $\mathbb{Z}^n$. Now apply Theorem 10.2 to $\ker \phi$ and note that $G \simeq \mathbb{Z}^n / \ker \phi$. Since G is finite, this kernel has rank n. The theorem follows.[29]

10.5.3 The Chinese Remainder Theorem for Commutative Rings

Let A be a commutative ring. Let I, J be ideals of A. Then I, J are coprime if

$$I + J = A .$$

THEOREM 10.5 (CHINESE REMAINDER THEOREM (CRT)) *Suppose that $I_1, \ldots, I_m \subset A$ are pairwise coprime ideals ($m > 1$); that is, $I_i + I_j = A$ if $i \neq j$. Then the map*

$$\psi : A/(I_1 \cdots I_m) \longrightarrow A/I_1 \times \ldots \times A/I_m$$

$$a \bmod I_1 \cdots I_m \mapsto (a \bmod I_1, \ldots, a \bmod I_m)$$

is an isomorphism of rings.

It is convenient to state the following trivial lemma for later use:

LEMMA 10.6 *If I, J are coprime ideals of A, then I^r, J^s are coprime ideals of A as well for each pair of integers $r, s \geq 1$.*

This is easy to verify. Namely, suppose that $a + b = 1$, with $a \in I$ and $b \in J$. Then work out $(a + b)^k = 1$ for some large enough positive integer k.

As an application of the CRT, if $n > 1$ is an integer and $n = p_1^{e_1} \cdots p_k^{e_k}$ is its factorization into positive powers of distinct positive prime numbers, we get the result that

$$\mathbb{Z}/n\mathbb{Z} \simeq \bigoplus_{\ell=1}^{k} \mathbb{Z}/p_\ell^{e_\ell}\mathbb{Z}$$

as rings.

10.6 Basic Field Theory

Let K be a field, and let L be an extension field. For a set $S \subset L$, the field generated by K and S, that is, the intersection of all subfields K' of L such that K is a subfield of K' and $S \subset K'$, is denoted by $K(S)$. The extension L is *finitely generated over K* if $L = K(S)$ for some finite set $S \subset L$. The extension L is simple (over K) if, additionally, $|S| = 1$. If $S = \{x_1, \ldots, x_m\}$, then we may write $K(x_1, \ldots, x_m)$ for $K(S)$.

10.6.1 Algebraic Extensions and Transcendental Extensions

Let $x \in L$, and consider the *evaluation map*

$$\phi : K[X] \longrightarrow K(x)$$

$$g(X) \mapsto g(x)$$

---

[29] For structure theorems on general finite groups (*Sylow Theorems*), please consult, for example, Rotman [163].

Note that ϕ is a ring morphism mapping the polynomial ring $K[X]$ to the field $K(x)$. Since ϕ fixes K pointwise, it is, in particular, a morphism of K-vector spaces. Since $K[X]$ is a PID, the kernel is a principal ideal (that is, generated by a single polynomial). The kernel of a ring morphism from a commutative ring to a field must be a prime ideal.[30] Here this means that the kernel is either trivial or generated by some irreducible polynomial $f(X) \in K[X]$.

In the latter case (that is, the kernel is nontrivial), without loss of generality, take $f(X)$ monic.[31] This polynomial $f(X)$ is the minimal polynomial of x over K. Or, equivalently, $f(X) \in K[X]$ is the monic polynomial of least degree such that x is a *root* of $f(X)$; that is, $f(x) = 0$.

If the kernel is nontrivial, then the image of ϕ is a field. Indeed, the image is isomorphic to $K[X]/(f(X))$, and this is a field because any nonzero prime ideal is maximal in $K[X]$. Furthermore, since the image contains both K and x, it must be equal to $K(x)$ by minimality. In other words, there is a K-isomorphism[32] of fields

$$\overline{\phi} : K[X]/(f(X)) \xrightarrow{\sim} K(x)$$

$$\overline{g(X)} \mapsto g(x)$$

In particular,

$$[K(x) : K] = \deg(f) < \infty$$

and

$$1, x, \ldots, x^{\deg(f)-1}$$

is a K-basis of $K(x)$ as a K-vector space, a power basis.[33]

However, if the kernel is trivial, then ϕ is injective. Since $[K[X] : K] = \infty$, it follows that $[K(x) : K] = \infty$.

This leads to the following definitions: an element $x \in L$ is algebraic over K if $[K(x) : K] < \infty$. By the preceding discussion, an element $x \in L$ is algebraic over K if and only if the element $x \in L$ is a root of some nonzero polynomial in $K[X]$. Furthermore, if $x \in L$ is algebraic over K, then the monic polynomial of least degree with that property is its minimal polynomial. If $x \in L$ is not algebraic over K, the element $x \in L$ is transcendental over K. The extension L is algebraic over K if each $x \in L$ is algebraic over K. Otherwise, the extension L is transcendental over K. Note that L is algebraic over K if $[L : K] < \infty$.

If K' is an intermediate extension $K \subset K' \subset L$, then the tower relation holds that L is algebraic over K if and only if L is algebraic over K' and K' is algebraic over K. If $[L : K] < \infty$, then the relation

$$[L : K] = [L : K'] \cdot [K' : K]$$

holds.[34]

---

[30] Otherwise, the image (which is contained in a field) has zero divisors, which is nonsense.

[31] A polynomial $f(X) \in K[X]$ is monic if its leading coefficient is equal to 1. In particular, a monic polynomial is nonzero.

[32] A *K isomorphism* is an isomorphism fixing K pointwise.

[33] It is clear that $1, \overline{X}, \ldots, \overline{X}^{\deg(f)-1}$ generate $K[X]/(f(X))$ as a K-vector space. If the dimension were strictly smaller than $\deg(f)$, this would mean that $f(X)$ divides some nonzero polynomial of degree strictly smaller than $\deg(f)$, which is nonsense.

[34] Note that this relation also holds if $[L : K] = \infty$.

Elements $x_1, \ldots, x_m \in L$ are algebraically independent over K if they do not jointly satisfy some nontrivial polynomial relation over K. Precisely, consider the evaluation map

$$K[X_1, \ldots, X_m] \longrightarrow L$$

$$f \mapsto f(x_1, \ldots, x_m)$$

Then $x_1, \ldots, x_m \in L$ are algebraically independent over K if this map is injective. A subset of L that is maximal with respect to algebraic independence over K is a transcendence basis. This notion of basis bears similarities to the notion of basis from linear algebra: any two transcendence bases have the same cardinality, and any algebraically independent set can be completed to a basis. The cardinality of a basis is the transcendence degree of L over K. If L is algebraic over K, any transcendence basis is empty, and hence the transcendence degree is 0. The field of rational functions $K(X)$, that is, the field of fractions of the polynomial ring $K[X]$, has transcendence degree 1 over K. If S is a transcendence basis of L over K, then L is algebraic over $K(S)$ by maximality, where $K(S)$ denotes the subfield of L generated by K and S.

10.6.2 Algebraic Closure

A field K is algebraically closed if each polynomial in $K[X]$ of degree ≥ 1 has at least one root in K. Equivalently, each polynomial $f(X) \in K[X]$ factorizes as a product of $\deg(f)$ linear terms in $K[X]$.[35] An algebraic closure of K is an algebraic extension field of K that is algebraically closed.

An algebraic closure of K exists, and it is unique, *up to K-isomorphism*, that is, a field isomorphism that fixes K pointwise. In particular, the set of distinct roots in an algebraic closure $\overline{K}$ of a polynomial $f(X) \in K[X]$ with $n := \deg(f) \geq 1$ is also unique up to such a K-isomorphism, whereas their multiplicities are unique. In particular, there are exactly n roots with multiplicities in an algebraic closure.

For example, the field of complex numbers $\mathbb{C}$ is an algebraic closure of the field of real numbers $\mathbb{R}$. An algebraic closure $\overline{\mathbb{Q}}$ of the field of rational numbers $\mathbb{Q}$ may be taken as a proper subfield of $\mathbb{C}$. An algebraic closure $\overline{\mathbb{F}}_q$ of $\mathbb{F}_q$ is an infinite extension field of $\mathbb{F}_q$ that essentially consists of the "union" of all its finite extensions properly "glued together" using a direct limit in order to make this precise.

A relevant relaxation is the following notion: let $\overline{K}$ be an algebraic closure of K. Let $f(X) \in K[X]$, and let $\mathcal{Z} \subset \overline{K}$ denote the set of its distinct roots. Then the *splitting field* of $f(X)$ is the field $K(\mathcal{Z})$, which is a finite-degree extension of K.[36]

10.6.3 Separable Extensions and Normal Extensions

Suppose that L is algebraic over K. Let $\overline{L}$ be an algebraic closure of L.[37] A K-embedding of L into $\overline{L}$ is a field morphism $\sigma : L \longrightarrow \overline{L}$ that fixes K pointwise. Note that a morphism between

---

[35] Use successive application of the Euclidean algorithm (see Theorem 11.125) to split off one linear term after another.

[36] It is unique up to K-isomorphism.

[37] This is an algebraic closure of any intermediate extension $K \subset K' \subset L$ as well because L is algebraic over K.

fields is always injective.[38] Also note that if $\sigma(L) \subset L$, then $\sigma(L) = L$ so that σ is in fact a K-automorphism of L.[39]

Let $x \in L$, and write $n = [K(x) : K]$. Let $f(X) \in K[X]$ denote its minimal polynomial over K. Note that $\deg(f) = n$ and that $f(X)$ factors into linear terms over $\overline{L}[X]$ (because $\overline{L}$ is an algebraic closure of K). Let $\mathcal{Z} \subset \overline{L}$ denote the set of its distinct roots, the conjugates of x. Write $n' = |\mathcal{Z}|$, and note that $1 \leq n' \leq n$. Each K-embedding σ of $K(x)$ into $\overline{L}$ sends x to some conjugate $z \in \mathcal{Z}$.[40] Since such an assignment completely determines an embedding, there are at most n' such embeddings. However, for each $z \in \mathcal{Z}$, there is such an embedding σ with $\sigma(x) = z$. In conclusion, there are exactly n' such embeddings. The element x is separable over K if $n' = n$, or in other words, if $f(X)$ has no repeated roots in $\overline{L}$.

The extension L is separable over K if each $x \in L$ is separable over K. Suppose that $[L : K] < \infty$. Then L is separable over K if and only if the number of distinct K-embeddings of L into $\overline{L}$ is exactly $[L : K]$. For separability, the tower property holds that if K' is an intermediate extension $K \subset K' \subset L$, then L is separable over K if and only if L is separable over K' and K' is separable over K. If $[L : K] < \infty$ and L is separable over K, then L is a simple algebraic extension of K.[41]

The field K is perfect if K' is separable over K for all finite-degree intermediate extension fields $K \subset K' \subset \overline{K}$, where $\overline{K}$ is an algebraic closure of K. For example, finite fields are perfect, as well as any field of characteristic 0.

The field L is normal over K if for each $x \in L$ it holds that each of the roots of its minimal polynomial over K is contained in L. If $n := [L : K] < \infty$, this is equivalent to requiring that each of the $\leq n$ distinct K-embeddings σ of L into $\overline{L}$ is a K-automorphism of L. This is the case if and only if $\sigma(L) \subset L$ for each of these embeddings σ.

10.6.4 Galois Correspondence

We state the main result of Galois theory for Galois field extensions of finite degree. As before, let $\overline{L}$ be an algebraic closure of L.

The field L is a finite-degree Galois extension of K if

1. $[L : K] < \infty$ (so L is algebraic over K).
2. L is separable over K.
3. L is normal over K.

Equivalently, each of the $[L : K]$ distinct K-embeddings of L into $\overline{L}$ is a K-automorphism of L; that is,

$$|\text{Aut}(L/K)| = [L : K] < \infty$$

This group is then the Galois group of the extension.

---

[38] Indeed, its kernel is an ideal, and out of the only two possibilities for this ideal, that is, the zero ideal and the whole field, the latter can be discarded because 1 must be mapped to 1.

[39] Indeed, the map σ is in particular an endomorphism of L as a finite-dimensional K-vector space, so σ is surjective.

[40] Namely, $f(x) = 0$ implies that $f(\sigma(x)) = 0$ because σ fixes K.

[41] More generally, the Primitive Element Theorem states that an algebraic extension of finite degree is simple if and only if the number of intermediate extensions is finite.

The Galois correspondence provides a complete description of the intermediate fields $K \subset K' \subset L$ in terms of the Galois group.

THEOREM 10.7 *Let K be a field, and let L be a finite-degree extension field. Suppose that L is Galois over K, with Galois group G. Then there is an inclusion-reversing bijection between the set of intermediate fields $K \subset K' \subset L$ and the set of intermediate groups H with $\{1\} \subset H \subset G$ characterized as follows.*

- *In the forward direction, an intermediate field K' is mapped to the subgroup H of G that fixes K' pointwise.*
- *In the other direction, a subgroup H is mapped to the intermediate field K' that is fixed pointwise by H.*

Additionally, K' is Galois over K if and only if the subgroup H of G corresponding to K' is a normal subgroup of G. In this case, G/H is isomorphic to the Galois group of the extension $K \subset K'$ (and the map $\overline{\sigma} \mapsto \sigma_{|K'}$ gives an isomorphism between these groups).

For example, let q be a prime power, and let $n \geq 1$ be an integer. A finite field $\mathbb{F}_{q^n}$ can be realized as the splitting field of the polynomial $X^{q^n} - X \in \mathbb{F}_q[X]$, as we sketch later. By the structure of this polynomial, it is not hard to see that its q^n distinct roots[42] form a finite field of order q^n that is essentially unique owing to the properties of a splitting field. Besides, its nonzero elements form a multiplicative group of order $q^n - 1$. Furthermore, it is a Galois extension of the finite field $\mathbb{F}_q$ of degree n.[43] Its Galois group is cyclic and is generated by the Frobenius automorphism of $\mathbb{F}_{q^n}$ given by $x \mapsto x^q$.

Suppose that L is separable over K and $n := [L : K] < \infty$. Fix some algebraic closure $\overline{L}$ of L. Let $\sigma_1, \ldots, \sigma_n$ be the distinct K-embeddings of L into $\overline{L}$. The norm map $\mathrm{N}_{L/K}$ and trace map $\mathrm{Tr}_{L/K}$ are as follows: for each $x \in L$, define

$$\mathrm{N}_{L/K}(x) = \prod_{i=1}^{n} \sigma_i(x) \in K$$

and

$$\mathrm{Tr}_{L/K}(x) = \sum_{i=1}^{n} \sigma_i(x) \in K$$

By Galois theory, both the norm and trace of $x \in L$ are indeed elements of K. In particular, their values do not depend on the choice of an algebraic closure of L. We verify this later. Consider the normal closure L' of L in $\overline{L}$, that is, the compositum of the subfields $\sigma_1(L), \ldots, \sigma_n(L)$ of $\overline{L}$. This contains L as a subfield (because the identity is among those K-embeddings). Observe that L' is a finite-degree Galois extension of K.[44] Write G' for its Galois group. Select an arbitrary $\tau \in G'$. Then $\tau \circ \sigma_1, \ldots, \tau \circ \sigma_n$ is a permutation of $\sigma_1, \ldots, \sigma_n$

---

[42] The formal derivative of the polynomial $X^{q^n} - X$ equals -1; hence it is coprime with it.

[43] Since the extension is finite and separable, it is simple. Hence, $\mathbb{F}_q(x) = \mathbb{F}_{q^n}$ for some $x \in \mathbb{F}_{q^n}$. The minimal polynomial $f(X) \in \mathbb{F}_q[X]$ of x has degree n. Hence, a finite field $\mathbb{F}_{q^n}$ can be realized as $\mathbb{F}_q[X]/(f(X))$ for some irreducible polynomial $f(X) \in \mathbb{F}_q[X]$ of degree n.

[44] Finiteness of the extension degree and separability are straightforward. The fact that any K-embedding τ of L' into some algebraic closure is a K-automorphism of L' follows directly from the definition of L' in combination with the fact that $\tau \circ \sigma_1, \ldots, \tau \circ \sigma_n$ is a permutation of $\sigma_1, \ldots, \sigma_n$ (see also below).

because each of those gives a different K-embedding of L into $\overline{L}$. Therefore, for each $x \in L$, the norm and trace of x are fixed under each $\tau \in G'$. The desired claim follows because an element of L' is fixed under all of G' if and only if it is an element of K.

The norm map is multiplicative on L; that is, $\mathrm{N}_{L/K}(xy) = \mathrm{N}_{L/K}(x) \cdot \mathrm{N}_{L/K}(y)$ for all $x, y \in L$. Note that $\mathrm{N}_{L/K}(1) = 1$. The trace map is a *nonzero* K-linear form on L.[45]

We give some examples. Suppose that $x \in L$ satisfies $L = K(x)$. This makes sense because L/K is a separable finite-degree extension by assumption. Let $f(X) \in K[X]$ be the minimal polynomial of x. Then the constant term of $f(X)$ equals $(-1)^n \cdot \mathrm{N}_{L/K}(x)$, and the coefficient of X^{n-1} in $f(X)$ equals $-\mathrm{Tr}_{L/K}(x)$.

As another example, suppose that $K = \mathbb{F}_q$ and $L = \mathbb{F}_{q^k}$ for some positive integer k. Then

$$\mathrm{Tr}_{L/K}(y) = \sum_{i=0}^{k-1} y^{q^i}$$

for all $y \in \mathbb{F}_{q^k}$ because the Galois group of $\mathbb{F}_{q^k}$ over $\mathbb{F}_q$ is generated by the Frobenius automorphism.

10.7 Algebraic Number Fields

10.7.1 Basic Definitions

An algebraic number field is an extension field K of the rational numbers $\mathbb{Q}$ such that $[K : \mathbb{Q}] < \infty$. Note that K is a simple algebraic extension of $\mathbb{Q}$. An element $y \in K$ is integral over the rational integers $\mathbb{Z}$ if its minimal polynomial $f(X) \in \mathbb{Q}[X]$ satisfies $f(X) \in \mathbb{Z}[X]$; that is, each coefficient of this monic polynomial is an integer.

The subset $\mathcal{O}_K \subset K$ consisting of all $y \in K$ that are integral over $\mathbb{Z}$ is a subring of K, the ring of integers of K. The field of fractions of $\mathcal{O}_K$ equals K.[46] If $\overline{\mathbb{Q}}$ is an algebraic closure of the rational numbers, then the set of elements $y \in \overline{\mathbb{Q}}$ such that y is integral over $\mathbb{Z}$, the integral closure of $\mathbb{Z}$ in $\overline{\mathbb{Q}}$, is a subring of $\overline{\mathbb{Q}}$. Trivially, if y is integral over $\mathbb{Q}$, then so are all of its conjugates over $\mathbb{Q}$.

For example, the ring of integers of $\mathbb{Q}$ is $\mathbb{Z}$ because no element in $\mathbb{Q} \setminus \mathbb{Z}$ is a zero of a monic polynomial with integer coefficients. As another example, let $K = \mathbb{Q}(i)$ with $i \in \mathbb{C}$ such that $i^2 = -1$; then $\mathcal{O}_K = \mathbb{Z}[i]$, the Gaussian integers $a + bi$ with $a, b \in \mathbb{Z}$. Even though a number field K is always a simple extension of $\mathbb{Q}$, it is typically not true that $\mathcal{O}_K$ is a simple extension of $\mathbb{Z}$.

10.7.2 Dedekind Domains and Class Groups

Let K be a number field. The first question about $\mathcal{O}_K$ is to what extent it resembles the rational integers $\mathbb{Z}$. An answer is given by the result that $\mathcal{O}_K$ is a Dedekind domain.

Let A be a domain that is not a field, and let $Q(A)$ be its field of fractions. Then A is a Dedekind domain if the following conditions are satisfied:

---

[45] This follows from a theorem by Artin on linear independence of characters. See, for example, Lang [126], Chapter VI, paragraph 5, page 286, Theorem 5.2.

[46] It is easy to see that for each $y' \in K$ there is some nonzero $\ell \in \mathbb{Z}$ such that $\ell \cdot y' \in \mathcal{O}_K$.

1. A is Noetherian; that is, each of its ideals is finitely generated as an A-module.
2. A is integrally closed within $Q(A)$; that is, if $f(X) \in A[X]$ is a monic polynomial and if $z \in Q(A)$ satisfies $f(z) = 0$, then $z \in A$.
3. Each nonzero prime ideal of A is maximal.

Basic examples of Dedekind domains are the ring of rational integers and a polynomial ring over a field. In each case, it is straightforward to show that the ring in question is integrally closed within its field of fractions, whereas the other properties are clear already. An immediate consequence of $\mathbb{Z}$ being integrally closed is that for all $x \in \mathcal{O}_K$ it holds that $N_{K/\mathbb{Q}}(x) \in \mathbb{Z}$ and $\text{Tr}_{K/\mathbb{Q}}(x) \in \mathbb{Z}$. That is, from the definition and from basic field theory, these values are in $\mathcal{O}_K \cap \mathbb{Q} = \mathbb{Z}$. It holds that $x \in \mathcal{O}_K$ is a unit if and only if $|N_{K/\mathbb{Q}}(x)| = 1$. In the forward direction, suppose that $x, x' \in \mathcal{O}_K$ satisfy $xx' = 1$. Then

$$1 = N_{K/\mathbb{Q}}(1) = N_{K/\mathbb{Q}}(xx') = N_{K/\mathbb{Q}}(x) \cdot N_{K/\mathbb{Q}}(x')$$

Since $N_{K/\mathbb{Q}}(x), N_{K/\mathbb{Q}}(x') \in \mathbb{Z}$, the claim follows. The other direction follows at once from the observation that for each $x \in \mathcal{O}_K$ there is $y \in \mathcal{O}_K$ such that $N_{K/\mathbb{Q}}(x) = x \cdot y$ (use the fact that one of the embeddings in the definition of the norm is the identity). Also, it can be shown that each ideal of $\mathcal{O}_K$ is generated as an $\mathcal{O}_K$-module by at most two elements of $\mathcal{O}_K$.

If A is a Dedekind domain, it enjoys unique factorization of ideals into products of prime *ideals*. Concretely, suppose that I is an ideal of A with $(0) \subsetneq I \subset A$. Then

$$I = \prod_P P^{e_P}$$

where the product ranges over all nonzero prime ideals P in A and where e_P is a *nonnegative integer* that is nonzero for at most finitely many of them. This expression is unique. Note that this "prime ideal factorization" is in fact a relaxation of the "prime *element* factorization" property enjoyed by unique factorization domains.[47]

A nonzero A-submodule I of $Q(A)$ is a fractional ideal of A if there exists $c \in A$ with $c \neq 0$ such that $cI \subset A$. The product of two fractional ideals, defined similarly as the product of two ideals, is a fractional ideal as well. It is clear that A acts as a neutral element: $AI = I$ because $1 \in A$. Hence, the fractional ideals form a (commutative) multiplicative monoid. It can be shown that the fractional ideals form a group if A is a Dedekind domain. Note that in order for the group property to hold, the only condition left to be verified is that for each fractional ideal I there is a fractional ideal J such that $IJ = A$.[48]

Suppose that A is a Dedekind domain. If $x \in Q(A)$ with $x \neq 0$, then xA is a principal fractional ideal. These principal fractional ideals form a subgroup of the group of fractional ideals. The ideal class group of A is then the group of fractional ideals taken modulo the principal fractional ideals. It is a theorem that the ideal class group of the number field K (i.e., that of $\mathcal{O}_K$) is a *finite* (commutative) group. Its cardinality h is the class number of K. To say that $\mathcal{O}_K$ is a PID is equivalent to saying that $h = 1$.

Finally, if $I \neq (0)$ is a fractional ideal of A, then

$$I = \prod_P P^{e'_P}$$

---

[47] It should be noted that in the case of number fields, $\mathcal{O}_K$ is typically *not* a unique factorization domain.

[48] Sure, there is $c \in A$ such that $(c) \cdot I \subset A$ by definition, but the point is existence of a fractional ideal J such that IJ achieves *equality* with A.

where the product ranges over all nonzero prime ideals P in A and where e'_p is an *integer* that is nonzero for at most finitely many of them. This expression is unique. In other words, the group of fractional ideals of a Dedekind domain is isomorphic to the free abelian group generated by its prime ideals.

As an aside, it can be shown that a Dedekind domain A can be equivalently defined as a domain A that is not a field such that its fractional ideals form a group.

10.7.3 The Fundamental Identity

A further important property is that $\mathcal{O}_K$ *is a free $\mathbb{Z}$-module of rank $n := [K : \mathbb{Q}]$.* Before we establish the consequences, we define the notion of an order, which is motivated by this fact. An order in a number field K of degree n is a subring of $\mathcal{O}_K$ that is of rank n as a $\mathbb{Z}$-module. Sometimes $\mathcal{O}_K$ is referred to as the maximal order.

Suppose that P is a nonzero prime ideal of $\mathcal{O}_K$. It follows easily that

$$P \cap \mathbb{Z} = p\mathbb{Z}$$

for some prime number $p \in \mathbb{Z}$ with $p > 0$. Consequently, $\mathcal{O}_K/P$ is the finite field $\mathbb{F}_{p^f}$ for some integer f with $1 \le f \le n$. That is, $\mathcal{O}_K/P$ is a field because P is maximal and $\mathbb{Z}/(P \cap \mathbb{Z})$ $(=\mathbb{F}_p)$ is a subring of $\mathcal{O}_K/P$ that is henceforth an $\mathbb{F}_p$-vector space of dimension at most n because it is generated by $\overline{b}_1, \ldots, \overline{b}_n$, where $b_1, \ldots, b_n$ is a $\mathbb{Z}$-basis of $\mathcal{O}_K$.

Now let $p \ge 2$ be a prime number. Consider the Dedekind factorization

$$p\mathcal{O}_K = P_1^{e_1} \cdots P_k^{e_k}$$

into positive powers of pairwise distinct prime ideals $P_1, \ldots, P_k$. We say that the prime number p ramifies in the number field if some $e_i > 1$, and we say that it is unramified otherwise.

By the CRT,

$$\mathcal{O}_K/p\mathcal{O}_K \simeq \mathcal{O}_K/P_1^{e_1} \times \cdots \times \mathcal{O}_K/P_k^{e_k}$$

Note that $\mathcal{O}_K/p\mathcal{O}_K$ is an $\mathbb{F}_p$-vector space of dimension n.[49] Let f_i be the positive integer such that

$$\mathcal{O}_K/P_i = \mathbb{F}_{p^{f_i}}$$

for $i = 1, \ldots, k$.[50] Then the Fundamental Identity states that

$$e_1 f_1 + \cdots + e_k f_k = n$$

10.7.4 Cyclotomic Number Fields

Here is an example that is relevant to our purpose. Let $p \in \mathbb{Z}$ be a prime number with $p > 2$.[51] Consider the polynomial $X^p - 1 \in \mathbb{Z}[X]$. Its roots in the complex numbers $\mathbb{C}$ are exactly the elements of the group of *pth roots of unity*. This is a cyclic group of order p generated by a primitive pth root of unity, say,

$$\omega = e^{2\pi i/p} \in \mathbb{C}$$

---

[49] In fact, it is an $\mathbb{F}_p$-algebra of dimension n. See Section 10.8.
[50] Note that $\mathcal{O}_K/P_i \cap \mathbb{Z} = p\mathbb{Z}$, for $i = 1, \ldots, k$.
[51] The discussion to follow is rather vacuous for $p = 2$ (but true).

(where $e = 2.71...$ is the base of the natural logarithm and where $i \in \mathbb{C}$ satisfies $i^2 = -1$). Next, consider the polynomial

$$f(X) = X^{p-1} + \cdots + X + 1 \in \mathbb{Z}[X]$$

which is irreducible in $\mathbb{Q}[X]$ (as follows after substituting $X = Y + 1$ and applying *Eisenstein's irreducibility criterion*). Since $(X-1)f(X) = X^p - 1$, the roots of $f(X)$ are exactly the pth roots of unity with 1 excluded; that is, its roots are $\omega, \ldots, \omega^{p-1}$.

The pth cyclotomic number field is the number field

$$K := \mathbb{Q}(\omega) \simeq \mathbb{Q}[X]/(f(X))$$

which is of degree $p - 1$ over $\mathbb{Q}$. It is immediate that K is a Galois extension of $\mathbb{Q}$ of degree $p - 1$ with a cyclic Galois group. The pth ring of cyclotomic integers is the ring $\mathcal{O}_K$, which is a simple extension of $\mathbb{Z}$ in this case. In fact,

$$\mathcal{O}_K = \mathbb{Z}[\omega]$$

that is, $\mathcal{O}_K$ is the ring generated by $\mathbb{Z}$ and ω. This ring has the special property that the only prime number that ramifies is the prime p itself (see Section 10.8.4). In fact, it ramifies *completely*; that is,

$$p\mathcal{O}_K = P^{p-1}$$

for some unique nonzero prime ideal P of $\mathcal{O}_K$ with

$$P \cap \mathbb{Z} = p\mathbb{Z}$$

It is not hard to show that

$$P = (1 - \omega)$$

From the Fundamental Identity,

$$p - 1 = e_1 f_1 = (p - 1) \cdot 1$$

and thus

$$\mathcal{O}_K/P \simeq \mathbb{F}_p$$

Finally, we state some further useful property concerning the primitive roots of unity. Note that

$$\mathrm{N}_{K/\mathbb{Q}}(1 - \omega^i) = p$$

for $i = 1, \ldots, p - 1$. This is easy to see because the polynomial $g(X) = f(-X + 1) \in \mathbb{Q}[X]$ is the minimal polynomial over $\mathbb{Q}$ for the complete set of conjugates $1 - \omega, \ldots, 1 - \omega^{p-1}$. Now just read off the constant term in $g(X)$. Next, observe that for $i = 1, \ldots, p - 1$, we have

$$\frac{1 - \omega^i}{1 - \omega} = 1 + \cdots + \omega^{i-1}$$

and, by multiplicativity of the norm,

$$\mathrm{N}_{K/\mathbb{Q}}\left(\frac{1 - \omega^i}{1 - \omega}\right) = 1$$

In conclusion, we have the following lemma:

LEMMA 10.8 *Let $p > 2$ be a prime number. Let $\mathcal{O}_K$ denote the ring of integers of the pth cyclotomic number field. Let $\omega \in \mathcal{O}_K$ be a primitive pth root of unity. Then, for $i = 0, \ldots, p-2$, it holds that $\sum_{j=0}^{i} \omega^j$ is a unit of $\mathcal{O}_K$.*

10.8 Algebras

10.8.1 Basic Definitions

Let K be a field. *For our purposes, a K-algebra A will mean a commutative ring A such that K is a subring.*[52] In particular, this means that A is a K-vector space of dimension ≥ 1. Note that $1_K = 1_A$.

Products of K-algebras, for example, the n-fold direct product K^n, where $n \geq 1$ is an integer, will be viewed as K-algebras with component-wise multiplication as ring multiplication and with K "diagonally embedded"; that is, $\lambda \in K$ is given by $(\lambda, \ldots, \lambda, \ldots)$ in the product. In particular, the multiplicative unity is the element $(1_K, \ldots, 1_K, \ldots)$.

A morphism $\phi : A \longrightarrow B$ of K-algebras is a map that is both a ring morphism and a K-vector space morphism. Note that this facilitates both ring-theoretic and linear algebraic arguments. Two K-algebras A, B are isomorphic if there are K-algebra morphisms $\phi : A \longrightarrow B$ and $\phi' : B \longrightarrow A$ such that $\phi \circ \phi'$ is the identity on B and $\phi' \circ \phi$ is the identity on A. A morphism is an isomorphism if and only if it is bijective.

10.8.2 Trace and Discriminant

Let V be an n-dimensional K-vector space ($1 \leq n < \infty$), and let ϕ be an endomorphism of V. Let $\Phi := (\phi_{ij})$ be the matrix representing ϕ with respect to some given basis. The characteristic polynomial of ϕ is defined as

$$f(X) := \det(X \cdot I_n - \Phi) \in K[X]$$

where I_n denotes the $n \times n$ identity matrix over K. The determinant of ϕ is $\det(\Phi)$. The trace of ϕ is defined as

$$\mathrm{Tr}(\phi) = \sum_{i=1}^{n} \phi_{ii} \in K$$

These definitions do not depend on the choice of basis. It holds that

$$f(X) = X^n - \mathrm{Tr}(\phi) \cdot X^{n-1} + \cdots + (-1)^n \cdot \det(\phi)$$

Suppose that A is a K-algebra with $n := \dim_K A < \infty$. For each $a \in A$, define

$$\mu_a : A \longrightarrow A$$

$$x \mapsto ax$$

the multiplication-by-a map on A. Note that this is a K-vector space endomorphism of A. The trace function on A/K is defined as

---

[52] Note that this definition is more restrictive than common definitions in the literature, where typically there is no a priori requirement concerning commutativity. Besides, algebras may be defined over rings instead of fields. There are further relaxations. See [126], Chapter III, paragraph 1, page 121.

$$\text{Tr}_{A/K} : A \longrightarrow K$$

$$a \mapsto \text{Tr}(\mu_a)$$

This is a K-linear form. Note that $(a,b) \mapsto \text{Tr}_{A/K}(ab)$ is a K-bilinear form on A (that is, it is a K-linear form in each of its arguments a,b).

LEMMA 10.9 *If A is an extension field of K of degree $n < \infty$, then the following statements are equivalent:*

1. *The trace function $\text{Tr}_{A/K}$ is not identically zero.*
2. *The K-bilinear form $(a,b) \mapsto \text{Tr}_{A/K}(ab)$ on A is nondegenerate.*
3. *For each K-linear form $\phi : A \longrightarrow K$, there is a unique $a \in A$ such that $\phi(x) = \text{Tr}_{A/K}(ax)$ for all $x \in A$.*

Proof The equivalence of the second and third claims is by definition of nondegeneracy. The equivalence of the first and second claims follows from the following trivial observation: since A is a field, for all $a,b \in A$ with $b \neq 0$, it holds that $\text{Tr}_{A/K}(a) = \text{Tr}_{A/K}((ab^{-1})b)$. ∎

PROPOSITION 10.10 *If A is a separable field extension of K of degree $n < \infty$, then the following statements hold:*

1. *The trace function as defined above coincides with the trace function as defined in Section 10.6.4. In particular, the trace function is not identically zero.*
2. *Let $a \in A$. The characteristic polynomial of μ_a equals the minimal polynomial of a over K taken to the $[A : K(a)]$-th power.*
3. *There exists a dual basis for each given basis. Concretely, if $e_1, \ldots, e_n \in A$ constitute a K-basis of A, then there is a K-basis $e'_1, \ldots, e'_n$ of A such that $\text{Tr}(e_i e'_j) = \delta_{ij}$ (Kronecker delta), for $1 \leq i,j \leq n$.*

As to the first and second claims, see, for example, Samuel [165].[53] For a proof that the trace function on a finite-degree separable extension field is not identically zero, see the reference in Section 10.6.4. The second claim implies that

$$\det(\mu_a) = \left(N_{K(a)/K}(a)\right)^{[A:K(a)]}$$

and that

$$\text{Tr}_{A/K}(a) = [A : K(a)] \cdot \text{Tr}_{K(a)/K}(a)$$

Note that if $A = K(a)$, then the minimal polynomial of a over K and the characteristic polynomial of μ_a are identical. The third claim is just linear algebra; it is an immediate consequence of the fact that $(a,b) \mapsto \text{Tr}(ab)$ is a nondegenerate K-bilinear form.

REMARK 10.11 *If A is a finite-degree extension field of K and A is not separable over K, then the trace function $\text{Tr}_{A/K}$ is identically zero.*[54]

---

[53] In Samuel [165], see Section 2.6, pages 36–8.
[54] See, for example, Stichtenoth [172], appendix A, page 333. The proof is not given there, but it can be shown using just basic theory of inseparability (note that inseparability can only occur in characteristic $p > 0$).

DEFINITION 10.12 (DISCRIMINANT OF A K-ALGEBRA) *Suppose that A is a K-algebra with $n := \dim_K A < \infty$. Then the discriminant of a set of elements $(a_1, \ldots, a_n) \in A^n$ is defined as*

$$D_{A/K}(a_1, \ldots, a_n) = \det(\mathrm{Tr}(a_i a_j))$$

which is an element of K.

The discriminant of A is the discriminant of a K-basis of A. This is only well defined up to multiplication by the square of a unit in K.[55] This follows immediately by linear algebra. The discriminant of A over K is said to differ from 0 if the discriminant of a K-basis differs from 0. Otherwise, the discriminant of A over K is said to equal 0. The discriminant is multiplicative in the sense that the discriminant of a finite direct product of K-algebras is nonzero if and only if the discriminant of each of the factors is nonzero.

PROPOSITION 10.13 *Suppose that A is a separable field extension of K of degree $n < \infty$. Let $a \in A$ be such that $A = K(a)$, then the following statements hold:*

1. *The discriminant of the K-basis $1, a, \ldots, a^{n-1}$ of A satisfies*

$$D_{A/K}(1, a, \ldots, a^{n-1}) = (-1)^{\frac{1}{2}n(n-1)} \cdot N_{A/K}(f'(a)) \neq 0$$

   where $f(X) \in K[X]$ is the minimal polynomial of a over K and $f'(X) \in K[X]$ is its formal derivative.[56]

2. *Alternatively, if $a_1, \ldots, a_n$ is the complete set of conjugates of a over K, then*

$$D_{A/K}(1, a, \ldots, a^{n-1}) = \prod_{i<j}(a_i - a_j)^2 \neq 0$$

3. *Let $a'_1, \ldots, a'_n \in A$. Then $D_{A/K}(a'_1, \ldots, a'_n) \neq 0$ if and only if $a'_1, \ldots, a'_n$ constitute a K-basis of A.*

Proof The first two claims follow by rather straightforward formula manipulations.[57] The third claim follows easily. If $a'_1, \ldots, a'_n \in A$ constitute a basis, then its discriminant differs from the discriminant of $a_1, \ldots, a_n$ by the square of a nonzero element. Therefore, the latter discriminant is nonzero by the first (second) claim. If $a'_1, \ldots, a'_n \in A$ do not constitute a basis, then the columns of the matrix $(\mathrm{Tr}(a'_i a'_j))$ are linearly dependent. Therefore, the discriminant is zero. ∎

Note that the preceding discriminant is uniquely determined as an element of the quotient group $K^*/(K^*)^2$.[58]

PROPOSITION 10.14 *Let A be a K-algebra with $n := \dim_K A < \infty$. Then the following statements hold:*

1. *Suppose that A is an extension field of K. Then A is separable over K if and only if the discriminant of A/K is nonzero.*

2. *If A contains a nonzero nilpotent, then the discriminant of A/K equals 0.*

---

[55] Namely, the square of the determinant of a base change.

[56] A dual basis can be made explicit as a function of a, $f(X)$, and $f'(X)$. For more information, see Lang [126], Chapter VI, paragraph 5.

[57] See, for example, Samuel [165], section 2.7.

[58] Here $(K^*)^2$ denotes the subgroup of squares.

Proof We start by verifying the first claim. The forward direction follows from Proposition 10.13. In the other direction, if A is not separable over K, then the trace function vanishes by Remark 10.11, and so does the discriminant.

As to the second claim, suppose that $a \in A$ is a nonzero nilpotent. Then μ_a is a nilpotent K-vector space endomorphism of A. In particular, it cannot have nonzero eigenvalues. Therefore, all the n roots of its characteristic polynomial are 0. Consequently, the trace equals 0. Now choose a K-basis of A that includes a. Then the product between a and any basis element y is nilpotent; hence, $\mathrm{Tr}_{A/K}(ay) = 0$. It follows directly that the discriminant vanishes because the matrix from its definition has a row consisting of zeros only. ∎

DEFINITION 10.15 (DISCRIMINANT OF A POLYNOMIAL) *The discriminant of a monic polynomial $f(X) \in K[X]$ of degree $n \geq 1$ is defined as*

$$D(f) = \prod_{1 \leq i < j \leq n} (a_i - a_j)^2 \in K$$

where $a_1, \ldots, a_n$ is a complete set of roots (with multiplicity) in some splitting field of $f(X)$.

By Galois theory, the discriminant of a polynomial is indeed an element of K and does not depend on the choice of splitting field. Note that $D(f) = 0$ if and only if $f(X)$ has roots with multiplicity greater than 1. Because $D(f)$ is a symmetric polynomial expression in the roots of $f(X)$, it follows by Galois theory that the discriminant can (in principle) be given as a polynomial expression in the coefficients of the polynomial.[59] Thus, the discriminant of a polynomial gives (important) information about its roots via a polynomial function of its coefficients.

We give an example of a class of polynomials for which this polynomial function has been made explicit. Suppose that $f(X) \in K[X]$ is an irreducible *trinomial*; that is, $f(X) = X^n + uX + v$ for some $u, v \in K$. Then a straightforward calculation[60] exploiting the preceding norm-derivative expression of the discriminant yields

$$D(f) = (-1)^{1/2n(n-1)}(n^n v^{n-1} + (-1)^{n-1}(n-1)^{n-1}u^n)$$

For $n = 2$, this gives the familiar expression

$$D(f) = u^2 - 4v$$

from high school algebra. For $n = 3$, this gives the expression

$$D(f) = -27v^2 - 4u^3$$

which is relevant when dealing with Weierstrass equations $Y^2 = X^3 + uX + v$ from the theory of elliptic curves (in characteristic $\neq 2, 3$).

---

[59] This follows from the basic result that symmetric polynomials can be expressed as polynomials in the elementary symmetric ones. See, for example, Lang [126], page 272, example 4. Note that in the case of norm and trace, which are similarly symmetric functions, this expression is particularly straightforward.

[60] For instance, see Samuel [165], section 2.7.

10.8.3 Basic Characterization Theorems

Finite products of finite-degree extension fields of K are among the most elementary examples of K-algebras. There is the following characterization:

THEOREM 10.16 *Let A be a K-algebra with $n := \dim_K A < \infty$. Then*

1. *A has 0 as its only nilpotent if and only if A is a finite direct product of finite-degree extension fields of K.*
2. *A has a nonzero discriminant over K if and only if A is a finite direct product of finite-degree separable extension fields of K.*

In particular, if K is a perfect field, then A has 0 as its only nilpotent if and only if A has nonzero discriminant.

Proof The first claim is shown as follows (forward direction only because the other is immediate): let P be any prime ideal of A. Then A/P is a domain. Also, A/P is a K-vector space of finite dimension. For a nonzero element $\mu \in A/P$, consider the multiplication-by-μ map on A/P, which is a vector-space isomorphism: it is injective because A/P is a domain and an injective endomorphism of a finite dimensional vector space is an isomorphism. Consequently, there is some $\mu' \in A/P$ such that $\mu\mu' = \mu'\mu = 1$. Thus, A/P is a field for each prime ideal P of A. Therefore, each prime ideal is maximal.

The nilradical (that is, the ideal of A consisting of all its nilpotents) is (0) by hypothesis. Since the nilradical of a commutative ring is the intersection of its prime ideals, it follows that the intersection taken over all maximal ideals in A equals (0) as well.

Next, observe that there are at most finitely many maximal ideals of A. Consider the canonical map of rings

$$A \longrightarrow A/P_1 \times \cdots \times A/P_\ell$$

where $P_1, \ldots, P_\ell$ are distinct maximal ideals of A. This is a morphism of K-algebras, and the terms on the right are finite-degree extension fields of K. By the Chinese Remainder Theorem, this map is surjective. By linear algebra, the K-dimension on the left (which equals n) is an upper bound for the total K-dimension on the right (which is at least ℓ). It follows that $\ell \leq n$. Therefore, A has at most finitely many maximal ideals.

Finally, assume that $P_1, \ldots, P_\ell$ enumerate all the maximal ideals of A. Then this canonical map is also injective because the intersection of the maximal ideals of A is (0), as established earlier. Hence, it is a K-algebra isomorphism.

The second claim follows by combining the first with Proposition 10.14 (also use multiplicativity of the discriminant). This concludes the proof.[61] ∎

10.8.4 An Application to Algebraic Number Theory

The discriminant of a number field is the discriminant of a $\mathbb{Z}$-basis of its ring of integers $\mathcal{O}$. This definition does not depend on the choice of the basis because a base change incurs a multiple equal to the square of the determinant of the base change, and this determinant

---

[61] For a general characterization of finite-dimensional K-algebras, see, for example, Lenstra [130], section 2.6. The proof of Theorem 10.16 given here is a special case.

equals ± 1 here. Reasoning as in the case of trace and norm, the discriminant of a number field is an integer. If the number field is the field of rational numbers itself, then the discriminant equals 1. If the degree of the number field is greater than 1, it holds that the discriminant is not equal to $-1, 0, 1$. By Stickelberger's Criterion,[62] it is 0 mod 4 or 1 mod 4. Using Theorem 10.2, it is not hard to see that the discriminant of an order in $\mathcal{O}$ equals the square of a nonzero integer times the discriminant of the number field. For example, the discriminant $D(p)$ of the pth cyclotomic number field ($p > 2$ prime) satisfies

$$D(p) = (-1)^{(p-1)/2} p^{p-2}$$

As an application, let $p \in \mathbb{Z}$ be a positive prime number. By inspection, we see that p is unramified if and only if $\mathcal{O}/p\mathcal{O}$ is a product of finite extension fields of $\mathbb{F}_p$, whereas the latter holds if and only if the discriminant of $\mathcal{O}/p\mathcal{O}$ is nonzero. Because this discriminant is obtained by reducing the discriminant of the number field modulo p, it follows, in particular, that a positive finite number of primes $p \in \mathbb{Z}$ ramify. For example, the discriminant of the pth cyclotomic number field ($p > 2$ prime) indeed shows that p itself is the only prime number that ramifies.

There is the following corollary: suppose that $a \in \mathbb{C}$ is integral over $\mathbb{Z}$ and $f(X) \in \mathbb{Z}[X]$ is its minimal polynomial. Then $D(f) \in \mathbb{Z}$, and by Proposition 10.13, the prime number p divides $D(f)$ if and only if the factorization of the polynomial $\bar{f}(X) \in \mathbb{F}_p[X]$, that is, $f(X)$ reduced modulo p, is not square-free. Moreover, if $\deg f(X) > 1$, then there is at least one prime number p such that the factorization in $\bar{f}(X) \in \mathbb{F}_p[X]$ is not square-free.

10.9 Tensor Products

Let A be a commutative ring.

10.9.1 Tensor Products of Modules

The tensor product of A-modules is defined by means of a *universal property*.

DEFINITION 10.17 (UNIVERSAL PROPERTY) *Let V, W be A-modules. A tensor product of V and W is a pair $(\mathcal{U}, \iota)$ such that the following statements hold:*

1. *$\mathcal{U}$ is an A-module and $\iota : V \times W \longrightarrow \mathcal{U}$ is an A-bilinear map.*
2. *Let Z be an A-module, and let $\psi : V \times W \longrightarrow Z$ be an A-bilinear map. Then there is a unique A-module morphism $f : \mathcal{U} \longrightarrow Z$ such that $\psi = f \circ \iota$.*

If a tensor product exists, it is *uniquely unique* in the following sense: if $(\mathcal{U}', \iota')$ is a tensor product of V and W as well, then there is a unique A-module isomorphism $g : \mathcal{U} \longrightarrow \mathcal{U}'$ such that $\iota' = g \circ \iota$.[63]

The existence of a tensor product is shown by a "canonical construction." This particular construction is then declared to be *the* tensor product of V and W. This makes sense because of strong equivalence, as mentioned earlier.

---

[62] See, for example, Lang [125].

[63] The property "uniquely unique" is stronger than the property "unique up to isomorphism." For instance, finite fields and algebraic closures satisfy the latter, weaker notion but not the former, stronger one.

THEOREM 10.18 *The tensor product exists.*

We verify this theorem as follows: consider the free A-module $\mathcal{M}$ generated by all pairs $(v,w) \in V \times W$, that is, $\mathcal{M}$ consists of all *formal* sums $\sum \lambda(v,w) \cdot (v,w)$ with $(v,w) \in V \times W$ and $\lambda(v,w) \in A$ such that $\lambda(v,w) \neq 0$ for at most a finite number of terms $(v,w) \in V \times W$. By convention, $1 \cdot (v,w)$ is denoted (v,w).

Also consider the submodule $\mathcal{N}$ of $\mathcal{M}$ generated by all elementary expressions of the form

1. $(\lambda \cdot v, w) - \lambda \cdot (v,w)$,
2. $(v, \lambda \cdot w) - \lambda \cdot (v,w)$,
3. $(v + v', w) - (v,w) - (v',w)$,
4. $(v, w + w') - (v,w) - (v,w')$,

where $\lambda \in A$, $v, v' \in V$, $w, w' \in W$.

The quotient $\mathcal{M}/\mathcal{N}$ is an A-module as well. Define

$$v \otimes w := \overline{(v,w)} = (v,w) + \mathcal{N} \ \in \ \mathcal{M}/\mathcal{N}$$

a tensor Each element of $\mathcal{M}/\mathcal{N}$ can be written as a finite A-sum of tensors (though such a decomposition is not unique in general).

Set

$$V \otimes_A W = \mathcal{M}/\mathcal{N}$$

and define

$$\iota : V \times W \longrightarrow V \otimes_A W$$

$$(v,w) \mapsto v \otimes w$$

DEFINITION 10.19 $(V \otimes_A W, \iota)$ *is the tensor product of the A-modules V and W.*

REMARK 10.20 If there is no ambivalence, we often drop the subscript A from the notation $V \otimes_A W$.

One sees at once that the tensor product admits the following "calculus":

THEOREM 10.21 *For all $\lambda \in A$, $v, v' \in V$, $w, w' \in W$, it holds that*

1. $(\lambda \cdot v) \otimes w = \lambda \cdot (v \otimes w)$.
2. $v \otimes (\lambda \cdot w) = \lambda \cdot (v \otimes w)$.
3. $(v + v') \otimes w = v \otimes w + v' \otimes w$.
4. $v \otimes (w + w') = v \otimes w + v \otimes w'$.

The calculus implies that ι is an A-bilinear map. It is left to argue that $(V \otimes W, \iota)$ is universal in the sense of Definition 10.17. Suppose that Z is an A-module and $\psi : V \times W \longrightarrow Z$ is an A-bilinear map. If there exists an A-module morphism $f : V \otimes W \longrightarrow Z$ such that $\psi = f \circ \iota$, then it must be *unique*. Indeed, since $f(v \otimes w) = \psi(v,w)$ for all tensors $v \otimes w$, and since, as remarked earlier, each element of $V \otimes W$ is a finite K-sum of tensors, the morphism f is uniquely defined by its action on the tensors.

Therefore, it remains to show that a factorization $f \circ \iota$ of ψ *exists*. The map ψ defines an A-module morphism $\mathcal{M} \to Z$ by sending a term $(v,w) \in \mathcal{M}$ to $\psi(v,w) \in Z$ and by extending this A-linearly. By inspection, the kernel of this morphism contains $\mathcal{N}$. Hence, this induces an A-module morphism f on $\mathcal{M}/\mathcal{N}$ such that $f(v \otimes w) = \psi(v, w)$ for each tensor $v \otimes w$ with $v \in V$, $w \in W$. This concludes the argument.

Tensor products often create a "larger space" (as we shall see shortly), but tensor products also may cause a "collapse." Here is an example: take the additive groups $\mathbb{Z}/2\mathbb{Z}$ and $\mathbb{Z}/3\mathbb{Z}$ as $\mathbb{Z}$-modules and let $x \otimes y \in \mathbb{Z}/2\mathbb{Z} \otimes \mathbb{Z}/3\mathbb{Z}$. Then $(x \otimes y) = (3x \otimes y) = (x \otimes 3y) = (x \otimes 0) = 0 \cdot (x \otimes 0) = 0$. So the tensor product is trivial in this case.

REMARK 10.22 The definition of tensor product extends in a straightforward way to tensor products of $n \geq 2$ terms, replacing bilinear maps by n-multilinear maps and adapting the other definitions accordingly.

REMARK 10.23 We make some general remarks about the use of the tensor product.

1. The point about the tensor product $V \otimes W$ is its (unique) existence according to the universal property. The construction of the module $\mathcal{M}/\mathcal{N}$ merely serves to show that the definition is not vacuous.
2. The fact that the tensor product establishes the stated one-to-one correspondence between A-bilinear maps $V \times W \longrightarrow Z$ and the A-module morphisms $F : V \otimes W \longrightarrow Z$ is often used to "linearize" a "bilinear problem" by passing to a tensor product.

10.9.2 Some Basic Theory of the Tensor Product

Commuting with Direct Sums

As a first result, we note that

$$A \otimes_A A \simeq A$$

In particular, this means that the tensor product is not trivial if A is nontrivial. We now verify the result: consider the A-bilinear map

$$\mu : A \times A \longrightarrow A$$
$$(a, b) \mapsto ab$$

By the universal property, there is a unique A-module morphism

$$f : A \otimes_A A \longrightarrow A$$

such that

$$\mu = f \circ \iota$$

Each element of $A \otimes_A A$ can be represented by some tensor $a \otimes 1$ with $a \in A$. So surjectivity follows because $f(a \otimes 1) = a$ for each $a \in A$. Likewise, injectivity follows because $f(a \otimes 1) = 0$ if and only if $a = 0$ (note that $0 \otimes 1 = 0 \otimes 0$). In conclusion, f is an A-module isomorphism. By a similar argument, if M is an A-module, then

$$A \otimes M \simeq M$$

If $\mathcal{I}$ is an index set, M_i is an A-module for each $i \in \mathcal{I}$, and N is an A-module, then it holds that

$$\left(\bigoplus_{i \in \mathcal{I}} M_i \right) \otimes N \simeq \bigoplus_{i \in \mathcal{I}} (M_i \otimes N)$$

Likewise,

$$N \otimes \left(\bigoplus_{i \in \mathcal{I}} M_i \right) \simeq \bigoplus_{i \in \mathcal{I}} (N \otimes M_i)$$

Hence the following lemma:

LEMMA 10.24 *Suppose that M is an A-module and N is a free A-module with basis $\{f_j\}_{j \in \mathcal{J}}$. Then the map*

$$\bigoplus_{j \in \mathcal{J}} M \longrightarrow M \otimes N$$

$$(\widehat{m}_j)_{j \in \mathcal{J}} \mapsto \sum_{j \in \mathcal{J}} \widehat{m}_j \otimes f_j$$

is an isomorphism of A-modules.

Note that the map is well defined because at most finitely many $\widehat{m}_j$s are nonzero by definition of a direct sum. We say that the elements of $M \otimes N$ are *uniquely expressed* in the preceding form. Of course, the lemma is easily adapted to the case where M is free.

REMARK 10.25 If M is free as well, with basis $\{e_i\}$, then this implies directly that $M \otimes N$ is free, with basis $\{e_i \otimes f_j\}$.

For example, let K be a field, and let M, N be finite-dimensional K-vector spaces with respective dimensions n and m. Then $M \otimes N \simeq K^{nm}$ as vector spaces. In particular, $K^n \otimes K^m \simeq K^{nm}$.

Base Extension

Let M be an A-module. Let B be a commutative extension ring of A. The A-module $B \otimes_A M$ may be viewed as a B-*module* in a natural way. Likewise, this holds for the A-module $M \otimes_A B$.

The idea is to define B-scalar multiplication on $B \otimes_A M$ simply by the assignment

$$b \cdot (b' \otimes m) = (bb' \otimes m)$$

and to extend it B-linearly to all of $B \otimes_A M$. We now sketch the proof that this works.

With a short argument that invokes the universal property twice, we show that there is a unique A-bilinear map from $B \times (B \otimes_A M)$ to $B \otimes_A M$ that sends $(b, (b' \otimes m))$ to $(bb' \otimes m)$. This immediately renders the (unique) B-module structure on $B \otimes_A M$ that is consistent with the preceding assignment.

Briefly, we consider the A-trilinear map from $B \times B \times M$ to $B \otimes_A M$ that sends (b, b', m) to $(bb' \otimes m)$. By the universal property,[64] this yields a unique A-linear map from $B \otimes_A (B \otimes_A M)$ to $B \otimes_A M$.[65] Once again by the universal property, this yields the claimed (unique) A-bilinear map from $B \times (B \otimes_A M)$ to $B \otimes_A M$.[66]

---

[64] Applied in the case of a tensor product with three terms.

[65] The brackets may be placed on account of *associativity* of the tensor product. For instance, if M, M', M'' are A-modules, then $M \otimes M' \otimes M'' \simeq (M \otimes M') \otimes M'' \simeq M \otimes (M' \otimes M'')$.

[66] Please refer to Lang [126], chapter XVI, paragraph 4, page 623. Base extension is actually more general. That is, the argument sketched here also works for each commutative ring B that may be viewed as an A-module. This includes, of course, the case we have presented, that is, where A is a subring of B.

Tensor Products of Algebras

Let K be a field. Let A, B be K-algebras. Then the K-vector space $A \otimes_K B$ may be viewed *as a K-algebra* in a natural way.

The idea is to induce a ring structure by defining

$$(a \otimes b) \cdot (a' \otimes b') = (aa') \otimes (bb')$$

and to extend this to all of $A \otimes_K B$. The field K is naturally embedded via

$$\lambda \mapsto \lambda \cdot (1 \otimes 1)$$

and the ring multiplication alluded to earlier is compatible with the K-scalar multiplication already enjoyed by $A \otimes_K B$. Using a similar style of reasoning as in the case of base extension, it is not so hard to verify that this works correctly.[67]

Tensor Products of Module Morphisms

Let A be a commutative ring, and let M, M', N, N' be A-modules. Suppose that

$$\phi : M \longrightarrow M' \quad \text{and} \quad \psi : N \longrightarrow N'$$

are A-module morphisms. Consider the tensor product $M \otimes N$ with the natural inclusion $\iota : M \times N \longrightarrow M \otimes N$ and the tensor product $M' \otimes N'$ with the natural inclusion $\iota' : M' \times N' \longrightarrow M' \otimes N'$.

Define the assignment

$$u \otimes v \mapsto \phi(u) \otimes \psi(v)$$

for all $u \in M, v \in N$. The A-linear extension of this assignment to all of $M \otimes N$ defines an A-module morphism from $M \otimes N$ to $M' \otimes N'$, denoted $\phi \otimes \psi$. But it requires a proof that this map is indeed well defined.

The map

$$\phi \times \psi : M \times N \longrightarrow M' \times N'$$
$$(u, v) \mapsto (\phi(u), \psi(v))$$

is an A-bilinear map. Composition with the natural inclusion ι' yields the A-bilinear map

$$\iota' \circ (\phi \times \psi) : M \times N \longrightarrow M' \otimes N'$$

By the universal property, it follows at once that, as desired, there is a unique A-linear map

$$F : M \otimes N \longrightarrow M' \otimes N'$$

such that

$$\iota' \circ (\phi \times \psi) = F \circ \iota$$

and

$$F(u \otimes v) = \phi(u) \otimes \psi(v)$$

for all $u \in M, v \in N$.

In the special case where M, N are free A-modules of finite rank, then

$$\mathrm{End}_A(M) \otimes_A \mathrm{End}_A(N) \simeq \mathrm{End}_A(M \otimes_A N)$$

[67] Please refer to Lang [126], chapter XVI, paragraph 6, pages 629–31.

where $\text{End}_A(M)$ (and $\text{End}_A(N)$) denotes the endomorphism ring of M (and N).

The following lemma is straightforward by the preceding discussion. Let M'', N'' be A-modules. Suppose that

$$\phi' : M' \longrightarrow M'' \quad \text{and} \quad \psi' : N' \longrightarrow N''$$

are A-module morphisms.

LEMMA 10.26 (COMPOSITION) *It holds that*

$$(\phi' \otimes \psi') \circ (\phi \otimes \psi) = (\phi' \circ \phi) \otimes (\psi' \circ \psi)$$

In particular, if ϕ, ψ are isomorphisms, then so is $\phi \otimes \psi$. Moreover,

$$(\phi \otimes \psi)^{-1} = \phi^{-1} \otimes \psi^{-1}$$

Proof The first claim follows at once from the definition. As to the remaining claims, just apply $\phi^{-1} \otimes \psi^{-1}$ after $\phi \otimes \psi$ (and vice versa). This gives the identity map on $M \otimes N$ (and $M' \otimes N'$). ∎

See Lang [126] for a generalization.[68]

10.9.3 *Examples*

Tensoring-Up of a Finite Abelian Group

Let G be a finite abelian group, viewed as a $\mathbb{Z}$-module. Let A be a commutative extension ring of $\mathbb{Z}$ that is free of rank n as a $\mathbb{Z}$-module. Select a $\mathbb{Z}$-basis $\{e_i\}_{i=1}^n$ of A. The elements of the $\mathbb{Z}$-module $G \otimes A$ can be uniquely expressed as $\sum_{i=1}^n g_i \otimes e_i$ with $g_1, \ldots, g_n \in G$. In particular, $G \otimes A$ is finite, and it has cardinality $|G|^n$, irrespective of the cardinality of A.

By base extension, this is an A-module. If $a \in A$, then

$$a \cdot \left(\sum_{i=1}^n g_i \otimes e_i \right) = \sum_{i=1}^n (g_i \otimes ae_i) = \sum_{i=1}^n g_i' \otimes e_i$$

for some $g_1', \ldots, g_n' \in G$. The g_i's in the latter equality are $\mathbb{Z}$-linear combinations of the g_is. The $\mathbb{Z}$-coefficients only depend on a and the $e_i \cdot e_j$s, and are easily obtained once a and the $e_i \cdot e_j$s are expressed as $\mathbb{Z}$-coordinate vectors with respect to the basis. This turns A-scalar multiplication into "linear algebra" (over $\mathbb{Z}$, that is).

Tensoring-Up of a Vector Space

In the second example, let K be a field, and let V be a K-vector space of finite dimension n. If L is an extension field of K, then L is a K-vector space. By base extension, $L \otimes_K V$ can be viewed as an L-vector space. We claim that $\dim_L L \otimes V = n$. So, in a sense, the vector space is just "scaled up" to include, more generally, L-multiples of vectors while the dimension does not change as a result. Moreover, V as a K-vector space is embedded in a natural way.

This can be verified as follows: let $\{\mathbf{e}_i\}_{i=1}^n$ be a K-basis for V. We have already seen that there is a one-to-one correspondence between the elements of $L \otimes V$ and the elements of the

---

[68] Chapter XVI, paragraph 1, pages 605–6.

form $\sum_i \lambda_i \otimes \mathbf{e}_i$. By base extension, this is an L-vector space, and we may equivalently state that the one-to-one correspondence is with elements of the form $\sum_i \lambda_i \cdot (1 \otimes \mathbf{e}_i)$ instead. The claim follows at once. The K-vector space V is naturally embedded via $v \mapsto 1 \otimes v$.[69]

Tensoring-Up of an Algebra

Let K be a field. Then

1. Let L be an extension field of K. Then

$$L \otimes_K K[X] \simeq L[X]$$

   as L-algebras.

2. If $f(X) \in K[X]$ is a polynomial of degree n and if K' is an extension field of K, then

$$K' \otimes_K (K[X]/(f(X) \cdot K[X])) \simeq K'[X]/(f(X) \cdot K'[X])$$

   as K'-algebras.

3. Let $\overline{K}$ be an algebraic closure of K. Let L be a finite-degree separable field extension of K. Then

$$\overline{K} \otimes_K L \simeq \overline{K}^{[L:K]}$$

   as $\overline{K}$-algebras.

We briefly comment on the first claim. There is one-to-one-correspondence between polynomials $f(X) = \sum_{i=0}^{\ell} \lambda_i X^i \in L[X]$ and expressions of the form $\sum_{i=0}^{\ell} \lambda_i \otimes X^i$. This gives a K-vector space isomorphism. Ring multiplication in $L \otimes_K K[X]$ mimics exactly the multiplication in $L[X]$ as well. Applying base extension and viewing L as embedded via $\lambda \mapsto (\lambda \otimes 1)$, it follows there is an L-algebra isomorphism.

We do not give a proof of the second claim; it follows from the first in combination with some further results on tensor products.[70]

As to the third claim, this is implied by the second example in combination with the following observations: write $L = K(x)$ for some $x \in L$ (which is possible by the assumptions on L), and take $f(X) \in K[X]$ as the minimal polynomial of x. When viewed as an element of $\overline{K}[X]$, it factors as a product of $[L:K]$ distinct linear polynomials. Then apply the Chinese Remainder Theorem (CRT) and use the fact that a polynomial ring over a field modulo an ideal generated by a linear polynomial is the field itself. In this way, it follows that $\overline{K}[X]/(f(X)) \simeq \overline{K}^{[L:K]}$.

---

[69] Using a similar argument, if A and B are both finite-dimensional K-algebras (of respective dimensions n and m), then the K-algebra A is mapped injectively into the K-algebra $A \otimes_K B$ via $a \mapsto a \otimes 1$. Likewise for B. Moreover, $A \otimes_K B$ may be viewed as a free A-module of rank m. Likewise, it may be viewed as a free B-module of rank n.

[70] Specifically, exactness properties. See, for example, Atiyah and Macdonald [1].

11

Secret Sharing

11.1 Introduction

A (t,n)-threshold secret-sharing scheme, where t,n are integers with $0 \leq t < n$, provides a means to "disperse" secret data s into a sequence of n pieces of data, called shares, such that any $\leq t$ shares jointly give *no information* on the secret s (*t-privacy*), whereas any $\geq t+1$ of these shares jointly determine the secret s *uniquely* (($t+1$)-reconstruction).

Thus, an adversary's uncertainty about the secret is not reduced by gaining access to t shares: from the point of view of the adversary, the a priori uncertainty about the secret is equal to the a posteriori uncertainty about the secret. In particular, if the adversary had no information before accessing t shares, then the adversary still has no information afterwards as a result. Moreover, if the adversary somehow manages to cause the loss (erasure) of t' shares, where $n - t' \geq t+1$, then the secret still can be reconstructed uniquely from $t+1$ remaining shares.

In the case $t = 0$, there is a trivial scheme by declaring each share to be equal to the secret.[1] The case $1 \leq t = n-1$ is more interesting. It has an elegant solution based on an idea similar to that underlying the *one-time pad* encryption scheme. Say that the secret s is encoded as an element of a given finite group G. Note that the group as such is *not* secret. Then the n shares $(s_1, \ldots, s_n) \in G^n$ are selected uniformly random subject to the condition that their product satisfies

$$s_1 \cdots s_n = s$$

This works, for instance, by selecting

$$(\rho_1, \ldots, \rho_{n-1}) \in G^{n-1}$$

uniformly at random and independent of the secret s and by defining the shares as

$$s_1 = \rho_1, \ldots, s_{n-1} = \rho_{n-1} \qquad s_n = \rho_{n-1}^{-1} \cdots \rho_1^{-1} \cdot s$$

Note that

$$s_1 \cdots s_n = \rho_1 \cdots \rho_{n-1} \cdot \left(\rho_{n-1}^{-1} \cdots \rho_1^{-1} \cdot s \right) = s$$

and that any vector of $n-1$ shares has the uniform distribution on G^{n-1} and is independently distributed of the secret s. If G is abelian, and if we use additive notation, then we may, of

---

[1] We find it convenient to allow this "pathetic" case $t = 0$. However, we do not find it convenient to allow the other pathetic case $t = n$.

course, define the nth share instead as

$$s_n = s - \left(\sum_{i=1}^{n-1} s_i \right)$$

which gives

$$s = \sum_{i=1}^{n} s_i$$

This scheme is sometimes referred to as the *n*-out-of-*n* secret-sharing scheme. The cases $1 \le t < n - 1$ require alternative ideas, which we explain later on. Note that the process of creating shares is *probabilistic*; that is, besides the secret itself, it requires (secret) "coin flips."

Secret sharing was invented in 1979 by Adi Shamir [167] and independently at the same time by Bob Blakley [22] to alleviate the single-point-of-failure problem for storage of secret data. Their respective solutions work for any threshold. Meanwhile, secret sharing has become a fundamental cryptographic primitive with a host of applications, most notably in threshold cryptography and secure multiparty computation (MPC), as we have seen in Part I.

Let K be a field, let p > 0 be a prime number, and let v be a positive integer. Define $q = p^v$. Let $\mathbb{F}_q$ be a finite field with q elements.

11.2 Notation

Let $\mathcal{F}$ be a nonempty set, and let $\mathcal{I}$ be a nonempty finite set. Then $\mathcal{F}[\mathcal{I}]$ denotes the set of functions

$$x : \mathcal{I} \longrightarrow \mathcal{F}$$

If $B \subset \mathcal{I}$ is nonempty, then the projection function

$$\pi_B : \mathcal{F}[\mathcal{I}] \longrightarrow \mathcal{F}[B]$$

maps each function $x \in \mathcal{F}[\mathcal{I}]$ simply to its restriction to the subdomain B. In other words, the function $\pi_B(x) \in \mathcal{F}[B]$ is defined such that it agrees with the function x on all of B. The dependence of projection maps on $\mathcal{F}$ and $\mathcal{I}$ is suppressed in the notation because this will always be clear from the context. For each set $B \subset \mathcal{I}$, its complement is defined as $\overline{B} = \mathcal{I} \setminus B$.

We may identify $\mathcal{F}[\mathcal{I}]$ with the Cartesian product of sets $\Omega := \prod_{i \in \mathcal{I}} \mathcal{F}$ in the obvious way. We say that $\mathcal{F}$ is the alphabet and $\mathcal{I}$ is the index set. For each $\mathbf{x} \in \Omega$, we write $\mathbf{x} = (x_j)_{j \in \mathcal{I}}$, the coordinate vector. Thus, $\mathbf{x} \in \Omega$ corresponds to $x \in \mathcal{F}[\mathcal{I}]$ with $x(i) = x_i$ for all $i \in \mathcal{I}$. Suppose that $B \subset \mathcal{I}$ is nonempty. For each $\mathbf{x} \in \Omega$, we may say that $\pi_B(\mathbf{x})$ corresponds to $(x_i)_{i \in B} \in \prod_{i \in B} \mathcal{F}$. As a shorthand for $\pi_B(\mathbf{x})$, the notation $\mathbf{x}_B$ is sometimes used.

For an integer $\ell \geq 1$, the notation $\mathcal{F}^\ell$ refers to the ℓ-fold Cartesian product of sets $\mathcal{F} \times \cdots \times \mathcal{F}$, leaving any index set implicit. When we say that $\mathcal{F}^\ell$ is indexed by a set $\mathcal{I}$, we mean that $|\mathcal{I}| = \ell$ and that $\mathcal{F}^\ell$ is identified with $\prod_{i \in \mathcal{I}} \mathcal{F}$. Often an index set $\mathcal{I}$ is a subset of the integers, for example, $\mathcal{I} = \{0, 1 \ldots, n\}$. In this case, an ordered tuple written as $(\cdot, \ldots, \cdot)$ is supposed to be indexed "with the indices increasing monotonically from left to right." This is convenient in some cases. When speaking of a projection function $\pi_B : \mathcal{F}^\ell \longrightarrow \mathcal{F}^{|B|}$, we tacitly assume that the image $\mathcal{F}^{|B|}$ is indexed by B.

In the context of linear algebra, specifically, in expressions involving multiplication of a matrix by a vector, it is convenient to treat a vector $\mathbf{x}$ as a *column vector*. The associated row vector, that is, its transpose, is denoted $\mathbf{x}^T$. Likewise, the transpose of a matrix M is denoted M^T. For example, if M is square matrix (over, say, some given ring) and $\mathbf{x}$ is a vector (defined over the same ring and of the appropriate length), then we have the products $\mathbf{x}^T M$ and $M\mathbf{x}$.

11.3 Interpolation Codes

Shamir's scheme was introduced in Chapter 3. We will explain the scheme in a different way, from a combinatorial perspective based on interpolation codes. This will help us generalize the approach later.

11.3.1 Definitions

DEFINITION 11.1 (CODE) *A code of length $\ell \geq 1$ over an alphabet $\mathcal{F}$ is a nonempty set $C \subset \mathcal{F}^\ell$. The elements of C are (code)words.*

Indexing $\mathcal{F}^\ell$ with some set $\mathcal{I}$, we may equivalently say that the code C is a nonempty set of functions $x : \mathcal{I} \longrightarrow \mathcal{F}$.

DEFINITION 11.2 (INTERPOLATION CODE) *Let C be a code of length $\ell \geq 1$ over a finite alphabet $\mathcal{F}$ of cardinality $\bar{q} \geq 2$. Write $\mathcal{I}$ for an index set of $\mathcal{F}^\ell$. Let r be an integer with $1 \leq r \leq \ell$. Then C is an $(r,\ell,\bar{q})$-interpolation code if, for each $B \subset \mathcal{I}$ with $|B| = r$, the projection map*

$$\pi_B : C \longrightarrow \mathcal{F}^r$$

$$\mathbf{x} \mapsto \pi_B(\mathbf{x})$$

is bijective. The class of all $(r,\ell,\bar{q})$-interpolation codes is denoted $\mathrm{IC}(r,\ell,\bar{q})$.

Equivalently, it is required that there is a *unique* $\mathbf{x} \in C$ with $\mathbf{x}_B = \mathbf{w}$ for each pair $(B,\mathbf{w})$, with $B \subset \mathcal{I}$, $|B| = r$, and $\mathbf{w} \in \mathcal{F}^r$. Note that if C is an $(r,\ell,\bar{q})$-interpolation code, then $|C| = \bar{q}^r$.

REMARK 11.3 Interpolation codes coincide with the orthogonal arrays $\mathrm{OA}(r,\ell,\bar{q})$, an extensively studied classical notion in combinatorics. See, for instance, Graham, Grötschel, and Lovász [102] and van Lint and Wilson [134]. For reasons to become clear shortly, the nomenclature used here suits our purposes better.

11.3.2 Basic Properties

In the "extreme cases" $r = 1, \ell$, the existence of interpolation codes is trivial to decide. Also, the case $r = \ell - 1$ is easy.

LEMMA 11.4 *Let $\ell, \bar{q}$ be integers with $\ell \geq 1$ and $\bar{q} \geq 2$. Then the following statements hold:*

1. $IC(1, \ell, \bar{q}) \neq \emptyset$.
2. $IC(\ell - 1, \ell, \bar{q}) \neq \emptyset$ if $\ell \geq 2$.
3. $IC(\ell, \ell, \bar{q}) \neq \emptyset$.

Proof As to the first claim, $C \in IC(1, \ell, \bar{q})$ if and only if any matrix whose rows are in one-to-one correspondence with the words of C has the property that, for each column, each of the $\bar{q}$ elements of the alphabet over which C is defined occurs exactly once in that column. As to the third claim, $C \in IC(\ell, \ell, \bar{q})$ if and only if C is equal to the ℓ-fold Cartesian product over its alphabet. As to the second claim, take the additive group of the ring $\mathbb{Z}/\bar{q}\mathbb{Z}$ of integers modulo $\bar{q}$ as the alphabet. Define the code C of length ℓ over this alphabet as the code consisting of all words $(g_1, \ldots, g_\ell) \in (\mathbb{Z}/\bar{q}\mathbb{Z})^\ell$ such that $g_1 = g_2 + \cdots + g_\ell$. Then $C \in IC(\ell - 1, \ell, \bar{q})$. ∎

It is a priori not clear for which other parameters $r, \ell, \bar{q}$ it holds that $IC(r, \ell, \bar{q}) \neq \emptyset$. The following straightforward reduction sometimes aids inductive proofs.

LEMMA 11.5 *Suppose that* $IC(r, \ell, \bar{q}) \neq \emptyset$. *Let k be an integer. Then*

1. *(Puncturing) If* $0 \leq k \leq \ell - r$, *then* $IC(r, \ell - k, \bar{q}) \neq \emptyset$.
2. *(Shortening) If* $0 \leq k \leq r - 1$, *then* $IC(r - k, \ell - k, \bar{q}) \neq \emptyset$.

Proof The claims are trivial if $k = 0$. So assume that $k > 0$. Let $C \in IC(r, \ell, \bar{q})$, and write $\mathcal{I}$ for an index set of $\mathcal{F}^\ell$. The first claim is immediate by puncturing: select a set $B \subset \mathcal{I}$ with $|B| = \ell - k$, and take the code $\pi_B(C) \subset \mathcal{F}^{|B|}$. Equivalently, remove all the $\overline{B}$-indexed coordinates. Since $1 \leq k \leq \ell - r$, the resulting code of length $\ell - k \geq r$ is $(r, \ell - k, \bar{q})$-interpolating. The second claim follows by shortening. Suppose that $k > 0$. Select a pair $(B, \mathbf{u})$ such that $B \subset \mathcal{I}$ with $|B| = k$ and $\mathbf{u} \in \mathcal{F}^k$. Take the subcode consisting of all $\mathbf{x} \in C$ with $\mathbf{x}_B = \mathbf{u}$, and remove all B-indexed coordinates. Since $1 \leq k \leq r - 1$, this code is $(r - k, \ell - k, \bar{q})$-interpolating. ∎

11.4 Secret Sharing from Interpolation Codes

Interpolation codes can be used to construct (t, n)-threshold secret-sharing schemes, as we now explain.[2]

11.4.1 The Scheme and Its Analysis

Suppose that C is a $(t + 1, n + 1, \bar{q})$-interpolation code such that $0 \leq t < n$. Write $\mathcal{F}$ for the alphabet, and take $\mathcal{I} = \{0, 1 \ldots, n\}$ as an index set for $\mathcal{F}^{n+1}$. Then C gives rise to a (t, n)-threshold secret-sharing scheme, where the secret can be chosen arbitrarily in $\mathcal{F}$ and where each share consists of a single element of $\mathcal{F}$ as follows: the code C as such is *public knowledge*.

1. Let $s \in \mathcal{F}$ be the secret.
2. Select $\mathbf{s} = (s_0, s_1, \ldots, s_n) \in C$ uniformly at random conditioned on $s_0 = s$.

---

[2] For the history of this idea, please see the references in Section 11.12.3.

3. The n shares are set to $(s_1, \ldots, s_n) \in \mathcal{F}^n$.

Here is an analysis of this scheme. Write $\mathcal{I}^* = \mathcal{I} \setminus \{0\}$. Consider, for each $B \subset \mathcal{I}$ with $B \neq \emptyset$, the map

$$\pi'_B : C \longrightarrow \mathcal{F}^{|B|}$$

$$\mathbf{s} \mapsto \mathbf{s}_B$$

If $|B| = t + 1$, then this map is bijective by definition of the interpolation property. If $|B| = t + 1$ and $0 \in B$, then, for each $s \in \mathcal{F}$, there are exactly $|\mathcal{F}|^t \geq 1$ words $\mathbf{s} \in C$ such that $s_0 = s$. Thus, the scheme is *well defined*, that is, given any $s \in \mathcal{F}$, there is indeed $\mathbf{s} \in C$ such that $s_0 = s$.

As for $(t+1)$-*reconstruction*, since $\mathbf{s}_B$ determines $\mathbf{s}$ uniquely for all sets $B \subset \mathcal{I}$ with $|B| = t + 1$, this holds in particular for all sets $B \subset \mathcal{I}^*$ with $|B| = t + 1$. Note that since $t < n$, there is at least one such set B, and hence the shares jointly determine the secret uniquely.

Finally, t-*privacy* can be argued as follows: the case $t = 0$ is not interesting because any single share in this scheme determines the secret uniquely. So assume that $t \geq 1$. Fix a pair (B, s) arbitrarily such that $B \subset \mathcal{I}^*$, $|B| = t$, and $s \in \mathcal{F}$. Consider the map

$$\pi'_{\{0\} \cup B} : C \longrightarrow \mathcal{F} \times \mathcal{F}^t$$

$$\mathbf{s} \mapsto (s_0, \mathbf{s}_B)$$

This is well defined because $t \geq 1$, and it is bijective, as argued earlier. Therefore, when fixing $s_0 \in \mathcal{F}$ arbitrarily, it induces a bijection between $\mathcal{F}^t$ and the subset of words $\mathbf{s} \in C$ with $s_0 = s$. It follows that $\mathbf{s}_B$ is distributed according to the uniform distribution on $\mathcal{F}^t$ if $s \in \mathcal{F}$ is fixed and if $\mathbf{s} \in C$ is chosen uniformly at random such that $s_0 = s$. Therefore, in particular, the distribution of $\mathbf{s}_B$ does not depend on the secret s. This independence means that any t shares jointly give no information on the secret, or rather, they do not decrease the uncertainty about the secret.

To be more precise, consider the following *Gedanken Experiment*, still assuming that $t \geq 1$. It is a "game" played between a challenger and a computationally unbounded party, the distinguisher.

1. The distinguisher selects a pair (B, s) such that $B \subset \mathcal{I}^*$, $|B| = t$, and $s \in \mathcal{F}$.
2. The distinguisher reveals their choice (B, s).
3. Secretly, the challenger proceeds as follows:

   - Select a challenge bit $b \in \{0, 1\}$ uniformly at random.
   - If $b = 0$, perform secret sharing. Select $\mathbf{s} \in C$ uniformly at random conditioned on $s_0 = s$, and set $\mathbf{u} = \mathbf{s}_B \in \mathcal{F}^t$.
   - If $b = 1$, refrain from secret sharing. Instead, select $\mathbf{u} \in \mathcal{F}^t$ uniformly at random.
   - Reveal $\mathbf{u}$ to the distinguisher.

4. The distinguisher selects a guessing bit $\widehat{b} \in \{0, 1\}$ and reveals it to the challenger.
5. Declare that the distinguisher wins if $\widehat{b} = b$. Otherwise, the distinguisher loses.

The distinguisher is not "psychic," so its best strategy is to select a guessing function

$$g : \mathcal{F}^t \longrightarrow \{0,1\}$$
$$\mathbf{u} \mapsto \widehat{b}$$

that optimizes their chances[3] given the initial choice (B,s). By the observation earlier, the distribution of $\mathbf{u}$ in the case $b = 0$ is the same distribution as in the case $b = 1$ (namely, the uniform distribution on $\mathcal{F}^t$). This implies that the guessing bit $\widehat{b}$ is distributed independently from the challenge bit b. Since b has a uniform distribution on $\{0,1\}$, the probability that $b = \widehat{b}$ is $\frac{1}{2}$, *no matter how the distinguisher plays*. So it is not possible to gain any advantage over "blind random guessing."

This means that the distinguisher cannot distinguish a "world" where t shares "arising from a correct secret sharing" were handed from a "world" where just "random garbage" was handed. Hence, we may say that the *a posteriori uncertainty* that a "t-bounded adversary" has about the secret is equal to the *a priori uncertainty* the adversary has about the secret *before* any secret sharing took place at all.

At this point we will not formally summarize our findings about secret sharing in a theorem. This will be done later on, after we have given a general and formal definition of secret sharing.

Finally, note that Lemma 11.4 in combination with the preceding construction gives an $(n-1,n)$-threshold secret-sharing scheme over an alphabet of cardinality $\bar{q}$ whenever $n,\bar{q} \geq 2$. Note that it also gives an (uninteresting) $(0,n)$-threshold secret-sharing scheme. This formalizes the schemes sketched in Section 11.1. More interesting schemes will follow after a closer look into the existence of interpolation codes.

11.4.2 A Variation: Multi-Secret Sharing

When given a $(t+k,n+k,\bar{q})$-interpolation code where n,t,k are integers such that $t \geq 0$, $k \geq 1$, and $t+k \leq n$, there is an alternative scheme that offers an interesting tradeoff.[4] Write $\mathcal{F}$ for the alphabet. Then, instead of having secrets in $\mathcal{F}$, the secrets can be taken in $\mathcal{F}^k$ instead. This is done by designating k special indices, say, $0,\ldots,k-1$, and selecting a random word such that the vector defined by those k coordinates equals the secret. This is well defined for similar reasons as earlier. This increases the "capacity" of the scheme in that the amount of data that can be secret shared in a single execution of the scheme has increased substantially while at the same time each of the shares still sits in $\mathcal{F}$.

However, there are also two drawbacks to this variation. First, the maximum number of players that can be handled in a scheme based on a given code decreases by $k-1$. Second, although there is t-privacy, there will be $(t+k)$-reconstruction rather than $(t+1)$-reconstruction. Hence, there is a gap of k between privacy and reconstruction. In particular, if $k > 1$, it is no longer a threshold scheme.

---

[3] Since there is no bound on the computational resources of the adversary, the adversary's best strategy here is deterministic. Indeed, for any probabilistic strategy such an adversary can simply determine in advance which particular sequence of coin flips in this strategy gives the highest chance of success.

[4] The construction we present is actually a special case of a more general construction for ramp schemes developed in references 23, 120, and 142 during the early 1980s. In Franklin and Yung [93], this idea was exploited as part of a powerful application to secure MPC with low amortized complexity.

11.5 Existence of Interpolation Codes

We shall investigate the existence of interpolation codes more thoroughly. So far we have only discussed the existence of interpolation codes in three extreme (and trivial) cases $r \in \{1, \ell - 1, \ell\}$ in Lemma 11.4 and two corresponding (t, n)-threshold secret-sharing schemes with $t = 0$ (from the case $r = 1$) or $t = n - 1$ (from the case $r = \ell - 1$). From the case $r = \ell$, no threshold secret-sharing scheme was derived.

We first construct interpolation codes for the whole range of values of r (and not just the extremes) under some conditions on the alphabet. These codes are obtained as *evaluation codes*, and their analysis is based on the classical Lagrange Interpolation Theorem, given later in a somewhat more modern form.

By combining these interpolation codes with the threshold secret-sharing scheme from Section 11.4, we will obtain Shamir's (t, n)-threshold secret-sharing scheme, which handles the full range $0 \leq t < n$.

11.5.1 Lagrange's Interpolation Theorem

DEFINITION 11.6 *Let $m \geq 0$ be an integer. Then $K[X]_{\leq m}$ denotes the K-vector space consisting of the polynomials $f(X) \in K[X]$ with $\deg(f) \leq m$.*[5]

THEOREM 11.7 (LAGRANGE) *Let $m \geq 1$ be an integer. Suppose that $\alpha_1, \ldots, \alpha_m \in K$ are pairwise distinct. Then the evaluation map*

$$\mathcal{E} : K[X]_{\leq m-1} \longrightarrow K^m$$

$$f(X) \mapsto (f(\alpha_1), \ldots, f(\alpha_m))$$

is an isomorphism of K-vector spaces.

A more classical formulation would state that if $(\alpha_1, y_1), \ldots, (\alpha_m, y_m)$ are arbitrary points in the plane K^2 such that $\alpha_1, \ldots, \alpha_m$ are pairwise distinct, then there exists a unique polynomial $f(X) \in K[X]$ such that $\deg(f) \leq m - 1$ and "the graph of $f(X) = Y$ passes through these m points," that is, $f(\alpha_i) = y_i$ for $i = 1, \ldots, m$.

Proof It is clear that $\mathcal{E}$ is a morphism of K-vector spaces. To show that the morphism $\mathcal{E}$ is an isomorphism, we show that it is surjective and injective. If $m = 1$, then $\mathcal{E}$ is the identity map: for each $y_1 \in K$, the unique polynomial f of degree at most 0 such that $\mathcal{E}(f) = y_1$ is the constant polynomial $f(X) \equiv y_1$.

Suppose that $m > 1$. Because the dimension of the K-vector space on the left equals that of the one on the right (namely, each equals m), by linear algebra, it suffices to prove that the morphism $\mathcal{E}$ is injective. If $\mathcal{E}(f) = \mathbf{0}$, then $f(X)$ has m distinct zeros, whereas its degree is at most $m - 1$. Because the number of zeros of a polynomial (over a field) of nonnegative degree is at most its degree, it follows that the polynomial identity $f(X) = 0$ holds. Hence, $\mathcal{E}$ is injective. This concludes the proof.

---

[5] Recall that if $f(X) \equiv c$, where $c \in K$, then $\deg(f) = 0$ if $c \neq 0$ and $\deg(f) = -\infty$ if $c = 0$.

For later use, it is convenient to construct the inverse of $\mathcal{E}$ explicitly. If $m = 1$, then $\mathcal{E}^{-1}$ is the identity map. Suppose that $m > 1$. For $i = 1, \ldots, m$, define the polynomial

$$\delta_i(X) = \prod_{1 \leq k \leq m, k \neq i} \frac{X - \alpha_k}{\alpha_i - \alpha_k} \in K[X]$$

Note that this is well defined because $\alpha_i - \alpha_k \neq 0$ if $i \neq k$. It is verified immediately that the polynomial $\delta_i(X)$ satisfies the following properties ($i = 1, \ldots, m$):

1. $\deg(\delta_i) = m - 1$.
2. $\delta_i(\alpha_i) = 1$.
3. $\delta_i(\alpha_j) = 0$ if $1 \leq j \leq m$ and $j \neq i$.

We claim that the inverse $\mathcal{E}^{-1}$ is given by

$$\mathcal{E}^{-1} : K^m \longrightarrow K[X]_{\leq m-1}$$

$$(y_1, \ldots, y_m) \mapsto \sum_{i=1}^{m} y_i \cdot \delta_i(X)$$

This is well defined because the polynomial on the right has degree at most $m - 1$.

To verify this claim, let $f(X) \in K[X]_{\leq m-1}$. Then

$$f(X) = \sum_{i=1}^{m} y_i \cdot \delta_i(X) \in K[X]$$

where

$$y_1 := f(\alpha_1), \ldots, y_m := f(\alpha_m)$$

Indeed, for $j = 1, \ldots, m$, we have

$$f(\alpha_j) = \sum_{i=1}^{m} y_i \cdot \delta_i(\alpha_j) = y_j \cdot 1 + \sum_{i \neq j} y_i \cdot 0 = y_j. \qquad \blacksquare$$

We will give alternative proofs in Section 11.6. In Section 11.13, we will generalize this result to commutative rings.

Notation being as in Theorem 11.7 and its proof, the following corollary is helpful later on:

COROLLARY 11.8 *Let $a \in K$. Then there exists a unique K-linear form $\phi : K^m \to K$ such that for all $f(X) \in K[X]_{m-1}$ it holds that*

$$\phi(f(\alpha_1), \ldots, f(\alpha_m)) = f(a)$$

Proof The claim is obvious if $m = 1$. Suppose that $m > 1$. If each of ϕ, ϕ' satisfies the requirement, then $\phi - \phi'$ is identically 0 on K^m because the image of $\mathcal{E}$ is equal to K^m. Therefore, ϕ, ϕ' are identical as K-linear forms. This settles uniqueness. As to existence, define ϕ as follows: for each $\mathbf{y} \in K^m$, $a \in K$, define

$$\phi(\mathbf{y}) := f(a)$$

where

$$f = \mathcal{E}^{-1}(\mathbf{y})$$

This is well defined because $\mathcal{E}$ is invertible. Moreover, this is a K-linear form that satisfies the requirement.

The coefficients of this form can be given explicitly as follows.

$$\phi : K^m \longrightarrow K$$

$$(Y_1, \ldots, Y_m) \mapsto \sum_{i=1}^{m} \delta_i(a) \cdot Y_i$$

with $\delta_i(X) \in K[X]$ $(i = 1, \ldots, m)$ as defined in the proof of Theorem 11.7. ∎

DEFINITION 11.9 (LINEAR CODE) *An $\mathbb{F}_q$-linear code of length $\ell \geq 1$ is a subspace C of the $\mathbb{F}_q$-vector space $\mathbb{F}_q^\ell$. Its dimension $\dim(C)$ is its dimension as a subspace.*

Note that $0 \in C$, so $C \neq \emptyset$.

An immediate consequence of Lagrange's Interpolation Theorem for the existence of (linear) interpolation codes is the following.

THEOREM 11.10 *Let q be a prime power. Suppose that r, ℓ are integers such that $1 \leq r \leq \ell \leq q$. Then there exists an $\mathbb{F}_q$-linear (r, ℓ, q)-interpolation code.*

Proof Select pairwise distinct elements $\alpha_1, \ldots, \alpha_\ell \in \mathbb{F}_q$. This is possible because $\ell \leq q$. Consider the polynomial evaluation code

$$C = \{(f(\alpha_1), \ldots, f(\alpha_\ell)) \mid f(X) \in \mathbb{F}_q[X], \deg(f) \leq r - 1\} \subset \mathbb{F}_q^\ell$$

This code is $\mathbb{F}_q$-linear because the evaluation map is a morphism of vector spaces and C is its image. Fix $\mathcal{I} = \{1, \ldots, \ell\}$ as the index set. Select an arbitrary pair $(B, \mathbf{v})$ with

$$B \subset \{1, \ldots, \ell\}, \quad |B| = r, \quad \text{and} \quad \mathbf{v} = (v_i)_{i \in B} \in \mathbb{F}_q^r$$

This is possible because $r \leq \ell$. By Theorem 11.7, there exists a unique polynomial $g(X) \in \mathbb{F}_q[X]$ such that

$$\deg(g) \leq r - 1 \quad \text{and} \quad g(\alpha_i) = v_i$$

for all $i \in B$. Hence, there is a unique word $\mathbf{x} \in C$ such that $\mathbf{x}_B = \mathbf{v}$, namely,

$$\mathbf{x} = (g(\alpha_1), \ldots, g(\alpha_\ell))$$

∎

In Section 11.7 we will relax the condition to $1 \leq r \leq \ell \leq q + 1$ by exploiting an extra evaluation point that was not visible so far, namely "the point at infinity."

11.5.2 Shamir's Scheme

Shamir's Threshold Secret-Sharing Scheme is obtained by instantiating the threshold secret-sharing scheme based on interpolation codes with the codes from Theorem 11.10. Concretely, Shamir's (t, n)-threshold scheme is as follows: suppose that $q > n$. Let t, n be integers with $0 \leq t < n$. Let $\alpha_1, \ldots, \alpha_n \in \mathbb{F}_q$ be pairwise distinct and nonzero. This makes sense because $q > n$. Note: $t, n, q, \alpha_1, \ldots, \alpha_n$ are *public data*.

- Let $s \in \mathbb{F}_q$ be the secret.
- Select a polynomial $f(X) \in \mathbb{F}_q[X]$ uniformly at random, conditioned on

1. $\deg(f) \leq t$.
2. $f(0) = s$.

Note that this is the same as selecting a coefficient vector

$$(a_0, a_1, \ldots, a_t) \in \mathbb{F}_q^{t+1}$$

uniformly at random, conditioned on $a_0 = s$, and setting

$$f(X) = s + a_1 X + \ldots + a_t X^t \in \mathbb{F}_q[X]$$

- The n shares in the secret s are

$$s_1 = f(\alpha_1) \in \mathbb{F}_q, \ldots, s_n = f(\alpha_n) \in \mathbb{F}_q$$

This scheme satisfies t-privacy and $(t+1)$-reconstruction with $t + 1 \leq n$.

REMARK 11.11 Using Corollary 11.8 and its proof, it follows how the secret s can be reconstructed from any $t + 1$ shares s_i. Indeed, for each set $B \subset \{1, \ldots, n\}$ with $|B| = t + 1$, there exists a linear form ϕ^B such that $\phi^B((s_i)_{i \in B})$ is equal to the secret with certainty. From the proof of Corollary 11.8, it follows that

$$s = \phi^B((s_i)_{i \in B}) = \sum_{i \in B} \delta_{i,B} \cdot s_i$$

where, for each $i \in B$,

$$\delta_{i,B} = \prod_{j \in B, j \neq i} \frac{-\alpha_j}{\alpha_i - \alpha_j} \in \mathbb{F}_q$$

11.6 Alternative Proofs of Lagrange's Theorem

Several key ideas in basic secret sharing are derived from Lagrange's Interpolation Theorem, variations thereof (e.g., over number fields), or more advanced generalizations of it (such as implied by the Riemann-Roch Theorem for algebraic function fields). Therefore, it makes sense to present alternative proofs of Lagrange's Interpolation Theorem in its most basic form.

11.6.1 Proof by Chinese Remainder Theorem

Lagrange's Interpolation Theorem also can be viewed as a special case of the Chinese Remainder Theorem (CRT). We verify this now.

For the statement of the CRT, please refer to Theorem 10.5. We start by including a proof sketch of the CRT for comparison with our first proof of the Lagrange Interpolation Theorem. Let A be a commutative ring. By definition, ideals I, J in A are co-prime if $I + J = A$. Restating the definition, ideals I, J of A are coprime if and only if there is $(x, y) \in I \times J$ such that $x + y = 1$, or equivalently, there is $y \in A$ such that $y \equiv 1 \mod I$ and $y \equiv 0 \mod J$. This extends trivially to $m \geq 2$ pairwise coprime ideals. With this reformulation in mind, under the hypothesis of the CRT, it is straightforward to craft $x_1, \ldots, x_m \in A$ such that for each x_j ($j = 1, \ldots, m$) it holds that $x_j \equiv 1 \bmod I_j$ and $x_j \equiv 0 \bmod I_k$ if $k \neq j$.[6]

If we consider the map defined by the assignment $a \mapsto (a \bmod I_1, \ldots, a \bmod I_m)$, then we see at once by the preceding discussion that it is surjective. We also see at once that its kernel equals $I_1 \cap \cdots \cap I_m$. We claim that this kernel is in fact equal to $I_1 \cdots I_m$. We verify this in the case $m = 2$; the general case follows similarly. First, the inclusion $IJ \subset I \cap J$ always holds. In the other direction, let $(x, y) \in I \times J$ be such that $x + y = 1$. This makes sense because I, J are pairwise coprime. Let $z \in I \cap J$. Then $xz + yz = z$, and we see that $z \in IJ$. This completes the proof sketch. In hindsight, the inverse of the isomorphism constructed is the map

$$\prod_{j=1}^{m} A/I_j \longrightarrow A / \prod_{j=1}^{m} I_j$$

$$(\bar{y}_1, \ldots, \bar{y}_m) \mapsto \bar{x}_1 \bar{y}_1 + \cdots + \bar{x}_m \bar{y}_m$$

where the x_is are the elements crafted earlier.

Now we apply the CRT to Lagrange Interpolation Theorem. Suppose that

$$\alpha_1, \ldots, \alpha_m \in K$$

are pairwise distinct ($m > 1$) Set

$$A = K[X]$$

and

$$I_1 = (X - \alpha_1) \cdot K[X], \ldots, I_m = (X - \alpha_m) \cdot K[X]$$

Note that these ideals are pairwise coprime. Indeed, $I_i + I_j$ contains the unit $\alpha_j - \alpha_i \in K \setminus \{0\}$ if $i \neq j$ because $(X - \alpha_i) - (X - \alpha_j) = \alpha_j - \alpha_i \neq 0$.

By the CRT,

$$K[X] / \prod_{i=1}^{m} (X - \alpha_i) \simeq K[X]/(X - \alpha_1) \times \cdots \times K[X]/(X - \alpha_m)$$

The residue classes on the left-hand side are represented exactly by the polynomials $f(X) \in K[X]$ of degree at most $m - 1$ because all is taken modulo the polynomial $\prod_{i=1}^{m} (X - \alpha_i)$ (which is of degree m).

The isomorphism ψ given by the CRT sends a polynomial f of degree at most $m - 1$ to

$$(f(X) \bmod (X - \alpha_1), \ldots, f(X) \bmod (X - \alpha_m))$$

But because α_j is a zero of the polynomial $f(X) - f(\alpha_j)$, it holds that $X - \alpha_j$ divides $f(X) - f(\alpha_j)$ and hence that

$$f(\alpha_j) \equiv f(X) \pmod{X - \alpha_j}$$

for $j = 1, \ldots, m$. Therefore, ψ sends a polynomial f of degree at most $m - 1$ to

$$(f(\alpha_1), \ldots, f(\alpha_m))$$

This concludes the proof.

---

[6] For each k, j with $k \neq j$, let x_{jk} be such that $x_{jk} \equiv 1 \bmod I_j$ and $x_{jk} \equiv 0 \bmod I_k$. Then, for each j, the element $x_j = \prod_{k \neq j} x_{jk}$ fits the bill.

Note that the preceding discussion on the inverse of the CRT isomorphism also puts the polynomials $\delta_i(X)$ from the proof of Theorem 10.5 or, more precisely, the inverse evaluation map $\mathcal{E}^{-1}$ into the perspective of the CRT; that is, when crafting the x_is from the preceding discussion in the specific setting of Lagrange interpolation, one obtains the $\delta_i(X)$s.

11.6.2 Proof by Vandermonde Determinant

Assume that $m > 1$. Theorem 11.7 also can be proved directly with linear algebra. Consider the square matrix M defined over K, with the vector $(1, \alpha_i, \alpha_i^2, \ldots, \alpha_i^{m-1})$ as its ith row, $1 \leq i \leq m$, a Vandermonde matrix. It is well known from algebra that

$$\det(M) = \prod_{1 \leq i < j \leq m} (\alpha_j - \alpha_i)$$

This identity is easily verified by "expanding the determinant of the matrix along the left most column" and by using induction.

Since the α_is are distinct by assumption, we have

$$\det(M) \neq 0$$

A moment's reflection reveals that

$$\mathcal{E}(f) = \mathbf{y} \in K^m$$

if and only if

$$M\mathbf{a} = \mathbf{y}$$

where

$$\mathbf{a} = (a_0, \ldots, a_{m-1})^T \in K^m$$

such that

$$f(X) = a_0 + a_1 X + \cdots + a_{m-1} X^{m-1} \in K[X]$$

Indeed, for $i = 1, \ldots, m$, the ith equation in the linear system is of the form

$$a_0 + a_1 \alpha_i + \ldots + a_{m-1} \alpha_i^{m-1} = y_i$$

Since $\det(M) \neq 0$, the result follows.

11.7 Using the Point at Infinity

There is one "extra point of evaluation" that can be added to Theorem 11.7. This is explained now.

DEFINITION 11.12 *Let $m \geq 1$ be an integer. For $f(X) \in K[X]$, define*

$$f(\infty_m) = a_{m-1}$$

where $a_{m-1} \in K$ is the coefficient of X^{m-1} in $f(X)$. Here ∞_m is to be treated as a formal symbol.

THEOREM 11.13 *Let $m \geq 1$ be an integer. Suppose that $\alpha_1, \ldots, \alpha_m \in K \cup \{\infty_m\}$ are pairwise distinct. Then the map*

$$\mathcal{E}' : K[X]_{\leq m-1} \longrightarrow K^m$$

$$f \mapsto (f(\alpha_1), \ldots, f(\alpha_m))$$

is an isomorphism of K-vector spaces.

Proof   If $\alpha_1, \ldots, \alpha_m \in K$, then the claim follows by Theorem 11.7. So assume, without loss of generality, that $\alpha_m = \infty_m$. It is clear that $\mathcal{E}'$ is a morphism of K-vector spaces. To show that it is an isomorphism, we show that it is surjective and injective. If $m = 1$, then $\mathcal{E}'$ is the identity map.

Suppose that $m > 1$. Since the dimension of the K-vector space on the left equals that of the one on the right (namely, each equals m), by linear algebra, it suffices to prove that the morphism $\mathcal{E}'$ is injective. Suppose that $\mathcal{E}'(f) = \mathbf{0}$. Since

$$f(\infty_m) = 0$$

it holds that the degree of $f(X)$ is at most $m - 2$. However, $f(X)$ has $m - 1$ zeros because

$$f(\alpha_1) = \cdots = f(\alpha_{m-1}) = 0$$

Therefore, $f(X)$ is identical to the zero-polynomial.

An explicit description of the inverse of $\mathcal{E}'$ can be easily extracted from the proof of Theorem 11.7. If $m = 1$, this is trivial. Suppose that $m > 1$. Consider the morphism

$$\mathcal{E} : K[X]_{\leq m-2} \longrightarrow K^{m-1}$$

$$g(X) \mapsto (g(\alpha_1), \ldots, g(\alpha_{m-1}))$$

and its inverse $\mathcal{E}^{-1}$. For each $(y_1, \ldots, y_m) \in K^m$, simply define

$$(g_0, \ldots, g_{m-2}) := \mathcal{E}^{-1}(y_1 - y_m \alpha_1^{m-1}, \ldots, y_{m-1} - y_m \alpha_{m-1}^{m-1})$$

Then

$$f(X) = g_0 + \cdots + g_{m-2} X^{m-2} + y_m X^{m-1}$$

is the $\mathcal{E}'$-inverse of $(y_1, \ldots, y_m)$.   ■

Using algebraic geometry (see Section 12.7.5), it can be justified in what way exactly $f(\infty_m)$ is in fact "an evaluation at the point at infinity."

An immediate consequence of this theorem is that we get the following relaxation for the conditions of Theorem 11.10.

THEOREM 11.14 *Let q be a prime power. Suppose that r, ℓ are integers such that $1 \leq r \leq \ell \leq q + 1$. Then there exists an $\mathbb{F}_q$-linear (r, ℓ, q)-interpolation code.*

With Theorem 11.13 in hand, the proof of the preceding theorem is essentially the same as that of Theorem 11.10.

11.8 Secret Recovery in the Presence of Corruptions

Shamir's (t,n)-threshold secret-sharing scheme is secure against a passive t-bounded adversary: t shares give no information about the secret, whereas $t+1$ shares determine it uniquely. We now consider an active t-bounded adversary, that is, one that gets to select a set B with $|B| = t > 0$, to inspect the shares $(s_i)_{i \in B}$ and to replace the original t shares $(s_i)_{i \in B}$ by corrupted shares $(\tilde{s}_i)_{i \in B} \neq (s_i)_{i \in B}$. Note that there is still t-privacy with respect to such an adversary.

In Chapter 5 we explained that for some values of n and t it is in principle possible to recover the original polynomial (and hence the secret) from the modified shares. Here we shall see that one can even do so efficiently.

11.8.1 Definitions and Basic Observations

Let $\mathcal{F}$ be a set with $|\mathcal{F}| \geq 2$, and let $\ell \geq 1$ be an integer. Fix some index set $\mathcal{I}$ for $\mathcal{F}^\ell$.

DEFINITION 11.15 (HAMMING DISTANCE) *Let* $\mathbf{x}, \mathbf{y} \in \mathcal{F}^\ell$. *The Hamming distance between* $\mathbf{x}$ *and* $\mathbf{y}$ *is defined as*

$$d_H(\mathbf{x}, \mathbf{y}) = |\{j \in \mathcal{I} \, : \, x_j \neq y_j\}|$$

If $\mathcal{F}$ *is a field, the Hamming weight of* $\mathbf{x} \in \mathcal{F}^\ell$ *is defined as*

$$w_H(\mathbf{x}) = |\{j \in \mathcal{I} \, : \, x_j \neq 0\}|$$

DEFINITION 11.16 (MINIMUM DISTANCE) *Let* $C \subset \mathcal{F}^\ell$ *be a code with* $|C| > 1$. *Its minimum distance is defined as*

$$d_{\min}(C) = \min_{\mathbf{x}, \mathbf{y} \in C : \mathbf{x} \neq \mathbf{y}} d_H(\mathbf{x}, \mathbf{y})$$

LEMMA 11.17 (MINIMUM DISTANCE OF A LINEAR CODE) *Suppose that* $C \subset \mathbb{F}_q^\ell$ *is an* $\mathbb{F}_q$-*linear code of positive dimension. Then*

$$d_{\min}(C) = \min_{\mathbf{x} \in C : \mathbf{x} \neq \mathbf{0}} w_H(\mathbf{x})$$

Proof It is easy to see that

$$d_H(\mathbf{x}, \mathbf{y}) = w_H(\mathbf{x} - \mathbf{y})$$

for all $\mathbf{x}, \mathbf{y} \in \mathbb{F}_q^\ell$. Since $\mathbf{x} - \mathbf{y} \in C$ whenever $\mathbf{x}, \mathbf{y} \in C$, the claim follows. ∎

LEMMA 11.18 (METRIC) *Hamming distance gives a metric on* $\mathcal{F}^\ell$. *In particular, it satisfies the triangle inequality; that is,*

$$d_H(\mathbf{x}, \mathbf{z}) \leq d_H(\mathbf{x}, \mathbf{y}) + d_H(\mathbf{y}, \mathbf{z})$$

for all $\mathbf{x}, \mathbf{y}, \mathbf{z} \in \mathcal{F}^\ell$.

Proof It is immediate that for all $\mathbf{x}, \mathbf{y} \in \mathcal{F}^\ell$, it holds that $d_H(\mathbf{x}, \mathbf{y}) \in \mathbb{R}$, $d_H(\mathbf{x}, \mathbf{y}) \geq 0$, $d_H(\mathbf{x}, \mathbf{y}) = d_H(\mathbf{y}, \mathbf{x})$, and $d_H(\mathbf{x}, \mathbf{y}) = 0$ if and only if $\mathbf{x} = \mathbf{y}$. Thus it remains to verify that the triangle inequality holds. The least sufficient number of coordinate modifications to pass from $\mathbf{x}$ to $\mathbf{z}$ directly equals $d_H(\mathbf{x}, \mathbf{z})$. First passing from $\mathbf{x}$ to $\mathbf{y}$ and then on to $\mathbf{z}$ requires in total $d_H(\mathbf{x}, \mathbf{y}) + d_H(\mathbf{y}, \mathbf{z})$ modifications. The claim follows. ∎

DEFINITION 11.19 (HAMMING SPHERE) *Let* $\mathbf{x} \in \mathcal{F}^\ell$, *and let* ρ *be a nonnegative real number. The Hamming sphere* $B(\mathbf{x}; \rho)$ *of radius* ρ *centered at* x *is the set*

$$B(\mathbf{x}; \rho) = \{\mathbf{x}' \in \mathcal{F}^\ell \; : \; d_{\mathrm{H}}(\mathbf{x}, \mathbf{x}') \leq \rho\} \subset \mathcal{F}^\ell$$

LEMMA 11.20 *Let* $C \subset \mathcal{F}^\ell$ *be a code with* $|C| > 1$. *Set*

$$\rho = \left\lfloor \frac{d_{\min}(C) - 1}{2} \right\rfloor$$

Then, for any $\mathbf{x}, \mathbf{x}' \in C$ *with* $\mathbf{x} \neq \mathbf{x}'$, *it holds that*

$$B(\mathbf{x}; \rho) \cap B(\mathbf{x}'; \rho) = \emptyset$$

Proof Suppose that there is $\mathbf{x}'' \in \mathcal{F}^\ell$ such that $\mathbf{x}'' \in B(\mathbf{x}; \rho) \cap B(\mathbf{x}'; \rho)$. Then

$$d_{\mathrm{H}}(\mathbf{x}, \mathbf{x}'') \leq \rho \quad \text{and} \quad d_{\mathrm{H}}(\mathbf{x}'', \mathbf{x}') \leq \rho$$

Hence, by the triangle inequality,

$$d_{\mathrm{H}}(\mathbf{x}, \mathbf{x}') \leq d_{\mathrm{H}}(\mathbf{x}, \mathbf{x}'') + d_{\mathrm{H}}(\mathbf{x}'', \mathbf{x}') \leq 2 \cdot \rho \leq d_{\min}(C) - 1 < d_{\min}(C)$$

a contradiction.   ∎

An immediate consequence of this lemma is the following: let an arbitrary vector $\mathbf{x} \in C$ be given, and suppose that $\mathbf{x}$ is replaced by some $\tilde{\mathbf{x}} \in \mathcal{F}^\ell$ with $d_{\mathrm{H}}(\mathbf{x}, \tilde{\mathbf{x}}) \leq \rho$: at most ρ *corruptions* have been introduced. Then, despite these corruptions, the vector $\tilde{\mathbf{x}}$ determines $\mathbf{x}$ uniquely: the vector $\mathbf{x}$ is the unique codeword that is closest to $\tilde{\mathbf{x}}$.[7] Note that this argument may fail if $\rho' > \rho$ corruptions are introduced.[8]

LEMMA 11.21 *Suppose that* $C \subset \mathcal{F}^\ell$ *is a* $(t+1, \ell, \bar{q})$*-interpolation code. Then* $d_{\min}(C) = \ell - t$.

Proof If $\mathbf{x}, \mathbf{y} \in C$ and $\mathbf{x} \neq \mathbf{y}$, then $\mathbf{x}, \mathbf{y} \in C$ can agree in at most t coordinates; otherwise, $\mathbf{x} = \mathbf{y}$ by the $(t+1)$-interpolation property. Hence, $d_{\min}(C) \geq \ell - t$. Fix an arbitrary $\mathbf{v} \in \mathcal{F}^t$ and an arbitrary set $B \subset \mathcal{I}$ such that $|B| = t$. Then, by the $(t+1)$-interpolation property, there are exactly $|\mathcal{F}| \geq 2$ vectors $\mathbf{x} \in C$ such that $\mathbf{x}_B = \mathbf{v}$. Any two distinct such words $\mathbf{x}, \mathbf{y} \in C$ satisfy $d_{\mathrm{H}}(\mathbf{x}, \mathbf{y}) \leq \ell - t$. The claim follows.   ∎

Now consider Shamir's (t, n)-threshold secret-sharing scheme $(t \geq 1)$. Write C for the underlying $(t+1, n+1, q)$-interpolation code and $C' \subset \mathcal{F}^{\ell-1}$ for "the part of C that corresponds to the shares," that is, C but without its 0th coordinate. Note that C' is a $(t+1, n, q)$-interpolation code and that there is an obvious bijection between C and C'. We have $d_{\min}(C') = n - t$. By the preceding considerations, $\lfloor (n-t-1)/2 \rfloor$ corruptions can be tolerated. Therefore, in order to tolerate a t-bounded adversary, it is a *sufficient* condition that

$$t \leq \left\lfloor \frac{n - t - 1}{2} \right\rfloor$$

---

[7] Of course, this observation is at the heart of the theory of error-correcting codes; see, for example, McWilliams and Sloane [143].

[8] Yet, if the number of corruptions is at most $d_{\min}(C) - 1$, then at least it can be *detected* that there are corruptions because such a number of corruptions will not transform any codeword to some other codeword.

which is equivalent to

$$t < \frac{n}{3}$$

It is easy to show that $t < n/3$ is also a *necessary* condition. Toward a contradiction, assume that t corruptions can be tolerated if $t \geq n/3$. Select two words $\mathbf{x}, \mathbf{y}$ in C such that $x_0 \neq y_0$ and such that they are at distance exactly $n - t + 1$ from one another. Let $\mathbf{x}', \mathbf{y}'$ be the corresponding words in C'. These are at the smallest possible distance $n - t$ from one another. Since $t \geq n/3$, there is

$$\mathbf{z}' \in B(\mathbf{x}', t) \cap B(\mathbf{y}', t)$$

Such $\mathbf{z}'$ gives rise to ambiguity because it could have arisen from "$\mathbf{x}'$ plus $\leq t$ corruptions" (in which case the secret would have been x_0), or it could have arisen from "$\mathbf{y}'$ plus $\leq t$ corruptions" (in which case the secret would have been $y_0 \neq x_0$).

11.8.2 The Welch/Berlekamp Algorithm

In the case of the Shamir's (t, n)-threshold secret-sharing scheme, the secret can be reconstructed *efficiently* in the presence of an active t-bounded adversary if $t < n/3$. Although the problem as such is of nonlinear nature, it can be linearized by means of a clever trick. The method we present is due to Welch and Berlekamp from the 1970s. In the late 1990s, Sudan [175] and Guruswami and Sudan [103] showed that a generalization of the mathematical idea behind this algorithm leads to a significantly better algorithm for the so-called list-decoding problem introduced by Elias in the 1950s.[9] Our presentation is based on Sudan.

Consider Shamir's secret-sharing scheme as presented in Section 11.5.2. Write $K = \mathbb{F}_q$. Assume that $t < n/3$. Consider a vector of shares for a secret $s \in K$

$$\mathbf{s}_f^* = (s_1, \ldots, s_n) = (f(\alpha_1), \ldots, f(\alpha_n)) \in K^n$$

where $f(X) \in K[X]_{\leq t}$. Let $\mathbf{e} \in K^n$ be an "error vector" subject to

$$w_H(\mathbf{e}) \leq t$$

Define

$$\tilde{\mathbf{s}}^* = \mathbf{s}_f^* + \mathbf{e} = (\tilde{s}_1, \ldots, \tilde{s}_n)$$

the corrupted share vector.

The method "interpolates" the n points $(\alpha_i, \tilde{s}_i)$ by a bivariate polynomial $Q(X, Y) \in K[X, Y]$ of a special form. From a computational point of view, this comes down to solving a system of linear equations. The polynomial $f(X)$ is extracted from $Q(X, Y)$ in a very simple way. Concretely, the method works as follows: let $Q(X, Y) \in K[X, Y]$ be any polynomial such that

1. $Q(\alpha_i, \tilde{s}_i) = 0$, for $i = 1, \ldots, n$.
2. $Q(X, Y) = f_0(X) - f_1(X) \cdot Y$, where

---

[9] For subsequent results in this area, please refer, for example, to Guruswami and Xing [104] and the references therein.

- $f_0(X), f_1(X) \in K[X]$,
- $f_1(0) = 1$,
- $\deg f_0(X) \leq 2t$, and
- $\deg f_1(X) \leq t$.

We will show the following:

- There exists at least one solution $Q(X, Y)$ satisfying these constraints.
- *Some* solution can be found by solving a system of linear equations.
- For *all* possible solutions $Q(X, Y)$ defined by some $f_0(X), f_1(X)$, it holds that

$$f(X) = \frac{f_0(X)}{f_1(X)}$$

First, note that the conditions on $Q(X, Y)$ can be stated equivalently in terms of a system of linear equations by taking its coefficients as the variables. To show that there exists at least one solution $Q(X, Y)$, let $B \subset \{1, \ldots, n\}$ be the set of indices i with $e_i \neq 0$.

If $B = \emptyset$, then

$$Q(X, Y) = f(X) - 1 \cdot Y$$

is a solution. Now suppose that $B \neq \emptyset$. Define

$$k(X) = \prod_{i \in B} \frac{(X - \alpha_i)}{-\alpha_i}$$

Note that

1. $k(X) \in K[X]$.
2. $k(0) = 1$.
3. $\deg k(X) \leq t$.
4. $k(\alpha_i) = 0$ if $i \in B$.

Now observe that

$$Q(X, Y) = k(X) \cdot f(X) - k(X) \cdot Y$$

is a solution. The only condition left to be verified is that it interpolates as required. If $i \in B$, then

$$Q(\alpha_i, \tilde{s}_i) = k(\alpha_i) \cdot f(\alpha_i) - k(\alpha_i) \cdot \tilde{s}_i = 0 \cdot s_i - 0 \cdot \tilde{s}_i = 0$$

However, if $i \notin B$, then

$$Q(\alpha_i, \tilde{s}_i) = k(\alpha_i) \cdot f(\alpha_i) - k(\alpha_i) \cdot \tilde{s}_i = k(\alpha_i) \cdot s_i - k(\alpha_i) \cdot s_i = 0$$

where we have used that $(\alpha_i, s_i) = (\alpha_i, \tilde{s}_i)$ if $i \notin B$.

It is left to show that for each solution $Q(X, Y)$ given by some $f_0(X), f_1(X)$ it holds that $f(X) = f_0(X)/f_1(X)$. By the fact that $f_1(0) = 1$, it follows that $f_1(X) \not\equiv 0$. Therefore, this fraction is well defined. It is left to show it equals $f(X)$, as desired. To this end, define

$$Q'(X) = Q(X, f(X)) \in K[X]$$

and note that

$$\deg Q'(X) \leq 2t$$

For $i \notin B$, it holds that

$$Q'(\alpha_i) = Q(\alpha_i, f(\alpha_i)) = Q(\alpha_i, s_i) = Q(\alpha_i, \tilde{s}_i) = 0$$

Therefore, $Q'(X)$ has at least $n - |B|$ roots. Since $t < n/3$ and $|B| \leq t$, it holds that

$$n - |B| \geq n - t > 2t$$

We conclude that the number of zeroes of $Q'(X)$ exceeds its degree. Therefore, $Q'(X)$ must be the zero-polynomial, and hence the identity

$$f_0(X) - f_1(X) \cdot f(X) = 0$$

holds in $K[X]$. This establishes the claim.

11.9 Formal Definition of Secret Sharing

We give a formal definition of secret sharing. Before doing so, we state some terminology concerning random variables and information theory. For an introduction to information theory, please refer to Cover and Thomas [56].[10]

11.9.1 Some Notions from Information Theory

Let $[0, 1]$ denote the interval of real numbers λ with $0 \leq \lambda \leq 1$.

DEFINITION 11.22 (PROBABILITY SPACE) *A finite probability space consists of a finite nonempty set Ω, the sample space, and a probability function*

$$P : \Omega \longrightarrow [0, 1]$$

with

$$\sum_{\omega \in \Omega} P(\omega) = 1$$

DEFINITION 11.23 (EVENTS) *A subset $\mathcal{E} \subset \Omega$ is an event. Its probability is*

$$P(\mathcal{E}) := \sum_{\omega \in \mathcal{E}} P(\omega)$$

By default, $P(\emptyset) = 0$.

DEFINITION 11.24 (RANDOM VARIABLE) *A random variable X defined on a finite probability space (Ω, P) consists of a finite nonempty set $\mathcal{X}$, the alphabet, and a map*

$$X : \Omega \longrightarrow \mathcal{X}$$

By definition, $X = x$ is the event

$$\{\omega \in \Omega : X(\omega) = x\}$$

---

[10] For a quick introduction to information theory from the point of view of cryptography, please refer to Cramer and Fehr [64]. For elementary calculus of (conditional) probabilities involving random variables, please refer to Shoup [168].

The probability distribution of X is defined as the function

$$P_X : \mathcal{X} \longrightarrow [0,1]$$

$$x \mapsto P(X = x)$$

REMARK 11.25 (ALPHABET NOTATION) In general, the alphabet of a random variable will be denoted by a calligraphic version of the name of the random variable. For instance, the alphabet of X is $\mathcal{X}$.

Let X, Y be random variables defined on a finite probability space (Ω, P).

DEFINITION 11.26 (UNIFORM DISTRIBUTION) *The random variable X has the uniform distribution if*

$$P_X(x) = \frac{1}{|\mathcal{X}|}$$

for all $x \in \mathcal{X}$.

DEFINITION 11.27 (PRODUCTS OF RANDOM VARIABLES) *The product*

$$XY : \Omega \longrightarrow \mathcal{X} \times \mathcal{Y}$$

is the random variable defined by

$$XY(\omega) = (X(\omega), Y(\omega))$$

DEFINITION 11.28 (INDEPENDENCE OF RANDOM VARIABLES) *The random variables X, Y are independent if*

$$P_{XY}(x,y) = P_X(x) \cdot P_Y(y)$$

for all $x \in \mathcal{X}, y \in \mathcal{Y}$.

LEMMA 11.29 *The random variable XY has the uniform distribution if and only if X and Y are independent and both X and Y have the uniform distribution.*

Proof We show the forward direction. The other direction is immediate. For all $(x,y) \in \mathcal{X} \times \mathcal{Y}$, the following holds. First,

$$P_{XY}(x,y) = \frac{1}{|\mathcal{X}| \cdot |\mathcal{Y}|}$$

because there is the uniform distribution on $\mathcal{X} \times \mathcal{Y}$. Second,

$$P_X(x) = \sum_{y \in \mathcal{Y}} P_{XY}(x,y) = |\mathcal{Y}| \cdot \frac{1}{|\mathcal{X}| \cdot |\mathcal{Y}|} = \frac{1}{|\mathcal{X}|}$$

and

$$P_Y(y) = \sum_{x \in \mathcal{X}} P_{XY}(x,y) = |\mathcal{X}| \cdot \frac{1}{|\mathcal{X}| \cdot |\mathcal{Y}|} = \frac{1}{|\mathcal{Y}|}$$

Therefore,

$$P_{XY}(x,y) = P_X(x) \cdot P_Y(y) \qquad \blacksquare$$

DEFINITION 11.30 (CONDITIONED RANDOM VARIABLE) *If $\mathcal{E}$ is an event with $P(\mathcal{E}) > 0$, then $P_{X|\mathcal{E}}$ denotes the probability distribution of X conditioned on $\mathcal{E}$. Precisely,*

$$P_{X|\mathcal{E}}(x) = \frac{P(X = x \cap \mathcal{E})}{P(\mathcal{E})}$$

for all $x \in \mathcal{X}$.

REMARK 11.31 It is sometimes convenient to speak of the random variable X conditioned on an event $\mathcal{E}$ with $P(\mathcal{E}) > 0$ as a random variable in its own right. This requires some care because the probability space must be adapted to do so. Precisely, the probability space is adapted to the pair $(\mathcal{E}, P')$, where P' is the probability function

$$P' : \mathcal{E} \longrightarrow [0,1]$$

$$\omega \mapsto \frac{P(\omega)}{P(\mathcal{E})}$$

We now define $X^{\mathcal{E}}$ as the random variable on the finite probability space $(\mathcal{E}, P')$ such that, as a function, $X^{\mathcal{E}}$ is simply the restriction of X to the subdomain $\mathcal{E}$. Note that $P'_{X^{\mathcal{E}}}$ is nothing other than the conditional probability distribution $P_{X|\mathcal{E}}$.

DEFINITION 11.32 (SUPPORT) *The support of the random variable X, denoted $\mathrm{supp}(X)$, is the set consisting of all $x \in \mathcal{X}$ such that $P_X(x) > 0$.*

Note that it is not assumed that $\mathcal{X} = \mathrm{supp}(X)$.

DEFINITION 11.33 (VECTOR OF RANDOM VARIABLES) *A vector of random variables is a vector $\mathbf{X} = (X_j)_{j \in \mathcal{I}}$ such that*

- *The index set $\mathcal{I} \subset \mathbb{Z}$ is finite and nonempty.*
- *Each of the X_js is a random variable, and all are defined on the same finite probability space.*

Note that a vector of random variables is in fact a nonempty finite product of random variables indexed by a set of integers.

DEFINITION 11.34 *Let $\mathbf{X} = (X_j)_{j \in \mathcal{I}}$ be a vector of random variables. If $B \subset \mathcal{I}$ with $B \neq \emptyset$, then $\mathbf{X}_B$ denotes the vector of random variables $(X_j)_{j \in B}$. Moreover, $\mathcal{X}_B$ denotes the Cartesian product $\prod_{j \in B} \mathcal{X}_j$. If $B = \mathcal{I}$, then $\mathcal{X}$ is a shorthand for $\mathcal{X}_B$.*

DEFINITION 11.35 (SHANNON ENTROPY) *Let $P : U \to [0,1]$ be a probability function defined on a nonempty finite set U. Its Shannon entropy is defined as*[11]

$$H(P) = -\sum_{\mathbf{u} \in U} P(\mathbf{u}) \cdot \log_2 P(\mathbf{u})$$

For the random variable X, we define

$$H(X) = H(P_X)$$

---

[11] We adhere to the usual convention that $0 \cdot \log_2 0 = 0$, which is justified by a simple continuity argument.

Shannon entropy can be interpreted essentially as the optimal encoding length $\lambda(P)$ of outcomes of a random process distributed according to P when prefix-free encoding is used and when optimality means minimizing the expected bit length of the encoding, where the expectation is taken over P.[12]

DEFINITION 11.36 (ENCODING LENGTH) *The average encoding length of a vector* $\mathbf{X} = (X_j)_{j \in \mathcal{I}}$ *of random variables is defined as* $\lambda(\mathbf{X}) = \frac{1}{|\mathcal{I}|} \cdot \sum_{j \in \mathcal{I}} H(X_j)$.

DEFINITION 11.37 (CONDITIONAL ENTROPY) *The entropy of X conditioned on Y is defined as*

$$H(X|Y) = \sum_{y \in \mathcal{Y}: P_Y(y) > 0} P_Y(y) \cdot H(X|Y=y)$$

where $H(X|Y=y) = H(P_{X|Y=y})$

In other words, $H(X|Y)$ is the expected entropy of $H(X|Y=y)$ with $P_Y(y) > 0$, where the expectation is taken over P_Y.

We will just need the basic facts from information theory given next.

LEMMA 11.38 *Let (X, Y, Z) be a vector of random variables. Then the following statements hold:*

1. $0 \le H(X) \le \log_2 |\mathcal{X}|$. *Equality on the left holds if and only if there exists $x \in \mathcal{X}$ with $P_X(x) = 1$. Equality on the right holds if and only if X has the uniform distribution.*
2. *(Monotonicity 1)* $H(X|Z) \le H(XY|Z)$.
3. *(Monotonicity 2)* $0 \le H(X|Y) \le H(X)$. *Equality on the left holds if and only if Y determines X with probability 1; that is, for each $y \in \mathcal{Y}$ with $P_Y(y) > 0$, there is a unique $x \in \mathcal{X}$ such that $P_{X|Y=y}(x) = 1$. Moreover, $H(X|Y) = 0$ implies $H(Y) \ge H(X)$. Equality on the right holds if and only if X and Y are independent.*
4. *(Chain rule)* $H(XY|Z) = H(X|Z) + H(Y|XZ)$.

The proofs of these claims can be found in Cover and Thomas [56]. Properties 1 and 3 are applied in Section 11.9.2 (formal definition of secret sharing). The other properties are only used in Section 11.12.1.

11.9.2 Defining Secret Sharing

Let $\mathbf{X}$ be a vector of random variables indexed by a set $\mathcal{I}$.

DEFINITION 11.39 (RECONSTRUCTING SET) *Let $B \subset \mathcal{I}$ with $B \ne \emptyset$, and let $j \in \mathcal{I}$. Then B is a reconstructing set for $\{j\}$ if $H(X_j|\mathbf{X}_B) = 0$; that is, $\mathbf{X}_B$ determines X_j.*

Trivially, if $j \in B$, then B is a reconstructing set for $\{j\}$. If B is not a reconstructing set for $\{j\}$, then

$$0 < H(X_j|\mathbf{X}_B) \le H(X_j)$$

that is, there is a positive amount of "uncertainty" about X_j when given $\mathbf{X}_B$.

---

[12] It holds that $H(P) \le \lambda(P) \le H(P) + 1$. In an appropriate asymptotic version of this problem, $\lambda(P) = H(P)$. See Cover and Thomas [56].

DEFINITION 11.40 (PRIVACY SET) *Let $B \subset \mathcal{I}$ with B, and let $j \in \mathcal{I}$. If $B \neq \emptyset$, then B is a privacy set for $\{j\}$ if $H(X_j | \mathbf{X}_B) = H(X_j)$; that is, $\mathbf{X}_B$ is independent of X_j. If $B = \emptyset$, then B is a privacy set by default.*

REMARK 11.41 A nonempty set $B \subset \mathcal{I}$ is both a reconstructing *and* a privacy set for $\{j\}$ if and only if $H(X_j) = 0$.

We now present a formal definition of secret sharing.

DEFINITION 11.42 (SECRET SHARING) *A secret-sharing scheme is a vector $\mathbf{S}$ of random variables indexed by a set $\mathcal{I}$ with $0 \in \mathcal{I}$ and $|\mathcal{I}| > 1$ such that the following statements hold:*

• *Uniformity of S_0:*

$$H(S_0) = \log_2 |\mathcal{S}_0| \geq 1$$

In other words, the random variable S_0 has the uniform distribution on $\mathcal{S}_0$, where $|\mathcal{S}_0| > 1$.
• *Reconstruction: the set $\mathcal{I}^* := \mathcal{I} \setminus \{0\}$ is a reconstructing set for $\{0\}$.*
• *Privacy: by default, the empty set is a privacy set for $\{0\}$.*[13]

DEFINITION 11.43 *The set $\mathcal{I}^*$ is the player set. Define $n(\mathbf{S}) = |\mathcal{I}^*|$, the number of players. The variable S_0 is the secret. For each $j \in \mathcal{I}^*$, the variable S_j is the share for player j. The set $\mathcal{S}_j$ is the corresponding share space.*

This definition can be stated in terms of (generalized) codes as follows: let $\mathcal{S}_0, \mathcal{S}_1, \ldots, \mathcal{S}_n$ be nonempty finite sets. Define $\mathcal{S} := \mathcal{S}_0 \times \mathcal{S}_1 \times \cdots \times \mathcal{S}_n$. Let $C \subset \mathcal{S}$ be nonempty, and let P be a probability distribution on C. Now sample $\mathbf{x} = (x_0, x_1, \ldots, x_n) \in C$ according to P. The uniformity condition from the definition says that x_0 has the uniform distribution on $\mathcal{S}_0$ and that $|\mathcal{S}_0| > 1$. Let $B \subset \mathcal{I}^*$ with $B \neq \emptyset$. Then B is a reconstructing set if x_0 can be guessed with probability 1 from $\mathbf{x}_B$ alone. The definition requires that $\mathcal{I}^*$ is a reconstructing set. The set B is a privacy set if $\mathbf{x}_B$ is independently distributed from x_0. By default, the empty set is a privacy set. There are no further a priori requirements. Note that if we cast secret sharing from interpolation codes in this framework, in particular, Shamir's scheme, then the distribution imposed on the code is the *uniform* one. For a strictly combinatorial treatment of secret sharing, see, for example, Stinson [174].

An equivalent definition of privacy sets is as follows: let $B \subset \mathcal{I}^*$ with $B \neq \emptyset$. Then B is a privacy set if $P_{\mathbf{S}_B | S_0 = s} = P_{\mathbf{S}_B}$ for each $s \in \mathcal{S}_0$. This means that if $\mathbf{s}$ is sampled from $\mathcal{S}$ conditioned on $S_0 = s$ for some secret $s \in \mathcal{S}_0$,[14] the shares $\mathbf{s}_B$ for a nonempty privacy set B have a distribution that does not depend on the particular secret s. For this reason, it should be clear that the explanation of privacy and reconstruction in secret sharing based on interpolation codes from Section 11.4 generalizes immediately to the general definition of secret sharing given here.

Note that the definition allows the secret and individual shares to be in different sets, not even necessarily of the same cardinality (as opposed to secret sharing based on interpolation codes from Section 11.4, where all are defined over the same alphabet $\mathcal{F}$).

---

[13] There are no a priori requirements concerning privacy sets. But, of course, secret sharing starts making sense when there are *nonempty* privacy sets.
[14] How this is done *algorithmically* depends, of course, on the details of the secret-sharing scheme.

DEFINITION 11.44 *The length of the secret is* $\lambda_0(\mathbf{S}) := \log_2 |\mathcal{S}_0|$. *The average length of the shares is* $\lambda^*(\mathbf{S}) := \lambda(\mathbf{S}^*)$, *where* $\mathbf{S}^* = (S_j)_{j \in \mathcal{I}^*}$.

REMARK 11.45 Some authors do not impose the uniform distribution on the secret but require that $H(S_0) > 0$ and that the support of S_0 is all of $\mathcal{S}_0$, all other requirements being the same. The resulting definition is essentially the same as the one given here. Briefly, one passes back to ours by conditioning on each secret separately and "gluing" these conditional distributions together by imposing the uniform probability distribution on the secret. See Blundo, De Santis, and Vaccaro [26] for details.

DEFINITION 11.46 (ACCESS STRUCTURE) *The access structure* $\Gamma(\mathbf{S})$ *consists of all reconstructing sets* $B \subset \mathcal{I}^*$.

By definition of a secret-sharing scheme, it holds that $\Gamma(\mathbf{S}) \neq \emptyset$ because $\mathcal{I}^* \in \Gamma(\mathbf{S})$.

DEFINITION 11.47 (*r*-RECONSTRUCTION) *Let r be a positive integer. The secret-sharing scheme* $\mathbf{S}$ *has r-reconstruction if for each subset* $B \subset \mathcal{I}^*$ *with* $|B| \geq r$ *it holds that* $B \in \Gamma(\mathbf{S})$. *The smallest positive integer r such that* $\mathbf{S}$ *has r-reconstruction is denoted* $r(\mathbf{S})$.

Note that $1 \leq r(\mathbf{S}) \leq n(\mathbf{S})$. Furthermore, for all integers r with $r(\mathbf{S}) \leq r \leq n(\mathbf{S})$, there is r-reconstruction.

DEFINITION 11.48 (ADVERSARY STRUCTURE) *The adversary structure* $\mathcal{A}(\mathbf{S})$ *consists of all privacy sets* $B \subset \mathcal{I}^*$.

By definition of a secret-sharing scheme, it holds that $\mathcal{A}(\mathbf{S}) \neq \emptyset$ because $\emptyset \in \mathcal{A}(\mathbf{S})$.

DEFINITION 11.49 (*t*-PRIVACY) *Let t be a nonnegative integer. The secret-sharing scheme* $\mathbf{S}$ *has t-privacy if for each subset* $B \subset \mathcal{I}^*$ *with* $|B| \leq t$ *it holds that* $B \in \mathcal{A}(\mathbf{S})$. *The largest nonnegative integer t such that* $\mathbf{S}$ *has t-privacy is denoted* $t(\mathbf{S})$.

As before, 0-privacy means by convention that "the empty set of shares does not decrease uncertainty about the secret," which makes sense. Note that $t(\mathbf{S}) = 0$ does not mean there is no nonempty privacy set. It just means that $H(X_0|X_j) < H(X_0)$ for some $j \in \mathcal{I}^*$; that is, there is some player whose share gives a positive amount of (partial) information about the secret. Clearly, in a perfect scheme, $t(\mathbf{S}) = 0$ means that there is a reconstructing player. The definition of secret sharing allows the "cryptographically noninteresting" case that there is no nonempty privacy set at all. However, it is useful to allow this case for technical reasons arising in proofs. Similarly, it is useful to allow $n(\mathbf{S}) = 1$. Note that for all integers t with $0 \leq t \leq t(\mathbf{S})$, there is t-privacy.

By the definitions and based on Remark 11.41, we have the following lemma:

LEMMA 11.50 $\mathcal{A}(\mathbf{S}) \cap \Gamma(\mathbf{S}) = \emptyset$. *In particular,* $0 \leq t(\mathbf{S}) < r(\mathbf{S}) \leq n(\mathbf{S})$.

DEFINITION 11.51 $\mathcal{A}'(\mathbf{S}) = 2^{\mathcal{I}^*} \setminus \Gamma(\mathbf{S})$.[15]

Note that $\mathcal{A}(\mathbf{S}) \subset \mathcal{A}'(\mathbf{S})$ by Lemma 11.50. Furthermore, note that if $\mathcal{A}(\mathbf{S}) \subsetneq \mathcal{A}'(\mathbf{S})$, then there is a set that is neither a privacy set nor a reconstructing set.

---

[15] The notation $2^{\mathcal{I}^*}$ refers to the collection of all subsets of the set $\mathcal{I}^*$.

The following straightforward lemma gives a sufficient condition for proving privacy. It is quite useful when analyzing certain schemes.

LEMMA 11.52 (SUFFICIENT CONDITION FOR PRIVACY) *Let $B \subset \mathcal{I}^*$ with $B \neq \emptyset$. If the distribution of $S_0 \times \mathbf{S}_B$ is the uniform distribution on $S_0 \times \mathrm{supp}(\mathbf{S}_B)$, then B is a privacy set.*

The proof follows by direct application of Lemma 11.29

11.9.3 Combinatorial Structures

There are several further relevant combinatorial structures associated with a secret-sharing scheme.

DEFINITION 11.53 (MONOTONE STRUCTURE) *A monotone structure is a pair (Γ, Ω) where Ω is a nonempty finite set, the domain, and Γ is a collection of subsets of Ω such that*

- $\emptyset \notin \Gamma$.
- $\Omega \in \Gamma$.
- *Γ is closed under taking supersets. This means that if $B \in \Gamma$ and $B \subset B' \subset \Omega$, then $B' \in \Gamma$.*

DEFINITION 11.54 (MINIMAL SET) *Let (Γ, Ω) be a monotone structure, and let $B \in \Gamma$. Then B is minimal if it is a minimal element in the partial order on Γ induced by set inclusion. In other words, $B \in \Gamma$ is minimal if for each proper subset $B'' \subsetneq B$ it holds that $B'' \notin \Gamma$.*

DEFINITION 11.55 (CONNECTED MONOTONE STRUCTURE) *A monotone structure (Γ, Ω) is connected if for each $i \in \Omega$ there is a minimal set $B \in \Gamma$ with $i \in B$.*

A secret-sharing scheme whose access structure is *not* connected contains some "dummy player(s)"; that is, each reconstructing set containing such a player remains reconstructing after removal of that player from the set.

DEFINITION 11.56 (ANTIMONOTONE STRUCTURE) *An antimonotone structure is a pair $(\mathcal{A}, \Omega)$ where Ω is a nonempty finite set, the domain, and $\mathcal{A}$ is a collection of subsets of Ω such that*

- $\emptyset \in \mathcal{A}$.
- $\Omega \notin \mathcal{A}$.
- *$\mathcal{A}$ is closed under taking subsets. This means that if $B \in \mathcal{A}$ and $B'' \subset B \subset \Omega$, then $B'' \in \mathcal{A}$.*

Note that if $\mathbf{S}$ is a secret-sharing scheme, then $\Gamma(\mathbf{S})$ is a monotone structure. Also note that both $\mathcal{A}(\mathbf{S})$ and $\mathcal{A}'(\mathbf{S})$ are antimonotone structures.

DEFINITION 11.57 (DUAL) *If (Γ, Ω) is a monotone structure, then its dual is the monotone structure (Γ^*, Ω) where*

$$\Gamma^* = \{B \subset \Omega \ : \ \Omega \setminus B \ \notin \Gamma\}$$

The following lemma is straightforward to prove.

LEMMA 11.58 $(\Gamma^*)^* = \Gamma$.

11.9.4 Perfect and Ideal Schemes

Throughout this section, let $\mathbf{S}$ be a secret-sharing scheme on the player set $\mathcal{I}^*$.

DEFINITION 11.59 (PERFECT SCHEMES) $\mathbf{S}$ *is perfect if* $\mathcal{A}(\mathbf{S}) = \mathcal{A}'(\mathbf{S})$*; that is,* $\Gamma(\mathbf{S}) \cup \mathcal{A}(\mathbf{S})$ *is a partition of* $2^{\mathcal{I}^*}$.

In other words, for each $B \subset \mathcal{I}^*$ with $B \neq \emptyset$, the corresponding shares either jointly give full information about the secret or do not reduce uncertainty at all. Note that $\mathcal{A} \cap \Gamma = \emptyset$ on account of Lemma 11.50.

DEFINITION 11.60 *Suppose that* $\mathbf{S}$ *is perfect. Then* $\mathbf{S}$ *is connected if* $\Gamma(\mathbf{S})$ *is connected.*

In other words, this definition excludes "dummy players" in a perfect secret-sharing scheme.

DEFINITION 11.61 (IDEAL SCHEMES) *Suppose that* $\mathbf{S}$ *is perfect and connected. Then* $\mathbf{S}$ *is ideal if* $|\mathcal{S}_j| = |\mathcal{S}_0|$ *for all* $j \in \mathcal{I}^*$*. Without loss of generality, we may assume that* $\mathcal{S}_i = \mathcal{S}_j$ *for all* $i,j \in \mathcal{I}$ *and define* $\mathcal{F} := \mathcal{S}_0$*. We say that* $\mathbf{S}$ *is defined over the alphabet* $\mathcal{F}$.

Note that this definition is motivated by the result in Theorem 11.97, which we show later. We are now in a position to adequately summarize the existence results on threshold secret sharing that we showed.

DEFINITION 11.62 (THRESHOLD SCHEMES) *The scheme* $\mathbf{S}$ *is a* (t,n)-*threshold secret-sharing scheme if* $n = n(\mathbf{S})$, $t = t(\mathbf{S})$*, and* $r(\mathbf{S}) = t(\mathbf{S}) + 1$.

Note that if $\mathbf{S}$ is a threshold secret-sharing scheme, then it is perfect and connected. It is perfect because each set $B \subset \mathcal{I}^*$ satisfies either $|B| \leq t(\mathbf{S})$ (in which case it is a privacy set) or $|B| \geq r(\mathbf{S}) = t(\mathbf{S}) + 1$ (in which case it is a reconstructing set). Moreover, $\Gamma(\mathbf{S})$ is connected because for each $j \in \mathcal{I}^*$ there is a set $B \subset \mathcal{I}^*$ with $j \in B$ and $|B| = r(\mathbf{S})$, and such a set B is minimal.

DEFINITION 11.63 (IDEAL THRESHOLD SECRET-SHARING SCHEME) *Let* $t, n, \bar{q}$ *be integers with* $\bar{q} \geq 2$ *and* $0 \leq t < n$*. The class of ideal* (t,n)-*threshold secret-sharing schemes over an alphabet of size* $\bar{q}$ *is denoted* $\mathrm{ITSS}(t,n,\bar{q})$.

THEOREM 11.64 *The secret-sharing scheme from Section 11.4 constructed from a* $(t + 1, n + 1, \bar{q})$-*interpolation code* $(0 \leq t < n)$ *over an alphabet of cardinality* $\bar{q} \geq 2$ *is an ideal* (t,n)-*threshold scheme on* n *players with secret space as well as each share space having cardinality* $\bar{q}$.

11.10 Linear Secret-Sharing Schemes

Linear secret-sharing schemes, first studied in generality by Brickell [29], can be defined in several ways. We find it convenient here to start by giving a definition and analysis based on linear codes inspired by Massey [139, 140], who first considered linear secret sharing from arbitrary linear codes. Afterwards, we cast Brickell's vector space construction in this light.

We start with a straightforward but useful lemma.

LEMMA 11.65 (REGULARITY OF FINITE MORPHISMS) *Let $\phi : G \longrightarrow H$ be a morphism of groups. Suppose that G is finite. Suppose that $x \in G$ is selected uniformly random. Then $\phi(x)$ is uniformly random on $\mathrm{im}\,\phi \subset H$, the image of ϕ. In particular, if ϕ is surjective, then $\phi(x)$ is uniformly random on H.*

Proof It is sufficient to show that ϕ is regular; that is, each element of $\mathrm{im}\,\phi$ has the same number of distinct preimages under ϕ. Let $h' \in \mathrm{im}\,\phi$. Define

$$\phi^{-1}(h') := \{g \in G : \phi(g) = h'\}$$

Let

$$g' \in \phi^{-1}(h')$$

Observe that

$$\phi^{-1}(h') = g' \cdot \ker\phi$$

Moreover,

$$|g' \cdot \ker\phi| = |\ker\phi|$$

because multiplication by g' induces a permutation of G. It follows that sets of the form $\phi^{-1}(h')$ with $h' \in \mathrm{im}\,\phi$ partition G into disjoint sets of equal cardinality. The claim follows. ∎

Throughout this section, if $\ell > 1$ is an integer, then, unless stated otherwise, it is assumed that $\mathbb{F}_q^\ell$ is indexed by the set $\mathcal{I} = \{0, 1, \ldots, \ell - 1\}$. Moreover $\mathcal{I}^* := \{1, \ldots, \ell - 1\}$. For a nonempty set $B \subset \mathcal{I}^*$, define $\overline{B} := \mathcal{I}^* \setminus A$. If $\mathbf{x} \in \mathbb{F}_q^\ell$ and $B = \emptyset$, then we write $\mathbf{x}_B = 0$ by default.

11.10.1 Massey's Scheme

DEFINITION 11.66 (LINEAR SECRET SHARING FOR $\mathbb{F}_q$ OVER $\mathbb{F}_q$) *Let $C \subset \mathbb{F}_q^{n+1}$ be an $\mathbb{F}_q$-linear code with $n \geq 1$. Then C is a linear secret-sharing scheme for $\mathbb{F}_q$ over $\mathbb{F}_q$ if the following conditions are satisfied.*

1. $\pi_0(C) \neq \{\mathbf{0}\} \subset \mathbb{F}_q$.
2. *For all $\mathbf{x} \in C$, it holds that if $\mathbf{x}_{\mathcal{I}^*} = \mathbf{0} \in \mathbb{F}_q^n$, then $x_0 = 0 \in \mathbb{F}_q$.*

This defines a secret-sharing scheme on n players in the sense of Definition 11.42 as follows: the projection $\pi_0 : C \longrightarrow \mathbb{F}_q$ is a morphism of $\mathbb{F}_q$-vector spaces. By the first condition, it is not identically zero. Because the image is one-dimensional, this projection is surjective. By Lemma 11.65, it holds that if $\mathbf{x} \in C$ is selected *uniformly at random*, then x_0 has the uniform distribution on $\mathbb{F}_q$, the secret space.

In addition, the second condition means that from the n shares $x_1, \ldots, x_n$ jointly, each of which sits in a share space $\mathbb{F}_q$, there is no ambivalence about the secret x_0: they jointly determine it with probability 1. Indeed, there is such ambivalence if and only if there are $\mathbf{x}', \mathbf{x}'' \in C$ such that $\mathbf{x}'_{\mathcal{I}^*} = \mathbf{x}''_{\mathcal{I}^*}$ but $x'_0 \neq x''_0$. Since the code is $\mathbb{F}_q$-linear, the latter is equivalent to the existence of $\mathbf{x} \in C$ such that $\mathbf{x}_{\mathcal{I}^*} = \mathbf{0}$ but $x_0 \neq 0$.

DEFINITION 11.67 (DUAL OF A LINEAR CODE) *Let $C \subset \mathbb{F}_q^\ell$ be an $\mathbb{F}_q$-linear code with $\ell \geq$ 1. Then its dual $C^\perp \subset \mathbb{F}_q^\ell$ is the $\mathbb{F}_q$-linear code consisting of all $\mathbf{y} \in \mathbb{F}_q^\ell$ such that $\langle \mathbf{x}, \mathbf{y} \rangle = 0$ for all $\mathbf{x} \in C$.*

LEMMA 11.68 *Let $C \subset \mathbb{F}_q^\ell$ be an $\mathbb{F}_q$-linear code with $\ell \geq 1$. Then the following statements hold:*

1. $\dim_{\mathbb{F}_q} C^\perp = \ell - \dim_{\mathbb{F}_q} C$.
2. $C = (C^\perp)^\perp$.

Proof This is implied by standard facts from linear algebra. Let V be a finite-dimensional K-vector space. Let V^* denote the space of K-linear forms $V \longrightarrow K$. If $W \subset V$ is a subspace, then the subspace of V^* consisting of maps that vanish on W has dimension $\dim_K V - \dim_K W$. This can be seen, for instance, by taking a basis of V that includes a basis of W. Furthermore, if ψ is a nondegenerate bilinear form on V, then ψ induces an isomorphism $a \mapsto \psi(\cdot, a)$ from V to V^*. Now set $V = \mathbb{F}_q^\ell$, $W = C$, and take as ψ the standard inner product on $\mathbb{F}_q^\ell$. Since $C^\perp$ corresponds (via the preceding isomorphism) to the K-linear forms vanishing on C, the first claim follows.

By definition of the dual code,

$$C \subset (C^\perp)^\perp$$

Since

$$\dim_{\mathbb{F}_q}(C^\perp)^\perp = \ell - \dim_{\mathbb{F}_q} C^\perp = \ell - (\ell - \dim_{\mathbb{F}_q} C) = \dim_{\mathbb{F}_q} C$$

it follows by linear algebra that

$$(C^\perp)^\perp = C$$

and the second claim follows follows as well.   ∎

LEMMA 11.69 *Let $C \subset \mathbb{F}_q^{n+1}$ be a linear secret-sharing scheme for $\mathbb{F}_q$ over $\mathbb{F}_q$ on $n \geq 1$ players. Then $C^\perp \subset \mathbb{F}_q^{n+1}$ is also a linear secret-sharing scheme for $\mathbb{F}_q$ over $\mathbb{F}_q$ on n players.*

Proof The dual code $C^\perp$ is an $\mathbb{F}_q$-linear code as well. We verify that it satisfies the conditions of Definition 11.66. Suppose that $\pi_0(C^\perp) = \{0\}$. Then $(1, 0 \ldots, 0) \in (C^\perp)^\perp$ by definition of the dual. By Lemma 11.68, it follows that $(1, 0 \ldots, 0) \in C$. This gives a contradiction with the second property of Definition 11.66 applied to C. Finally, suppose that there is $\mathbf{x}^* \in C^\perp$ such that $x_0^* = 1$ but $\mathbf{x}_{\mathcal{I}^*}^* = \mathbf{0}$. Then, by definition of the dual code, this implies that $\pi_0(C) = \{0\}$. This gives a contradiction with the first property of Definition 11.66 applied to C.   ∎

11.10.2 Basic Results by Dualization

LEMMA 11.70 *Let $C \subset \mathbb{F}_q^{n+1}$ be a linear secret-sharing scheme for $\mathbb{F}_q$ over $\mathbb{F}_q$ on $n \geq 1$ players. Let $B \subset \mathcal{I}^*$ be a nonempty set. Then the following statements are equivalent:*

1. $B \in \Gamma(C)$.
2. *For all $\mathbf{x} \in C$, it holds that if $\mathbf{x}_B = \mathbf{0}$, then $x_0 = 0$.*
3. *There is $\mathbf{x}^* \in C^\perp$ with $x_0^* = 1$ and $\mathbf{x}_{\overline{B}}^* = \mathbf{0}$.*

Proof The equivalence of the first and second claims is argued in a similar way as it has already been argued for $B = \mathcal{I}^*$ right after Definition 11.66. We now argue that the first claim implies the third. Fix some $B \in \Gamma(C)$. Define the map

$$\rho : \pi_B(C) \longrightarrow \mathbb{F}_q$$

$$\mathbf{x}_B \mapsto x_0$$

This is well defined because $B \in \Gamma(C)$: if $\mathbf{x}_B = \mathbf{x}'_B$ for some $\mathbf{x}, \mathbf{x}' \in C$, then $x_0 = x'_0$. This map is clearly $\mathbb{F}_q$-linear. The third claim now follows by basic linear algebra. For instance, extend ρ arbitrarily to an $\mathbb{F}_q$-linear form on $\mathbb{F}_q^{|B|}$. Suppose that this form is given as $\sum_{i \in B} u_i X_i$, where $u_i \in \mathbb{F}_q$ for each $i \in B$. Then the vector $(u_i)_{i \in \mathcal{I}} \in \mathbb{F}_q^{n+1}$ with $u_0 = -1$ and $u_i = 0$ if $i \notin B$ satisfies the requirements.

To argue that the third claim implies the first claim, note that

$$x_0 = -\sum_{i \in B} x_i x_i^*$$

for all $\mathbf{x} \in C$. Hence, $B \in \Gamma(C)$. ∎

LEMMA 11.71 *Let $C \subset \mathbb{F}_q^{n+1}$ be a linear secret-sharing scheme for $\mathbb{F}_q$ over $\mathbb{F}_q$ on n players. Let $B \subset \{1, \ldots, n\}$ be a nonempty set. Then the following statements are equivalent.*

1. $B \in \mathcal{A}(C)$.
2. *There is $\mathbf{x} \in C$ such that $x_0 = 1$ and $\mathbf{x}_B = \mathbf{0}$.*

Proof If $B \in \mathcal{A}(C)$, there is ambivalence; that is, there are $\mathbf{x}', \mathbf{x}'' \in C$ with $\mathbf{x}'_B = \mathbf{x}''_B$ but $x'_0 \neq x''_0$. By linearity, this means that there is $\mathbf{x} \in C$ such that $x_0 = 1$ and $\mathbf{x}_B = \mathbf{0}$. However, the existence of $\mathbf{x} \in C$ such that $x_0 = 1$ and $\mathbf{x}_B = \mathbf{0}$ implies that the map $C \longrightarrow \mathbb{F}_q \times \pi_B(C)$ defined by the assignment $\mathbf{x}' \mapsto (x'_0, \mathbf{x}'_B)$ is a surjective morphism. Indeed, $\mathbf{x}' + \lambda \mathbf{x}$ maps to $(x'_0 + \lambda, \mathbf{x}'_B)$ for all $\mathbf{x}' \in C$ and for all $\lambda \in \mathbb{F}_q$. By Lemma 11.52, it follows that $B \in \mathcal{A}(C)$. ∎

COROLLARY 11.72 *Let $C \subset \mathbb{F}_q^{n+1}$ be a linear secret-sharing scheme for $\mathbb{F}_q$ over $\mathbb{F}_q$ on n players. Let $B \subset \mathcal{I}^*$. Then*

- $B \in \Gamma(C)$ *if and only if* $\overline{B} \in \mathcal{A}(C^\perp)$.
- $B \in \mathcal{A}(C)$ *if and only if* $\overline{B} \in \Gamma(C^\perp)$.

THEOREM 11.73 (DUALIZATION) *Let $C \subset \mathbb{F}_q^{n+1}$ be a linear secret-sharing scheme for $\mathbb{F}_q$ over $\mathbb{F}_q$ on n players. Then*

1. *The linear secret-sharing scheme C is perfect.*
2. $\Gamma(C^\perp) = (\Gamma(C))^*$.

Proof Suppose that $B' \subset \mathcal{I}^*$ is nonempty. The statement that there is $\mathbf{x} \in C$ such that $x_0 = 1$ and $\mathbf{x}_{B'} = \mathbf{0}$ is the negation of the statement that for all $\mathbf{x} \in C$ it holds that if $\mathbf{x}_{B'} = \mathbf{0}$, then $x_0 = 0$. Therefore, for all $B \subset \mathcal{I}^*$, it holds that

$$B \in \mathcal{A}(C) \quad \text{if and only if} \quad B \notin \Gamma(C)$$

This proves the first claim. Applying Corollary 11.72, it follows that for all $B \subset \mathcal{I}^*$,

$$B \in \Gamma(C^\perp) \quad \text{if and only if} \quad \overline{B} \notin \Gamma(C)$$

This proves the second claim.   ∎

REMARK 11.74 If the access structure of a linear secret-sharing scheme is connected, then the scheme is ideal.

Dualization in the context of secret sharing was introduced by Karchmer and Wigderson [119] and Simmons, Jackson, and Martin [171].

DEFINITION 11.75 *Let $C \subset \mathbb{F}_q^\ell$ be an $\mathbb{F}_q$-linear code with $\ell \geq 1$. Then $w_0(C)$ is the minimum of $w_H(\mathbf{x})$ taken over all $\mathbf{x} \in C$ with $x_0 = 1$, if such $\mathbf{x}$ exists. If not, $w_0(C) = 0$ by default.*

REMARK 11.76 As opposed to the minimum distance $d_{\min}(C)$, the parameter $w_0(C)$ depends on how the code is indexed. More precisely, it depends on which coordinate is labeled by 0.

THEOREM 11.77 (PARAMETER CONTROL FROM LINEAR CODES) *Let $C \subset \mathbb{F}_q^{n+1}$ be an $\mathbb{F}_q$-linear code with $n \geq 1$. If*

$$w_0(C) \geq 2$$

then C is a linear secret-sharing scheme for $\mathbb{F}_q$ over $\mathbb{F}_q$ on n players with t-privacy and r-reconstruction such that

$$t = w_0(C^\perp) - 2 \quad \text{and} \quad r = n - w_0(C) + 2$$

which is sharp in both cases. In particular, if

$$d_{\min}(C) \geq 2 \quad \text{and} \quad d_{\min}(C^\perp) \geq 2$$

then there is t-privacy and r-reconstruction with

$$t = d_{\min}(C^\perp) - 2 \quad \text{and} \quad r = n - d_{\min}(C) + 2$$

Proof From $w_0(C) \geq 2$, it follows that each $\mathbf{x} \in C$ with $x_0 \neq 0$ satisfies $\mathbf{x}_{\mathcal{I}^*} \neq \mathbf{0}$ and that such $\mathbf{x} \in C$ exists. From this observation, it follows that C is a linear secret-sharing scheme. Note that $w_0(C) \geq 2$ implies that $w_0(C^\perp) \geq 2$ because $w_0(C^\perp) = 1$ implies that $w_0(C) = 0$ and $w_0(C^\perp) = 0$ implies that $w_0(C) = 1$.

As to reconstruction, let $\mathbf{x} \in C$. Suppose that $\mathbf{x}_B = \mathbf{0}$ for some $B \subset \mathcal{I}^*$ with $|B| \geq n - w_0(C) + 2$. Then

$$w_H(\mathbf{x}) \leq w_H(x_0) + w_0(C) - 2 \leq w_0(C) - 1$$

Therefore, it holds that $x_0 = 0$. However, suppose that $\mathbf{x} \in C$ satisfies $x_0 = 1$ and $w_H(\mathbf{x}) = w_0(C)$. Then there is a set $B \subset \mathcal{I}^*$ with $|B| = n - w_0(C) + 1$ such that $\mathbf{x}_B = \mathbf{0}$. Therefore, $B \in \mathcal{A}(C)$. Thus there is no r'-reconstruction with $r' < n - w_0(C) + 2$. In other words, there is reconstruction as claimed, and the bound is sharp.

As to privacy, this follows immediately by dualizing the result on reconstruction. By Corollary 11.72, there is t-privacy in C if and only if there is $(n-t)$-reconstruction in $C^\perp$.

Finally, the conditions on minimum distance of C, and $C^\perp$, imply that $w_0(C) \geq 2$. To conclude, note that $d_{\min}(C) \leq w_0(C)$ and $d_{\min}(C^\perp) \leq w_0(C^\perp)$.   ∎

This theorem is not stated in Massey [139, 140], but it follows from the results. Moreover, it appears to have been part of the "folklore." See also the discussion and constructions in Cascudo et al. [38], Chen et al. [50], and Duursma and Park [89].

LEMMA 11.78 (UNIFORMITY) *Let $C \subset \mathbb{F}_q^{\ell}$ be an $\mathbb{F}_q$-linear code with $\ell \geq 1$. Fix some index set $\mathcal{I}$ for $\mathbb{F}_q^{\ell}$. Suppose that*

$$d_{\min}(C^{\perp}) \geq 2$$

Let $B \subset \mathcal{I}$ with $|B| = d_{\min}(C^{\perp}) - 1$. Then

$$\pi_B : C \longrightarrow \mathbb{F}_q^{|B|}$$

is a surjective $\mathbb{F}_q$-vector space morphism.

Proof For any $\mathbf{x}^* \in \mathbb{F}_q^{\ell}$ with

$$\mathbf{x}_B^* \in (\pi_B(C))^{\perp} \subset \mathbb{F}_q^{|B|} \quad \text{and} \quad \mathbf{x}_{\overline{B}}^* = \mathbf{0} \in \mathbb{F}_q^{\ell - |B|}$$

it holds that

$$\mathbf{x}^* \in C^{\perp}$$

Since

$$w_H(\mathbf{x}^*) \leq |B| < d_{\min}(C^{\perp})$$

it must hold that $\mathbf{x}^* = \mathbf{0}$. Thus $(\pi_B(C))^{\perp} = \{\mathbf{0}\}$, or equivalently, $\pi_B(C) = \mathbb{F}_q^{|B|}$. This proves the lemma. ∎

COROLLARY 11.79 (UNIFORMITY OF SHARES) *Let $C \subset \mathbb{F}_q^{n+1}$ be a linear secret-sharing scheme for $\mathbb{F}_q$ over $\mathbb{F}_q$ on $n \geq 1$ players. Suppose that $d_{\min}(C^{\perp}) > 2$. Write $t = d_{\min}(C^{\perp}) - 2$. Then each set of t shares in the corresponding secret-sharing scheme is uniformly random in $\mathbb{F}_q^t$.*

REMARK 11.80 In applications, it is convenient to employ a generator matrix for the code C of a linear secret-sharing scheme, that is, a matrix G such that its (say, $e \geq 2$) columns form a basis of C (or at least generate C). In this way, it is straightforward to sample shares for a given secret. Without loss of generality, G has the vector $(1, 0, \ldots, 0)$ as its first row. Then

$$G(s, \rho_1, \ldots, \rho_{e-1})^T = (s, x_1, \ldots, x_n)^T$$

where $s \in \mathbb{F}_q$ is the secret and $\rho_1, \ldots, \rho_{e-1} \in \mathbb{F}_q$ are chosen independently and uniformly at random. The elements $x_1, \ldots, x_n$ are shares for the secret s.

DEFINITION 11.81 (IDEAL LINEAR THRESHOLD SCHEMES) *Let t, n be integers with $0 \leq t < n$. Then $\mathrm{ITSS}_{\mathrm{lin}}(t, n, q)$ denotes the set of linear secret-sharing schemes for $\mathbb{F}_q$ over $\mathbb{F}_q$ with t-privacy and $(t+1)$-reconstruction.*

The following theorem summarizes the results presented so far.

THEOREM 11.82 *Let q be a prime power. Let t, n be integers with $0 \leq t < n$. Then $\mathrm{ITSS}_{\mathrm{lin}}(t, n, q) \neq \emptyset$ if one of the following two conditions is satisfied:*

- *$t = 0$ or $t = n - 1$.*
- *$1 \leq t < n - 1$ and $n \leq q$.*

Proof The first claim follows by combining Theorem 11.64 with Lemma 11.4. The second claim follows by combining Theorem 11.64 with Theorem 11.14. ∎

11.10.3 Brickell's Scheme

Cast in Massey's framework, Brickell's earlier (but equivalent) *vector space construction* [29] of linear secret-sharing schemes is as follows:

DEFINITION 11.83 *Let V be an $\mathbb{F}_q$-vector space with $\dim_{\mathbb{F}_q} V < \infty$. Let V^* denote the dual space of V, that is, the space of $\mathbb{F}_q$-vector space morphisms $\phi : V \longrightarrow \mathbb{F}_q$. Let $z_0, z_1, \ldots, z_n \in V$ for some positive integer n. Then the $\mathbb{F}_q$-linear code $C \subset \mathbb{F}_q^{n+1}$ is defined as*

$$C = \{(\phi(z_0), \phi(z_1), \ldots, \phi(z_n)) \mid \phi \in V^*\} \subset \mathbb{F}_q^{n+1}$$

Clearly, this notion captures exactly the $\mathbb{F}_q$-linear codes. However, this definition enables an instructive analysis of the associated secret-sharing scheme in terms of linear algebra. First, we state a lemma from basic linear algebra.

LEMMA 11.84 *Let V be a finite-dimensional vector space over a field K. Let $U \subset V$ be a subspace, and let $x \in V$. Then $x \notin U$ if and only if there is a linear form $\phi \in V^*$ such that ϕ vanishes on U (that is, ϕ is identically 0 on U) but $\phi(x) = 1$.*

Proof The claim in the forward direction can be verified as an immediate consequence of the fact that there is a basis of V that contains x as well as a basis of U. The other direction is trivial. ∎

LEMMA 11.85 *Let C be as defined earlier. It is an $\mathbb{F}_q$-linear secret-sharing scheme on n players if and only if $z_0 \neq 0$ and the $\mathbb{F}_q$-span of $z_1, \ldots, z_n$ includes z_0.*

Proof As to the proof that it is an $\mathbb{F}_q$-linear secret-sharing scheme, it should be clear that the condition $\pi_0(C) = \mathbb{F}_q$ holds if and only if $z_0 \neq 0$. By inspection, the condition that for all $\mathbf{x} \in C$ it holds that if $\mathbf{x}_{\mathcal{I}^*} = \mathbf{0} \in \mathbb{F}_q^n$, then $z_0 = 0 \in \mathbb{F}_q$ is equivalent to the condition that for all $\phi \in V^*$ such that $\phi(z_i) = 0$ for $i = 1, \ldots, n$ it holds that $\phi(z_0) = 0$. By Lemma 11.84, the latter is equivalent to z_0 being in the $\mathbb{F}_q$-span of $z_1, \ldots, z_n$. ∎

LEMMA 11.86 *Let C be as in Definition 11.83. Suppose that $z_0 \neq 0$ and the $\mathbb{F}_q$-span of $z_1, \ldots, z_n$ includes z_0. Let $B \subset \{1, \ldots, n\}$ be nonempty. Then*

1. $B \in \Gamma(C)$ *if and only if the $\mathbb{F}_q$-span of the $z_i s$ with $i \in B$ includes z_0.*
2. $B \in \mathcal{A}(C)$ *if and only if there is $\phi \in V^*$ such that $\phi(z_i) = 0$ for all $i \in A$ and $\phi(z_0) = 1$.*

Proof The proof of the first claim follows from the combination of Lemmas 11.70 and 11.84. The proof of the second claim follows directly from Lemma 11.71. ∎

In the other direction, a linear secret-sharing scheme in the sense of Massey implies one in the sense of Brickell. That is, choose some matrix such that the columns form a basis for the linear code, and take its $n + 1$ rows as $z_0, z_1, \ldots, z_n$. Thus the two definitions are equivalent. However, Massey's formulation makes it easier to draw on results from coding theory when constructing secret-sharing schemes with sufficient control over the t-privacy and r-reconstruction parameters. However, for certain specialized classes of access structures, it is often more convenient to think in terms of Brickell's original definition.

11.11 Generalizations of Linear Secret Sharing

We now discuss some generalizations of linear secret-sharing schemes.

11.11.1 Linear Secret Sharing with a Large Secret Space

DEFINITION 11.87 (LINEAR SECRET-SHARING FOR $\mathbb{F}_q^k$ OVER $\mathbb{F}_q$) *Let* $C \subset \mathbb{F}_q^{n+k}$ *be an* $\mathbb{F}_q$-linear code where n,k are positive integers. Define $\mathcal{I} = \{-k+1,\ldots,0,1,\ldots,n\}$ as the index set. Define $\mathcal{I}^* = \{1,\ldots,n\}$, and define $\mathcal{Z} = \{-k+1,\ldots,0\}$. Then C is a linear secret-sharing scheme for $\mathbb{F}_q^k$ over $\mathbb{F}_q$ if the following conditions are satisfied:

1. $\pi_{\mathcal{Z}}(C) = \mathbb{F}_q^k$.
2. For all $\mathbf{x} \in C$, it holds that if $\mathbf{x}_{\mathcal{I}^*} = \mathbf{0} \in \mathbb{F}_q^n$, then $\mathbf{x}_{\mathcal{Z}} = \mathbf{0} \in \mathbb{F}_q^k$.

By a similar analysis to the one following Definition 11.66, this gives rise to a secret-sharing scheme.

As before, if $B \subset \mathcal{I}^*$, then $\overline{B} := \mathcal{I}^* \setminus B$. For $i = 1,\ldots,k$, let $\mathbf{u}_i \in \mathbb{F}_q^k$ denote the ith vector in the standard basis of $\mathbb{F}_q^k$; that is, there is 1 in the ith coordinate and 0 in all others. An easy adaptation of the arguments in the proofs of Lemmas 11.70 and 11.71 implies the following:

LEMMA 11.88 *Let* $B \subset \mathcal{I}^*$ *be a nonempty set. Then*

- $B \in \Gamma(C)$ *if and only if, for each integer i with $1 \le i \le k$, there is* $\mathbf{x}^* \in C^\perp$ *such that*

$$\mathbf{x}_{\mathcal{Z}}^* = \mathbf{u}_i \quad and \quad \mathbf{x}_{\overline{B}}^* = \mathbf{0} \in \mathbb{F}_q^{n-|B|}.$$

Equivalently, $B \in \Gamma(C)$ if and only if, for each $\mathbf{x} \in C$, it holds that $\mathbf{x}_B = \mathbf{0}$ implies $\mathbf{x}_{\mathcal{Z}} = \mathbf{0}$.
- $B \in \mathcal{A}(C)$ *if and only if, for each integer i with $1 \le i \le k$, there is* $\mathbf{x} \in C$ *such that*

$$\mathbf{x}_{\mathcal{Z}} = \mathbf{u}_i \quad and \quad \mathbf{x}_B = \mathbf{0} \in \mathbb{F}_q^{|B|}$$

Theorem 11.73 (dualization) does not hold for a scheme satisfying Definition 11.87 if $k > 1$ because it is not a perfect secret-sharing scheme in that case. Indeed, the second condition is not the negation of the first. In fact, using these two conditions, it is easy to prove that if B is a privacy set and B' is a reconstructing set with $B \subset B'$, then $|B'| - |B| \ge k$.

REMARK 11.89 Using similar reasoning as in the proof of Theorem 11.73, the claim in Corollary 11.72 still holds.

REMARK 11.90 There is an immediate translation of Definition 11.87 into the language of Brickell's scheme from Section 11.10.3. Clearly, this involves elements $z_{-k+1},\ldots,z_0,z_1,\ldots,z_n$ instead of just the elements $z_0,z_1,\ldots,z_n$. The characterizations of $\Gamma(C)$ and $\mathcal{A}(C)$ in Lemma 11.88 translate in the obvious way. The condition that $\pi_{\mathcal{Z}}(C) = \mathbb{F}_q^k$ translates to the condition that $z_{-k+1},\ldots,z_0$ are linearly independent.

Theorem 11.77 in combination with Lemma 11.78 implies the following result (see also Chen et al. [50]).

THEOREM 11.91 (GENERALIZED PARAMETER CONTROL FROM LINEAR CODES) *Let* n,k *be positive integers. Let* $C \subset \mathbb{F}_q^{n+k}$ *be an* $\mathbb{F}_q$-linear code. If

$$d_{\min}(C) \ge k+1 \quad and \quad d_{\min}(C^\perp) \ge k+1$$

then it is a linear secret-sharing scheme for $\mathbb{F}_q^k$ over $\mathbb{F}_q$ with t-privacy and r-reconstruction such that

$$t = d_{\min}(C^\perp) - k - 1 \quad and \quad r = n - d_{\min}(C) + k + 1$$

Moreover, in the corresponding secret-sharing scheme, any vector of t shares is uniformly random in $\mathbb{F}_q^t$.

REMARK 11.92 Sharp bounds for the privacy and reconstruction parameters in this construction are obtained by replacing distance by a straightforward generalization of the weights from Definition 11.75 and following a similar approach as in Theorem 11.77. Equivalently, linear secret-sharing schemes for $\mathbb{F}_q^k$ over $\mathbb{F}_q$ can be conveniently captured in terms of *pairs of codes*. See theorem 10 in Chen et al. [50].

11.11.2 Further Generalizations

We now turn to a generalization in a different direction.

DEFINITION 11.93 *A generalized linear secret-sharing scheme $\Sigma := (C, \Pi)$ for $\mathbb{F}_q$ over $\mathbb{F}_q$ on $n \geq 1$ players consists of a linear secret-sharing scheme C on $m \geq n$ players, indexed by the set $\mathcal{J} = \{0, 1, \ldots, m\}$, and a disjoint partition Π of the set $\mathcal{J}^* = \{1, \ldots, m\}$ by n nonempty subsets $I_1, \ldots, I_n \subset \mathcal{J}$. Define $\mathcal{I} = \{0, 1, \ldots, n\}$ and $\mathcal{I}^* = \{1, \ldots, n\}$, the player set.*

The idea is that in a linear secret-sharing scheme according to Definition 11.66, the m share coordinates are subdivided into n consecutive blocks, each of which corresponds to a different player in the generalization. In particular, the number of field elements a player gets as a share equals the cardinality of the block corresponding to that player.

In Chapter 6 this generalization also was considered, and there we showed that such schemes can be used for multiparty computation (MPC) in much the same way as Shamir's scheme. The advantage of the generalized schemes is that they can be constructed for any monotone access structure and over any field, as we shall see next.

We denote the access structure on the total of n players in the generalization as $\Gamma(\Sigma)$. Let $B \subset \mathcal{I}^*$ be a nonempty set. Observe that Σ is a *perfect* secret-sharing scheme with

$$B \in \Gamma(\Sigma) \quad \text{if and only if} \quad \cup_{j \in B} I_j \in \Gamma(C)$$

If we cast this generalization in the language of Brickell's scheme, we obtain monotone span programs, a notion introduced by Karchmer and Wigderson [119] that is well studied in complexity theory. This connection was first noted by Beimel [11]. Even further generalization of this notion where the secret space can have dimension greater than 1 were studied by Bertilsson and Ingemarsson [20] and van Dijk [82].

THEOREM 11.94 *Let $\Sigma = (C, \Pi)$ be a generalized linear secret-sharing scheme for $\mathbb{F}_q$ over $\mathbb{F}_q$. Define $\Sigma^* = (C^\perp, \Pi)$. Then*

1. *Σ is perfect.*
2. *$\Gamma(\Sigma^*) = (\Gamma(\Sigma))^*$.*

This theorem follows from the characterization of $\Gamma(\Sigma)$ earlier in combination with the results in Section 11.10.2. It is equivalent to the well-known fact that for any monotone

Boolean function and for any finite field, it holds that its monotone span program complexity equals that of its dual [119].

The relevance of generalized linear secret-sharing schemes becomes apparent from the following theorem:

THEOREM 11.95 *Let Γ be a monotone access structure on $n \geq 1$ players. Then there is a generalized linear secret-sharing scheme Σ for $\mathbb{F}_q$ over $\mathbb{F}_q$ on n players such that $\Gamma(\Sigma) = \Gamma$ [18, 116].*

There are several ways in which this result can be shown. Typically, the access structure is decomposed into smaller pieces for which schemes are known, and then these schemes are "glued" together to get a scheme for the composition.[16] The simplest (yet a rather "expensive") approach is that of Ito, Saito, and Nishizeki [116], which works as follows:[17]

- Enumerate all the minimal sets of Γ, say; this results in the sets $B_1, \dots, B_\ell$.
- Let $s \in \mathbb{F}_q$ be the secret. For $i = 1, \dots, \ell$, do the following: select a fresh random $|B_i|$-out-of-$|B_i|$ additive secret sharing over $\mathbb{F}_q$ (see Section 11.1) of the secret s. Call this the ith sharing. Assign each of the $|B_i|$ resulting shares to a different player in B_i.

Note that the length of the share vector for a player is exactly the number of minimal sets this player sits in. The access structure is what it should be, as we verify later. By definition of a minimal set, it holds that $B \in \Gamma$ if and only if there is some integer j with $1 \leq j \leq \ell$ such that $B_j \subset B$. Therefore, if $B \notin \Gamma$, then $B_i \setminus B$ is nonempty for all $1 \leq i \leq \ell$. Therefore, B *lacks* at least one out of the $|B_i|$ shares resulting from the ith sharing (for all $1 \leq i \leq \ell$). Since these sharings are independently generated, this means that B gets no information on the secret s from the total information available to B. However, if $B \in \Gamma$, then there is some integer j with $1 \leq j \leq \ell$ such that $B_j \subset B$. Hence, B has in particular all the $|B_j|$ shares from the jth sharing of s and can reconstruct the secret s.

Generally, this leads to very inefficient secret-sharing schemes. For instance, consider the (t, n)-threshold access structure with, say, $t \approx n/2$. Then the share length in the preceding scheme is *exponential* in n because of the sheer magnitude of the quantity $\binom{n}{t}$ for these values of the parameters.

An approach [18] that is in several cases much better in this respect is based on monotone Boolean formulas from complexity theory. A monotone Boolean formula is a finite directed acyclic graph such that

- At the top, there are precisely $n \geq 1$ vertices without any incoming edges, the input vertices. These vertices are numbered $1, \dots, n$, and each of them may have an arbitrary number of outgoing edges going down.
- At the bottom, there is precisely one vertex without any outgoing edges. It has just a single incoming edge from above. This is the output vertex.
- In between, each computation vertex has two incoming edges from above and one outgoing edge going down. Such a vertex is labeled either with the Boolean logical AND operator or with the Boolean logical OR operator.

---

[16] See Stinson [173] for results on composition.
[17] In Chapter 6 an alternative proof based on so-called replicated secret sharing can be found. This is not more efficient in general, however.

By definition, the logical AND and OR operate on bits $b, b' \in \{0, 1\}$. The AND produces $c = 1$ as the outgoing bit if the incoming bits $b, b' \in \{0, 1\}$ satisfy $b = b' = 1$, and it produces $c = 0$ as the outgoing bit otherwise. An OR operator produces $c = 1$ if $b = 1$ or $b' = 1$, and it produces $c = 0$ otherwise. If a bit is represented as an element of, say, the finite field $\mathbb{F}_2$, the AND corresponds to $c := bb' \in \mathbb{F}_2$ and the OR corresponds to $c := bb' + b + b' \in \mathbb{F}_2$.

Under this definition, a monotone Boolean formula represents a Boolean function f: $\{0, 1\}^n \longrightarrow \{0, 1\}$ as follows: given $(b_1, \ldots, b_n) \in \{0, 1\}^n$, label the ith input vertex with b_i for $i = 1, \ldots, n$. Now start the "computation" by pushing the bits $b_1, \ldots, b_n$ inductively down the graph: each time a logical operator is encountered, the incoming bits b, b' are converted to an outgoing bit c that represents the result of the respective logical operation on b, b'. This process is continued until the output vertex receives a bit, which is declared $f(b_1, \ldots, b_n)$.

Note that the simplest examples are just those formulas that consist of a single AND or a single OR: two input vertices, one computation vertex, and one output vertex. In general, formulas are just compositions of these two basic building blocks, leading to a single output vertex. Disregarding the directedness, as a graph, it is a tree. By basic graph theory, this means that the total number of edges equals the number of vertices minus 1. The *size* of a formula is the number of computation vertices.

This function f computed by the formula is monotone in the sense that if $(b_1, \ldots, b_n) \in \{0, 1\}^n$ is such that $f(b_1, \ldots, b_n) = 1$, then flipping any 0-bit among $b_1, \ldots, b_n$ (if there is any 0-bit there) to a 1-bit does not affect the f value; that is, it remains 1. Each monotone Boolean function $f: \{0, 1\}^n \longrightarrow \{0, 1\}$ is computed by some monotone Boolean formula.

One way to see this is to note first that monotone access structures correspond naturally with monotone Boolean functions simply by representing a set by its characteristic bit vector and declaring the f value to be 1 if and only if the set in question sits in the access structure. It is an easy task to construct a monotone Boolean formula computing a given monotone access structure (i.e, if one does not care too much about the resulting size). For instance, a construction can be based on a slight generalization of the idea behind the preceding scheme [116]: construct the formula as "a (multi-input) OR over the minimal sets, each of which is in turn given as a (multi-input) AND." The conversion to a formula in which the computation gates have incoming degree 2 is straightforward.

Working inductively in the *reverse* direction, that is, from the bottom to the top in a monotone Boolean formula, a linear secret-sharing scheme can be constructed whose access structure corresponds to the monotone Boolean function computed by the formula in question. Place the secret s at the output vertex. If the output vertex receives the output of a computation from an AND computation vertex directly above it, generate a random two-out-of-two additive secret sharing for s, and send share s_0 up the left input edge of that preceding computation vertex and send s_1 up the right one. If it was an OR instead, just send the secret s up instead on both the left and the right. Now repeat this process for s_0 and, independently, for s_1 and so on until each input vertex at the top has received an element through each one of its outgoing edges. The vector of elements an input vertex thus receives constitutes its share in the secret s. It is not so hard to prove by induction that this generalized linear secret-sharing scheme has the access structure as claimed.

To illustrate why this approach is more powerful than that of Ito, Saito, and Nishizeki [116], consider the following example: because it is known [178] that the majority function, that is, the Boolean function $f: \{0, 1\}^n \longrightarrow \{0, 1\}$ that gives 1 if and only if the Hamming weight of the argument is strictly greater than $n/2$, can be computed by a polynomial (in n) size monotone Boolean formula, this results in a generalized linear secret-sharing scheme for the majority access structure in which each of the n individual share vectors has length polynomial in n.[18]

The approach can be further extended by allowing more general types of monotone gates in the formula, not just ORs and ANDs. For instance, if in addition small threshold gates are allowed (such as two-out-of-three or two-out-of-four), the formula-based approach sketched here has applications to MPC secure against a general adversary, that is, one that is not necessarily constrained by a threshold condition on which subsets of the network may be corrupted.[19]

By a counting argument, most access structures admit only exponentially inefficient linear secret-sharing schemes. This is generally believed to be true for nonlinear schemes as well, although a proof is lacking at present. More precisely, the minimal length of the shares in secret-sharing schemes for general (nonthreshold) access structures has been conjectured to grow exponentially in the number of players. Nevertheless, the best known lower bounds are still very far from establishing this. Another related open problem is to determine which access structures admit an ideal secret-sharing scheme. These open problems have attracted considerable attention during the last few decades, and a rich theory has been developed in which matroid theory plays a pivotal role. For more information on this, refer to Beimel [12] and Padró [153].

11.11.3 Extension Field Interpolation

Toward an improvement of the multi-secret-sharing scheme from Section 11.4.2, we generalize Theorem 11.7, Lagrange's Interpolation Theorem. Other applications are given in Chapter 12.

THEOREM 11.96 *Fix an algebraic closure $\overline{K}$ of K. Let $\alpha_1, \ldots, \alpha_m \in \overline{K}$. For $i = 1, \ldots, m$, write $h_i(X) \in K[X]$ for the minimal polynomial of α_i over K. Suppose that if $m > 1$, the polynomials $h_1(X), \ldots, h_m(X) \in K[X]$ are pairwise distinct.[20] For $i = 1, \ldots, m$, define*

$$\delta_i = \deg h_i(X) \ (= \dim_K K(\alpha_i))$$

Moreover, define

$$M = \sum_{i=1}^{m} \delta_i$$

As before, let $K[X]_{\leq M-1}$ denote the K-vector space of polynomials $f(X) \in K[X]$ such that $\deg f \leq M - 1$. Then the evaluation map

$$\mathcal{E} : K[X]_{\leq M-1} \longrightarrow \bigoplus_{i=1}^{m} K(\alpha_i)$$

$$f(X) \mapsto (f(\alpha_i))_{i=1}^{m}$$

is an isomorphism of K-vector spaces.

---

[18] Of course, Shamir's scheme gives a much better result, but our point here is just to show a separation.

[19] For applications, see Cramer, Damgård, and Maurer [61]. An application to security against threshold adversaries is given by Cohen et al. [52].

[20] Equivalently, α_i, α_j are not Galois-conjugate over K if $i \neq j$.

Proof Since the K-dimensions on both sides are identical, it is sufficient to argue injectivity. Let $f(X) \in K[X]_{\leq M-1}$ with $f(X) \not\equiv 0$. Suppose that for $i = 1, \ldots, m$, it holds that

$$f(\alpha_i) = 0$$

Since the polynomials $h_1(X), \ldots, h_m(X)$ are pairwise coprime, it is the case that

$$h_1(X) \cdots h_m(X) \mid f(X)$$

that is, their product divides $f(X)$ in $K[X]$. But this implies that

$$\deg f \geq M$$

a contradiction. Alternatively, the theorem also can be shown easily using the Chinese Remainder Theorem.

For completeness, we give a direct construction of the inverse $\mathcal{E}^{-1}$. Suppose first that $m = 1$, and set $\alpha_1 = x$. If $x \in K$, then $K(x) = K$ and $M = 1$. Hence, the claim is a special case of Theorem 11.7. If $x \notin K$, then the claim follows directly from the fact that there is the basis

$$1, x, \ldots, x^{k-1} \in K(x)$$

of $K(x)$ as a K-vector space, where

$$k = \dim_K K(x) > 1$$

If $y \in K(x)$, then $\mathcal{E}(f) = y$, where $f(X)$ is the polynomial whose coefficient vector is the coordinate vector of y according to the preceding basis.

Now suppose that $m > 1$. For $i = 1, \ldots, m$, define

$$\delta_i'(X) = \prod_{1 \leq k \leq m, k \neq i} h_k(X) \in K[X]$$

and

$$z_i = \delta_i'(\alpha_i) = \prod_{1 \leq k \leq m, k \neq i} h_k(\alpha_i) \in K(\alpha_i)$$

For all $1 \leq i, j \leq m$ with $i \neq j$, it follows that

$$\delta_i'(\alpha_j) = 0 \quad \deg(\delta_i') = M - \dim_K K(\alpha_i)$$

Moreover, by assumption on the α_is, it holds that $h_j(\alpha_i) \neq 0$ if $i \neq j$. Therefore,

$$z_i \neq 0$$

for $i = 1, \ldots, m$.

Let

$$\mathbf{y} \in \bigoplus_{i=1}^{m} K(\alpha_i)$$

For $i = 1, \ldots, m$, select

$$f_i(X) \in K[X]$$

such that

$$\deg(f_i) \leq \dim_K K(\alpha_i) - 1 \quad f_i(\alpha_i) = \frac{y_i}{z_i}$$

By the result for the case $m = 1$, these exist. Then define

$$f(X) = \sum_{i=1}^{m} \delta_i'(X) f_i(X) \in K[X]$$

It follows that

$$\deg(f) \leq \max_{1 \leq i \leq m} \deg(\delta_i' \cdot f_i) \leq \max_{1 \leq i \leq m} \left((M - \dim_K K(\alpha_i)) + (\dim_K K(\alpha_i) - 1) \right) = M - 1$$

and that, for $j = 1, \ldots, m$,

$$f(\alpha_j) = \sum_{i=1}^{m} \delta_i'(\alpha_j) f_i(\alpha_j) = \delta_j'(\alpha_j) f_j(\alpha_j) = z_j \frac{y_j}{z_j} = y_j \qquad \blacksquare$$

11.11.4 Multi-Secret Sharing Revisited

We give an example of a secret-sharing scheme in the sense of Definition 11.87. In the "multi-secret sharing scheme" from Section 11.4.2, the length of the secret can be increased at the expense of the following two consequences:

- A growing gap between privacy and reconstruction
- A decrease in the maximum number of players that can be accommodated

We show that the latter of these two consequences can be avoided.

Theorem 11.96 gives rise to the following improvement [49] of the "multi-secret-sharing scheme" from Section 11.4.2: Suppose that t, k, n are integers with $t \geq 1$, $k > 1$ and $t + k < n \leq q$. Let $\alpha_0 \in \mathbb{F}_{q^k}$ be such that $\mathbb{F}_q(\alpha_0) = \mathbb{F}_{q^k}$, and let $\alpha_1, \ldots, \alpha_n \in \mathbb{F}_q$ be pairwise distinct. Consider

$$C = \{ (f(\alpha_0), f(\alpha_1), \ldots, f(\alpha_n)) \mid f(X) \in \mathbb{F}_q[X], \deg(f) \leq t + k \} \subset \mathbb{F}_{q^k} \oplus \left(\bigoplus_{i=1}^{n} \mathbb{F}_q \right)$$

Define $\mathcal{I} = \{0, 1, \ldots, n\}$ as the index set, and define $\mathcal{I}^* = \{1, \ldots, n\}$. The secret-sharing scheme is defined by selecting $\mathbf{x} \in C$ uniformly at random. The secret equals $x_0 \in \mathbb{F}_{q^k}$, and $x_1, \ldots, x_n \in \mathbb{F}_q$ are the shares. By combining Theorem 11.96 with Lemma 11.88, it is immediate that there is $(t + k + 1)$-reconstruction and t-privacy. Note that for each $B \subset \mathcal{I}^*$ with $|B| = t$, it holds that $\pi_B(C) = \mathbb{F}_q^k$. Therefore, by Lemma 11.65, any vector of t shares is uniformly random in $\mathbb{F}_q^t$.

11.12 Bounds for Secret Sharing

We show several limitations on the parameters of a secret-sharing scheme.

11.12.1 Lower Bound on the Length of Shares

In a perfect, connected secret-sharing scheme, the length of a share is at least the length of the secret, as is shown in the following theorem:

THEOREM 11.97 *[120] Let* **S** *be a secret-sharing scheme indexed by a set* $\mathcal{I}$. *Suppose that* **S** *is perfect and connected. Let* $j \in \mathcal{I}^*$. *Then*

$$H(S_j) \geq H(S_0)$$

In particular,

$$|\mathcal{S}_j| \geq |\mathcal{S}_0|$$

Proof Let $j \in \mathcal{I}^*$. If $\{j\} \in \Gamma(\mathbf{S})$, then $H(S_0|S_j) = 0$, and the claim follows directly by Lemma 11.38. Now suppose that $\{j\} \notin \Gamma(\mathbf{S})$, and let $B \in \Gamma(\mathbf{S})$ be a minimal set such that $j \in B$. Then

$$H(S_0|\mathbf{S}_B) = 0$$

and

$$H(S_0) = H(S_0|\mathbf{S}_{B\setminus\{j\}})$$

By Lemma 11.38, it follows that

$$H(S_0) = H(S_0|\mathbf{S}_{B\setminus\{j\}}) \leq H(S_0 S_j|\mathbf{S}_{B\setminus\{j\}})$$
$$= H(S_j|\mathbf{S}_{B\setminus\{j\}}) + H(S_0|S_j \mathbf{S}_{B\setminus\{j\}}) = H(S_j|\mathbf{S}_{B\setminus\{j\}}) \leq H(S_j) \quad \blacksquare$$

REMARK 11.98 This theorem motivates Definition 11.63.

Again by Lemma 11.38, we have the following corollary:

COROLLARY 11.99 *Suppose that* **S** *is an ideal secret-sharing scheme defined over an alphabet* $\mathcal{F}$ *of cardinality* $\bar{q}$. *Then* S_j *gives the uniform distribution on* $\mathcal{F}$ *for all* $j \in \mathcal{I}$.

11.12.2 *Shortening of a Secret-Sharing Scheme*

We explain the general principle of shortening of secret-sharing schemes. This is often a useful handle for proofs by induction. Throughout this section, let **S** be a secret-sharing scheme indexed by a set $\mathcal{I}$.

DEFINITION 11.100 (SHORTENING) *Suppose that* $B \in \mathcal{A}(\mathbf{S})$ *with* $B \neq \emptyset$ *and* $\mathbf{u} \in \mathcal{S}_B$ *satisfy* $P(\mathbf{S}_B = \mathbf{u}) > 0$. *Then* $\mathbf{S}^{B;\mathbf{u}}$ *is the secret-sharing scheme obtained by conditioning the random variable* **S** *on the event* $\mathbf{S}_B = \mathbf{u}$ *and deleting the random variables corresponding to* B. *Thus there are* $|\mathcal{I}^*| - |B| \geq 1$ *players left. We say that* **S** *is shortened at* $(B; \mathbf{u})$.

This is well defined on account of Remark 11.31. An alternative way of describing the construction of $\mathbf{S}^{B;\mathbf{u}}$ is as follows[21]: Suppose that B is a nonempty privacy set, and suppose that $\mathbf{u}$ is a share vector for B that is assigned with nonzero probability when sampling from **S**. The shortened scheme then samples from **S** conditioned on the event that B gets $\mathbf{u}$. The corresponding shares for $\mathcal{I}^* \setminus B$ are assigned, but the ones for B are deleted.

---

[21] For secret sharing, this notion was first introduced by Jackson and Martin [117] and Martin [138] under the name of contraction. Our treatment here is from Cascudo, Cramer, and Xing [43] and has been inspired by a classic notion from the theory of linear codes that goes by the same name (not to be confused with *puncturing*, which just means ignoring selected coordinates). See, for example, Huffmann and Pless [110].

It is easy to see that this is in fact a secret-sharing scheme. Since S_0 is independently distributed from $\mathbf{S}_B$, it holds that $P(S_0 = s|\mathbf{S}_B = \mathbf{u}) = P(S_0 = s)$ for all $s \in \mathcal{S}_0$. Thus the secret space is unchanged, and there is still the uniform probability distribution on it. The share spaces are unchanged as well.

Finally, the set $\mathcal{I}^* \setminus B$ clearly reconstructs in $\mathbf{S}^{B;\mathbf{u}}$: by construction, any "full share vector" according to $\mathbf{S}^{B;\mathbf{u}}$ determines a unique "full share vector" according to $\mathbf{S}$ with $\mathbf{S}_B = \mathbf{u}$. This, in turn, determines the secret because $\mathbf{S}$ is a secret-sharing scheme. In particular, $r(\mathbf{S}^{B;\mathbf{u}}) \le r(\mathbf{S}) - |B|$ for this reason. We argue about privacy next.

LEMMA 11.101 *[43] If $t(\mathbf{S}) \ge 1$ and $1 \le |B| \le t(\mathbf{S})$, then*

- $r(\mathbf{S}^{B;\mathbf{u}}) \le r(\mathbf{S}) - |B|$,
- $t(\mathbf{S}^{B;\mathbf{u}}) \ge t(\mathbf{S}) - |B|$.

Proof The statement about $r(\mathbf{S}^{B;\mathbf{u}})$ was argued earlier. If $|B| = t(\mathbf{S})$, then $t(\mathbf{S}^{B;\mathbf{u}}) \ge 0$ by definition. Now suppose that $|B| < t(\mathbf{S})$. Let $B' \subseteq \mathcal{I}^* \setminus B$ be such that $|B'| = t(\mathbf{S}) - |B|$. Since $|B \cup B'| = t(\mathbf{S})$, it holds that $\mathbf{S}_{B \cup B'}$ is independent of S_0. Then, for each $\mathbf{v} \in \mathcal{S}_B$ satisfying $P(\mathbf{S}_{B'} = \mathbf{v}|\mathbf{S}_B = \mathbf{u}) > 0$, it holds that

$$P(S_0 = s, \mathbf{S}_{B'} = \mathbf{v}|\mathbf{S}_B = \mathbf{u}) = P(S_0 = s|\mathbf{S}_{B'} = \mathbf{v}, \mathbf{S}_B = \mathbf{u}) \cdot P(\mathbf{S}_{B'} = \mathbf{v}|\mathbf{S}_B = \mathbf{u})$$

$$= P(S_0 = s|\mathbf{S}_B = \mathbf{u}) \cdot P(\mathbf{S}_{B'} = \mathbf{v}|\mathbf{S}_B = \mathbf{u})$$

where the first equality follows from elementary calculus of conditional probabilities and the second because $B, B \cup B'$ are privacy sets of $\mathbf{S}$. We have proved that S_0 and $\mathbf{S}_{B'}$ are independent when conditioned on the event $\mathbf{S}_B = \mathbf{u}$, and this is the same as saying that B' is a privacy set in the scheme $\mathbf{S}^{B;\mathbf{u}}$. ∎

REMARK 11.102 More generally, suppose that the pair $(B, \mathbf{u})$ with $B \in \mathcal{A}(\mathbf{S})$ and $B \ne \emptyset$ and with $\mathbf{u} \in \mathcal{S}_B$ satisfies $P(\mathbf{S}_B = \mathbf{u}) > 0$. Then $\Gamma(\mathbf{S}^{B;\mathbf{u}})$ includes all sets $B' \subset \mathcal{I}^* \setminus B$ such that $B \cup B' \in \Gamma(\mathbf{S})$, and $\mathcal{A}(\mathbf{S}^{B;\mathbf{u}})$ includes all sets $B' \subset \mathcal{I}^* \setminus B$ such that $B \cup B' \in \mathcal{A}(\mathbf{S})$.

11.12.3 ITSS–IC–MDS Equivalence

We now show the well-known result that ideal threshold secret-sharing (ITSS), interpolation codes (ICs), and maximum-distance separable codes (MDS codes) are all essentially equivalent. We will use these equivalences later on to show bounds on ideal threshold secret sharing.

THEOREM 11.103 *[24, 137] Let $t, n, \bar{q}$ be integers with $0 \le t < n$ and $\bar{q} \ge 2$. Suppose that $\mathbf{S} = (S_0, S_1, \ldots, S_n)$ is an ideal (t, n)-threshold secret-sharing scheme defined over an alphabet $\mathcal{F}$ of cardinality $\bar{q}$. Then*

1. *The code $C := \{x \in \mathcal{F}^{n+1} : P(\mathbf{S} = x) > 0\}$ corresponding to $\mathbf{S}$ is a $(t + 1, n + 1, \bar{q})$-interpolation code.*
2. *$\mathbf{S}_B$ gives the uniform distribution on $\mathcal{F}^{t+1}$ for each $B \subset \{0, 1, \ldots, n\}$ with $|B| = t + 1$. Consequently, because C is a $(t + 1, n + 1, \bar{q})$-interpolation code, $\mathbf{S}$ gives the uniform distribution on C.*

Proof We give a proof sketch. The argument is by induction on t. Suppose that $t = 0$. By assumption, for each $j \in \mathcal{I}^*$, the random variable S_j determines the random variable S_0. But S_0 also determines S_j (and hence S_j has the uniform distribution on $\mathcal{F}$ just as S_0) for each $j \in \mathcal{I}^*$. That is, consider the induced "reconstruction" map from the support of S_j to the support of S_0, the latter of which is all of $\mathcal{F}$. Since this map is surjective, and since $\mathrm{supp}(S_j) \subset \mathcal{F}$, it follows that $\mathrm{supp}(S_j) = \mathcal{F}$ and that the map is injective as well. Therefore, each of the $n + 1$ random variables determines each of the n other ones (and has the uniform distribution on $\mathcal{F}$).

Now suppose that $t > 0$. As to the first claim, select arbitrary $j \in \mathcal{I}^*$, $u \in \mathcal{F}$. Now shorten the scheme at $(\{j\}, u)$. By Corollary 11.99, this is well defined. By Lemma 11.101, this results in an ideal $(t-1, n-1)$-threshold scheme over the alphabet $\mathcal{F}$ of cardinality $\bar{q}$. By the induction hypothesis, the code $C^{\{j\};u}$ corresponding to this scheme is a $(t, n, \bar{q})$-interpolation code. It follows that C is a $(t+1, n+1, \bar{q})$-interpolation code, because $j \in \mathcal{I}^*$ and $u \in \mathcal{F}$ are arbitrary and $t > 0$. As to the second claim, this follows similarly by induction. Briefly, S_j gives the uniform distribution on $\mathcal{F}$ by Corollary 11.99, and after shortening, there is "t-wise uniformity" on $\mathbf{S}^{\{j\};u}$ by the induction hypothesis. This implies "$(t+1)$-wise uniformity" for $\mathbf{S}$. ∎

Note that combining this with Theorem 11.64 gives a strong equivalence between ideal threshold secret sharing and interpolation codes (orthogonal arrays).

Lemma 11.104 (Singleton Bound) *Let C be a code of length $\ell \geq 1$ over an alphabet of cardinality $\bar{q} \geq 2$. Suppose that $|C| > 1$. Then*

$$|C| \leq \bar{q}^{\ell - d + 1}$$

where $d := d_{\min}(C)$.

Proof Write $\mathcal{F}$ for the alphabet, and write $\mathcal{I}$ for an index set. If $d = 1$, the bound is trivial because $C \subset \mathcal{F}^\ell$. Now suppose that $d > 1$. Fix $B \subset \mathcal{I}$ arbitrarily with $|B| = \ell - d + 1$. Consider the projection map that sends $\mathbf{x} \in C$ to $\mathbf{x}_B \in \mathcal{F}^{\ell - d + 1}$. This map is injective; otherwise, there are $\mathbf{x}, \mathbf{y} \in C$ with $\mathbf{x} \neq \mathbf{y}$ and $d_H(\mathbf{x}, \mathbf{y}) \leq d - 1$, which is nonsense. The bound follows. ∎

Definition 11.105 (MDS Code) *A code C with $|C| > 1$ of length ℓ and minimum distance d over an alphabet of cardinality $\bar{q}$ is maximum distance separable (MDS) if it attains the singleton bound; that is, $|C| = \bar{q}^{\ell - d + 1}$. The class of all MDS codes with length ℓ and minimum distance d defined over an alphabet of cardinality $\bar{q}$ is denoted $\mathrm{MDS}(k, \ell, \bar{q})$, where $k := \ell - d + 1$.*

It is straightforward that interpolation codes and MDS codes are equivalent, as shown in the following lemma:

Lemma 11.106 *Let $r, \ell, \bar{q}$ be integers with $1 \leq r \leq \ell$ and $\bar{q} \geq 2$. Then $C \in \mathrm{IC}(r, \ell, \bar{q})$ if and only if $C \in \mathrm{MDS}(r, \ell, \bar{q})$.*

Proof In the forward direction, let $C \in \mathrm{IC}(r, \ell, \bar{q})$. Then $|C| = \bar{q}^r$. By Lemma 11.21, the minimum distance of C equals $\ell - r + 1$. In the other direction, let $C \in \mathrm{MDS}(r, \ell, \bar{q})$. Write $d = \ell - r + 1$. By definition, it holds that $d = d_{\min}(C)$. The case $r = \ell$ is trivial because this means that $C = \mathcal{F}^\ell$. Now suppose that $r < \ell$ so that $d > 1$. Select $B \subset \mathcal{I}$ arbitrarily such that

$|B| = \ell - d + 1$. Consider the projection map that sends $\mathbf{x} \in C$ to $\mathbf{x}_B \in \mathcal{F}^{\ell-d+1}$. This map is injective for the same reason as in the proof of Lemma 11.104. Since $|C| = \bar{q}^r = \bar{q}^{\ell-d+1}$ by definition, this projection map constitutes a bijection. ∎

On account of Theorem 11.103, Theorem 11.64, and Lemma 11.106, we have the following equivalences:

THEOREM 11.107 (ITSS-IC-MDS EQUIVALENCE) *Let $t, n, \bar{q}$ be integers with $0 \leq t < n$ and $\bar{q} \geq 2$. Then the following three statements are equivalent*[22]:

- ITSS$(t, n, \bar{q}) \neq \emptyset$.[23]
- IC$(t + 1, n + 1, \bar{q}) \neq \emptyset$.
- MDS$(t + 1, n + 1, \bar{q}) \neq \emptyset$.

This result also holds when restricted to the $\mathbb{F}_q$-linear case.

11.12.4 Upper Bounds on Length for Fixed Alphabet Size in ITSS

We show the fundamental limitation that the number of players n in an ideal (t, n)-threshold secret-sharing scheme is bounded as a function of the cardinality $\bar{q}$ of the alphabet if the trivial cases $t = 0, n - 1$ are excluded.

We present two results. The first, which asserts that $n < 2\bar{q} - 1$ whether the scheme is linear or not, combines the fact that ideal threshold secret-sharing schemes are *equivalent* to interpolation codes with an application of the classical Bush bound [32] for orthogonal arrays $O(r, \ell, \bar{q})$ (= interpolation codes) and a bound on pairwise orthogonal Latin squares.[24] We also provide an alternative proof of the same bound but assuming linearity.

The second result is a direct application of S. Ball's breakthrough result [2] in combinatorics and coding theory that affirms the long-standing linear MDS Conjecture *in the case of prime fields*, in combination with the fact that ideal (linear) threshold secret-sharing schemes are equivalent to (linear) *maximum distance separable (MDS) codes*. As a consequence, the existence of ideal $\mathbb{F}_p$-linear threshold schemes (p prime) is completely understood. That is, excluding the trivial case $t = 0, n - 1$, a (t, n)-scheme exists if *and only if $n \leq p$*.

We start with some preparations for the first result.

DEFINITION 11.108 *Let $\bar{q} \geq 2$ be an integer. A Latin square of order $\bar{q}$ is a square matrix M with entries in the set $[\bar{q}] := \{1, \ldots, \bar{q}\}$ such that each element of $[\bar{q}]$ occurs exactly once in each column (and row).*

Note that M is a $\bar{q} \times \bar{q}$ matrix.

DEFINITION 11.109 *Suppose that M, M' are Latin squares of order $\bar{q}$. Then M, M' are orthogonal if the $\bar{q}^2$ ordered pairs (M_{ij}, M'_{ij}) with $1 \leq i, j \leq \bar{q}$ are all distinct; that is, there is a bijection with the set $[\bar{q}] \times [\bar{q}]$.*

---

[22] We have refrained from repeating the explicit correspondences between the equivalent classes later.
[23] For the definition, see Section 11.9.4.
[24] We thank Andries Brouwer for suggesting this proof to us (2010).

There is the following classical bound for orthogonal Latin squares (see, e.g., van Lint and Wilson [134]).

LEMMA 11.110 *Suppose $M_1, M_2, \ldots, M_w$ are pairwise orthogonal Latin squares of order $\bar{q}$. Then $w < \bar{q}$.*

Proof Having a permutation act on the symbols $\{1, \ldots, \bar{q}\}$ of some M_i and replacing M_i by the resulting Latin square does not affect pairwise orthogonality. Therefore, we may assume without loss of generality that the top row of each M_i is the vector $(1, 2, \ldots, \bar{q})$. Now consider the entries $x_1, \ldots, x_w$, where x_i is the $(2,1)$-entry in M_i ($1 \leq i \leq w$). The following two observations together justify the claimed bound: (1) by the Latin-square property, none of the x_is is equal to 1 because the top left corner of each M_i is 1, and (2) because the top rows are identical, pairwise orthogonality implies that $x_i \neq x_j$ for all $1 \leq i < j \leq w$. ∎

THEOREM 11.111 (BUSH BOUND [32]) *Suppose that $\mathrm{IC}(r, \ell, \bar{q}) \neq \emptyset$, for some integers $r, \ell, \bar{q}$ with $2 \leq r \leq \ell - 2$ and $\bar{q} \geq 2$. Then $r < \bar{q}$.*

Proof By application of Lemma 11.5 (puncturing), we may assume that $\mathrm{IC}(r, r+2, \bar{q}) \neq \emptyset$ as well. Select some code in this class, and consider the subcode consisting of the following words. Without loss of generality, the symbols $0, 1$ are in the alphabet.

1. (*Category I*) Among the first $r - 1$ coordinates, there are exactly $r - 2$ occurrences of 0, whereas the rth coordinate is 0.
2. (*Category II*) The first $r - 1$ coordinates are 0, and the rth coordinate is 0 as well.   '
3. (*Category III*) The first $r - 1$ coordinates are 0, whereas the rth coordinate is 1.

For each of these categories, it is by the interpolation property that the "tail," that is, the pair consisting of the last two coordinates (the $(r+1)$st and the $(r+2)$nd), is uniquely determined by the first r coordinates. Thus, categories II and III each contain a single element. Write (a, b) and (a', b') for their respective tails. Again by interpolation, $a \neq a'$ and $b \neq b'$. By counting, category I consists of exactly $(\bar{q} - 1)(r - 1)$ words. For each of those, if its tail is given by (x, y), then $x \neq a$ and $y \neq b$ and $(x, y) \neq (a', b')$ by interpolation. Since, in category I, distinct words have distinct tails (again by interpolation), the cardinality of category I is upper bounded by the number of possible tails, taking into account the tail restrictions for category I derived earlier. Concretely, it holds that

$$(\bar{q} - 1)(r - 1) \leq (\bar{q} - 1)^2 - 1$$

which is equivalent to the claimed bound. ∎

LEMMA 11.112 *Let $\ell, \bar{q}$ be integers $\ell \geq 2$ and $\bar{q} \geq 2$. Suppose that $\mathrm{IC}(2, \ell, \bar{q}) \neq \emptyset$. Then $\ell < \bar{q} + 2$.*

Proof If $\ell < 4$, then the claim is trivially true. So assume that $\ell \geq 4$. Consider any code in $\mathrm{IC}(2, \ell, \bar{q})$. Such a code gives rise to $\ell - 2 \geq 2$ pairwise orthogonal Latin squares of order $\bar{q}$ as follows: interpret its words $\mathbf{x}$ as vectors of the form $(i, j, L_1(i,j), \ldots, L_{\ell-2}(i,j))$, where (i,j) indicates the (i,j) position in a $\bar{q} \times \bar{q}$ matrix and $L_u(i,j)$ gives the entry in the uth matrix at the (i,j) position ($u = 1, \ldots, \ell - 2$). The interpolation property implies that these are well defined, are Latin squares, and are pairwise orthogonal. The claimed bound now follows by application of Lemma 11.110. ∎

We are now in a position to state and prove the first bound.

THEOREM 11.113 (UPPER BOUND ON LENGTH IN ITSS) *Let $t, n, \bar{q}$ be integers with $1 \leq t < n - 1$ and $\bar{q} \geq 2$. Suppose that* ITSS$(t, n, \bar{q}) \neq \emptyset$. *Then $n < 2\bar{q} - 2$.*

Proof Apply Theorem 11.103, and let $C \in$ IC$(t + 1, n + 1, \bar{q})$. Since $(n + 1) - (t + 1) \geq 2$ and $t + 1 \geq 2$, by Theorem 11.111, it follows that

$$t + 1 < \bar{q}$$

Next, apply Lemma 11.5 (shortening) to obtain a code $C'' \in$ IC$(2, n + 2 - t, \bar{q})$. By Lemma 11.112,

$$n + 2 - t < \bar{q} + 2 .$$

The claimed bound follows by combining these two bounds. ∎

We remark that *in the $\mathbb{F}_q$-linear case*, there is the following alternative proof: it is straightforward that the existence of an $\mathbb{F}_q$-linear MDS code of length ℓ and dimension k implies the existence of a set of ℓ vectors in $\mathbb{F}_q^k$ such that each subset of k of them constitutes an $\mathbb{F}_q$-basis of $\mathbb{F}_q^k$, and vice versa. That is, in the forward direction, construct a matrix whose collection of rows constitutes an $\mathbb{F}_q$-basis for the given MDS code. The set of column vectors has the claimed property. In the other direction, appropriately reverse this process.

Suppose that we are given a set of ℓ vectors in $\mathbb{F}_q^k$ such that each subset of k of them constitutes an $\mathbb{F}_q$-basis of $\mathbb{F}_q^k$, with $2 \leq k \leq \ell$. Then there is the fundamental bound that $\ell \leq q + k - 1$. Indeed, select any $k - 2 \geq 0$ vectors and observe (from Ball [2]) that there are exactly $q + 1$ hyperplanes H containing those $k - 2$ vectors (select $\mathbf{0}$ when $k = 2$). That is, complement the selected $k - 2$ vectors with two extra vectors to get an $\mathbb{F}_q$-basis of $\mathbb{F}_q^k$; the hyperplanes H in question correspond one to one with the $q + 1$ lines (passing through the origin) in the plane spanned by those two extra vectors. Moreover, each of those $q + 1$ hyperplanes H contains at most one of the other $\ell - k + 2$ vectors (because otherwise the dimension of H would be k instead of $k - 1$), whereas for each of those vectors there is clearly such a hyperplane H containing it, by construction. In conclusion, $\ell - k + 2 \leq q + 1$ or, equivalently, $\ell \leq q + k - 1$.

Taking the dual of a linear MDS code gives a linear MDS code, as is easy to see.[25] Assuming that the condition $k < \ell - 1$ also holds, the dimension of the dual is $\ell - k \geq 2$. Applying the bound derived earlier to the dual of C, it follows that $\ell \leq q + (\ell - k) - 1$. Combining the two, it follows that $\ell \leq 2q - 2$.[26]

We will state (but not prove – this is beyond the present scope) a bound for ideal linear threshold sharing that is a direct consequence of S. Ball's recent breakthrough result [2] in combinatorics and coding theory that affirms the long-standing linear MDS Conjecture *in the case of prime fields*.

---

[25] See, for instance, van Lint and Wilson [132], page 101, theorem 6.8.3.

[26] Yet another proof is by inspection of the weight distribution of linear MDS codes (which is well known) in combination with a similar dualization argument. See van Lint [132], pages 102–3 (combine theorem 6.8.8 with corollary 6.8.9).

CONJECTURE 11.114 *Let q be a prime power. Suppose that C is an $\mathbb{F}_q$-linear code of length $\ell \geq 4$ and dimension k with $1 < k < \ell - 1$. If C is an MDS code, then $\ell \leq q + 1$ except when q is even and (k = 3 or k = q − 1), in which case $\ell \leq q + 2$ (see, e.g., Huffman and Pless [110], page 265).*

THEOREM 11.115 [2] *The linear MDS Conjecture holds for all finite fields $\mathbb{F}_q$ where q is a prime number.*

Combining this with Theorems 11.107 and 11.82, the case of ideal linear secret sharing over prime fields is completely solved.

THEOREM 11.116 (FULL CHARACTERIZATION OF THE $\mathbb{F}_p$-LINEAR CASE) *Let t,n,p be integers with $0 \leq t < n$ and $p \geq 2$ a prime number. Then $\mathrm{ITSS}_{\mathrm{lin}}(t,n,p) \neq \emptyset$ if and only if one of the following two conditions is satisfied:*

1. $t = 0$ *or* $t = n − 1$.
2. $1 \leq t < n − 1$ *and* $n \leq p$.

11.12.5 A Lower Bound on the Threshold Gap

Theorem 11.111 shows that the number n of players in an ideal (t,n)-threshold secret-sharing scheme is bounded as a function of the cardinality $\bar{q}$ of the alphabet if $1 \leq t < n − 1$. Therefore, if the number of players in a secret-sharing scheme is sufficiently large compared with the cardinality of the alphabet, there must be a "gap" between privacy and reconstruction that is greater than 1. We now show some general bound on the magnitude of this gap [43]. In Section 12.6.4, we show some consequences of this bound.

Let $\mathbf{S}$ be a secret-sharing scheme indexed by some set $\mathcal{I}$. As in Section 11.9.2, let $r(\mathbf{S})$ (and $t(\mathbf{S})$) denote the minimum r (and maximum t) such that $\mathbf{S}$ has r-reconstruction (and t-privacy). Furthemore, let $n(\mathbf{S})$ denote the cardinality of the player set $\mathcal{I}^*$. Also, $\lambda^*(\mathbf{S})$ denotes the average Shannon entropy of the shares.

DEFINITION 11.117 (THRESHOLD GAP) *The threshold gap of $\mathbf{S}$ is*

$$g(\mathbf{S}) := r(\mathbf{S}) - t(\mathbf{S})$$

Note that $\mathbf{S}$ is a threshold secret-sharing scheme if $g(S) = 1$.

THEOREM 11.118 *[43] Suppose that $t(\mathbf{S}) \geq 1$. Then*

$$g(\mathbf{S}) \geq \frac{n(\mathbf{S}) - t(\mathbf{S}) + 1}{2^{\lambda^*(\mathbf{S})}}$$

REMARK 11.119 This bound becomes invalid if $t(\mathbf{S})$ is substituted by a lower bound. For instance, the trivial lower bound $1 \leq t(\mathbf{S})$ would give $g(\mathbf{S}) \geq n(\mathbf{S})/\bar{q}$. This is false in the case of ideal $(n − 1, n)$-threshold secret-sharing schemes with $n > \bar{q}$.

We will prove the following weaker corollary:

COROLLARY 11.120 *[43] Suppose that $t(\mathbf{S}) \geq 1$. Furthermore, suppose that each share space has cardinality $\bar{q}$ for some positive integer $\bar{q}$. Then*

$$g(\mathbf{S}) \geq \frac{n(\mathbf{S}) - t(\mathbf{S}) + 1}{\bar{q}}$$

Proof Write $\mathbf{S}^*$ for the joint shares, that is, the vector of random variables $(S_j)_{j \in \mathcal{I}^*}$. We first show that

$$r(\mathbf{S}) \geq \frac{n(\mathbf{S})}{\bar{q}} + 1$$

Let s, s' be distinct elements of the secret space $\mathcal{S}_0$. Since $t(\mathbf{S}) \geq 1$, the probability distributions of $S_j | (S_0 = s)$ and $S_j | (S_0 = s')$ coincide for each $j \in \mathcal{I}^*$.

For each $j \in \mathcal{I}^*$, this implies that if we sample $x_j \in \mathcal{S}_j$ according to $S_j | (S_0 = s)$ and $y_j \in \mathcal{S}_j$ according to $S_j | (S_0 = s')$, then the collision probability satisfies[27]

$$P(x_j = y_j) \geq \frac{1}{|\mathcal{S}_j|} = \frac{1}{\bar{q}}$$

Therefore, if $\mathbf{x} \in \prod_{j \in \mathcal{I}^*} \mathcal{S}_j$ is sampled according to $\mathbf{S}^* | (S_0 = s)$, and independently, $\mathbf{y} \in \prod_{j \in \mathcal{I}^*} \mathcal{S}_j$ is sampled according to $\mathbf{S}^* | (S_0 = s')$, then the expected Hamming distance between $\mathbf{x}$ and $\mathbf{y}$ satisfies

$$\mathrm{E}(d_{\mathrm{H}}(\mathbf{x}, \mathbf{y})) \leq (1 - \frac{1}{\bar{q}}) \cdot n(\mathbf{S})$$

by linearity of expectation.

Consequently, there are $\mathbf{x}, \mathbf{y}$ such that

1. $\mathbf{x}$ (and $\mathbf{y}$) has a positive probability of showing up when sampling from $\mathbf{S}^* | (S_0 = s)$ (and $\mathbf{S}^* | (S_0 = s')$).
2. The Hamming distance between $\mathbf{x}, \mathbf{y}$ is at most $(1 - \frac{1}{\bar{q}}) \cdot n(\mathbf{S})$; that is, $\mathbf{x}, \mathbf{y}$ have at least $n(\mathbf{S})/\bar{q}$ coordinates in common.

Since their respective secrets differ, it must hold that $r(\mathbf{S}) \geq (n(\mathbf{S})/\bar{q}) + 1$, as desired. Note that $r(\mathbf{S}) \geq (n(\mathbf{S})/\bar{q}) + 1$ is equivalent to $g(\mathbf{S}) \geq (n(\mathbf{S}) - t(\mathbf{S}) + 1)/\bar{q}$ if $t(\mathbf{S}) = 1$.

Now assume that $t(\mathbf{S}) > 1$. Shorten the scheme arbitrarily at some $t(\mathbf{S}) - 1$ coordinates, resulting in a scheme $\mathbf{S}'$ on $n(\mathbf{S}) - t(\mathbf{S}) + 1$ players. By Lemma 11.101,

$$r(\mathbf{S}') \leq r(\mathbf{S}) - t(\mathbf{S}) + 1$$

and

$$t(\mathbf{S}') \geq 1$$

Application of the preceding bound then yields

$$r(\mathbf{S}') \geq \frac{n(\mathbf{S}) - t(\mathbf{S}) + 1}{\bar{q}} + 1$$

---

[27] This is verified at once using the Cauchy-Schwarz Inequality, a special case of which says that for all $\mathbf{x}, \mathbf{y} \in \mathbb{R}^n$, it holds that $\langle \mathbf{x}, \mathbf{y} \rangle \leq \langle \mathbf{x}, \mathbf{x} \rangle \cdot \langle \mathbf{y}, \mathbf{y} \rangle$.

Therefore,

$$g(\mathbf{S}) = r(\mathbf{S}) - t(\mathbf{S}) = (r(\mathbf{S}) - t(\mathbf{S}) + 1) - 1 \geq r(\mathbf{S}') - 1 \geq \frac{n(\mathbf{S}) - t(\mathbf{S}) + 1}{\bar{q}}$$

which is the claimed bound. ∎

We note that some earlier lower bounds on the gap are implied by references [25, 83, 117, and 152] (see Cascudo, Cramer, and Xing [43] for a discussion). The bound given here, however, gives a better result for small alphabets (which is what we are interested in here).[28]

The bound from Theorem 11.118 can be improved for linear secret-sharing schemes, as follows:

COROLLARY 11.121 *[43] Suppose that* $\mathbf{S}$ *is an* $\mathbb{F}_q$*-linear secret-sharing scheme. Further-more, suppose that* $1 \leq t(\mathbf{S}) < r(\mathbf{S}) \leq n(\mathbf{S}) - 1$. *Then*

$$g(\mathbf{S}) \geq \frac{n(\mathbf{S}) + 2}{2q - 1}$$

Proof Let $C \subset \mathbb{F}_q^{n+1}$ be an $\mathbb{F}_q$-linear code realizing the scheme. Applying Theorem 11.73, the gap of the scheme $\mathbf{S}^{\perp}$ induced by $C^{\perp}$ equals $g(\mathbf{S})$ and $t(\mathbf{S}^{\perp}) = n(\mathbf{S}) - r(\mathbf{S}) \geq 1$. Application of the bound from Corollary 11.120 gives

$$g(\mathbf{S}) \geq \frac{r(\mathbf{S}) + 1}{q}$$

Combining this with the bound from Corollary 11.120 applied to $\mathbf{S}$ gives

$$2g(\mathbf{S}) \geq \frac{n(\mathbf{S}) - t(\mathbf{S}) + 1 + r(\mathbf{S}) + 1}{q} = \frac{n(\mathbf{S}) + 2 + g(\mathbf{S})}{q}$$

and the desired bound follows. ∎

REMARK 11.122 (GENERALIZATIONS) The bound from this corollary also applies to the linear secret-sharing schemes for $\mathbb{F}_q^k$ over $\mathbb{F}_q$ from Definition 11.87 on account of Remark 11.89. It also applies to the generalized linear secret-sharing schemes for $\mathbb{F}_q$ over $\mathbb{F}_q$ from Definition 11.93 on account of Theorem 11.94 (dualization). In the latter case, the share spaces do not necessarily have the same cardinality. Therefore, in Corollary 11.121, the definition of the parameter q must be replaced by the average over the values q^{m_i}, where m_i is the cardinality of the ith set from the disjoint partition Π defined there ($i = 1, \ldots, n$).

This leads, for instance, to an alternative proof of the fact [119] that the binary monotone span program complexity of the majority function on n input bits is $\Omega(n \log n)$.

11.13 Interpolation over Algebraic Number Fields and Black Box Secret Sharing

So far we have considered interpolation over fields and secret sharing over finite fields. We now study interpolation over general commutative rings and present an application of interpolation over algebraic number fields to black box secret-sharing schemes.

---

[28] A special case of this bound, namely, when $g(\mathbf{S}) = 1$, was shown previously in unpublished work by Joe Kilian and Noam Nisan in 1990. See Cascudo, Cramer, and Xing [43].

11.13.1 Admissible Sets and Interpolation over Commutative Rings

Throughout this section, let A be a nontrivial commutative ring.

The main purpose of this section is to show that Lagrange interpolation over general commutative rings can be characterized exactly in terms of admissible sets, which are defined next. This characterization will follow by a combination of Theorem 11.124 and Lemma 11.128. Moreover, we show some relevant bounds involving admissible sets.

DEFINITION 11.123 (ADMISSIBLE SET) *Let $T \subset A$ be a nonempty set. Then T is admissible if, for all $\alpha, \beta \in T$, it holds that if $\alpha \neq \beta$, then $\alpha - \beta$ is a unit in A. If $|T| = 1$, the set T is admissible by default.*

As a generalization of Definition 11.6, for each integer $m \geq 0$, let $A[X]_{\leq m}$ denote the set consisting of polynomials $f(X) \in A[X]$ such that $\deg f(X) \leq m$. Note that $A[X]_{\leq m}$ is a free A-module of rank $m + 1$.

THEOREM 11.124 (LAGRANGE INTERPOLATION OVER COMMUTATIVE RINGS)
Suppose that $T \subset A$ is admissible. Then the evaluation map

$$\mathcal{E} : A[X]_{\leq |T|-1} \longrightarrow \bigoplus_{\alpha \in T} A$$

$$f(X) \mapsto (f(\alpha))_{\alpha \in T}$$

is an isomorphism of A-modules.

Proof The claim is trivial if $|T| = 1$. So assume that $|T| > 1$. We follow the approach from Section 11.6.1, based on the CRT. We only point out the differences. Since T is admissible, the ideals $I_\alpha := (X - \alpha) \subset A[X]$ with $\alpha \in T$ are pairwise coprime in $A[X]$. That is, if $\alpha \neq \alpha'$, then the ideal $I_\alpha + I_{\alpha'} \subset A[X]$ contains the unit $\alpha - \alpha'$. By the CRT,

$$A[X]/\prod_{\alpha \in T}(X - \alpha) \simeq \prod_{\alpha \in T} A[X]/(X - \alpha)$$

It is sufficient to show the following:

1. The A-module morphism from $A[X]_{\leq |T|-1}$ to $A[X]/\prod_{\alpha \in T}(X - \alpha)$ that sends a polynomial to its class (that is, the natural inclusion of $A[X]_{\leq |T|-1}$ into $A[X]$ followed by the canonical morphism) is an isomorphism.
2. For all $f(X) \in A[X]$, and for all $\beta \in A$, it holds that $f(X) \equiv f(\beta) \pmod{X - \beta}$.

As to the first property, by Theorem 11.125, each element on the l.h.s. is represented by some polynomial of degree at most $|T| - 1$. By Corollary 11.127, exploiting the fact that the difference of any two distinct elements of the admissible set T is, in particular, nonzero and not a zero divisor, it follows that distinct polynomials of degree at most $|T| - 1$ represent distinct classes. The second property follows by Corollary 11.126. This concludes the proof.

On the constructive side, for each $\alpha \in T$, consider the polynomial

$$\delta_\alpha(X) = \prod_{\substack{\alpha' \in T: \\ \alpha' \neq \alpha}} \frac{X - \alpha'}{\alpha - \alpha'} \in Q(A)[X]$$

where $Q(A)$ is the field of fractions of A. By assumption on T, the denominators are units in A. Therefore, for each $\alpha \in T$,

$$\delta_\alpha(X) \in A[X]$$

It follows that the inverse of $\mathcal{E}$ is the map

$$\mathcal{E}^{-1} : \bigoplus_{\alpha \in T} A \longrightarrow A[X]_{\leq |T|-1}$$

$$(z_\alpha)_{\alpha \in T} \mapsto \sum_{\alpha \in T} z_\alpha \cdot \delta_\alpha(X)$$

Note that by the discussion in Section 11.6.1, the definition of the inverse map also can be viewed as an immediate inheritance of the CRT. ∎

Of course, the preceding theorem also can be proved via Vandermonde determinants in combination with basic results on linear systems of equations over rings. Moreover, the theorem can be easily generalized so as to "include evaluations at the point at infinity," just as in Theorem 11.13.

THEOREM 11.125 (EUCLIDEAN ALGORITHM) *Let $f(X), g(X) \in A[X]$ be such that $f, g \neq 0$. Suppose that the leading coefficient of $g(X)$ is a unit in A. Then there exist unique $q(X), r(X) \in A[X]$ such that*

1. $f(X) = r(X) + q(X)g(X)$.
2. $\deg r(X) < \deg g(X)$.

For a proof, see, for example, Lang [126].

The following corollary is a special case of this theorem.

COROLLARY 11.126 *Suppose that $f(X) \in A[X]$ and $a \in A$ are such that $f \neq 0$ and $f(a) = 0$. Then $f(X) = (X - a)q(X)$ for a unique polynomial $q(X) \in A[X]$.*

Note that $\deg q(X) = \deg f(X) - 1$ in the preceding corollary.

COROLLARY 11.127 *Let $f(X) \in A[X]$ with $f \neq 0$. Suppose that $T' \subset A$ is a nonempty set such that the following statements hold:*

1. *If $a, b \in T'$ and $a \neq b$, then $a - b$ is not a zero divisor in A.*
2. *For each $a \in T'$, it holds that $f(a) = 0$.*

Then $|T'| \leq \deg f(X)$.

Proof Proof is by induction on $|T'|$. The claim is trivial if $|T'| = 1$. So assume that $|T'| > 1$. Applying Corollary 11.126, let $b \in T'$, and let $q(X) \in A[X]$ be such that $f(X) = (X - b)q(X)$. Let $a \in T' \setminus \{b\}$. Then

$$0 = f(a) = (a - b)q(a)$$

Since $a - b$ is nonzero and not a zero divisor in A, it follows that $q(a) = 0$. Now apply the induction hypothesis to the pair $(q(X), T' \setminus \{b\})$. It follows that $|T'| - 1 \leq \deg q(X)$. Hence, $|T'| \leq \deg q(X) + 1 = \deg f(X)$. ∎

Assuming that Corollary 11.127 is understood for the case of fields, here is how one can argue the remaining cases without further recourse to the Euclidean algorithm: if A is a field, then the corollary expresses nothing other than the fact that a polynomial of degree $n \geq 0$ has at most n distinct zeros.[29] If A is a domain (that is, it has no zero divisors), the claim follows by passing to its quotient field $Q(A)$. If A is not a domain, let $Z(A) \subset A$ consist of its zero divisors together with 0.[30] Then $Z(A)$ contains a prime ideal P of A.[31] Consider the quotient ring A/P. Write $\bar{f}(X)$ for the image of $f(X)$ in $(A/P)[X]$ under reduction modulo P. Similarly, write $\bar{T}'$ for the image of T' in A/P. Clearly, it holds that $\bar{f}(\bar{a}) = 0$ in A/P, for all $\bar{a} \in \bar{T}'$. By the conditions of the corollary, for all $a, b \in T'$ with $a \neq b$, it holds that $\bar{a} - \bar{b} \neq 0$ in A/P. Hence, each element of $\bar{T}'$ is a root of $\bar{f}(X)$ and $|\bar{T}'| = |T'|$. Since A/P is a domain and $\deg \bar{f}(X) \leq \deg f(X)$, the claim follows.

LEMMA 11.128 (NECESSITY OF ADMISSIBILITY) *Let $\widetilde{T} \subset A$ be a nonempty set. Replace the admissible set $T \subset A$ in Theorem 11.124 by $\widetilde{T}$. Suppose that the corresponding map $\widetilde{\mathcal{E}}$ is an isomorphism. Then $\widetilde{T}$ is admissible.*

Proof We may assume that $|\widetilde{T}| > 1$. We give two proofs. Let J be a maximal ideal in A. The map $\widetilde{\mathcal{E}}$ induces an isomorphism of A/J-vector spaces

$$(A/J)[X]_{|\widetilde{T}|-1} \longrightarrow \bigoplus_{\alpha \in \widetilde{T}} A/J$$

that works just by "reduction modulo J." Indeed, the map is well defined (i.e., a polynomial with coefficients in J is sent to the all-zero vector), and it inherits surjectivity from $\widetilde{\mathcal{E}}$. Since the dimensions on both sides are finite and the same, the map must be injective as well. Hence it is an isomorphism. It follows at once that the pairwise differences of the elements in $\widetilde{T}$ are units. Indeed, if not, then some difference is contained in some maximal ideal, and the preceding induced map is not an isomorphism: the evaluation points are not pairwise distinct, and hence, the dimension of the image is strictly smaller than $|\widetilde{T}|$.

We now give a more explicit proof. Let $x \in \widetilde{T}$. Consider the polynomial

$$g(X) = \prod_{\substack{x' \in \widetilde{T}: \\ x' \neq x}} (X - x') \in A[X]$$

By the hypothesis, let $f(X) \in A[X]$ be the unique polynomial of degree at most $|\widetilde{T}| - 1$ such that for all $x' \in \widetilde{T}$ with $x \neq x'$,

$$f(x) = 1 \quad \text{and} \quad f(x') = 0$$

Then, for all $z \in \widetilde{T}$,

$$g(x) \cdot f(z) = g(z)$$

---

[29] Note that the zero-polynomial $f = 0$ has $|A|$ distinct zeroes, but its degree is $-\infty$ by definition. Hence, this does not contradict the claim.

[30] This is in general *not* an ideal. For instance, in $\mathbb{Z}/6\mathbb{Z}$, the element $\bar{2} + \bar{3}$ is a unit and, hence, not a zero divisor.

[31] If a set $S \subset A$ is closed under multiplication and $0 \notin S$, the set of ideals that avoid S is not empty because it contains (0). Moreover, a maximal element P (in the sense of the partial ordering by inclusion) is a prime ideal of A. If A is finite, then the existence of a such a maximal element is clear. Otherwise, it follows from Zorn's Lemma. For the details, see, for example, Lang [126] (associated primes on page 416). Now set $S = A \setminus Z(A)$ (that is, S consists of the nonzero elements that are not zero divisors), and note that, by Lemma 10.1, the set S is multiplicatively closed.

By the hypothesis, this means that the polynomial identity

$$g(x) \cdot f(X) = g(X)$$

holds. Since $\deg g(X) = |\widetilde{T}| - 1$ and $\deg f(X) \leq |\widetilde{T}| - 1$, it holds that $\deg f(X) = |\widetilde{T}| - 1$ as well. Since $g(X)$ is monic, it follows that $g(x)$ is a unit. Hence, $x - x'$ is a unit, for all $x' \in \widetilde{T}$ with $x \neq x'$. Since $x \in \widetilde{T}$ is arbitrary, the claim follows.   ∎

11.13.2 Interpolation over Algebraic Number Fields

We now show explicit bounds on the cardinality of admissible sets for some given rings A, most notably the case where A is the ring of integers of a cyclotomic number field.

DEFINITION 11.129 (LENSTRA CONSTANT) *The quantity $\lambda(A)$ denotes the supremum of $|T|$, where T ranges over all admissible subsets of A.*

We first give some straightforward examples. In general, $\lambda(A) \geq 2$ because $0, 1 \in A$ and $0 \neq 1$ by assumption. If A is a field, then A itself is admissible. Thus, for example, $\lambda(\mathbb{Q}) = \infty$, and $\lambda(\mathbb{F}_q) = q$. It is immediate that $\lambda(\mathbb{Z}) = 2$ because, by the pigeonhole principle, among any three integers there are at least two that have the same residue class modulo 2. Hence the difference of such two is an even number and therefore not a unit.

Let $p \geq 2$ be a prime, and let $k \geq 1$ be an integer. Then $\lambda(\mathbb{Z}/p^k\mathbb{Z}) = p$. That is, the set consisting of the classes of $0, 1, \ldots, p - 1$ is admissible. Once again by the pigeonhole principle, any set of size $> p$ is not admissible. Applying the Chinese Remainder Theorem, it follows that $\lambda(\mathbb{Z}/n\mathbb{Z}) = p'$, where $n \geq 2$ is an integer, and $p' > 0$ is the smallest prime number with $p' | n$. If A is an $\mathbb{F}_q$-algebra such that $\dim_{\mathbb{F}_q} A < \infty$ and such that 0 is its only nilpotent, then A is a product of finite extension fields of $\mathbb{F}_q$ by Theorem 10.16. Hence $\lambda(A)$ equals the cardinality of the smallest of these fields.

In general, the quantity $\lambda(A)$ may be upper bounded as follows:

LEMMA 11.130 *For each proper ideal I in A, it holds that*

$$\lambda(A) \leq |A/I|$$

Proof   Without loss of generality, assume that $|A/I| < \infty$. By the pigeonhole principle, a set $T \subset A$ with $|T| > |A/I|$ contains distinct elements $a, b \in T$ such that $a \equiv b \bmod I$ or, equivalently, $a - b \in I$. Since I is a proper ideal, this implies that such $a - b$ is not a unit.   ∎

REMARK 11.131 Since each proper ideal I is contained in some maximal ideal J, and since $|A/J| \leq |A/I|$ for such I, J, it follows that attention may be restricted to the maximal ideals when upper bounding $\lambda(A)$ by the approach of Lemma 11.130.

We give an application to the theory of algebraic number fields. Let K be a number field of degree n. Since $\mathcal{O}_K$ is a free $\mathbb{Z}$-module of rank n, it follows that

$$|\mathcal{O}_K/2\mathcal{O}_K| \leq 2^n$$

Hence,

$$\lambda(\mathcal{O}_K) \leq 2^n < \infty$$

Let $p \geq 2$ be a prime number, and let K be the pth cyclotomic number field, with ring of integers $\mathcal{O}_K$. If $p = 2$, then $K = \mathbb{Q}$. Hence, $\lambda(\mathcal{O}_K) = 2$ in this case. If $p > 2$, then $\lambda(\mathcal{O}_K)$ can be determined as follows: let $\omega \in \mathbb{C}$ be a primitive pth root of unity. Consider the set

$$T = \{0, 1, 1 + \omega, \ldots, 1 + \omega + \cdots + \omega^{p-2}\} \subset \mathcal{O}_K$$

This is an admissible set of cardinality p. Indeed, the difference between any two distinct elements in this set is of the form $1 + \cdots + \omega^i$ for some i with $0 \leq i \leq p - 2$ or of the form $\omega^j + \cdots + \omega^i$ for some i, j with $1 \leq j < i \leq p - 2$. Dividing the latter by ω^j, they fall into the former category. By Lemma 10.8, it follows that T is an admissible set. Hence $\lambda(\mathcal{O}_K) \geq p$.

Let P be the unique prime ideal of $\mathcal{O}_K$ that lies above p. Since p is totally ramified in $\mathcal{O}_K$ (see Section 10.7.4), the Fundamental Identity (see Section 10.7.3) gives $|\mathcal{O}_K/P| = p$. By Lemma 11.130, it follows that $\lambda(\mathcal{O}_K) \leq p$. Combining the two bounds, it follows that

$$\lambda(\mathcal{O}_K) = p$$

REMARK 11.132 Suppose that we restrict, in Definition 11.129, the admissible sets T to those with the additional property that each element of T is a unit. Writing $\lambda'(A)$ for the corresponding constant, it is easy to see that

$$\lambda(A) = \lambda'(A) + 1$$

That is, let T be an admissible set with $|T| > 1$, and fix $a \in T$. Then the set

$$U_a = \{a - b \mid b \in T, b \neq a\}$$

fits the requirements. In the other direction, set $T = U \cup \{0\}$. In the case of the ring of integers in a number field, such sets of units whose pairwise differences are units are called (sets of) exceptional units.[32]

11.13.3 Interpolation over A-Modules

For applications to black box secret sharing, we need a slightly more general version of Theorem 11.124, which we present next. Let M be an A-module.[33] Since $A[X]_{\leq w-1}$ is a free A-module of rank w with basis $1, X, \ldots, X^{w-1}$, Lemma 10.24 implies that each element of $M \otimes A[X]_{\leq w-1}$ is uniquely expressed as $\sum_{i=0}^{w-1} f_i \otimes X^i$ with $f_i \in M$ ($i = 0, \ldots, w - 1$).

DEFINITION 11.133 *Let M be an A-module. Let w be a positive integer. For all $\mathbf{f} \in M \otimes A[X]_{\leq w-1}$ and $x \in A$, define*

$$\mathbf{f}(x) = \sum_{i=0}^{w-1} f_i \cdot x^i \ \in M$$

where

$$\mathbf{f} = \sum_{i=0}^{w-1} f_i \otimes X^i$$

with $f_i \in M$ ($i = 0, \ldots, w - 1$)

---

[32] These play a significant role in the theory of *Euclidean number fields* [128].

[33] For our purposes, it will be convenient to write here the A-scalar multiplication of the A-module M "on the right" (i.e., $m \cdot a$), instead of "on the left" (i.e., $a \cdot m$). Thus M is (tacitly assumed to be a) right-A-module.

THEOREM 11.134 (LAGRANGE INTERPOLATION OVER A-MODULES) *Let M be an A-module. Suppose that $T \subset A$ is an admissible set. Consider the evaluation map*

$$\mathcal{E}_\otimes : M \otimes_A A[X]_{\leq |T|-1} \longrightarrow \bigoplus_{\alpha \in T} M$$

$$\mathbf{f} \mapsto (\mathbf{f}(\alpha))_{\alpha \in T}$$

Then $\mathcal{E}_\otimes$ is an isomorphism of A-modules.

Proof The proof of the theorem essentially comes down to a straightforward combination of Theorem 11.124 with Lemma 10.26: in the notation of that lemma, set $M' = M$, $N = A[X]_{\leq |T|-1}$ and $N' = \bigoplus_{\alpha \in T} A$, set the map ϕ to the identity map Id on M, and set the map ψ to the isomorphism $\mathcal{E} : A[X]_{\leq |T|-1} \longrightarrow \bigoplus_{\alpha \in T} A$ from Theorem 11.124. This yields an isomorphism

$$\text{Id} \otimes \mathcal{E} : M \otimes_A A[X]_{\leq |T|-1} \longrightarrow M \otimes_A \bigoplus_{\alpha \in T} A$$

Moreover, once again by Lemma 10.24, there is the isomorphism

$$\chi : M \otimes_A \bigoplus_{\alpha \in T} A \longrightarrow \bigoplus_{\alpha \in T} M$$

by A-linear extension of the assignment

$$m \otimes (a_\alpha)_{\alpha \in T} \mapsto (m \cdot a_\alpha)_{\alpha \in T}$$

Therefore, the map

$$\chi \circ (\text{Id} \otimes \mathcal{E}) : M \otimes_A A[X]_{\leq |T|-1} \longrightarrow \bigoplus_{\alpha \in T} M$$

is an isomorphism. By inspection,

$$\chi \circ (\text{Id} \otimes \mathcal{E}) = \mathcal{E}_\otimes$$

This concludes the proof. Note that the inverse of $\mathcal{E}_\otimes$ is the map

$$\mathcal{E}_\otimes^{-1} : \bigoplus_{\alpha \in T} M \longrightarrow M \otimes_A A[X]_{\leq |T|-1}$$

$$(z_\alpha)_{\alpha \in T} \mapsto \sum_{\alpha \in T} z_\alpha \otimes \delta_\alpha(X)$$

where the $\delta_\alpha(X)$s are as in the proof of Theorem 11.124. ∎

As is the case with Theorem 11.124, the preceding theorem also can be proved via Vandermonde determinants in combination with basic results on linear systems of equations over rings.

11.13.4 Black Box Secret Sharing

A (t,n)-threshold black box secret-sharing scheme provides a "universal" method for performing (t,n)-threshold secret sharing over an *arbitrary finite abelian group G*. Given a secret element of G and uniformly random elements of G, each share (or share vector) is obtained by $\mathbb{Z}$-linear combination(s) of the secret and those random elements. Similarly, reconstruction of the secret from shares is done by taking $\mathbb{Z}$-linear combinations. This makes sense because G is a $\mathbb{Z}$-module.

The salient feature of black box secret sharing, however, is that the $\mathbb{Z}$-linear combinations are *oblivious* of the actual finite abelian group over which the secret sharing is performed. In particular, there is no information required on further structural properties of the group, such as its order, decomposition, and so on, to operate the scheme. It is in this sense that we have called such a scheme "universal" (with respect to the class of finite abelian groups).

Note that $\mathbb{Z}$-scalar multiplication can be achieved by repeated addition.[34] It is more efficient, however, to apply the "double-and-add" method, which is the additive version of the well-known "square-and-multiply" method for fast exponentiation.[35] In this way, the number of group operations is logarithmic in the absolute value of the (nonzero) integer scalar.

A *toy example* to illustrate the principle is provided by the additive two-out-of-two secret-sharing scheme discussed earlier. Let G be an arbitrary finite abelian group. Suppose that $s \in G$ is the secret. Now draw a uniformly random element $u \in G$ and take $\mathbb{Z}$-linear combinations to determine shares s_0, s_1, as follows: $s_0 := u \in G$, and $s_1 := s + u \in G$. To reconstruct s from s_0, s_1, take the following $\mathbb{Z}$-linear combination: $s = s_1 - s_0$. Neither s_0 or s_1 alone gives any information about s, whereas s can be reconstructed given both. So there is 1-privacy and 2-reconstruction. This is a black box secret-sharing scheme because the only property of G used is that it is a finite abelian group. This extends trivially to $(n-1, n)$-threshold black box secret sharing ($n \geq 2$), where there is $(n-1)$-privacy and n-reconstruction.

Let t, n be arbitrary integers with $1 \leq t < n - 1$. The question is: *does there exist a (t, n)-threshold black box secret-sharing scheme?* We give an affirmative answer. However, the equivalent of an ideal scheme does not exist: universality (i.e., a single instance works for any finite abelian group as discussed earlier) comes at the price of a share being necessarily "larger" than the secret. In other words, the *expansion factor*, that is, the total number of group elements (assigned to the n players in a secret sharing) divided by n, is *greater* than 1.

This can be argued as follows: observe that a (t, n)-threshold black box secret-sharing scheme in particular implies a generalized (t, n)-threshold secret-sharing scheme over $\mathbb{F}_2$ in the sense of Definition 11.93. A result from Karchmer and Wigderson [119] on the complexity of monotone span programs for threshold functions implies that in such secret-sharing schemes, a full-share vector has length $\Omega(n \log n)$ if $1 \leq t < n - 1$. For details, please refer to Cramer and Fehr [65] and Cramer et al. [66]. This can also be verified using Corollary 11.121, taking into account Remark 11.122 and setting $g = 1$.

On the constructive side, as in the case of general linear secret sharing over finite fields, a straightforward adaptation of the approach of Ito, Saito, and Nishizeki [116] gives a black box secret-sharing scheme for each (t, n)-threshold access structure, where t is the privacy threshold and n is the number of players. However, unless t is close to 1 or close to n, the share vector of G-elements a player gets suffers from expansion to a very large length,

---

[34] That is, for each $a \in \mathbb{Z}$ and $g \in G$, the operation $a \cdot g$ can be computed as $g + \cdots + g$ (a times) if $a \geq 0$ and as $(-g) + \cdots + (-g)$ ($|a|$ times) if $a < 0$.

[35] Also known as *repeated-squaring algorithm*. See, for example, Shoup [168].

namely, *exponential* in n if $t \approx n/2$. This can be brought down to *polynomial* (in n) expansion for any majority threshold access structure (that is, where $t + 1 > n/2$) by using an approach outlined in Section 11.11.2, which combines the work of Benaloh and Leichter [18] with that of Valiant [178].

However, there are vastly superior solutions. We first present a solution [81] that achieves expansion as small as *linear* (in n), which already substantially improves the approach referred to earlier. This solution is based on algebraic number theory. Then we present two solutions [65, 66] that achieve the minimal logarithmic expansion. These are also based on algebraic number theory but work around what seems to be a difficult obstacle in Desmedt and Frankel [81] to achieving smaller than linear expansion by that method.

Before doing so, we note that black box secret sharing was originally motivated by threshold public-key cryptography [79, 80], that is, cryptosystems where the decryption capability is securely distributed among a number of servers. In the case of the RSA cryptosystem, the problem arises that the order of the group in which the decryption (or signing) key lives has to remain secret from each quorum of t servers. Black box secret sharing provides a way to secret share the RSA secret key in such a way that the decryption (or signature) process can be handled by an efficient secure computation among the servers. In the case of RSA better solutions were later found that avoid black box secret sharing altogether. However, for certain other relevant threshold cryptography scenarios, black box secret sharing is required [76, 77].

A General $\mathbb{Z}$-Module Theoretical Definition

We give a formal definition in terms of matrices (a reader who so prefers can move on to the coordinate-free definition we present later). Let t, n be integers with $1 \leq t < n$. A (t, n)-threshold black box secret-sharing scheme is captured by a sequence of integer matrices $M, M_0, M_1, \ldots, M_n$ as follows: there are positive integers $e, d_1, \ldots, d_n$ such that the matrix M has $e \geq 1$ columns and $d := d_1 + \cdots + d_n + 1$ rows. The matrix M_0 corresponds to the submatrix of M consisting of its first row, which is the vector $\mathbf{u}_1^T := (1, 0, \ldots, 0) \in \mathbb{Z}^e$. The matrix M_1 corresponds to the submatrix of M consisting of the next d_1 rows of M, the matrix M_2 corresponds to the submatrix of M consisting of the d_2 rows directly thereafter, and so on. By extension, for a nonempty subset $B \subset \{1, \ldots, n\}$, let M_B be the submatrix M restricted to those blocks M_i with $i \in B$. Also, define $d_B = \sum_{i \in B} d_i$.

DEFINITION 11.135 (BLACK BOX SECRET SHARING) *Let t, n be integers with $1 \leq t < n$. The sequence of integer matrices*

$$(M_0, M_1, \ldots, M_n)$$

introduced earlier is a (t, n)-threshold black box secret-sharing scheme if, for each $B \subset \{1, \ldots, n\}$, the following statements hold:

1. *If $|B| = t + 1$, then there is a vector $\mathbf{r} \in \mathbb{Z}^{d_B}$, depending on B, such that*

$$M_B^T \mathbf{r} = \mathbf{u}_1 \in \mathbb{Z}^e$$

2. *If $|B| = t$, then there exists a vector $\mathbf{k} \in \mathbb{Z}^e$, depending on B, such that*

$$M_0 \mathbf{k} = \mathbf{u}_1^T \mathbf{k} = 1 \in \mathbb{Z} \quad \text{and} \quad M_B \mathbf{k} = \mathbf{0} \in \mathbb{Z}^{d_B}$$

The expansion factor of the scheme is the fraction

$$\frac{\sum_{i=1}^{n} d_i}{n} \in \mathbb{Q}$$

With the $(n-1,n)$-threshold black box secret-sharing scheme discussed earlier in mind, we now explain how schemes satisfying this definition can be similarly used, but now in the general case of (t,n)-threshold black box secret sharing.

For each finite abelian group G, the matrix M induces a morphism of finite $\mathbb{Z}$-modules

$$M : G^e \longrightarrow G \times G^{d_1} \times \cdots \times G^{d_n}$$

$$\mathbf{g} \mapsto (\mathbf{u}_1^T \mathbf{g}, M_1 \mathbf{g}, \ldots, M_n \mathbf{g})$$

The first coordinate (the G coordinate) will be viewed as the "secret" and the remaining n coordinates as the "shares." By Lemma 11.65, the map M is a regular map onto its image $M(G^e)$; that is, each element in the image has the same (finite) number of preimages. Select a uniformly random element $\gamma \in M(G^e)$. Note that this is the same as selecting a uniformly random element $\mathbf{g} \in G^e$ and setting $\gamma := M\mathbf{g}$. In particular, the uniform distribution on G is thereby attained by the secret because $M_0 \mathbf{g}$ just "picks" the first coordinate $\mathbf{u}_1^T \mathbf{g}$ of $\mathbf{g}$. Moreover, if $|B| = t + 1$, then

$$\mathbf{r}^T (M_B \mathbf{g}) = (\mathbf{r}^T M_B) \mathbf{g} = \mathbf{u}_1^T \mathbf{g} = M_0 \mathbf{g}$$

Hence, there is $(t+1)$-reconstruction. Finally, if $|B| = t$, then for each $s \in G$ there is an element in $M(G^e)$ such that the secret equals s and, for each $i \in B$, the share for i is $\mathbf{0} \in G^{d_i}$. This is easy to see as follows: for a vector $\mathbf{x} = (x_1, \ldots, x_e)^T \in \mathbb{Z}^e$ and an element $g \in G$, let $\mathbf{x} * g$ denote the vector $(x_1 g, \ldots, x_e g) \in G^e$. Then

$$M(\mathbf{x} * g) = (M\mathbf{x}) * g$$

By the properties of the vector $\mathbf{k}$, the secret of $M(\mathbf{k} * s) \in M(G^e)$ equals s, and for each $i \in B$, the share for i equals $\mathbf{0} \in G^{d_i}$. Combining this observation with the fact that the map induced by M is a regular map onto its image $M(G^e)$, it follows using Lemma 11.52 that there is t-privacy. Note that the distribution on t shares does not depend on the secret.

Furthermore, the integer matrices and vectors involved in the definition of black box secret-sharing schemes are the same for all finite abelian groups G. Please refer to Cramer and Fehr [65] for a discussion arguing that the definition just given is "minimal" in a precise and meaningful way.

For completeness, we also give an equivalent *coordinate-free* definition as follows:

DEFINITION 11.136 (ALTERNATIVE, EQUIVALENT DEFINITION) *Let t,n be integers with $1 \le t < n$. A (t,n)-threshold black box secret-sharing scheme consists of a free $\mathbb{Z}$-module $\mathcal{M}$ of finite rank and submodules*

$$\mathcal{M}_0, \mathcal{M}_1, \ldots, \mathcal{M}_n \subset \mathcal{M}$$

For each nonempty subset $B \subset \{1, \ldots, n\}$, define

$$\mathcal{M}_B = \sum_{i \in B} \mathcal{M}_i$$

that is, $\mathcal{M}_B \subset \mathcal{M}$ is the submodule spanned by the $\mathcal{M}_i$ with $i \in B$. For each $B \subset \{1, \ldots, n\}$, the following are required:

1. Rank($\mathcal{M}_0$) = 1.
2. *If $|B| = t + 1$, then*

$$\mathcal{M}_0 \subset \mathcal{M}_B$$

3. *If $|B| = t$, then there is a $\mathbb{Z}$-linear form*

$$\phi^B : \mathcal{M} \longrightarrow \mathbb{Z}$$

   depending on B such that

$$\phi^B(\mathcal{M}_B) = \{0\} \quad and \quad \phi^B(\mathcal{M}_0) = \mathbb{Z}$$

The expansion factor of the scheme is the ratio

$$\frac{\sum_{i=1}^{n} \operatorname{rank}(\mathcal{M}_i)}{n} \in \mathbb{Q}$$

LEMMA 11.137 *Definitions 11.136 and 11.135 are equivalent.*

Proof   It is straightforward that a scheme in the sense of Definition 11.135 implies a scheme in the sense of Definition 11.136 with the same parameters. The other direction follows from an application of Theorem 10.2. Since rank($\mathcal{M}_0$) = 1, and since there is a $\mathbb{Z}$-linear form on $\mathcal{M}$ whose image of $\mathcal{M}_0$ equals $\mathbb{Z}$, namely, any of the forms ϕ^B with $|B| = t$ from the definition, there is $z \in \mathcal{M}_0$ such that z is a $\mathbb{Z}$-basis of $\mathcal{M}_0$ and there is a $\mathbb{Z}$-basis of $\mathcal{M}$ that includes z. Without loss of generality, we may assume that $\phi^B(z) = 1$ for each B with $|B| = t$ (by updating ϕ^B with a sign, where necessary). This means that when embedding $\mathcal{M}$ into $\mathbb{Z}^e$ for some large enough integer e, it is possible to choose $\mathbf{z} = (1, 0, \ldots, 0) \in \mathbb{Z}^e$ without loss of generality. To revert to the matrix-based definition, choose a basis (or generating set) for each submodule $\mathcal{M}_i$.   ∎

In comparison with the definition of general linear secret sharing over a finite field, one of the important differences is the technical handle for proving t-privacy. Whereas in the former case it is sufficient to require that if $|B| = t$, then $z \notin \mathcal{M}_B$, this is not sufficient in the latter: because we are working over $\mathbb{Z}$ here, all that can be concluded with certainty from $z \notin \mathcal{M}_B$ is that there is a $\mathbb{Z}$-linear form $\phi^B : \mathcal{M} \longrightarrow \mathbb{Z}$, depending on B, such that $\phi^B(\mathcal{M}_B) = 0$ and $\phi^B(z) = \lambda \neq 0$ for some integer λ. This is not sufficient for black box secret sharing. That is, for fixed B with $|B| = t$, consider the ideal $I \subset \mathbb{Z}$ generated by all such integers λ, and write $I = (a)$ for some integer a. If $I \subsetneq \mathbb{Z}$, and if p is a prime number dividing a, then this means that the set B can reconstruct the secret in the case $G = \mathbb{Z}/p\mathbb{Z}$. For a full technical discussion, please refer to Cramer and Fehr [65].

11.13.5 Constructions Based on Algebraic Number Theory

We present the results from Cramer and Fehr [65] and Desmedt and Frankel [81].[36] Suppose that A is a nontrivial commutative ring that is free and of finite rank as a $\mathbb{Z}$-module.[37] Its $\mathbb{Z}$-rank is denoted $k(A)$. Let G be an arbitrary finite abelian group. Set

$$M = G \otimes_{\mathbb{Z}} A$$

---

[36] Our exposition here differs significantly from the respective expositions of these authors, though.

[37] Note that A contains $\mathbb{Z}$ as a subring in a unique way. That is, 0 is mapped to 0_A, and 1 is mapped to 1_A. Since A is free, this is an injective ring morphism. In particular, $k(A) \geq 1$.

We view M as an A-module by base extension (see Section 10.9.2).

Let t, n be integers with $0 \leq t < n$. Suppose that

$$n + 1 \leq \lambda(A)$$

Fix an admissible set $T \subset A$ with $|T| = n + 1$. Let $\alpha_0, \ldots, \alpha_n$ denote the distinct elements of T. Consider the A-module morphism

$$\mathcal{E}' : M \otimes_A A[X]_{\leq t} \longrightarrow \bigoplus_{i=0}^{n} M$$

$$\mathbf{f} \mapsto (\mathbf{f}(\alpha_0), \ldots, \mathbf{f}(\alpha_n))$$

see Definition 11.133.

On account of Lemma 10.24, it holds that

$$|M| = |G|^{k(A)}$$

because A is a free $\mathbb{Z}$-module of rank $k(A)$ and

$$\left| M \otimes_A A[X]_{\leq t} \right| = |M|^{t+1} = |G|^{k(A) \cdot (t+1)}$$

because $A[X]_{\leq t}$ is a free A-module of rank $t + 1$.

For each $B \subset \{0, 1, \ldots, n\}$ with $|B| = t + 1$ and for each vector

$$(z_i)_{i \in B} \in \bigoplus_{i \in B} M$$

there is a unique

$$\mathbf{f} = \sum_{j=0}^{t} f_j \otimes X^j \in M \otimes_A A[X]_{\leq t}$$

with $f_j \in M$ $(j = 0, \ldots, t)$ such that for each $i \in B$,

$$\mathbf{f}(\alpha_i) = z_i \in M$$

This follows from Theorem 11.134, instantiated with the admissible set $T_B = \{\alpha_i\}_{i \in B}$. Note that this unique $\mathbf{f}$ can be computed from the vector $(z_i)_{i \in B}$ by applying the inverse of the isomorphism in question, whose explicit description is given at the very end of the proof of Theorem 11.134. In conclusion, the image of the map $\mathcal{E}'$ is a $(t + 1, n + 1, |G|^{k(A)})$-interpolation code over the finite alphabet M. This gives an ideal (t, n)-threshold secret-sharing scheme defined over M by Theorem 11.107.

We now discuss how to base a (t, n)-black box secret-sharing scheme on these observations. Without loss of generality, we may assume that $0 \in T$ (say, $\alpha_0 = 0$).[38] Fix a basis $e_1, \ldots, e_k$ of A as a free $\mathbb{Z}$-module where $k = k(A)$. Maintain the elements of $M = G \otimes_{\mathbb{Z}} A$ by their unique representation as $\sum_{\ell=1}^{k} g_\ell \otimes e_\ell$ with $(g_1, \ldots, g_k) \in G^k$.

Because $\alpha_0 = 0$, it is immediately clear that a uniformly random $\mathbf{f} \in M \otimes_A A[X]_{\leq t}$ leads to $\mathbf{f}(0)$ having uniform distribution on M. Decomposing $\mathbf{f}(0) \in M$ as

$$\mathbf{f}(0) = f_0 = \sum_{\ell=1}^{k} g_\ell \otimes e_\ell$$

---

[38] That is, replace T by the set consisting of the differences with one fixed element of T. The resulting set contains 0, has the same cardinality as T, and is admissible as well.

the value

$$s \otimes e_1 \in M \quad \text{with} \quad s := g_1 \in G$$

is declared to be the secret. Note that this is essentially the same as saying that the secret is the "first coordinate" of the vector in G^k that represents $\mathbf{f}(0) \in M$.

As to the computations, all inputs, intermediary results, and outputs are represented as elements in G^k. Choosing a uniformly random element in M then just comes down to sampling k independent uniformly random elements from G. Additions of elements in M amounts to addition of the respective vectors in G^k representing them.

By inspection of the proof of Theorem 11.134, particularly the evaluation map and its inverse, it follows that computation of the shares and the reconstruction of the secret are by A-scalar operations completely oblivious of the specific finite abelian group involved. By the discussion in Section 10.9.3, it follows that A-scalar multiplications are composed of $\mathbb{Z}$-scalar multiplications. Hence, this gives a black box secret-sharing scheme as required.[39] Finally, it is clear that the expansion factor is $k(A)$, the rank of A as a free $\mathbb{Z}$-module. These considerations lead to the following theorem:

THEOREM 11.138 *Suppose that A is a nontrivial commutative ring such that as a $\mathbb{Z}$-module, A is free and of finite rank $k(A)$. Suppose that $\lambda(A) \geq 4$. Let t,n be integers such that $1 \leq t < n - 1 \leq \lambda(A) - 2$. Then there exists a (t,n)-threshold black box secret-sharing scheme with expansion factor $k(A)$.*

REMARK 11.139 Recall that in the case $t = n - 1$, there is black box secret sharing with expansion factor 1, that is, no expansion.[40]

The solution from Desmedt and Frankel [81] is retrieved by selecting a prime number p with $p > n$ and by setting A as the ring of integers of the pth cyclotomic number field. This ring A satisfies $\lambda(A) = p$, as shown in Section 11.13.1. By Bertrand's Postulate[41] from number theory, for all integers $n \geq 1$, there is a prime number p with $n < p \leq 2n$. This ensures that expansion $O(n)$ is achievable by this method.

THEOREM 11.140 *[81] Let t,n be integers such that $1 \leq t < n - 1$. Then there exists a (t,n)-threshold blackbox secret-sharing scheme with expansion factor $O(n)$.*

It appears to be a difficult problem whether or not there exist nontrivial commutative rings A that are free and of finite rank as $\mathbb{Z}$-modules and that achieve $\lambda(A)$ *exponential* in $k(A)$.[42] This is an obstacle to improving black box secret sharing via the method of Desmedt and Frankel [81].

This obstacle is circumvented by Cramer and Fehr [65], who exploit the observation that black box secret sharing may as well be based on admissible pairs. After a suitable choice of rings A, this leads to $O(\log n)$ expansion, which is minimal.

---

[39] It is not hard to show that the conditions from Definition 11.135 are satisfied, but we omit the details.
[40] Of course, the same holds for the pathetic case $t = 0$.
[41] See, for instance, Hardy and Wright [105].
[42] It appears that for orders in number fields, the best-known result is *linear* in the rank.

DEFINITION 11.141 *Let R be a nontrivial commutative ring. Let $T \subset R$ be a finite set with $|T| > 1$. Then*

$$\Delta(T) = (-1)^{\frac{1}{2}|T|(|T|-1)} \cdot \prod_{\substack{\alpha, \alpha' \in T: \\ \alpha \neq \alpha'}} (\alpha - \alpha')$$

Note that $\Delta(T)$ is the *square* of a Vandermonde determinant defined by the elements in the set T. Also note that $T \subset R$ with $|T| > 1$ is admissible if and only if $\Delta(T)$ is a unit in R.

DEFINITION 11.142 (ADMISSIBLE PAIRS) *Let R be a nontrivial commutative ring. Let $T, T' \subset R$ be sets. Then $\{T, T'\}$ is an admissible pair (in R) if*

1. $1 < |T| = |T'| < \infty$.
2. *The ideals $(\Delta(T))$ and $(\Delta(T'))$ are coprime in R.*

If $|T| = |T'| = 1$, then $\{T, T'\}$ is by default an admissible pair in R. The cardinality $c(T, T')$ of an admissible pair $\{T, T'\}$ is the integer $(|T| + |T'|)/2 \ (= |T| = |T'|)$.

We may assume, without loss of generality, that

$$0 \in T \quad \text{and} \quad 0 \in T'.$$

That is, select $\beta \in T$, and replace T by the set consisting of all elements $\alpha - \beta \in R$ with $\alpha \in T$ (similarly for T'). Note that neither the cardinalities nor the Δ values have changed in the process.

DEFINITION 11.143 *Let R be a nontrivial commutative ring. Then $\widehat{\lambda}(R)$ is the supremum of $c(T, T')$, where $\{T, T'\}$ ranges over all admissible pairs in R.*

Note that $\widehat{\lambda}(R) \geq 2$.

We now explain the construction from Cramer and Fehr [65]. As before, A is a nontrivial commutative ring such that as a $\mathbb{Z}$-module, A is free and of finite rank $k(A)$. Select a $\mathbb{Z}$-basis $e_1, \ldots, e_k$ of A where $k = k(A)$. Let G be an arbitrary finite abelian group, and define

$$M = G \otimes_{\mathbb{Z}} A$$

where M is viewed again as an A-module. Suppose that t, n are integers with $0 \leq t < n$. For the moment, let $T \subset A$ be an arbitrary set such that $|T| = n + 1$ and $0 \in T$. Let $\alpha_0, \alpha_1, \ldots, \alpha_n$ denote the distinct elements of T where $\alpha_0 = 0$.

Define

$$\delta = \prod_{0 \leq j < i \leq n} (\alpha_i - \alpha_j) \ \in A$$

Note that

$$\delta^2 = \Delta(T)$$

Slightly modify the preceding "polynomial evaluation" as

$$\mathbf{f}^{(\delta)}(x) := f_0 \cdot \delta + \sum_{i=1}^{t} f_i \cdot x^i \ \in M$$

for all $x \in A$. Note the multiplication by δ in the "lowest-order coefficient."

Define the A-module morphism

$$\mathcal{E}'' : M \otimes_A A[X]_{\leq t} \longrightarrow \bigoplus_{i=0}^{n} M$$

$$\mathbf{f} \mapsto (\mathbf{f}^{(\delta)}(\alpha_0), \ldots, \mathbf{f}^{(\delta)}(\alpha_n))$$

Consider the (t, n)-threshold black box scheme discussed earlier but with T as selected here, taking into account these slight modifications and the fact that T is not promised to be admissible. As before, the secret is declared to be the "first coordinate" of f_0. However, note that this is no longer equal to $\mathbf{f}(0)$ because of the factor δ.

Using similar reasoning as before, this scheme is "black box" and has t-privacy. However, only a *weak form* of $(t + 1)$-reconstruction holds. That is, there is $(t + 1)$-reconstruction only of a δ^2-multiple of the secret; that is, the element $(s \otimes \delta^2 e_1)$ is reconstructed instead of $s \otimes e_1$.[43] If δ is not a unit in A, depending on the order of the group G, this may cause an irreversible loss of information about the secret s.[44] Clearly, this is in violation of the "black box principle."

To remedy this, suppose that

$$\widehat{\lambda}(A) \geq n + 1$$

Let $\{T, T'\}$ be an admissible pair in A of cardinality $n + 1$. Without loss of generality, assume that $0 \in T$ and $0 \in T'$. Since the ideals $(\Delta(T)), (\Delta(T')) \subset A$ are coprime, there are $\rho, \rho' \in A$ such that

$$\rho \cdot \Delta(T) + \rho' \cdot \Delta(T') = 1$$

Now consider two instances of the "weak scheme" in parallel: one instance based on T and another instance based on T', *independent* of each other under the constraint that the secret in one equals that in the other. Then the joint scheme is "black box" and has t-privacy.[45] This time, however, there is $(t + 1)$-reconstruction; the secret $s \otimes e_1$ is recovered as

$$\rho \cdot (s \otimes \Delta(T) \cdot e_1) + \rho' \cdot (s \otimes \Delta(T') \cdot e_1) = (s \otimes (\rho \cdot \Delta(T) + \rho' \cdot \Delta(T'))e_1) = s \otimes e_1$$

These considerations lead to the following theorem:

THEOREM 11.144 *[65] Suppose that A is a nontrivial commutative ring such that as a $\mathbb{Z}$-module, A is free and of finite rank $k(A)$. Suppose that $\widehat{\lambda}(A) \geq 4$. Let t, n be integers such that $1 \leq t < n - 1 \leq \widehat{\lambda}(A) - 2$. Then there exists a (t, n)-threshold black box secret-sharing scheme with expansion factor at most $2 \cdot k(A)$.*

To circumvent the obstacle in the approach from Desmedt and Frankel [81], and to reach minimal $O(\log n)$ expansion, it remains to prove the claim that there exist nontrivial commutative rings A such that, as a $\mathbb{Z}$-module, the ring A is free of finite rank $k(A)$ and such that, $\widehat{\lambda}(A)$ is exponential in $k(A)$. This can be shown as follows: suppose that $f(X) \in \mathbb{Z}[X]$ is

---

[43] Privacy as well as weak reconstruction can be easily verified by considering Lagrange interpolation over $Q(A)$ and by clearing denominators. See Cramer and Fehr [65] for more details.

[44] In this way, one also sees that black box secret sharing based on "interpolation over the rational integers" fails.

[45] We skip the straightforward formalization of this parallelization as an appropriately defined product of black box secret-sharing schemes.

monic and irreducible. Let $v \in \mathbb{C}$ be a root of $f(X)$, and define $K = \mathbb{Q}(v)$. Consider the order $\mathbb{Z}[v]$ in the number field K. Suppose that $f(X)$ has the following two additional properties:

1. $d := \deg f(X) = \lceil \log_2(n+1) \rceil$.
2. For each prime number p with $2 \leq p \leq n$, it holds that the polynomial $\bar{f}(X) \in \mathbb{F}_p[X]$ is irreducible, where $\bar{f}(X)$ is the image of $f(X)$ under reduction modulo p.

Define

$$T = \{0, 1 \ldots, n\} \subset \mathbb{Z}$$

Then there exists $T' \subset \mathbb{Z}[v]$ $|T'| = n+1$ and $(\Delta(T))$ and $(\Delta(T'))$ are coprime ideals in $\mathbb{Z}[v]$. Note that the $\mathbb{Z}$-rank of $\mathbb{Z}[v]$ equals $\lceil \log_2(n+1) \rceil$.[46] The existence of such T' can be argued as follows: define

$$N = \prod_{\substack{2 \leq p \leq n, \\ p \text{ prime}}} p$$

Because $\Delta(T)$ is a rational integer that factorizes over the prime numbers p with $2 \leq p \leq n$ (and with each such prime number p occurring in its factorization), some large enough positive power of N is divisible by $\Delta(T)$. In other words, as ideals in $\mathbb{Z}[v]$, some large enough power of (N) is contained in $(\Delta(T))$. Hence, applying Lemma 10.6, it is sufficient to show the existence of distinct elements $\alpha_0', \alpha_1', \ldots, \alpha_n' \in \mathbb{Z}[v]$ such that the ideals (N) and $(\Delta(T'))$ are coprime in $\mathbb{Z}[v]$.

We now show the existence of such a set T'. By the assumptions on $f(X)$, it holds that for each prime number p with $2 \leq p \leq n$,

$$\mathbb{Z}[v]/p\mathbb{Z}[v] \simeq \mathbb{F}_{p^d}$$

and

$$p^d \geq n+1$$

Therefore,

$$\mathbb{Z}[v]/N\mathbb{Z}[v] \simeq \prod_{\substack{2 \leq p \leq n, \\ p \text{ prime}}} \mathbb{F}_{p^d}$$

which follows by the Chinese Remainder Theorem, and hence,

$$\lambda(\mathbb{Z}[v]/N\mathbb{Z}[v]) = 2^d \geq n+1$$

Hence, there exists $T' = \{\alpha_0', \alpha_1', \ldots, \alpha_n'\} \subset \mathbb{Z}[v]$ with $|T'| = n+1$ such that (the class of) $\Delta(T')$ is a unit in the ring $\mathbb{Z}[v]/N\mathbb{Z}[v]$. Equivalently, $(\Delta(T'))$ and (N) are coprime ideals in $\mathbb{Z}[v]$.

All that remains to be shown is the existence of polynomials $f(X)$ that satisfy the hypotheses. For each prime number p with $2 \leq p \leq n$, choose an irreducible monic polynomial $f^{(p)}(X) \in \mathbb{F}_p[X]$ of degree $d = \lceil \log_2(n+1) \rceil$. Once again using the Chinese Remainder Theorem, it is easy to construct an integer monic polynomial $f(X)$ of degree d such that modulo each prime number p with $2 \leq p \leq n$ it equals $f^{(p)}(X)$. Because such a

---

[46] It is possible to slightly weaken the conditions on $f(X)$ while still guaranteeing the same conclusion, but the conditions stated here simplify the ensuing arguments somewhat.

polynomial $f(X)$ is (automatically) irreducible in $\mathbb{Z}[X]$, each of the hypotheses is satisfied. Note that the expansion factor of the resulting scheme equals $d = O(\log n)$, which is minimal.

REMARK 11.145 If the constructions based on algebraic number theory from Cramer and Fehr [65] and Desmedt and Frankel [81] are represented by integer matrices in the way just indicated, the integers occurring in these matrices have bit-length polynomial in n.

The constant in the $O(\log n)$ expansion factor has been improved by Cramer, Fehr, and Stam [66] via use of a more refined approach. It is based on sets T defining a Vandermonde determinant that is primitive; that is, its only rational integer divisors are $-1, 1$. The existence of an order A in a number field of degree $k(A)$ such that A admits a set T with a primitive Vandermonde determinant and such that $|T|$ is exponential in $k(A)$ has been shown by Cramer, Fehr, and Stam [66] using a combination of arguments from algebraic number theory and algebraic geometry.

THEOREM 11.146 *[65, 66] There exists a positive real constant c such that the following holds: let t, n be integers with $1 \leq t < n - 1$. Then there exists a (t, n)-threshold black box secret-sharing scheme with expansion factor at most $c + \log_2 n$.*

This is tight up to an additive constant.

12

Arithmetic Codices

12.1 Introduction

We introduce the notion of an arithmetic codex [43, 57], or codex for short, and develop its basic theory. Codices encompass several well-established notions from cryptography (various types of *arithmetic* secret-sharing schemes, which all enjoy additive as well as multiplicative properties) and from algebraic complexity (bilinear complexity of multiplication in algebras) in a single mathematical framework. Arithmetic secret-sharing schemes have important applications to secure multiparty computation (MPC) and even to *two*-party cryptography. One such application, known as "MPC-in-the-head," can be found in Chapter 8.

Interestingly, several recent applications to two-party cryptography (including the one we present in this book) rely crucially on the existence of certain *asymptotically good* schemes. It is intriguing that their construction requires asymptotically good towers of algebraic function fields over a finite field: no elementary (probabilistic) constructions are known in these cases. Besides introducing the notion, we discuss some of the constructions, as well as some limitations.

Throughout this chapter, let K be a field, let p > 0 be a prime number, let v be a positive integer, and define $q = p^v$. Let $\mathbb{F}_q$ be a finite field with q elements.

12.2 The Codex Definition

For our purposes, a K-algebra is a commutative ring such that K is a subring (see Section 10.8). By definition of a subring, the multiplicative unity of a K-algebra is precisely the multiplicative unity of K. It is henceforth denoted by 1. Recall that a K-algebra is in particular a K-vector space.

12.2.1 Powers of a Space

Taking *powers* of a subspace of a K-algebra R plays a fundamental role in the definition and study of codices. Suppose that $C \subset R$ is a K-vector subspace of R, with R viewed as a K-vector space. In general, of course, the space C is *not* closed under multiplication. For example, take $R = K[X]$, the polynomial ring over K, and let C be the subspace of polynomials of degree $\leq t$ for some positive integer t.

We define, for each positive integer d, the "closure" of C under "d-multiplication" as the subspace $C^{*d} \subset R$ generated by the elements of R that can be written as a product of d elements selected from C. Formally, we have the following:

DEFINITION 12.1 (SET OF d-PRODUCTS) *Let R be a K-algebra. Let $C \subset R$ be a K-vector subspace. Let $d \geq 0$ be an integer. The set $m_d(C) \subset R$ consists of all $z \in R$ such that*

$$z = \prod_{i=1}^{d} x^{(i)}$$

for some $(x^{(1)}, \ldots, x^{(d)}) \in C^d$.

By the convention that the empty product equals 1, it follows that $m_0(C) = \{1\}$.

DEFINITION 12.2 (POWERS OF A SPACE) *Let R be a K-algebra. Let $C \subset R$ be a K-vector subspace. Let $d \geq 0$ be an integer. The space C^{*d} is the K-vector subspace of R spanned by the set $m_d(C)$.*

Concretely, the space C^{*d} consists of all finite sums $\left(\sum \lambda x \right) \in R$ with $\lambda \in K$ and $x \in m_d(C)$. In particular, $C^{*0} = K$.

REMARK 12.3 If $1 \in C$, then
$$K \subset C \subset \ldots \subset C^{*d}$$

If $K = \mathbb{F}_q$ and the Frobenius map (i.e., the qth power map) *fixes R* (i.e., $x^q = x$ for all $x \in R$), then
$$C \subset C^{*q}$$

We view K^n as a K-algebra in the natural way, that is, as an n-fold direct product of the K-algebra K. Thus ring multiplication is component-wise. Moreover, K is embedded "diagonally"; that is, $\lambda \in K$ corresponds to $(\lambda, \ldots, \lambda) \in K^n$. In particular, $\mathbf{1} := (1, \ldots, 1)$ is the multiplicative unity.[1] The space K^n is indexed by the set $\{1, \ldots, n\}$. If $\mathbf{x} \in K^n$, then we write $\mathbf{x} = (x_i)_{i=1}^n$ for its coordinate vector. See the conventions in Section 11.2.

For each $\mathbf{x}, \mathbf{y} \in K^n$, their component-wise product in K^n is denoted by $\mathbf{x} * \mathbf{y}$. Thus
$$\mathbf{x} * \mathbf{y} = (x_1 y_1, \ldots, x_n y_n) \in K^n$$

for all $\mathbf{x}, \mathbf{y} \in K^n$. If $\mathbf{x} \in K^n$ and m is a nonnegative integer, then $\mathbf{x}^m$ denotes $\mathbf{x} * \cdots * \mathbf{x} \in K^n$ (m times). The empty product ($m = 0$) yields $\mathbf{1}$ by default. Thus
$$\mathbf{x}^m = (x_1^m, \ldots, x_n^m)$$

for all $\mathbf{x}, \mathbf{y} \in K^n$ and for all integers $m \geq 0$. The standard inner product on K^n is denoted by $\langle \cdot, \cdot \rangle$. Thus
$$\langle \mathbf{x}, \mathbf{y} \rangle = \sum_{i=1}^{n} x_i y_i \in K$$

for all $\mathbf{x}, \mathbf{y} \in K^n$.

[1] So, for example, if $K = \mathbb{F}_q$ and $R = \mathbb{F}_q^n$, then Remark 12.3 means that $C \subset C^{*q}$ always.

Let A be a K-algebra, and let n be a positive integer. Let t, d, r be integers with $d \geq 1$ and $0 \leq t < r \leq n$. Informally, an (n, t, d, r)-*codex for A over K* consists of a K-vector subspace

$$C \subset K^n$$

and a K-vector space morphism

$$\psi : C \longrightarrow A$$

such that the following statements hold:

1. Each element $a \in A$ is "presented" in the sense that $\psi(\mathbf{x}) = a$ for some $\mathbf{x} \in C$; that is, ψ is surjective. In particular, this means that[2]

$$\dim_K A < \infty$$

2. The product $\mathbf{z} \in K^n$ of any d C-elements uniquely determines the product $a \in A$ of the d respective A-elements presented by them. Moreover, any selection of r coordinates of $\mathbf{z}$ suffices to determine this product a. In fact, for each such selection of r coordinates, there exists a K-*vector space morphism* from K^r to A such that when applied to the selected r coordinates of $\mathbf{z}$, the element a is obtained.
3. If $t > 0$, any t coordinates of a generic ("random") C-element are jointly independent from ("give no information about") the A-element that this C-element presents.

Note that if $K = \mathbb{F}_q$, then the preceding case $d = 1$ essentially describes a linear secret-sharing scheme for $\mathbb{F}_q^k$ over $\mathbb{F}_q$ with t-privacy and r-reconstruction where $k := \dim_K A$. Not surprisingly, we will be more interested in the case $d > 1$ here.

REMARK 12.4 Recall that if $\dim_K A < \infty$ and 0 is the only nilpotent in A, then A is isomorphic (as a K-algebra) to a finite direct product of finite-degree extension fields of K. Moreover, if the discriminant of A over K is nonzero, then, additionally, each of these extensions is separable over K (see Theorem 10.16). An example with $\dim_K A < \infty$ and nontrivial nilpotents is the K-algebra $K[X]/(X^2)$, which has $\overline{X}^2 = 0$. It is easy to generate other elementary (multi-variate) examples along these lines.

We shall now develop the formal definition of a codex.[3] *We use the notational conventions from Section 11.2 (indexing, coordinates, projection). By default, we will assume that K^n is indexed by the set $\mathcal{I} = \{1, \ldots, n\}$.* Recall that for a nonempty set $B \subset \{1, \ldots, n\}$, the map projecting the elements of K^n onto their B-indexed coordinates is denoted by π_B. Also recall that for $\mathbf{x} \in K^n$, the notation $\mathbf{x}_B$ may be used as a shorthand for $\pi_B(\mathbf{x})$.

DEFINITION 12.5 *For a subspace $C \subset K^n$ and a nonempty set $B \subset \{1, \ldots, n\}$, we define $C_{\mathbf{0} \downarrow B} = C \cap \ker \pi_B$.*

In other words, the subspace $C_{\mathbf{0} \downarrow B} \subset C$ consists of all elements in C with B-indexed coordinates all equal to zero.

---

[2] As K-vector spaces, $A \simeq C / \ker \psi$ because ψ is surjective. Therefore, $\dim_K A \leq n$. Note that $\dim_K A \geq 1$ because the field K is contained in A as a subring.

[3] Reading "multiplication" into the symbol $\mathbf{x}$, the term *codex* signals a code with "multiplicative properties."

12.2.2 Multiplicativity

DEFINITION 12.6 ((*d,r*)-MULTIPLICATIVITY) *Let A be a K-algebra. Let n,d,r be integers with $d \geq 1$ and $1 \leq r \leq n$. Let $C \subset K^n$ be a K-vector subspace, and let*

$$\psi : C \longrightarrow A$$

be a K-vector space morphism. Then (C, ψ) has (d,r)-multiplicativity if there is a unique K-vector space morphism

$$\overline{\psi} : C^{*d} \longrightarrow A$$

such that the following conditions are satisfied:

1. $\overline{\psi}$ *satisfies the multiplicative relation*

$$\overline{\psi}(x_1 * \cdots * x_d) = \prod_{j=1}^{d} \psi(x_j)$$

 for all $x_1, \ldots, x_d \in C$.
2. $\overline{\psi}$ *is r-wise determined; that is,*

$$\bigcup_{\substack{B \subset \{1,\ldots,n\}: \\ |B|=r}} \left(C^{*d}\right)_{0 \downarrow B} \subset \ker \overline{\psi}$$

Note that at this point the morphism ψ is not necessarily surjective. In particular, the trivial morphism is not excluded from the definition here. Also, strictly speaking, it is not necessary to state the uniqueness of $\overline{\psi}$ as a separate condition; because C^{*d} is generated as a K-vector space by $m_d(C)$, and because the multiplicative relation holds, mere existence means that the K-vector space morphism $\overline{\psi}$ is determined by its action on $m_d(C)$, which is, in turn, determined by ψ.

By inspection, the condition of being r-wise determined is equivalent to the condition that $\overline{\psi}(\mathbf{z}) = \overline{\psi}(\mathbf{z}')$ for all $\mathbf{z}, \mathbf{z}' \in C^{*d}$ with $\pi_B(\mathbf{z}) = \pi_B(\mathbf{z}')$ for some $B \subset \{1, \ldots, n\}$ with $|B| = r$. This motivates the terminology because this means that "$\overline{\psi}(\mathbf{z})$ is uniquely determined by any r coordinates of $\mathbf{z}$, for each $\mathbf{z} \in C^{*d}$." In alternative language, the restriction of C^{*d} to those elements whose Hamming weight is at most $n - r$ is contained in the kernel of $\overline{\psi}$.

In the case $d = 1$, the map ψ is r-wise determined by definition because ψ and $\overline{\psi}$ coincide in this case. This is also true in the uninteresting case $d \geq 1$ and $\psi \equiv 0$. We now give a general condition that guarantees that (d,r)-multiplicativity implies that ψ is r-determined. This condition is trivially satisfied in the cases of our interest later on. See also Remark 12.8.

Recall that the set consisting of all $z \in A$ such that $z = 0$ or z is a zero divisor in A is denoted $Z(A)$. By Lemma 10.1, its complement $A \setminus Z(A)$ is multiplicatively closed.

LEMMA 12.7 *Suppose that at least one of the following conditions is satisfied.*

1. *The only nilpotent in A is 0.*
2. *im $\psi \not\subset Z(A)$.*

Then (d,r)-multiplicativity in Definition 12.6 implies that ψ is r-determined as well; that is,

$$\bigcup_{\substack{B \subset \{1,\ldots,n\}: \\ |B|=r}} C_{0 \downarrow B} \subset \ker \psi$$

Proof We may assume that $d > 1$. Suppose that $\mathbf{x} \in C$ is such that $\mathbf{x}_B = \mathbf{0}$ for some $B \subset \{1, \ldots, n\}$ with $|B| = r$. We show that $\psi(\mathbf{x}) = 0$. Since $\mathbf{x}^d \in C^{*d}$, $(\mathbf{x}^d)_B = \mathbf{0}$ and $|B| = r$, and the identity

$$\overline{\psi}(\mathbf{x}^d) = (\psi(\mathbf{x}))^d = 0$$

holds by definition of (d,r)-multiplicativity. Hence, $\psi(\mathbf{x})$ is a nilpotent. If the first condition of the lemma is satisfied, it follows that $\psi(\mathbf{x}) = 0$ as desired.

Now assume that the second condition of the lemma is satisfied. Let $\mathbf{y} \in C$ be such that $\psi(\mathbf{y}) \in A \setminus Z(A)$. Define

$$\mathbf{z} = \mathbf{x} * \mathbf{y}^{d-1}$$

Since $\mathbf{z} \in C^{*d}$, $\mathbf{z}_B = \mathbf{0}$ and $B = r$, the identity

$$0 = \overline{\psi}(\mathbf{z}) = \overline{\psi}(\mathbf{x} * \mathbf{y}^{d-1}) = \psi(\mathbf{x}) \cdot (\psi(\mathbf{y}))^{d-1}$$

holds by definition of (d,r)-multiplicativity. By Lemma 10.1, it holds that

$$(\psi(\mathbf{y}))^{d-1} \in A \setminus Z(A)$$

Hence $\psi(\mathbf{x}) = 0$ as desired. ∎

REMARK 12.8 If A is a product of fields, for instance, then the first condition of the lemma is satisfied. If ψ is surjective (so that 1 has a ψ-inverse), then the second condition of the lemma is satisfied.

DEFINITION 12.9 *Suppose that (C, ψ) has (d,r)-multiplicativity. Then (C, ψ) is unital if $\mathbf{1} \in C$ and $\psi(\mathbf{1}) = 1$.*

REMARK 12.10 Suppose that (C, ψ) has (d,r)-multiplicativity, and suppose that it is unital. Then

1. $C \subset C^{*d}$.
2. The restriction of $\overline{\psi}$ to C coincides with ψ. In other words, the map $\overline{\psi}$ extends the map ψ to C^{*d}. By convention, this extension is denoted by ψ as well.
3. For all integers d' with $1 \leq d' \leq d$, and for all $\mathbf{x}_1, \ldots, \mathbf{x}_{d'} \in C$, it holds that

$$\psi(\mathbf{x}_1 * \cdots * \mathbf{x}_{d'}) = \prod_{j=1}^{d'} \psi(\mathbf{x}_j)$$

The first property follows on account of Remark 12.3. The second property follows from the fact that for all $\mathbf{x} \in C$, it holds that

$$\overline{\psi}(\mathbf{x}) = \overline{\psi}(\mathbf{1}^{d-1} * \mathbf{x}) = \left(\prod_{j=1}^{d-1} \psi(\mathbf{1})\right) \cdot \psi(\mathbf{x}) = \psi(\mathbf{x})$$

The third property follows because for all integers d' with $1 \leq d' \leq d$ and for all $\mathbf{x}_1, \ldots, \mathbf{x}_{d'} \in C$, it holds that

$$\psi(\mathbf{x}_1 * \cdots * \mathbf{x}_{d'} * \mathbf{1}^{d-d'}) = \left(\prod_{j=1}^{d'} \psi(\mathbf{x}_j)\right) \cdot \psi(\mathbf{1})^{d-d'} = \prod_{j=1}^{d'} \psi(\mathbf{x}_j)$$

12.2.3 Disconnection

DEFINITION 12.11 (*t*-DISCONNECTION) *Let A be a K-algebra. Let n,t be integers with $0 \le t < n$. Let $C \subset K^n$ be a K-vector subspace, and let*

$$\psi : C \longrightarrow A$$

be a K-vector space morphism. If $t = 0$, then (C, ψ) is 0-disconnected by default. Suppose that $t > 0$. Then (C, ψ) is t-disconnected if, for each $B \subset \{1,\dots,n\}$ with $|B| = t$, the projection map

$$\pi_{\psi,B} : C \longrightarrow \psi(C) \times \pi_B(C)$$

$$\mathbf{x} \mapsto (\psi(\mathbf{x}), \pi_B(\mathbf{x}))$$

is surjective. If, in addition, $\pi_B(C) = K^t$, there is t-disconnection with uniformity.

In the case where K is a finite field (so that C and $\psi(C)$ are finite), there is the following interpretation: suppose that $t > 0$, and let $B \subset \{1,\dots,n\}$ with $|B| = t$. By Lemma 11.65, the map $\pi_{\psi,B}$ is regular, and if $\mathbf{x}$ is uniformly random on C, then $\pi_{\psi,B}(\mathbf{x})$ is uniformly random on $\psi(C) \times \pi_B(C)$. By elementary probability, this is equivalent to saying that $\psi(\mathbf{x})$ is uniformly random on $\psi(C)$, the vector $\pi_B(\mathbf{x})$ is uniformly random on $\pi_B(C)$, and $\psi(\mathbf{x})$ and $\pi_B(\mathbf{x})$ are *independently distributed*. In particular, if $\psi \not\equiv 0$, then $\psi(\mathbf{x}) \in A$ can be guessed from $\pi_B(\mathbf{x}) \in K^t$ with probability ϵ, where $\epsilon = 1/|\psi(C)| \le 1/|K|$, but no better. Note that $\epsilon = 1/|A|$ if ψ is surjective. Uniformity means that, in addition, $\pi_B(\mathbf{x})$ is uniformly random on K^t.

It is sometimes convenient to work with the following equivalent formulations of disconnection.

LEMMA 12.12 *Let A be a K-algebra. Let n,t be integers with $1 \le t < n$. Let $C \subset K^n$ be a K-vector subspace, and let $\psi : C \longrightarrow A$ be a K-vector space morphism. The following statements are equivalent.*

1. *(C, ψ) is t-disconnected.*
2. *For each $B \subset \{1,\dots,n\}$ with $|B| = t$, the restricted map*

$$\psi_{|C_{\mathbf{0}\downarrow B}} : C_{\mathbf{0}\downarrow B} \longrightarrow \psi(C)$$

   is surjective.
3. *For each $B \subset \{1,\dots,n\}$ with $|B| = t$, and for each $a \in \psi(C)$, there is $\mathbf{x} \in C$ with $\psi(\mathbf{x}) = a$ and $\mathbf{x}_B = \mathbf{0} \in K^t$.*

Proof The equivalence between the second and third statements is clear. The first implies the third by definition. To show that the third implies the first, we argue as follows: let $B \subset \{1,\dots,n\}$ with $|B| = t$. Let $a' \in \psi(C)$, and let $\mathbf{x}' \in C$. Then $a' - \psi(\mathbf{x}') \in \psi(C)$. Let $\mathbf{x}'' \in C$ be such that $\psi(\mathbf{x}'') = a' - \psi(\mathbf{x}')$ and $\mathbf{x}''_B = \mathbf{0} \in K^t$. Define

$$\mathbf{z} = \mathbf{x}' + \mathbf{x}'' \in C$$

Then

$$\psi(\mathbf{z}) = \psi(\mathbf{x}' + \mathbf{x}'') = \psi(\mathbf{x}') + \psi(\mathbf{x}'') = \psi(\mathbf{x}') + (a' - \psi(\mathbf{x}')) = a'$$

and

$$\mathbf{z}_B = \mathbf{x}'_B$$

This shows that the image of $\pi_{\psi,B}$ is all of $\psi(C) \times \pi_B(C)$. ■

12.2.4 Codices

We are now ready to define codices.

DEFINITION 12.13 (CODEX) *[43, 57] Let A be a K-algebra with* $\dim_K A < \infty$. *Let* n,t,d,r *be integers with* $d \geq 1$ *and* $0 \leq t < r \leq n$. *An* (n,t,d,r)-codex *for A over K is a pair* (C, ψ) *where*

$$C \subset K^n$$

is a K-vector subspace and

$$\psi : C \longrightarrow A$$

is a K-vector space morphism such that

1. *ψ is surjective.*
2. *(C, ψ) satisfies (d,r)-multiplicativity.*
3. *(C, ψ) satisfies t-disconnection.*

An (n,t,d,r)-codex *for A over K has uniformity if it satisfies the stronger property of t-disconnection with uniformity. It is unital if (C, ψ) is unital.*

DEFINITION 12.14 (ARITHMETIC SECRET SHARING) *If K is a finite field, $d \geq 2$ and $t \geq 1$, then the codex in Definition 12.13 is called an* (n,t,d,r)-arithmetic secret-sharing scheme *with secret space A and share space K.*

These general definitions of codices and arithmetic secret-sharing schemes grew out of a series of results [38, 41, 48, 50, 61], starting with the results on linear secret sharing with (strong) multiplication in Cramer, Damgård, and Maurer [61]. The latter were, in turn, inspired by the way the multiplicative properties of Shamir's scheme have been exploited in secure multiparty computation (MPC) in references [14], [46] and [93].

As opposed to the notion of "plain secret sharing," which is very suggestive as to how it actually may be used in cryptographic protocols, the notion of arithmetic secret sharing is less intuitive. For instance, the way the properties of these schemes are exploited in secure computation can hardly be guessed straight from their definition. Please refer to Section 12.5 or to Cascudo, Cramer, and Xing [41] for a high-level explanation of two of the main applications of arithmetic secret-sharing to secure computation. See also the references in Section 12.8.

DEFINITION 12.15 (ARITHMETIC EMBEDDING) *In Definition 12.13, if ψ is a K-vector space isomorphism, and if $d \geq 2$, then the codex is an* (n,d)-arithmetic embedding *(of A over K).*

Note that $t > 0$ is not possible in the case of an arithmetic embedding. If $d = 2$, then the smallest n such that an $(n,2)$-arithmetic embedding of A over K exists is the bilinear multiplication complexity of A over K, a classical notion from algebraic complexity theory (see, e.g., Bürgisser, Clausen, and Shokrullahi [31]). Especially the case where K is a finite field, $\mathbb{F}_q$ and A is an extension field, $\mathbb{F}_{q^k}$ (for some integer $k > 1$) has been studied extensively during the last four decades.

The case where K is a finite field and A is a finite-degree extension field of K, the codex notion generalizes this classical notion of bilinear multiplication algorithms in finite fields in two ways if both $t > 0$ and $r < n$. Also note that arithmetic secret-sharing schemes with secret space $\mathbb{F}_q^k$ and share space $\mathbb{F}_q$ have particularly important cryptographic applications (see the references in Cascudo, Cramer, and Xing [41] and Section 12.5), whereas bilinear complexity is trivial here. From a cryptographic point of view, our notion encompasses all known relevant variations on arithmetic secret sharing.[4]

Finally, for favorable settings of the parameters, codices support "efficient decoding" of the A-element even if a presentation $\mathbf{x} \in C$ comes with some errors, by a linearization argument that makes generic use of the properties of the codex. An explanation is given in Section 12.5.4.

12.3 Equivalent Definitions

12.3.1 A Definition in Terms of Generalized Codes

We give an equivalent definition of codices in terms of generalized codes in Theorem 12.18. This definition is particularly useful when analyzing certain explicit constructions.

Let A be a K-algebra, and let n be a positive integer. Consider the $(n + 1)$-fold direct product $A \times K^n$, and index it with the set $\mathcal{I} = \{0, 1 \ldots, n\}$.[5] Define $\mathcal{I}^* = \{1, \ldots, n\}$. For $B \subset \mathcal{I}^*$ nonempty, define the following: the projection functions $\pi_0 : A \times K^n \longrightarrow A$ and $\pi_B : A \times K^n \longrightarrow K^{|B|}$ are defined in the obvious way. The notation $\pi_{0,B}$ is shorthand for the projection $\pi_{\{0\} \cup B}$.

If $\widetilde{C} \subset A \times K^n$ is a K-vector subspace, then $C \subset K^n$ denotes the K-*part of* $\widetilde{C}$, that is, the K-vector subspace consisting of all $\mathbf{x} \in K^n$ such that $(a, \mathbf{x}) \in \widetilde{C}$ for some $a \in A$. Equivalently, $C = \pi_{\mathcal{I}^*}(\widetilde{C})$.

Conversely, if $C \subset K^n$ is a K-vector subspace and $\psi : C \longrightarrow A$ is a K-vector space morphism, then $\widetilde{C} \subset A \times K^n$ is the K-vector subspace consisting of all $(\psi(\mathbf{x}), \mathbf{x}) \in A \times K^n$ with $\mathbf{x} \in C$, the A-*extension of* (C, ψ).

LEMMA 12.16 *Let A be a K-algebra. Let n, d, r be integers with $d \geq 1$ and $1 \leq r \leq n$. Then*

1. *Let $\widetilde{C} \subset A \times K^n$ be a K-vector subspace. Assume that the only nilpotent in A is 0 or that there exists $(u, \mathbf{y}) \in \widetilde{C}$ such that $u \in A \setminus Z(A)$.[6] Suppose that there is a K-vector subspace*

---

[4] As an aside, using the theory of quadratic forms, it is shown in Cascudo, Cramer, and Mirandola [39] that dropping the linearity condition on the map $\overline{\psi}$ in Definition 12.6 ((d, r)-multiplicativity) leads to a strictly weaker notion of arithmetic secret sharing. Note that when dropping this linearity condition, the property of being r-wise determined requires a rephrasing as a strictly combinatorial property, which is straightforward to carry out.

[5] To avoid confusion, we mean that index 0 refers to the A-coordinate, whereas indices $1, \ldots, n$ refer to the n K-coordinates, as usual.

[6] See Remark 12.8; this condition is naturally satisfied in the cases of our interest here.

$\widetilde{D} \subset A \times K^n$ *such that*

$$\widetilde{C}^{*d} \subset \widetilde{D}$$

and such that for all $\widetilde{\mathbf{z}} \in \widetilde{D}$ *it holds that*

$$\widetilde{z}_0 = 0 \ \ if \ \widetilde{\mathbf{z}}_B = \mathbf{0} \quad for \ some \quad B \subset \mathcal{I}^* \quad with \quad |B| = r$$

Then (C, ψ) *has* (d,r)-*multiplicativity where* $C \subset K^n$ *is the K-part of* $\widetilde{C}$ *and the K-vector space morphism*

$$\psi : C \longrightarrow A$$

$$\mathbf{x} \mapsto a$$

is such that $a \in A$ *is the unique element with* $(a,\mathbf{x}) \in \widetilde{C}$.

2. *Conversely, let* $C \subset K^n$ *be a K-vector subspace, and let* $\psi : C \longrightarrow A$ *be a K-vector space morphism. Suppose that* (C, ψ) *has* (d,r)-*multiplicativity. Let* $\overline{\psi}$ *be the associated map from Definition 12.6. Then its A-extension* $\widetilde{C} \subset A \times K^n$ *satisfies*

$$\widetilde{C}^{*d} = \{(\overline{\psi}(\mathbf{z}), \mathbf{z}) \mid \mathbf{z} \in C^{*d}\} \subset A \times K^n$$

REMARK 12.17 The reader may as well set $\widetilde{D} = \widetilde{C}^{*d}$ in this lemma and the subsequent Theorem 12.18. However, the actual statement of the lemma reflects the fact that in concrete situations, one typically proves bounds on the parameters of $\widetilde{C}^{*d}$ by finding a (larger) code $\widetilde{D}$ whose relevant parameters can be more easily analyzed. Therefore, it is useful to have the lemma already taking care of this situation.

Proof (of Lemma 12.16) Let $\mathbf{z} \in K^n$. If there is $a \in A$ such that $(a,\mathbf{z}) \in \widetilde{C}^{*d}$, then this value a is unique. That is, suppose that $(a',\mathbf{z}) \in \widetilde{C}^{*d}$ with $a' \in A$. Then $(a - a', \mathbf{0}) \in \widetilde{C}^{*d}$. By the conditions on $\widetilde{D}$, taking $B = \{1, \ldots, n\}$ and noting that $r \leq n$, it follows that $a = a'$. Therefore, the K-vector space morphism

$$\overline{\psi} : C^{*d} \longrightarrow A$$

$$\mathbf{z} \mapsto a$$

such that $(a,\mathbf{z}) \in \widetilde{C}^{*d}$ is well defined.

Furthermore, let $\mathbf{x} \in K^n$. If there is $a \in A$ such that $(a,\mathbf{x}) \in \widetilde{C}$, then this value a is unique as well. We may assume that $d > 1$. Suppose that $\widetilde{\mathbf{x}} := (b,\mathbf{0}) \in \widetilde{C}$ for some $b \in A$. We show that $b = 0$. Since

$$\widetilde{\mathbf{x}}^d = (b^d, \mathbf{0}) \in \widetilde{C}^{*d}$$

it follows from the conditions on $\widetilde{D}$ that

$$b^d = 0$$

Hence b is a nilpotent of A. Therefore, if the only nilpotent in A is 0, it follows that $b = 0$.

If A does have nontrivial nilpotents, let $(u,\mathbf{y})$ be as in the statement of the lemma. Then

$$\widetilde{\mathbf{x}} * (u^{d-1}, \mathbf{y}^{d-1}) = (bu^{d-1}, \mathbf{0}) \in \widetilde{C}^{*d}$$

By the conditions on $\widetilde{D}$, it follows that

$$bu^{d-1} = 0$$

By Lemma 10.1, it follows that

$$u^{d-1} \in A \setminus Z(A)$$

Hence $b = 0$. In conclusion, the K-vector space morphism

$$\psi : C \longrightarrow A$$

$$\mathbf{x} \mapsto a$$

such that $(a, \mathbf{x}) \in \widetilde{C}$ is well defined.

Next, note that for all $\mathbf{x}_1, \ldots, \mathbf{x}_d \in C$, it holds that

$$(\psi(\mathbf{x}_1), \mathbf{x}_1) * \cdots * (\psi(\mathbf{x}_d), \mathbf{x}_d) = (\psi(\mathbf{x}_1) \cdots \psi(\mathbf{x}_d), \mathbf{x}_1 * \cdots * \mathbf{x}_d)$$

$$= (\overline{\psi}(\mathbf{x}_1 * \cdots * \mathbf{x}_d), \mathbf{x}_1 * \cdots \mathbf{x}_d)$$

The first identity holds by the definition of the $*$-product. The second identity holds by a combination of the definition of $\overline{\psi}$ with the fact that the element from the penultimate expression is contained in $\widetilde{C}^{*d}$. From the second identity, we see that the multiplicative relation holds for (C, ψ). Finally, $\overline{\psi}$ is r-wise determined by the condition on $\widetilde{D}$. This proves the first claim.

The proof of the second claim is straightforward from the definition of multiplicativity. ∎

Combining Lemmas 12.12 and 12.16, we get the following theorem (see also Remark 12.17):

THEOREM 12.18 (CODEX AS GENERALIZED CODE) *Let A be a K-algebra with $\dim_K A < \infty$. Let n, t, d, r be integers with $d \geq 1$ and $0 \leq t < r \leq n$. Let*

$$\widetilde{C} \subset A \times K^n$$

be a K-vector subspace. Suppose that the following statements hold:

- $\pi_0(\widetilde{C}) = A$.
- *If $t > 0$, then for each $B \subset \mathcal{I}^*$ with $|B| = t$ and for each $a \in A$, there is $\widetilde{\mathbf{x}} \in \widetilde{C}$ with $\widetilde{\mathbf{x}}_B = \mathbf{0}$ and $\widetilde{x}_0 = a$.*

Furthermore, suppose that there is a K-vector subspace

$$\widetilde{D} \subset A \times K^n$$

such that

- $\widetilde{C}^{*d} \subset \widetilde{D}$.
- *For all $\widetilde{\mathbf{z}} \in \widetilde{D}$, it holds that $\widetilde{z}_0 = 0$ if $\widetilde{\mathbf{z}}_B = \mathbf{0}$ for some $B \subset \mathcal{I}^*$ with $|B| = r$.*

Then (C, ψ) is an (n, t, d, r)-codex for A over K, where $C := \pi_{\mathcal{I}^*}(\widetilde{C}) \subset K^n$ and $\psi : C \longrightarrow A$ is the K-vector space morphism such that $\widetilde{C}$ consists of all $(a, \mathbf{x}) \in A \times K^n$ with $\mathbf{x} \in C$ and $a = \psi(\mathbf{x})$.

There is also a natural converse, but we do not state that here.

12.3.2 A Definition in Terms of Multi-Linear Algebra

It is also natural to develop an equivalent codex definition in the language of multilinear algebra, more precisely, linear algebra in the space of symmetric tensors.[7] We sketch next how this works out for an important class of arithmetic secret-sharing schemes, namely, $(n,t,2,n-t)$-codices for $\mathbb{F}_q^k$ over $\mathbb{F}_q$ with $t \geq 1$, although we shall not use the resulting definition further on.[8]

We make some ("coordinate-free") preparations first. The reader who prefers a "matrix-based" view can easily extract a complete analogy in such terms. Let V be a finite-dimensional K-vector space. Furthermore, let $\mathrm{Bil}(V)$ denote the space of K-bilinear forms $\Phi : V \times V \longrightarrow K$. Also, for $\Phi \in \mathrm{Bil}(V)$, define its transpose $\Phi^T \in \mathrm{Bil}(V)$ by declaring $\Phi^T(x,y) = \Phi(y,x)$ for all $x,y \in V$. Let $\mathrm{Sym}(V)$ denote the subspace of $\mathrm{Bil}(V)$ consisting of the symmetric forms Φ', that is, $\Phi'(x,y) = \Phi'(y,x)$ for all, $x,y \in V$. Let $\mathrm{Alt}(V)$ denote the subspace of $\mathrm{Bil}(V)$ consisting of the alternating forms Φ'', that is, $\Phi''(x,x) = 0$, for all $x \in V$.

Consider the tensor product $V \otimes_K V$. By universality, we have a vector space isomorphism

$$\mathrm{Bil}(V) \overset{\sim}{\longrightarrow} (V \otimes_K V)^*$$

$$\Phi \mapsto \phi$$

with ϕ being the unique map in $(V \otimes_K V)^*$ such that $\phi(x \otimes y) = \Phi(x,y)$ for all $x,y \in V$.

Let

$$S^2(V) \subset V \otimes_K V$$

denote the K-vector subspace of symmetric tensors, that is, the K-span of all tensors $x \otimes x$ with $x \in V$. By linear algebra, it follows as a corollary that we have a vector space isomorphism

$$\mathrm{Bil}(V)/\mathrm{Alt}(V) \overset{\sim}{\longrightarrow} (S^2(V))^*$$

$$\Phi + \mathrm{Alt}(V) \mapsto \phi$$

with ϕ being the unique map in $(S^2(V))^*$ with

$$\phi(x \otimes x) = \Phi(x,x)$$

for all $x \in V$.

Now suppose for simplicity that the characteristic of K is different from 2. Then $\mathrm{Sym}(V) \cap \mathrm{Alt}(V) = \{0\}$. Hence, taking into account that for all $\Phi \in \mathrm{Bil}(V)$ it holds that

$$\Phi = \left(\frac{\Phi + \Phi^T}{2} \right) + \left(\frac{\Phi - \Phi^T}{2} \right)$$

we have the (internal) direct sum decomposition of vector spaces

$$\mathrm{Bil}(V) \simeq \mathrm{Sym}(V) + \mathrm{Alt}(V)$$

---

[7] See also the definition of tensor rank of multiplication in finite fields, for example, in Bürgisser, Clausen, and Shokrollahi [31].

[8] It also can be easily restated in the language of *quadratic forms* (see, e.g., Lam [123]). Our presentation here is inspired by the definitions in Cascudo et al. [39] (which build on those in Cramer et al. [63]).

In particular, each class $\Phi + \text{Alt}(V) \in \text{Bil}(V)/\text{Alt}(V)$ contains a unique symmetric form $\Phi' \in \text{Sym}(V)$, and moreover, we have a vector space isomorphism

$$\text{Sym}(V) \simeq (S^2(V))^*$$

$$\Phi \mapsto \phi$$

with ϕ being the unique map in $(S^2(V))^*$ with

$$\phi(x \otimes x) = \Phi(x,x)$$

for all $x \in V$.

We now define the rank of $\phi \in (S^2(V))^*$ as the rank of this unique symmetric form $\Phi' \in \Phi + \text{Alt}(V)$. That is, consider the K-vector space morphism

$$V \longrightarrow V^*$$

$$x \mapsto \Phi'(\cdot, x)$$

Then the rank of Φ' is the rank of this map, that is, the dimension of its image. In other words, if we view Φ' as defining some (possibly degenerate) "inner product" on V, then the rank of Φ' is the codimension of the space consisting of elements "orthogonal" (under Φ') to *all* of V.

It is not hard to verify that ϕ is of rank 1 if and only if there is some $\Psi_0 \in V^*$ and $\lambda \in K$ with $\lambda \neq 0$ such that

$$\Phi'(x,y) = \lambda \cdot \Psi_0(x)\Psi_0(y)$$

for all $x,y \in V$,[9] which is a fact we shall use later.

LEMMA 12.19 (TENSOR-PRODUCT CHARACTERIZATION) *Suppose that the characteristic p of $\mathbb{F}_q$ satisfies $p > 2$. Let k,n,t be integers with $k \geq 1$ and $1 \leq t < n - t$. Index $\mathbb{F}_q^k \times \mathbb{F}_q^n$ with the set $\mathcal{I} = \{-k+1, \ldots, 0, 1, \ldots, n\}$. Define $\mathcal{Z} = \{-k+1, \ldots, 0\}$ and $\mathcal{I}^* = \{1, \ldots, n\}$.*

There exists an $(n,t,2,n-t)$-arithmetic secret-sharing scheme for $\mathbb{F}_q^k$ over $\mathbb{F}_q$ if and only if there exists a finite-dimensional $\mathbb{F}_q$-vector space V and a set of elements

$$\{z_\ell\}_{\ell \in \mathcal{I}} \subset V$$

such that for each $B \subset \mathcal{I}^*$ and each $j \in \mathcal{Z}$, the following conditions hold:

1. *The set of elements $\{z_u\}_{u \in \mathcal{Z}} \subset V$ is linearly independent over $\mathbb{F}_q$.*
2. *If $|B| = t$, then there is $\phi \in (S^2(V))^*$ of rank 1 such that $\phi(z_i \otimes z_i) = 0$ for all $i \in (\mathcal{Z} \setminus \{j\}) \cup B$ and such that $\phi(z_j \otimes z_j) = 1$.*
3. *If $|B| = n - t$, then there is no $\phi \in (S^2(V))^*$ such that $\phi(z_i \otimes z_i) = 0$ for all $i \in B$ and such that $\phi(z_j \otimes z_j) = 1$.*

---

[9] Briefly, if $W \subset V$ is the codimension-1 kernel, choose $\Psi_0 \in V^*$ such that Ψ_0 vanishes on W but $\Psi_0(z) \neq 0$ for some $z \in V$. Note that V is the (internal) direct sum of W and the line spanned by z. Now set $\lambda = \Phi'(z,z)/\Phi_0(z)^2$. It is easy to check that the resulting form agrees with Φ' on V.

Proof   We only show the "if" part. We verify that the conditions of Theorem 12.18 are satisfied. Consider the $\mathbb{F}_q$-linear code

$$C := \{(\phi(z_{-k+1}),\ldots,\phi(z_0),\phi(z_1),\ldots,\phi(z_n)) \mid \phi \in V^*\} \subset \mathbb{F}_q^k \times \mathbb{F}_q^n$$

Fix any $B \subset \mathcal{I}^*$ and $j \in \mathcal{Z}$.

By the first condition it holds that $\pi_{\mathcal{Z}}(C) = \mathbb{F}_q^k$. Suppose that $|B| = t$. Then the postulated map ϕ in the second condition corresponds to a symmetric form $\lambda \cdot \Phi_0(x)\Phi_0(y)$ for some $\Phi_0 \in V^*$ and some nonzero $\lambda \in K$. Hence, for each $i \in (\mathcal{Z} \setminus \{j\}) \cup B$, it holds that

$$0 = \phi(z_i \otimes z_i) = \lambda \cdot \Phi_0(z_i)^2$$

so that

$$\Phi_0(z_i) = 0$$

whereas

$$1 = \phi(z_j \otimes z_j) = \lambda \cdot \Phi_0(z_j)^2$$

so that

$$\Phi_0(z_j) \neq 0$$

Finally, suppose that $|B| = n - t$. By the third condition, Lemma 11.84 implies that the $\mathbb{F}_q$-span of any $n - t$ tensors $z_i \otimes z_i$ ($i \in \mathcal{I}^*$) contains $z_j \otimes z_j$. Therefore, there are $(\lambda_i)_{i \in B} \in \mathbb{F}_q^{n-t}$ such that

$$z_j \otimes z_j = \sum_{i \in B} \lambda_i \cdot (z_i \otimes z_i)$$

Hence,

$$\chi(z_j)\chi'(z_j) = \sum_{i \in B} \lambda_i \cdot \chi(z_i)\chi'(z_i)$$

for all $\chi, \chi' \in V^*$. This is justified by universality of the tensor product because the product $\chi(v)\chi'(v')$ with $(v,v') \in V \times V$ defines a bilinear form on V. Since C^{*2} is the $\mathbb{F}_q$-span of all vectors of the form $(\chi(z_a)\chi'(z_a))_{-k+1 \leq a \leq n}$, the immediate consequence is that for all $\mathbf{u} \in C^{*2}$, if $\mathbf{u}_B = \mathbf{0}$, then $u_j = \mathbf{0}$.   ∎

12.4 Basic Constructions

12.4.1 Polynomial Codices

THEOREM 12.20 (POLYNOMIAL CODICES) *Suppose that A is a simple algebraic extension field of K. Write $k = [A : K]$, the degree of the extension. Let n, t, d be integers such that*

1. *$n \geq 1$, $d \geq 1$, and $t \geq 0$.*
2. *$0 < d(t + k - 1) < n$.*
3. *$n + 1 \leq |K|$ if $k = 1$ and $n \leq |K|$ if $k > 1$.*

Then there exists an $(n, t, d, d(t + k - 1) + 1)$-codex for A over K. Moreover, it is unital and has uniformity.

Proof By the conditions on A, the extension degree k is finite, and there is $\alpha_0 \in A$ such that $A = K(\alpha_0)$. Let $\alpha_1, \ldots, \alpha_n \in K$ be such that $\alpha_0, \alpha_1, \ldots, \alpha_n$ are pairwise distinct. For each integer m, consider the polynomial evaluation code

$$E(m) = \{(f(\alpha_0), f(\alpha_1), \ldots, f(\alpha_n)) \mid f(X) \in K[X]_{\leq m}\} \subset A \times K^n$$

where $K[X]_{\leq m}$ denotes the K-vector space of polynomials of degree at most m. Using Theorem 11.96, we shall argue that the code

$$\widetilde{C} := E(t+k-1) \subset A \times K^n$$

satisfies the conditions of Theorem 12.18. Define $\mathcal{I} = \{0, 1, \ldots, n\}$ as the index set of $A \times K^n$, and define $\mathcal{I}^* = \{1, \ldots, n\}$. First, since $K(\alpha_0)$ and $K[X]_{\leq k-1}$ are isomorphic as K-vector spaces, it follows at once that $\pi_0(\widetilde{C}) = K(\alpha_0) = A$. Second (assuming that $t > 0$), for each $B \subset \mathcal{I}^*$ with $|B| = t$, it follows similarly that $\pi_{0,B}(\widetilde{C}) = A \times K^{|B|}$ because $K(\alpha_0) \bigoplus K^t$ and $K[X]_{\leq t+k-1}$ are isomorphic as K-vector spaces. Third, by definition,

$$\widetilde{C}^{*d} \subset E(d(t+k-1)) \subset A \times K^n$$

Finally, if $\widetilde{\mathbf{z}} = (g(\alpha_j))_{j \in \mathcal{I}} \in E(d(t+k-1))$ with $g(X) \in K[X]_{d(t+k-1)}$ satisfies $\widetilde{\mathbf{z}}_B = \mathbf{0}$ for some set $B \subset \mathcal{I}^*$ with $|B| = d(t+k-1)+1$, then $g = 0$, and hence, $g(\alpha_0) = 0$. ∎

REMARK 12.21 (USING THE POINT AT INFINITY) The condition $n+1 \leq |K|$ if $k = 1$ (and $n \leq |K|$ if $k > 1$) can be weakened to $n \leq |K|$ if $k = 1$ (and $n \leq |K| + 1$ if $k > 1$). This is done by introducing one extra evaluation in the definition of evaluation code, namely, the evaluation $f(\infty)$ defined as the coefficient of X^{t+k-1} in $f(X)$. See Section 11.7 for details, which are easily adapted to the present case.

We also have the following important variation.

THEOREM 12.22 (POLYNOMIAL CODICES (VARIATION)) *Let k be a positive integer, and let $A = K^k$. Let n, t, d be integers such that*

1. $n \geq 1$, $d \geq 1$, and $t \geq 0$.
2. $0 < d(t+k-1) < n$.
3. $n+k \leq |K|$.

Then there exists an $(n, t, d, d(t+k-1)+1)$-codex for A over K. Moreover, it is unital and has uniformity.

The proof of this theorem is very similar to that of Theorem 12.20. Remark 12.21 applies here as well.

COROLLARY 12.23 *Let $p > 0$ be a prime number, and let v be a positive integer. Define $q = p^v$. Let $\mathbb{F}_q$ be a finite field of cardinality q. Let n, d, k be integers with $n \geq 1$, $d \geq 1$, $t \geq 0$, and $d(t+k-1)+1 \leq n$. Then*

- *There is an $(n, t, d, d(t+k-1)+1)$-codex for $\mathbb{F}_q^k$ over $\mathbb{F}_q$ if $n+k \leq q$.*
- *There is an $(n, t, d, d(t+k-1)+1)$-codex for $\mathbb{F}_{q^k}$ over $\mathbb{F}_q$ if $n \leq q$ and $k > 1$.*

In each case, the codex is unital and there is uniformity if $t \geq 1$.

12.4.2 A Remark on Codices from Linear Codes

There are sufficient conditions for the existence of (n,t,d,r)-codices for $\mathbb{F}_q^k$ over $\mathbb{F}_q$ that can be conveniently stated in terms of the theory of error-correcting codes. By combining Theorem 11.91 with Theorem 12.18, we obtain the following result:

THEOREM 12.24 *Let n,t,d,r,k be integers such that $0 \leq t < r \leq n$ and $k \geq 1$. Suppose that $C \subset \mathbb{F}_q^{n+k}$ is an $\mathbb{F}_q$-linear code such that*

1. $d_{\min}(C^\perp) \geq t+k+1$.
2. $d_{\min}(C^{*d}) \geq n-r+k+1$.

Then there exists an (n,t,d,r)-codex for $\mathbb{F}_q^k$ over $\mathbb{F}_q$.

12.4.3 Connection with Known Schemes

We now have the following examples. Let n,t,d,k be integers such that $0 \leq t < n$ and $d,k \geq 1$.

1. Suppose that $q \geq 2k-1$. For any $k > 1$, there is a $(2k-1,2)$-arithmetic embedding for $\mathbb{F}_{q^k}$ over $\mathbb{F}_q$. This corresponds to a bilinear multiplication algorithm for $\mathbb{F}_{q^k}$ over $\mathbb{F}_q$. This is a classical notion in algebraic complexity theory (see Bürgisser, Clausen, and Shokrollahi [31]).
2. Suppose that $n < q$ and $1 \leq t < n$. Shamir's secret-sharing scheme [167] is an $(n,t,1,t+1)$-codex for $\mathbb{F}_q$ over $\mathbb{F}_q$.
3. Suppose that $n < q$ and $1 \leq t < \frac{1}{2}n$ (and $1 \leq t < \frac{1}{3}n$). If $t < \frac{1}{2}n$, Shamir's scheme has *multiplication*. If, in fact, $t < \frac{1}{3}n$, then it has strong multiplication (see Cramer, Damgård, and Maurer [61]). This corresponds to an $(n,t,2,n)$-arithmetic secret-sharing scheme for $\mathbb{F}_q$ over $\mathbb{F}_q$ and an $(n,t,2,n-t)$-arithmetic secret-sharing scheme for $\mathbb{F}_q$ over $\mathbb{F}_q$. These properties were first used by Ben-Or, Goldwasser, and Wigderson [14] and Chaum, Crépeau and Damgård [46] in the context of secure multiparty computation.
4. Suppose that $k \geq 1$, $n+k-1 < q$, and $1 \leq t < \frac{1}{3}(n-2k+2)$. Franklin-Yung's variation [93] on Shamir's scheme, also known as a "packed secret-sharing scheme" (with strong multiplication), corresponds to an $(n,t,2,n-t)$-arithmetic secret-sharing scheme for $\mathbb{F}_q^k$ over $\mathbb{F}_q$.
5. Suppose that $k > 1$, $n \leq q$, and $1 \leq t < \frac{1}{3}(n-2k+2)$. A variation on Franklin-Yung's scheme [49] where $\mathbb{F}_q^k$ is replaced by $\mathbb{F}_{q^k}$ corresponds to an $(n,t,2,n-t)$-arithmetic secret-sharing scheme for $\mathbb{F}_{q^k}$ over $\mathbb{F}_q$.
6. *Construction from self-dual codes* [50, 61]. Another type of elementary example is as follows [50]. Instantiating Theorem 12.24 with self-dual codes of length $n+1$ and minimum distance $d' > 2$ gives rise to an $(n,d'-2,2,n)$-arithmetic secret-sharing scheme for $\mathbb{F}_q$ over $\mathbb{F}_q$.

   Various other constructions based on general linear codes (e.g., high-information-rate ramp schemes with or without multiplicative properties) also can be found in Chen et al. [50]. These results were inspired by the monotone span program-based construction of linear secret-sharing schemes with multiplication from Cramer, Damgård and Maurer [61]. In Duursma and Shen [90] construction from Reed-Muller codes is discussed.

Note that Remark 12.21 about using the point of infinity applies here as well, giving slightly weaker requirements in some cases.

12.5 Applications

We briefly sketch some applications of codices. First, it is useful to discuss some basic properties of codices.

12.5.1 Basic Properties of Codices

Let A be a K-algebra. Let n, d, r be integers with $d \geq 1$ and $1 \leq r \leq n$. Let $C \subset K^n$ be a K-vector subspace and let $\psi : C \longrightarrow A$ be a K-vector space morphism.

DEFINITION 12.25 (HOMOGENIZATION OF POLYNOMIALS) *Let $m \geq 1$ be an integer, and let $f \in K[X_1, \ldots, X_m]$. Then $f^{\dagger} \in K[X_0, X_1, \ldots, X_m]$ is the unique homogeneous polynomial*[10] *with $\deg f^{\dagger} = \deg f$ (total degree) such that*

$$f^{\dagger}(1, X_1, \ldots, X_m) = f(X_1, \ldots, X_m)$$

in $K[X_1, \ldots, X_m]$.

Most of the applications in which multiplicativity plays a role rely, in part, on the following property:

LEMMA 12.26 *Suppose that (C, ψ) has (d, r)-multiplicativity. Let $m \geq 1$ be an integer, and let $f \in K[X_1, \ldots, X_m]$ with $\deg f \leq d$. Then the following statements hold:*

1. *If (C, ψ) is unital, define the map*

$$\mathcal{F} : \bigoplus_{\ell=1}^{m} K^n \longrightarrow K^n$$

$$(\mathbf{x}_1, \ldots, \mathbf{x}_m) \mapsto (\ldots, f(x_{1j}, \ldots, x_{mj}), \ldots)$$

where x_{ij} denotes the jth coordinate of $\mathbf{x}_i$ $(i = 1, \ldots, m, \ j = 1, \ldots, n)$. Then, for all $\mathbf{x}_1, \ldots, \mathbf{x}_m \in C$, it holds that

$$\mathcal{F}(\mathbf{x}_1, \ldots, \mathbf{x}_m) \in C^{*d}$$

and

$$\psi(\mathcal{F}(\mathbf{x}_1, \ldots, \mathbf{x}_m)) = f(\psi(\mathbf{x}_1), \ldots, \psi(\mathbf{x}_m))$$

2. *More generally, assume that $1 \in \operatorname{im} \psi$.*[11] *Let $\mathbf{u} \in C$ be such that $\psi(\mathbf{u}) = 1$. Define the map*

$$\mathcal{F}_{\mathbf{u}}^{\dagger} : \bigoplus_{\ell=1}^{m} K^n \longrightarrow K^n$$

$$(\mathbf{x}_1, \ldots, \mathbf{x}_m) \mapsto (\ldots, f^{\dagger}(u_j, x_{1j}, \ldots, x_{mj}), \ldots)$$

---

[10] That is, the monomials with nonzero coefficient all have the same degree.
[11] Of course, this condition is satisfied if ψ is surjective.

where x_{ij} denotes the jth coordinate of $\mathbf{x}_i$ $(i = 1,\ldots,m,\ j = 1,\ldots,n)$. Then for all $\mathbf{x}_1,\ldots,\mathbf{x}_m \in C$, it holds that

$$\mathcal{F}_{\mathbf{u}}^{\dagger}(\mathbf{x}_1,\ldots,\mathbf{x}_m) \in C^{*d}$$

and

$$\overline{\psi}(\mathcal{F}_{\mathbf{u}}^{\dagger}(\mathbf{x}_1,\ldots,\mathbf{x}_m)) = f(\psi(\mathbf{x}_1),\ldots,\psi(\mathbf{x}_m))$$

The proof of this lemma follows at once from the definition of (d,r)-multiplicativity. In the unital case, also take Remark 12.10 into account. Note that since A is a K-algebra, the evaluation $f(a_1,\ldots,a_m) \in A$ is well defined for all $a_1,\ldots,a_m \in A$.

The next lemma is also useful in some protocol applications where it is desirable to have an explicit representation of $\overline{\psi}$ as a matrix that only picks the coordinates indexed by a set $B \subset \{1,\ldots,n\}$ with $|B| = r$.

LEMMA 12.27 (C,ψ) *has (d,r)-multiplicativity if and only if, for each set $B \subset \{1,\ldots,n\}$ with $|B| = r$, there exists a K-vector space morphism*

$$\rho^B : K^n \longrightarrow A$$

such that the following conditions are satisfied:

1. $\rho^B(\prod_{i=1}^d \mathbf{x}_i) = \prod_{i=1}^d \psi(\mathbf{x}_i)$ *for all $(\mathbf{x}_1,\ldots,\mathbf{x}_d) \in C^d$; that is, ρ^B satisfies the same multiplicative relation as $\overline{\psi}$ does.*
2. $\ker \pi_B \subset \ker \rho^B$; *that is, ρ^B "ignores all coordinates $i \notin B$".*

Proof The proof is by elementary linear algebra. In the forward direction, select an arbitrary $B \subset \{1,\ldots,n\}$ with $|B| = r$. The map $\overline{\psi}$ is defined on C^{*d} and vanishes on $C^{*d} \cap \ker \pi_B$ by definition. Now extend it to the K-vector subspace $C^{*d} + \ker \pi_B \subset K^n$ such that it vanishes on $\ker \pi_B$. This extension is, of course, unique. The required map ρ^B now can be taken as an arbitrary extension of the latter to all of K^n.

In the other direction, select an arbitrary $B \subset \{1,\ldots,n\}$ with $|B| = r$ and define $\overline{\psi}$ as the restriction of the map ρ^B to C^{*d}. It follows at once that $\overline{\psi}$ satisfies the multiplicative relation. This definition of $\overline{\psi}$ is independent of B because the action of ρ^B on $m_d(C)$ (and hence that on all of C^{*d}) depends only on ψ. Therefore, if $\mathbf{z} \in C^{*d}$ satisfies $\pi_{B'}(\mathbf{z}) = \mathbf{0}$ for some $B' \subset \{1,\ldots,n\}$ with $|B'| = r$, it holds that $\overline{\psi}(\mathbf{z}) = \rho^{B'}(\mathbf{z}) = 0$. ∎

REMARK 12.28 (RECOMBINATION VECTORS) Write $k := \dim_K A$, and suppose that $k < \infty$. Once a K-basis for A is fixed (as well as, say, the standard basis for K^n), each ρ^B may be given by a matrix with k rows and n columns and entries in K. If $A = K$, for instance, each ρ^B thus is representable by a K-linear form $\langle \mathbf{r}^B, \cdot \rangle$, with $r_i^B = 0$ if $i \notin B$.

The definition of a recombination vector originates from Cramer, Damgård, and Maurer [61], where multiplicative properties of linear secret-sharing schemes were first formalized and the first general results were obtained.

12.5.2 Multiparty Computation Secure against a Passive Adversary

Consider an $(n,t,2,n)$-arithmetic secret-sharing scheme (C,ψ) for $\mathbb{F}_q^k$ over $\mathbb{F}_q$. Index $\mathbb{F}_q^k \times \mathbb{F}_q^n$ with the set $\mathcal{I} = \{-k+1,\ldots,0,1,\ldots,n\}$. Define $\mathcal{Z} = \{-k+1,\ldots,0\}$ and $\mathcal{I}^* = \{1,\ldots,n\}$.

Such a scheme can be used to reduce n-party secure multiplication to secure addition in the case of a *passive adversary* at the cost of one round of interaction. This is done by taking the protocol we presented in Chapter 3 for Shamir's scheme and generalizing it in the natural way.

On account of Remark 12.28, there is a matrix ρ with k rows and n columns and entries in $\mathbb{F}_q$ such that for all $\mathbf{x}, \mathbf{x}' \in C$,

$$\rho(x_1 x_1', \ldots, x_n x_n')^T = \psi(\mathbf{x}) * \psi(\mathbf{x}') \in \mathbb{F}_q^k$$

The reduction works as follows: as in Chapter 3, we have n players arranged in a complete communication network of perfectly private channels between each pair of players. There is a passive adversary and a bound t on the number of players it can corrupt. Recall that a passive adversary knows all about each of the at most t players it corrupts but cannot modify their actions. If a player is not corrupted, it is honest and executes its required actions faithfully.

The purpose of the protocol to follow is to establish a secret sharing of the product of two secrets given secret sharings of these secrets. Of course, no information should leak in the process. Moreover, the secret sharing of the product should be in the same scheme as that of the two secrets so that it facilitates an ongoing secure computation.

Suppose that the network has access to secret sharings $\mathbf{x}, \mathbf{x}' \in C$, with respective secrets $\psi(\mathbf{x}), \psi(\mathbf{x}') \in \mathbb{F}_q^k$. It does not matter how these sharings have come into existence: for instance, perhaps they were obtained from some external source or from different players in the network, or they may have resulted from a previous secure computation. We assume that for $i = 1, \ldots, n$, player P_i holds share x_i in secret $\psi(\mathbf{x}) \in \mathbb{F}_q^k$ and share x_i' in secret $\psi(\mathbf{x}') \in \mathbb{F}_q^k$.

Now, for $i = 1, \ldots, n$, player P_i secret shares the locally computable secret value

$$(\rho_{1i} x_i x_i', \ldots, \rho_{ki} x_i x_i') \in \mathbb{F}_q^k$$

where the coefficient vector is the ith column of the matrix ρ, by choosing a uniformly random element $\mathbf{x}^{(i)} \in C$ such that

$$\psi(\mathbf{x}^{(i)}) = (\rho_{1i} x_i x_i', \ldots, \rho_{ki} x_i x_i')^T$$

and, for $j = 1, \ldots, n$, sending the jth share $x_j^{(i)}$ to player P_j over the private channel connecting the two.

Next, for $j = 1, \ldots, n$, player P_j sums the n received shares. This gives a secret sharing of $\psi(\mathbf{x}) * \psi(\mathbf{x}')$ according to C (see, e.g., Chen et al. [49]). This generalizes Shamir-based solutions from references [14], [46] and [93] (see also Cramer, Damgård, and Maurer [61]).[12]

12.5.3 Zero-Knowledge Verification of Secret Multiplications

Consider an $(n, t, 2, n - t)$-arithmetic secret-sharing scheme (C, ψ) for $\mathbb{F}_q^k$ over $\mathbb{F}_q$. Such a scheme can be used for "zero-knowledge verification of secret multiplications." In a nutshell, the main idea is as follows: suppose that a prover and a verifier have access to

---

[12] The "local share multiplication plus resharing" simplification (in the case of Shamir's scheme) has been attributed to Michael Rabin.

an $\mathbb{F}_q$-linear cryptographic commitment scheme, allowing them to commit to a value in $\mathbb{F}_q$. Before the commitment is opened, the verifier gains no knowledge about the $\mathbb{F}_q$ value committed to (hiding property), whereas the prover can open the commitment later only to reveal the original value (binding property). Linearity means that $\mathbb{F}_q$-linear combinations of commitments can be taken noninteractively.[13]

Suppose that a prover gives (coordinate-wise) commitments to secrets $\mathbf{x}_0, \mathbf{y}_0, \mathbf{z}_0 \in \mathbb{F}_q^k$, and claims that $\mathbf{x}_0 * \mathbf{y}_0 = \mathbf{z}_0$. The purpose of the following protocol is for the prover to convince a skeptical verifier that this is indeed true (correctness), without revealing the secrets in the process (privacy).

To prove the claim, the prover gives (coordinate-wise) commitments to random $\mathbf{x}, \mathbf{y} \in C$ such that $\psi(\mathbf{x}) = \mathbf{x}_0$ and $\psi(\mathbf{y}) = \mathbf{y}_0$ and a (coordinate-wise) commitment to some $\mathbf{z} \in C^{*2}$ such that $\overline{\psi}(\mathbf{z}) = \mathbf{z}_0$. If the commitment scheme is $\mathbb{F}_q$-linear, it is easy to design a mechanism such that regardless of the prover's honesty, the correctness constraints are satisfied that, indeed, $\mathbf{x}, \mathbf{y} \in C$ and $\mathbf{z} \in C^{*2}$ and indeed $\psi(\mathbf{x}) = \mathbf{x}_0$, $\psi(\mathbf{y}) = \mathbf{y}_0$, and $\overline{\psi}(\mathbf{z}) = \mathbf{z}_0$.

Moreover, the mechanism allows the prover to select $\mathbf{x}, \mathbf{y}, \mathbf{z}$ such that $\mathbf{z} = \mathbf{x} * \mathbf{y}$, and in fact, this is exactly what the *honest* prover is required to do. Note that this gives

$$\mathbf{z}_0 = \overline{\psi}(\mathbf{z}) = \overline{\psi}(\mathbf{x} * \mathbf{y}) = \psi(\mathbf{x}) \cdot \psi(\mathbf{y}) = \mathbf{x}_0 * \mathbf{y}_0$$

Meanwhile, the mechanism protects the privacy of the honest prover's secrets. However, in case of a *cheating* prover, there is no guarantee that $\mathbf{z} = \mathbf{x} * \mathbf{y}$. See, for instance, Cramer, Damgård, and Maurer [61] to fill in the details of this mechanism.

Now, if $\mathbf{z} = \mathbf{x} * \mathbf{y}$ (as in the case of an honest prover), then indeed $\mathbf{x}_0 * \mathbf{y}_0 = \mathbf{z}_0$, as verified earlier. Inspection by the verifier (after opening by the prover) of any t "share triples" (x_i, y_i, z_i) then gives no information on the "secret triple" $(\mathbf{x}_0, \mathbf{y}_0, \mathbf{x}_0 * \mathbf{y}_0)$, by t-privacy. Moreover, $z_i = x_i y_i$ for *each* of those t share triples.

However, suppose that there is a cheating prover at work and that $\mathbf{z}_0 \neq \mathbf{x}_0 * \mathbf{y}_0$. Then there are at most $n - t - 1$ share triples (x_i, y_i, z_i) such that $z_i = x_i y_i$, and hence, there are at least $t + 1$ share triples for which there is an *inconsistency*. This follows from $(2, n - t)$-multiplicativity.

If t is not too small compared with n, and if the verifier chooses t distinct positions i at random, it is with high probability that this cheating prover is exposed. By the preceding observations, there are no inconsistencies in the case an honest prover, and moreover, the prover's privacy is guaranteed. This procedure is essentially from Cramer, Damgård, and Maurer [61], building on ideas from Ben-Or, Goldwasser, and Wigderson [14] and Chaum, Crépeau and Damgård [46].

These facts together give a handle for probabilistic private checking that $\mathbf{z}_0 = \mathbf{x}_0 * \mathbf{y}_0$ in several different application scenarios, most notably perfect information-theoretically secure general MPC in the case of a *malicious adversary*. In Cramer, Damgård, and Pastro [62], a quite efficient method is given for checking in zero-knowledge that a private vector of committed values satisfies a given arithmetic circuit. This involves arithmetic secret-sharing schemes with $d > 2$.

---

[13] That is, any secret value taken in $\mathbb{F}_q$ can be committed to, and just given two commitments to respective secrets s, s' and given a scalar $\lambda \in \mathbb{F}_q$ as inputs, a commitment to $s + \lambda s' \in \mathbb{F}_q$ can be efficiently computed. Moreover, given opening information for the input commitments, opening information for the output commitment can be efficiently computed.

12.5.4 Error Correction in Codices

The important subclass of arithmetic secret-sharing schemes that satisfy $r = n - t$ offers efficient recovery of the secret even if a given full-share vector contains some (malicious) errors. The method, given next, can be understood as a variation on a decoding method based on error correcting pairs [87, 122, 155], that in itself is a generalization of the *Welch-Berlekamp algorithm* (Section 11.8.2).

THEOREM 12.29 *[41, 63] Let A be an $\mathbb{F}_q$-algebra with $\dim_{\mathbb{F}_q} A < \infty$. Suppose that (C, ψ) is an $(n, t, d, n - t)$-arithmetic secret-sharing scheme for A over $\mathbb{F}_q$. On input $(i, \tilde{\mathbf{x}})$, where i is an integer with $1 \le i \le d - 1$ and where*

$$\tilde{\mathbf{x}} := \mathbf{x} + \mathbf{e} \in \mathbb{F}_q^n$$

with $\mathbf{x} \in C^{*(d-i)}$ and with $\mathbf{e} \in \mathbb{F}_q^n$ such that $w_H(\mathbf{e}) \le t$, the value

$$a := \psi(\mathbf{x}) \in A$$

is recovered deterministically by linear algebra.

Proof Recall that $d \ge 2, t \ge 1$ by definition of an arithmetic secret-sharing scheme. For convenience of exposition, suppose that it is unital. The map $\overline{\psi}$ is an extension of the map ψ because in this case $C \subset C^{*(d-1)} \subset C^{*d}$ (see Section 12.5.1). It is now sufficient to show the case $i = 1$.

Consider the system of equations

$$\tilde{\mathbf{x}} * \mathbf{z}' = \mathbf{z} \quad \text{and} \quad \psi(\mathbf{z}') = 1$$

in the pair of unknowns

$$(\mathbf{z}', \mathbf{z}) \in C \times C^{*d}$$

Note that this is in fact a *linear* system of equations (taking into account that, of course, membership of a subspace can be captured by a linear system of equations). If a generator matrix of C is given, an $\mathbb{F}_q$-basis for A is selected, and ψ is given by a matrix, then this system can be made explicit.

We prove that, first, this system has *some* solution $(\mathbf{z}', \mathbf{z}) \in C \times C^{*d}$ and that, second, *any* solution $(\mathbf{y}', \mathbf{y}) \in C \times C^{*d}$ satisfies

$$\psi(\mathbf{y}) = a$$

First, define $B \subset \{1, \ldots, n\}$ as the set of all js with $e_j \ne 0$. Let $\overline{B}$ denote its complement. If $B \ne \emptyset$, let $\mathbf{z}' \in C$ be such that $\psi(\mathbf{z}') = 1$ and $\mathbf{z}'_B = \mathbf{0}$. Otherwise, let $\mathbf{z}' \in C$ be such that $\psi(\mathbf{z}') = 1$. Since $|B| \le t$, this is possible from the assumptions in either case.

Then

$$(\mathbf{z}', \mathbf{z}) \in C \times C^{*d} \quad \text{with} \quad \mathbf{z} := \mathbf{x} * \mathbf{z}'$$

is a solution because $\psi(\mathbf{z}') = 1$ and

$$\tilde{\mathbf{x}} * \mathbf{z}' = \mathbf{x} * \mathbf{z}' = \mathbf{z}$$

Second, let $(\mathbf{y}', \mathbf{y}) \in C \times C^{*d}$ be *any* solution. Since

$$(\tilde{\mathbf{x}} * \mathbf{y}')_{\overline{B}} = (\mathbf{x} * \mathbf{y}')_{\overline{B}} = \mathbf{y}_{\overline{B}}$$

$$\mathbf{x} * \mathbf{y}' \in C^{*d}$$

and $|\overline{B}| \geq n - t$, it follows that

$$\psi(\mathbf{y}) = \psi(\mathbf{x} * \mathbf{y}') = \psi(\mathbf{x})\psi(\mathbf{y}') = a \cdot 1 = a$$

as desired. ∎

Theorem 12.29 differs from the result in references [122] and [155] in that, first, it is not the classical error-correction scenario for linear codes that is considered here but rather recovery of just the algebra element presented by a corrupted codex element. Second, the method from references 122 and 155 is given in terms of minimum distance, whereas the method here relies in essence on a measure closely related to the weights from Theorem 11.77. Third, recovery in higher powers is considered here, not just in the "base code." Fourth, the respective requirements do not appear to be easily comparable.

That said, the spirit of the proof of Theorem 12.29 bears similarity to that of references [122] and [155]. In Duursma [86], the method from Cramer et al. [63] for the special case of strongly multiplicative linear secret-sharing schemes is explained from the perspective of references [122] and [155]. For relaxed conditions under which the theorem holds, please refer to Cascudo, Cramer, and Xing [41].

12.5.5 Bilinear Multiplication Algorithms

We conclude with a classical application from algebraic complexity theory. If (C, ψ) is an $(n, 2)$-arithmetic embedding, say, for $\mathbb{F}_{q^k}$ over $\mathbb{F}_q$, then it may be interpreted as a specialized "vectorial representation" of the extension field $\mathbb{F}_{q^k}$ over $\mathbb{F}_q$. Extension field addition (and scalar multiplication) amounts to vector addition (and multiplication of a vector by a scalar). Extension field multiplication requires just the coordinate-wise product of vectors followed by a linear map. All these operations are over the base field $\mathbb{F}_q$.

Concretely, this interpretation can be extracted from the definition of an arithmetic embedding as follows: by definition, the map

$$\psi : C \longrightarrow \mathbb{F}_{q^k}$$

is an isomorphism of $\mathbb{F}_q$-vector spaces. By Remark 12.28, there is an $\mathbb{F}_q$-vector space morphism

$$\rho : \mathbb{F}_q^n \longrightarrow \mathbb{F}_{q^k}$$

such that for all $\mathbf{x}, \mathbf{y} \in C$,

$$\psi^{-1} \circ \rho(\mathbf{x} * \mathbf{y}) \in C$$

presents

$$\psi(\mathbf{x}) \cdot \psi(\mathbf{y}) \in \mathbb{F}_{q^k}$$

Note that all operations (addition and scalar multiplication, on the one hand, and multiplication, on the other hand) are over the base field $\mathbb{F}_q$ and that multiplications only arise in the product $\mathbf{x} * \mathbf{y}$, which gives n of them in total. In a model where the resources needed for addition as well as scalar multiplication (each over the base field) can be neglected, it makes sense to consider multiplication algorithms that minimize just the number of multiplications over the base field. For an in-depth treatment and history, please consult Bürgisser, Clausen, and Shokrollahi [31].

In Theorem 12.20 we have given a method for constructing arithmetic embeddings for finite field extensions. In general, there is the following classical generic construction of arithmetic embeddings, once again stated and analyzed in our framework. It works for *all* finite-dimensional K-algebras at the price of a *quadratic* embedding length.

THEOREM 12.30 *Let A be a K-algebra with $1 \leq \dim_K A < \infty$. Define $k := \dim_K A$. There exists a $(\frac{1}{2}k(k+1), 2)$-arithmetic embedding of A over K.*

Proof The statement is trivial for $k = 1$. So assume that $k > 1$. Choose a K-basis $e_1, \ldots, e_k$ of A as a K-vector space. For $a \in A$, let $\mathbf{a} \in K^k$ denote the coordinate vector of a with respect to this basis; that is,

$$a = a_1 e_1 + \cdots + a_k e_k$$

Consider the K-vector space morphism

$$\phi : A \longrightarrow K^{\frac{1}{2}k(k+1)}$$

$$a \mapsto (a_1, \ldots, a_k, \ldots, a_i + a_j, \ldots)$$

where $1 \leq i < j \leq k$. Note that this map is injective. Define

$$C = \phi(A) \subset K^{\frac{1}{2}k(k+1)}$$

Furthermore, define

$$\psi : C \longrightarrow A$$

as the unique K-vector space morphism such that

$$\psi \circ \phi(a) = a$$

for all $a \in A$. This is possible because ϕ is injective. Note that ψ essentially "picks" the first k coordinates $x_1, \ldots, x_k$ of $\mathbf{x} \in C$ and sets

$$\psi(\mathbf{x}) = x_1 e_1 + \cdots + x_k e_k$$

For all $a_1, \ldots, a_k, b_1, \ldots, b_k \in K$, it holds that

$$(a_1 e_1 + \cdots + a_k e_k) \cdot (b_1 e_1 + \cdots + b_k e_k)$$

$$= \sum_{1 \leq i \leq k} a_i b_i e_i^2 + \sum_{1 \leq i < j \leq k} (a_i b_j + a_j b_i) e_i e_j$$

$$= \sum_{1 \leq i \leq k} a_i b_i e_i^2 + \sum_{1 \leq i < j \leq k} ((a_i + a_j)(b_i + b_j) - a_i b_i - a_j b_j) e_i e_j$$

One now quickly sees that there is a K-vector space morphism $\overline{\psi} : C^{*2} \longrightarrow A$ as required in Definition 12.15. In fact, Lemma 12.27, in combination with the subsequent Remark 12.28, renders the conclusion immediate by inspection of the latter identity. ∎

For advanced results, consult the references given in Section 12.8.

12.6 Basic Limitations on Codices

We show some basic limitations on realizable codex parameters. In particular, we give some initial remarks about asymptotic properties.

12.6.1 Remarks on the Powering Operation

It is worth noting that (n,t,d,r)-codices involve subspaces "whose dth power does not fill the whole space."

LEMMA 12.31 *Let A be a K-algebra. Let n,d,r be integers with $d \geq 1$ and $1 \leq r \leq n$. Let $C \subset K^n$ be a K-vector subspace, and let $\psi : C \longrightarrow A$ be a K-vector space morphism. If (C, ψ) has (d,r)-multiplicativity, then*

$$\widetilde{C}^{*d} \subsetneq A \times K^n$$

Suppose that the only nilpotent in A is 0 or that $\operatorname{im} \psi \not\subset Z(A)$.[14] If $r < n$ and $\psi \not\equiv 0$, then the stronger property holds that

$$C^{*d} \subsetneq K^n$$

Proof The first part of the remark is trivial: since $\overline{\psi}(\mathbf{0}) = 0$, there is in particular no element $(a, \mathbf{0}) \in \widetilde{C}^{*d}$ with $a \neq 0$. As to the second part, write $\mathbf{e}_1, \ldots, \mathbf{e}_n \in K^n$ for the vectors of the standard basis. Toward a contradiction, suppose that $C^{*d} = K^n$. It follows that $\mathbf{e}_1, \ldots, \mathbf{e}_n \in C^{*d}$ and that

$$\overline{\psi}(\mathbf{e}_1) = \cdots = \overline{\psi}(\mathbf{e}_n) = 0$$

because the Hamming weight w of each of these $\mathbf{e}_i$s satisfies $1 = w \leq n - r$. Therefore,

$$\overline{\psi} \equiv 0$$

We show that this leads to the contradiction that

$$\psi \equiv 0$$

Let $\mathbf{x} \in C$ with $\mathbf{x} \neq \mathbf{0}$. Then

$$0 = \overline{\psi}(\mathbf{x}^d) = (\psi(\mathbf{x}))^d$$

If $d = 1$, then $\psi(\mathbf{x}) = 0$. So assume that $d > 1$. If the only nilpotent in A is 0, it follows that $\psi(\mathbf{x}) = \mathbf{0}$. Otherwise, let $\mathbf{y} \in C$ be such that

$$\psi(\mathbf{y}) \in A \setminus Z(A)$$

Then

$$0 = \overline{\psi}(\mathbf{x} * \mathbf{y}^{d-1}) = \psi(\mathbf{x}) \cdot (\psi(\mathbf{y}))^{d-1}$$

By Lemma 10.1, it follows that $(\psi(\mathbf{y}))^{d-1} \in A \setminus Z(A)$. Hence $\psi(\mathbf{x}) = \mathbf{0}$. The claim follows. ∎

If $r = n$, then it does *not* necessarily hold that $C^{*d} \subsetneq K^n$. For instance, if $K = \mathbb{F}_2$ and $A = \mathbb{F}_4$, then the construction from Theorem 12.20 (assuming that the subsequent instruction from Remark 12.21 is implemented) gives a $(3,2)$-arithmetic embedding (C, ψ) of $\mathbb{F}_4$ over $\mathbb{F}_2$ if we set $k = 2, n = 3, d = 2$, and $t = 0$. However, one checks by hand that $C^{*2} = \mathbb{F}_2^3$.

The powering operation is *not benign* in a sense. For instance, $C^{*2} = K^n$ for a generic subspace $C \subset K^n$ of dimension $\gg \sqrt{n}$ when K is a fixed finite field. We give here just one elementary reason pointing in that direction. The general result [40] hinted at here involves some nontrivial facts from the theory of quadratic forms over finite fields.

---

[14] See Remark 12.8.

LEMMA 12.32 *Suppose that $C \subset K^n$ $(n > 2)$ is a K-vector subspace with $C \neq \{0\}, K^n$. Suppose that t is an integer such that $d_{\min}(C^\perp) > t > 1$. Then $C^{*\lceil (n-1)/(t-1) \rceil} = K^n$.*

Proof   Observe that the conditions imply that $\pi_B(C) = K^t$ for all $B \subset \{1, \ldots, n\}$ with $|B| = t$. This fact is easily seen to imply that each of the standard basis vectors $\mathbf{e}_1, \ldots, \mathbf{e}_n \in K^n$ is contained in $C^{*\lceil (n-1)/(t-1) \rceil}$ as follows: without loss of generality, consider just $\mathbf{e}_1 = (1, 0, \ldots, 0) \in K^n$. Select a vector in C such that its "leftmost" coordinate equals 1, followed by a window of $t - 1 > 0$ consecutive 0s. Next, do as before, except that the window of 0s starts right after where the preceding ended. Repeat this until the "end of the vector has been reached" (where, in the very last step, the window may possibly be of smaller size than $t - 1$, of course). In this way, $\lceil \frac{n-1}{t-1} \rceil$ vectors in C are obtained whose coordinate-wise product equals $\mathbf{e}_1$.   ∎

From the lemma one sees, for instance, that if $K = \mathbb{F}_q$ with q constant and $t = \Omega(n)$, then some constant power of C fills up all of K^n. We now show an upper bound on the parameter d in the case where $A = \mathbb{F}_{q^k}$.[15]

THEOREM 12.33 *[42] Suppose that (C, ψ) is an (n, t, d, r)-codex for $\mathbb{F}_{q^k}$ over $\mathbb{F}_q$ with $k \geq 2$. Then*

$$d \leq q$$

Proof   Toward a contradiction, suppose that $d \geq q + 1$. Since the Frobenius map, that is, the qth power map, acts on $\mathbb{F}_q^k$ as the identity, it follows that

$$\mathbf{x}^q * \mathbf{y}^{d-q} = \mathbf{x} * \mathbf{y}^{d-1}$$

for all $\mathbf{x}, \mathbf{y} \in C$. Define

$$a := \psi(\mathbf{x}) \quad b := \psi(\mathbf{y})$$

Then this implies that

$$a^q b^{d-q} = \overline{\psi}(\mathbf{x}^q * \mathbf{y}^{d-q}) = \overline{\psi}(\mathbf{x} * \mathbf{y}^{d-1}) = \psi(\mathbf{x}) \cdot \psi(\mathbf{y})^{d-1} = ab^{d-1}$$

If $a \neq 0$ and $b \neq 0$, this implies that

$$a^{q-1} = b^{q-1}$$

However, since $k \geq 2$, there are $a_0, b_0 \in \mathbb{F}_{q^k} \setminus \{0\}$ with

$$a_0^{q-1} \neq b_0^{q-1}$$

Since ψ is surjective, there are $\mathbf{x}, \mathbf{y} \in C$ such that

$$\psi(\mathbf{x}) = a_0 \quad \psi(\mathbf{y}) = b_0$$

and a contradiction arises.   ∎

REMARK 12.34 (A GENERALIZATION)   From references [30] and [161], the stronger result follows that $d \leq q$ for any finite-dimensional $\mathbb{F}_q$-algebra A such that $A \not\cong \mathbb{F}_q^k$, where $k = \dim_K A$.

---

[15] See Bürgisser, Clausen, and Shokrollahi [31] for lower bounds on bilinear complexity.

We verify this by combining the preceding proof strategy with the algebra classification from Theorem 10.16. Let A be a finite-dimensional $\mathbb{F}_q$-algebra. Suppose that there is an (n,t,d,r)-codex for A over $\mathbb{F}_q$. Conducting the preceding argument with $\mathbb{F}_{q^k}$ replaced by A, it follows that $d \leq q$ if the property holds that the Frobenius map does not act as the identity on A.[16] Suppose that A *does* have the property that the Frobenius map acts as the identity on A. Then A also has the property of having 0 as its only nilpotent.[17] Thus Theorem 10.16 applies, and A is a finite product of finite extensions of $\mathbb{F}_q$. Since the Frobenius map acts as the identity on A, each of these extensions has degree 1. This concludes the proof.

On a historical note, mathematical considerations on products of codes or powers of codes in the sense of the $*$-product have been present, for example, in work from the 1980s on *a proof of the Roos bound for cyclic codes* [133], on *secure multiparty computation* [14, 46] (essentially, the square of certain Reed-Solomon codes or Shamir's secret-sharing scheme), and *bilinear complexity of extension field multiplication* [51] and in work from the 1990s on *error correction algorithms* [122, 155] (so-called error-correcting pairs) and once again *secure multiparty computation* [61] ((strongly) multiplicative properties of general linear secret-sharing schemes). Some years later, motivated in part by *asymptotics of secure multiparty computation* (see the overview in Section 12.8), further systematic study of the notion has been conducted, starting with reference [48] and followed by references [38, 41, 43, 44, 50, 57, 145, and 159–161]. Novel applications have been proposed in references [54, 55, 62, 69, 78, 106, 113–115, 118, and 135]. Most of these deal with various aspects of secure two-party (or multiparty) cryptography, whereas some others are concerned with cryptanalysis of public-key cryptosystems based on error-correcting codes or geometry of numbers.

It is interesting to observe that so far the most striking applications of codices in secure MPC or in two-party cryptography make requirements not only on powers of the code but also on its *dual*.

12.6.2 Bound on Arithmetic Embeddings

We discuss a classical bound for arithmetic embeddings (see, e.g., Bürgisser, Clausen, and Shokrollahi [31]) stated and analyzed in our framework.

THEOREM 12.35 *Let A be an extension field of K with $k := \dim_K A < \infty$. Let n be a positive integer. Suppose that (C, ψ) is an $(n, 2)$-arithmetic embedding of A over K. Then $n \geq 2k - 1$.*

Proof We claim that the minimum distance of C is at least k. Hence, by the Singleton Bound, $k \leq n - k + 1$, and the desired result follows. We now prove the claim. Toward a contradiction, suppose that there is $\mathbf{x} \in C$ with $\mathbf{x} \neq \mathbf{0}$ and $w_{\mathrm{H}}(\mathbf{x}) \leq k - 1$. Consider the K-vector space $\mathbf{x} * C \subset K^n$. Because $w_{\mathrm{H}}(\mathbf{x}) \leq k - 1$, it follows that this space has dimension at most $k - 1$. However, a contradiction arises because it follows from $\mathbf{x} \neq \mathbf{0}$ that the K-vector space morphism $\overline{\psi}$ restricted to $\mathbf{x} * C$ is a surjection onto A, which has dimension k. Indeed,

---

[16] To see this, select $\mathbf{y} \in C$ such that $\psi(\mathbf{y}) = 1$, and define $b = 1$ at the start of the proof.

[17] Namely, $x^q = x$ and $x^m = 0$ for some $x \in A$ and for some positive integer m implies that $x = 0$. This is clear if $m \leq q$. If $m > q$, it is reduced inductively until $m < q$.

$\overline{\psi}(\mathbf{x} * \mathbf{y}) = \psi(\mathbf{x}) \cdot \psi(\mathbf{y})$ for all $\mathbf{y} \in C$ and $\psi(\mathbf{x}) \neq 0$ because ψ is an isomorphism of K-vector spaces. This proves the claim.   ∎

Generally, if there is an (n,d)-arithmetic embedding of the extension field A over K with $d \geq 2$, then $n \geq dk - (d-1)$.

12.6.3 General Bounds on Codices

LEMMA 12.36 *Let A be a K-algebra with $\dim_K A < \infty$. If (C, ψ) is an (n,t,d,r)-codex for A over K, then $(C^{*d}, \overline{\psi})$ is an $(n, dt, 1, r)$-codex for A over K. In particular,*

$$dt < r$$

Proof We first show that the hypothesis on (C, ψ) implies that $dt < r$. If $t = 0$, this holds by default. So assume that $t > 0$. Toward a contradiction, suppose that $dt \geq r$. Index K^n with the set $\mathcal{I} = \{1, \ldots, n\}$. Choose sets $B_1, \ldots, B_d \subset \mathcal{I}$ and elements $\mathbf{y}^{(1)}, \ldots, \mathbf{y}^{(d)} \in C$ such that

- For $i = 1, \ldots, d$, it holds that $|B_i| = t$.
- $|\cup_{i=1}^{d} B_i| \geq r$.
- For $i = 1, \ldots, d$, it holds that $\mathbf{y}_{B_i}^{(i)} = \mathbf{0}$ and $\psi(\mathbf{y}^{(i)}) = 1$. Note that this makes sense on account of Lemma 12.12.

Then

$$\overline{\psi}\left(\prod_{i=1}^{d} \mathbf{y}^{(i)}\right) = \prod_{i=1}^{d} \psi(\mathbf{y}^{(i)}) = 1$$

However,

$$w_{\mathrm{H}}\left(\prod_{i=1}^{d} \mathbf{y}^{(i)}\right) \leq n - r \quad \text{and} \quad \prod_{i=1}^{d} \mathbf{y}^{(i)} \in C^{*d}$$

Hence, by (d,r)-multiplicativity,

$$\overline{\psi}\left(\prod_{i=1}^{d} \mathbf{y}^{(i)}\right) = 0$$

a contradiction. Therefore, $dt < r$ as desired.

We now show the claim about $(C^{*d}, \overline{\psi})$. It is easy to see that the map

$$\overline{\psi} : C^{*d} \longrightarrow A$$

is surjective. If $d = 1$, then $C^{*d} = C$, and $\overline{\psi}$ is the same as ψ. Hence, the claim follows from the codex definition in this case. Now assume that $d > 1$. For given $a \in A$, choose $\mathbf{v} \in C$ such that $\psi(\mathbf{v}) = a$. Furthermore, choose $\mathbf{u} \in C$ such that $\psi(\mathbf{u}) = 1$. Now define

$$\mathbf{z} = \mathbf{u}^{d-1} * \mathbf{v}$$

and note that

$$\overline{\psi}(\mathbf{z}) = \overline{\psi}(\mathbf{u}^{d-1} * \mathbf{v}) = (\psi(\mathbf{u}))^{d-1} * \psi(\mathbf{v}) = a$$

by the codex definition. Therefore, the pair $(C^{*d}, \overline{\psi})$ constitutes an $(n, t', 1, r)$-codex for A over K for some integer $t' \geq 0$.

We now show that we can take $t' = dt$. If $t = 0$, then this is trivial. So assume that $t > 0$. Let $B \subset \mathcal{I}$ be such that $|B| = dt$. Since $dt < r \leq n$, this makes sense. Select some disjoint partition of B into subsets $B_1, \ldots, B_d$, each of cardinality t. Then select $\mathbf{y}^{(1)}, \ldots, \mathbf{y}^{(d)} \in C$ such that $\psi(\mathbf{y}^{(i)}) = 1$ and $\pi_{B_i}(\mathbf{y}^{(i)}) = \mathbf{0}$ for $i = 1, \ldots, d$. This makes sense on account of Lemma 12.12. Finally, define

$$\mathbf{y} = \mathbf{y}^{(1)} * \cdots * \mathbf{y}^{(d)}$$

and note that

$$\overline{\psi}(\mathbf{y}) = \overline{\psi}(\mathbf{y}^{(1)} * \cdots * \mathbf{y}^{(d)}) = \psi(\mathbf{y}^{(1)}) * \cdots * \psi(\mathbf{y}^{(d)}) = 1$$

and

$$\pi_{B_i}(\mathbf{y}) = \mathbf{0}$$

The claim follows from Lemma 12.12. ∎

A small variation of the preceding argument implies the following:

LEMMA 12.37 *Let A be a K-algebra with $\dim_K A < \infty$. If (C, ψ) is an (n, t, d, r)-codex for A over K, then it is an $(n, t, 1, r - (d-1)t)$-codex for A over K.*

Proof If $t = 0$, then the claim follows from Lemma 12.7. So assume that $t > 0$. Index K^n with the set $\mathcal{I} = \{1, \ldots, n\}$. Let $\mathbf{x} \in C$ and $B \subset \mathcal{I}$ such that

$$\mathbf{x}_B = \mathbf{0} \quad \text{and} \quad |B| = r - (d-1)t$$

By Lemma 12.36, it holds that $r - (d-1)t > 0$. Therefore, the preceding selection makes sense. We have to show that $\psi(\mathbf{x}) = 0$.

Choose sets $B_1, \ldots, B_{d-1} \subset \mathcal{I}$ and elements $\mathbf{y}^{(1)}, \ldots, \mathbf{y}^{(d-1)} \in C$ such that

- For $i = 1, \ldots, d-1$, it holds that $|B_i| = t$.
- $B, B_1, \ldots, B_{d-1}$ are pairwise disjoint (so their union has cardinality $r \leq n$).
- For $i = 1, \ldots, d-1$, it holds that $\mathbf{y}^{(i)}_{B_i} = \mathbf{0}$ and $\psi(\mathbf{y}^{(i)}) = 1$.

Then

$$\mathbf{x} * \prod_{i=1}^{d-1} \mathbf{y}^{(i)} \in C^{*d} \quad \text{and} \quad w_{\mathrm{H}}\left(\mathbf{x} * \prod_{i=1}^{d-1} \mathbf{y}^{(i)}\right) \leq n - r$$

Hence, by (d, r)-multiplicativity,

$$0 = \overline{\psi}\left(\mathbf{x} * \prod_{i=1}^{d-1} \mathbf{y}^{(i)}\right) = \psi(\mathbf{x}) \cdot \prod_{i=1}^{d-1} \psi(\mathbf{y}^{(i)}) = \psi(\mathbf{x})$$

Thus ψ is $(r - (d-1)t)$-determined. ∎

Combining Lemmas 12.36 and 12.37, whose proof ideas are inspired by results from Cramer, Damgård, and Maurer [61], with the gap bound from Corollary 11.120 from Cascudo, Cramer, and Xing [43] or its refinements, implies nontrivial bounds on codices with $t > 0$.

12.6.4 An Asymptotical Bound

The bound $dt < r$ from Lemma 12.36 can be strengthened substantially by application of Theorem 11.118 (which originates from Cascudo, Cramer, and Xing [43]) as follows:

THEOREM 12.38 *[42] Let A be an $\mathbb{F}_q$-algebra with $\dim_{\mathbb{F}_q} A < \infty$. If there is an (n,t,d,r)-codex for A over $\mathbb{F}_q$ with $d > 1$ and $t > 0$, then*

$$r - dt > \frac{n+2}{2q-1}$$

In particular, if $r = n - t$, then

$$(d+1)t < n - \frac{n+2}{2q-1}$$

If, additionally, $d = 2$, then

$$3t < n - \frac{n+2}{2q-1}$$

For example, suppose that $A = \mathbb{F}_q$ and $t > 0$ such that $n := 3t + 1 < q$. Then Shamir's scheme gives an $(n,t,2,n-t)$-arithmetic secret-sharing scheme for $\mathbb{F}_q$ over $\mathbb{F}_q$ (use Theorem 12.20). Shamir's scheme with these parameters plays a central role in secure MPC [14, 61]. It follows from the preceding inequality for $r = n - t$ and $d = 2$ that the ratio $3t/(n-1) = 1$ is *not* attainable if q is *small* compared with n, that is, if

$$q < \frac{n+3}{2}$$

In fact, this inequality has a stronger implication. For fixed q and for n tending to infinity, we see that, asymptotically, this ratio is upper bounded by a constant *strictly smaller than 1*. Thus it is not even possible to get this ratio arbitrarily close to 1.

DEFINITION 12.39 *For each $n \geq 1$, let $T(n,q)$ denote the largest integer t such that there exists an $(n,t,2,n-t)$-codex for $\mathbb{F}_q$ over $\mathbb{F}_q$. Then*

$$\widehat{\tau}(q) := \limsup_{n \to \infty} \frac{3 \cdot T(n,q)}{n-1}$$

Note that this is well defined because $t = 0$ is allowed here, and for each $n \geq 1$, there exists a trivial $(n,0,2,n)$-codex for $\mathbb{F}_q$ over $\mathbb{F}_q$.[18]

THEOREM 12.40 *[43] For each finite field $\mathbb{F}_q$, it holds that*

$$\widehat{\tau}(q) < 1 - \frac{1}{2q-1} < 1$$

See Cascudo, Cramer, and Xing [43] for improvements of this bound.

At this point it is not clear *at all* whether it holds that $\widehat{\tau}(q) > 0$ for some finite field $\mathbb{F}_q$: in the polynomial codex construction, n is bounded as a function of q. But, for sure, *if* it

---

[18] Namely, the code C is just the diagonal in $\mathbb{F}_q^n$, and the map ψ projects onto its first component.

does (and we shall see shortly *that* it does), then the rate $t/(n-1)$ is asymptotically strictly smaller than $1/3$.[19]

To show that positive rates can indeed be achieved is more involved. Before we can do so in Section 12.8, we need to discuss some results on towers of algebraic function fields.

12.7 Towers of Algebraic Function Fields

We give an overview of the basic theory of algebraic function fields, and we discuss fundamental asymptotical results on towers of algebraic function fields over finite fields. Our exposition follows mostly Stichtenoth [172], but at some places we follow Neukirch [147] or Rosen [162].

12.7.1 Definition of an Algebraic Function Field

Let K be a field. An algebraic function field F/K (in one variable) is an extension field F of K such that F is a finite-degree algebraic extension of $K(x)$ for some $x \in F$ that is transcendental over K. Equivalently, F is finitely generated over K as a field, with transcendence degree 1. Note that the field $K(x)$ is isomorphic to the field of rational functions $K(X)$, that is, the field of fractions of the polynomial ring $K[X]$. In particular, $|F| = \infty$. Such a transcendental element x can always be chosen such that F is a finite-degree, separable field extension of $K(x)$ if K is perfect.[20] If F/K is an algebraic function field, we always assume that K is the full field of constants; that is, if $z \in F$ is algebraic over K, then $z \in K$.

12.7.2 Valuation Rings

Let F/K be an algebraic function field. Let A be a valuation ring of F, that is, a subring of F such that

- $K \subsetneq A \subsetneq F$.
- For all $f \in F$ with $f \neq 0$, it holds that $f \in A$ or $f^{-1} \in A$.

There are infinitely many valuation rings in F.

The ring A is a PID with a single nontrivial prime ideal P, its corresponding place. Let $t \in A$ be such that $P = tA$, a uniformizer. It holds that each nonzero $f \in A$ can be uniquely expressed as $f = ut^m$, where $u \in A$ is a unit and m is a nonnegative integer. Note that the element t is prime and that the set of uniformizers consists of all $u't$ with $u' \in A$ a unit. The units $U(A)$ of A coincide with the set $A \setminus P$. It is verified at once that P is maximal. Also note that F is the field of fractions of A.

The ring A is determined by P because $f \in A$ if and only if $f^{-1} \notin P$. As a consequence, this gives a bijection between the valuation rings of F and the places of F. From now on,

---

[19] For stronger bounds as well as generalizations, for example, for arithmetic secret-sharing where the secret space is $\mathbb{F}_q^k$ with k "much larger" than 1, please refer to Cascudo, Cramer, and Xing [42]. The case $k > 1$ additionally exploit classical bounds from the theory of error-correcting codes (such as the Griesmer bound).

[20] See Stichtenoth [172], chapter 3, proposition 3.10.2.

we denote the set of places of F by $\mathbb{P}(F)$ and the valuation ring corresponding to $P \in \mathbb{P}(F)$ by $\mathcal{O}_P$.

The valuation ring $\mathcal{O}_P$ gives rise to a discrete valuation

$$\vartheta_P : F \longrightarrow \mathbb{Z} \cup \{\infty\}$$

on F. Let $t \in \mathcal{O}_P$ be a uniformizer. For $f \in F$, define $\vartheta_P(f)$ as follows: first, $\vartheta_P(0) = \infty$ by default. Second, if $f \in \mathcal{O}_P$ with $f \neq 0$, define $\vartheta_P(f) = m$, where m is the unique nonnegative integer such that $f = ut^m$ for some unit $u \in \mathcal{O}_P$. Note that $\vartheta_P(f)$ does not depend on the choice of uniformizer. Third, if $f \notin \mathcal{O}_P$, then $f^{-1} \in \mathcal{O}_P$ and define $\vartheta_P(f) = -\vartheta_P(f^{-1})$.

This discrete valuation ϑ_P satisfies the following basic properties. For all $f, g \in F$, it holds that

- $\vartheta_P(fg) = \vartheta_P(f) + \vartheta_P(g)$ (multiplicativity).
- $\vartheta_P(f+g) \geq \min\{\vartheta_P(f), \vartheta_P(g)\}$ (triangle inequality).
- $\vartheta_P(f+g) = \min\{\vartheta_P(f), \vartheta_P(g)\}$ if $\vartheta_P(f) \neq \vartheta_P(g)$ (strong triangle inequality).

Note that

$$\mathcal{O}_P = \{f \in F : \vartheta_P(f) \geq 0\}$$

$$P = \{f \in F : \vartheta_P(f) > 0\}$$

$$U(\mathcal{O}_P) = \{f \in F : \vartheta_P(f) = 0\}$$

$$F \setminus \mathcal{O}_P = \{f \in F : \vartheta_P(f) < 0\}$$

Since $K \subset \mathcal{O}_P$, $K \cap P = \{0\}$, and P is maximal, it follows that $\mathcal{O}_P/P$ is an extension field of K, the residue class field of P. The degree of this extension is finite. The degree of the place P is defined as

$$\deg P := [\mathcal{O}_P/P : K]$$

Let $f \in F$. If $f \in \mathcal{O}_P$, then

$$f(P) := (f \bmod P) \in \mathcal{O}_P/P$$

the evaluation of f at P. Note that $f(P) = 0$; that is, f has a zero at P if and only if $f \in P$. If $f \notin \mathcal{O}_P$, then f has a pole at P, and we write $f(P) = \infty$.

The rational places are the places of degree 1. Therefore, if P is a rational place, and if $f \in \mathcal{O}_P$, then $f(P) \in K$. If $f \in K$, then $f(P) = f$ for all places P. Hence, the elements of K are *constants*. There are no other constants, as is implied by the following property.

Let $f \in F$ and $f \notin K$. Then

- There exists a place $P' \in \mathbb{P}(F)$ such that f has a zero at P'; that is, $f(P') = 0$.
- There exists a place $P'' \in \mathbb{P}(F)$ such that f has a pole at P''; that is, $f(P'') = \infty$.
- At all places $Q \in \mathbb{P}(F)$, except for a finite, positive number of them, f has neither a pole nor a zero; that is, $f(Q) \neq 0, \infty$.

More precisely, *counting multiplicities, f* has *as many zeros as poles*. That is, it holds that

$$\sum_{P \in \mathbb{P}(F)} \vartheta_P(f) \cdot \deg P = 0$$

Note that this identity also holds if $f \in K$ with $f \neq 0$ because all valuations are equal to zero for such functions f.

12.7.3 Divisors and the Divisor Class Group

Define $\mathrm{Div}(F)$ as the free abelian group generated by the set $\mathbb{P}(F)$. Its elements are called divisors. If $D \in \mathrm{Div}(F)$, then it is represented by a formal sum

$$D = \sum_{P \in \mathbb{P}(F)} \lambda_P \cdot P$$

such that $\lambda_P \in \mathbb{Z}$ for all $P \in \mathbb{P}(F)$ and $\lambda_P = 0$ except for a finite number of $P \in \mathbb{P}(F)$. The divisor with $\lambda_P = 0$ for all $P \in \mathbb{P}(F)$, that is, the neutral element of the group $\mathrm{Div}(F)$, is denoted by 0. The degree of $D \in \mathrm{Div}(F)$ is defined as

$$\deg D = \sum_{P \in \mathbb{P}(F)} \lambda_P \cdot \deg P \in \mathbb{Z}$$

Note that the map

$$\mathrm{Div}(F) \longrightarrow \mathbb{Z}$$

$$D \mapsto \deg D$$

is a group morphism.

Let $f \in F$ with $f \neq 0$. Then the divisor of f is defined as

$$(f) = \sum_{P \in \mathbb{P}(F)} \vartheta_P(f) \cdot P \in \mathrm{Div}(F)$$

Since $\vartheta_P(f) = 0$ for almost all $P \in \mathbb{P}(F)$, this is indeed a divisor. Note that

$$\deg(f) = 0$$

The following result gives additional information. Let Z_0 (and Z_∞) denote the set of zeros (and poles) of f. Define the zero divisor $(f)_0$ (and pole divisor $(f)_\infty$) of f as

$$(f)_0 = \sum_{P \in Z_0} \vartheta_P(f) \cdot P \qquad (f)_\infty = \sum_{P \in Z_\infty} (-\vartheta_P(f)) \cdot P$$

Then, if f is not constant,

$$\deg(f)_0 = \deg(f)_\infty = [F : K(f)] < \infty$$

The subgroup of $\mathrm{Div}(F)$ consisting of all divisors with degree 0 is denoted $\mathrm{Div}_0(F)$. The set of all divisors (f), the principal divisors, is a subgroup of $\mathrm{Div}_0(F)$, and it is denoted by $\mathrm{Prin}(F)$. The (degree-zero) Picard group[21] of F is the quotient group

$$\mathrm{Cl}(F) := \mathrm{Div}_0(F)/\mathrm{Prin}(F)$$

If $K = \mathbb{F}_q$, the order of this group, the class number of F, is *finite*.

A divisor $D = \sum_{P \in \mathbb{P}(F)} \lambda_P \cdot P \in \mathrm{Div}(F)$ is effective if $\lambda_P \geq 0$ for all $P \in \mathbb{P}(F)$. If $D' \in \mathrm{Div}(F)$, then we write $D \geq D'$ if $D - D' \in \mathrm{Div}(F)$ is effective. In this notation, $D \in \mathrm{Div}(F)$ is effective if $D \geq 0$, where $0 \in \mathrm{Div}(F)$. The support of D is the finite set $\mathrm{supp}(D)$ consisting of all $P \in \mathbb{P}(F)$ such that $\lambda_P \neq 0$.

---

[21] Or (degree-zero) divisor class group.

12.7.4 The Weak Approximation Theorem

The Weak Approximation Theorem states the following:

THEOREM 12.41 *Let F/K be an algebraic function field. Let $P_1,\ldots,P_m \in \mathbb{P}(F)$ be distinct places. Let $f_1,\ldots,f_m \in F$ and $r_1,\ldots,r_m \in \mathbb{Z}$. Then there exists $f \in F$ such that*

$$\vartheta_{P_1}(f - f_1) = r_1,\ldots,\vartheta_{P_m}(f - f_m) = r_m$$

In a sense, this is a Chinese Remainder Theorem for algebraic function fields.

The Strong Approximation Theorem states that if S is a *proper* subset $S \subsetneq \mathbb{P}(F)$ such that $P_1,\ldots,P_m \in S$, then we can *additionally* enforce $\vartheta_P(f) \geq 0$ for all $P \in S \setminus \{P_1,\ldots,P_m\}$.

12.7.5 The Riemann–Roch Theorem

Let $D \in \mathrm{Div}(F)$. Define

$$\mathcal{L}(D) = \{f \in F \setminus \{0\} : (f) + D \geq 0\} \cup \{0\}$$

the Riemann–Roch space of D. Note that $\mathcal{L}(D)$ is a K-vector space. Define

$$\ell(D) := \dim_K(\mathcal{L}(D))$$

Elementary properties of Riemann–Roch spaces include the following:

- $\mathcal{L}(D) = \{0\}$ if $\deg D < 0$.
- If $D \leq D'$, then $\mathcal{L}(D) \subset \mathcal{L}(D')$.
- For all $f \in \mathcal{L}(D)$, it holds that $f(P) \neq \infty$ for each $P \notin \mathrm{supp}(D)$.

The first follows at once. Indeed, if $f \in \mathcal{L}(D)$ with $f \neq 0$, then $0 \leq \deg((f) + D) = \deg(f) + \deg D = \deg D < 0$, a contradiction. The second and third follow from the definitions.

Divisors $D_0, D_1 \in \mathrm{Div}(F)$ are linearly equivalent, denoted $D_0 \sim D_1$, if

$$D_1 = (f) + D_0$$

for some $f \in F$ with $f \neq 0$. If $D_0 \sim D_1$, then $\deg D_0 = \deg D_1$ and $\mathcal{L}(D_0) \simeq \mathcal{L}(D_1)$. In particular, $\ell(D_0) = \ell(D_1)$. Each divisor $D \in \mathrm{Div}(F)$ with $\ell(D) > 0$ is linearly equivalent to some effective divisor. That is, let $f \in \mathcal{L}(D)$ with $f \neq 0$. Then $(f) + D \geq 0$ by definition.

It holds that

$$\ell(D) \leq \deg D + 1$$

if $\deg D \geq 0$. We briefly sketch the proof of this claim. Under the stated condition the claim is true in either of the cases $\ell(D) = 0$ or $D = 0$. Consider the case $\ell(D) > 0$ and $D \geq 0$. It is not hard to show that if $D' \in \mathrm{Div}(F)$ and $P \in \mathbb{P}(F)$, then $\ell(D' + P) \leq \ell(D') + \deg P$.[22] Applying induction, the claim follows in this case. For general $D \in \mathrm{Div}(F)$ with $\ell(D) > 0$, apply the latter to some effective divisor that is linearly equivalent to D.

Consider the "defect" $\deg D + 1 - \ell(D)$. By the preceding discussion, this is nonnegative if $\deg D \geq 0$. Clearly, it is not positive if $\deg D < 0$.

---

[22] See Stichtenoth [172], chapter 1, lemma 1.4.8, page 18.

DEFINITION 12.42 (GENUS) *Let F/K be an algebraic function field. The genus of F is defined as*

$$g(F) := \max_{D \in \mathrm{Div}(F)} \{\deg D + 1 - \ell(D)\}$$

So far it is only clear that $0 \leq g(F) \leq \infty$. Riemann's Inequality essentially shows that $g(F) < \infty$. The latter fact, in combination with the definition of the genus, immediately gives a nontrivial lower bound on the Riemann–Roch dimension of divisors with degree at least $g(F)$.

THEOREM 12.43 (RIEMANN'S INEQUALITY) *Let F/K be an algebraic function field. Then $0 \leq g < \infty$, where g is the genus of F. Consequently, for all $D \in \mathrm{Div}(F)$, it holds that*

$$\ell(D) \geq \deg D + 1 - g$$

The classical Riemann–Roch Theorem[23] turns Riemann's Inequality into an equality for all $D \in \mathrm{Div}(F)$ by adding the "missing term" into the inequality.

A canonical divisor is a divisor $W \in \mathrm{Div}(F)$ such that

- $\deg W = 2g - 2$ and
- $\ell(W) \geq g$,

which exists.[24]

The Riemann–Roch Theorem states the following.

THEOREM 12.44 (RIEMANN–ROCH) *Let F/K be an algebraic function field. Let $W \in \mathrm{Div}(F)$ be a canonical divisor. For all $D \in \mathrm{Div}(F)$, it holds that*

$$\ell(D) = \deg D + 1 - g + \ell(W - D)$$

where g is the genus of F.

It follows in particular that $\ell(W) = g$ by setting $D = W$.

COROLLARY 12.45 *For all $D \in \mathrm{Div}(F)$ with $\deg D > 2g - 2$, it holds that*

$$\ell(D) = \deg D + 1 - g$$

The simplest example of an algebraic function field is the rational function field $K(X)$, that is, the field of fractions of the polynomial ring $K[X]$. Its elements can be represented as $a(X)/b(X) \in K(X)$, with $a(X), b(X) \in K[X]$ relatively prime and $b(X)$ nonzero. It is easy to describe the places and valuations. Let $P(X) \in K[X]$ be a polynomial of degree $d \geq 1$, and suppose that it is irreducible.

Let $f \in K(X)$. Suppose that $f \neq 0$, and write $f = (a(X)/b(X))P(X)^m$ such that $P(X)$ divides neither $a(X)$ nor $b(X)$ as polynomials, with $a(X), b(X) \in K[X]$ relatively prime and $m \in \mathbb{Z}$. Then $f \in \mathcal{O}_P$, the valuation ring corresponding to $P(X)$, if and only if $m \geq 0$. Furthermore, $f \in P$, where P is the place corresponding to $\mathcal{O}_P$, if and only if $m > 0$. Finally, f is a unit in $\mathcal{O}_P$ if $m = 0$. The polynomial $P(X)$ is a uniformizer, and the valuation $\vartheta_P(f)$ equals m.

---

[23] See Stichtenoth [172], chapter 1, paragraph 5, pages 24–31.
[24] See Stichtenoth [172], sections 1.5 and 1.6.

The ring $\mathcal{O}_P$ is the localization of $K[X]$ at the maximal ideal $(P(X))$, that is, the ring consisting of the elements of $K(X)$ with denominator not divisible by $P(X)$. Moreover, $K[X]/(P(X))$ is an extension field of K of degree d, and it is isomorphic to $\mathcal{O}_P/P$ via the assignment $\overline{f(X)} \mapsto f(X)(P)$. If $P(X) = X - z$ ($z \in K$), then P is a rational place, and $a(X)/b(X) \in \mathcal{O}_P$ evaluated at P is just $a(z)/b(z)$.

This accounts for all places except one: the infinite place P_∞. Let $f \in K(X)$. Suppose that $f \neq 0$, and write $f = a(X)/b(X)$. Then $f \in \mathcal{O}_\infty$ if and only if $\deg b(X) \geq \deg a(X)$. Furthermore, $f \in P_\infty$ if and only if $\deg b(X) > \deg a(X)$. Finally, f is a unit if these degrees are equal. The rational function $1/X$ is a uniformizer of $\mathcal{O}_\infty$.

The valuation $\vartheta_{P_\infty}(f)$ equals $\deg b(X) - \deg a(X)$. If $f \in \mathcal{O}_\infty$, then $f(P_\infty) = 0$, if $f \in P_\infty$ and $f(P_\infty) = a_k/b_k$ otherwise, where a_k (and b_k) is the leading coefficient of $a(X)$ (and $b(X)$). In particular, P_∞ is a rational place.

The genus of the rational function field equals 0. This is easy to verify. First, it holds that $\ell(m \cdot P_\infty) \geq m + 1$ for any integer $m \geq 0$. Indeed, $1, X, \ldots, X^m \in \ell(m \cdot P_\infty)$. Second, by the Riemann–Roch Theorem, this gives $m + 1 \leq \ell(m \cdot P_\infty) = \deg(m \cdot P_\infty) + 1 - g = m + 1 - g$ for large enough m. Thus $g = 0$. Note that if $K = \mathbb{F}_q$, then there are exactly $q + 1$ rational places in the rational function field over $\mathbb{F}_q$.

If F has at least one rational place, and if $g = 1$, then F is an *elliptic function field*.

12.7.6 The Hasse-Weil Theorem

From here on, $K = \mathbb{F}_q$. Let $N(F)$ be the number of rational places of F. For each nonnegative integer n, define

$$A_n = |\{D \in \mathrm{Div}(F) \mid D \geq 0 \text{ and } \deg D = n\}|$$

It holds that $A_n < \infty$ for each $n \geq 0$. The zeta function of $F/\mathbb{F}_q$ is the power series

$$Z(t) = \sum_{n=0}^{\infty} A_n t^n \in \mathbb{C}[[t]]$$

which converges for $|t| < 1/q$. The L-polynomial is defined as

$$L(t) := (1 - t)(1 - qt)Z(t) \in \mathbb{C}[[t]]$$

It can be shown that

$$L(t) \in \mathbb{Z}[t] \quad \text{and} \quad \deg L(t) = 2g$$

Writing

$$L(t) = a_0 + a_1 t + \cdots + a_{2g} t^{2g}$$

it follows that

$$a_1 = N - (q + 1)$$

where $N := N(F)$, the number of rational places. Now $L(t)$ is identical to 1 if $g = 0$, and otherwise, it factors in $\mathbb{C}[t]$ as

$$L(t) = \prod_{i=1}^{2g} (1 - \alpha_i t)$$

where $\alpha_1, \ldots, \alpha_{2g} \in \mathbb{C}$ are, of course, reciprocals of algebraic integers. Hence

$$N = q + 1 + \sum_{i=1}^{2g} \alpha_i$$

The celebrated Hasse-Weil Theorem,[25] also known as the Riemann Hypothesis for Function Fields, gives the absolute values of the α_is.

THEOREM 12.46 (HASSE-WEIL) *Let $F/\mathbb{F}_q$ be an algebraic function field. Let g denote its genus. Then the 2g roots $\alpha_1, \ldots, \alpha_{2g}$ of the L-polynomial $L(t) \in \mathbb{Z}[t]$ satisfy*

$$|\alpha_i| = \sqrt{q}$$

for $i = 1, \ldots, 2g$.

An upper bound on the number of rational places in F follows at once.

THEOREM 12.47 (HASSE-WEIL BOUND) *Let $F/\mathbb{F}_q$ be an algebraic function field. Let g denote its genus. Then*

$$N \leq q + 1 + 2g\sqrt{q}$$

where N denotes the number of rational places of F.

In particular, the number of rational places of $F/\mathbb{F}_q$ is bounded as a function of q and g. Actually, it holds that

$$|N - (q + 1)| \leq 2g\sqrt{q}$$

which gives the additional information that if g is *small* compared with q, there cannot be too few rational places.

Serre improved this bound as follows:

THEOREM 12.48 (SERRE) *Notation being as earlier,*

$$|N - (q + 1)| \leq g\lfloor 2\sqrt{q} \rfloor$$

12.7.7 Bounds on Ihara's Constant

For each finite field $\mathbb{F}_q$, and for each integer $g \geq 0$, define $N_q(g)$ as the maximum of the number of rational places $N(F)$, where F ranges over all the algebraic function fields whose full field of constants is $\mathbb{F}_q$ and whose genus is g.

DEFINITION 12.49 (IHARA'S CONSTANT) *For each finite field $\mathbb{F}_q$, define*

$$A(q) := \limsup_{g \to \infty} \frac{N_q(g)}{g}$$

where $g > 0$.

By the Hasse-Weil Bound, it follows that

$$0 \leq A(q) \leq 2\sqrt{q} < \infty.$$

---

[25] See Stichtenoth [172], chapter 5, paragraph 2, pages 197–212, theorem 5.2.1.

By Theorem 12.48, we may replace $2\sqrt{q}$ by $\lfloor 2\sqrt{q} \rfloor$ in the preceding bound.

Note that $A(q) \geq \ell$ for some nonnegative real number ℓ if and only if, for each real number $\epsilon > 0$, there is an infinite family of algebraic functions fields $\{F_i/\mathbb{F}_q\}_{i=0}^{\infty}$ such that

1. The sequence $g_0, g_1, g_2, \ldots$ is strictly increasing, where $g_i := g(F_i)$ for all $i \geq 0$.
2. For all $i \geq 0$, it holds that $N_i/g_i \geq (1 - \epsilon) \cdot \ell$, where $N_i := N(F_i)$.

The upper bound on $A(q)$ is improved as follows:

THEOREM 12.50 (DRINFELD-VLADUT BOUND) *For each finite field* $\mathbb{F}_q$, *it holds that*

$$A(q) \leq \sqrt{q} - 1$$

It is a priori not clear at all whether $A(q) > 0$ for some finite field $\mathbb{F}_q$. Using the theory of modular curves, Ihara [111] showed the following result.

THEOREM 12.51 (IHARA) *Suppose that* $\mathbb{F}_q$ *is a finite field such that* q *is a square. Then*

$$A(q) \geq \sqrt{q} - 1$$

Combining this with the Drinfeld-Vladut Bound, we obtain the *exact* value of $A(q)$ if q is a square.

THEOREM 12.52 *Suppose that* $\mathbb{F}_q$ *is a finite field such that* q *is a square. Then*

$$A(q) = \sqrt{q} - 1$$

In 1982, Tsfasman, Vlăduţ, and Zink [176] used this result[26] to show that *error-correcting codes* exist that exceed the *asymptotic Gilbert-Varshamov bound*. See, for example, Stichtenoth [172] and Tsfasman, Vlăduţ, and Nogin [177]. This has spawned substantial research into algebraic function fields with many rational points that continues to date.

Finally, Serre [166] showed, using class field theory, that $A(q)$ is *positive* in all cases.

THEOREM 12.53 (SERRE) *There exists an absolute positive real constant c such that*

$$A(q) > c \cdot \log(q) > 0$$

for each finite field $\mathbb{F}_q$.

One can take $c = 1/96$.[27]

12.7.8 *Garcia-Stichtenoth's Explicit Optimal Towers*

Garcia and Stichtenoth [95, 96] were first to present an *explicit* construction that shows $A(q) = \sqrt{q} - 1$ when q is square, using *recursive towers*. It is beyond the scope here to give the full proof. Yet we wish to give a taste of it by a high-level overview. We restrict our attention to an overview of an explicit proof of the weaker result that $A(q) > 0$ for some finite fields $\mathbb{F}_q$. Their general (and optimal) result is more involved.[28]

---

[26] In fact, they exhibited their own proof of a weaker result.
[27] See Niederreiter and Xing [148], page 133, theorem 5.2.9.
[28] See chapter 1 of Garcia and Stichtenoth [97] for a more advanced overview. Our overview is mostly based on the detailed proof from "first principles" in Stichtenoth [172]. For an overview of a nonconstructive proof

A tower over $\mathbb{F}_q$ is an infinite sequence $\mathcal{F} = (F_0, F_1, F_2, \ldots)$ of algebraic function fields $F_i/\mathbb{F}_q$ such that the following statements hold:

- $F_0 \subsetneq F_1 \subsetneq F_2 \subsetneq \ldots \subsetneq F_m \subsetneq \ldots$.
- Each field extension F_{i+1} of F_i is finite and separable ($i = 0, 1, 2, \ldots$).
- The genera $g(F_i)$ tend to infinity when i tends to infinity.

Recall that, by our definition, the full field of constants of $F_i/\mathbb{F}_q$ equals $\mathbb{F}_q$ for all $i \geq 0$.

Define the (Ihara) limit of a tower as

$$\lambda(\mathcal{F}) := \lim_{i \to \infty} \frac{N(F_i)}{g(F_i)}$$

its splitting rate as

$$\nu(\mathcal{F}) := \lim_{i \to \infty} \frac{N(F_i)}{[F_i : F_0]}$$

and its genus as

$$\gamma(\mathcal{F}) := \lim_{i \to \infty} \frac{g(F_i)}{[F_i : F_0]}$$

These limits exist. Moreover,

$$\lambda(\mathcal{F}) \in \mathbb{R}_{\geq 0}, \; \nu(\mathcal{F}) \in \mathbb{R}_{\geq 0}, \; \gamma(\mathcal{F}) \in \mathbb{R}_{>0} \cup \{\infty\}$$

and

$$\lambda(\mathcal{F}) = \frac{\nu(\mathcal{F})}{\gamma(\mathcal{F})}$$

with

$$0 \leq \lambda(\mathcal{F}) \leq A(q)$$

Therefore, in order to achieve $\lambda(\mathcal{F}) > 0$, it is necessary and sufficient that

$$0 < \nu(\mathcal{F}) \quad \gamma(\mathcal{F}) < \infty$$

In particular, splitting and genus can be treated separately.

Before continuing, we discuss some very helpful basic facts about extensions of algebraic function fields. Along the way, we point out some of the well-known strong similarities with algebraic number fields.[29]

Let $F/\mathbb{F}_q$ and $F'/\mathbb{F}_q$ be algebraic function fields such that F' is a finite-degree separable extension of F. Write $n := [F' : F]$. There is the following relation between the places of F' and those of F: each place P of F' yields a place of F when intersected with F. If $P \cap F = \wp$, we say that the place P of F' lies above the place $\wp$ of F. Moreover, for each place of F, there is a place of F' that lies above it, and there are at most n of them.

The places of F' lying above a place of F obey the Fundamental Identity. Let $\wp$ be a place of F, with corresponding valuation ring $\mathfrak{o}_\wp$. Let P be a place of F', with corresponding valuation ring $\mathcal{O}_P$. Suppose that P lies above $\wp$.

---

based on the theory of modular curves, see Moreno [146]. See also Niederreiter and Xing [148] and Tsfasman, Vlăduţ, and Nogin [177].

[29] For an in-depth treatment of the similarities between algebraic function fields and algebraic number fields, see Neukirch [147] and Rosen [162].

The relative degree f of P with respect to $\wp$ is the positive integer defined as

$$f(P|\wp) := [\mathcal{O}_P/P : \mathfrak{o}_\wp/\wp]$$

Note that $\mathcal{O}_P/P$ is a finite-degree extension of $\mathbb{F}_q$ that contains $\mathfrak{o}_\wp/\wp$ as an intermediate extension, so this is well defined.

The ramification index of $\wp$ at P is the positive integer defined as

$$e(P|\wp) = \vartheta_P(t)$$

where ϑ_P is the valuation in F' induced by P, and $t \in \mathfrak{o}_\wp$ is any uniformizer of $\mathfrak{o}_\wp$. Note that $e(P|\wp) = 1$ if and only if t is a uniformizer not only of $\mathfrak{o}_\wp$ but also of $\mathcal{O}_P$.

Let $P_1, \ldots, P_k$ be the set of places of F' lying above the place $\wp$ of F. Then the Fundamental Identity states that

$$e_1 f_1 + \cdots + e_k f_k = n$$

where $e_j = e(P_j|\wp)$ and $f_j = f(P_j|\wp)$ for $j = 1, \ldots, k$.

We say that $\wp$ splits completely in F' if there are exactly n places P' above $\wp$. On account of the Fundamental Identity, each of these has relative degree $f(P'|\wp) = 1$.

Kummer's Theorem[30] implies information about splitting as follows: let $z \in F'$ be such that $F' = F(z)$, and consider the minimal polynomial $f(X) \in F[X]$ of z over F. Suppose that $f(X) \in \mathfrak{o}_\wp[X]$; that is, z is integral over $\mathfrak{o}_\wp$. If $f(X)$ is reduced modulo $\wp$ and its factorization in $(\mathfrak{o}_\wp/\wp)[X]$ is square-free,[31] then $\wp$ is unramified, and there is bijection between the factors and the places above $\wp$. Moreover, for each factor, the corresponding place above $\wp$ has relative degree equal to the degree of the factor. In particular, if it factors in distinct linear terms, there are precisely n distinct places above $\wp$, and each of those is of relative degree 1. Therefore, this gives a sufficient criterion for complete splitting.

We say that $\wp$ ramifies in F' at P if $e(P|\wp) > 1$. If $\wp$ ramifies at P, and if p, the characteristic of $\mathbb{F}_q$, divides $e(P|\wp)$, then we say that $\wp$ wildly ramifies at P. If $\wp$ ramifies at P, and if p does not divide $e(P|\wp)$, then we say it tamely ramifies at P.

We say that $\wp$ is ramified in F' if it is ramified at some place of F' lying above it. If $\wp$ is not ramified in F', we say that $\wp$ is unramified in F'. If no place of F ramifies wildly in F', then the extension F'/F is tame. Otherwise, it is wild. A tower is tame if each of the extensions F_i/F_0 is tame. It is wild if it is not tame.

It is useful to develop a different perspective on these definitions. The ring $\mathfrak{o}_\wp$ is a Dedekind domain with F as its field of fractions. Let $\mathcal{O}'$ denote its integral closure in F', that is, the subring of F' consisting of those elements $x \in F'$ such that the minimal polynomial $f(X) \in F[X]$ of x over F satisfies $f(X) \in \mathfrak{o}_\wp[X]$. This is also a Dedekind domain, with F' as its field of fractions. Moreover, $\mathcal{O}'$ is a free $\mathfrak{o}_\wp$-module of rank n.

Consider the Dedekind factorization of the ideal $\wp \cdot \mathcal{O}'$ of $\mathcal{O}'$. There is a bijection between the prime ideals of $\mathcal{O}'$ occurring in this factorization and the places P of F' lying above the place $\wp$ of F. That is, in one direction, the localization of $\mathcal{O}'$ at a prime ideal of $\mathcal{O}'$ that appears in the Dedekind factorization of the ideal $\wp \cdot \mathcal{O}'$ gives a valuation ring $\mathcal{O}_P$ of F' such that P lies above $\wp$. In the other direction, the intersection with $\mathcal{O}'$ of a valuation ring

---

[30] See, for example, Stichtenoth [172], chapter 3, paragraph 3, pages 86–90, theorem 3.3.7.
[31] Note that this is just factorization in a polynomial ring over a finite extension field of $\mathbb{F}_q$.

$\mathcal{O}_P$ of F' such that P lies above $\wp$ gives a prime ideal of $\mathcal{O}'$ that appears in the Dedekind factorization of the ideal $\wp \cdot \mathcal{O}'$. Moreover, the relative degree of a place P of F' lying above the place $\wp$ of F is the relative degree of the prime ideal $I(P) := \mathcal{O}_P \cap \mathcal{O}'$ of $\mathcal{O}'$ lying above $\wp$; that is, it equals the degree of the field extension $\mathcal{O}'/I(P) \supset \mathfrak{o}_\wp/\wp$. As an aside, in this way, one sees that the Fundamental Identity for algebraic function fields over $\mathbb{F}_q$ is in essence the same as the corresponding one for algebraic number fields.

This perspective allows us to describe which places of F ramify and at which places of F' this happens (and how badly!) because this is all captured by the different. Since F' is a finite separable extension of F by assumption, the trace $\mathrm{Tr}_{F'/F}$ is nontrivial. As remarked earlier, this implies that the dual space of F' (as an F-vector space), that is, the space of F-linear forms $F' \longrightarrow F$, coincides with the F-vector space of maps $\phi_a : F' \longrightarrow F$ defined by the assignment $x \mapsto \mathrm{Tr}_{F'/F}(ax)$, where $a \in F'$.

Now consider the set of elements $a \in F'$ such that the F-linear form ϕ_a associated with a according to this correspondence satisfies $\phi_a(\mathcal{O}') \subset \mathfrak{o}_\wp$. This set happens to constitute a fractional ideal $\mathcal{C}_\wp^{-1}$ of $\mathcal{O}'$ containing $\mathcal{O}'$. If we now invert this fractional ideal in the group of fractional ideals of $\mathcal{O}'$, we get an ideal $\mathcal{C}_\wp$ of $\mathcal{O}'$. Its Dedekind factorization is nontrivial if and only if $\wp$ ramifies in F'. If it ramifies, this factorization gives a bijection with the places of F' lying above $\wp$ at which $\wp$ ramifies.

For example, if $\mathcal{O}'$ is a simple extension of $\mathfrak{o}_\wp$, that is, $\mathcal{O}' = \mathfrak{o}_\wp[z]$ for some $z \in \mathcal{O}'$, then $\mathcal{C}_\wp$ is very easy to describe. If $f(X) \in \mathfrak{o}_\wp[X]$ denotes the minimal polynomial of z over F, then $\mathcal{C}_\wp$ is the ideal $f'(z) \cdot \mathcal{O}'$ of $\mathcal{O}'$, where $f'(X) \in \mathfrak{o}_\wp[X]$ denotes the formal derivative of $f(X)$.[32]

The Dedekind Different Theorem gives more information about the factorization of $\mathcal{C}_\wp$. As before, let P be a place of F' above the place $\wp$ of F. If this factorization is nontrivial, that is, $\mathcal{C}_\wp \neq \mathcal{O}'$, and if P corresponds to some prime ideal in its Dedekind factorization (that is, $e(P|\wp) > 1$), denote its exponent in this factorization by $d(P|\wp)$, the different exponent of $\wp$ at P. Then $d(P|\wp) = e(P|\wp) - 1$ if and only if $\wp$ ramifies tamely at P. If it ramifies wildly, then $d(P|\wp) > e(P|\wp) - 1$. If $\wp$ does not ramify at P, define $d(P|\wp) = 0$ $(= e(P|\wp) - 1)$.

At most finitely, many places of F ramify in F'. We sketch a proof of this claim. Fix an arbitrary F-basis $z_1, \ldots, z_n$ of F'. If $z_1, \ldots, z_n \in \mathcal{O}'$, then it can be shown that

$$\sum \mathfrak{o}_\wp \cdot z_i \subset \mathcal{O}' \subset \sum \mathfrak{o}_\wp \cdot z_i^*$$

where $z_1^*, \ldots, z_n^*$ denotes the dual basis. If, additionally, $z_1^*, \ldots, z_n^* \in \mathcal{O}'$, then it follows directly that this basis as well as its dual constitutes a basis of the free $\mathfrak{o}_\wp$-module $\mathcal{O}'$. The claim now follows from two further facts. First, it can be shown that the dual basis of a basis of the free $\mathfrak{o}_\wp$-module $\mathcal{O}'$ generates $\mathcal{C}_\wp^{-1}$ as $\mathfrak{o}_\wp$-module. Therefore, under the preceding conditions,

$$\mathcal{C}_\wp^{-1} = \mathcal{C}_\wp = \mathcal{O}'$$

and $\wp$ is unramified in F'. Second, the preceding conditions are satisfied for all except finitely many valuations rings of F. This follows immediately by inspection of the coefficients of the minimal polynomials in $F[X]$ of each of the elements in this basis and in its dual.

The claim also can be verified using Kummer's Theorem. Let $z \in F'$ be such that $F' = F(z)$, and consider the minimal polynomial $f(X) \in F[X]$ of z over F. The discriminant of

---

[32] See, for example, Naor [147], chapter 3, paragraph 2, page 197, proposition 2.4.

$1, z, \ldots, z^{n-1}$ with respect to F'/F equals $N_{F'/F}(f'(z)) \in F$ (up to a sign), where $f(X) \in F[X]$ is the formal derivative of $f(X)$. Since z is integral over almost all valuation rings of F, and since for almost all of those this discriminant is not contained in the corresponding place $\wp$, it follows that the factorization of (the class of) $f(X)$ in $(\mathfrak{o}_\wp/\wp)[X]$ is square-free for each of those places $\wp$. The claim follows.

Define the different as

$$\mathrm{Diff}(F'/F) := \sum_{P|\wp} d(P|\wp) \cdot P \ \in \mathrm{Div}(F')$$

where $\wp$ runs through all places of F and P runs through all places of F' above $\wp$. Note that this is indeed a divisor: at most, finitely many places of F ramify in F' and $d(P|\wp) > 0$ if and only if $\wp$ ramifies at P.

If the extension F'/F is tame, then

$$\mathrm{Diff}(F'/F) = \sum_{P|\wp} (e(P|\wp) - 1) \cdot P \ \in \mathrm{Div}(F')$$

The different plays a crucial role in the Hurwitz Genus Formula. This basically expresses that the genus evolves linearly in $[F' : F]$ and in the genus $g(F)$, except for an additive "error term" caused by the different. Precisely, it says that

$$2g(F') - 2 = (2g(F) - 2)[F' : F] + \deg \mathrm{Diff}(F'/F)$$

For example, if F is the rational function field over $\mathbb{F}_q$ (which has genus 0), then F'/F is ramified. Also, in order to show that the genus tends to infinity in a proposed tower, it is sufficient to identify some F_i with $g(F_i) \geq 2$.

Note that application of the Dedekind Different Theorem gives the following lower bound:

$$2g(F') - 2 \geq (2g(F) - 2)[F' : F] + \deg \left(\sum_{P|\wp} (e(P|\wp) - 1) \cdot P \right)$$

with equality if and only if the extension F'/F is tame.

From the Hurwitz Genus Formula, it is clear that in order for the genus of the tower to satisfy $\gamma(\mathcal{F}) < \infty$, the ramification in the tower needs to be controlled. A neat trick toward this end uses the Fundamental Identity in combination with the Hurwitz Genus Formula to show that it suffices that the number of places $\wp$ of F_0 that ramify in *some* extension F_i in the infinite tower is finite (that is, there is a "finite ramification locus") and that no such $\wp$ ramifies wildly.

There is also a version for the wild case, where in addition to a finite ramification locus it is required that for each $\wp$ in the finite ramification locus, all different exponents $d(P|\wp)$ occurring in the tower are upper bounded by $a_\wp \cdot e(P|\wp)$, with $a_\wp \in \mathbb{R}$ a constant depending on $\wp$.[33] It follows that

$$\gamma(\mathcal{F}) \leq g(F_0) - 1 + \frac{1}{2} \sum_\wp a_\wp \cdot \deg \wp < \infty$$

---

[33] See Stichtenoth [172], chapter 7.2, page 249, theorem 7.2.10.

where $\wp$ runs through the finite ramification locus. In the tame case, of course, all $a_\wp$s can be taken equal to 1.

In order for the splitting rate to satisfy $v(\mathcal{F}) > 0$, it is sufficient that its splitting locus is nonempty. This is the set of *rational* places $\wp$ of F_0 such that $\wp$ *splits completely* in *each* extension F_i of F_0; that is, for each such extension F_i, there are exactly $[F_i : F_0]$ places above $\wp$. These all must be rational on account of the Fundamental Identity. It follows that

$$v(\mathcal{F}) \geq s > 0$$

where $s > 0$ is the cardinality of the splitting locus. Putting this together, it follows that

$$\lambda(\mathcal{F}) = \frac{v(\mathcal{F})}{\gamma(\mathcal{F})} > 0$$

So it remains to enforce the sufficient conditions on the ramification locus, on the one hand, and on the splitting locus, on the other hand. A main handle to achieve this is to consider *recursively defined* towers. Let $f(Y) \in \mathbb{F}_q(Y)$ and $h(X) \in \mathbb{F}_q(X)$ be nonconstant rational functions. Write $f(Y) = f_0(Y)/f_1(Y)$ with $f_0(Y), f_1(Y) \in \mathbb{F}_q[Y]$ and with $f_0(Y), f_1(Y)$ relatively prime. Define

$$\deg f(Y) = \max\{\deg f_0(Y), \deg f_1(Y)\}$$

Let $\mathcal{F} = (F_0, F_1, F_2, \ldots)$ be a sequence of algebraic functions fields over $\mathbb{F}_q$. Then $\mathcal{F}$ is *recursively defined* by the equation

$$f(Y) = h(X)$$

if there are elements $x_i \in F_i$ for all $i \geq 0$ such that

- x_0 is transcendental over $\mathbb{F}_q$, and $F_0 = \mathbb{F}_q(x_0)$.
- For all $i \geq 0$, it holds that $F_{i+1} = \mathbb{F}_q(x_0, \ldots, x_i, x_{i+1})$ or, equivalently, $F_{i+1} = F_i(x_{i+1})$.
- For all $i \geq 0$, it holds that $f(x_{i+1})$, $h(x_i)$ are well defined and satisfy $f(x_{i+1}) = h(x_i)$.
- $[F_1 : F_0] = \deg f(Y)$.

Note that $x_1, x_2, \ldots$ may be selected in an algebraic closure of $\mathbb{F}_q(x_0)$. For $i \geq 0$, define

$$\widehat{f_i}(Y) := f_0(Y) - h(x_i) f_1(Y) \in F_i[Y]$$

The condition $[F_1 : F_0] = \deg f(Y)$ on the first step in the tower (which will play a distinguished role later on) is equivalent to the condition that the polynomial $\widehat{f_0}(Y)$ is irreducible in the polynomial ring $\mathbb{F}_q(x_0)[Y]$. It follows that $[F_{i+1} : F_i] \leq \deg f(Y)$ for all $i \geq 1$ because $\widehat{f_i}(Y)$ may no longer be irreducible in some $F_i[Y]$.

The first question is, which recursively defined sequences constitute a tower? Separability, which is required for each extension $F_i \subset F_{i+1}$, is easy: $\widehat{f_i}(Y) := f_0(Y) - h(x_i) f_1(Y) \in F_i[Y]$ has no multiple roots if $f_0(Y), f_1(Y) \notin \mathbb{F}_q(Y^p)$, where p is the characteristic of $\mathbb{F}_q$; that is, $f(Y) \notin \mathbb{F}_q(Y^p)$. For example, if $\deg f(Y) < p$, then this is automatically satisfied ($f(Y)$ is not constant!).

The conditions that each extension $F_i \subset F_{i+1}$ is strict and that for each F_i the full field of constants is $\mathbb{F}_q$ can be enforced with a single condition, namely, that for each $i \geq 0$ there exists a place $P \in \mathbb{P}(F_i)$ and a place $Q \in \mathbb{P}(F_{i+1})$ lying above it such that $e(Q|P) = [F_{i+1} : F_i] > 1$. This is easy to justify. The required strict inclusion already follows from $e(Q|P) > 1$

by the Fundamental Identity. By the basic theory of constant field extensions,[34] the relative degree $f(Q|P)$ must satisfy $f(Q|P) > 1$ if the field of constants of F_{i+1} is a strict extension of $\mathbb{F}_q$. However, the ramification degree $e(Q|P)$ "eats up" the entire degree of the extension, so there is "no room" in the Fundamental Identity for this to happen.

Finally, the condition that the genus tends to infinity often can be shown using either of the following two handles: if the number of rational points in the tower tends to infinity, then the genus also must tend to infinity on account of the Hasse-Weil Bound. Another option is to show that $g(F_i) \geq 2$ for some $i \geq 0$ and to draw the desired conclusion by successive applications of the Hurwitz Genus Formula.

A pivotal aspect of recursive towers is the following observation. For all $i \geq 0$, it holds that

- $\mathbb{F}_q(x_i, x_{i+1}) \simeq \mathbb{F}_q(x_0, x_1) = F_1$ and $\mathbb{F}_q(x_i) \simeq \mathbb{F}_q(x_0) = F_0$.
- There is the parallelogram of inclusions where F_{i+1} is the compositum of F_i and $\mathbb{F}_q(x_i, x_{i+1})$ and where the rational function field $\mathbb{F}_q(x_i)$ is a subfield of each of the latter two.

A main reason why this is so useful is that it opens the door to reducing the issues about splitting locus and ramification locus of the tower, by means of inductive arguments, to issues about the extension F_1 of the rational function field F_0 *at the bottom of the tower*, which is much easier to analyze. To this end, various "parallelogram laws" come in handy.

It is beyond the scope of this work to detail all of this here. But we do give a flavor as follows: let us view the parallelogram such that F_{i+1} sits in the north corner, F_i in the west, $\mathbb{F}_q(x_i, x_{i+1})$ in the east, and the rational function field $\mathbb{F}_q(x_i)$ in the south. It makes sense to speak of the lower-left extension, the upper-right extension, and so on. The main diagonal is the north viewed as an extension of the south.

Abhyankar's Lemma,[35] for instance, implies that if a place of the west ramifies in the north, then the place of the south it lies above ramifies in the east; this is an upper-left versus lower-right connection. From Galois theory it follows that if a place of the south splits completely in the east *and* in the west, then it splits completely in the north. This is a lower-left + lower-right versus main diagonal connection. Note that Kummer's Theorem, mentioned earlier, implies a criterion for complete splitting in terms of factorization of polynomials over finite extension fields of $\mathbb{F}_q$.

Facts such as the ones just discussed make it possible to reduce the delicate selection of the polynomials $f(Y)$ and $h(X)$ required to enforce a nontrivial splitting locus *and* a finite ramification locus to establishing a particular favorable situation just in the extension F_1/F_0 at the bottom of the tower, which is much more manageable. Besides, the resulting conditions on $f(Y), h(X)$ are typically easily stated in terms of basic algebra and are oblivious of the towers once stated.[36]

Here is an example of a tower crafted in this way: for a finite field $\mathbb{F}_q$ with q square and $\ell := \sqrt{q} > 2$, set

$$Y^{\ell-1} = 1 - (X+1)^{\ell-1}$$

---

[34] See Stichtenoth [172], theorem 3.6.3, page 114.
[35] See Stichtenoth [172], chapter 3.9, page 137, theorem 3.9.1.
[36] See, for instance, Stichtenoth [172], chapter 7.3, page 259, theorem 7.3.1.

Then the recursive tower induced by this relation has a positive limit.[37] In the case of $\mathbb{F}_9$, this is *optimal*; that is, its limit is $\sqrt{9} - 1 = 2$.

To reach the Drinfeld-Vladut Bound for *each* finite field $\mathbb{F}_q$ with q square, Garcia and Stichtenoth [96] constructed a recursive tower such that

- $N(F_i) \geq (q - \sqrt{q})\sqrt{q^{i-1}}$.
- $g(F_i) \leq \sqrt{q^i}$.

Note that, indeed, this means that

$$\lim_{i \to \infty} \frac{N(F_i)}{g(F_i)} \geq \sqrt{q} - 1$$

while equality follows from the Drinfeld-Vladut Bound. Setting $q = \ell^2$, this works with the recursive tower defined by the relation[38]

$$Y^\ell - Y = \frac{X^\ell}{1 - X^{\ell-1}}$$

12.7.9 Other Lower Bounds on Ihara's Constant

No single value of $A(q)$ is known if q is a nonsquare. However, there are several dedicated lower bounds that improve on Theorem 12.53 in this case.

For instance, by using modular curves and explicit function fields, Zink [181], van der Geer and van der Vlugt [98], Bezerra, Garcia, and Stichtenoth [21], and Bassa, Garcia, and Stichtenoth [6] showed that

$$A(q^3) \geq \frac{2(q^2 - 1)}{q + 2}$$

Recently, Bassa et al. [5] showed an explicit tower of algebraic function fields over finite fields $\mathbb{F}_{p^{2m+1}}$ for any prime p and integer $m \geq 1$ and proved that this tower gives

$$A(p^{2m+1}) \geq \frac{2(p^{m+1} - 1)}{p + 1 + \epsilon} \quad \text{with} \quad \epsilon = \frac{p - 1}{p^m - 1}$$

Lower bounds on $A(q)$ have been shown for small primes q such as $q = 2, 3, 5, 7, 11, 13, \ldots$. For instance, Duursma and Mak [88] showed that

$$A(2) \geq 0.316999\ldots$$

and

$$A(3) \geq 0.492876\ldots$$

Finally, note that for the case $\mathbb{F}_p$ with p prime, no construction of any explicit tower with a positive limit is known. In fact, there exists a certain class of recursions that does give positive results whenever $q \neq p$ [94] but this *necessarily* fails to give any such result if $q = p$, as shown by Lenstra [129].

---

[37] See Stichtenoth [172], chapter 7.4, page 260, theorem 7.3.2.
[38] See Stichtenoth [172], chapter 7.4, page 265, theorem 7.4.7.

12.8 Asymptotically Good Arithmetic Secret-Sharing Schemes

The history of asymptotically good arithmetic secret-sharing schemes is preceded by that of asymptotic study of bilinear complexity of multiplication in extensions of a finite field, that is, arithmetic embeddings in our language. This was initiated by Chudnovsky and Chudnovsky [51] in the mid-1980s. Here the finite field $\mathbb{F}_q$ is fixed, and an unbounded number of finite extensions of $\mathbb{F}_q$ is considered. The purpose is to derive upper bounds on the asymptotic ratio between bilinear complexity of multiplication in an extension and its degree.

Using a variation on the techniques of Tsfasman, Vlăduţ, and Zink [176] from their 1982 breakthrough improvement of the Gilbert-Vashamov error-correcting bound (which relies on deep results from algebraic geometry [111] in combination with Goppa's idea [101] of algebraic geometry codes), they showed that, surprisingly, this ratio is bounded from above by a *constant* (depending on q). More precisely, set $d = 2$, and fix a finite field $\mathbb{F}_q$. Then there is a real number $c > 1$ with $c = c(q)$ such that

$$\liminf_{k \geq 1} n_0/k \leq c$$

where, in our language, n_0 is the length of the shortest arithmetic $(n, 2)$-embedding of $\mathbb{F}_{q^k}$ over $\mathbb{F}_q$.[39]

This work was continued by Shparlinski, Tsfasman, and Vlăduţ [169]. See Bürgisser, Clausen, and Shokrollahi [31] for the history of the topic up to the late 1990s, as well as for definitions (nonasymptotic), bounds, and generalizations. Papers discussing more recent improvements on explicit bounds include references [45], [159] and [164].

Motivated by showing a suitable asymptotic version of the "Fundamental Theorem on Information–Theoretically Secure Multiparty Computation" by Ben-Or, Goldwasser, and Wigderson [14] and Chaum, Crépeau, and Damgård [46] from 1988, Chen and Cramer [48] initiated in 2006 a study of *asymptotically good arithmetic secret-sharing schemes* and showed the first positive results for the strongest notions using yet another variation on the algebraic geometric techniques of Tsfasman, Vlăduţ, and Zink [100].

In 2007, the results of Chen and Cramer [48] played a central role in the surprising work of Ishai et al. [118] on the "secure multiparty computation in the head" paradigm and its application to communication-efficient zero knowledge for circuit satisfiability. This caused nothing less than a paradigm shift that perhaps appears even as counterintuitive: secure *multiparty* computation (and in particular, asymptotically good arithmetic secret sharing) is a very powerful abstract primitive for *communication-efficient two-party cryptography*. Subsequent fundamental results that also rely on the asymptotics from Chen and Cramer [48] include *two-party secure computation* [69, 78, 115], *OT combiners* [106], *correlation extractors* [114], *amortized zero knowledge* [62], and *OT from noisy channels* [113].

The results of Chen and Cramer [48] were strengthened by Cascudo et al. [38]. A more powerful paradigm for the construction of arithmetic secret-sharing schemes based on novel algebraic geometric ideas was presented by Cascudo, Cramer, and Xing [42] and Cascudo et al. [44]. We first explain the results from Chen and Cramer [48]. This is followed by an overview in Section 12.9 of the results from Cascudo, Cramer, and Xing [41, 44].

---

[39] It is also interesting to consider the lim sup of this ratio.

We will show the result from Chen and Cramer [48] that for some fixed finite fields $\mathbb{F}_q$ and for $d \geq 2$ a constant, there exists an unbounded family of $(n,t,d,n-t)$-arithmetic secret-sharing schemes for $\mathbb{F}_q^k$ over $\mathbb{F}_q$ with uniformity such that $n \to \infty$, $k = \Omega(n)$, and $t = \Omega(n)$. The only known proof of existence of such a family crucially exploits good towers of algebraic function fields; no "elementary" proof of existence is known.

Before continuing, it should be noted that if

- $(d,n-t)$-multiplicativity is replaced by (d,n)-multiplicativity and
- the restrictions $k = 1$ and $d = 2$ are made,

then there *is* an elementary proof of existence of the corresponding family: combine the construction from Section 12.4.3 based on self-dual codes with the basic fact from classical coding theory that asymptotically good self-dual codes exist.[40] This idea [50] does have some interesting applications, but unfortunately, it does not support the powerful applications mentioned earlier.

We start with a "dualization" lemma that will prove helpful.

LEMMA 12.54 *Let K be a field. Let F be an algebraic function field of genus g with full field of constants K. Let $X, X_0 \in \mathrm{Div}(F)$. Let $W \in \mathrm{Div}(F)$ be a canonical divisor. Then*

$$\ell(X + X_0) = \ell(X) + \deg X_0$$

if and only if

$$\ell(W - X - X_0) = \ell(W - X)$$

Proof This is a direct consequence of Theorem 12.44 (Riemann–Roch): in the first equality of the statement of the lemma, substitute $\ell(X + X_0) = \deg X + \deg X_0 + 1 - g + \ell(W - X - X_0)$ and $\ell(X) = \deg X + 1 - g + \ell(W - X)$. It follows at once that the first equality holds if and only if $\ell(W - X - X_0) = \ell(W - X)$. ∎

Next we generalize Theorem 11.96 to work over algebraic function fields.

THEOREM 12.55 (LAGRANGE OVER ALGEBRAIC FUNCTION FIELDS) *Let F/K be an algebraic function field of genus g. Let $\mathbb{P}(F)$ denote the set of places of F. Let*

$$P_1, \ldots, P_m \in \mathbb{P}(F)$$

be distinct places of F. For $= 1, \ldots, m$, define

$$L_i := \mathcal{O}_{P_i}/P_i$$

which is an extension field of K of degree $\deg P_i$. Also define

$$P := \sum_{i=1}^{m} P_i \in \mathrm{Div}(F)$$

Let $X \in \mathrm{Div}(F)$ be such that

$$\mathrm{supp}(X) \cap \mathrm{supp}(P) = \emptyset$$

---

[40] That is, for each finite field, there is an infinite family of self-dual $\mathbb{F}_q$-linear codes such that the minimum distance is linear in the length. See, for example, McWilliams and Sloane [143], chapter 19, paragraph 6, pages 629–33.

Let $W \in \mathrm{Div}(F)$ be a canonical divisor of F. Then the K-vector space morphism

$$\mathcal{E} : \mathcal{L}(X) \to \bigoplus_{i=1}^{m} L_i$$

$$f \mapsto (f(P_i))_{i=1}^{m}$$

has the following properties:

- *It is injective if and only if $\ell(X - P) = 0$.*
- *It is surjective if and only if $\ell(W - X + P) = \ell(W - X)$.*

In particular, it is surjective if $\ell(W - X + P) = 0$.

Proof   Since $\mathrm{supp}(X) \cap \mathrm{supp}(P) = \emptyset$, the map $\mathcal{E}$ is well defined. Its injectivity is equivalent to $\ker \mathcal{E}$ being trivial. Since

$$\ker \mathcal{E} = \mathcal{L}(X - P)$$

the injectivity claim follows.

Surjectivity of the map $\mathcal{E}$ is equivalent to $\mathrm{im}\,\mathcal{E}$ having K-dimension $\deg P$, which, in turn, is equivalent to the condition that

$$\deg P = \ell(X) - \dim_K \ker \mathcal{E}$$

Since $\dim_K \ker \mathcal{E} = \ell(X - P)$, the first surjectivity claim now follows by substitution of the latter equality into the former and subsequent application of Lemma 12.54.

The second surjectivity claim is an immediate consequence. Because P is an effective divisor, it holds that $W - X \leq W - X + P$. Hence,

$$0 \leq \ell(W - X) \leq \ell(W - X + P)$$

In conclusion, it is a sufficient condition for surjectivity that $\ell(W - X + P) = 0$.   ∎

From this point on, let F be an algebraic function field with a full field of constants $\mathbb{F}_q$. Let g denote the genus of F, and let $\mathbb{P}(F)$ denote the set of places of F.

The following theorem gives a sufficient condition for the existence of codices in terms of the solvability of certain systems of *Riemann–Roch equations*:

THEOREM 12.56 *[41, 48] Let n, d, t, r, k be integers such that $d \geq 1$, $0 \leq t < r \leq n$, and $k \geq 1$. Suppose that F has at least $n + k$ distinct rational places $P_1, \ldots, P_n, Q_1, \ldots, Q_k \in \mathbb{P}(F)$. Let $W \in \mathrm{Div}(F)$ be a canonical divisor. Define*

$$Q := \sum_{i=1}^{k} Q_i \in \mathrm{Div}(F)$$

and, for each set $B \subseteq \{1, \ldots, n\}$, define

$$P_B := \sum_{i \in B} P_i \in \mathrm{Div}(F)$$

with $P_\emptyset := 0 \in \mathrm{Div}(F)$.

If the system of "Riemann–Roch equations"

$$\begin{cases} \ell(W - X + Q + P_B) = 0 & \text{for all } B \subset \{1,\ldots,n\}, |B| = t \\ \ell(dX - P_B) = 0 & \text{for all } B \subset \{1,\ldots,n\}, |B| = r \end{cases}$$

has a solution $X := G$, *where* $G \in \mathrm{Div}(F)$, *then there exists an* (n,t,d,r)*-codex for* $\mathbb{F}_q^k$ *over* $\mathbb{F}_q$ *with uniformity.*

Proof   Note that if there is a solution $G \in \mathrm{Div}(F)$, we assume without loss of generality that the support of G avoids each of the places $P_1,\ldots,P_n,Q_1,\ldots,Q_k$: just replace G by the equivalent divisor $G + (f)$, where f is selected using Theorem 12.41 (Weak Approximation Theorem) in such a way that the support of $G + (f)$ avoids each of $P_1,\ldots,P_n,Q_1,\ldots,Q_k$. Clearly, the latter divisor is a solution of the system if G is.

Now let $G \in \mathrm{Div}(F)$ be a solution to the system, subject to the preceding assumption. The theorem is shown by verifying that the conditions from Theorem 12.18 are satisfied. Define the $\mathbb{F}_q$-linear code

$$\widetilde{C} := \{(f(Q_1),\ldots,f(Q_k),f(P_1),\ldots,f(P_n)) \mid f \in \mathcal{L}(G)\} \subseteq \mathbb{F}_q^k \times \mathbb{F}_q^n$$

Define $\mathcal{I} = \{-k+1,\ldots,0,1,\ldots,n\}$ as the index set for $\mathbb{F}_q^k \times \mathbb{F}_q^n$. Also define $\mathcal{Z} = \{-k+1,\ldots,0\}$ and $\mathcal{I}^* = \{1,\ldots,n\}$. Since

$$0 \le \ell(W - G + Q) \le \ell(W - G + Q + P_B) = 0$$

for all $B \subset \mathcal{I}^*$ with $|B| = t$, it follows by Theorem 12.55 on account of the equality $\ell(W - G + Q) = 0$ that

$$\pi_{\mathcal{Z}}(\widetilde{C}) = \mathbb{F}_q^k$$

Note that, in particular, this means that $\ell(G) > 0$ and $\deg G \ge 0$. Similarly, it follows by Theorem 12.55 on account of the equality $\ell(W - G + Q + P_B) = 0$ that if $t \ge 1$, then for all $B \subset \mathcal{I}^*$ with $|B| = t$, it holds that

$$\pi_{\mathcal{Z},B}(\widetilde{C}) = \mathbb{F}_q^k \times \mathbb{F}_q^t$$

Finally, define

$$\widetilde{D} := \{((\widetilde{f}(Q_1),\ldots,\widetilde{f}(Q_k)),(\widetilde{f}(P_1),\ldots,\widetilde{f}(P_n))) \mid \widetilde{f} \in \mathcal{L}(dG)\} \subseteq \mathbb{F}_q^k \times \mathbb{F}_q^n$$

Since for all $f_1,\ldots,f_d \in \mathcal{L}(G)$ it holds that

$$\widetilde{f} := \prod_{i=1}^d f_i \in \mathcal{L}(dG)$$

it follows that

$$\widetilde{C}^{*d} \subset \widetilde{D}$$

Let $B \subset \mathcal{I}^*$ with $|B| = r$. By Theorem 12.55, the condition $\ell(dG - P_B) = 0$ implies that if $\widetilde{\mathbf{z}}_B = \mathbf{0}$ for some $\widetilde{\mathbf{z}} \in \widetilde{D}$, then the only possible defining function $\widetilde{f} \in \mathcal{L}(dG)$ underlying $\widetilde{\mathbf{z}}$ is the function $\widetilde{f} = 0$. Hence, $\widetilde{\mathbf{z}}_{\mathcal{Z}} = \mathbf{0}$.   ∎

Note that it is not guaranteed that these schemes are unital. However, if G is effective, that is, $G \ge 0$, then the constants are contained in $\mathcal{L}(G)$. This is a sufficient condition for being unital.

We now discuss a straightforward approach to solving the Riemann–Roch system from Theorem 12.56. Observe that

$$\deg(W - G + Q + P_B) = 2g - 2 - \deg G + k + t$$

for all sets $B \subset \mathcal{I}^*$ with $|B| = t$, and that

$$\deg(dG - P_B) = d \cdot \deg G - r$$

for all sets $B \subset \mathcal{I}^*$ with $|B| = r$. Since a divisor of negative degree has Riemann–Roch dimension equal to 0, it suffices to *force*

$$2g - 2 - \deg G + k + t < 0 \quad \text{and} \quad d \cdot \deg G - r < 0$$

This works as follows: assuming, in addition, that the conditions

1. $r = d(2g - 1 + k + t) + 1$ and
2. $d(2g - 1 + k + t) < n$

hold, it follows that *any* divisor $G \in \mathrm{Div}(F)$ with degree

$$\deg G = 2g - 1 + k + t$$

is a solution to the system.

Indeed, we get

$$2g - 2 - \deg G + k + t = 2g - 2 - (2g - 1 + k + t) + k + t = -1 < 0$$

and

$$d \cdot \deg G - r = d(2g - 1 + k + t) - d(2g - 1 + k + t) - 1 = -1 < 0 \,.$$

Note that there always exist divisors of any given degree m. That is, for each algebraic function field over $\mathbb{F}_q$, there is a divisor of degree 1, and a divisor of degree m is obtained by multiplying such a divisor by m.[41]

REMARK 12.57 (ONE-POINT DIVISORS) If we assume that F has at least $n + k + 1$ rational places, then there is a rational place P' distinct from $P_1, \ldots, P_n, Q_1, \ldots, Q_k$. In this case, we can define

$$G = (2g - 1 + k + t) \cdot P'$$

so that the resulting scheme is unital.

Thus we have shown the following theorem.

THEOREM 12.58 (SOLUTION BY DEGREE) *[48] Let F be an algebraic function field with* $\mathbb{F}_q$ *as its full field of constants. Let g denote its genus. Let n,d,t,k be integers. Suppose that*

1. $k \geq 1$, $d \geq 1$ *and* $0 \leq t < n$.
2. *F has at least* $n + k$ *distinct rational places.*
3. $d(2g + k + t - 1) < n$.

Then there exists an $(n,t,d,d(2g + k + t - 1) + 1)$-*codex for* $\mathbb{F}_q^k$ *over* $\mathbb{F}_q$ *with uniformity.*

---

[41] See Stichtenoth [172], chapter 5, proposition 5.1.11.

In comparison with Theorem 12.20, the condition $q + 1 \geq n + k$ has been replaced by the condition that F has at least $n + k$ rational places, which is weaker. However, this does not come entirely for free because the second condition $d(2g + k + t - 1) + 1 \leq n$ involves the genus of F. Before we study these results asymptotically, let us point out that a result similar to that in Theorem 12.58 holds for codices for $\mathbb{F}_{q^k}$ over $\mathbb{F}_q$.

THEOREM 12.59 *[49] Let F be an algebraic function field with $\mathbb{F}_q$ as its full field of constants. Let g denote its genus. Let n, d, t, k be integers. Suppose that*

1. *$k \geq 2$, $d \geq 1$ and $0 \leq t < n$.*
2. *F has at least n distinct rational places.*
3. *F has a place of degree k.*
4. *$d(2g + k + t - 1) < n$.*

Then there exists an $(n, t, d, d(2g + k + t - 1) + 1)$-codex for $\mathbb{F}_{q^k}$ over $\mathbb{F}_q$ with uniformity.

Note that if $k \geq 4g + 3$, then F has at least one place of degree k.[42] A similar observation as in Remark 12.57 applies here as well if we assume that F has at least $n + 1$ rational places.

We now turn to asymptotics. We focus on $(n, t, d, n - t)$-arithmetic secret-sharing schemes for $\mathbb{F}_q^k$ over $\mathbb{F}_q$ with uniformity because these represent the subclass of codices with the most interesting and powerful applications so far.[43]

THEOREM 12.60 *[48] Let $d \geq 2$ be an integer. Suppose that Ihara's constant satisfies*

$$A(q) > 2d$$

Then there exists an infinite family of $(n, t, d, n - t)$-arithmetic secret-sharing schemes for $\mathbb{F}_q^k$ over $\mathbb{F}_q$ with uniformity, such that

1. *$n \longrightarrow \infty$.*
2. *$k = \Omega(n)$.*
3. *$t = \Omega(n)$.*

Proof Select a real number δ such that

$$A(q) > \frac{2d}{1 - \delta(1 + 2d)} > 2d$$

By the condition $A(q) > 2d$, such δ exists, and it is necessarily positive.

Select an infinite sequence of algebraic function fields $F_0, F_1, F_2, \ldots$ over $\mathbb{F}_q$ such that the respective genera g_i and the respective numbers of rational places N_i ($i = 0, 1, 2, \ldots$) satisfy the following conditions:

1. g_i tends to infinity as i tends to infinity.
2. $N_i / g_i > 2d / (1 - \delta(1 + 2d))$ for all large enough i.

Note that this is possible by the definition of $A(q)$ and the choice of δ.

---

[42] For this result as well as a generalization, please refer to Stichtenoth [172], chapter 5, corollary 5.2.10.

[43] For an asymptotical result on $(n, t, d, n - t)$-arithmetic secret-sharing schemes for $\mathbb{F}_{q^k}$ over $\mathbb{F}_q$, please refer to Chen et al. [49].

Set

$$k_i = \lfloor \delta N_i \rfloor, \quad t_i = \lfloor \delta N_i \rfloor, \quad n_i = N_i - k_i$$

for $i = 0, 1, 2, \ldots$. Since N_i tends to infinity as i tends to infinity and $n_i \geq (1 - \delta)N_i$, it follows at once that, as required, n_i tends to infinity, and k_i, t_i are linear in n_i. Furthermore,

$$d(2g_i + k_i + t_i - 1) + 1 \leq 2dg_i + 2d\delta N_i + 1 - d < N_i - \delta N_i \leq N_i - k_i = n_i$$

for all large enough i. Indeed, the first and third inequalities follow by definition and the second follows because $2dg_i < (1 - \delta(1 + 2d))N_i$ for all large enough i. Now apply Theorem 12.58. ∎

These schemes can be efficiently constructed and operated for certain asymptotically good (optimal) towers [170]; that is, there is an efficient algorithm to construct a generator matrix for the code C and a matrix representing ψ for each codex (C, ψ) in this family.[44]

Implementing Remark 12.57 (one-point divisors) does not affect the asymptotic result. Thus, if it is deemed convenient, the schemes may be assumed *unital* as well.[45]

By the result from Section 12.5.4, these codices allow for efficient "recovery of the secret given a full vector of shares with t malicious errors" (even in "higher powers" of the codices). See Cascudo, Cramer, and Xing [41] for a statement of Theorem 12.60 that takes this into account. See Chen et al. [49] for an asymptotic version of Theorem 12.59.

REMARK 12.61 (SUFFICIENT CONDITIONS) The conditions of this theorem are satisfied if q is a square and $q > (2d + 1)^2$, as follows from Theorem 12.51 (Ihara) as well as from Garcia and Stichtenoth's results (see Section 12.7.8). Alternatively, by Theorem 12.53 (Serre), the conditions are satisfied if q is very large. Additional sufficient conditions can be extracted from Section 12.7.9.

COROLLARY 12.62 *[48] If q is square and $q \geq 49$, it holds that $\widehat{\tau}(q) \geq 1 - (4/(\sqrt{q} - 1)) > 0$.*

Proof Since $k = 1$ in this case, the conditions can be relaxed to $0 < \delta < 1/(1 + d)$ and $A(q) > 2d/(1 - \delta(1 + d))$ after a slight adaptation of the proof. Substituting $A(q) = \sqrt{q} - 1$ and $d = 2$, we get the conditions $0 < \delta < 1/3$ and $3\delta < 1 - (4/(\sqrt{q} - 1))$. Then set $t_i = \lfloor \delta N_i \rfloor$ and $n_i = N_i - 1$. Because 3δ can be selected arbitrarily close to $1 - (4/(\sqrt{q} - 1))$, the desired result follows. ∎

12.9 The Torsion Limit and Its Applications

An interesting question is whether the contention of Theorem 12.60 holds for *any* finite field, that is, whether it holds without the condition $A(q) > 2d$. A version of Theorem 12.60 that is valid for *any* finite field $\mathbb{F}_q$ in the case $d = 2$ is shown in Cascudo et al. [38]. The idea is to combine Theorem 12.60 over an extension field $\mathbb{F}_{q^\ell}$ for which $A(q^\ell) > 4$ with (one or more steps of) a dedicated field descent[46] involving an arithmetic embedding of $\mathbb{F}_{q^\ell}$ over

---

[44] See also Noseda, Oliveira, and Quoos [151] and the references therein.
[45] Methods such as the one from Shum et al. [170] even *require* one-point divisors for efficiency.
[46] In the language of coding theory, a field descent refers to a *concatenation* method.

$\mathbb{F}_q$. Unfortunately, it has some drawbacks. First, this type of descent removes *uniformity*, a property required in some applications such as that by Ishai et al. [113]. Second, the result does not generalize to all finite fields $\mathbb{F}_q$ when $d > 2$. Third, the descent incurs substantial overhead, thereby affecting the magnitude of the constant factors in the expressions for k, t. However, it *does* show that $\hat{\tau}(q) > 0$ for *all* finite fields $\mathbb{F}_q$.[47]

For the construction of the arithmetic secret-sharing schemes in Theorem 12.60, the method of "solving by degree" of the relevant Riemann–Roch systems has been combined with the existence of certain asymptotically good towers of algebraic function fields. This approach has been substantially improved in Cascudo, Cramer, and Xing [41, 44],[48] leading to a relaxation of the condition $A(q) > 2d$ in Theorem 12.60. This time, however, uniformity is *preserved*. As it turns out, it follows that Theorem 12.60 holds for much smaller values of q. Moreover, because overhead incurred by the dedicated field descent is avoided, the constant factors in the expressions for k, t are also improved.

The improvement consists of two parts. First, the solving strategy for the Riemann–Roch systems has been refined with the aid of the *torsion limit* of a tower. For a given tower $\mathcal{F}/\mathbb{F}_q$, this strategy exploits not only information on the Ihara limit of $\mathcal{F}$[49] but also information on the asymptotics of the (degree-0 divisor) class group $\mathrm{Cl}(F)$, concretely, the ratio between (the base-q logarithm of) the order of the d-torsion subgroup[50] $\mathcal{J}_F[d] \subset \mathrm{Cl}(F)$ and the genus $g(F)$, because F ranges over $\mathcal{F}$. More precisely, the d-torsion limit of $\mathcal{F}$ is defined as

$$J_d(\mathcal{F}) = \liminf_{F \in \mathcal{F}} \frac{\log_q |\mathcal{J}_F[d]|}{g(F)}$$

This strategy allows for identification of solutions with a smaller degree than the ones selected in the "solving-by-degree method," which is a key factor behind the relaxed condition mentioned earlier.

Second, new parameters are shown that satisfy this relaxed condition. This involves further results from algebraic geometry, notably about torsion subgroups of abelian varieties and about p-rank in certain Artin-Schreier extensions of functions fields. It leads to the conclusion that Theorem 12.60 holds for much smaller values of q. We now present an outline.

For the moment, take a fixed function field $F/\mathbb{F}_q$. It is useful to start by recalling the following facts: write h for the order of the class group $\mathrm{Cl}(F)$. Let $r \geq 0$ be an integer. The set $\mathrm{Div}_r(F)$ of divisors of degree r is partitioned into exactly h equivalence classes when taken modulo the principal divisors $\mathrm{Prin}(F)$. A divisor of degree r has positive Riemann–Roch dimension if and only if each element of its equivalence class does, which is, in turn, equivalent to the statement that it contains some effective divisor of degree r. In other words, taking $\mathrm{Div}_r(F)$ modulo $\mathrm{Prin}(F)$, the number of classes having positive Riemann–Roch dimension is at most A_r, the number of *effective* divisors of degree r.

---

[47] Note that Cascudo et al. [38] deals with the case $k = 1$ only; however, the result generalizes to $k = \Omega(n)$ in a straightforward way. It also can be generalized easily to the case $2 \leq d \leq q$.

[48] The article by Cascudo, Cramer, and Xing [44] is the extended version of that in reference 41. In addition, it includes applications to frameproof codes and arithmetic embeddings.

[49] Recall that this is the limit of the ratio between the number of rational points and the genus, with the genus tending to infinity.

[50] The subgroup of elements annihilated when multiplied by d.

Consider the Riemann–Roch system at hand, and let X be the "variable" divisor of degree denoted by s. Attention may be restricted to the class of X modulo the group of principal divisors. The idea is to (greedily) estimate the number m of classes in $\text{Div}_s(F)$ modulo $\text{Prin}(F)$ that represent "nonsolutions" and then to derive a manageable condition under which $h > m$, thereby automatically giving a sufficient condition for the existence of a solution and, hence, for the existence of the desired codex.

Now consider the relevant system underlying Theorem 12.60, dictated by Theorem 12.56. Each of the equations is of the form $\ell(-X+U)=0$ or of the form $\ell(dX+V)=0$. We focus on the latter type of equation; the treatment of the former is essentially a special case. Write $r = \deg(dX+V)$. Suppose that X is a nonsolution; that is, $\ell(dX+V) > 0$. Then there are at most A_r possibilities for the class of dX. Consequently, there are at most $A_r \cdot |\mathcal{J}_F[d]|$ possibilities for the class of X: the difference of any two is an element of the class group, and this element is annihilated when multiplied by d. Using a "greedy union" argument, an upper bound is obtained on the number of classes in $\text{Div}_s(F)$ modulo $\text{Prin}(F)$ representing a nonsolution to *some* equation in the system. This leads to the sufficient condition that

$$h > \binom{n}{t}(A_{r_1} + A_{r_2}|\mathcal{J}_F[d]|)$$

where $r_1 := 2g - s + t + k - 2$ and $r_2 := ds - n + t$.[51]

Careful inspection of the zeta function of F yields an upper bound on the ratio A_r/h whenever $0 \le r < g$ and $g \ge 1$, given as a function of g, r, q. That is,

$$\frac{A_r}{h} \le \frac{g}{q^{g-r-1}(\sqrt{q}-1)^2}$$

Substitution of this upper bound turns the sufficient condition into another one just involving the parameters s, k, n, t, g, as well as d, q: the class number h has dropped out.

Now consider a tower $\mathcal{F}/\mathbb{F}_q$ with Ihara limit $A > 0$, and let $d = 2$. After some calculus, the ideas discussed earlier lead to the conclusion that this tower gives rise to the desired schemes from Theorem 12.60 if

$$A > 1 + J_2(\mathcal{F})$$

See Cascudo, Cramer, and Xing [44] for the precise condition in the case $d > 2$.

Now, for given real number A with $0 < A \le A(q)$, let the quantity $J_d(q,A)$ denote the lim inf of $J_d(\mathcal{F})$ taken over all towers over $\mathbb{F}_q$ with Ihara limit at least A.[52] It is now possible to finally state the relaxed condition for Theorem 12.60. For instance, in the case $d = 2$, it holds for a given finite field $\mathbb{F}_q$ if there is a real number A such that $0 < A \le A(q)$ and such that

$$A > 1 + J_2(q,A)$$

Note that, in particular, an asymptotically good tower is required, as before. Again, see Cascudo, Cramer, and Xing [44] for the precise condition in the case $d > 2$.

---

[51] The method of showing existence of certain codes by solving appropriate (what we call) "Riemann–Roch systems" is due to Vlăduţ [179] and has been followed by several authors since. A novelty in the systems discussed here is treatment of d-torsion considerations arising from $d > 1$.

[52] With some care, this definition can be generalized to infinite *families* of function fields, not just towers. The stated results will still hold.

The second step is to investigate when the condition is satisfied. Generally, the order of the d-torsion subgroup can be upper bounded using a theorem of Weil on d-torsion in abelian varieties or by a method involving the Weil pairing for abelian varieties. This leads to the following "generic" bounds in the case that d is *prime*:

- If $d \mid (q-1)$, then

$$J_d(q, A(q)) \leq \frac{2}{\log_d q}$$

- If $d \nmid (q-1)$, then

$$J_d(q, A(q)) \leq \frac{1}{\log_d q}$$

However,[53] certain Artin-Schreier towers admit a dedicated analysis of d-torsion, as shown by Cascudo, Cramer, and Xing [41, 44]. Under the restriction that $d = p$, where p is the characteristic of $\mathbb{F}_q$, the idea is to apply a combination of the Deuring-Shafarevich formula for p-rank with the Riemann-Hurwitz genus formula so as to obtain a recursion involving p-ranks and genera only (as well as q).[54] Since the p-rank of F equals $\log_p q \cdot \log_q |\mathcal{J}_F[p]|$, this gives in principle an alternative way to access information about the torsion limit for such towers.

Briefly, for this idea to work, it is a convenient requirement that in consecutive steps of the tower, the "error terms" in both formulas (arising from ramification in the tower) differ by a nonzero constant so that the desired recursion is simply obtained from the two formulas by Gaussian elimination. Precise knowledge of the genus in each step of the tower is another convenient requirement. Once substituted into the recursion, the recursion thus can be solved, and precise knowledge of the p-rank in each step of the tower is obtained.

Applying this approach to a specific, optimal tower given by Garcia and Stichtenoth [95] leads to a substantial improvement on the "generic" approach.

THEOREM 12.63 *[41, 44] If d is a prime, q is a square, and $d|q$, then*

$$J_d(q, \sqrt{q} - 1) \leq \frac{1}{(\sqrt{q} + 1) \log_d q}$$

There are some other asymptotically good (optimal) towers known where this approach applies as well, but there the result is not nearly as good [4].

All in all, this leads to the following results:

THEOREM 12.64 *[41, 44] Let q be a prime power, and let $d = 2$. Suppose that there exists a real number A such that $0 < A \leq A(q)$ and $A > 1 + J_2(q, A)$. Then there exists an infinite*

---

[53] The torsion limit [41, 44] just described has been introduced independently by Randriambololona [158], in the context of bounds on frameproof codes. The generic bounds are also discussed, but not the superior bounds for the Artin-Schreier case from Cascudo, Cramer, and Xing [41, 44] given next. See Cascudo, Cramer, and Xing [41, 44] for additional applications to bilinear complexity of extension field multiplication and frameproof codes.

[54] The p-rank of a function field $F/\mathbb{F}_q$, a.k.a. the Hasse-Witt invariant, is the dimension of the finite dimensional $\mathbb{F}_p$-vector space $\mathcal{J}_{\widehat{F}}[p]$, where $\widehat{F}$ is the function field obtained by extending the field of constants of F to an algebraic closure $\overline{\mathbb{F}}_q$ of $\mathbb{F}_q$; that is, $\widehat{F} = F \cdot \overline{\mathbb{F}}_q$.

family of $(n,t,2,n-t)$-arithmetic secret-sharing schemes for $\mathbb{F}_q^k$ over $\mathbb{F}_q$ with uniformity such that

1. $n \longrightarrow \infty$.
2. $k = \Omega(n)$.
3. $t = \Omega(n)$.

COROLLARY 12.65 *The conditions of Theorem 12.64 are satisfied for all finite fields $\mathbb{F}_q$ with $q \geq 8$ and $q \neq 11, 13$.*

See, Cascudo, Cramer, and Xing [44] for statements in the case $d > 2$.

The proof of Theorem 12.64 also directly implies the following result:

COROLLARY 12.66 *Let $\mathbb{F}_q$ be a finite field with $q \geq 8$ and $q \neq 11, 13$. Then there exists an infinite family of $\mathbb{F}_q$-linear codes C such that C, $C^\perp$, and C^{*2} are simultaneously asymptotically good.*

The case where just C, C^{*2} are considered (so the dual $C^\perp$ is left out of consideration) has been shown to hold for all finite fields [160] using an algebraic geometric argument in combination with a refined field descent method. Corollary 12.66 also has a formulation for the case $d > 2$. Techniques similar to the ones employed in the proofs of Theorem 12.64 and Corollary 12.66 also lead to improved results on frameproof codes and arithmetic embeddings of finite fields (see Cascudo, Cramer, and Xing [44]).

REMARK 12.67 In principle, Theorem 12.64 and Corollary 12.66 are nonconstructive. However, a plausibly efficient *randomized* construction is discussed by Cascudo, Cramer, and Xing [44], based in part on the observation that given a suitable tower, a random divisor class of a certain degree constitutes a solution of the relevant Riemann–Roch system with overwhelming probability: the number of nonsolutions is a negligible fraction of the class number.

Finally, it is interesting to note that, at present, there is no *elementary* proof for the existence of the asymptotically good arithmetic secret-sharing schemes shown in Theorem 12.60, whose proof is algebraic geometric and requires asymptotically good towers of functions fields.[55] This is, so far, in contrast with the theory of error-correcting codes, where the existence of asymptotically good codes can be shown by elementary (probabilistic) methods.

12.10 Outlook

There are several meaningful ways to extend the codex notion. We mention a few. Presently, one of the most promising extensions, both from a technical and from an application point of view, is to study *symmetries* of codices, that is, their automorphism groups. This is motivated by recent results [16, 17, 67]. Motivated by a technical argument in Randriambololona [160], it is relevant to consider a generalization of the codex notion where not only multiplication in the presented K-algebra A is considered but, *simultaneously*, several other multilinear

---

[55] The situation is the same for asymptotically good arithmetic embeddings of finite fields.

maps. It also makes sense to define a codex over K-algebras, not just over fields K; that is, the coordinates of the code take value in a K-algebra rather than in the field K.[56] Moreover, so far the codex notion is inherently commutative. It is natural to bring non-commutativity into play. On the application side, new uses of codices keep coming up time and again.

The most powerful way to construct asymptotically good arithmetic secret-sharing schemes in the subclass addressed in Theorem 12.60 is by using the torsion-limit approach from Theorem 12.64 and Corollary 12.66. Is this approach anywhere *close to optimal?* Or can it be improved, possibly by some alternative approach or a further refinement? An interesting question is whether the asymptotically good arithmetic secret-sharing schemes in the subclass addressed in Theorem 12.60 *exist over* $\mathbb{F}_2$. Moreover, with a few exceptions, there has been very little emphasis on the study of *nonasymptotic codex constructions* so far.

For small fields and in the case $k = 1$, the constructive bound from Corollary 12.62 is still *far removed* from the numerical limitations imposed by Theorem 12.40 (and its improvements).[57] A sizeable portion of this gap may be caused by the fact that the techniques for proving limitations are still rather *crude*. Yet major improvements seem to require new approaches, algebraic-combinatorial or otherwise: known bounding techniques (including those inspired by bounds from the theory of error-correcting codes) lack sensitivity to capture well enough the substantial influence of the powering operation.

Improvement of the known *descent methods* is another direction. For instance, it would be interesting to *preserve dual distance* by a descent method. However, the paradigm as we know it works "locally" in that, in particular, it replaces each coordinate by some (necessarily) redundant expansion and thus turns any good dual distance very bad. Therefore, to solve this, an entirely new idea is required that works in a more *global* way, so to speak. In addition, presently known descent techniques do not suffice to show the existence of codes C such that both C and C^{*d} are asymptotically good *in the case $d > 2$*.

On the strictly algebraic geometric side, research on the torsion limit has just started. A major question is *whether it is possible that $J_d(q,A) = 0$ for some finite field $\mathbb{F}_q$, some integer $d \geq 2$, and some real number $A > 0$. Improving the nontrivial bounds known so far is also important, but a particularly intriguing question is whether there are (many?) *other good towers of the Artin-Schreier type* than just the one from Garcia and Stichtenoth [95] that give such bounds (or perhaps even better ones) using the Deuring-Shafarevich approach when compared with Theorem 12.63.

Although the understanding of explicit equations for recursive towers from *modular curves* is steadily improving,[58] it is presently not clear whether the result from Theorem 12.63 can be explained from the theory of modular curves or whether it can perhaps even be improved using that theory. Moreover, are there good bounding techniques dedicated to good towers of *another type* than Artin-Schreier? Finally, there are important questions in *computational algebraic geometry* about the *efficiency of solving Riemann–Roch systems* (see Remark 12.67 for a possible direction).

---

[56] A special case has been defined and studied in Cramer, Damgård, and Maurer [61]. Another motivation for such an extension is given by the results of Beimel et al. [13].

[57] See the discussion in Cascudo, Cramer, and Xing [41, 44].

[58] See Bassa et al. [5], where curves on higher dimensional (Drinfeld) modular varieties are used to obtain equations for good recursive towers over all nonprime finite fields.

List of Algorithms

List of Exercises

References

1. M. F. Atiyah and I. G. Macdonald. *Introduction to Commutative Algebra*. Addison-Wesley, Reading, MA, 1969.
2. Simeon Ball. On sets of vectors of a finite vector space in which every subset of basis size is a basis. *J. Eur. Math. Soc.*, 14:733–48, 2012.
3. Boaz Barak, Ran Canetti, Jesper Buus Nielsen, and Rafael Pass. Universally composable protocols with relaxed setup assumptions. In *FOCS*, pp. 186–95. IEEE Computer Society, Washington DC, 2004.
4. Alp Bassa and Peter Beelen. The Hasse-Witt invariant in some towers of function fields over finite fields. *Bull. Brazil. Math. Soc.*, 41:4:567–82, 2010.
5. Alp Bassa, Peter Beelen, Arnaldo Garcia, and Henning Stichtenoth. Towers of function fields over non-prime finite fields. *Acta Arith.*, 164:163–79, 2014.
6. Alp Bassa, Arnaldo Garcia, and Henning Stichtenoth. A new tower over cubic finite fields. *Moscow Math. J.*, 8(3):401–18, September 2008.
7. Donald Beaver. Efficient multiparty protocols using circuit randomization. In Joan Feigenbaum, ed., *Advances in Cryptology: CRYPTO '91*, vol. 576 of *Lecture Notes in Computer Science*, pp. 420–32. Springer-Verlag, Berlin, 1991.
8. Donald Beaver. Foundations of secure interactive computing. In Joan Feigenbaum, ed., *Advances in Cryptology: CRYPTO '91*, vol. 576 of *Lecture Notes in Computer Science*, pp. 377–91. Springer-Verlag, Berlin, 1991.
9. Donald Beaver and Silvio Micali and Phillip Rogaway. The Round Complexity of Secure Protocols (Extended Abstract). In Harriet Ortiz, editor, *Proceedings of the 22nd Annual ACM Symposium on Theory of Computing, May 13–17, 1990, Baltimore, Maryland, USA*, pp. 503–513, 1990.
10. Zuzana Beerliová-Trubíniová and Martin Hirt. Perfectly-secure mpc with linear communication complexity. In Ran Canetti, ed. *Theory of Cryptography, Fifth Theory of Cryptography Conference*, vol. 4948 of *Lecture Notes in Computer Science*. Springer-Verlag, Berlin, 2008, pp. 213–30.
11. Amos Beimel. Secure schemes for secret sharing and key distribution. PhD thesis, Department of Computer Science, Technion, 1996.
12. Amos Beimel. Secret-sharing schemes: A survey. In Yeow Meng Chee, Zhenbo Guo, San Ling, Fengjing Shao, Yuansheng Tang, Huaxiong Wang, and Chaoping Xing, eds., *IWCC*, Vol. 6639 of *Lecture Notes in Computer Science*, pp. 11–46. Springer-Verlag, Berlin, 2011.
13. Amos Beimel, Aner Ben-Efraim, Carles Padró, and Ilya Tyomkin. Multi-linear secret-sharing schemes. In Yehuda Lindell, ed., *TCC*, Vol. 8349 of *Lecture Notes in Computer Science*, pp. 394–418. Springer-Verlag, Berlin, 2014.
14. Michael Ben-Or, Shafi Goldwasser, and Avi Wigderson. Completeness theorems for noncryptographic fault-tolerant distributed computation (extended abstract). In *Proceedings of the Twentieth Annual ACM Symposium on Theory of Computing (STOC'88)*, ACM, New York, 1988, pp. 1–10.
15. Eli Ben-Sasson, Serge Fehr, and Rafail Ostrovsky. Near-linear unconditionally-secure multiparty computation with a dishonest minority. *Advances in Cryptology–CRYPTO 2012*, pp. 663–680. Springer Berlin Heidelberg, 2012.
16. Eli Ben-Sasson, Ariel Gabizon, Yohay Kaplan, Swastik Kopparty, and Shubhangi Saraf. A new family of locally correctable codes based on degree-lifted algebraic geometry codes. In Dan Boneh,

Tim Roughgarden, and Joan Feigenbaum, eds. *Symposium on Theory of Computing Conference (STOC'13)*. ACM, New York, 2013, pp. 833–42.

17. Eli Ben-Sasson, Yohay Kaplan, Swastik Kopparty, Or Meir, and Henning Stichtenoth. Constant rate PCPs for Circuit-SAT with sublinear query complexity. In *FOCS*, pp. 320–9. IEEE Computer Society, Washington, DC, 2013.

18. Josh Cohen Benaloh and Jerry Leichter. Generalized secret sharing and monotone functions. In Shafi Goldwasser, ed., *CRYPTO*, vol. 403 of *Lecture Notes in Computer Science*, pp. 27–35. Springer-Verlag, Berlin, 1988.

19. Rikke Bendlin, Ivan Damgård, Claudio Orlandi, and Sarah Zakarias. Semi-homomorphic encryption and multiparty computation. In Kenneth G. Paterson, ed. *Advances in Cryptology: EUROCRYPT 2011, 30th Annual International Conference on the Theory and Applications of Cryptographic Techniques*, vol. 6632 of *Lecture Notes in Computer Science*. Springer-Verlag, Berlin, 2011, pp. 169–88.

20. Michael Bertilsson and Ingemar Ingemarsson. A construction of practical secret sharing schemes using linear block codes. In Jennifer Seberry and Yuliang Zheng, eds., *AUSCRYPT*, vol. 718 of *Lecture Notes in Computer Science*, pp. 67–79. Springer-Verlag, Berlin, 1992.

21. J. Bezerra, A. Garcia, and H. Stichtenoth. An explicit tower of function fields over cubic finite fields and Zink's lower bound. *J. Reine Angew. Math.*, 589:159–199, December 2005.

22. G. R. Blakley. Safeguarding cryptographic keys. Proceedings of the 1979 AFIPS National Computer Conference, AFIPS Conference Proceedings, vol. 48, AFIPS Press, 1979, pp. 313–317. AFIPS is "http://en.wikipedia.org/wiki/American_Federation_of_Information_Processing_Societies"

23. G. R. Blakley and C. Meadows. Security of ramp schemes. In G. R. Blakley and David Chaum, eds., *CRYPTO*, vol. 196 of *Lecture Notes in Computer Science*, pp. 242–68. Springer, Berlin, 1984.

24. G. R. Blakley and G. A. Kabatianski. Ideal perfect threshold schemes and MDS codes. In *Proceedings of IEEE International Symposium on Information Theory*, p. 488. IEEE, New York, 1995.

25. Carlo Blundo, Alfredo De Santis, and Ugo Vaccaro. Efficient sharing of many secrets. In Patrice Enjalbert, Alain Finkel, and Klaus W. Wagner, eds., *STACS*, vol. 665 of *Lecture Notes in Computer Science*, pp. 692–703. Springer-Verlag, Berlin, 1993.

26. Carlo Blundo, Alfredo De Santis, and Ugo Vaccaro. On secret sharing schemes. *Inf. Process. Lett.*, 65(1):25–32, 1998.

27. Peter Bogetoft, Dan Lund Christensen, Ivan Damgård, Martin Geisler, Thomas P. Jakobsen, Mikkel Krøigaard, Janus Dam Nielsen, Jesper Buus Nielsen, Kurt Nielsen, Jakob Pagter, Michael I. Schwartzbach, and Tomas Toft. Secure multiparty computation goes live. In Roger Dingledine and Philippe Golle, eds., *Financial Cryptography*, vol. 5628 of *Lecture Notes in Computer Science*, pp. 325–43. Springer-Verlag, Berlin, 2009.

28. G. Bracha. An $o(\log n)$ expected rounds randomized Byzantine generals protocol. *J. ACM*, 34(4): 910–20, 1987.

29. Ernie Brickell. Some ideal secret sharing schemes. *J. Combin. Math. Combin. Comput.*, 9:105–13, 1989.

30. Nader H. Bshouty. Multilinear complexity is equivalent to optimal tester size. *Electronic Colloquium on Computational Complexity (ECCC)*, 20:11, 2013.

31. Peter Bürgisser, Michael Clausen, and Amin Shokrollahi. *Algebraic Complexity Theory*. [Grundlehren der mathematischen Wissenschaften]. Springer, Berlin, 1997.

32. K. A. Bush. Orthogonal arrays of index unity. *Ann. Math. Stat.*, 23:426–34, 1952.

33. Ran Canetti. Universally composable security: A new paradigm for cryptographic protocols. In *42nd Annual Symposium on Foundations of Computer Science*, pp. 136–45. IEEE, New York, 2001. Full version available on the eprint archive.

34. Ran Canetti, Yevgeniy Dodis, Rafael Pass, and Shabsi Walfish. Universally composable security with global setup. In Salil P. Vadhan, ed., *TCC*, vol. 4392 of *Lecture Notes in Computer Science*, pp. 61–85. Springer-Verlag, Berlin, 2007.

35. Ran Canetti, Uri Feige, Oded Goldreich, and Moni Naor. Adaptively secure multi-party computation. In *Proceedings of the Twenty-Eighth Annual ACM Symposium on the Theory of Computing*, pp. 639–48, ACM, New York, 1996.

36. Ran Canetti, Eyal Kushilevitz, and Yehuda Lindell. On the limitations of universally composable two-party computation without set-up assumptions. *J. Cryptology*, 19(2):135–67, 2006.

37. Ran Canetti, Yehuda Lindell, Rafail Ostrovsky, and Amit Sahai. Universally composable two-party and multi-party secure computation. In *Proceedings of the Thirty-Fourth Annual ACM Symposium on the Theory of Computing*, pp. 494–503, ACM, New York, 2002.

38. Ignacio Cascudo, Hao Chen, Ronald Cramer, and Chaoping Xing. Asymptotically good ideal linear secret sharing with strong multiplication over *any* fixed finite field. In Shai Halevi, ed., *CRYPTO*, vol. 5677 of *Lecture Notes in Computer Science*, pp. 466–86. Springer-Verlag, Berlin, 2009.

39. Ignacio Cascudo, Ronald Cramer, Diego Mirandola, Carles Padró, and Chaoping Xing. On secret sharing with nonlinear product reconstruction. *SIAM Journal on Discrete Mathematics*, 2015.

40. Ignacio Cascudo, Ronald Cramer, Diego Mirandola, and Gilles Zémor. Squares of Random Linear Codes. *IEEE Transactions on Information Theory*, 61(3):1159–1173, 2015.

41. Ignacio Cascudo, Ronald Cramer, and Chaoping Xing. The torsion-limit for algebraic function fields and its application to arithmetic secret sharing. In Phillip Rogaway, ed. *Advances in Cryptology: CRYPTO 2011, 31st Annual Cryptology Conference*, vol. 6841 of *Lecture Notes in Computer Science*. Springer-Verlag, Berlin, 2011, pp. 685–705. Early versions had been widely circulated since November 2009.

42. Ignacio Cascudo, Ronald Cramer, and Chaoping Xing. The arithmetic codex. *IACR Cryptology ePrint Archive*, 2012:388, 2012. A five-page summary also appeared in *Proceedings of IEEE Information Theory Workshop (ITW)*. IEEE, New York, 2012.

43. Ignacio Cascudo, Ronald Cramer, and Chaoping Xing. Bounds on the threshold gap in secret sharing and its applications. *IEEE Transactions on Information Theory*, 59(9):5600–12, 2013.

44. Ignacio Cascudo, Ronald Cramer, and Chaoping Xing. Torsion limits and Riemann-Roch systems for function fields and applications. *IEEE Transactions in Information Theory*, 60(7):3871–88, 2014.

45. Ignacio Cascudo, Ronald Cramer, Chaoping Xing, and An Yang. Asymptotic bound for multiplication complexity in the extensions of small finite fields. *IEEE Transactions on Information Theory*, 58(7):4930–35, 2012.

46. David Chaum, Claude Crépeau, and Ivan Damgård. Multiparty unconditionally secure protocols (extended abstract). In *Proceedings of the Twentieth Annual ACM Symposium on Theory of Computing (STOC'88)*, ACM, New York, 1988, pp. 11–19.

47. David Chaum, Ivan Damgård, and Jeroen van de Graaf. Multiparty computations ensuring privacy of each party's input and correctness of the result. In Carl Pomerance, ed., *Advances in Cryptology: CRYPTO '87*, Vol. 293 of *Lecture Notes in Computer Science*, pp. 87–119, Springer-Verlag, Berlin, 1987.

48. Hao Chen and Ronald Cramer. Algebraic geometric secret sharing schemes and secure multi-party computations over small fields. In Cynthia Dwork, ed., *CRYPTO*, vol. 4117 of *Lecture Notes in Computer Science*, pp. 521–36. Springer-Verlag, Berlin, 2006.

49. Hao Chen, Ronald Cramer, Robbert de Haan, and Ignacio Cascudo Pueyo. Strongly multiplicative ramp schemes from high degree rational points on curves. In Nigel P. Smart, ed., *EUROCRYPT*, vol. 4965 of *Lecture Notes in Computer Science*, pp. 451–70. Springer-Verlag, Berlin, 2008.

50. Hao Chen, Ronald Cramer, Shafi Goldwasser, Robbert de Haan, and Vinod Vaikuntanathan. Secure computation from random error correcting codes. In Moni Naor, ed. *Advances in Cryptology: EUROCRYPT 2007, 26th Annual International Conference on the Theory and Applications of Cryptographic Techniques*, vol. 4515 of *Lecture Notes in Computer Science*. Springer-Verlag, Berlin, 2007, pp. 291–310.

51. D. V. Chudnovsky and G. V. Chudnovsky. Algebraic complexities and algebraic curves over finite fields. *J. Complexity*, 1988:285–316, 1988.

52. Gil Cohen, Ivan Bjerre Damgård, Yuval Ishai, Jonas Kölker, Peter Bro Miltersen, Ran Raz, and Ron D. Rothblum. Efficient multiparty protocols via log-depth threshold formulae (extended abstract). In Ran Canetti and Juan A. Garay, eds., *CRYPTO (2)*, vol. 8043 of *Lecture Notes in Computer Science*, pp. 185–202. Springer-Verlag, Berlin, 2013.

53. Henri Cohen. *A Course in Computational Algebraic Number Theory*, vol. 138 of *GTM*. Springer-Verlag, Berlin, 1993.

54. Alain Couvreur, Philippe Gaborit, Valérie Gauthier-Umaña, Ayoub Otmani, and Jean-Pierre Tillich. Distinguisher-based attacks on public-key cryptosystems using Reed–Solomon codes. *Designs, Codes and Cryptography*, 2013:1–26, 2013.

55. Alain Couvreur, Ayoub Otmani, and Jean-Pierre Tillich. Polynomial time attack on wild mceliece over quadratic extensions. In Phong Q. Nguyen and Elisabeth Oswald, eds., *EUROCRYPT*, vol. 8441 of *Lecture Notes in Computer Science*, pp. 17–39. Springer-Verlag, Berlin, 2014.

56. Thomas Cover and Joy Thomas. *Elements of Information Theory*. Wiley, New York, 1991.

57. Ronald Cramer. The arithmetic codex: Theory and applications. In Kenneth G. Paterson, ed. *Advances in Cryptology: EUROCRYPT 2011, 30th Annual International Conference on the Theory and Applications of Cryptographic Techniques*, vol. 6632 of *Lecture Notes in Computer Science*. Springer-Verlag, Berlin, 2011, p. 1. Abstract of invited talk.

58. Ronald Cramer, Ivan Damgård, and Jesper Buus Nielsen. Multiparty computation from threshold homomorphic encryption. In *Advances in Cryptology: EUROCRYPT 2001*, vol. 2045 of *Lecture Notes in Computer Science*, pp. 280–300. Springer-Verlag, Berlin, 2001.

59. Ronald Cramer, Ivan Damgård, and Stefan Dziembowski. On the complexity of verifiable secret sharing and multiparty computation. In *Proceedings of the Thirty-Second Annual ACM Symposium on the Theory of Computing*, pp. 325–34, ACM, New York, 2000.

60. Ronald Cramer, Ivan Damgård, Stefand Dziembowski, Martin Hirt, and Tal Rabin. Efficient multiparty computations secure against an adaptive adversary. In Jacques Stern, ed., *Advances in Cryptology: EUROCRYPT '99*, vol. 1592 of *Lecture Notes in Computer Science*, pp. 311–26. Springer-Verlag, Berlin, 1999.

61. Ronald Cramer, Ivan Damgård, and Ueli M. Maurer. General secure multi-party computation from any linear secret-sharing scheme. In Bart Preneel, ed., *EUROCRYPT*, vol. 1807 of *Lecture Notes in Computer Science*, pp. 316–34. Springer-Verlag, Berlin, 2000.

62. Ronald Cramer, Ivan Damgård, and Valerio Pastro. On the amortized complexity of zero knowledge protocols for multiplicative relations. In Adam Smith, ed., *ICITS*, vol. 7412 of *Lecture Notes in Computer Science*, pp. 62–79. Springer-Verlag, Berlin, 2012.

63. Ronald Cramer, Vanesa Daza, Ignacio Gracia, Jorge Jiménez Urroz, Gregor Leander, Jaume Martí Farré, and Carles Padró. On codes, matroids, and secure multiparty computation from linear secret-sharing schemes. *IEEE Transactions on Information Theory*, 54(6):2644–57, 2008. Preliminary version in *CRYPTO 2005*.

64. Ronald Cramer and Serge Fehr. The mathematical theory of information and its applications to privacy amplification (and more). Course notes, Mathematical Institute, Leiden University, version 2.0, 2011. Available from www.cwi.nl/crypto/docs.html.

65. Ronald Cramer and Serge Fehr. Optimal black-box secret sharing over arbitrary abelian groups. In Moti Yung, ed., *CRYPTO*, vol. 2442 of *Lecture Notes in Computer Science*, pp. 272–87. Springer-Verlag, Berlin, 2002.

66. Ronald Cramer, Serge Fehr, and Martijn Stam. Black-box secret sharing from primitive sets in algebraic number fields. In Victor Shoup, ed., *CRYPTO*, vol. 3621 of *Lecture Notes in Computer Science*, pp. 344–60. Springer-Verlag, Berlin, 2005.

67. Ronald Cramer, Carles Padró, and Chaoping Xing. Optimal Algebraic Manipulation Detection Codes in the Constant-Error Model. In *Proceedings of 12th IACR TCC 2015*, Springer LNCS, vol. 9014, pp. 481–501, 2015.

68. Ivan Damgård, Matthias Fitzi, Eike Kiltz, Jesper Buus Nielsen, and Tomas Toft. Unconditionally secure constant-rounds multi-party computation for equality, comparison, bits and exponentiation. In Shai Halevi and Tal Rabin, eds., *TCC*, vol. 3876 of *Lecture Notes in Computer Science*, pp. 285–304. Springer-Verlag, Berlin, 2006.

69. Ivan Damgård, Yuval Ishai, and Mikkel Krøigaard. Perfectly secure multiparty computation and the computational overhead of cryptography. In Henri Gilbert, ed., *EUROCRYPT*, vol. 6110 of *Lecture Notes in Computer Science*, pp. 445–65. Springer-Verlag, Berlin, 2010.

70. Ivan Damgård, Yuval Ishai, Mikkel Krøigaard, Jesper Buus Nielsen, and Adam Smith. Scalable multiparty computation with nearly optimal work and resilience. In David Wagner, ed. *Advances in*

Cryptology: CRYPTO 2008, 28th Annual International Cryptology Conference, vol. 5157 of *Lecture Notes in Computer Science*. Springer-Verlag, Berlin, 2008, pp. 241–61.

71. Ivan Damgård and Jesper Buus Nielsen. Improved noncommitting encryption schemes based on a general complexity assumption. In Mihir Bellare, ed., *Advances in Cryptology: CRYPTO 2000*, vol. 1880 of *Lecture Notes in Computer Science*, pp. 432–50. Springer-Verlag, Berlin, 2000.

72. Ivan Damgård and Jesper Buus Nielsen. Universally composable efficient multiparty computation from threshold homomorphic encryption. In D. Boneh, ed., *Advances in Cryptology: CRYPTO 2003*, vol. 2729 of *Lecture Notes in Computer Science*, pp. 247–64. Springer-Verlag, Berlin, 2003.

73. Ivan Damgård and Jesper Buus Nielsen. Scalable and unconditionally secure multiparty computation. In Alfred Menezes, ed., *CRYPTO*, vol. 4622 of *Lecture Notes in Computer Science*, pp. 572–90. Springer-Verlag, Berlin, 2007.

74. Ivan Damgård and Jesper Buus Nielsen. Adaptive versus static security in the UC model. In Sherman S. M. Chow, Joseph K. Liu, Lucas Chi Kwong Hui, and Siu-Ming Yiu, eds., *Provable Security: 8th International Conference, ProvSec 2014*, vol. 8782 of *Lecture Notes in Computer Science*, pp. 10–28. Springer-Verlag, Berlin, 2014.

75. Ivan Damgård, Valerio Pastro, Nigel Smart, and Sarah Zakarias. Multiparty computation from somewhat homomorphic encryption. *Cryptology ePrint Archive*, 2011:535, 2011.

76. Ivan Damgård and Rune Thorbek. Linear integer secret sharing and distributed exponentiation. In Moti Yung, Yevgeniy Dodis, Aggelos Kiayias, and Tal Malkin, eds., *Public Key Cryptography*, vol. 3958 of *Lecture Notes in Computer Science*, pp. 75–90. Springer-Verlag, Berlin, 2006.

77. Ivan Damgård and Rune Thorbek. Noninteractive proofs for integer multiplication. In Moni Naor, ed. *Advances in Cryptology: EUROCRYPT 2007, 26th Annual International Conference on the Theory and Applications of Cryptographic Techniques*, vol. 4515 of *Lecture Notes in Computer Science*. Springer-Verlag, Berlin, 2007, pp. 412–29.

78. Ivan Damgård and Sarah Zakarias. Constant-overhead secure computation of boolean circuits using preprocessing. *Theory of Cryptography*, pp. 621–41. Springer Berlin Heidelberg, 2013.

79. Yvo Desmedt. Society and group oriented cryptography: A new concept. In Carl Pomerance, ed., *CRYPTO*, vol. 293 of *Lecture Notes in Computer Science*, pp. 120–7. Springer-Verlag, Berlin, 1987.

80. Yvo Desmedt and Yair Frankel. Threshold cryptosystems. In Gilles Brassard, ed., *CRYPTO*, vol. 435 of *Lecture Notes in Computer Science*, pp. 307–15. Springer-Verlag, Berlin, 1989.

81. Yvo Desmedt and Yair Frankel. Perfect homomorphic zero-knowledge threshold schemes over any finite abelian group. *SIAM J. Discrete Math.*, 7(4):667–79, 1994.

82. Marten van Dijk. Secret key sharing and secret key generation. Ph.D. Thesis, Eindhoven University of Technology, The Netherlands, 1997.

83. Yevgeniy Dodis, Amit Sahai, and Adam Smith. On perfect and adaptive security in exposure-resilient cryptography. In Birgit Pfitzmann, ed., *EUROCRYPT*, vol. 2045 of *Lecture Notes in Computer Science*, pp. 301–24. Springer-Verlag, Berlin, 2001.

84. Danny Dolev, Ruediger Reischuk, and H. Raymond Strong. Early stopping in Byzantine agreement. *ACM Transactions on Programming Languages and Systems*, 37(4):720–41, 1990.

85. Danny Dolev and Raymond H. Strong. Polynomial algorithms for multiple processor agreement. In *Proceedings of the Fourteenth Annual ACM Symposium on Theory of Computing*, pp. 401–7, ACM, New York, 1982.

86. Iwan Duursma. Algebraic geometry codes: general theory. In D. Ruano, E. Martínez-Moro, and C. Munuera, eds., *Advances in Algebraic Geometry Codes*, pp. 1–48. World Scientific, New York, 2008.

87. Iwan Duursma and Ralf Kötter. Error-locating pairs for cyclic codes. *IEEE Transactions on Information Theory*, 40(4):1108–21, 1994.

88. Iwan Duursma and Kit-Ho Mak. On lower bounds for the Ihara constants $A(2)$ and $A(3)$. *Compositio Mathematica*, 149(7):1108–28, 2013.

89. Iwan Duursma and Seungkook Park. Coset bounds for algebraic geometric codes. *Finite Fields and Their Applications*, 16(1):36–55, 2010.

90. Iwan Duursma and Jiashun Shen. Multiplicative secret sharing schemes from Reed-Muller type codes. In *ISIT*, pp. 264–8. IEEE, New York, 2012.

91. Matthias Fitzi, Martin Hirt, and Ueli M. Maurer. Trading correctness for privacy in unconditional multi-party computation (extended abstract). In Hugo Krawczyk, ed., *CRYPTO*, vol. 1462 of *Lecture Notes in Computer Science*, pp. 121–36. Springer-Verlag, Berlin, 1998.

92. Matthias Fitzi and Ueli M. Maurer. Efficient Byzantine agreement secure against general adversaries. In Shay Kutten, ed., *DISC*, vol. 1499 of *Lecture Notes in Computer Science*, pp. 134–48. Springer-Verlag, Berlin, 1998.

93. Matthew K. Franklin and Moti Yung. Communication complexity of secure computation (extended abstract). In S. Rao Kosaraju, Mike Fellows, Avi Wigderson, and John A. Ellis, ed., *STOC*, pp. 699–710. ACM, New York, 1992.

94. A. Garcia, H. Stichtenoth, and M. Thomas. On towers and composita of towers of function fields over finite fields. *Finite Fields and Their Applications*, 3:257–74, 1997.

95. Arnaldo Garcia and Henning Stichtenoth. A tower of Artin-Schreier extensions of function fields attaining the Drinfeld-Vlăduţ bound. *Invent. Math.*, 1995:211–22, 1995.

96. Arnaldo Garcia and Henning Stichtenoth. On the asymptotic behavior of some towers of function fields over finite fields. *J. Number Theory*, 61:248–73, 1996.

97. Arnaldo Garcia and Henning Stichtenoth, eds. *Topics in Geometry, Coding Theory and Cryptography*. Springer, New York, 2007.

98. Gerard van der Geer and Marcel van der Vlugt. An asymptotically good tower of curves over the field with eight elements. *Bulletin of the London Mathematical Society*, 34(3):291–300, 2002.

99. Craig Gentry. Fully homomorphic encryption using ideal lattices. In Michael Mitzenmacher, ed., *STOC*, pp. 169–78. ACM, New York, 2009.

100. Oded Goldreich, Silvio Micali, and Avi Wigderson. How to play any mental game or a completeness theorem for protocols with honest majority. In *Proceedings of the Nineteenth Annual ACM Symposium on Theory of Computing*, pp. 218–29, ACM, New York, 1987.

101. V. D. Goppa. Codes on algebraic curves. *Soviet Math. Dokl*, 24:170–2, 1981.

102. Ron Graham, Martin Grötschel, and Laszlo Lovász, editors. *Handbook of Combinatorics*. MIT Press, Cambridge, MA, 1995.

103. Venkatesan Guruswami and Madhu Sudan. Improved decoding of Reed-Solomon and algebraic-geometry codes. *IEEE Transactions on Information Theory*, 45(6):1757–67, 1999.

104. Venkatesan Guruswami and Chaoping Xing. List decoding Reed-Solomon, algebraic-geometric, and Gabidulin subcodes up to the Singleton bound. In Dan Boneh, Tim Roughgarden, and Joan Feigenbaum, eds. *Symposium on Theory of Computing Conference (STOC'13)*. ACM, New York, 2013, pp. 843–52.

105. G. H. Hardy and E. M. Wright. *An Introduction to the Theory of Numbers*. Oxford University Press, 1979.

106. Danny Harnik, Yuval Ishai, Eyal Kushilevitz, and Jesper Buus Nielsen. OT-combiners via secure computation. In Ran Canetti, ed. *Theory of Cryptography, Fifth Theory of Cryptography Conference*, vol. 4948 of *Lecture Notes in Computer Science*. Springer-Verlag, Berlin, 2008, pp. 393–411.

107. Martin Hirt and Ueli Maurer. Player simulation and general adversary structures in perfect multiparty computation. *Journal of Cryptology*, 13(1):31–60, 2000.

108. Paul G. Hoel, Sidney C. Port, and Charles J. Stone. *Introduction to Probability Theory*. Houghton Mifflin, Boston, 1971.

109. Dennis Hofheinz and Victor Shoup. Gnuc: A new universal composability framework. *Journal of Cryptology*, 1–86, 2013.

110. W. C. Huffman and V. Pless. *Fundamentals of Error Correcting Codes*. Cambridge University Press, 2003.

111. Y. Ihara. Some remarks on the number of rational points of algebraic curves over finite fields. *J. Fac. Sci. Tokyo*, 3:721–4, 1981.

112. Yuval Ishai, Joe Kilian, Kobbi Nissim, and Erez Petrank. Extending oblivious transfers efficiently. In Dan Boheh, ed., *Advances in Cryptology: CRYPTO 2003*, vol. 2729 of *Lecture Notes in Computer Science*, pp. 145–61. Springer-Verlag, Berlin, 2003.

113. Yuval Ishai, Eyal Kushilevitz, Rafail Ostrovsky, Manoj Prabhakaran, Amit Sahai, and Jürg Wullschleger. Constant-rate oblivious transfer from noisy channels. In Phillip Rogaway, ed. *Advances*

in Cryptology: CRYPTO 2011, 31st Annual Cryptology Conference, vol. 6841 of *Lecture Notes in Computer Science*. Springer-Verlag, Berlin, 2011, pp. 667–84.

114. Yuval Ishai, Eyal Kushilevitz, Rafail Ostrovsky, and Amit Sahai. Extracting Correlations, FOCS, pp. 261–270, 2009. http://doi.ieeecomputersociety.org/10.1109/FOCS.2009.56

115. Yuval Ishai, Manoj Prabhakaran, and Amit Sahai. Founding cryptography on oblivious transfer – efficiently. In David Wagner, ed. *Advances in Cryptology: CRYPTO 2008, 28th Annual International Cryptology Conference*, vol. 5157 of *Lecture Notes in Computer Science*. Springer-Verlag, Berlin, 2008, pp. 572–91.

116. M. Ito, A. Saito, and T. Nishizeki. Secret sharing schemes realizing general access structures. In *Proc. IEEE GlobeCom '87*, pp. 99–102, IEEE, New York, 1987.

117. Wen-Ai Jackson and Keith Martin. A combinatorial interpretation of ramp schemes. *Australasian Journal of Combinatorics*, 14:51–60, 1996.

118. Yuval Ishai, Eyal Kushilevitz, Rafail Ostrovsky, and Amit Sahai. Zero-knowledge from secure multiparty computation. STOC, pp. 21–30, 2007. http://doi.acm.org/10.1145/1250790.1250794, *SIAM J. Comput.*, 39(3):1121–52 2009.

119. Mauricio Karchmer and Avi Wigderson. On span programs. In *Structure in Complexity Theory Conference*, pp. 102–11, 1993.

120. Ehud D. Karnin, J. W. Greene, and Martin E. Hellman. On secret sharing systems. *IEEE Transactions on Information Theory*, 29(1):35–41, 1983.

121. Joe Kilian. Founding cryptography on oblivious transfer. In *Proceedings of the Twentieth Annual ACM Symposium on Theory of Computing (STOC'88)*, ACM, New York, 1988, pp. 20–31.

122. Kötter, R. A unified description of an error locating procedure for linear codes. In *Proceedings of Algebraic and Combinatorial Coding Theory*, Voneshta Voda, pp. 113–17, 1992.

123. Tsit-Yuen Lam. *Introduction to Quadratic Forms over Fields*. American Mathematical Society, Washington, DC, 2005.

124. Leslie Lamport, Robert Shostak, and Marshall Pease. The Byzantine generals problem. *ACM Transactions on Programming Languages and Systems*, 4(3):381–401, 1982.

125. Serge Lang. *Algebraic Number Theory*. Springer, New York, 1994.

126. Serge Lang. *Algebra, Graduate Texts in Mathematics*. Springer, New York, 2002.

127. Serge Lang. *Undergraduate Algebra*. Springer, New York, 2002.

128. H. W. Lenstra, Jr. Euclidean number fields of large degree. *Invent. Math.*, 38:237–54, 1977.

129. H. W. Lenstra, Jr. On a problem of Garcia, Stichtenoth, and Thomas. *Finite Fields and Their Applications*, 8:166–70, 2002.

130. H. W. Lenstra, Jr. *Galois Theory for Schemes*, 2008; available at: `websites.math.leidenuniv.nl/algebra/`.

131. Yehuda Lindell and Benny Pinkas. A proof of security of Yao's protocol for two-party computation. *J. Cryptology*, 22(2):161–88, 2009.

132. J. H. van Lint. *Introduction to Coding Theory*, 3rd, ed., *Graduate Texts in Mathematics*. Springer, New York, 1999.

133. J. H. van Lint and R. M. Wilson. On the minimum distance of cyclic codes. *IEEE Transactions on Information Theory*, 32(1):23–40, 1986.

134. J. H. van Lint and R. M. Wilson. *A Course in Combinatorics*, 2nd ed. Cambridge University Press, 2001.

135. Irene Marquez Corbella and Ruud Pellikaan. Error-correcting pairs for a public-key cryptosystem. *CoRR*, abs/1205.3647, 2012.

136. John Martin. *Introduction to Languages and the Theory of Computation*. McGraw-Hill, New York, 2003.

137. Keith Martin. Discrete structures in the theory of secret sharing. Ph.D. thesis, University of London, 1991.

138. Keith Martin. New secret sharing schemes from old. *J. Combin. Math. Combin. Comput.*, 14:65–77, 1993.

139. Jim Massey. Minimal codewords and secret sharing. In *Proceedings of the 6th Joint Swedish-Russian Workshop on Information Theory*, pp. 269–79, Institutionen för informationsteori, Tekniska högsk. Lund, Sweden, 1993.

140. Jim Massey. Some applications of coding theory in cryptography. *Codes and Ciphers: Cryptography and Coding IV*, pp. 33–47, 1995.

141. Ueli Maurer. Constructive cryptography: a new paradigm for security definitions and proofs. In Sebastian Mödersheim and Catuscia Palamidessi, eds., *TOSCA*, vol. 6993 of *Lecture Notes in Computer Science*, pp. 33–56. Springer-Verlag, Berlin, 2011.

142. Robert J. McEliece and Dilip V. Sarwate. On sharing secrets and Reed-Solomon codes. *Commun. ACM*, 24(9):583–4, 1981.

143. F. J. McWilliams and N. J. A. Sloane. *The Theory of Error-Correcting Codes*. North-Holland, Amsterdam, 1977.

144. Silvio Micali and Phillip Rogaway. Secure computation. In Joan Feigenbaum, ed., *Advances in Cryptology: CRYPTO '91*, Vol. 576 of *Lecture Notes in Computer Science*, pp. 392–404. Springer-Verlag, Berlin, 1991.

145. Diego Mirandola and Gilles Zémor. Schur products of linear codes: a study of parameters. Master's thesis, Univ. Bordeaux, 2012.

146. Carlos Moreno. *Algebraic Curves over Finite Fields*. Cambridge Tracts in Mathematics. Cambridge University Press, 1991.

147. Jürgen Neukirch. *Algebraic Number Theory*. Graduate Texts in Mathematics. Springer, New York, 1999.

148. Harald Niederreiter and Chaoping Xing. *Rational Points on Curves over Finite Fields*. Cambridge University Press, 2001.

149. Jesper Buus Nielsen. On protocol security in the cryptographic model. Dissertation Series DS-03-8, BRICS, Department of Computer Science, University of Aarhus, August 2003.

150. Jesper Buus Nielsen, Peter Sebastian Nordholt, Claudio Orlandi, and Sai Sheshank Burra. A new approach to practical active-secure two-party computation. In Reihaneh Safavi-Naini and Ran Canetti, eds., *CRYPTO*, vol. 7417 of *Lecture Notes in Computer Science*, pp. 681–700. Springer-Verlag, Berlin, 2012.

151. Francesco Noseda, Gilvan Oliveira, and Luciane Quoos. Bases for Riemann-Roch spaces of one-point divisors on an optimal tower of function fields. *IEEE Transactions on Information Theory*, 58(5): 2589–98, 2012.

152. Wakaha Ogata and Kaoru Kurosawa. Some basic properties of general nonperfect secret sharing schemes. *J. UCS*, 4(8):690–704, 1998.

153. Carles Padró. Lecture notes in secret sharing. Eprint 2012/674, available at: eprint.iacr.org, 2012.

154. Pascal Paillier. Public-key cryptosystems based on composite degree residue classes. In Jacques Stern, ed., *Advances in Cryptology: EUROCRYPT '99*, vol. 1592 of *Lecture Notes in Computer Science*, pp. 223–38. Springer-Verlag, Berlin, 1999.

155. Ruud Pellikaan. On decoding by error location and dependent sets of error positions. *Discrete Mathematics*, 106–7:369–81, 1992.

156. Birgit Pfitzmann, Matthias Schunter, and Michael Waidner. Secure reactive systems. Technical Report RZ 3206, IBM Research, Zürich, May 2000.

157. Tal Rabin and Michael Ben-Or. Verifiable secret sharing and multiparty protocols with honest majority. In *Proceedings of the Twenty First Annual ACM Symposium on Theory of Computing*, pp. 73–85. ACM, New York, 1989.

158. Hugues Randriambololona. Hecke operators with odd determinant and binary frameproof codes beyond the probabilistic bound? *IEEE Information Theory Workshop (ITW 2010)*, pp. 1–5. IEEE, New York, 2010.

159. Hugues Randriambololona. Bilinear complexity of algebras and the Chudnovsky-Chudnovsky interpolation method. *J. Complexity*, 28(4):489–517, 2012.

160. Hugues Randriambololona. Asymptotically good binary linear codes with asymptotically good self-intersection spans. *IEEE Transactions on Information Theory*, 59(5):3038–45, 2013.

161. Hugues Randriambololona. On products and powers of linear codes under componentwise multiplication. *arXiv preprint arXiv:1312.0022*, 2013.
162. Michael Rosen. *Number Theory in Function Fields. Graduate Texts in Mathematics.* Springer, New York, 2002.
163. Joseph J Rotman. *An Introduction to the Theory of Groups*, vol. 148. Springer, New York, 1995.
164. S. Ballet and R. Rolland. On the bilinear complexity of the multiplication in finite fields. In *Arithmetic, Geometry and Coding Theory (AGCT 2003), Séminaires et Congrès 11*, Société Mathématique de France, pp. 179–88, 2005.
165. Pierre Samuel. *Algebraic Theory of Numbers.* Hermann, Paris, 1970.
166. Jean-Pierre Serre. Rational points on curves over finite fields. Notes of lectures at Harvard University, 1985.
167. Adi Shamir. How to share a secret. *Communications of the ACM*, 22(11):612–13, 1979.
168. Victor Shoup. *A Computational Introduction to Number Theory and Algebra.* Cambridge University Press, 2005.
169. Igor Shparlinski, Michael Tsfasman, and Serge Vlăduţ. Curves with many points and multiplication in finite fields. *Lecture Notes in Mathematics*, 1518:145–69, 1992.
170. Kenneth W. Shum, Ilia Aleshnikov, P. Vijay Kumar, Henning Stichtenoth, and Vinay Deolalikar. A low-complexity algorithm for the construction of algebraic-geometric codes better than the Gilbert-Varshamov bound. *IEEE Transactions on Information Theory*, 47(6):2225–41, 2001.
171. G. Simmons, W.-A. Jackson, and K. Martin. The geometry of shared secret schemes. *Bull. Inst. Combin. Appl.*, 1:71–88, 1991.
172. Henning Stichtenoth. *Algebraic Function Fields and Codes*, 2nd ed. *Graduate Texts in Mathematics.* Springer, New York, 2008.
173. Douglas R. Stinson. Decomposition constructions for secret-sharing schemes. *IEEE Transactions on Information Theory*, 40(1):118–25, 1994.
174. Douglas R Stinson. *Cryptography: Theory and Practice.* CRC Press, Boca Raton, FL, 2005.
175. Madhu Sudan. Decoding of Reed-Solomon codes beyond the error-correction bound. *J. Complexity*, 13(1):180–93, 1997.
176. M. Tsfasman, S. Vlăduţ, and Th. Zink. Modular curves, Shimura curves, and Goppa codes, better than Varshamov Gilbert bound. *Math. Nachr.*, 1982:21–8, 1982.
177. Michael Tsfasman, Serge Vlăduţ, and Dmitry Nogin. *Algebraic Geometric Codes: Basic Notions*, vol. 139 of *Mathematical Surveys and Monographs.* American Mathematical Society, Washington, DC, 2007.
178. Leslie G. Valiant. Short monotone formulae for the majority function. *J. Algorithms*, 5(3):363–6, 1984.
179. S. Vlăduţ. An exhaustion bound for algebraic-geometric modular code. *Probl. Inf. Transm*, 23:22–34, 1987.
180. Andrew Chi-Chih Yao. How to generate and exchange secrets (extended abstract). In *27th Annual Symposium on Foundations of Computer Science*, pp. 162–7. IEEE, New York, 1986.
181. Th. Zink. Degeneration of Shimura surfaces and a problem in coding theory. In Lothar Budach, ed., *FCT*, vol. 199 of *Lecture Notes in Computer Science*, pp. 503–11. Springer-Verlag, Berlin, 1985.

Index

CPSIA information can be obtained
at www.ICGtesting.com
Printed in the USA
LVHW101448250620
658991LV00021B/409

9 781107 043053